Cloud Computing Service and Deployment Models:

Layers and Management

Alberto M. Bento
University of Baltimore, USA

Anil K. Aggarwal
University of Baltimore, USA

BUSINESS SCIENCE Reference

Managing Director:	Lindsay Johnston
Editorial Director:	Joel Gamon
Book Production Manager:	Jennifer Romanchak
Publishing Systems Analyst:	Adrienne Freeland
Development Editor:	Myla Merkel
Assistant Acquisitions Editor:	Kayla Wolfe
Typesetter:	Erin O'Dea
Cover Design:	Nick Newcomer

Published in the United States of America by
Business Science Reference (an imprint of IGI Global)
701 E. Chocolate Avenue
Hershey PA 17033
Tel: 717-533-8845
Fax: 717-533-8661
E-mail: cust@igi-global.com
Web site: http://www.igi-global.com

Library of Congress Cataloging-in-Publication Data

  Cloud computing service and deployment models: layers and management / Alberto M. Bento and Anil K. Aggarwal, editors.
   p. cm.
   Includes bibliographical references and index.
   Summary: "This book presents a collection of diverse perspectives on cloud computing and its vital role in all components of organizations, improving the understanding of cloud computing and tackling related concerns such as change management, security, processing approaches, and much more"--Provided by publisher.
ISBN 978-1-4666-2187-9 (hbk.) -- ISBN 978-1-4666-2188-6 (ebook) -- ISBN 978-1-4666-2189-3 (print & perpetual access) 1. Cloud computing. 2. Management information systems. 3. Information technology--Management. I. Bento, Alberto M., 1943- II. Aggarwal, Anil, 1949-

 QA76.585.C583 2013
 004.6782--dc23

                           2012019839

British Cataloguing in Publication Data
A Cataloguing in Publication record for this book is available from the British Library.

All work contributed to this book is new, previously-unpublished material. The views expressed in this book are those of the authors, but not necessarily of the publisher.

This book is dedicated to our families and friends, especially Ana, Regina, Nick, Eleanor, Nick Sr., Sharda, Bimal, Shefali, Sonali and Savita without whose support this book could not have been completed.

List of Reviewers

Cecelia Wright Brown, *University of Baltimore, USA*
Deans, P. Candace, *University of Richmond, USA*
Alpana Desai, *University of Alaska Anchorage, USA*
Shamim Hossain, *IBM Corporation, Australia*
Wei Nein "William" Lee, *Webydesign.com*
Marc Rabaey, *Europalaan 16, Belgium*
Venky Shankararaman, *Singapore Management University, Singapore*
Haibo Yang, *Victoria University of Wellington, New Zealand*
Minnie Yi-Miin Yen, *University of Alaska Anchorage, USA*

Table of Contents

Section 1
Cloud Computing Services

Detailed Table of Contents

Section 1
Cloud Computing Services

Chapter 1

    Shamim Hossain, IBM Corporation, Australia

This chapter introduces terms and terminologies associated with cloud computing from a vendor neutral perspective. Readers are gradually introduced to cloud computing elements, which paves the way for better understanding in later chapters.

Chapter 2

    Shamim Hossain, IBM Corporation, Australia

In this chapter, the author takes a closer look at this important service which is considered as the backbone of cloud computing.

Chapter 3

    Cecelia Wright Brown, University of Baltimore, USA
    Kofi Nyarko, Morgan State University, USA

The purpose of this chapter is to discuss the origin and evolution of SaaS, as well as to describe its role in today's enterprise environment. This chapter begins with a description of the evolution of SaaS, followed by the architecture, implementation, and associated business model.

Chapter 4

    Haibo Yang, Victoria University of Wellington, New Zealand
    Sid Huff, Victoria University of Wellington, New Zealand
    Mary Tate, Victoria University of Wellington, New Zealand

This research aims at providing a conceptualization of IS agility based on research to date, and examining how cloud computing might facilitate such agility. Based on a literature review, cloud computing services (IaaS, PaaS, and SaaS) are analyzed against multiple aspects of IS agility. Only IaaS is found to have the potential providing consistent agility, whereas agility at PaaS and SaaS levels is more determined by human/organization factors. Lastly suggestions for businesses and directions to future research are proposed.

Chapter 5

This chapter presents an investment framework, which takes into account global, business, IT, and operational strategies, so that cloud computing projects have more chance to succeed. The need for flexibility in the investments is addressed by the real option valuation, which is placed in the context of the authors' holistic investment framework for cloud computing.

Section 2
Cloud Services Development and Framework

Chapter 6

This chapter presents a systems approach to cloud computing services. Specifically, it examines issues in the context of the system development life cycle (SDLC). For completeness purposes, the author discusses issues in relation to SDLC; however, in practice, each user will have to customize this approach to suit one's application(s).

Chapter 7

This chapter examines selected, established requirements engineering methods in order to study the extent to which they can be applied to the specific requirements of cloud-based solutions. Furthermore, it develops a comparison framework containing the features of cloud computing.

Chapter 8

This chapter develops a preliminary decision framework to assist managers who are determining which cloud solution matches their specific requirements and evaluating the numerous commercial claims (in many cases unsubstantiated) of a cloud's value.

Chapter 9

Venky Shankararaman, Singapore Management University, Singapore
Lum Eng Kit, Singapore Management University, Singapore

In this chapter, the author briefly introduces the various cloud computing architecture layers, provides detailed cloud integration scenarios, and discusses some of the challenges and present some integration solutions. The author also provides points for consideration to help organizations decide appropriate integration solutions to suit their needs.

Section 3
Security and Legal Issues in Cloud Computing

Chapter 10

Shantanu Pal, The University of Calcutta, India

The objective of this chapter is to discuss and understand the basic security and privacy challenges of a cloud computing environment as the security of cloud computing is the greatest challenge for delivering a safer cloud environment for both the service providers and the service customers.

Chapter 11

Alpana M. Desai, University of Alaska Anchorage, USA
Kenrick Mock, University of Alaska Anchorage, USA

In this chapter, the authors discuss the technical, legal, and policy/organizational security risks of cloud computing. They review recommendations/strategies for managing and mitigating security threats in cloud computing. The authors also present vendor-specific solutions and strategies that cloud service providers are implementing for mitigating security risks in cloud computing.

Chapter 12

Yoshito Kanamori, University of Alaska Anchorage, USA
Minnie Yi-Miin Yen, University of Alaska Anchorage, USA

In this chapter, the authors first clarify misperceptions by introducing the new threats and challenges involved in cloud environments. Specifically, security issues and concerns are depicted in three practical scenarios designed to illuminate the different security problems in each cloud deployment model.

Section 4
Legal Issues in Cloud Computing

Chapter 13

Sam De Silva, Manches LLP, UK

The chapter considers the key legal issues with cloud computing including: (1) liability for service failure; (2) service levels and service credits; (3) intellectual property issues; and (4) jurisdiction and governing law.

Chapter 14

Michael L. Kemp, University of Richmond, USA
Shannon Robb, University of Richmond, USA
P. Candace Deans, University of Richmond, USA

The purpose of this chapter is to examine the current legal environment of cloud computing. As the cloud platform continues to evolve, companies will find the need to address the business risks, particularly legal issues which will be of paramount concern. This chapter discusses the legal dimensions of cloud computing from the perspective of three L's: Location, Litigation, and Liability.

Section 5
Economic Impact of Cloud Computing

Chapter 15

Cameron Deed, Yellowfin, Australia
Paul Cragg, University of Canterbury, New Zealand

This chapter explores the business impacts associated with the adoption of a cloud-based business intelligence application. A generic benefits management framework was adopted to guide the study of five firms. Numerous types of benefit were identified, including strategic, managerial, operational, and functional and support.

Chapter 16

Wei Nein "William" Lee, University of Houston, USA

This chapter provides specific return on investment analysis and business case studies leveraging the application and value proposition of these solutions. In summary, the analysis presented suggests that an inevitable shift from legacy network architectures to SaaS and VDI computing is the path forward.

Chapter 17

Federico Etro, University of Venice, Ca' Foscari, Italy

This chapter examines the economic impact of the diffusion of a new technology as cloud computing. This will allow firms to rent computing power and storage from service providers, and to pay on demand, with a profound impact on the cost structure of all the industries, turning some of the fixed costs in marginal costs of production.

Section 6
Applications and Advances in Cloud Computing

Chapter 18

In this chapter, the author describes findings and prototypes of emerging tactical networking services, which he was able to identify based on unique experimental studies of tactical networking. The described findings should be helpful in structuring tactical cloud services for the variety manned-unmanned sensor networking applications.

Foreword

A cloud does not know why it moves in just such a direction and at such a speed...It feels an impulsion... this is the place to go now. But the sky knows the reasons and the patterns behind all clouds, and you will know, too, when you lift yourself high enough to see beyond horizons.

Cloud Computing has been a part of humankind's vision of the future for at least 70 years. In the late 1930s the futurist and novelist H.G Wells envisioned a World Brain, "a complete planetary memory for all mankind." "The time is close at hand," Wells wrote, "when any student, in any part of the world, will be able to sit with his projector in his own study at his or her own convenience to examine any book, any document, in an exact replica." (1938). That time has come.

Since Wells made his prediction, society has been on a steady quest for information ubiquity. The main driving force has been advances in computers and communication networks. It began with heavy tonnage, minimal function, and sluggish mainframes -- computers anchored in a single isolated location. Since then, the information industry has consistently expanded the scope, power, and flexibility of computing and communication services.

As the technology has changed, so too have the organizational structures used to deploy it. The early stand-alone systems – in 1949 Edmund Berkeley called them "Giant Brains" – were almost always owned and operated by the using organization. In 1951, the U. S. Census Bureau was the first organization to employ a Remington Rand UNIVAC, a computer designed by J. Presper Eckert and John Mauchly. In 1954, General Electric was the first company to use a general application computer for its business operations. At that time the editors of the Harvard Business Review hailed these developments as the coming of the next age of industry.

Yet, even during these inaugural days some visionaries were looking forward to a much different and broader, more Wellsian, based application of the technology. For example, about 1950, Herb Grosch, one of the first computer gurus, envisioned a time in which the entire world would eventually operate using dumb terminals powered by just 15 large – i.e. supercomputer – data centers (Ryan et al., 2010). In 1990 the late Max Hopper, who at American Airlines pioneered the strategic use of computers and the corporate role of CIO, made a notable and controversial forecast. In a Harvard Business Review article, "Rattling SABRE – New Ways to Compete on Information," Hopper echoed John McCarthy's 1960s observation by proclaiming: "The game is shifting from who can build the newest proprietary electronic tools to who can use and modify available tools more effectively" (1990). Hopper argued that computer utilities – such as what is now called "the cloud" – were the future of information systems.

Cloud computing may be defined as a technological arrangement in which software, information, skilled personnel and other shared resources are provided to operate on computers and other devices whose services are made available over a widespread network such as the Internet. With the advent of the cloud the visionaries' forecasts are coming true. A strong current trend has emerged for parties to acquire information services from other providing organizations rather than to own and manage all of the factors of information production themselves. In this model a client's information and processing capacity is not resident at a fixed location but rather is made available on demand virtually anywhere and anytime.

In the domain of cloud computing the concept of service – basically providing for someone else's needs by another party – is taking center stage. A new relationship called "as a service" has emerged. Indeed, an acronym, XaaS, has been coined to stand for "anything" or "everything as a service" when offered through a cloud. Services subsumed under XaaS include: Software as a Service (SaaS), Infrastructure as a Service (IaaS), Platform as a Service (PaaS), Storage as a Service (also SaaS), Communications as a Service (CaaS), Network as a Service (NaaS), Monitoring as a Service (MaaS), and likely many more to come. Underlying this alphabetic potage is a dramatic change in the accessibility, agility, and cost to performance ratio of information processing. In effect the service orientation of cloud computing foretells a whole new way of doing business.

This new capability comes not a moment too soon. The cloud is becoming the weapon of choice in what might be called strategic "data wars," or the war of analytics. This battlefield is predicated on developing insights and decision recommendations from the results of "data mining" and the application of statistical models and mathematical analysis to increasingly large masses of data. In general, the world and organizations are creating and transmitting data – so called "big data" – much faster than they are able to efficiently and effectively process it. Moreover, information is flowing faster as more customers need to be accommodated and all parties are demanding faster turnaround times.

The overall impact is staggering. International Data Corporation estimates that in 2011 the amount of data created globally was 1.2 zettabytes per annum, seemingly a huge number. When IDC assesses the new growth potential they forecast that by 2020 global volume will reach an astounding 35 zettabytes. Indeed we are rapidly running out of metric prefixs – kilo (10^3), mega, giga, tera, peta, exa, zetta, and on to yotta (10^{24}) – to measure the explosion in data. Diamandis and Kotler (2012) estimate that five exabytes of data are now being created every two days. That is about equivalent to all of the words written and images created from the beginning of civilization up to the year 2003. The growth continues to be exponential. By 2013 they predict that five exabytes of data will be created every 10 minutes.

These may be conservative estimates. Retrospective history shows that many such forecasts end up under estimating the actual growth. Recall that in 1943 IBM's Thomas Watson allegedly said, "I think there is a world market for maybe five computers."

Increased volume is accompanied by a faster tempo. The speed with which data is coming in (its velocity) is also increasing rapidly. At the same time the data elements being processed are more varied and comprehensive in nature – alphanumeric text, graphics, photos, audio, music, movies, videos, measurement data from numerous sensors of various types, et cetera. The value proposition has also changed. Importantly, by using data mining techniques just a few nuggets plucked from within these massive data streams can be of immense strategic and tactical value.

How can all this data be dealt with? The current proprietary technological platforms that many organizations employ are simply unable to cope with these demands, at least in a timely and cost/effective basis. Moving to the cloud with its increased flexibility, elasticity, scalability, speed, offers a solution. The cloud's improved economic model is based more on incremental costs (in some cases "metered" costs based on actual use) rather than on incurring large fixed costs promises great advantages for responding to this challenging environment economically. For these reasons all organizations and many individuals should be considering a cloud solution.

Drs. Alberto Bento and Anil Aggarwal have brought together a group of practitioners and thinkers who have worked in and reflected upon the many facets of change that cloud computing – though still in its infancy – is bringing about. The book's first five parts address many vital aspects of cloud computing: What services are offered? (Section 1), How are these services developed? (Section 2), How are security issues addressed? (Section 3), What legal issues must be dealt with? (Section 4), and What is the appropriate economic model for evaluating cloud computing? (Section 5). A sixth section deals with applications and advances.

Let this book be your sky. It can help you "lift yourself high enough to see beyond the horizons" and learn more about the "reasons and patterns" behind cloud computing.

Richard O. Mason
Southern Methodist University, USA

Richard O. Mason *is Carr P. Collins Professor of Management Information Sciences at the Edwin L. Cox School of Business at Southern Methodist University. He received his B.S. degree (1956) from Oregon State University in Business and Technology and his Ph.D. degree (1968) from the University of California, Berkeley, in Business Administration. Mason's current areas of teaching include Business Ethics and Social Responsibility, Electronic Commerce, Managing Emerging Technologies and Global Business Environments. His current areas of research include business strategy and information systems, social and ethical implications of information systems, ethics and genetics, and the history of information systems. He recently completed a three-year term on the GMAC Commission to examine the future role of graduate management education and was selected in 1989 to be a delegate to the USSR to review Soviet plans for the "Informatization of Soviet Society." In 1992, Mason was elected as a foreign member of the Russian Academy of Natural Sciences in the Information and Cybernetics section. He was awarded a Fulbright Fellowship in 1993 to do research at Umea University in Sweden.*

REFERENCES

Berkeley, E. C. (1949). *Giant brains or machines that think*. New York, NY: John Wiley & Sons.

Diamandis, P. H., & Kolter, S. (2012). *Abundance*. New York, NY: Free Press.

Hopper, M. D. (1990, May 1). Rattling SABRE – New ways to compete on information. *Harvard Business Review*.

Ryan, P., Merchant, R., & Falvey, S. (2011). Regulation of the Cloud in India. *Journal of Internet Law*, *15*(4), 7.

Wells, H. G. (1938). *World brain* (p. 54). London, UK: Ayer.

ENDNOTES

[1]   Attributed to Richard Bach author of *Jonathan Livingston Seagull* http://thinkexist.com/quotation/a_cloud_does_not_know_why_it_moves_in_just_such_a/143436.html

[2]   IBM's mid 1950s development of its "service bureaus" and H. Ross Perot establishment of Electronic Data Systems in 1962 are exceptions that pioneered some of the business concepts currently being followed by cloud providers.

[3]   One zettabyte is 10^{21} bytes or one billion terabytes. An exabyte is one quintillion bytes or 1 followed by 18 zeros.

Preface

Cloud computing is an emerging discipline which is changing the way corporate computing is and will be done in the future. The National Institute of Standards and Technology (NIST) defines cloud computing as a "model for enabling convenient, on-demand network access to a shared pool of configurable computing resources (e.g., networks, servers, storage, applications, and services) that can be rapidly provisioned and released with minimal management effort or service provider interaction." The architecture of Cloud Computing is comprised of four layers: Infrastructure as a Service (comprised of servers, hypervisor, storage and network), Platform as a Service (development environment including data base, integration and development tools), Software as a Service (ready-made applications), and Business Process as a Service (applications plus services). In addition, there are different types of clouds: private, public, hybrid and community clouds, with different capabilities and requirements. As with any new area, cloud computing raises many conceptual, technical, and managerial issues that need to be addressed by both academicians and practitioners.

OBJECTIVE OF THE BOOK

The book aims to provide relevant theoretical frameworks and practical applications in the area. Chapters were written for the benefit of professionals who want to improve their understanding of cloud computing and address many of the issues related to change management, security, management and processing approaches related to cloud computing. A key objective is to provide a systematic source of reference for all aspects of cloud computing. Another key objective is to understand the changes cloud computing will have on organizations and management. Most of what has been written about cloud computing is either about its technical aspects, or are descriptions of products and services, many by providers of these products and services. This book brings many different perspectives to start a more serious discussion about what cloud computing is and its impacts in the many facets of organizations.

Content

The book is organized in six sections with following emphasis:

1. **Cloud computing services:** The definition of cloud computing terms and taxonomy, detailed review of Infrastructure as A Service, Software as a Service, managing the cloud for agility, and a holistic investment framework for cloud computing.

2. **Cloud services development framework:** A systems approach and requirements engineering for cloud applications, a decision framework for small businesses, and integrating cloud scenarios and solutions.

3. **Security in cloud computing:** Security concerns and issues, security in cloud computing, and cloud security and risk management.

4. **Legal issues in cloud computing:** Key issues and legal implications of cloud computing in US and UK.

5. **Economic impact of cloud computing:** The business impacts, economics of cloud computing, and an economic analysis of cloud and VDI models.

6. **Applications and advances in cloud computing:** An advanced example on the pattern of tactical networking services.

The book includes in seventeen chapters with contributions from twenty-nine authors from seven different countries providing a global, broad perspective on cloud computing topics. This book is an excellent starting point for both practitioners and academicians that want to migrate to cloud computing or engage in cloud computing research. As already mentioned, cloud computing is an emerging discipline and new concepts, methodologies, and applications are constantly emerging making this a challenging and rewarding area of research. We invite our colleagues to research further in this area to build the ever increasing knowledge base of cloud computing.

Al Bento
University of Baltimore, USA

Anil Aggarwal
University of Baltimore, USA

Section 1
Cloud Computing Services

Chapter 1
Cloud Computing Terms, Definitions, and Taxonomy

Shamim Hossain
IBM Corporation, Australia

ABSTRACT

Cloud computing has taken the IT industry by storm. It has ushered a new era of computing and IT delivery model. This chapter introduces terms and terminologies associated with cloud computing from a vendor neutral perspective. Readers are gradually introduced to cloud computing elements which pave the way for better understanding in later chapters.

INTRODUCTION

For the last few years we have seen the reverberation of cloud computing in global IT field. Although some have seen it as a hype and most common buzz word, cloud computing appeared as a valuable driver of growth for business, cost saving, reducing energy usage and extricating the headache of IT infrastructure administration and maintenance. Not only has it been the linchpin of low cost delivery model but also a highly powerful tool to intercept market with a much quicker time for valuable businesses. It is fascinating to see how organizations can configure and use cloud based offerings, also known as services (will be discussed later), in a matter of minutes or hours as opposed to days, weeks or months in conventional IT system. It is no embellishment to say the businesses need to adopt cloud computing to cater for on-demand services delivery that arises from Service Oriented Architecture (SOA), Unified Computing (UC), integrated application architectures and distributed computing. Application architecture has expanded far beyond the very early client server model. High performance and distributed computing model was visualized by grid computing earlier. Cloud computing has added few more dimension to this era to make an epoch making revolution. Now it is not just a hyped technology but a disruptive technology shaping the IT industry. Companies have become global and so are their IT infrastructures. IT resources (servers, storage, network etc) are spread all over the world and these are connected through internet.

DOI: 10.4018/978-1-4666-2187-9.ch001

Industries have never seen such a revolutionized architecture. To the end user the whole thing is just one network. Internet has been the weaver to bring the IT resources together. As cloud computing definitions are revealed progressively in this chapter, readers will gain more insight into this.

BACKGROUND

There is a plethora of definitions available for cloud computing. Many different sources have defined cloud computing from different perspective and the definitions have been the subject of debate. We will present several definitions in this section and will unfold cloud computing with detailed description of its traits and features. Cloud computing has attracted attentions from academia, industries, tech-savvy individuals and analytic firms. This positive attitude and rumination towards cloud computing resulted in many definitions.

Cloud has often been used as a metaphor for internet. In network diagram blocks of network and transport mechanism are often represented by a cloud (Rittinghouse & Ransome, 2010). However, cloud computing has got some additional new meanings. To start with, it can be stated that cloud computing is the culmination of grid computing, utility computing, unified communication (UC), Service Oriented Architecture (SOA), Web 2.0 and many other similar technologies. It has been described as the new age of computing, adopting a "pay as you go" or utility model, similar to electricity, water and other common place utilities. To an end user, cloud computing is an illusion of a pool of infinite computing resources on demand. These resources are served by a sprawl of servers, networking equipments and storage systems from a data center. This new consumption and delivery model displays a shift from a Capital Expenditure (CAPEX) to an Operating Expenditure (OPEX).

From the myriads of definitions available, the definition by National Institute of Standards and Technology (NIST) has been widely accepted (NIST, 2010).

Cloud computing is a model for enabling convenient, on-demand network access to a shared pool of configurable computing resources (e.g., networks, servers, storage, applications, and services) that can be rapidly provisioned and released with minimal management effort or service provider interaction.

Cloud computing is an elastically scalable, virtualized system which can be rapidly provisioned with flexible pricing model (pay as you go) (Rimal, Eunmi, & Lumb, 2009; Sarna, 2011).

According to Reliable Adaptive Distributed Systems Laboratory, UC Berkeley, cloud computing is the aggregation of application delivered as services over internet and hardware and systems software in the datacenters that provide those services (Armbrust, et al., 2009).

Nicholas Carr in his Wall Street Journal bestseller (Carr, 2008) portrayed a very insightful discussion of technological transformation and an insight into cloud computing. He has analyzed how disruptive technology like cloud computing is shaping the world. Following is an excerpt from his famous book "The big switch: rewiring the world, from Edison to Google":

A hundred years ago, companies stopped generating their own power with steam engines and dynamos and plugged into the newly built electric grid. The cheap power pumped out by electric utilities didn't just change how businesses operate. It set off a chain reaction of economic and social transformations that brought the modern world into existence. Today, a similar revolution is under way. Hooked up to the Internet's global computing grid, massive information-processing plants have begun pumping data and software code into our homes and businesses. This time, it's computing that's turning into a utility.

The shift is already remaking the computer industry, bringing new competitors like Google and Salesforce.com to the fore and threatening stalwarts like Microsoft and Dell. But the effects will reach much further. Cheap, utility-supplied computing will ultimately change society as profoundly as cheap electricity did. We can already see the early effects — in the shift of control over media from institutions to individuals, in debates over the value of privacy, in the export of the jobs of knowledge workers, even in the growing concentration of wealth. As information utilities expand, the changes will only broaden, and their pace will only accelerate."

Maximilien and et al. has defined cloud computing as the natural progression of Service Oriented Architecture (SOA) (Maximilien, Ranabahu, Engehausen, & Anderson, 2009). In this model of computing, all aspects of compute stack (software and hardware) are exposed as a service (Maximilien, et al., 2009).

Cloud should exhibit certain characteristics, attributes, deployment models and service models at a minimum to make it distinguished from grid or distributed computing (NIST, 2010). These have been summarized in Table 1. More than three service models have become popular. These will be covered in Cloud Services section shortly.

Cloud computing may also showcase following additional attributes (Mall & Grance, 2009). However these are not essential to define cloud computing.

- Massive scale
- Homogeneity
- Virtualization

Table 1. Attributes of cloud computing

Characteristics	On-demand Self service	This means provisioning of computing resources as needed without human interaction with each service's provider
	Ubiquitous access	It means access over the network using any thin or thick client (e.g., mobile phones, laptops, and PDAs)
	Resource pooling	This means that computing resources are pooled and resources are dynamically assigned and reassigned according to demand.
	Rapid elasticity	Computing resources can be rapidly and elastically provisioned and scaled up or down as needed.
	Measured service	Cloud computing resource usage can be monitored using metering facility. Providers will bill the customers based on the usage.
Service models	Infrastructure as a Service (IaaS)	This means providing service to a customer for processing power, storage, networks and other fundamental computing resources.
	Platform as a Service (PaaS)	It includes middlewares, programming tools, application runtimes, operating systems and any other tools.
	Software as a Service (SaaS)	It means a provider's application hosted on its cloud infrastructure.
Deploy Model	Public cloud	This infrastructure is owned by a provider selling or providing cloud services to other organizations. Multiple organizations can share the resources using multi-tenancy model.
	Private cloud	This type of cloud infrastructure is solely owned by an organisation. It is managed by this organization or a third party, located on site or off-site.
	Community Cloud	This type of model is owned and shared by multiple organizations who has a shared concern (e.g., mission, security requirements, policy, and compliance considerations)
	Hybrid cloud	This type of cloud is a combination of any of the above clouds which are bound together by standardized or proprietary technology.

- Resilient computing
- Low cost software
- Geographic distribution
- Service orientation
- Advanced security technologies

Research Analyst Firm Gartner has described cloud computing as a revolutionary style of computing emerging from evolutionary changes (Gartner, 2010). Social and market trends, Service Oriented architecture, Web 2.0, exponential growth in connected devices, collaboration and social networking are fuelling these evolutionary changes. Gartner has specified following characteristic for cloud computing (Gartner, 2011).

- Service based offerings
- Scalable and elastic
- Shared resources for better utilization
- Measured service
- Predominant use of internet and communication technologies

These attributes are in resonance with NIST. With these attributes above Gartner has defined cloud computing as a "style of computing in which scalable and elastic IT-enabled capabilities are provided as a service to consumers using Internet technologies".

We are embarking into an era where devices are being instrumented, interconnected and intelligent to perform tasks in a smarter and efficient way and reshape the way every business operates to make a smarter planet (IBM, 2011b). Internet has started to talk to a large number of devices that we see around us. Smart mobiles, personal digital assistance, gaming consoles, RFID enabled devices, medical devices, vehicles, smart utility grids, household devices like refrigerators, washing machines, home monitoring etc are just to name a few. Figure 1 illustrates this scenario in a pictorial manner. As more and more devices are being connected to internet, explosive data growth will be observed. Experts will agree that

dynamic computing platform like cloud computing is ready for this new epoch as we start to embrace the change.

Cloud computing has its application almost in every industry we can think of. Banking, telecommunications, data mining and warehousing, entertainment, education, energy and utilities and many more public and private sectors are embracing cloud computing. Healthcare industry is among others which can be greatly benefited by this nascent technology (Hossain & Luby, 2010). Mobile computing and wireless sensor networks are also being integrated with cloud network (Dijiang, Xinwen, Myong, & Jim, 2010). More and more technologies will evolve around cloud computing in coming days. We will not be surprised when this happens as this change is inevitable.

Some Clarifications around Cloud Misconceptions

Some confusing definitions of cloud computing has made meaning of cloud computing extremely nebulous. We will try to dispel the misconception here with some myths around cloud (Parekh, 2011; Sridhar, 2009).

Myth 1: Cloud computing should satisfy all the requirements: scalability, pay per use model, on demand, resiliency, multi-tenancy and workload migration.

It may be highly beneficial to satisfy all the requirements of cloud computing. However based on the services offered a cloud computing may fulfill a subset of the requirements and it will still suffice to be called a cloud computing system. For example, a cloud computing environment may be fully dedicated to one organization. It may be a private cloud hosted at a customer's premise or data center or a server managed by another provider. This cloud displays traits like scalability, pay per use model, on demand, resiliency and workload

Figure 1. Numerous devices connected to internet

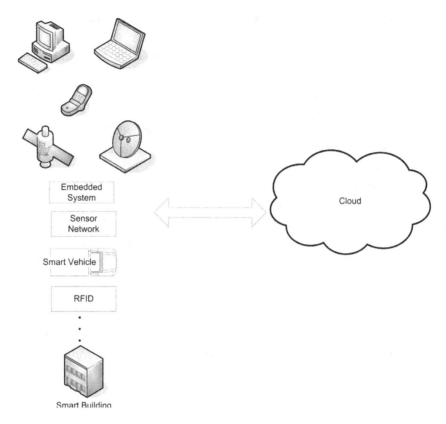

migration. But it does not possess a multi tenancy model. It is still considered a cloud computing environment. Characteristics displayed by cloud computing may differ in varying contexts.

Myth 2: Cloud computing requires virtualization.

Virtualization in a cloud solution can improve IT efficiency and utilization significantly. However it is not a mandatory requirement for a cloud solution. There are some examples of small scale systems or even large scale systems where servers are provisioned directly rather than using virtual machines. For example, Google has claimed that they do not use virtualization for their cloud platform (Procopio, 2011). However this solution may be very expensive. IT decision makers in an organization need to decide which the best option might be for their organization.

Myth 3: Cloud computing requires exposing an organization's data to outside world.

This is not true. With proper design and architecture, an organization can keep their sensitive and confidential information in their on premise data center or private cloud and expose the web front end in the public cloud. With the advancements of firewalls, intrusion detection and prevention systems, an organization can protect their information in a private cloud without exposing it to the outside world. Many companies are just frightened to adopt cloud computing because of their lack of knowledge about cloud computing and misconception of risk of exposing sensitive information.

Myth 4: Cloud computing is only useful if an organization is outsourcing IT facilities to a cloud service provider.

This is not true. Many organization use internal cloud for their in house application. This way computing resource usage by different business units of the organization can be measured and departments can be charged accordingly. A department does not require capacity planning in advance. Demand can scale up or down and the department is charged for what it uses. Internal private cloud can also be used for research and development of innovative solutions. Cloud will be particularly useful during development and testing of prototypes which requires a huge surge in demand of infrastructure capacity. These are some of the examples which demonstrate that a business can reap the benefits of cloud computing without outsourcing to a cloud service provider.

Myth 5: There is only one way to do cloud computing.

This is a misconception around cloud computing. There are many different ways a cloud service can be delivered. SaaS, IaaS and PaaS are cloud services model, just to name a few. Section Cloud Services describes commonly available cloud services offered over internet. Readers are encouraged to look at that section later in the book chapter.

Myth 6: Cloud computing and web hosting are the same.

Perhaps this is the most widespread misconception. A cloud computing platform can be a web site hosting service. On the contrary a web site hosting service may not necessarily be a cloud computing system. Web site hosting or exposing a web service is obviously not cloud computing. A computing system should showcase certain attributes, characteristics, services and deployment

models to call it a cloud. Readers are urged to refer to cloud definition earlier from this chapter.

Myth 7: Everything should be on the cloud.

This is not true. Not all workloads are suitable and ready to run on clouds. Elaboration on this point can be found later in the chapter in "Areas not yet ready for cloud adoption" section.

Emergence of Cloud Computing

Cloud Computing is not a technology revolution, but rather a process and business evolution on how we use those technologies that enables Cloud Computing as it exists today: SaaS, inexpensive storage, REST, AJAX, SOA(service-oriented architectures), On Demand Computing, Grid Computing, Utility computing, virtualization, etc. – Maria Spinola (Spinola, 2009)

Technology advancements in computing systems, internet and innovation in software in the last decades have bolstered cloud computing. The idea of cloud computing dates back to 1961 when Professor John McCarthy publicly suggested that computer time-sharing technology might lead to a platform in future when computing power and even applications could be offered or sold by a utility based business model. It is like selling electricity, water etc. to customers (Rittinghouse & Ransome, 2010). The concept of time sharing was embraced by many and became popular in the late 1960s. However lack of technologies (software, hardware and networking) to support this new computing model made this idea faded away. Since the advent of new millennium (2000) we have seen proliferation of technology advancement in networking, software and hardware and the old concept has been reincarnated. Many experts define that cloud computing is the reincarnation of the time-sharing systems of 1960s and network and grid computing of the 1990s (Kim, Kim,

Lee, & Lee, 2009). As a result cloud computing may be touted as the old wine in a new bottle (Voas & Zhang, 2009). Six phases of computing paradigm shift of the last half century have been presented Jeffrey et al (Voas & Zhang, 2009). In phase 1, many people shared powerful mainframes via a dummy terminal to perform computation. Technology giant IBM was the pioneer in offering mainframe services via time sharing in the 1960s. In phase 2, there was a shift to personal computers (PCs) from mainframes as PCs became power enough to perform most of the tasks that a user needed. Phase 3 has seen a collection of computers connected within a local network to share resources. In phase 4, these local networks were interconnected to create a global network. This heralded the birth of internet. In this phase users utilized this internet to access remote application and resources. In phase 5, grid computing emerged and computer power and storage were shared though distributed computing. Phase 6 has ushered the strength of cloud computing where computing resources can be shared via internet in a flexible, scalable and automated way.

We will conclude this section with an analogy made by Irving Wladawsky-Berger, Chairman Emeritus, IBM Academy of Technology and a visiting Lecturer at MIT. He has compared evolution around cloud computing to the Cambrian explosion which happened more than 500 million years ago (Economist, 2008). During this period rate of evolution speeded up due to cell perfection and standardization among other reasons. Thus evolution to more complex organism took place. Similarly with the maturity, development and advancements of technologies over the last 50 years, the building blocks to make a complex IT system have been standardized. These technologies coupled with the drive to increase IT efficiency are acting as a catalyst for the evolution of cloud computing.

Cloud Services

With the prevalence of Service Oriented Architecture and cloud's modular and reusable approach, many IT offerings can be provided as Service. The term "XaaS" has been coined to mean Anything as a Service (Linthicum, 2009) (Bose, 2008). Technologies have proliferated many facets of our lives. We are in a world where almost anyone can access internet and anything can connect to internet. IT industry has been observing a pattern of repeatable use of hardware and software as services for the last two decades. Popularity of internet, commoditization and standardization of technologies, virtualization and emergence of web services has been the accelerator for this change. Users have been demanding information and applications delivered via internet. This is acting as a catalyst to the rise of XaaS.

An increasing number of services are being offered through cloud or internet. The most commons services from XaaS categories are:

- Software as a Service
- Platform as a Service
- Infrastructure as a Service

Software as a Service (SaaS)

In traditional application distribution model, an application is purchased and then installed on a computing device locally. This model is often known as Software as a Product (SaaP). Here a consumer is burdened with the complexity of installation, management, maintenance, upgrade and licensing cost.

With the maturity of Service Oriented Architecture (SOA), web services and other web technologies, there is a stride towards SaaS model. Also better and faster internet connection has made it possible to access business, academic and scientific applications hosted on data centers as opposed application installed locally on a computer. This is a new application delivery model in which the consumers use an application hosted on a cloud infrastructure over internet. The providers install, manage and maintain the application and provide an interface to access it. Normally the interface to the software is through a thin client interface (e.g. a web browser). Ubiquitous network access is one of the essential characteristics of Cloud Computing. Ideally consumers should be able to run the interface to cloud applications in any type of devices (e.g. netbooks, notebooks, PCs, smart phones, mobiles, gaming consoles, Kiosk etc) with an internet connection and a web browser. Figure 2 illustrates how a magnitude of client devices can retrieve software services from cloud SaaS provider over internet.

The consumer does not manage or control the underlying cloud infrastructure including network, servers, operating systems, storage, or even individual application capabilities, with the possible exception of limited user-specific application configuration settings (NIST, 2010). This cloud computing model is Software as a Service and the provider is known as SaaS providers. There are many SaaS providers in the market. Google, Salesforce.com, IBM etc are few of them. Saleforce.com's offering of Customer Relationship Management (CRM) products as SaaS has been exemplary. Their brilliant idea of application over the internet or cloud has reshaped and revamped the software delivery model. This has also turned their organization into a billion dollar company (Benioff & Adler, 2009).

SaaS model alleviates the headache of software applications, ongoing maintenance, patches, performance monitoring and upgrades for an enterprise. SaaS providers are often equipped with large data centers and leverage these large economies of scale for their applications offerings. A provider typically provides a service to multiple consumers. Google web based email Gmail is one example of SaaS. LotusLive online collaborations suite by technology giant IBM is another example (IBM, 2011a).

"Pay as you go" model exists for the pricing of SaaS like any other services of cloud computing. Users are charged based on per-use or subscription for a given bandwidth and storage. There is no upfront cost from the providers. It is a measured service. However terms and conditions may vary from one provider to another.

Platform as a Service (PaaS)

In this model consumers use a hosting environment provided by providers. Providers deliver not only infrastructure but also middlewares (databases, messaging engines etc) and solution stack for application build, development and deploy. This capability allows the consumers to deploy consumer-created or applications created using programming languages, tools (e.g. middlewares) and runtime environments supported by providers (NIST, 2010). In few words we can refer this model as an application framework. The consumer has control over the application deployed and its configurations but the consumer does not control the underlying layer (operating system, hardware, storage and network) on which the application is running. PaaS platform will assure the scalability and elasticity of an application created using PaaS provider's application framework. This process happens transparently to the consumer. Examples of PaaS are Google App Engine, IBM WebSphere Cloudburst service, Force.com from Saleforce.com etc. Programming languages which have gained popularity in cloud domain are Java, PHP, Python, Ruby, Perl and some others which support platform independence. C/C++ and.Net applications have also become popular in Microsoft Azure platform (Jennings, 2009). Figure 3 depicts this delivery model. Clients leverage this service through internet.

Figure 2. Software as a service

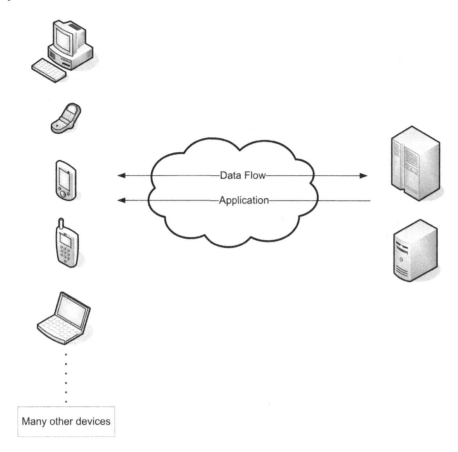

Many other devices

Infrastructure as a Service (IaaS)

IaaS means the delivery of computing infrastructure as a service. The consumer rent data center space, processing power, storage, networking and other required computing resources as a fully outsourced service instead of purchasing and installing these in their own data center. Components for IaaS include, but are not limited to, the following (Rittinghouse & Ransome, 2010)

- Servers
- Communication network (including routers, switches, firewalls, load balancer etc.)
- High Speed internet connectivity (often on OC 192 backbones)
- Platform virtualization environment

- Service-level agreements
- Utility computing billing

In Figure 4 we can see how customers using many client devices can access infrastructure in a cloud over internet. The consumer is charged for the resources used. In this model the consumer is provided with required raw computing resources on which the consumer can deploy and run own software including operating systems, middleware and applications (NIST, 2010). The consumer has control over operating systems, storage, deployed applications and in some cases limited access to networking components like firewall and load balancer. However, the consumer has no access to underlying cloud infrastructure. Amazon EC2 is one example of IaaS.

Figure 3. Platform as a service

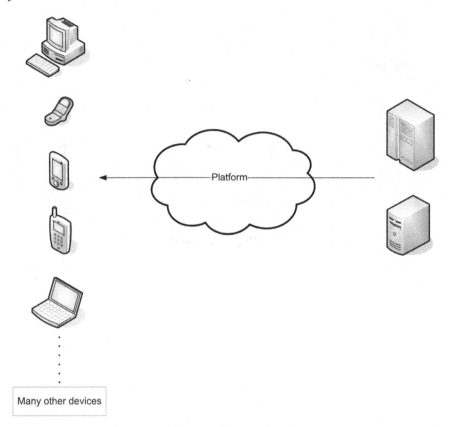

There is soaring interests for other cloud based services in IT industry. These services are some variations and add-ons to SaaS, PaaS and IaaS. The other common place examples are:

Communication as a Service (CaaS)

This is a model of providing communication technologies as cloud based solution to the consumer (Rittinghouse & Ransome, 2010). The provider manages the hardware and software for communication services like Voice over IP (VoIP), video conferencing and Instant Messaging (IM). The provider is also responsible for maintaining a minimum Quality of Service (QoS) under a service level agreement (SLA). Similar to other services consumers are billed according to their usage. Analyst Firm Gartner defined CaaS as IP

telephony located within a third-party data center and also managed and owned by a third party. This service can be provided to multiple customers in a multi-tenancy model (Gartner, 2007). According to this article, CaaS market is projected to total $2.3 billion in 2011 which means a compound annual growth rate (CAGR) at more than 105% for the period.

Storage as a Service (STaaS)

This is a delivery model by which any storage resources can be accessible to an application for use by a consumer. The application does now have any knowledge of the actual location of storage. It is also indiscernible to the user. An application uses the storage as if it were a local storage. High speed internet connection and cut-

Figure 4. Infrastructure as a service

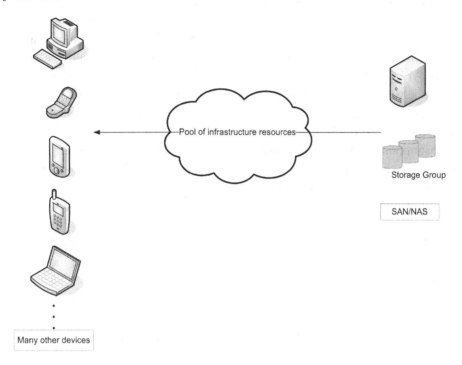

ting edge networking equipments and interfaces have made the obstacles to access a long distance storage slither away. Local jurisdiction, rules and regulation may impose a restriction on storing sensitive and classified information outside a geographical area. However it is possible to offer customers Storage as a Service which will meet a customer's requirement to keep data in a particular geographical area.

Security and Data Protection as a Service (SDPaaS)

This is the delivery model by which a set of tools delivered via internet to the customer by the provider for security management. SDPaaS may include, but are not limited to, the following (SearchSecurity.com, 2011):

- Anti-virus, anti-spyware and anti-spam tools offered over internet and ongoing support and maintenance provided by the

provider. The consumers will not be responsible for updating and downloading security patch, virus definition like they do for software installed on their PC or laptops.
- Identity management software
- Administrative tasks performed by a outsourced company, e.g. monitoring servers logs
- Services for email filtering, web content filtering and vulnerability management (Mather, Kumaraswamy, & Latif, 2009)
- Offering a web console to the consumer to gain an overview of security of the environments and other security related activities.

Providers in this regime are Ping Identity (Corporation, 2011), McAfee, Kapersky Labs, Panda Software, Symantec, Trend Micro, Cisco and VeriSign. Big Blue offers IBM Vulnerability Management Service in this space (IBM, 2009c).

Information as a Service (INFaaS)

This means offering useful information to the customer over internet by means of a web service or an agreed API. Examples of Information as a Service include weather information, stock exchange information, online credit check etc. Providers in this space offer the information to the customer on subscription basis or free of charge. As providers are using cloud based solution, their service dynamically scale up or down according to demand.

Database as a Service (DaaS)

This is a delivery model by which any database independent of geographical location can be accessible to an application for use by a consumer. The customer gets the illusion of a local database. DaaS is highly flexible, scalable and offers high availability. There is not yet an open standard in this space in the market. Different providers offer different flavors of their databases and different access mechanism, e.g. API, web services etc. Some DaaS products are Amazon SimpleDB, Microsoft's SSDS etc.

Process as a Service (PRaaS)

This is a delivery model by which some business functions are exposed as services to the customer. This is an interesting area as customers are often interested in certain processes and also integration of different independent processes together similar to Service Oriented Architecture (SOA). PRaaS is hosted on cloud to provide high scalability. We have been seen the trend of Business Process Outsourcing (BPO) for last few decades. IT companies often send the backend tasks to some providers to save money. PRaaS has combined this BPO and cloud computing together to achieve this goal. With PRaaS customers can accelerate their move towards BPO for specialized process oriented tasks and focus more on their front of-

fice tasks (Wainewright, 2009). Customers will have better agility in solving business problems with readily available process as a service. On the other hand, a company with specialized skill in developing complex business process can be a PRaaS provider by offering their solution to the consumers and be financially very profitable. The provider can leverage the large economies of scale of its cloud computing solution. Appian is an example of PRaaS provider (Appian, 2011).

Integration as a Service (INaaS)

This service offers an integration framework over the internet to enable integration of systems and enterprise applications. In essence this is similar to Enterprise Application Integration (EAI) but delivered as a service (Linthicum, 2009). Integration as a Service can provide support for routing, mediation, transformation, business event handling and other required integration services directly from the cloud. Amazon SQS is an example of Integration as a Service product.

Mobility as a Service (MaaS)

This is a nascent but very promising technology and service being offered through cloud. This service provides ubiquitous access and connectivity to enterprise data and applications from any device and any place (Winthrop, 2011). MaaS simplifies all aspects deploying, managing, supporting, connecting and protecting data and thus helps mobile workers within the enterprise (MaaS360, 2011).

THE NEED FOR CLOUD COMPUTING

There are miscellaneous articles and literatures explaining the benefits of cloud computing. According to Economist (Economist, 2008)

The rise of the cloud is more than just another platform shift that gets geeks excited. It will un-

doubtedly transform the information technology (IT) industry, but it will also profoundly change the way people work and companies operate. It will allow digital technology to penetrate every nook and cranny of the economy and of society, creating some tricky political problems along the way.

Benefits of cloud computing coupled with market demand and trend can bring upon a colossal of promises to IT industry. Let's look at some of the business and operational benefits.

Agility

An organization can be greatly benefited from the faster deployment of infrastructure and applications when using cloud based solution. Automated provisioning in a consolidated and virtualized environment enables an organization to realize increased IT agility to meet challenging and changing business requirements. In traditional model, when the business decision makers want to increase capacity by expanding their infrastructure, there is a long waiting or lead time. This non-standard and non-automated process is error prone and associated with costly delay where skilled resources wait for infrastructure to become available. This process distracts skilled resources from productive works to accelerate new projects and confines them to mundane manual administration of IT systems. Often an organization needs to wait for weeks or months for purchasing, configuring and installing hardware. With cloud computing model, an organization can use on-demand computing from different providers or in house cloud data center and set up the required software and hardware environment in a matter of hours or days. This model of provisioning frees skilled resources that can be leveraged over many productive and innovative business developments. This enhanced delivery model enables better customer retention, growth of business (horizontal market expansion) and faster time to market. Deployment speed of resources

offered by cloud computing is very hard to match in conventional IT systems. Furthermore, cloud computing can be used as a test bed to develop and test application prototype. This gives an organization a competitive advantage to invent a product with low cost and less spending and makes the organization more responsive to growing business needs. Thus cloud computing also drives innovation and helps an organization keep pace with market trends and demands.

Reduced Capital Expenditure

Companies often struggle or do not have the budget to build their own data centers or expand their existing IT infrastructure to grow their business. Even if they have bought new infrastructures, new resources may be under utilized and may not deliver return on investment. If companies could purchase or rent just only the required amount of processing power and dynamically increase or decrease the amount of resources to rent, this problem would be solved. Cloud provides dynamic, resilient and cost-effective IT systems than previous generations of technologies allowed. Companies now can simply rent computing and networking resources from a cloud vendor to accomplish their tasks and avoid huge up front cost. The consumers pay for what they have used and pay on a month basis. Thus the capital expenses (CapEx) can be consolidated into ongoing operational expenses (OpEx) and other investment to grow their business.

Low Ongoing Cost

Cloud computing can dramatically reduce ongoing cost of infrastructure management for an organization. Research shows that power and cooling cost have skyrocketed by 800% since 1996. However data center resources have utilization as low as 5% (IBM, 2009a). Furthermore administrative staffs are needed to maintain a data center for an organization. According to Clabby Analytics

(Analytics, 2008), IT labor costs alone constitute 70% of IT operating budget. With cloud computing an organization can forget the headache of maintaining the infrastructure and rent the resources as they need. Also as cloud computing requires less human intervention through its autonomic nature, it reduces the time required for requisition and provision of IT resources. Thus an organization can free their staffs for innovation and new business development. Cloud computing can bolster IT asset utilization through virtualization, workload management and consolidation of multiple physical servers into less physical server. Server consolidation reduces IT infrastructure costs and increase operational efficiency by reducing under utilized servers. Large scale of economies from massive data centers can save customers an enormous amount of on-going cost (See Table 2). Following table has been adapted from (Hamilton, 2008) and (Armbrust, et al., 2009). It illustrates what economies of scale can offer.

Another important point to notice is that as fewer servers are required in a cloud computing environment through server consolidation and virtualization, physical server depreciation cost will be reduced. Of course fewer servers also mean less energy consumption and less floor space in a data center. System administration cost is significantly reduced due to efficiency gain in system administration with advanced service management software. An administrator can maintain and manage more system by leveraging the management tool which was not previously possible with manual system administration. It is interesting to see how cost savings is achieved through automated provision. A cloud solution comes with a self service portal and a service catalogue of deployable system images. A requestor (e.g. a developer/tester) can request for an image from the catalogue and specifies the start date, period of time the image will be required and other relevant information (e.g. if image is required for development, test or system integration). An automated workflow management is integrated with self service portal which forwards the request to an approver. This whole automation expedites the process which is free from human error and environments may be ready in minutes as opposed to weeks or months. In a traditional IT delivery model, when an environment used for development or testing or any other purpose is not required any more, it often remain unused or under utilized for no good reason. This is known as "Limbo" state. As none has clear visibility because of too many manual processes, this trend adds operational cost. Cloud's automation can thus reduce operational cost by de-provisioning or returning unused resources to resource pool.

A study by IBM shows that in a non-cloud environment 30% of all defects are caused by wrongly configured test environments (IBM, 2009b). While 30% to 50% of all servers in traditional IT infrastructure are dedicated to test, it provides little real business value because of poor utilization of the resources. Cloud computing improves quality by reducing defects due to poor modeling and faulty configuration as much as 15 to 30%. This results in a huge cost savings. Cloud computing reduces capital and licensing costs as much as 50 to 75% using virtualization (IBM, 2011c). Operating and labor costs are reduced by a substantial 30 to 50% through automatic provisioning and configuration of development and test environment.

Scalability and Economies of Scale

In traditional IT delivery model an organization needs to forecast growing demand and perform a rigorous processing and storage capacity planning. It will be immensely difficult to make an accurate estimate in today's complex IT environment and when data produced is exponentially growing. Subsequently over estimation or under estimation often occurs. This results in under utilizations of resources and dissatisfied customers respectively. We are currently experiencing growth of information from a myriad of data sources, mobile

Table 2. Economies of scale in 2006 for medium-sized datacenter (1000 servers) vs. very large datacenter (50,000 servers)

Technology	Cost in medium-sized data center	Cost in very large data center	Improvement ratio in large data center
Network	$95 per Mbit/sec/month	$13 per Mbit/sec/month	7.1
Storage	$2.20 per GByte/month	$0.40 per Gbyte/month	5.7
Administration	~ 140 servers/Administrator	>1000 servers/Administartor	7.1

devices, unified communications, RFID systems, Web 2.0 and mashups. World global IP traffic will exceed half a zettabyte by 2013 (Cisco, 2008). We will soon see an example which will justify how a cloud computing environment is superior to conventional data center in terms of growth. The agility and scalability of cloud computing comes from the massive data center that cloud providers have built. With this juggernaut of resources and scalability an organization can forget the solicitude of capacity planning and take advantage of autonomic provisioning of IT resources as demand increases.

Let's look at the success stories of Animoto, a Facebook application provider. Animoto converts the music and images that a customer uploads to this application to a web-based video slide show. This application became immediately popular when it was launched in March 2008. More and more people started to use it and share it. It experienced its peak demand in mid April 2008 and 250,000 people signed up in three days. Animoto scaled up from 50 servers to 3500 servers using Amazon AWS in three days to handle this load (Armbrust, et al., 2009). After the peak subsided Animoto was able to release the servers without much effort. This dynamic provisioning and de-provisioning helped them provide service to the growing customer base and cope up with the unpredictable nature of data traffic and workload.

Sustainability

In today's world an organization has to try hard to sustain the growth of the business and retain customers. This organization has to understand market and social trends and come to the market with innovative products. IT has been an inseparable part of any business to drive business process improvement and innovation. In a traditional IT model an organization has to be very careful in their service delivery as there are many points of failure in current IT systems. Furthermore, CIOs are struggling to manage their IT environments as old data centers are environmentally and economically unsustainable due to less efficiency, poor design and asset utilization. As cloud service providers have invested an immense amount of money, planning and knowledge into designing resilient cloud architecture, an organization will be better off transferring the responsibility of running IT resources to cloud providers. There will be limited points of failures which will be the responsibility of the cloud provider. The time and resources thus the organization saved can be invested into other productive and business critical areas rather than just performing mundane infrastructure administration.

Skilled Vendors in Market

Nurturing of Cloud Computing is being done by all the big brands in the industries who are putting forward their efforts and experience of many years into cloud development. Some of these vendors are also members of cloud computing bodies who are working on solicitation of cloud standards along with the customers. No other technologies have taken IT industry by such a storm that cloud computing did. This disruptive technology has got academia, industry and every tech-savvy person very excited. Technology giants involved in cloud development from the beginning. They have successfully demonstrated their products in solving business problems. This has earned the trust of customers. Not all workloads are suitable to be moved to the cloud. Skilled vendors can perform an assessment of a customer's current situation and advise if cloud computing should be adopted. Organizations can rely on the skilled cloud provider with peace of mind.

Reliability

Improved reliability is offered in cloud computing environments. An organization has less to worry about data recovery, redundancy and backup as because service providers utilize multiple redundant sites. With this built in reliability an organization can trust the cloud providers to seamlessly provide service.

Improved Efficiency

IT industry has always contemplated better energy usage in order to reduce energy costs and green house gas emissions. Cloud computing has made this dream come true by improving utilization of data centers resources efficiently. In traditional IT model, a server utilization ranges from 5% to 20% (Armbrust, et al., 2009). Energy consumption can be attributed to CPU utilization, storage devices, memory and networking equipments. It is shocking that a server which is idle may still use up to 60% of it's peak power (Berl, et al., 2009). Most traditional data centers also spent most of the data center power on cooling (between 60% and 70%) (Berl, et al., 2009). However in some reports power spent on cooling has been defined as 50%. Irrespective of this value, a savings of 20% can be achieved by increasing energy efficiency in server and network energy consumption and an organization should rather spend money saved this way on some productive areas. According to

a technical paper by Big Blue, cloud computing can save 80% on floor space and 60% on power, while tripling asset utilization (IBM, 2009a). Large-scale cloud providers efficiently use each server to achieve highest utilization rate possible without impacting response time. Cloud providers have moved to a "many applications on a single server model" as opposed to "an application per server" model. With virtualization technologies many applications can be run on multiple virtual machines without impacting performance but it increases the server utilization significantly. A typical on-premise application may run only at 5 to 10% average utilization. This same application when hosted in cloud can achieve 40 to 70% utilization (Accenture, 2010; Grid, 2008). According to the report by Accenture (Accenture, 2010) cloud computing can reduce carbon emission by 30 to 90% for major business applications.

Forcing Standardization

At the same time organizations have started to realize the business benefits of cloud computing, they have discovered the fact that open standards should emerge in cloud space. In absence of open standards, an organization can not easily move their workloads or services from one cloud to another or integrate the solutions from multiple cloud providers. User of proprietary solutions will result in vendor lock-in. Industries have already realized this and this realization and needs have been driving the cloud providers to work on open standards and interoperability. Many advocacy groups have been formed. A notable advocacy group named Cloud Standards Customer Council (Council, 2011) by Object Management Group (OMG) has been newly formed. This nascent group currently formed by more than 45 leading organizations worldwide will work on cloud adoption, standards, interoperability and security. Other initiatives for cloud standardization include DMTF Open Cloud Standards Incubator and Open Cloud Manifesto.

As cloud connects heterogeneous systems and uses a modular approach, open standards will emerge rapidly in industry.

High Performance Computing

High performance computing (HPC) and parallel computing will find its home in a cloud platform. Cloud's flexible, scalable and dynamic platform can be used for solving critical problems that require faster processing nodes. Let us assume that one task can be completed in a computer with certain configuration in five hours. Processing of task can be carried out in parallel. If a user can run the task in a cloud with five computing instances of equivalent configuration, it will be finished in just an hour.

CHALLENGES TO ADOPT CLOUD COMPUTING

With benefits and advantages of any technology, there are some disadvantages and challenges as well. The same applies to cloud computing. These challenges can be market inhibitors for cloud computing. In this section we will look at some of the challenges that this nascent technology is facing.

Security

With proliferation of Service Oriented Architecture (SOA), Web 2.0, Unified Communication, online collaboration, real time data streams and wireless and mobile computing traffic pattern on the internet has changed. A single request from an application may hit multiple servers and databases and get involved in multiple sessions before a response is sent back to the client. This traffic pattern imposes some security risks. If not properly designed a cloud data may be susceptible to security risks. Hackers try to break into any computer system and cloud system will not be an exception (Kim, et al., 2009). Leading cloud providers in the market have the ability to take care of security services like access control, firewall, activity monitoring etc. Still security concern is considered as the biggest challenges to adopt cloud computing. As such many organizations do not feel comfortable about hosting their confidential and sensitive information on the cloud. Multi-tenancy model of cloud computing further adds to the fear of the customers. Although cloud providers offer logical separation of resources in a multi-tenancy model, some customers have very low confidence in sharing the same infrastructures with others. Shared infrastructure increases the risk of unauthorized access.

Immaturity

Cloud is a new technology. It is quickly evolving around some pre-existing and new cutting edge infrastructure and smart software components. Many organizations are scared to move their workload into cloud until the technology has matured and successfully been demonstrated in solving many business problems.

Network Performance

Communication network and high speed internet is vein and artery of a cloud computing system. It is the network which connects users and all components of cloud together. In many places of world there is lack of high speed internet which will limit the adoption of cloud computing. Cloud data may be spread at different geographically distributed areas around the globe. Low internet speed will be a bottleneck in system performance and ultimately make cloud computing unusable.

Interoperability and Portability

Lack of open standards is curbing the adoption of cloud. If two heterogeneous cloud systems can not talk to each other, there is a high risk of integrating two systems. Without industry standards solution from one cloud provider may not be integrated to that of another provider. Many providers use proprietary hardware and software. Use of these technologies will result in vendor lock-in. For example, applications hosted on one cloud infrastructure may not be ported to another cloud infrastructure because of non-standard and different Application Programming Interface (API). Furthermore many organizations have legacy systems and applications which they do not want to throw away. They would rather want to enhance their IT infrastructure by purchasing or rent additional resources and then integrate with legacy systems. With lack of interoperability this integration will never be realized.

Legislative and Regulatory Issues

Legislative and regulatory issues may prohibit adoption of cloud computing. Government organizations may not allow sharing infrastructure with other organizations or host data outside a country's boundary.

We have challenges to overcome to adopt cloud computing as we have with any new technologies. As technologies, standards and maturity revolving cloud computing enhance, it will not be long when it will be a more common practice in IT industry to have cloud based solution as a standard. There are already some areas which are ready to adopt cloud computing. However, there are some areas which is not yet ready because of maturity of cloud technologies and business and operation model of certain businesses. The following two sections cover both ready and unready scenarios. It may be noted that strict regulations and laws in a certain geographic area can always restrict the use of public cloud to protect sensitive information of citizens. This has been described in "Areas not yet ready for cloud adoption" section.

AREAS READY FOR CLOUD ADOPTION

Some areas in businesses are better suited and almost ready for cloud computing, while some are not until rigorous assessments are done by an organization.

Following areas are readily available to adopt cloud computing:

Application Development and Testing

Development and testing will be greatly benefited from cloud computing. Small and medium size businesses (SMB) and Independent Software Vendors (ISV) do not need to invest upfront on expensive data center infrastructure for development and test environment. Establishing a data center is often lengthy process and it can take up to weeks or months. Cloud computing can make the daunting task of setting up infrastructures easier; alleviate the need to have own infrastructure and offers on-demand provision of virtual and physical resources. Development and test environments can be set up in a matter of hours or days. Organization can be benefited with very quick time to market their products and offerings and a quicker return on investment.

Some advantages are:

- Virtualized development and testing environments are highly scalable
- Production equivalent development and test environments can set up with less manual steps
- Automated provisioning and configuration enables to meet challenging development and testing cycle times, reduce IT labor costs and configuration errors, streamline the environment and improve solution quality

Big Blue's Smart Development and Test Cloud is one of the most prominent tools in the market(IBM, 2010).

Online Collaboration and Networking Application

Cloud computing has already sparked huge interest and change in online collaboration and networking applications. Social networking sites like Facebook, Twitter etc are already using cloud infrastructures. Popular web based email Gmail is based on cloud computing. Organizations will be benefited by switching their emails and messaging applications to cloud. Web 2.0 based internal web sites, Project WiKi, collaborating web applications, online chat and video conferencing can leverage the tremendous scalability and flexibility feature of cloud computing and reap the benefit.

Backup and Disaster Recovery

In traditional computing model, organizations need a big capital investment for backup and disaster recovery. Cloud computing has come to rescue by offering a dynamic and on-demand model for backup and recovery. It will be appropriate for startup and small and medium size businesses that do not have huge capital to invest but can readily take advantage of cloud storage from different providers. However as cloud security management is still maturing, organizations may not be very keen to store their sensitive information in another provider's data center.

Cloud Desktop and Other Productivity Applications

Organizations provide employees with workstations. In current conventional model, a system administration or IT support person has to configure and install operating systems and other applications on every single PC. An organization also needs to pay for licensing fee for operating systems and other applications. Moreover the employee or IT support person is required to perform upgrade, install security patches and maintenance. The whole process is very costly and daunting. Many organizations have recently started to move towards desktop cloud or desktop in the cloud. It is based on centralized and virtualized desktop architectures. From a catalogue of virtual images, the right desktop image can immediately or in a matter of few minutes be made available to the employee. The employee accesses the desktop through a web browser. Virtual images are preconfigured with required software. Another added advantage of this cloud desktop is that it does not require a high end PC to access the desktop. All that needs is a browser. Employees can even access the desktop from any thin or thick client. Similarly, students in academic institutes can also use desktop cloud in laboratories, classes and libraries.

Besides cloud desktop, productivity applications like e-learning, calendar etc can also be moved to cloud. Academic institutes can be benefited by hosting their leaning management system on cloud.

Enterprise and Web Applications

Interaction-intensive Web 2.0 applications, mashups and data-intensive applications like analytics, mining and business intelligence are suitable candidates for cloud deployments (Maximilien, et al., 2009).

Businesses can run applications like customer relationship management (CRM), accounting, HR, management tools and business analytics on the cloud. Many organizations have already moved these applications onto cloud and getting good return on investment. Cloud solution is faster to setup, requires less management and administration by the organization and saves a signification amount of money and licensing cost. Websites for conferences or events (e.g. sporting event, father's day etc), promotional and seasonal (e.g.

websites operational during holiday) websites and also websites that are operational during day and inactive at night are perfect examples of applications that may run on the cloud (Varia, 2008).

Batch Processing

Cloud computing is very well suited to be used in processing pipelines and batch processing (Varia, 2008). Cloud processing power can be used to convert documents from one format to another. For examples, millions of Microsoft word documents can be easily converted to PDF, millions of images or documents can be converted into raw searchable text using optical character recognition (OCR). Image processing can be performed with cloud. Examples may be resizing millions of images. Cloud compute power can also be used for video processing (e.g. transcoding from one format to another), creating an index of web crawl data and data mining. Some other batch processing examples are (Varia, 2008)

- Generate and analyze daily/weekly/monthly report
- Perform nightly automated builds of source code in parallel and thus save a lot of productive hours
- Perform nightly automated Unit Testing and Deployment Testing of different configurations

AREAS NOT YET READY FOR CLOUD ADOPTION

Following are some of the cases when an organization should not adopt cloud computing:

1. Public Cloud may not be suitable when there is a high concern for handling of highly sensitive health data. This data is covered by Health Insurance Portability and Accounting Act (HIPAA). Multi-tenancy model of cloud computing will not be suitable for storing health data from several organizations. Strict rules and regulations have already been set by several organizations to restrict storage of their sensitive data outside their corporate data centers. However these data centers may be based on premise or off premise and managed by the corporations themselves or a third party. In general, when data is regulated by some acts, e.g. HIPAA, Sarbanes-Oxley, an organization should not store data on a public cloud (Velte, Velte, & Elsenpeter, 2010).

2. Cloud computing has a dynamic infrastructure and data can stored in any geographical location. When there is a geopolitical concern and compliance issue, public cloud should not be used.

3. Applications which are tightly bound to a particular type of hardware, chips or drivers are not a good candidate for cloud computing. Generally applications which need to access low level hardware resources and also depend on specific type of resources, will not work in cloud computing infrastructure.

4. A cloud provider normally provides particular services like SaaS, PaaS or IaaS or others. Underlying infrastructure is abstracted from the consumer. If a consumer needs detailed control of cloud infrastructure, a public cloud may not be suitable. In this case the consumer should go private cloud.

5. Application integration can often impose a challenge in adopting cloud computing. If resources hosted on existing infrastructure and cloud infrastructure are dependent on each other but can not run in sync, there may be a serious problem.

6. Sometimes it is not possible to abandon existing legacy applications and equivalent cloud applications do not exist. In this scenario an organization can not switch to cloud. In some cases an application is also not ready

to be moved to cloud. It has been discussed in point 2 above.

7. Cloud computing requires high speed internet backbone. Customers are connected to the cloud data center through internet. Cloud computing has a very complex architecture and distributed servers are connected by layers of networking equipments, communication links etc. Although it is imperceptible to the customer, data can be stored in one location and processing power can be provided from another location which is hundreds of miles away. With the advent of high speed internet, it does not matter where different components are located. However, in absence of a high speed internet connection, there will be latency issue and it will impact business transactions. Also there may be situations when a large amount of data needs to moved from one location to another. This process will take some time even with the fastest internet connection. Cloud computing should not be used when latency is an issue. Cloud is not always suitable for mission critical real time application.

FUTURE RESEARCH DIRECTIONS

Cloud computing has entered into its early teenage years from a toddler. Over the years we have seen developments and maturity in cloud technologies including security and standardization. This gradual development needs to continue for coming years as more and more industries are adopting cloud computing. Both industries and academia need to nurture cloud computing in its teenage years. While this chapter provides the basic of cloud computing, readers are also urged to keep abreast of current developments in clouds by reading industry and academic technical papers on a regular basis. This technology is rapidly evolving. New technologies are coming to markets and new terms are often being coined. In future all these new terminologies along with existing ones will be covered in a book chapter like this.

CONCLUSION

Cloud computing is the culmination of decades of research in distributed computing, utility computing, virtualization, communications networks and efficient software. These technologies have evolved in the last 50 years. We have now reached an era where most of these technologies have been standardized and these are driving the evolution of more complex systems at a faster rate. Cloud computing is rapidly intercepting IT industry and emerging as a disrupting technology. It represents a new tipping point in transforming IT industry. With the global presence of internet, cloud computing has contributed to the globalization of IT resources. As a result cloud computing is very complex in nature. In this chapter terms and terminologies associated with cloud computing were presented. The materials covered here will hopefully dispel the misconception and misnomer around cloud computing. Business benefits, market inhibitors to adopt cloud, workload readiness, cloud services delivery and deployment model have also been discussed. Cloud is a promising paradigm shift in IT industry which promises to increase dynamicity, business agility and innovation. IT business decision makers will be relieved from their burdened IT infrastructure suffering from growing operational cost, decreasing IT efficiency and utilization by making a successful move to cloud platform. It can bestow upon an organization a quick Return on Investment (ROI) by reducing total cost of ownership (TCO) and payback from productivity improvements, hardware, software, automation and many other useful byproducts. Reduction in costs and energy budget is achieved without sacrificing Service Level Agreement. Thus cloud computing is much more than cheaper computing.

An organization need to assess their readiness before adopting cloud computing. Workload, portability, interoperability, security, performance and disaster recovery are some of the areas that an organization should be aware of (Russell, 2010). There is still some concerns as this technology is still maturing. Cloud computing models and architectures will evolve and mature in the next few years. All these hinge upon joint collaboration among industries, standard bodies and academia. Cloud computing has tremendous potential. Not only cloud computing will bring upon innovative technological solutions and applications, it will also offer a green IT solution by means of higher server utilization and reduced carbon foot print.

REFERENCES

Accenture. (2010). *Cloud computing and sustainability: The environmental benefits of moving to the cloud.* Retrieved from http://www.microsoft.com/click/services/Redirect2.ashx?CR_EAC=300012377

Appian. (2011). *BPM is the cloud.* Retrieved February 27, 2011, from http://www.appian.com/bpm-software/cloudbpm.jsp

Armbrust, M., Fox, A., Griffith, R., Joseph, A. D., Katz, R. H., & Konwinski, A. (2009). *Above the clouds: A Berkeley view of cloud computing (No. UCB/EECS-2009-28).* Berkeley: EECS Department, University of California.

Benioff, M. R., & Adler, C. (2009). *Behind the cloud: the untold story of how Salesforce.com went from idea to billion-dollar company--And revolutionized an industry* (1st ed.). San Francisco, CA: Jossey-Bass.

Berl, A., Gelenbe, E., Di Girolamo, M., Giuliani, G., De Meer, H., & Dang, M. Q. (2009). Energy-efficient cloud computing. *The Computer Journal, 53*(7), 1045–1051. doi:10.1093/comjnl/bxp080

Bose, S. (2008). *Gathering clouds of XaaS!* Retrieved March 26, 2011, from https://www.ibm.com/developerworks/mydeveloperworks/blogs/sbose/entry/gathering_clouds_of_xaas?lang=en

Carr, N. G. (2008). *The big switch: Rewiring the world, from Edison to Google* (1st ed.). New York, NY: W. W. Norton & Co.

Cisco. (2008). *Approaching the zettabyte era: Visual networking index - Cisco Systems.* Retrieved February 26, 2010, from http://www.cisco.com/en/US/solutions/collateral/ns341/ns525/ns537/ns705/ns827/white_paper_c11-481374_ns827_Networking_Solutions_White_Paper.html

Clabby Analytics. (2008). *The data center 'implosion explosion'.* Retrieved from http://www-03.ibm.com/press/us/en/attachment/23540.wss?fileId=ATTACH_FILE4&fileName=Clabby%20Analytics%20Implosion%20Explosion.pdf

Clouds Standard Customer Council. (2011). *Website.* Retrieved from http://www.cloud-council.org/

Dijiang, H., Xinwen, Z., Myong, K., & Jim, L. (2010, 4-5 June 2010). *MobiCloud: Building secure cloud framework for mobile computing and communication.* Paper presented at the 2010 Fifth IEEE International Symposium on Service Oriented System Engineering (SOSE).

Economist. (2008). *Let is rise.* Retrieved January 10, 2011, from http://www.economist.com/node/12411882?story_id=12411882

Gartner. (2007). *Gartner forecasts worldwide communications-as-a-service revenue to total $252 million in 2007.* Retrieved March 1, 2011, from http://www.gartner.com/it/page.jsp?id=518407

Gartner. (2010). *Key issues for cloud computing*

Gartner. (2011). *Cloud computing.* Retrieved January 1, 2011, from www.gartner.com/technology/initiatives/cloud-computing.jsp.

Hamilton, J. (2008). *Internet-scale service efficiency.* Paper presented at the Large-Scale Distributed Systems and Middleware (LADIS) Workshop.

Hossain, S., & Luby, D. (2010). *Cloud computing in healthcare Industry.* Paper presented at the Annual International Conference on Cloud Computing and Virtualization, Singapore.

IBM. (2009a). The benfits of cloud computing Retrieved Feb 1, 2011, from http://www-304.ibm.com/businesscenter/cpe/download0/202011/cloud_benefitsofcloudcomputing.pdf

IBM. (2009b). *Cloud computing: Save time, money, and resources with a private test cloud.* Retrieved from http://www.redbooks.ibm.com/redpapers/pdfs/redp4553.pdf

IBM. (2009c). *IBM point of view: Security and cloud computing.*

IBM. (2010). *IBM smart business development and test cloud.* Retrieved Jan 12, 2011, from http://www-935.ibm.com/services/au/gts/pdf/IBM_Smart_Business_Dev_Test_Cloud.pdf

IBM. (2011a). *Cloud computing and IBM LotusLive.* Retrieved January 10, 2011, from https://www.lotuslive.com/styles/tours/cloud_computing_datasheet.pdf

IBM. (2011b). *IBM smarter planet.* Retrieved Jun 7, 2010, from http://www.ibm.com/smarterplanet/us/en/

IBM. (2011c). *Smart business development and test cloud.* Retrieved Jan 15, 2011, from http://www-935.ibm.com/services/us/en/it-services/smart-business-development-and-test-cloud.html

Jennings, R. J. (2009). *Cloud computing with the Microsoft Azure services platform* (1st ed.). Indianapolis, IN: Wiley Pub., Inc.

Kim, W., Kim, S. D., Lee, E., & Lee, S. (2009). Adoption issues for cloud computing. *The Proceedings of the 11th International Conference on Information Integration and Web-based Applications & Services.*

Linthicum, D. (2009). *Defining the cloud computing framework.* Retrieved March 22, 2011, from http://cloudcomputing.sys-con.com/node/811519

MaaS360. (2011). *Mobility-as-a-service.* Retrieved March 30, 2011, from http://www.maas360.com/fiberlink/en-US/mobilityAsAService/

Mall, P., & Grance, T. (2009). Effectively and securely using the cloud computing paradigm. Retrieved January 31, 2011, from http://csrc.nist.gov/groups/SNS/cloud-computing/cloud-computing-v26.ppt

Mather, T., Kumaraswamy, S., & Latif, S. (2009). *Cloud security and privacy* (1st ed.). Beijing, China: O'Reilly.

Maximilien, E. M., Ranabahu, A., Engehausen, R., & Anderson, L. C. (2009). *Toward cloud-agnostic middlewares.* Paper presented at the 24th ACM SIGPLAN Conference Companion on Object Oriented Programming Systems Languages and Applications.

NIST. (2010). *NIST definition of cloud computing v15.* Retrieved May 1, 2011, from http://csrc.nist.gov/groups/SNS/cloud-computing/

Parekh, H. (2011). *Defining what the cloud is not – Myths and misnomers.* Retrieved Jan 15, 2011, from http://hareshparekh.ulitzer.com/node/1772591

Ping Identity Corporation. (2011). *Website.* Retrieved March 2, 2011, from http://www.pingidentity.com/

Procopio, M. (2011). *Cloud computing does not require virtualization.* Retrieved August 8, 2011, from http://www.enterprisecioforum.com/en/blogs/michaelprocopio/cloud-computing-does-not-require-virtualization

Rimal, B. P., Eunmi, C., & Lumb, I. (2009, 25-27 Aug. 2009). *A taxonomy and survey of cloud computing systems.* Paper presented at the Fifth International Joint Conference on INC, IMS and IDC, 2009. NCM '09.

Rittinghouse, J. W., & Ransome, J. F. (2010). *Cloud computing: Implementation, management, and security.* Boca Raton, FL: CRC Press.

Russell, D. (2010). *Weather report: Considerations for migrating to the cloud.* Retrieved December 1, 2010, from http://www.ibm.com/developerworks/cloud/library/cl-wr1migrateapps-tocloud/index.html

Sarna, D. E. Y. (2011). *Implementing and developing cloud computing applications.* Boca Raton, FL: CRC Press.

SearchSecurity.com. (2011). Retrieved February 20, 2011, from http://searchsecurity.techtarget.com/sDefinition/0,sid14_gci1381571,00.html

Spinola, M. (2009). *An essential guide to possibilities and risks of cloud computing.*

Sridhar, T. (2009). Cloud computing - A primer part 1: Models and technologies. *The Internet Protocol Journal Cisco, 12*(3), 2–19.

The Green Grid. (2008). Five ways to reduce data center server power consumption. Retrieved from http://www.thegreengrid.org/Global/Content/white-papers/Five-Ways-to-Save-Power

Varia, J. (2008). *Building GrepTheWeb in the cloud, part 1: Cloud architectures.* Retrieved June 30, 2010, from http://aws.amazon.com/articles/1632?_encoding=UTF8&jiveRedirect=1

Velte, A. T., Velte, T. J., & Elsenpeter, R. C. (2010). *Cloud computing: A practical approach.* New York, NY: McGraw-Hill.

Voas, J., & Zhang, J. (2009). Cloud computing: New wine or just a new bottle? *IT Professional, 11*(2), 15–17. doi:10.1109/MITP.2009.23

Wainewright, P. (2009). *PRaaS: Process as a service.* Retrieved February 5, 2011, from http://nauges.typepad.com/my_weblog/2009/08/praas-process-as-a-service.html

Winthrop, P. (2011). *Ruminating on MaaS: Mobility as a service.* Retrieved April 5, 2011, from http://theemf.org/2011/03/16/ruminating-on-maas-mobility-as-a-service

KEY TERMS AND DEFINITIONS

Cloud Bursting: The technique of acquiring additional IT resources on demand besides an organization's existing IT resources to fulfill a short term requirement when there is a surge in demand. This concept is used in hybrid cloud model. When an internal IT system (private cloud) has sufficient resources to handle workloads, hybrid cloud is not used. However when there is a peak demand and private cloud can not handle the workloads, excess workloads is managed by the hybrid cloud. Cloud bursting can be of two types – loosely coupled and tightly coupled. In a loosely coupled model, only results processed by additional IT resources are provided to the private cloud. On the other hand, in a tightly coupled model, additional IT resources and private cloud work together to solve the same problem. This process requires frequent data sharing and communication between private cloud and extra resources (Sridhar, 2009).

Cloud Broker: There is a multitude of cloud products in the market. It may be an overwhelming and daunting task for an organization to choose the right product for its need. Cloud broker works as a facilitator to help customers choose the right cloud products. Broker has no cloud resources of its own. Based on a customer's requirements and Service Level Agreement (SLA) a broker can find the right cloud platform for the customer or gives the customer the option of choosing from a collection of suitable cloud platforms fulfilling the requirements criteria. Cloud broker also assists the customer with migration and integration of applications and services.

Federation: The process of sharing data and identity information across multiple cloud platforms. For federation to work there is a need of open industry standards and interoperability. Otherwise heterogeneous cloud platforms from different provider can not communicate with each other and leverage cloud federation. Cloud federation focuses on consistency and access controls for two or more geographically distributed clouds when authentication, data, computing resources, access and storage resources are shared among them.

Cloudsourcing: A new term coined to refer to the delivery model in which an organization migrate or source their IT solutions to the cloud of a third party. In this model an organization's complete IT solution runs from the cloud through a combination of cloud applications, platforms and infrastructure. Simply put, it can be defined as running one's business from the cloud. An organization does not possess any server to host their application but still can execute their IT operations by leveraging this outsourcing model. The main advantage of adopting this model is to save huge capital investment required to set up IT infrastructure. An organization does need only fewer resources (in some cases none) for infrastructure administration. The time and resources saved by utilizing this model can be used in other productive and critical areas for the business.

Chapter 2
Infrastructure as a Service

Shamim Hossain
IBM Corporation, Australia

ABSTRACT

Infrastructure as a Service is the pillar on which a cloud computing architecture is built. With the advancement of technologies in communications, computing, and storage devices, IaaS has emerged as a highly efficient platform to construct SaaS and PaaS layer on top of it. IaaS solutions vary from an organization to another. One single solution does not fit all. This chapter looks at the general constituents of IaaS.

INTRODUCTION

Infrastructure as a Service is one of the building blocks of cloud computing. It is the linchpin which revamps the cloud solution by offering underlying IT infrastructure. In this chapter we will take a closer look at this important service which is considered as the backbone of cloud computing. Massive data centers and servers farms comprise the cloud's underlying infrastructure on which SaaS and PaaS run. According to Matthieu (Hug, 2008) from his online article -

An emerging computing paradigm where data and services reside in massively scalable data centers and can be ubiquitously accessed from any connected devices over the internet.

From a very high level these massive data centers are cloud IaaS. We will see cloud data center architecture later in the chapter. These data centers provide large scale of economies and dynamic scalability among others.

In many different literatures, several different versions of definition for IaaS exist. The definition from NIST has been widely accepted. Let us revisit the definition of IaaS as defined by NIST (NIST, 2010).

The capability provided to the consumer is to provision processing, storage, networks, and other fundamental computing resources where the consumer is able to deploy and run arbitrary software, which can include operating systems and applications. The consumer does not manage or control the underlying cloud infrastructure but has control over operating systems, storage, deployed applications, and possibly limited control of selected networking components (e.g., host firewalls).

DOI: 10.4018/978-1-4666-2187-9.ch002

IaaS itself is comprised of many different components. A list of components is provided here. Detailed discussion will follow throughout the chapter. Components for IaaS include, but are not limited to, the following (Rittinghouse & Ransome, 2010) (Reese, 2009):

- Servers (both physical and virtual)
- Storage systems by means of NAS and SAN
- Network segmentation using different network blocks and VLANs
- Communication network (including routers, switches, firewalls, load balancer, etc.)
- High Speed Internet connectivity (often on OC 192 backbones)
- Platform virtualization environment
- Service-level agreements
- Utility computing billing
- Security by means of hardware or VM based firewall and intrusion detection & prevention system
- Hardware load balancer
- DNS, DHCP and other management and support services
- Power, cooling and disaster recovery system

Many of terms and jargons above will be discussed throughout this chapter. In this chapter we first present a background of cloud data centers so that users can get an overview of them before looking at technical details. It is followed by a detailed description of cloud components and some energy efficiency metrics to measure data center energy usage. Cloud Components section discusses about access devices, high-speed broadband access, virtualization and functional areas of a data center (network, computing and storage infrastructure and security services). Later in this section we provide a complete picture of a generic cloud data center. Then we discuss different additional attributes of IaaS in the Section IaaS

Characteristics. Before conclusion we present a section on Cloud Standard Bodies. These standard bodies have been working for the emergence of open standards and interoperability of technologies around cloud computing.

BACKGROUND

Before we delve into the details, let us look at the massive scale and size of some of the cloud data centers by Internet Powerhouses like Google, Microsoft, Amazon and Yahoo. Technology provider IBM, Google and others are investing huge amount of money to spur innovation of cloud computing. Cloud's scalability and elasticity emanates from its massive scale of economies. Gigantic data centers from the tech titans are leveraging the economies of scale in computing power, energy consumption, cooling, site operations and administration (Erdogmus, 2009). Cloud service providers are acquiring more and more computing powers and expanding their data centers (Economist, 2008). According to this report from Economist, Google has more than 30 data centers comprised of over 1 million servers. Organizations tend to build large-scale data centers in areas where affordable land, good communications (e.g. optical fiber connections), water for cooling and cheap electricity are readily available. It is not surprising that today's large-scale cloud data center hosts even million servers (Katz, 2009). Following is an excerpt from this paper.

These new data centers are the physical manifestation of what Internet companies are calling cloud computing. The idea is that sprawling collections of servers, storage systems, and network equipment will form a seamless infrastructure capable of running applications and storing data remotely, while the computers people own will provide little more than the interface to connect to the increasingly capable Internet.

Microsoft's data center based in Quincy occupies an area of over 43600 square meters (almost 10 American football fields) and uses 4.8 kilometers of chiller pipes, 965 km of electrical wire, 92900 square meters of drywall and 1.5 metric tons of batteries for backup power. These figures are mind boggling and bewildering. Another example is Yahoo's 13000 square meters datacenter based in Sunnyvale, California. This data center will operate with a zero carbon footprint and hydropower, water-based chillers and cold air will be used for cooling (Katz, 2009).

While most of the servers use rack configuration, technology giants IBM, HP, Oracle and others are now also building data centers using identical building blocks with integrated computing, electric power and cooling. This modular approach is highly efficient in terms of saving space and administration. These modules are integrated inside a shipping container and can be delivered by a truck. One module can fit up to 3000 servers which is more than ten times a typical data center can house in the same space. Other advantages are these are easy to deploy. Modules just need to be delivered, lowered to the floor and powered up. It gives an organization the opportunity to upgrade their technology very easily. They can refresh their technology by sending the container to the vendor and getting the upgraded version back. Randy H. Katz has provided an architectural overview of a large scale data center utilizing modular approach. According to his technical paper (Katz, 2009), a data center with 24000 square meters can fit 400 containers. Two power stations supply a total of 300 megawatts. 100 megawatts is used for cooling and wasted in electrical losses. Other 200 megawatts is used for computing equipment. As a backup source of electricity, generators and batteries are used. Water based cooling systems circulate cold water through the containers to remove heat. This water based cooling systems have been described as more energy efficient than conventional chillers. There is no need for raised floor or air conditioned room. Containers

are delivered to the facility by trucks and then lowered to the floor space. These containers are then attached to a spine infrastructure that feeds network connectivity, power and water based cooling. Each 67.5 cubic-meter container can fit 2500 servers. This gives rise to a total of a million (400 x 2500) servers.

Million-server data centers are not very rare in this era of computing. These large scale data centers are the main driver to provide enormous elasticity and flexibility in cloud computing. We started this chapter with the discussion on data centers as these data centers are the lifeblood of cloud computing. Many IT professionals often neglected data centers in the past. Cloud computing has brought data centers to lime light. Data centers operators are seeing cloud computing as a boon for their business. As more and more people are adopting cloud computing, there is need for more data centers to provide the infrastructure and network for public, private or hybrid cloud. Cloud market is maturing very quickly. IDC forecasted that there will be a growth rate six times the rate of IT spending between 2009 and 2013 (Patrizio, 2010) in cloud computing space. Approximately $17 billion was spent on cloud related technologies, hardware and software in 2009. IDC projected that spending will grow to $45 billion by 2013.

By now readers will get a high level overview of cloud Infrastructure as a Service (IaaS). Progressively in this chapter we will look at components comprising IaaS.

CLOUD COMPONENTS

"One size does not fit all" is very appropriate for cloud computing. One cloud computing solution can not cater the need for different customers. As a result there is no single cloud architecture that can be used without tailoring to meet a particular demand. In this section we will look at the basic architectures that can be used as a basis for most cloud solutions. At the end of this section we also discuss briefly about the energy efficiency that can be achieved from a cloud data center. Because of advanced technological building blocks each of which are very energy efficient, smart software and on-demand nature, a cloud data center will be energy efficient for both a service provider and a consumer.

Cloud computing is not a totally new technology. Many pre-existing technologies combined with technological advancements in broadband internet, computing systems and innovative software have paved the way to create a storm for cloud computing.

Cloud Computing is not a technology revolution, but rather a process and business evolution on how we use those technologies that enables Cloud Computing as it exists today: SaaS, inexpensive storage, REST, AJAX, SOA(service-oriented architectures), On Demand Computing, Grid Computing, Utility computing, virtualization, etc. – Maria Spinola (Spinola, 2009)

From a bird's eye view, cloud computing components are client devices, internet and data center. Processing is mainly done in the servers of a data center or a collection of data centers which are connected by a multitude of networking equipments (e.g. routers, switches etc) and internet. The servers may be physical or virtualized. It is virtualization which has made self-service, auto provisioning and de-provisioning possible in cloud computing, reduced energy usage and operating costs significantly. The data center acts as a big centralized computer which is the producer of information. Where as end users are consumers of information.

Access Devices

End users use a multitude of thick or thin client devices and web interfaces to access the cloud services. Traditionally both software and data reside on a user's computer (thick client). In ideal scenario of a cloud computing model, no data and software is installed on a user's access device. We have replaced the term computers with access devices as there are endless possibilities of accessing internet from heterogeneous devices. These heterogeneous devices may just have the bare minimum to run an operating system and a web browser. Based on this discussion client devices can be categorized in two different types.

Thick Client

These are computing devices with enough processing power and storage that can carry out heavy duty tasks on their own. These devices normally consume more energy than thin clients. Examples are regular personal computers, laptops etc.

Thin Client

Any computing device with a bare minimum of processing power and storage to access internet and display graphical user interface and web pages are considered as thin client. These are basically low end computing device and depend significantly on another computer to perform heavy duty activities. These devices are mainly used for displaying results and providing end user with an interface to invoke activities and retrieve results. Examples are netbooks, smart mobile phones, portable and handheld devices, tablets etc. These devices normally consume less energy. New types of thin clients are always emerging in the markets. Two recent trends in the market are ultra-thin clients and web thin clients (Wikipedia). Ultra-thin client or zero-client does not have a full-fledged operating system. The kernel initializes network and networking protocol and displays a server's output. Web thin client runs a Web OS (Tech, 2009). These clients solely depend on web based software and applications for their operations. Thin clients can offer up to 80% more energy efficiency than traditional desktop personal computers with similar capabilities (Velte, Velte, & Elsenpeter, 2010).

Data Center

Data center is the heart of a cloud computing system. Data center acts as a big computer which performs all the heavy duty tasks and results are dispatched to client devices. Data center is a large sprawl of servers. User applications are hosted in these servers. In introduction of this chapter we discussed briefly about data centers. Servers are housed in a building. However, all the servers do not need to be in a same building. These can reside in geographically different locations. Distributed servers are connected by high speed communication network. Servers are also distributed for redundancy and disaster recovery. Many cloud service providers prefer to have distributed servers in different locations for redundancy, high availability, flexibility and security. This ensures seamless delivery of service to end users in case of one data center being non-operational due to some disasters or accidents. Other data centers would still be operational and thus businesses would be less impacted.

From a very high level, a cloud data center should possess servers, storage, networking equipments and connections, load balancers, firewall and many others. Some key software components are cloud service managements software (for metering, measurement and billing), business applications for service orchestration, middleware like databases and application and web servers. Key facilities components are power and cooling system, racks, cables and data center physical construction components (Cisco, 2009a).

High-Speed Broadband Access

Broadband internet is the arteries and veins of a cloud computing system. It is the internet which connects myriad of devices together and creates a mammoth cloud. High bandwidth and low la-

tency communication link at a low cost is a key consideration for cloud. Fiber to the home, passive optical network, PtP (point to point) optical system, DSL (digital subscriber line), satellite and wireless broadband have acted as a catalyst to make cloud computing popular. Most of mobile devices and phones are now shipped with wireless interfaces. This has made it possible to use these devices for accessing internet. With the proliferation of technologies many people now have access to internet in some ways. Users now prefer to perform most of their tasks on the web, use web applications and collaborate with others online. This trend is making cloud computing very popular.

Virtualization

Virtualization is not a prerequisite for cloud computing. However it will be very hard to see a cloud computing system without virtualization these days. This is a very powerful and fundamental technology which is reshaping the IT infrastructure and is a key enabler of cloud computing. Virtualization is the process of abstraction of computing resources (CPU, network, storage, memory, application stack, databases, other useful tools etc) from applications and end users (Mather, Kumaraswamy, & Latif, 2009) (Ruest & Ruest, 2009). In simple words, virtualization means using a computer's resources to imitate another computer's resources or whole computer (Hurwitz, 2009). Some experts have cited virtualization as the main ingredient of cloud computing (Sarna, 2011). It provides the platform for consolidation and optimization of complex IT resources and offers infinite agility. The history of virtualization dates back to early 1960s when IBM invented virtualization to run multiple software contexts on a mainframe. Virtualization started to lose its popularity in 1980s and 1990s. In the last decade when organization realized that physical servers in data centers were operating at very low utilization rate (15% or below), they started to think about virtualization again. Server virtualization allowed an organization to run multiple virtual servers on a single physical server by means of partitioning. This created an opportunity to reduce hardware acquisition, administration and management cost and increase utilization and energy efficiency by consolidating physical servers.

In this section, we will look at technology enablers and different aspects of virtualization. First we look at hypervisor which performs the abstraction of computing resources. Then in sub-section A, B and C, we present characteristics exhibited by virtualization, advantages and types respectively.

Hypervisor is a type of virtualization software which allows multiple operating systems to run on a single physical server. These operating systems are known as guest OS (Operating System) and the physical server is known as host server. Hypervisor is also known as Virtual Machine Manager (VMM). It is the hypervisor which performs abstraction of the underlying hardware from the VMs. There are two types of hypervisors. Native or bare metal or type 1 hypervisor runs directly on the host's hardware to control the hardware and manage guest operating systems. Guest operating systems run directly on the hypervisor (Wikipedia, 2011b). Examples are IBM z/VM, VMWare ESXi, Citrix XenServer etc. Type 2 or hosted hypervisor runs on top an operating system (known as host operating system). In this scenario hypervisor exists as second level software layer and guest operating systems run as third level software layer. VMWare Server is an example of type 2 hypervisor. Figure 1 shows the hierarchy of physical servers, host operating system, hypervisor and virtual machines. This figure has been adapted from (IBM, 2007) and (Sridhar, 2009a). Two VMs have been depicted here for both type 1 and type 2 hypervisor as a matter of illustration. The actual number of VMs will depend on physical server capacity, memory and storage constraints. A VM has an operating system of its known. This is known as guest operating system. As we can see from Figure 1, in

case of a type 2 hypervisor, both the hypervisor and traditional (non-virtualized) applications run on the host operating system as level 2 software. Normally applications running on VMs do not have any knowledge that these are running on a hosted environment.

Characteristics of Virtualization

Virtualization exhibits following three characteristics suitable for cloud computing (Hurwitz, 2009).

Partitioning

This is the feature which enables multi-tenancy in a cloud environment. Virtualization facilitates multiple operating systems and applications to reside on the same physical server by partitioning available resources. This enables serving multiple customers from a single physical server but still providing separation of resources.

Isolation

Virtual machines (VM) reside on the same physical server in different partitions. As a result each virtual instance is isolated from other virtual machines. Failure of one virtual machine does not impact other virtual machines. This isolation property also helps with troubleshooting of a virtual machine without impacting other virtual machines and ensuring seamless operation of the physical server and other VMs. This feature is also useful for workload migration between different servers.

Encapsulation

Each virtual machine appears as a single complete entity to applications and end users. This encapsulation enables applications inside a virtual machine communicating to the right application outside the virtual machine and not interfering with another application.

Figure 1. Host OS, guest OS, hypervisors, and virtual machines

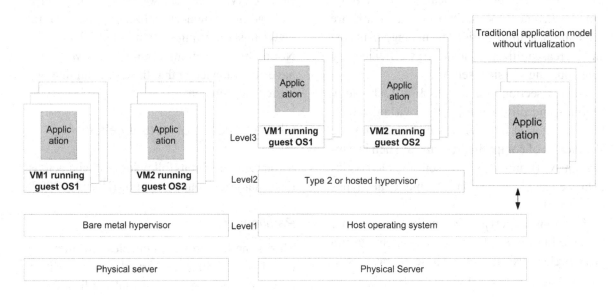

Type 1 Native or bare metal hypervisor based solution   Type 2 or hosted hypervisor based solution

Advantages of Virtualization

Maintenance

It is relatively very easy to administer virtualized server than a physical server. Virtual servers can be quickly shutdown and started up with less effort and time than that required for a physical server. Snapshots of virtual machines can be maintained as file backup. In case of emergency or hardware failure it is very easy to restore a virtual server from the snapshot.

Workload Migrations

Virtual machines can be easily migrated from one physical server to another by simply copying files associated with the machines. Thus virtual workload migrations require less effort than workload migration across physical servers.

Reducing Costs

Virtualization has the largest potential to cut cost through server virtualization and consolidation.

According to Gartner IT Infrastructure and Operations constitute 60% of annual IT spending for an organization. 21% of the total spending is from data center alone (Pultz, 2009). According to the same report organizations have reported 20% reduction in Infrastructure and Operations costs through consolidation. Gartner suggested CIOs to adopt the following projects for cost cutting (Pultz, 2009).

- Utilizing mainframe as server consolidation platform
- Moving storage to Network attached storage (NAS) or Storage area network
- Progressively moving towards unified communications
- Adopting enterprise service bus (ESB) as middleware
- Integrating security platforms
- Adopting all-Ethernet solution and terabit switching in data center
- Converging to IP network in Metropolitan-area network (MAN)/WAN

Gartner's research has shown that virtualization is the most effective contributor among all projects to cut cost. As many physical servers can be consolidated to one physical server through virtualization, utilization and energy efficiency is increased significantly. This also reduces carbon footprint. Gartner report shows that 90% of the cost saving is achieved from savings in power.

Resiliency

In case of a physical server failure virtual machine can be easily restored from the snapshot. A snapshot is the emulated copy of a server (VM image) taken at a certain point of time. A physical machine with a virtual machine can be easily restored to this point by file system copy. Also a virtual machine can be migrated from one physical server to another within same data center or to a different data center. Offline and live migration have been discussed in detail in Section Virtual Workload Migration later in this chapter. Also administrators can identify problems at physical server level by migrating the running VMs to a different physical server (Sridhar, 2009a). All these features provide an increased resiliency.

Types of Virtualizations

Two flavors of virtualization exist. One is known as full virtualization and the other is known as para- virtualization. In full virtualization a whole system (disk drive, BIOS, network interface card, processor etc.) is emulated. In this mode of virtualization, guest operating systems have no control of system resources. In paravirtualization multiple guest operating systems run by sharing system resources (e.g. processors, memory etc.) more efficiently (Velte, et al., 2010). The operating system (OS) inside a VM is aware of virtualization in paravirtualization mode. Full virtualization does not require any modification to the guest operating system. However, in the case of paravirtualization operating system requires modification to run on hypervisor or virtual machine manager.

Guest operating systems run better with paravirtualization than full virtualization. Paravirtualization consumes less processing power (less overhead) and hosts more virtual machines than a full virtualization environment can host on the same hardware. However paravirtualization offers decreased flexibility as OS requires modification to run on hypervisor. There is also security risk as the guest operating systems have more control of the underlying hardware.

VMWare is an example of a hypervisor to enable full virtualization. To achieve paravirtualization it is necessary to have paravirtualization capable hypervisors. Some examples of hypervisors in this category are Xen, Virtuozzo, OpenVZ, and Vserver (Wikipedia, 2011c).

The selection of a type of virtualization has to be determined based on the requirement and performance of an application. Let us discuss a case when near-native performance is required from a VM and portability and security risk is not an issue (perhaps because it is a private cloud). A modified version of guest OS, which is aware of virtualization, is also readily available in this scenario. As discussed before, paravirtualization will be the preferred solution in this scenario. However when security and portability are major concerns and virtualization overhead is not a concern, full virtualization will be preferred.

As explained above an OS and applications run on a VM. Applications are totally ignorant and independent of the virtualized situation. This feature provides flexibility as applications do not need to be changed to run in another virtualized environment.

Virtualizations are new atomic units of computing. Data center technologies possess virtualization across storage, servers and network. Virtualization has its application in security as well. A VM can be used as a virtual firewall. The VM contains the appropriate operating system and firewall and antivirus software. This configuration is known as firewall virtual appliance. Every packet is verified and checked by the virtual firewall before it gets dispatched to the required VM.

Virtualization exists in the space of computing resources. However, not much work has progressed for optical communication link virtualization. It is interesting and promising to see that concepts developed by some researchers from Japan for a virtualized optical network (VON). According to this model, a virtualized optical link will be allocated between two servers on demand. This VON will be able to automatically create any to any connectivity with appropriate optical bandwidth (Masahiko & Yukio, 2009). VON can also help with load balancing when there is an extreme demand from a particular data center. VON will engage additional servers located at other data center by allocating appropriately sized optical paths. This way valuable optical bandwidth will not be wasted. Also there is no need for a pre-established dedicated link between two data centers. When implemented, VON will revolutionize optical communication technology in cloud computing space.

Functional Areas of Cloud Computing Data Center

A cloud-ready data center has the following four functional areas in general. Different vendor solutions may vary from each other but the following four are prerequisites (Juniper, 2010a).

- **Network infrastructure:** This is the infrastructure which provides the connectivity and communication mechanism for all required cloud services between users and the data centers, across multiple data centers and for servers within a data center. More discussion on data center network infrastructure will follow.
- **Compute and storage infrastructure:** This provides the necessary computing power and storage required for applications to provide service to the customers.

Computing infrastructure is the workhorse of a cloud computing system.
- **Services:** This provides security, identity management, application acceleration, deep packet inspections (DPI) and load balancing.
- **Management and orchestration:** This component is responsible for efficient monitoring, management and planning of cloud computing infrastructure.

For the purpose of this chapter we provide detailed discussion about some of the components from the above four catergories. In subsection A, B, C and D below we present network infrastructure, storage infrastructure, computing infrastructure and security services respectively. Then we provide a complete picture of a cloud IaaS infrastructure emanated from these components.

Network Infrastructure

Network architecture and infrastructure is a core component for cloud services delivery. Thousands of compute and storage nodes are connected to data centers through data center network fabric (Oberle, et al., 2010). Network infrastructure consists of a combination of equipments in three domains, knows as

- Access network
- Core network
- Edge network

Access network is responsible for providing connectivity to enterprise servers, storage devices and IP or office automation devices in a data center. Data center access switches are generally located at the top of the rack or at the end of the row of server racks (Juniper, 2010a).

The core network is responsible for high speed packet switching between multiple access network devices. It takes care of all data going in and out of the data center. As a result it must be capable of high speed throughput (normally 10 GbE interface) and provide robust and fail-safe Layer 3 connection to access layer devices. Core network is very important as it is the gateway where other modules like WAN (Wide Area Network) edge connect (Juniper, 2010a).

The edge network is responsible for providing connectivity to end user networks. End user networks can be a private Wide Area Network (WAN) or campus backbones, VPNs, mobile access networks or other types of internet access (Juniper, 2010a). Edge network ensures high performance, reliability, agility and multilayered controls for improved user experience.

Besides the network based classification above, data center network (DCN) follows a hierarchical or layered design approach. The layers which complete the networking stack are known as

- Access layer
- Aggregation layer
- Core layer

Functionality of access layer is similar to access network as discussed above. In this layer servers get attached to the network and network policies like access control list (ACL), quality of service (QoS), VLANs etc are enforced (Cisco, 2009b). When designing the access layer some factors should be taken into consideration. These factors dictate the capacity of the equipments in this layer. Server density, form factor and server virtualization are critical decision criteria. With the adoption of virtualization, multiple physical servers are consolidated into one physical server in the form of VMs. The data traffic from multiple VMs is now multiplexed into one physical Ethernet connection. As a result an improved throughput (10 Gbps) is required from Ethernet network interface card (NIC). Access layer switch can appear in few different configurations. Most common are end-of-row (EOR, where switch is located at the end of row of servers rack) and top-of-rack (TOR, where switch is located at the

top of servers rack). Integrated switch, where a blade switch inside a modular blade server chassis is used, exists in some configurations. In virtual domain software based Virtual Ethernet Switch is used. Virtual switch is often realized as a plug-in to the hypervisor. Its main functionality is to switch between virtual machines within a physical server according to some policies and aggregate traffic from all virtual machines to forward to an external physical switch. Every virtual machine has a virtual Ethernet adapter (Virtual network interface card - vNIC) which connects to the virtual switch. If two virtual machines (VM) connected to the same virtual switch need to communicate with each other, virtual switch performs the layer 2 switching without involving the physical switch and network. This virtual switch connects to the external physical switch by means of a physical Ethernet adapter located in the physical server. Figure 2 illustrates this in a pictorial manner. For illustration purpose here, only two VMs and two virtual Ethernet adapters have been shown. Normally one hypervisor possesses one virtual switch. However, it is not uncommon to have more than one switch to provide more logical segmentation of network with a VM. A physical server may also have more than one physical Ethernet adapter.

The physical connection between the virtual switch and physical switch is known as uplink. In some cases a hypervisor may have more than one virtual switch for better logical segmentation and hence more than one uplink to the external physical switch (Sridhar, 2009b). Each virtual machine requires a Media Access Control (MAC) address and IP address. As the number of VM increases, switching starts to become complicated. Virtual switches take care of switching between VMs inside a physical server according to policy. Virtual switches differ slightly from physical switches from operational point of view. They do not need to run network protocols and do not treat all the ports the same way. They do not need to learn MAC address for the ports connected to the VMs. Virtual switch forwards all

Figure 2. Operation of physical and virtual switch and adapter

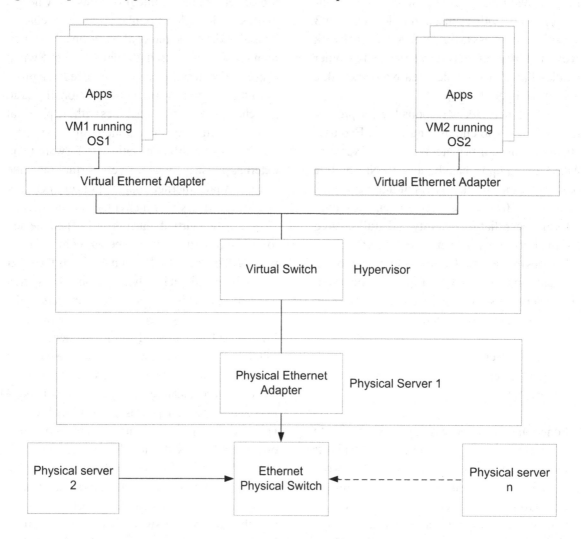

destination-unknown frames over uplink to the physical switch. An external management entity is used for network operation configuration (Sridhar, 2009a). For example, an administrator can configure the access control list on the virtual switch to prohibit some VMs on the same physical server from communication with one another. Multiple virtual machines can be managed by an external node which may be a VM or a physical server. This management node provides a view which facilitates administration of all the switches. This node can run control or management plane protocols for multiple virtual switches.

During migration of VMs, this feature helps easier migration of policies and access control lists (Sridhar, 2009b). Simple Network Management Protocol (SNMP) is used for managing physical or virtual network devices.

Aggregation layer switches sit between access layer switches and core switches. Access layer switches connect to aggregation switches. One aggregation switch connects to another aggregation switch. Thus aggregation layer switches interconnect access layer switches across racks and provide connectivity between servers and multi-tiered applications. Aggregation layer behaves as a boundary between Layer 3 routed links and Layer 2 Ethernet broadcast domain. Access switches leverage IEEE 802.1Q Virtual LAN (VLAN) trunks to connect to aggregation layer. VLAN trunks provide the capability to connect servers belonging to different VLANs and IP subnets to the same physical switch (Furht & Escalante, 2010). Aggregation layer is responsible for providing integration of network-hosted services, e.g. load balancing, intrusion detection, firewalls, SSL offload, network analysis etc (Cisco, 2009b).

A core switch connects to multiple aggregation switches and expose the data center to the outside world through Layer 3 IP. Core layer is responsible for layer 3 switching of IP traffic between the data center and the Internet Service Provider's edge and backbone (Furht & Escalante, 2010). In case of a private cloud an organization may own more than one data centers in geographically distributed areas. These data centers are connected via a private wide area network (WAN) or a metropolitan area network (MAN). In this scenario the best approach is to connect the data centers through Layer 2 networks. In case of a public cloud, data traffic is carried over public internet. Layer 3 networking topologies are utilized to connect core switches of multiple distributed data centers. Figure 4 (found later in this chapter) displays three layers of data center networks.

Storage Infrastructure

Storage infrastructure plays a significant role in any data center. Storage can be connected locally to a physical server and by means of a network interface. The fixed direct access storage device (DASD) is not very efficient and flexible and as such new data centers are focusing more on storage connected to network. According to a technical report by IBM and Cisco, storage utilization is 10% in Windows environments and 30% in Unix environments for many organizations (IBM/CISCO, 2008). With storage virtualization, utilization can be increased significantly.

Cloud storage infrastructure mainly consists of a shared storage. It may be distributed or centralized. Again it comes in two flavors -

- File based such as Network access Storage (NAS)
- Block based such as Storage Area Network (SAN)

Storage system is basically a disk array. Two types of storage virtualizations exist in the storage domain. These are –

- Block virtualization
- File virtualization

Storage virtualization offers location independence by abstracting the physical location of the storage. Storage virtualization creates the illusion of a single monolithic storage device by connecting multiple scattered and independent storage devices in the data center. Thus an administrator can manage the storage with greater flexibility.

Cloud based storage services was one of the early offerings from the cloud providers. Cloud storage has emerged as a model of networked online storage where data is stored in a multitude of scattered virtual servers rather than dedicated physical servers (Wikipedia, 2011a). Cloud service providers offer storage to customers based on their requirements. The provider virtualizes storage and exposes these as storage pools. Customers utilize these pools to store their files and data objects. To the end user it may look like a centralized storage. However, storage resources may be scattered across multiple servers. Cloud storage services are normally accessed through SOAP or REST API (Orenstein, 2010). Cloud storage gateways are network appliances which are often installed at customer premises. The purpose of cloud storage gateway is to expose the storage services in such a way that the customers can treat these as local storage devices (Wikipedia, 2011a).

Storage is mainly accessed over a network in a cloud data center. File based data storage leverages Network File System (NFS) or Common Internet File System (CIFS) protocol as access mechanism. Block based storage is accessed via Fiber Channel (FC), Internet Small Computer System Interface (iSCSI), Serial Attached SCSI (SAS), Fiber Connection (FICON) or other protocols. Fiber Channel and Ethernet interfaces are two most popular network technologies for storage. Physical servers are fitted with several I/O cards or interfaces to connect to multiple network segments or completely separate network infrastructures. With advancement of technologies and I/O convergence, the number of interfaces required in a server has reduced. This results in lower cost of data center operation and better manageability. Storage or disk arrays are connected to a Fiber Channel or Ethernet switch which in turn connects to physical servers by means of Fiber Channel or Ethernet adapters. Besides Fiber Channel and Ethernet interfaces, iSCSI has also become popular (Sridhar, 2009a). iSCSI runs SCSI protocol on a TCP/IP over Ethernet connection. Fiber Channel over Ethernet (FCoE) is a converged network interface which relieves a physical server from having a separate Fiber Channel adapter and an Ethernet adapter to communicate to storage systems with Fiber Channel interfaces. Normally Ethernet interface is used for server to server or server to client communication and Fiber Channel for server to storage communication. With FCoE a physical server is only equipped with an Ethernet adapter. This type of Ethernet adapter which performs both Ethernet and FCoE functions is known as Converged Network Adapter (CNA). FC based traffic encapsulated within an Ethernet frame is forwarded to FCoE gateway. This gateway does the necessary Ethernet to Fiber Channel conversion and connects to FC channel storage arrays. Figure 3 illustrates this. If storage systems are also equipped with FCoE features, Ethernet frame can easily be sent to storage arrays from the server without the need of FCoE gateway (Sridhar, 2009a).

Computing Infrastructure

Computing infrastructure is the brain of a cloud computing solution. There are solutions to provide computing power from a variety of technologies. Mainframe, midrange server and x86 based server are ideal candidates for compute cloud. In this section we will briefly look at some cloud computing platforms. Many experts often define mainframe as the original cloud platform. The mainframe is a cloud computing differentiator (IBM, 2011d). Mainframes have started to gain its popularity in cloud computing domain (Harbert, 2011). Massive reduction in operating cost and huge improvement in utilization are achieved by implementing a cloud solution with mainframe. For example, IBM's System z mainframe can simplify a data-center by reducing its components by 90% with its unique virtualization capability and design principle (IBM, 2011d). The new mainframes are so powerful and advanced that these can be ideal platform for cloud computing. Some advantages of mainframes (Barnett, 2010) are:

- By means of consolidation new mainframes can reduce energy usage, floor

Figure 3. FCoE based storage

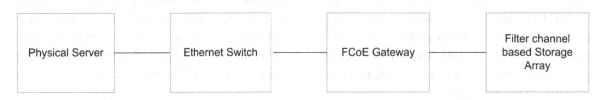

Figure 4. Cloud data center network architecture

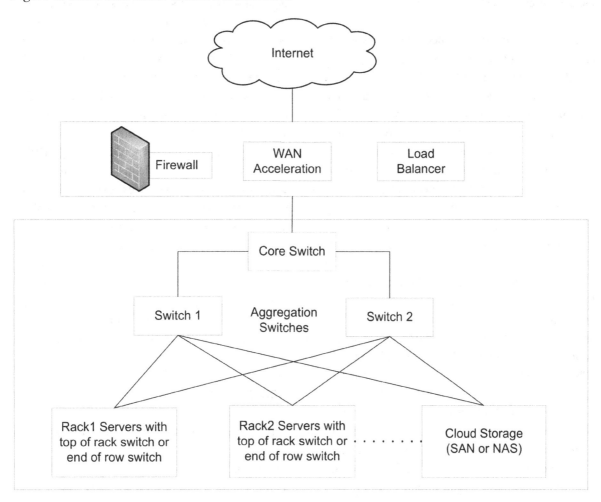

space, labor costs and software licensing costs by up to 90%
- It provides a virtualization environment (LPAR, z/VM) that support thousands of mainframe, Linux and Java environments within one physical machine
- IBM mainframe zEnterprise adds POWER and x86 servers onto mainframe-refined workload management. This is achieved through zEnterprise BladeCenter Extension (zBX) chassis. This will facilitate to run a variety of workloads like AIX, Linux and Windows in the mainframe in near term (Partridge, 2011).

- By shifting cloud platform from old x86 servers to newer mainframes 80% to 100% utilization can be achieved

However, x86-virtualization has become matured in the last decade and as such x86 based servers in a massive scaled out architecture will be the mainstream cloud solution for many businesses in near term. Mainframe cloud solution will take off at a faster pace than x86-platform once technologies for running x86 based workload on mainframe become matured.

Security Services

Internet traffic pattern has become very complicated and challenging because of Service Oriented Architecture (SOA), Web 2.0, rich media application and others. More will be discussed in the following section (Cloud Computing Traffic Pattern). A single request may involve multiple servers over multiple sessions. As more servers are involved, this traffic pattern also imposes some security risks. As such it is necessary to secure data and user identity, maintain data integrity and protect every node from malicious attack. Commonly used technologies to ensure a data center security are routers, firewalls, intrusion prevention system (IPS), Virtual Private Network (VPN) for secure remote access and Network Access Control (NAC). However for a robust and secured cloud platform additional security services is necessary (Juniper, 2010b). Stateful firewalls, IPS, application and identity awareness, secure remote access, NAC, DNS/DHCP services and Authentication, Authorization and Accounting (AAA) services are required for a cloud platform. Cloud system is vulnerable to Distributed Denial of Service (DDoS). This can make the cloud services unavailable to the intended users. This type of lockout is known as DDoS lockout. Cloud follows distributed infrastructure architecture. A prevention mechanism of DDoS lockout may be moving to workloads to another data center and redirect users traffic there.

Secure remote access leverages virtual private network (VPN) technology. VPN establishes a virtual network by which employees or remote offices can get secured access to corporate network using public internet. This is an alternate cheaper option than having dedicated or leased line between two branch offices. Companies with global presence may have branch offices all over the world. Leased line is not feasible solution in this case. VPN creates a virtual tunnel between two end points. All data inside the tunnel is encrypted to turn public internet into a secured private network so that only authorized users can access an organization's network. Two types of secure remote access technologies are prevalent in the industry. These are IPSec VPN and SSL VPN (Velte, et al., 2010). Internet Protocol Security (IPSec) works on Layer 3 (Network Layer) of OSI model. IPSec VPN uses IPSec protocol for tunneling. Upon connection on a IPSec VPN, authorized computer node virtually becomes a part of the corporate network. IPSec client software needs to be installed on the client computing device to get access to IPSec VPN. On the contrary Secured Sockets Layer (SSL) VPN does not require any specialized software installed on client device. It leverages SSL protocol which most web browsers support. SSL VPN provides granular and better access control. It creates a tunnel between end points of two specific applications. Thus authorized users get access only to a specific application rather than the whole corporate network.

Complete Picture

Separation of application architectures in three layers or three-tier model is also followed in cloud computing paradigm. The tiers are known as presentation tier (web front end), application tier (processing application and business logic and functionalities) and finally database tier (database management and data manipulation). This three-tier model is often a simplified version of an N-tier architecture. Three layers are not necessarily implemented in separate servers. Two layers may share the same physical server. For instance, application tier and database tier can be mapped into the same physical server (Sridhar, 2009b). Presentation layer is normally exposed to the outside world in a data center. As such, web and application servers face internet to handle request from users. Presentation tier normally finds its home in Demilitarized Zone (DMZ) and other tiers are secured by firewalls, intrusion prevention system and other measures. Traditionally there are two network segments (Virtual Local

Area Network – VLAN) in a data center. Public front end is located one VLAN which uses public IP address. Other tiers are situated in another VLAN using private IP addresses. All layers may securely access database tier. Figure 4 depicts a data center network architecture. It displays three layers – access layer, aggregation layer and core layer. These layers have been discussed in detail in Network Infrastructure Section earlier. Figure 4 has been presented later in this section to show other components that exist between core switch and the public internet. As we can see in this figure multiple servers (physical/virtual) and storage arrays are interconnected via aggregation switch. A core switch connects to multiple aggregation switches and expose the data center to the outside world through Layer 3 IP. As a security measure and performance improvement a cloud data center deploys Firewall, WAN Acceleration and Load Balancer between core switch and public internet. Firewall is used to filter unwanted traffic from entering the data center network. WAN Acceleration leverages a number of acceleration technologies

like low level compression, intelligent bitwise compression and specific protocol optimization to accelerate applications and protocol over WAN (Riverbed, 2011). This technology also addresses latency issue. Load balancing technology is used to distribute workload across the data center network and computing nodes to achieve optimal resource utilization, maximize throughput and avoid overload.

Two distinct cloud networks are connected via dedicated optical links, MPLS/VPLS network or public internet. Figure 5 depicts a hybrid cloud architecture and illustrates how components are connected together.

As we can see from Figure 5, a secure Virtual Private Network (VPN) tunnel is first formed between the private cloud and the public cloud. The private cloud shown on the left hand side of Figure 5 is a block diagram representation of Figure 4. Servers, access switches and aggregation switches are shown together in a box for simplicity. Core switch with the help of Firewall, WAN Acceleration and Load Balancer exposes the data

Figure 5. Hybrid cloud architecture

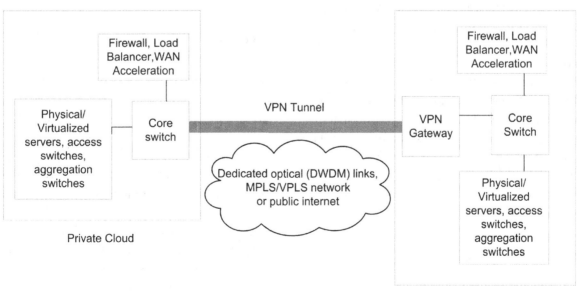

center to the outside world or public internet. On the right hand side of Figure 5, we see the same configuration for a public cloud except the addition of a VPN gateway. Core switch of the private cloud connects to VPN gateway of the public cloud. VPN tunnel uses public IP addresses to create VPN link between public cloud and private cloud. VPN gateway is assigned with private IP addresses for internal data center network of the public cloud. Datacenter servers are normally segmented into multiple VLANs or IP networks according to policy, applications and multi-tenancy requirements.

Now we will look at one of most important benefits that can result from a cloud data center. IT business decision makers and operators need to understand energy efficiency metric so that they can take valuable decisions to constantly improve the efficiency of their data centers.

Energy Efficiency of Cloud Data Center

Organizations all over the world have become concerned about green house gas reduction and efficient energy usage. High energy efficiency is one of the most important incentives offered by cloud computing. To measure data center efficiency the term Power Usage Effectiveness (PUE) has been coined. It is an efficiency metric measured as the ratio of total power consumed by a data center to the power consumption of IT equipments (Belady, Rawson, Pfleuger, & Cader, 2008). It includes power spent or wasted on cooling, transformation of grid power, mechanical losses and other non-IT usage. Power usage of IT equipments can be attributed to CPU, memory, networking equipments, storage and security services (firewall, intrusion prevention system etc).

$$PUE = \frac{Power\_drawn\_by\_a\_datacenter}{Power\_consumed\_by\_IT\_equipments}$$

As we can see from the equation above the more efficient a data center is, the closer PUE will get towards 1. Take for example a PUE of 1.8. This means for every 1 watt of power used by IT equipments in a data center, 0.8 is used for non-IT purpose. In a situation of old data centers, where 60% to 70% of total power is spent on cooling (Berl, et al., 2009), PUE can easily go beyond 3. This is a very bad figure for a data center to have.

Another term is often used as data center efficiency metric. This is called Data Center Infrastructure Efficiency (DCiE) (Belady, et al., 2008). DCiE is the reciprocal value of PUE. For example, a PUE of 2 means DCiE is 0.5. This means data center infrastructure is 50% efficient.

It is interesting to see that cloud service providers have been able to achieve an improved PUE or DCiE with their massive data centers by leveraging innovative, smart and efficient technologies and large scale of economies. Technology giant IBM has demonstrated a PUE of 1.19 or DCiE value of 84% (IBM, 2011b). This is a very inspiring figure as we want to embark into a world of smarter computing and smarter energy. A study shows that organizations can reduce carbon emissions by 30% to 90% by switching to a cloud infrastructure (Accenture, 2010).

IAAS CHARACTERISTICS

Cloud Computing Traffic Pattern

Service Oriented Architecture (SOA), Web 2.0, real-time data streams, online collaboration, Unified Communications (UC) and explosive growth of mobile and wireless devices are driving the traffic pattern in the internet now-a-days. These features present the network with a challenging pattern. Simple client –server application architecture has become a thing of the past. In client-server model a request is originated from a client, request is processed by the server and the response is sent to the client. This is known as north-south traffic scheme. Now-a-days bi-directional traffic pattern has become omni-directional. A request originated from a client travels to a server, information is shared among multiple servers and storage, result is processed by a server and the result is sent to the client. A single request hits more than one server for processing of request. It is needless to say that these servers may be scattered in geographically different locations. SOA, Virtualization and cloud computing have introduced server to server or server to storage traffic pattern. This is known as east-west traffic scheme. 75% of traffic in a data center can be attributed to east-west traffic in recent days (Juniper, 2010c). Three classes of traffic dominate a data center. User/application traffic is growing in the data center. Storage traffic is significantly growing because of generation of data from a multitude of sources and more usage of networked storage. The final category is inter-process communications (IPC) traffic. IPC traffic is due to SOA and resource pool management for virtualization and cloud computing (Juniper, 2010c).

Virtual Workload Migration

VM migration means moving a VM from one physical server to another and continuing the operation of VM in the latter. It may be often necessary to perform workload migration. The reasons may be

- When performing maintenance or upgrade of a physical server, administrators need to shut down the application before bringing down the server. It will adversely impact application availability. Moving a virtual machine to another server will ensure seamless operation of services
- An organization can move its workload to data centers located at areas with lower power and infrastructure cost. Operational cost of a data center may force an organi-

zation to move a workload to certain geographic locations at certain time of the day. For example, at night the cooling cost of a server will be less as temperature is cooler than day time. During peak time of the day electricity usage rate may be higher than off peak time. When it is night in a country, it may be day time in some other countries. Cloud data can be moved to a cloud data center somewhere in the world which is observing night time in rotation on a 24-hour basis. Thus moving a VM to a data center in an area where operational cost is lower makes sense in terms of cost cutting. Many people call it "Follow-the-moon" model (Higginbotham, 2009). Another model has emerged which is known as "follow-the-sun" model. In this scheme an organization migrate workload around the world where solar cell are used for producing electricity from sun light at day time. Use of other renewable energy can cut power cost significantly if VM can be migrated to the right data center at the right time.

- Servers in a particular data center may experience a huge surge in demand, while servers in another data center may remain under-utilized. It only makes sense to migrate workload from the former data center to the latter. Also sometimes virtual machines need to be transferred from a physical server to another within the same data center for load balancing. Workload migration thus plays an important role in load balancing.

VM migration can be of two types. Offline migration is the situation when a VM is suspended or frozen on the source server, moved to the destination server and started again. This process requires some downtime. Another alternative is live migration where VM is transferred from source to destination without suspending it on the source server. When the migration is completed, the VM on the second server becomes operational immediately after a short hiccup. This process requires less downtime. When migrating a VM from a physical server to another within the same data center, VM data needs to be accessible to both source and destination. However it requires less effort as physical servers (hosts) are situated within the same data center and data can be accessed from networked storage devices. If VM migration is between two separate data centers, then data needs to be moved across the data centers. Migration introduces some level of difficulty to network operation. VM migration may involve the same access layer switch or a different access layer switch belonging to same or a different data center. Aggregation layer services need to be modified in some cases to support this migration. In case of a live migration IP and TCP packets associated with the VM need to be resolved to a different or same MAC address so that operation can continue with non-disruptive connection. As virtual machines are mobile, network policies like access control list needs to be reviewed consistently regardless of their location in the network (Cisco, 2009b).

Huge amount of transferable data during VM migration can easily overwhelm a network. It can be often in the range of gigabytes. During live migration VM data is transferred incrementally. Thus there is less pressure on the network. The scenario is different in the case of offline migration. As whole VM is moved over the network, it creates huge pressure on the network and impacts performance of network operation and other physical or virtualized server. This impact can however be reduced by throttling the amount of data in a certain period of time, bandwidth reservation and monitoring intermediate network devices (Sridhar, 2009b).

Nature of Scaling in Cloud Computing

Flexibility and dynamic scalability offered by cloud computing has become an intriguing factor for IT decision makers to adopt this nascent technology. Cloud provides a user the capability to meet the demand for resources by dynamically scaling up or down. This change can occur manually or programmatically. Manual intervention will negate the advantages of cloud's dynamic scalability feature. It is the dynamic scaling which has taken IT industry by storms. In this section we discuss about dynamic scaling and two other sub types that fall under dynamic scaling (Reese, 2009).

Dynamic Scaling

This type of scaling does not require attention from an administrator. Rather it is controlled by a special type of service management software. Big Blue's offering "IBM Service Delivery Manager" is a cloud management platform which facilitates automatic provisioning and de-provisioning, resource monitoring and cost management (IBM, 2011c).

Dynamic scaling can be either proactive or reactive.

Proactive Scaling

This requires some input from human but rest is taken care of by software to provision/de-provision IT resources based on a plan. An administrator configures a management tool to create a schedule and plan to alter infrastructure resources at different times and the management software does it automatically at appropriate time.

Reactive Scaling

In this model infrastructure reacts to changing demand by altering IT resources on its own with the help of management software. No human intervention is necessary in this regard. When a demand surge is detected, this management software will automatically provision additional resources to cope up with the demand. As the peak subsides, these additional resources will be released automatically.

Explosive growth of mobile and connected devices and wireless technologies have also added some degrees of complexity and fueled the necessity to have dynamic infrastructure that cloud computing offers (Glisic, 2011).

CLOUD STANDARD BODIES

Cloud interoperability and open standards are major concerns for the enterprises and users. In absence of portability, proprietary technologies can lead to vendor lock-in. Industry is focusing on Cloud federation as cloud computing is being matured. As industries realized that cloud must evolve as an open system, several standard bodies have been formed who are working with providers and customers for standardization and interoperability of technologies and addressing security aspects.

Cloud Standards Customer Council has recently been formed by a joint venture of more than 45 world leading organizations. This end user advocacy group is managed by Object Management Group (OMG). It is a fastest growing council which is looking at cloud adoption prioritizing key interoperability issues such as management, reference architectures, hybrid cloud, as well as security and compliance (IBM, 2011a). This council will combine vendor-led cloud standards efforts and clients requirements to ensure end user has freedom of choice, flexibility and openness that they have with traditional IT environments.

With a common goal of achieving cloud openness more than 400 organizations signed up for Open Cloud Manifesto. It is not an organization as such. The Open Cloud Manifesto establishes a core set of principles to ensure that organizations will have freedom of choice, flexibility, and openness as they take advantage of cloud computing (CloudComputingUseCaseGroup, 2011). This

openness will provide them with choice, flexibility, speed and agility. The six principles of Open Cloud Manifesto are:

- Cloud providers must work together to ensure that the challenges to cloud adoption are addressed through open collaboration and the appropriate use of standards.
- Cloud providers must use and adopt existing standards wherever appropriate. The IT industry has invested heavily in existing standards and standards organizations; there is no need to duplicate or reinvent them.
- When new standards (or adjustments to existing standards) are needed, we must be judicious and pragmatic to avoid creating too many standards. We must ensure that standards promote innovation and do not inhibit it.
- Any community effort around the open cloud should be driven by customer needs, not merely the technical needs of cloud providers, and should be tested or verified against real customer requirements.
- Cloud computing standards organizations, advocacy groups, and communities should work together and stay coordinated, making sure that efforts do not conflict or overlap.
- Cloud providers must not use their market position to lock customers into their particular platforms and limiting their choice of providers.

The Desktop Management Task Force (DMTF) has been working on a standardized portable format of VM. This is known Open Virtualization Format (OVF). This will ensure VM can be copied from one server to another and still operate on all infrastructure without any issue. If an organization choose multiple cloud vendors and use their services, this standardized VM will guarantee that it will be compatible everywhere. Open Cloud Incubator by DMTF focuses on architectural semantics and implementation details to achieve interoperable cloud management between cloud service providers (CSP) and consumers (DMTF, 2011). Cloud Management Work Group (CMWG) and Cloud Audit Data Federation (CADF) Work Group are addressing this work by DMTF.

Other groups formed to address cloud standards are Cloud Security Alliance (CSA), Organization for the Advancement of Structured Information Standards (OASIS) and The Open Group (TOG). The Storage Networking Industries Association (SNIA) addresses the issues around cloud based storage. Cloud Data Management Interface (CDMI) is the outcome of their effort (SNIA, 2011).

FUTURE RESEARCH DIRECTIONS

It is not just a cool factor to jump into cloud band-wagon these days. It is becoming a necessity to sustain one's existence in the highly competitive industry. As cloud technology is being matured with advanced technologies, security and open standards, more and more users are adopting cloud computing. Almost everywhere a big revolution in IT industry is being observed as cloud rapidly penetrates technology arena. Industry and academia are collaborating for continual enhancement of this technology. As a result of this nurturing cloud computing has entered into its teenage years from a toddler. More and more technology providers and academic researchers are putting significant efforts for cloud's rapid advancements. So it is very important to continue learning about new cloud building blocks and technologies that are being developed. This book chapter has covered a significant amount technical detail from a plethora of sources. Readers are also encouraged to read industry and academic technical papers and articles from analysts to be aware of the re-

cent developments. In future a book chapter like this will incorporate the new developments and refreshed technologies that build up cloud along with the existing material. This will ensure that readers can grasp the evolution in the technological developments of cloud computing.

CONCLUSION

Cloud computing simplifies IT conundrum by offering an on-demand, scalable and flexible infrastructure. IaaS builds the foundation for services delivery. Understanding of IaaS is important for both the service provider and the consumer. With smart design of IaaS, under utilization of servers and high operating costs will be a thing of the past. Small and medium size business can leverage the large economies of scale form data centers managed by service providers. Thus they can afford to drive new innovations and accelerate new products development just by renting required computing resources from the providers. This results in no upfront capital investment and smaller operating expenses. These benefits are applicable to any organizations regardless of their size. Big organizations that need to keep sensitive and confidential information on premise may build their own private data center and efficiently use the resource on demand across its multiple line of business (LOB). Most importantly, the payback from hardware, software, productivity improvements, automated provisioning and maintenance and administration justify the initial investment on cloud computing. As multiple physical servers are consolidated into fewer servers, an organization can reap benefit by reduced hardware depreciation cost and less energy cost due to improved utilization. Automated provisioning frees valuable skilled resources in an organization to focus on innovative and new developments and foster the growth of business. Automated provisioning also means reduced cost due to elimination of human errors in configurations and deployments. Self service portal and service catalogues coupled with automated workflows reduces provisioning time from months to days or hours. This helps an organization with faster time to market. To achieve these operational and financial benefits, a cloud solution needs to have a solid Infrastructure as a Service. Energy efficient networks, computing and storage, supporting devices and smart management software form a highly robust IaaS which in turn drives a smart cloud data center. In this chapter we looked at different IaaS components and how these fit together. IT decision makers and service implementers will be beneficial by gaining insight into cloud architectures. Readers are encouraged to keep abreast themselves of latest developments in cloud computing space as technologies are evolving very rapidly. If Moore's law holds, we will progressively see improvements in infrastructure components and as a result IaaS fitted with better equipments in coming days. In fine, it is better late than never to adopt cloud computing. IT decision makers should seriously review the need of their organizations, assess their existing infrastructure and solution and consider cloud solution as appropriate. Cloud can be a key differentiator in realizing a company's growth in the fierce competition of recent days. Most importantly with advanced IaaS in a cloud data center, organizations can have possess greener data centers and reduce carbon dioxide emission and environment footprint (Berl, et al., 2009). Thus IT industry along with others can contribute to make our beautiful planet greener and a sustainable environment for us and future generations. With adoption of cloud computing carbon footprint per user will shrink over time. Weather forecast for cloud looks very promising. It will herald a new era to transform the whole IT industry and make a sustainable business world.

REFERENCES

Accenture. (2010). Cloud computing and sustainability: The environmental benefits of moving to the cloud. Retrieved from http://www.microsoft.com/click/services/Redirect2.ashx?CR_EAC=300012377

Barnett, G. (2010). *The mainframe and the cloud. (No. BC-INF-W-00068UK-EN-00)*. The Bathwick Group.

Belady, C., Rawson, A., Pfleuger, J., & Cader, T. (2008). Green grid data centr power efficiency metrics: PUE and DCiE. Retrieved from http://www.thegreengrid.org/~/media/WhitePapers/White_Paper_6_-_PUE_and_DCiE_Eff_Metrics_30_December_2008.pdf?lang=en

Berl, A., Gelenbe, E., Di Girolamo, M., Giuliani, G., De Meer, H., & Dang, M. Q. (2009). Energy-efficient cloud computing. *The Computer Journal, 53*(7), 1045–1051. doi:10.1093/comjnl/bxp080

Cisco. (2009a). Cisco cloud computing - Data center strategy, architechture, and solutions. Retrieved April 25, 2011, from http://www.cisco.com/web/strategy/docs/gov/CiscoCloudComputing_WP.pdf

Cisco. (2009b). *Cisco VN-link: Virtualization-aware networking*. Retrieved from http://www.cisco.com/en/US/solutions/collateral/ns340/ns517/ns224/ns892/ns894/white_paper_c11-525307.pdf

Cloud Computing Use Case Group. (2011). *Open cloud manifesto*. Retrieved January 1, 2011, from http://www.opencloudmanifesto.org

Desizn Tech. (2009). *Top 5 web operating systems*. Retrieved January 26, 2011, from http://desizn-tech.info/2009/08/top-5-web-operating-systems/

DMTF. (2011). *Cloud: DMTF.* Retrieved Mar 24, 2011, from http://dmtf.org/standards/cloud

Economist. (2008). *Down on the server farm.* Retrieved December 21, 2010, from http://www.economist.com/node/11413148

Erdogmus, H. (2009). Cloud computing: Does Nirvana hide behind the nebula? *Software, 26*(2), 4–6. doi:10.1109/MS.2009.31

Furht, B., & Escalante, A. (2010). *Handbook of cloud computing* (1st ed.). New York, NY: Springer. doi:10.1007/978-1-4419-6524-0

Glisic, S. G. (2011). *Advanced wireless communications & Internet: Future evolving technologies* (3rd ed.). Chichester, UK: Wiley. doi:10.1002/9781119991632

Harbert, T. (2011). *New job for mainframes: Cloud platform.* Retrieved April 5, 2011, from http://www.computerworld.com/s/article/9214913/New_job_for_mainframes_Cloud_platform

Higginbotham, S. (2009). Google gets shifty with its data center operations. Retrieved November 29, 2010, from http://gigaom.com/2009/07/16/google-gets-shifty-with-its-data-center-operations/

Hug, M. (2008). *Will cloud-based multi-enterprise information systems replace extranets?* Retrieved Dec 7, 2010, from http://www.infoq.com/articles/will-meis-replace-extranets

Hurwitz, J. D. (2009). *Cloud computing for dummies* (1st ed.). Indianapolis, IN: Wiley Pub., Inc.

IBM. (2007). *Virtualization in education.* Retrieved from http://www-07.ibm.com/solutions/in/education/download/Virtualization%20in%20Education.pdf

IBM. (2011a). *IBM joins forces with over 45 organizations to launch cloud standards customer council for open cloud computing.* Retrieved April 10, 2011, from http://www-03.ibm.com/press/us/en/pressrelease/34198.wss

IBM. (2011b). *IBM Poughkeepsie green data center.* Retrieved April 2, 2011, from http://www-01.ibm.com/software/success/cssdb.nsf/CS/LWIS-8FEUFH?OpenDocument&Site=default&cty=en_us

IBM. (2011c). *IBM service delivery manager.* Retrieved March 1, 2011, from http://www-01.ibm.com/software/tivoli/products/service-delivery-manager/

IBM. (2011d). *IBM Systems z - News: Cloud computing with System z.* Retrieved Jan 31, 2011, from http://www-03.ibm.com/systems/z/news/announcement/20090915_annc.html

IBM/CISCO. (2008). *Virtualized storage infrastructure solution from IBM and Cisco.* Retrieved from http://www.cisco.com/web/partners/pr67/pr30/pr220/docs/IBM_Cisco_Virtualized_Storage_042808_SB.pdf

Juniper. (2010a). *Cloud-ready data center reference architecture.* Retrieved from http://www.juniper.net/us/en/local/pdf/reference-architectures/8030001-en.pdf

Juniper. (2010b). *Government data center network reference architecture.* Retrieved from http://www.juniper.net/us/en/local/pdf/reference-architectures/8030004-en.pdf

Juniper. (2010c). *Network fabrics for modern data center.* Retrieved from http://www.juniper.net/us/en/local/pdf/whitepapers/2000327-en.pdf

Katz, R. H. (2009). Tech titans building boom. *Spectrum, IEEE, 46*(2), 40-54.

Masahiko, J., & Yukio, T. (2009). *Virtualized optical network (VON) for agile cloud computing environment.* Paper presented at the Optical Fiber Communication Conference.

Mather, T., Kumaraswamy, S., & Latif, S. (2009). *Cloud security and privacy* (1st ed.). Cambridge, MA: O'Reilly.

NIST. (2010). *NIST definition of cloud computing* v15 Retrieved May 1, 2011, from http://csrc.nist. gov/groups/SNS/cloud-computing/

Oberle, K., Stein, M., Voith, T., Gallizo, G., Ku, X., et al. (2010, 11-14 October). *The network aspect of infrastructure-as-a-service.* Paper presented at the 2010 14th International Conference on Intelligence in Next Generation Networks (ICIN).

Orenstein, G. (2010). *Show me the gateway - Taking storage to the cloud.* Retrieved December 21, 2010, from http://gigaom.com/2010/06/22/show-me-the-gateway-taking-storage-to-the-cloud/

Partridge, R. (2011). *Are mainframe the original cloud platform?* Retrieved April 6, 2011, from http://ideasint.blogs.com/ideasinsights/2011/04/ are-mainframes-the-original-cloud-plat-forms.html?utm_source=feedburner&utm_ medium=feed&utm_campaign=Feed%3A+Idea sInsights+%28IDEAS+Insights%29

Patrizio, A. (2010). *IDC sees cloud market maturing quickly.* Retrieved December 1, 2010, from http://itmanagement.earthweb.com/netsys/ article.php/3870016/IDC-Sees-Cloud-Market-Maturing-Quickly.htmhttp:/itmanagement. earthweb.com/netsys/article.php/3870016/IDC-Sees-Cloud-Market-Maturing-Quickly.htm

Pultz, J. E. (2009). *10 key actions to reduce IT infrastructure and operations cost structure. (No. G00170304).* Gartner.

Reese, G. (2009). *Cloud application architectures: Building applications and infrastructure in the Cloud.* Sebastopol, CA: O'Reilly Media, Inc.

Rittinghouse, J. W., & Ransome, J. F. (2010). *Cloud computing: Implementation, management, and security.* Boca Raton, FL: CRC Press.

Riverbed (2011). WAN acceleration. Retrieved April 2, 2011, from http://www.wan-acceleration. org

Ruest, D., & Ruest, N. (2009). *Virtualization: A beginner's guide.* New York, NY: McGraw Hill.

Sarna, D. E. Y. (2011). *Implementing and developing cloud computing applications.* Boca Raton, FL: CRC Press.

SNIA. (2011). *SNIA - SNIA cloud storage initiative.* Retrieved March 1, 2011, from http://www. snia.org/cloud

Spinola, M. (2009). *An essential guide to possibilities and risks of cloud computing.*

Sridhar, T. (2009a). Cloud computing - A primer part 1: Models and technologies. *The Internet Protocol Journal Cisco, 12*(3), 2–19.

Sridhar, T. (2009b). Cloud computing - A primer part 2: Infrastructure and implementation topics. *The Internet Protocol Journal Cisco, 12*(4).

Velte, A. T., Velte, T. J., & Elsenpeter, R. C. (2010). *Cloud computing: A practical approach.* New York, NY: McGraw-Hill.

Wikipedia. (2011a). *Cloud storage.* Retrieved March 1, 2011, from http://en.wikipedia.org/wiki/ Cloud_storage

Wikipedia. (2011b). *Hypervisor.* Retrieved January 15, 2011, from http://en.wikipedia.org/wiki/ Hypervisor

Wikipedia. (2011c). *Virtual private server.* Retrieved August 25, 2011, from http://en.wikipedia. org/wiki/Virtual_private_server

Wikipedia. (n.d.). *Thin client.* Retrieved February 1, 2011, from http://en.wikipedia.org/wiki/ Thin_client

Chapter 3
Software as a Service (SaaS)

Cecelia Wright Brown
University of Baltimore, USA

Kofi Nyarko
Morgan State University, USA

ABSTRACT

SaaS, short for Software-as-a-Service, is quickly becoming the dominant approach for software delivery as a Web-based service. It is a software deployment model in which an enterprise application is delivered and managed as a service by a software vender to simultaneously meet the needs of multiple customers. By enabling remote access to software and its associated functions, SaaS allows organizations and individuals to access business and commercial functionality at a cost typically less than paying for licensed applications. The purpose of this chapter is to discuss the origin and evolution of SaaS, as well as to describe its roll in today's enterprise environment. This chapter begins with a description of the evolution of SaaS, followed by the architecture, implementation, and associated business model.

INTRODUCTION

SaaS is considered both a business model and application delivery model. As such, it encompasses a wide array of business, marketing and technical opportunities, issues, and challenges. The flexibility of SaaS implementations also means organizations can be charged on a Pay-as-you-go basis. One of the key benefits of SaaS, is that since it is a hosted application, users do not need to invest in costly hardware. In general, it removes the need for organizations to handle installation,

set-up and the daily maintenance of servers and software. An aggregator may also bundle software by several providers in order to provide customers with a broad range of services that provide significant value to those with specific needs. This chapter will discuss the evolution of SaaS with considerations given to the independent software vender and the various methods of delivery. The architecture from which SaaS is derived is then discussed, followed by its present architecture. This chapter also discusses the process of implementing a SaaS model as well as the associated business model.

DOI: 10.4018/978-1-4666-2187-9.ch003

BACKGROUND

SaaS is a technological invention dating back to the 1990s that initially went unnoticed due to the rapid adoption of web services that was taking place during that time. Software applications during this period mainly operated in isolation on a single machine. Internet connections had very low bandwidths in the 1990s, which severely limited the adoption of software delivery over the Internet. The subscription approach to software delivery was later employed to provide software services to multiple systems without requiring the users to purchase and maintain locally installed applications. Even though SaaS implementations were becoming more prevalent in the late 90s, it was still impractical due to old prevailing web technologies and limits in data communication technologies. Furthermore, major software vendors like Microsoft and Oracle did not view SaaS as a reliable alternative for mission critical services. Thus, SaaS found its use in practical small-medium markets, where it was employed as a solution to software problems of limited scope. When larger vendors like Salesforce and Netsuite began to show interest in the subscription model of SaaS, its popularity began to improve significantly. Businesses quickly learned that SaaS afforded them the liberty to access entire system services or subscribe to only the essential ones. Other reasons why SaaS started to be widely adopted include:

1. Higher internet bandwidth and restructuring of data networks
2. Internet speeds increased exponentially, thus reducing SaaS latency
3. Internet became more affordable
4. Businesses possessed significantly higher bandwidths

Furthermore, as people became more comfortable with conducting just about everything online, the SaaS model became more familiar.

Initially software vendors found it hard to accept the subscription model commonly employed by SaaS vendors. However, as the number of internet subscribers exploded in the early millennium, vendors began to realize the untapped potential of recurring revenue with relatively low overhead offered by the subscription based SaaS model (Menken, 2008; 2010).

Today, the typical method by which customers access a SaaS application is through a Web browser or a thin client over the Internet. If any customization capabilities are provided, they are generally available to all customers in a consistent manner. While this presents obvious benefits to the customer, such as ongoing support and upgrades, there is also significant benefit to the independent software vendor. From the perspective of the vendor, this model inherently provides strong protection of intellectual property, while offering strict control of the software-operating environment. In addition, the SaaS model generally provides a repeatable revenue stream from the service subscription fees. Furthermore, while software vendors may have various applications with varying capabilities, it is generally not necessary to have unique instances of applications for each customer who has special needs. Often, all that's necessary is a single SaaS application instance that can support many unique customers. This concept, called multi-tenancy, is discussed in more depth further in the chapter. These characteristics of the SaaS model make it a ubiquitous network-based solution, which is perfectly suited to serve the needs of a highly dispersed workforce (Menken, 2008; 2010).

The Four Waves of SaaS

While many concepts have been used to describe the emergence and future of the SaaS model, the most enduring one is the Four Waves concept. Understanding this concept may help software vendors who are considering moving an existing application service provider (ASP) or client-server application to a SaaS enabled one. The SaaS vendor's approach in the first wave is very simple, typically involving a stand-alone application. In this implementation, the focus is generally cost savings due to the ease of deployment and maintenance. Typically only about 20% of IT budgets are allocated for software, with the lion's share spent on people, services and hardware required to operate the software. By taking responsibility for operating the software on behalf of the customer, a larger portion of the IT budget may be applied to the software itself while reducing the overall size of the budget necessary, thereby increasing profitability, even after hosting fees are paid.

In the second wave, there is a more mainstream adoption of SaaS services, where the solutions tend to be more sophisticated. In the current state of the SaaS offerings, which can be clearly identified as the second wave, there is an emphasis on more customization capabilities and integration. With SaaS gaining in popularity in the corporate ecosystem, it will become increasingly important to integrate these solutions as part of a comprehensive corporate software strategy. When this point arrives, SaaS will have entered the third wave where it evolves, matures and gains widespread acceptance in a manner where it becomes integrated into the fabric of existing corporate data structure. Consequently it becomes a critical component spurring business transformation and streamlining existing processes to be more efficient and cost effective. In some cases, new business processes are created that would otherwise have been unfeasible.

Finally, the fourth wave encompasses the cloud-computing paradigm. Cloud computing extends the concept of on-demand software, embodied by SaaS, to include on-demand infrastructure. It provides more flexibly deployed and managed solutions, which compliment the impact of the third wave by accelerating business transformation. In order to reach this level of in-

tegration, the independent software vendor must adopt SaaS as the primary means for delivering enterprise application solutions.

Benefits of SaaS

The SaaS model offers tremendous benefits for both the independent software vendor (ISV) and the customer. In the case of the customer, they benefit from the vendor's latest technological features without the disruption and costs associated with traditional software updates and upgrades. Even though the SaaS vendor now has the responsibility for ensuring the availability, reliability, security and scalability of the software solution, they also benefit from the demise of some of the traditional software development and distribution processes such as support for varying hardware platforms as well as the logistics involved in physical deployment of the software. Customers do not need to pay for software maintenance agreements that place the burden on them to notify the vendor when a problem arises. Rather the SaaS vendor provides the service level agreement (SLA) that clearly states how the vendor will proactively support the software services to ensure their availability, security, and performance. In this way the vendor's success is closely aligned with how effectively the agreed level of service is provided, which is facilitated by the tight control the vendor holds over the physical and software platform upon which the service exists.

An ISV embracing the SaaS model needs to ensure their overall business plan includes a 'dual mode' operation: on premises software and SaaS application. Generally speaking, this often requires additional R&D investment in the software being delivered as well as revised budgets for many departments, including Sales, Marketing Development and Support. The business plan will most likely have to be adjusted to reflect a percentage of income being delivered through recurring subscriptions, as opposed to the single charge for software license fees and annual maintenance payments.

Well Known SaaS Vendors

Recently, Adobe, a software company that focuses on tools for content creation and delivery, announced that its entire software offering will adopt a SaaS model. The reason cited for adapting this model is the notion of keeping things simple, requiring a focus on usability and experience rather than features alone. Expanding on this shift Adobe has launched stripped down online versions of some of its popular applications, such as Premiere Express, which powers the video mashups at sites like Photobucket and YouTube. The general principle being adopted by Adobe is to offer a subset of features, which fall short of their traditional software packages, but are useful and usable by the broader community while cleverly applying the 80/20 rule (20% of your customers generate 80% of your revenue).

Google is one of the leaders of the SaaS revolution. The company was incorporated in 1998, and introduced a well-known email service, called "Gmail", in 2004. With such productivity tools, Google made significant contributions to introducing the SaaS model to a vast majority of the world's population. Most Google productivity tools are offered in two ways:

1. Free, with limited functionality
2. Paid, with complete functionality

Google's many online offerings of productivity tools have started to rival their competitor's desktop counterparts. While it is widely conceived that these products do not rival their competitor's in features, they often succeed due to the convenience of adoption and the free price tag.

Microsoft is another renowned company, providing SaaS facilities, which were established in 1997. Like Google, it has also introduced free

and paid software packages, however due to its legacy as a traditional software company, most of its software offerings are traditional desktop applications. However, Microsoft has been dedicating significant resources to moving key enterprise applications, such as Microsoft Office, to "the Cloud".

The company most often associated with SaaS is Salesforce. Its business model is managing customer relationship management (CRM) tools, which counts as one of the largest SaaS products. A close second is Content Software Services, which include marketing services, sales services and call centre operation service. Salesforce was started by Marc Benioff, a former Oracle executive, in 1999. Salesforce is expanding rapidly and diversifying swiftly. This means they are quickly becoming a dominating force in the SaaS market. They have the unique ability to offer their clients complete packages of services in contrast to separate and small services as they are usually marketed in SaaS.

MAIN FOCUS OF THE CHAPTER

SaaS Delivery Model and Architecture

SaaS systems can be configured and delivered using various delivery models. Generally, they can be deployed in a matter of hours to support time-sensitive and business-critical processes. As mentioned earlier, the software can be hosted off-premises (in the cloud), on-premises (at the end user organization), or even as a "hybrid" configuration with the database-hosted on-premises while the application is hosted in the cloud. A well-engineered SaaS system should offer a number of these installation/configuration options in order to satisfy the various customer security, governance and control requirements.

Some SaaS ISV's host their services on their own data centers, although the number of ISVs taking this path is quickly dwindling. While this delivery method is still more efficient than delivering software to the customer's site, it burdens the ISV with operational responsibilities, such as building a datacenter, providing availability, performance, security, reliability etc. An increasing number of ISVs can now take advantage of emerging Cloud Computing platforms, such as Microsoft Azure and Amazon EC2, which permit them to bring new SaaS applications to market without a heavy investment in hardware infrastructure and a minimum involvement in operational processes. The cloud computing platforms provide "elastic" resources, which are often priced at utility levels, on a subscription bases designed to cope with fluctuations in demand. This is an ideal platform for both start-up and established ISVs entering the SaaS market.

With the hybrid delivery model, the SaaS vendor hosts the application, while the database is located on the customer's site. This model is most ideal for organizations that have database security or compliance issues but still desire the low hassle benefits of a SaaS solution. The hybrid model is especially well suited for dealing with government regulations that impose restrictions on the location of the databases.

Some organizations have specific high value applications with security or compliance requirements that do not permit off-premises storage of corporate data. For such organizations, the on-premises model is the most ideal. With this model, the application is either run on the customer's servers or on servers furnished by the SaaS vendor. In this case, the application is generally treated as a conventional application that accomplishes a specific objective, thus it is deployed as a Single-Instance, Single Tenant (SIST) application. However, the customer may choose to switch on the multi-tenant capabilities of the SaaS application to have the software used in other parts of the organization. International companies could rely on this method to have SaaS applications on-premises, while each branch, located in different countries, operates as a tenant

of the overall system. Even though the application could be running behind a firewall on vendor supplied appliances on the customer's premises (as opposed to the cloud), the appliances are still considered part of the vender's cloud, and is thus still maintained and updated by the vendor.

Platform as a Service (PaaS) has recently emerged as an underlying layer, supporting SaaS applications. Currently, there are two main types of PaaS offerings: platforms that have emerged from successful SaaS applications and platforms that have been designed, from the beginning, to provide a generic software platform for SaaS application developers. The PaaS vendor reduces the effort, development cost, and time involved in creating SaaS applications by providing key resources and services. Examples of these services and resources include extensible databases, role based security, screen generation, and report generation. However, SaaS applications built on a PaaS becomes dependent on that PaaS, which reduces the independence of the ISV. This may in turn devalue the ISV in the eyes of investors. Furthermore, depending on the nature of the PaaS, SaaS applications may not be able to be deployed as on-premise applications.

The current SaaS architecture is an extension of the distributed application architecture, illustrated in Figure 1. The User tier simply consists of thin client applications, such as the web browser, which handles input and output from the server. The application tier houses the application server, which among other things, handles HTTP/HTTPS requests and communicates with the Data Access Engine tier. The data access tier provides a level of abstraction between the business logic and the data itself by handling the processing of data requests. Lastly, there is the data storage tier, where the physical storage of data resides.

SaaS can be considered as both an application delivery model and a business model. In that regard, the distributed application architecture is extended to include components that facilitate and enhance the business model. In the case of a

Figure 1. Distributed application architecture

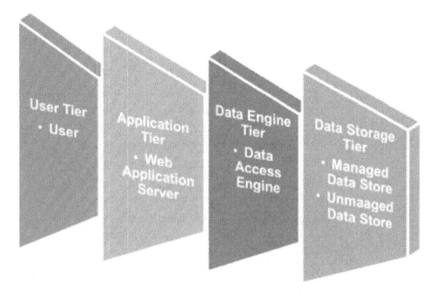

traditional software vender, the primary concern is with application functionality. Customers are often taxed with the responsibility of operating and managing the respective environments in which their software resides (SaaS Attack, 2008). This is typically not the case with a SaaS vendor. They are equally concerned with the operation and management of the environment that supports their customers.

A typical SaaS architecture is depicted in Figure 2. In this architecture, an additional distribution tier is included to represent the fact that service requests may not be contained to a single physical operating environment, but rather they may be routed between several environments for various reasons. Additionally, the application tier now contains additional components that take into account the additional functionality required of a mature SaaS offering. Administration and monitoring, which are critical to the efficient operation of a SaaS business, are presented as components that operate across tiers.

The distribution tier is responsible for handling load balancing. The term load balancing represents a set of techniques for distributing tasks across multiple systems in order to optimize resource utilization, throughput or response time. This is a critical aspect for SaaS businesses since it ensures that customers are provided with the best level of service possible under severe resource loads. There are other reasons why it may be advantageous to route service requests to different physical operating environments. One such reason is to ensure resiliency by leveraging multiple, geographically disparate data centers. Each data center provides a similar set of services to one another, so that customer requests can be routed among them as governed by the local resources available at each center. In this way, resources are efficiently utilized while providing high availability to the customers. This process is part of a broader topic on hosting and replication.

Yet another reason to route certain service requests to specific environments maybe to comply with international data privacy laws. Data privacy is a pervasive issue that every country seems to handle differently. There are certification programs, such as Safe Harbor, instituted by the U.S. Department of Commerce, to facilitate compliance with the privacy laws of other nations. However, even with these programs, there is no guarantee that customers in other countries will not require

Figure 2. Typical SaaS architecture

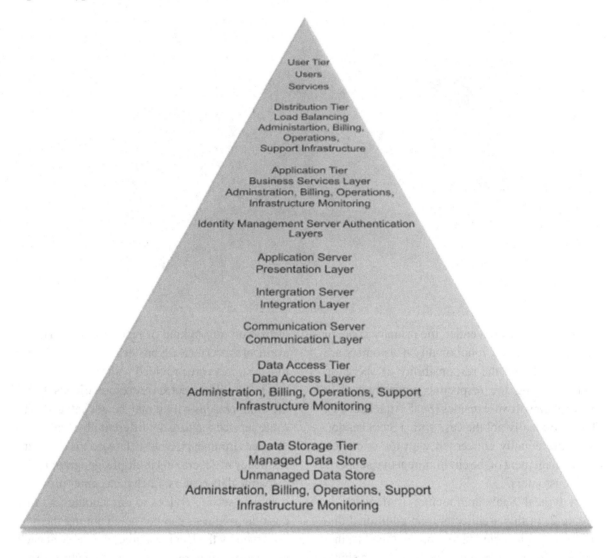

that their corporate data be physically housed in their own country. This is a very complex topic that is outside the scope of this text. For SaaS vendors wishing to develop businesses in such countries, it may be necessary to support multiple production environments in disparate locations, where service requests are routed as necessary.

In this architecture, the application tier has also been revised. The SaaS architecture model provides quite a bit of detail regarding the application tier. This tier has evolved from a general application server running an application to one that represents various types of specialized servers, each of which provides specific services and functionality.

An often-overlooked component of the SaaS architecture is outbound/inbound communication. At the very least, it is a useful way to reach customers to inform them that the SaaS application requires their input. This communication could occur through methods like email, which use a mail/message transport agent, or MTA. Although it is a simple process to run, it often requires more thought and design.

Implementation

In recent years, an increasing number of customers have come to recognize the benefits of the SaaS model, it is no longer considered a buzzword, but rather a mainstream solution. Consequently, it is becoming imperative for ISVs that have traditional on-premise software to seriously consider SaaS implementations. However, while transitioning to SaaS may make long-term business sense, it requires a fair amount of planning and organization. ISVs with traditional offerings must undergo several significant organization-wide changes to successfully transition to an on-demand model. There is no particular silver bullet approach for implementing SaaS, yet, any approach should consider the fundamental requirements of scalability and multi-tenancy.

Scalability and Multi-Tenancy

Scalability is an important requirement to consider since customers rely on the SaaS vendor to reliably provide solutions, regardless of the load of the vendor's current and future customer base. In addition, it is critical that the SaaS be able to handle growth from an administrative perspective, otherwise, the business management may quickly become chaotic. Load scalability deals with the system's ability to effectively handle increasing levels of demand and throughput in a non-disruptive manner. Administrative scalability addresses the vendor's ability to manage multiple customers in a single environment in a manner that delivers consistent levels of service to each customer as the customer base grows.

There are two primary methods for achieving scalability. A SaaS vendor can choose to scale vertically also referred to as scaling up, by adding more resources to a node (a device connected to a network, such as a server or router) in system. This type of planning often includes adding redundancy of all components to insure the systems remain operational if a given component fails. The other option available is horizontal scalability. This method is sometimes referred to as scaling out and involves the addition of more nodes to an application server cluster. A cluster is a group of systems that are coupled together over a fast Ethernet backbone. Work is distributed to individual nodes in the cluster in accordance with resource availability and demand.

Mult-tenancy is the architectural model that allows a SaaS vendor to serve multiple customers from a single shared instance of an application. This model allows the SaaS vendor to control the cost structure of the business. For example, it is impractical to have thousands of customers who each operate a separate instance of an application; rather each customer has a customized configuration of the application.

Considerations for ISVs

An ISV may prepare an existing application for SaaS deployment by retro-fitting it with a degree of multi-tenancy. While this option requires changes to the source code, and is thereby considered more intrusive, the result is a more sophisticated approach to SaaS in which simpler application management is provided in addition to more robust application monetization. Furthermore, it provides a good trade-off between the level of investment required and the return on investment. Rather than retro-fit an existing application, an ISV may choose to re-develop the application to produce a true single-instance/multi-tenant application that takes advantage of new opportunities that require a variant of the existing application. If performed well, this could result in a very efficient multi-tenanted application that offers full automatic operation of execution, operation, subscriber management, provisioning, trial creation/conversion, monetization and billing.

In considering the appropriate approach for SaaS implementation, the ISV should consider the following six steps: assessment, proof of concept, detailed analysis, solution design, solution execution, and support/monitor. Before the ISV proceeds with adopting the SaaS model, some thought should be given to if it truly benefits the goals and objectives of the business. It is important to assess whether the current and future user base will be able to provide a return on investment within a practical time frame. Depending where users will be located and how they will access the application, it might be necessary to consider outsourcing the hosting of the infrastructure. A process of carrying out a proof of concept validates key assumptions that were made in the prior assessment step, such as the technical challenges involved, hosting and scalability issues that may arise, the potential impact on business processes and the state of the current architecture.

One of the most crucial steps for SaaS implementation is a detailed analysis involving infrastructure requirements (hardware, network, security, backup etc.), developing the SLA, determining an appropriate revenue model, and defining appropriate support mechanisms. The findings from this analysis feeds into the solution design step in which a design is architected that best suits the SaaS offering. The successful architecture should include considerations for security management, application usage (single vs. multi-tenant), performance and scalability, fail over mechanism, exposing application through web services, and the use of federated servers (virtualization).

Finally, the last two steps for considering SaaS implementation involve solution execution and support. For solution execution, the actual enablement of the application via the SaaS model is considered. Depending on the complexity of the application, this can be planned in a phased approach. Two of the key success factors in this step include having Agile development practices, and testing the software functionality under various stress conditions. Lastly, it is essential to have a monitoring mechanism in place that gauges the usage of the application and handles support ser-

vices. Monitoring the application for performance and availability is vital to meet the SLA.

Even though the SaaS transition path varies, it is critical to understand the influences within a company, such as: engineering, sales, support and finance to name a few. Here are a few considerations: 1) Taking a team approach can garner support and knowledge; 2) Familiarization with the products on the market will help to develop product standards; 3) Examining how to manage cost is an excellent tool to establish a strategy; 4) Decide on the most applicable business model that will enhance initiatives; 5) Be strategic with the SaaS plan, permit time for the transition, inform and assure customers of mutual SaaS benefits; 6) Consider the SLA accountabilities, duties and obligations associated with the SaaS delivery model; 7) Ensure that obligations are met, maintained and measured to reflect the strength of the system; 8) An option for outsourcing can provide flexibility; 9) Advance to a service oriented architecture by distinguishing product functionalities which are scalable within the SaaS architecture; 10) Develop a plan to transition customers from on-premise deployment; 11) Use technology to automate (Wtoll, 2011).

Maturity Level

In order for ISVs to effectively capitalize on the SaaS business model, they must be able to sufficiently gauge maturity level. A suitable maturity model provides an assessment of the solutions and ensures the decisions that must be made by vendors are based on realistic strategies. Targeting the highest maturity level is not necessarily the best fit for every vendor. The first widely accepted maturity model emerged from Microsoft. Their model places SaaS architectures in one of four maturity levels, who's key attributes are configurability, multi-tenant efficiency, and scalability as seen in Figure 3. Another widely accepted SaaS maturity model comes from Forrester Research

Figure 3. Maturity model

Inc (Sorenson & Chen, 2008). They classify the maturity of SaaS solutions on six levels. Each level is defined in response to the question "who provides what to whom" as illustrated in Table 1 (Ried, Rymer, & Iqbal, 2008).

Impact Cycle

Keeping the user at the forefront is critical to the success of SaaS. As companies migrate to SaaS, applications must be sound and employees should

Table 1. Maturity of SaaS solutions on six levels

Levels	Description
Level 0: Outsourcing is not SaaS	With outsourcing, a major application or a unique application landscape for a large enterprise customer is operated by a service provider. The outsourcing company can't leverage this application for a second customer, outsourcing does not qualify as SaaS.
Level 1: Manual ASP business models target midsize companies	A hosting provider runs packaged applications like SAP's ERP 6.0, which require significant IT skills, for multiple midsize enterprises. The client has a dedicated server running its instance of the application and is able to customize the installation in the same way as self-hosted applications.
Level 2: Industrial ASPs cut the operating costs of packaged applications to a minimum	An ASP uses sophisticated IT management software to provide identical software packages with customer-specific configurations to many SMB customers. The software package is the original software created for self-hosted deployment.
Level 3: Single-app SaaS is an alternative to traditional packaged applications	Software vendors create new generations of business applications that have SaaS capabilities built in. Web-based user interface (UI) concepts and the ability to serve a number of tenants with scalable infrastructure are typical characteristics. Customization is restricted to configuration. Single-app SaaS adoption focusing on SMBs. Salesforce.com's (CRM) applications initially entered the market at this level.
Level 4: Business-domain SaaS provides all the applications for an entire business domain	Advanced SaaS vendors provide a well-defined business applications and a platform for additional business logic. This complements the original single application of the previous level with third-party packaged SaaS solutions and custom extensions. The model satisfies the requirements of a large enterprise, which can migrate a complete business domain like "customer care" toward SaaS.
Level 5: Dynamic Business Apps-as-a-service is the visionary target	Forrester's Dynamic Business Application imperative embraces a new paradigm of application development: "design for people, build for change." Advanced SaaS vendors coming from level 4 will provide a comprehensive application and integration platform on demand, which they will pre-populate with business applications or business services. They can compose tenant-specific and user-specific business applications on various levels. The resulting process agility will attract customers, including large enterprise.

be well versed on performance and procedures (IXDA 2007). This can reduce the probability of employee disputes over business application performance (Hoffman, 2007). A survey by Kaminario, showed that employee productivity due to poor application performance was cited as a critical issue by 25% of the respondents. It would be suitable to integrate employee efficiency with page load, page refresh, data entry and system performance metrics. ISVs are increasingly investing time in web applications to ensure performance metrics are acceptable so that business efficiency and user approval is not compromised. The SaaS influence in business is evident within industry, operational and engineering cycles as presented in Figure 4, a SaaS Business Impact Cycle (Wtoll, 2011; Menken, 2008)

Administration

The administration of a SaaS system is influenced by the service distribution and the affective administration of the business within an architecture. There are a few concepts to consider when examining SaaS administration. The billing model is most feasible when an assessment of customer metering has been performed. A metering solution should advance usage data to a billing system that accurately generates and presents customer invoices for payment. Where applicable, billing can be managed within the SaaS setting or by an external billing service. For example, a billing process which accepts usage input from metering or contractual details with a fixed recurring fee would be practical. With this type of metering process a recurring invoice can be created and

Figure 4. SaaS business impact cycle

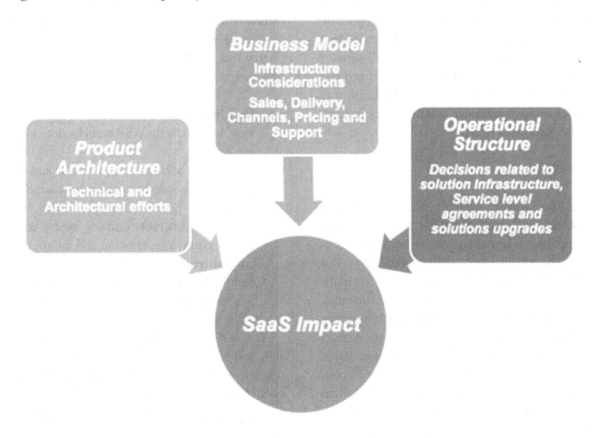

given to the customer for payment. Operations are generally responsible for maintaining and ensuring that the SaaS environment provides quality service. Preferably, the support, help desk or ticketing system is fused into the administration component. If a ticketing system is incorporated into a SaaS application, clients can submit tickets directly from the application or phone the help desk where the status can be tracked.

Infrastructure Monitoring

A SaaS infrastructure should contain hardware redundancy and data recovery failover capacity to a remote location as part of data back-up. A number of methods are available to assist with monitoring the SaaS environment, such as SLA reporting. Automating reporting and providing fast access to generated reports can effectively manage SLAs. In addition, a monitoring component can help assess the efficiency of support staff, which is critical in determining when and how to increase staff in response to business growth. By implementing tracking support metrics that include the management of the overall support function, the number of support calls, and per client ticket figures, it is easier to build customer assurance and confidence, which ensures stability in the SaaS environment.

Configuration

The Four Waves Evolution Model, provides a high level of constructability and adaptability where dissimilar methods can work for dissimilar customers using the same methodology. For example, a hierarchical data structure that traditionally would consider a user interface tree may not be as practical as a paginated table interface for a customer that has volumes of data. A SaaS solution can support more than one application implementation and allow the customer to construct an application to perform in a manner that is acceptable. Contemplating how to implement configurable functionality is as important as using

a variety of customized versions of the application to accomplish the goal of maturity in SaaS implementation.

A consistent approach has become the technology norm for web-based user interface through cascading style sheets (CSS), where customers have options to customize and develop the SaaS application. The SaaS model requires customers to use a single version of an application as opposed to separate customized versions. In some instances this can be problematic for SaaS vendors because, they need to continue to provide customers customizable tools for the application. One approach is to permit extensions of system objects via custom fields. The custom fields should be clearly defined and utilized in a manner that eliminates the need to change the database schema.

Saas Business and Pricing Model

SaaS services, also considered on-demand solutions or services, are considered the next generation of Application Service Provision (ASP) services (Kang et al., 2010; TripleTree, 2004; Cherry Tree, 2000). The advantages of SaaS over ASP include,

- SaaS integrates an e-commerce point-of-view instead of the ASP model's outsourcing view
- The SaaS model focus on the skills and requirements needed to customize customer solutions
- SaaS is a coherent business model concerned with value creation and appropriation whereas ASP is more of a technical definition as depicted in Figure 5, a generic SaaS business model

The SaaS model is different from the development and release business model, of which ISVs customers had become accustomed. As indicated by SIIA (2001), from the vendor's point-of-view there are three primary benefits in moving to the SaaS model:

Figure 5. Generic SaaS business model

- It reduces the substantial costs of code delivery to the customer (also updates can be provided faster and more often)
- Recurring-revenue models, traditionally enjoyed by the ISPs, are extremely appealing to software developers (Cusumano, 2003; Nambisan, 2001)
- Online service model greatly expands the potential customer base of the ISV

Other reasons for moving to a software service model are that firms may want to change their "traditional" business model to a more Internet focused approach, offer better online services and information to customers, limit the costs of implementing and configuring software for customers, and/or attract new customers, partners, and investors (TripleTree, 2004; Cherry Tree, 2000).

As related to an ISV, the SaaS model is considered to be a new sale or distribution channel, which would not necessitate a complete renewal of the company's strategy. For an ISV with es-

tablished customers, the key issue centers around bringing software services to market with the least disruption to any current sales or distribution channels, while achieving a maximum additive effect on sales.

SaaS pricing tends to differ from traditional software, which typically relies on a perpetual license process with an up-front fee. Depending on the nature of the software, and its deployment, venders may charge additional smaller ongoing support fees. On the other hand, SaaS pricing is generally based on one of two service models:

1. Subscription model
2. "Fremium" model

With the general subscription, or "pay-as-you-go," model SaaS providers charge a monthly or annual fee for access to their services, where the initial setup costs tend to be low. SaaS providers may choose to provide granular subscription fees based on usage parameters, such as the number

Table 2. Benefits and risks for SaaS provider

Benefits for the SaaS provider	Risks for the SaaS provider
SaaS enables economies of scale in production and distribution (one-to many offering)	It is difficult to manage the complex network of suppliers, which is required for integrating the product and service businesses
The cash flows from SaaS are more predictable than in traditional software sales (recurring revenue)	Moving to the SaaS model initially reduces the turnover as the revenue comes from monthly/quarterly service fees instead of license sales
SaaS expands the potential customer base	Performance and scalability issues are to be expected, depending on the technical solution used
The sales cycle of SaaS services is shorter than that of traditional software sales	High initial investment in starting the SaaS business (building and maintaining the required IT infrastructure and costs of buying 3rd party software)
SaaS lowers version management and maintenance costs	The customization of the SaaS applications typically incurs extra costs
By successfully integrating products and services into a SaaS offering, provider creates barriers to entry for competitors	Requires commitment to a more frequent release/upgrade cycle

of users, sometimes referred to as seats, or on a unit basis, such as per transaction or event. The advantage to this pricing model in general, is that it allows companies to modify cost associated with acquiring software, from capital budgets to operating budgets. Companies can remunerate the cost of software, providing additional flexibility to alter software fees to compliment business needs. In a SaaS pay-as-you-go subscription pricing model customers pay for the level of service needed, as opposed to paying the full cost for a software license in advance without full deployment. What make this model feasible are the cost and the reduced risks associated with deploying an enterprise application. A SaaS model passes the responsibility of effectively deploying and maintaining applications from the customer to the vendor. SaaS vendors maintain accessibility, consistency and safety, which allow a user to leverage the software's functionality without worrying about management. Companies can avoid hidden costs of additional hardware, which

may be needed to fully support an application or dedicate additional staff to support the application on an ongoing basis. Table 2 outlines a few of the benefits and risk a SaaS provider may face (SaaS Attack, 2008).

The other general SaaS pricing model is typically termed "Fremium". With this model, SaaS providers essentially provide free access to their services, albeit with limited functionality or scope. This is made possible due to the low cost of setting up a new user in a multi-tenant environment, also referred to as user provisioning. The long-term goal of this approach is to attract as many users as possible, based on freely available services that provide sufficient functionality. As users become more comfortable with the offerings and integrate the services within their workflow, they elect to upgrade their service to obtain enhanced functionality and broader scope.

For ISVs, there are several points to consider when migrating to a SaaS pricing model:

- ISVs have to retrofit into the SaaS existing product portfolio regardless of the limited visibility associated with customer value. Hence, established ISVs should distinguish their products, service solutions and establish a method to support the new pricing model. This can be accomplished by deploying a software monitoring and metering mechanism which automatically measure and bill for software use.

- It can be challenging to determine how to package and price new offerings for ISVs seeking to implement SaaS. The ISVs will need to limit the risk of customers discarding existing software products in favor of the SaaS solutions. Which many not be completely undesirable when the alternative could be losing the customer entirely.

- What are the financial implications of the SaaS model on revenue recognition? Customary ISVs are straightforward in acknowledging the full value of their perpetual licensing agreements. Keep in mind SaaS revenue is only recognized as it is earned.

- SaaS has a low price point. Many SaaS providers offer a free single-user licenses in hopes that their starter sets will quickly gain market share and convert users to more profitable enterprise packages. However, it is has been difficult generating the add-on and up-sell prospects which was anticipated to offset the low-cost solution.

- This is not a one size fit all model. Traditionally, ISVs who balance their solution pricing and existing product pricing schedules can experience difficultly when determining a customer's price-sensitivity for SaaS. So, ISVs with channel partners that sell and support end-users will become problematic because a means to gauge customers pricing preferences is missing.

FUTURE RESEARCH DIRECTIONS

As SaaS evolves it will remain increasingly significant to enterprise and a highly dispersed workforce. As such, how will the future look for SaaS? For starters, SaaS applications will not be limited to a particular business, but will rather be more applicable to a user's network. This will most likely result in a more user-friendly model, as opposed to a business friendly one. In addition, even though a variety of product marketing and management strategies for SaaS exist, the trend to emphasis more comprehensive product features will be essential to business processes. If businesses allow financial metrics to continue to drive the technology strategy, the ability to strengthen a dependable, accessible service at a low cost will serve as a serious business advantage. It is also likely that SAAS products will begin to utilize more digital and social media strategies as customers become more accustomed to this sort of interaction.

CONCLUSION

It has been established that SaaS has a track record of success and has become a mainstream movement. SaaS has ascended a generation of SaaS-based IT management software. SaaS is easy to deploy, use and maintain. Many SaaS customers have expressed a high degree of satisfaction, which often translates to referrals through social networks. This type of unsolicited customer satisfaction is paramount to the continuation and diversity of SaaS service offerings, which will continue to expand.

REFERENCES

Cherry Tree. (2000, September). *Framing the IT services industry: 2nd generation ASPs*. Spotlight Report, Cherry Tree & Co. Retrieved from www.cherrytreeco.com

Cusumano, M. (2003). Finding your balance in the products and service debate. *Communications of the ACM, 46*(3), 15–17. doi:10.1145/636772.636786

Hoffman, R. (2007, March 11). *Why being embarrassed is critical to the success of your startup*. Retrieved from http://www.cambrianhouse.com/blog/startups-entrepreneurship/why-being-embarrassed-is-critical-to-the-success-of-your-startup/

IXDA Interaction Design Association. (2007, November 27). Define the "user centered design" process. Retrieved from http://www.ixda.org/node/15599

Menken, I. (2008, November 20). *SaaS - The complete cornerstone guide to software as a service best practices concepts, terms, and techniques for successfully planning, implementing and managing saas solutions*, (pp. 12, 18, 19, 34, 36, 39). Emereo Pty. Ltd.

Menken, I., & Blokdijk, G. (2009, October 10). Cloud computing best practice guide specialist, software as a service & web applications, (pp. 11-19, 43, 45, 46). Emereo Pty. Ltd.

Menken, I., & Blokdijk, G. (2010, September 8). Cloud computing: SaaS and Web applications specialist level complete certification kit - Software as a service study guide book and online course, (2nd ed, pp. 11-21, 38-42, 43). Emereo Pty. Ltd.

Nambisan, S. (2001). Why service business are not product businesses. *MIT Sloan Management Review, 42*(4), 72–81.

Ried, S., Rymer, J. R., & Iqbal, R. (2008). *Forrester's SaaS maturity model*. Forrester Research.

SaaS-Attack. (2008). *SaaS maturity model*. Retrieved from http://www.saas-attack.com/saasmaturitymodel.aspx

SaaS-Attack. (2008). *SaaS business model*. Retrieved from http://www.saas-attack.com/SaaSModel/SaaSBusinessModels/tabid/60/Default.aspx

SaaS-Attack. (2008). *SaaS pricing model*. Retrieved from http://www.saas-attack.com/SaaSModel/SaaSPricingModel/tabid/216/Default.aspx

Seungseok, K., Jaeseok, M., Jongheum, Y., Seong-Wook, H., Taehyung, C., Ji-man, C., & Sang-Goo, L. (2010). *General maturity model and reference architecture for SaaS service* (pp. 337–346).

Sorenson, P., & Chen, X. (2008 October, 28). *Towards SaaS (software as a service) evaluation model*. Department of Computing Science, University of Alberta. Retrieved from http://ssrg.cs.ualberta.ca/images/3/35/CASCON2008-Sorenson.pdf

TripleTree. (2004). *Software as a service: Changing the paradigm in the software industry*. Washington, DC: SIIA and TripleTree Industry Analysis Series. Retrieved from www.siia.net

Wtoll. (2011, April 15). *The SaaS transition and the importance of web performance*. Retrieved from http://blog.yottaa.com/2011/04/the-saas-transition-and-the-importance-of-web-performance

ADDITIONAL READING

Aramand, M. (2008). Software products and services are high tech? New products development strategy for software products and services. *Technovation, 28*(3), 154–160. doi:10.1016/j.technovation.2007.10.004

Baca, F. (2009). Considering HR outsourcing? Consider SaaS. *Financial Executive, 25*(8), 59–60.

Biddick, M. (2010, January 18). Time for a SaaS strategy. *InformationWeek, 1254,* 27–32.

Blokdijk, G. (2008). *SaaS 100 success secrets – How companies successfully buy, manage, host and deliver software as a service (SaaS).* Brisbane, Australia: Emereo Pty Ltd.

Braude, E. (2008). Software-as-a-service and offshoring. *International Journal of Business Insights & Transformation, 2*(1), 93–95.

Brereton, O. P. (1999, December). The future of software. *Communications of the ACM, 42*(12), 78–84. doi:10.1145/322796.322813

Campbell-Kelly, M. (2009). Historical reflections: The rise, fall, and resurrection of software as a service. *Communications of the ACM, 52*(5), 28–30. doi:10.1145/1506409.1506419

Chia, E. (2008). Matheting firm adopts software-as-a-service path. *Enterprise Innovation, 4*(1), 23.

Choudhary, V. (2007). Comparison of software quality under perpetual licensing and software as a service. *Journal of Management Information Systems, 24*(2), 141–165. doi:10.2753/MIS0742-1222240206

Choudhary, V., Tomak, K., & Chaturvedi, A. (1998). Economic benefits of software renting. *Journal of Organizational Computing and Electronic Commerce, 8*(4), 277–305. doi:10.1207/s15327744joce0804_2

Concha, D., Espadas, J., Romero, D., & Molina, A. (2010). The e-HUB evolution: From a custom software architecture to a Sofware-as-a-Service implementation. *Computers in Industry, 61*(2), 145–151. doi:10.1016/j.compind.2009.10.010

Fan, M., Kumar, S., & Whinston, A. B. (2009). Short-term and long-term competitions between providers of shrink-wrap software and software as a service. *European Journal of Operational Research, 196*(2), 661–671. doi:10.1016/j.ejor.2008.04.023

Goth, G. (2008). Software-as-a-service: The spark that will change software engineering? *IEEE Distributed Systems Online, 9*(7).

Greer, M. B. (2009). *Software as a service inflection point: Using cloud computing to achieve business agility.* Bloomington, IN: iUniverse.

Guptill, B., & McNee, W. S. (2008). SaaS sets the stage for 'cloud computing'. *Financial Executive, 24*(5), 37–44.

Gurnami, H., & Karlapalem, K. (2001). Optimal pricing strategies for Internet-based software dissemination. *The Journal of the Operational Research Society, 52*(1), 64–70. doi:10.1057/palgrave.jors.2601046

Hatch, R. (2008). *SaaS architecture, adoption and monetization of SaaS projects using best practices service strategy, service design, service transition, service operations and continual service improvement processes.* Brisbane, Australia: Emereo Pty Ltd.

Hoch, F., et al. (2001). *Software as a service: "A to Z" for ISVs.* Washington, DC: Software & Information Industry Association (SIIA).

Huang, K. W., & Sundararajan, A. (2005 November). *Pricing models for on-demand computing.* Working Paper CeDER-05-26, Center for Digital Economy Research, Stern School of Business, New York University.

Kern, T. (2002). Exploring ASP as sourcing strategy: Theoretical perspectives, propositions for practice. *The Journal of Strategic Information Systems, 11,* 153–177. doi:10.1016/S0963-8687(02)00004-5

Krafzig, D., Banke, K., & Slama, D. (2004). *Enterprise SOA: Service-oriented architecture best practices.* Prentice Hall Publishing.

Lamont, J. (2010). SaaS: Integration in the cloud. *KM World, 19*(1), 12–22.

Mietzner, R., Leymann, F., & Papazoglou, M. (2008). *Defining composite configurable SaaS application packages using SCA, variability descriptors and multi-tenancy patterns.* ICIW. doi:10.1109/ICIW.2008.68

Naedele, M. (2003, April). Standards for XML and Web services security. *Computer*, *11*(3), 96–98. doi:10.1109/MC.2003.1193234

Orr, B. (2006). SaaS just may be the end of software as we know it. *ABA Banking Journal*, *98*(8), 51–52.

Pallatto, J. (2006 February 23). IBM recruiting ISVs, partners to SaaS. *The Channel Insider.*

Scheibler, T., Mietzner, R., & Leymann, F. (2008). EAI as a service – Combining the power of executable EAI patterns and SaaS. In *Proceedings of Enterprise Distributed Object Computing.*

Shirky, C. (2002, September). Web services and context horizons. *Computer*, *35*(9), 98–100. doi:10.1109/MC.2002.1033037

Surala, A., Barua, A., & Whinston, A. B. (2009). A transaction cost perspective of the 'software-as-a-service' business model. *Journal of Management Information Systems*, *26*(2), 205–240. doi:10.2753/MIS0742-1222260209

Thompson, J. K. (2009). Business intelligence in a SaaS environment. *Business Intelligence Journal*, *14*(4), 50–55.

Vorisek, J., & Feuerlicht, G. (2004). Is it the right time for the enterprise to adopt software-as-a-service model? *Information & Management*, *17*(3-4), 18–21.

Waters, B. (2005). Software as a service: A look at the customer benefits. *Journal of Digital Asset Management*, *1*(1), 32–39. doi:10.1057/palgrave.dam.3640007

Wong, K. (2008). SaaS vendors buying innovation rather than developing it themselves. *Network-World Asia*, *4*(8), 35.

KEY TERMS AND DEFINITIONS

ASP: Application service provider (ASP) is a term that describes an alternative application deployment model. Applications deployed in an ASP model are most often hosted by a service provider outside of the end customer's premises, and accessed via client-side application or Web browser over a private connection. Traditional application licensing and maintenance conventions apply in this model.

CSS: Cascading style sheets (CSS) is a style sheet language used to describe the presentation of a document written in a markup language.

Customer/Tenant: Customer/Tenant is a term in this document that refers to the company or business that subscribes to the SaaS offering.

Customization: In the context of a SaaS enabled application, customization is defined as changes to the business logic, user interface, and/or database on behalf of a single customer, and requires application code to be recompiled. In practice, most SaaS enabled applications either do not allow for customization, as it 'breaks' the scalability model by requiring the service provider to support multiple code bases, increasing costs, or customization provided to one customer is made available to all customers and users.

HTTP: Hypertext Transfer protocol is a communications protocol used to transfer data on the Web.

HTTPS: Hypertext Transfer protocol over secure socket Layer is a secure HTTP connection, combining a normal HTTP interaction over an encrypted Secure Sockets Layer (SSL) or Transport Layer Security (TLS) connection.

ISV: An independent software vendor which makes and sells software products that run on one or more computer hardware or operating system platform.

Mail/Message Transport Agent: An MTA is an email agent that forwards email from one location to another. Under X.400 ITU-T which recommendation defines standards for Data Communication Networks for Message Handling Systems. If an MTA is unable to transfer email to the next designated step, it will hold and periodically reattempt to send the email for a specified period of time.

Multi-Tenancy: Multi-Tenancy is an architectural design concept used to maximize customer and user scalability. As well as to provide maximum operational scalability and lower support costs for the service provider by leveraging common user interface, business logic, and/or databases for all customers and users. Multi-tenancy at all layers of the application is considered an architectural ideal but not required at all layers to realize benefits. The cost savings often associated with multi-tenancy are often considered key to building and maintaining lower cost service offerings.

Personalization: Personalization in the context of a SaaS-enabled application relates to minor 'tweaks' to the configuration to support the business process of customers and users. The ability to personalize some elements of a SaaS- enabled application are most often designed into the application at the time it was built.

RAM: Random access memory is a type of computer data storage in which data items can be accessed in any order versus requiring the movement of the recording medium or a reading head. This generally refers to the volatile computer memory where the operating system and applications run as opposed to the non-volatile disk drives where data is stored.

SaaS: Software-as-a-service (saas) shares the distinction of being both a business model and an application delivery model. SaaS enables customers to utilize an application on a pay-as-you-go basis and eliminates the need to install and run the application on the customer's own hardware. Customers generally access the application via a Web browser or thin client over the Internet. SaaS is most often subscription-based and all ongoing support, maintenance, and upgrades are provided by the software vendor as part of the service. Application customization capabilities, if available at all, are generally provided to all customers in a consistent manner. From the perspective of the software vendor, the SaaS model provides stronger protection of its intellectual property, operational control of the environment running the software, and generally a repeatable revenue stream from the service subscription fees. Software vendors have varying capabilities and applications can come in varying flavors but SaaS applications most typically support many unique customers using a single instance of that application also known as multi-tenancy.

SaaS Offering: A Saas offering in this document is defined as a turnkey service offering, which includes the application license, maintenance, application support, subscription pricing, and hosting and associated delivery infra- structure.

SaaS-Enabled Application: A saas-enabled Application is defined as an application that has been designed and built to be deployed and consumed in a service model, and incorporates many of the attributes previously defined above.

SAN: Storage Area network is an architecture to attach remote computer storage devices to servers in such a way that, to the operating system, the devices appear as locally attached. SANs are generally optimized for the storage of large amounts of data and contain functionality to improve resilience.

SQL: Structured Query Language is a standardized programming language for querying and modifying data and managing databases.

Chapter 4
Managing the Cloud for Information Systems Agility

Haibo Yang
Victoria University of Wellington, New Zealand

Sid Huff
Victoria University of Wellington, New Zealand

Mary Tate
Victoria University of Wellington, New Zealand

ABSTRACT

Change is endemic in modern business competition. In an age of globalization, with the rapid develop-ment of Internet technologies, changes occur at a much faster pace, and are also more unpredictable. Being agile in a turbulent environment has been ranked highly by executives in surveys of business issues conducted in past five years. Today nearly all organizations rely on information systems (IS) to operate. Agility in IS is critical in achieving overall agility in business. However, despite the interest from the practitioner community, IS agility (sometimes termed IT agility) in academia has received limited recognition and represents an under-researched area. The recent adoption of cloud computing services has presented a major change in the way IS are delivered, in the hope of creating more agile and responsive IS. However, whether or not cloud computing, as promised by the providers, increases IS agility, is still unclear. This research aims at providing a conceptualization of IS agility based on research to date, and examining how cloud computing might facilitate such agility. Based on a literature review, cloud computing services (IaaS, PaaS, and SaaS) are analyzed against multiple aspects of IS agility. Only IaaS is found to have the potential providing consistent agility, whereas agility at PaaS and SaaS levels is more determined by human/organization factors. Lastly, suggestions for businesses and directions to future research are proposed.

DOI: 10.4018/978-1-4666-2187-9.ch004

INTRODUCTION

In the competitive business world, change has become the rule of the game. Firms have to adapt to changing business conditions (Chonko & Jones, 2005). Indeed, the whole concept of entrepreneurship has long been described as the search for change, response to change, and exploitation of change as opportunity (Drucker, 1968). Furthermore, the rate of change has been dramatically increasing due to unprecedented phenomena such as globalisation and revolutionary Internet technologies.

Not only are the changes occurring faster, they are becoming increasingly unpredictable (Sharifi & Zhang, 2001); including unpredictability about when a certain change will take place; what a particular change will look like; or a combination of both (Pankaj, Hyde, Ramaprasad, & Tadisina, 2009). Such changes in the business environment can threaten businesses with rigid established infrastructures and processes (SEO & Paz, 2008). However, organizations with flexible, easily reconfigured infrastructures – i.e., agile businesses - are able to leverage the threats into opportunities and greater profits (Sull, 2010).

Agility is defined as the ability of an organization to handle changes, in particular unpredictable ones, with ease and appropriate speed, so as to thrive in a dynamic market (Dove, 2001). Surveys of executives have found that agility is rated as one of the most critical features organizations should possess. In a global survey, 89 percent of over 1500 respondents indicated that agility is "very" or "extremely" important for business performance, while 91 percent perceived that the importance of agility has increased in the five years preceding the survey (McKinsey, 2006). More recently, a survey conducted by the Society for Information Management (SIM) ranked agility third among the top ten IT management concerns (Luftman & Ben-Zvi, 2010).

Agility in information systems (IS) is often seen as a critical component of business agility (Bhatt, Emdad, Roberts, & Grover, 2010; Caswell & Nigam, 2005; Goodhue, Chen, Boudreau, Davis, & Cochran, 2009). In today's digital economy, IS pervades all aspects of business. In particular, information systems often play a critical role in areas where organizational agility is most required (Oosterhout, Waarts, & Hillegersberg, 2006). IS deployments once measured in years now must be completed in much shorter time spans - months or weeks, or sometimes just days. Furthermore, the accelerating pace of business demands that IS respond to changes in business conditions quickly and effectively. Therefore, to have an agile business, a firm requires agility in its IS function (Hugoson, Magoulas, & Pessi, 2009; Weill, Subramani, & Broadbent, 2002); non-agile, difficult-to-adapt IT systems hinder the overall agility of the business (SEO & Paz, 2008).

To achieve agility in IS, IT practitioners have devoted considerable effort to bring about innovations in technical architectures and frameworks. In particular, the service-oriented paradigm has become increasingly popular in recent years (Chang, He, & Castro-Leon, 2006). This paradigm proposes that IT systems should be built based on loosely coupled and reusable modular services which can be quickly constructed and deconstructed to support changing requirements in IS and business requirements (Setia, Sambamurthy, & Closs, 2008). Out of the notion of service orientation has emerged a new approach for converting conventional IT resources into public online services – an approach commonly called cloud computing.

Cloud computing,[1] which delivers IT resources in a service-oriented model, is intended to provide agile and responsive computing power to organizations. The necessary underlying computing power is provided by large data centers, each typically operating tens of thousands of servers (Katz, 2009), which brings about economies of scale. Hence cloud computing providers can rent out their computing resources and services to clients at a low price. These resources and services are delivered via the Internet, often in a self-service model (Mell & Grance, 2010). Therefore cloud computing adopters no longer need to maintain and manage local IT infrastructures and systems to support their business applications. Instead they can focus more on their core businesses, and leave many IT-related activities such as server operation and maintenance to be handled by remote providers who are more experienced and efficient in managing such technologies.

IS agility, while important in practice, has received limited attention by IS academic researchers. (Mathiassen & Pries-Heje, 2006). Among other reasons, researching the concept has traditionally been difficult. Part of the difficulty lies in the complex and multifaceted nature of the very concept of IS agility, which makes it hard to agree on how it should be investigated and from whose perspective (MacCormack, 2008). The situation can become even more complicated if a diversity of technologies is introduced. Cloud computing, as a unified IT delivery model with a focus on agility, provides a valuable context for IS researchers to better understand issues surrounding IS agility.

This chapter intends to analyze the impact of cloud computing on IS agility from a user perspective. It is structured as following: First a conceptualisation of IS agility and its antecedents is provided, based on research literature. Next an overview of the characteristics of major cloud computing services is presented. Then an analysis of the antecedents of IS agility against each level of cloud computing services is conducted. The chapter concludes with some suggestions for businesses and directions for future research.

INFORMATION SYSTEMS AGILITY

Conceptualization of IS Agility

Research in agility is still evolving and a mature definition is yet to emerge. The general concept of agility was introduced into the mainstream business literature in a report titled *21st Century*

Manufacturing Enterprise Strategy (Goldman, Preiss, Nagel, & Dove, 1991). Within this report the term agile manufacturing was coined, defined as the ability to respond quickly to customer needs and market changes while still controlling costs and quality. IS agility is often examined via analogical reasoning, drawing from other (non-IS) studies of agility in organisations (Pankaj, et al., 2009). Hence when discussing IS agility it is common practice to draw upon concepts established in previous agile manufacturing research (Dove, 2001; Goldman, Nagel, & Preiss, 1995; Sharifi & Zhang, 2001) and interpret them from an IS standpoint.

From a technology perspective, IS agility is considered to be the ability of an IS to provide cost- and time-efficient response to changes (Ngo-Ye & Ahsan, 2005). In other words, it is "about reconfiguring or replacing your IT systems when new marketplace realities change the way you have to do business" (Sengupta & Masini, 2008, p.43). Managerially, IS agility has been proposed as the capacity of the IS function to rapidly adapt to changing line function demands (Tiwana & Konsynski, 2010). Though the particular focuses may differ, the existing conceptualizations echo a common theme, that is, agility is about responding to change with ease and speed; and that achieving agility is especially challenging when changes are unpredictable.

Early conceptualizations of IS agility stress the reactive capability of IS, namely, responding to changes. This is in line with the COBIT (Control Objectives for Information and related Technology) framework (IT_Governance_Institute, 2007) which specifies agility as the capability of an IT function to respond to received changes in business requirements and strategy. However, academic researchers have not stopped there. Recent theoretical development has suggested that IS agility should be not only a reactive capability in responding, but should also include a proactive capacity concerned with sensing changes (Hobbs & Scheepers, 2009). Sensing or detecting changes in the business environment is argued to be essential to speeding the subsequent responses, as sensing determines what changes are emerging and will need to be acted on (Overby, Bharadwaj, & Sambamurthy, 2006; Sambamurthy, Bharadwaj, & Grover, 2003).

As an emerging construct, the conceptualization of IS agility has been developed in an incremental manner. Initially, "sensing" and "responding" have been identified as two key aspects of IS agility. More recently still, the IS agility concept has been enlarged to include "diagnosing" and "real-time" aspects, necessary for providing a complete conceptualization (Pankaj, et al., 2009). Table 1 summarizes the emerging components of the construct "IS agility."

When a change in the environment occurs, an agile IS function (including IT personnel and IT systems) first senses the emerging change, then diagnoses the stimulus which involves interpreting or analyzing such stimulus to understand the nature, cause and impact of change. Finally, it responds to the stimulus, by selecting and executing appropriate responses. And, importantly, it is considered critical that all these actions should take place in real time (Pankaj, et al., 2009).

"Real-time" response is the essence of agility. The activities of sensing and diagnosing a change, selecting and executing an action should all happen in a time-span that is equivalent to the one in which the process of interest is happening (Pankaj, et al., 2009). Real-time is a key property that distinguishes agility from other related concepts such as flexibility[2]. In the context of IS agility, real-time response does not necessarily mean things happening in an instant; rather it should be interpreted in relation to the context of the underlying business change (Pankaj, et al., 2009). Depending on the time-frame of the relevant business processes, the actual time taken for an action can vary from minutes to hours or days in an operational context, and from weeks to months in a strategic context, and still be considered to have occurred in "real time." If the time requirements of the underlying business change are not met, even if the tasks were performed eventually, the IS could not be deemed to be agile (Pankaj, et al., 2009).

While a complete delineation of IS agility is still evolving, in this chapter the conceptualisation discussed above, derived from Pankaj, Hyde et al. (2009), is adopted as the most inclusive. In the next section, certain characteristics of IS which potentially enable IS agility will be discussed.

Characteristics of IS Enabling Agility

For the purpose of discussion in this chapter, "IS" can be viewed as a combination of two interrelated parts: the underlying IT infrastructure, along with supporting personnel and procedures (Byrd & Turner, 2000). The IT infrastructure includes various electronic assets such as hardware, software, data, and networking that are designed to support a business. The personnel apply the infrastructure within the context of certain work processes (procedures) to fulfil the purposes of the organisation. Based on the literature, this section discusses some specific characteristics of these two parts that can enable agility in IS.

Table 1. Components of IS agility

Sense	Ability of the IS to sense the stimuli for change in real time	
Diagnose	Ability of the IS to interpret or analyze stimuli in real time to determine the nature, cause, and impact of change.	
Respond	Ability of the IS to respond to a change in real time. Response is further disaggregated into Select and Execute.	Select: Ability of the IS to select a response in real time (very short planning time) to capitalize on opportunity or counter the threat.
		Execute: Ability of the IS to execute the response in real time

Source: (Pankaj, et al., 2009)

Agility-Enabling IT Personnel Capabilities

In order to enable IS agility, IT personnel should be able to work cooperatively in cross-functional teams and embrace various kinds of technologies. The literature suggests that certain factors contribute to such ability. IT staff need four types of knowledge and skills to handle IS changes quickly and effectively: 1) technology management knowledge and skills; 2) technical knowledge and skills; 3) interpersonal and management skills; and 4) business functional knowledge and skills (Byrd & Turner, 2000; Lee, Trauth, & Farwell, 1995). This range of skills and knowledge can be summarized into three capabilities, shown in Table 2: technical capability, business capability, and behavioral capability (Fink & Neumann, 2007).

- **Technical capability:** Refers not only to the specific technical specialties (including programming, understanding software development processes and knowledge of operating systems, database systems, and other such areas), but is also concerned with the understanding of where and how to deploy IT effectively in order to support the strategic goals and objectives of an organization (Lee, et al., 1995). IT personnel with stronger technical capability are more likely to provide effective technical solutions faster.

- **Business capability:** Relates to the ability of IT personnel to comprehend the business processes they support as well as the organizational consequences associated with the technical solutions they implement. Such ability requires general business knowledge, organization-specific knowledge, and knowledge to learn about business functions (Lee, et al., 1995). Strong business capability helps IT personnel to better interpret business problems and develop appropriate technical solutions.

- **Behavioral capability:** Denotes a set of interpersonal and management knowledge and skills which are especially critical to IT personnel who frequently assume a boundary spanning role in their organizations (Lee, et al., 1995). Such capability includes team collaboration, project management, presentation and communication, planning, organizing and leading projects etc (Fink & Neumann, 2007). IT personnel with strong behavioral capability are often sensitive to organizational culture and politics, which makes them work efficiently and effectively across business functions.

Agility-Enabling IT Infrastructure Characteristics

To enable IS agility, IT infrastructure should be change-friendly, and capable of adding, removing, and modifying components and functionalities

Table 2. Capabilities of IT personnel enabling IS agility

	Definition	References
Technical Capability	The technical ability of IT personnel based on their specific expertise in technical areas	Byrd and Turner (2001); Lee et al.(1995)
Business Capability	The ability of IT personnel to understand the overall business environment and the specific organizational context	Byrd and Turner (2001); Lee et al.(1995)
Behavioral Capability	The interpersonal and management ability of IT personnel to interact with and manage others	Byrd and Turner(2001); Lee et al.(1995)

Source: (Fink & Neumann, 2007)

easily and quickly. The literature has indicated that several characteristics can contribute to such capability, namely, connectivity, compatibility, interoperability, modularity, scalability, and standardization, as summarized in Table 3.

- **Connectivity and compatibility:** Have become basic characteristics of a robust IS. Being compatible with, and easily connected to, other system components as required is a big advantage in terms of handling system changes, especially when these changes are unpredictable. Compatibility can be achieved at various levels: "at one extreme, only simple text messages can be shared, while at the other extreme any document, process, service, video, image, text, audio, or a combination of these can be used by any other system, regardless of manufacturer, make, or type" (Byrd & Turner, 2000).

- **Interoperability:** Is a relatively recent requirement that has arisen from the global trend of operating business applications over the Internet. The essence of interoperability is that two or more systems or components can exchange and share information or even functionalities in order to solve a business problem. In general, interoperability is required at two levels: the inter-enterprise level and the intra-enterprise level (Camarinha-Matos, et al., 2003). In modern businesses relying on IS to operate, the degree of inter-enterprise interoperability impacts progress when partnering with new suppliers or retailers, whereas the degree of intra-enterprise interoperability can influence the speed and quality of cross-functional efforts.

- **Modularity:** Is a general design principle that intentionally divides a complex system into subsystems which exhibit limited interdependence (Tiwana & Konsynski,

Table 3. Characteristics of IT infrastructure enabling IS agility

Attribute	Definition	References
Connectivity	The ability of any technology component to attach to any of the other components inside and outside the organisational environment (Byrd & Turner, 2000).	(Byrd & Turner, 2000) (Ngo-Ye & Ahsan, 2005)
Compatibility	The ability to share any type of information across any technology component (Byrd & Turner, 2000);	(Byrd & Turner, 2000) (Ngo-Ye & Ahsan, 2005) (Bhatt, et al., 2010)
Interoperability	The ability for two heterogeneous components to communicate and cooperate with one another despite differences in languages, interfaces, and platforms (Izza, Imache, Vincent, & Lounis, 2008)	(Hugoson, et al., 2009) (Camarinha-Matos, Afsarmanesh, & Rabelo, 2003) (Izza, et al., 2008)
Modularity	The ability to add, modify, and remove any software, hardware, or data components of the infrastructure with ease and with no major overall effect (Byrd & Turner, 2000).	(Byrd & Turner, 2000) (Ngo-Ye & Ahsan, 2005) (Bhatt, et al., 2010) (Pankaj, et al., 2009) (Nazir & Pinsonneault, 2008)
Standardization	The degree to which standards and policies pre-specify how IT infrastructures operate (Weill, et al., 2002).	(Pankaj, et al., 2009) (Gallagher & Worrell, 2008); (Nazir & Pinsonneault, 2008); (Weill, et al., 2002)
Scalability	The ability of a system, a network, or a process, which indicates its ability to either handle growing amounts of work in or to be enlarged in a graceful manner (Bondi, 2000).	(Bhatt, et al., 2010) (Pankaj, et al., 2009) (Bondi, 2000)

2010). Modularity applies to both application and data components of an IS (Byrd & Turner, 2000). In theory, advances in modularity should allow rapid changes to both the data and applications without major economic penalty. Modularity is a key aspect of service-orientation: SOA solutions are generally based on loosely coupled modules (Christopher, 2000).

- **Standardisation:** Has long been argued as a way of increasing efficiency in technology management (Tassey, 2000). To achieve agility in IS, "standards for processes, practices, functions, and activities that can be incorporated into IS; standards for decomposition of functionality into lower level modules or components; standards for information exchange between module/components; standards (like naming of variables) for building of the modules and/or components; and even standards for assessing and certifying the skills of IS staff/contractors" need to be established (Pankaj, et al., 2009). IS agility is about dealing with mostly unpredicted changes with ease and speed, and the existence of standards can ease the panic when unpredicted changes occur.

- **Scalability:** Refers to the ability of easily expanding and shrinking capacity when resources are added or removed, in order to deal with changing demands on a system (Bondi, 2000). When a particular aspect of a business succeeds and experiences rapid growth in demand for services, if the underlying infrastructure does not scale well, it will fail to provide sufficient capacity to keep the system response time in an acceptable range. The direct consequences are compromised service quality and dissatisfied users, which may lead to the loss of clients or business opportunities (Bondi, 2000). By the same token, reducing capacity is important for resource optimisation

and cost control. An application does not stay at peak resource utilisation all the time. Once the number of requests goes down, the system should be able to release the resources assigned to an application and reassign them to other applications which are demanding additional resources. An agile infrastructure should consist of scalable hardware and software which allow it to handle changing demand from the business frontline with ease and speed.

Research literature suggests that the aforementioned capabilities of IT personnel and characteristics of infrastructure potentially enable IS agility, but it does not explain exactly how they contribute to the process of sensing, diagnosing, and responding to changes in real time. It has been suggested that "the agility of IS is often studied through IT solutions that compose IS" (Izza, et al., 2008, p.5). Without a specific IT solution in mind, conceptually incorporating all the discussed IS agility elements together lacks focus. Cloud computing is an IT solution with high relevance for the study of IS agility. Next an overview of cloud computing will be presented and followed with an analysis of its potential IS agility effects.

CLOUD COMPUTING

Cloud Computing Definition

Cloud computing as an emerging paradigm is challenging the traditional way in which IT is provisioned. Instead of operating servers and applications on the premises, cloud computing offers an alternative to businesses by providing on-demand computing power via the Internet, with quick implementation, little local maintenance, and less local IT staffing (Truong, 2010). This potentially results in reduced cost and improved agility, according to leading providers such as Microsoft and IBM.

The National Institute of Standards and Technology (NIST) defines cloud computing as a "model for enabling convenient, on-demand network access to a shared pool of configurable computing resources (e.g., networks, servers, storage, applications, and services) that can be rapidly provisioned and released with minimal management effort or service provider interaction" (Mell & Grance, 2009). This cloud model lists five essential characteristics:

1. **On-demand self-service:** A consumer can unilaterally provision computing capabilities, such as server time and network storage, as needed automatically without requiring human interaction with each service's provider.

2. **Broad network access:** Capabilities are available over the network and accessed through standard mechanisms that promote use by heterogeneous thin or thick client platforms (e.g., mobile phones, laptops, and PDAs).

3. **Resource pooling:** The provider's computing resources are pooled to serve multiple consumers using a multi-tenant model, with different physical and virtual resources dynamically assigned and reassigned according to consumer demand. Examples of resources include storage, processing, memory, network bandwidth, and virtual machines.

4. **Rapid elasticity:** Capabilities can be rapidly and elastically provisioned, in some cases automatically, to quickly scale out and rapidly released to quickly scale in.

5. **Measured Service:** Cloud systems automatically control and optimize resource use by leveraging a metering capability at some level of abstraction appropriate to the type of service (e.g., storage, processing, bandwidth, and active user accounts) (Mell & Grance, 2009).

Depending on the provider and consumer of cloud services, there are generally four types of cloud:

1. **Public cloud:** Most commonly referred to; is owned and operated by independent vendors and accessible to the general public.

2. **Private cloud:** An internal utilization of cloud technologies which is maintained in house and solely accessible to internal users within an organization.

3. **Community cloud:** Shared by several organizations and supports a specific community that has shared concerns. (e.g., mission, security requirements, policy, and compliance considerations). It may be managed by the organizations or a third party and may exist on premise or off premise.

4. **Hybrid cloud:** A combination of two or more types of clouds (private, community, or public). For example, an organization may bridge its internally operated private cloud with other public clouds together by standardized or proprietary technology in order to satisfy business needs (Mell & Grance, 2009).

This chapter focuses on the public cloud which is what the variant the term "cloud computing" commonly refers to.

Cloud Computing Services

With cloud computing, there are generally three types of service models:

1. IaaS (Infrastructure-as-a-Service)
2. PaaS (Platform-as-a-Service), and
3. SaaS (Software-as-a-Service).

Table 4 illustrates some representative cloud providers by service types.

Table 4. Cloud service levels and providers

Cloud Services	Examples of Cloud Providers
IaaS	Amazon EC2, Amazon S3, IBM Blue Cloud, HP Flexible Computing, Sun & Microsoft Network.com, Nimbus, Eucalyptus
PaaS	Google App Engine, Microsoft Azure, LongJump, Bungee Lab's Bungee Connect
SaaS	Salesforce CRM, Oracle SaaS platform, Google Apps, NetSuite, Workday Human Capital Management, Zoho

Source: Adapted from (Leavitt, 2009)

IaaS provides the raw materials of cloud computing, the infrastructures, such as processing, storage and other forms of network and hardware resources in a virtual, on demand manner via the Internet (Leavitt, 2009). Developments in virtualization and network management have meant that cloud infrastructures can scale up and down dynamically according to user demand. Infrastructure utilisation is monitored by the cloud management system and the users are charged for what has been used. IaaS users do not manage or control the underlying cloud infrastructure but have control over operating systems, storage, deployed applications, and possibly limited control of select networking components (e.g., host firewalls) (Mell & Grance, 2009).

Typical IaaS examples include Amazon EC2 (Elastic Cloud Computing) and S3 (Simple Storage Service) where computing and storage infrastructure are open to public access in a utility fashion. For a fee, a user can easily access thousands of virtual servers from EC2 to run a business analysis and then release them as soon as the computational work is done. Some researchers further divide IaaS into HaaS (Hardware as a Service) and DaaS (Data as a Service) (Wang et al., 2008), but it is more common that IaaS is referred to as a whole concept.

PaaS focuses on enabling SaaS applications (discussed next) (Candan, Li, Phan, & Zhou, 2009). PaaS moves one step further than IaaS by providing programming and execution environments to the user. A PaaS product acts as an integrated design, develop, test, and deploy platform. The PaaS user can create applications using programming languages and APIs supported by the provider, and then directly deploy the applications onto the provider's cloud infrastructure within a few clicks. The PaaS user does not manage or control the underlying cloud infrastructure including network, servers, operating systems, or storage, but has control over the deployed applications and possibly application hosting environment configurations (Mell & Grance, 2009). Such an approach can reduce most of the system administration burden (e.g. manually setting up the development environment and the deployment runtime) traditionally carried by the developers who can then concentrate on more productive problems. PaaS typically provides a complete set of development tools, from the interface design, to process logic, and to integration (Lawton, 2008). Some other appealing features of PaaS include built-in instruments for measuring the usage of the deployed applications for billing purposes, and established online communities for collaboration and problem solving..

An example of PaaS is Google's App Engine, which allows users to build applications on the same scalable systems that power Google applications (Foster, Yong, Raicu, & Lu, 2008). PaaS offerings tend to lower the entry level for software development. WaveMaker, recently acquired by VMware, is providing an easy and intuitive way of building web sites, enabling non-expert developers to build their own online applications in the cloud. Such platforms comprise a modern instantiation of the End User Computing (EUC) paradigm which has long been envisioned by generations IS researchers (Huff, Munro, & Martin, 1988). PaaS users will likely become providers of SaaS once their products are mature. However, unlike IaaS, PaaS providers may choose to focus on a narrow market and support specialised development in certain industry segments. For example, Long-Jump's platform is only for developing CRM systems for newspapers.

SaaS provides users with complete, turnkey applications, even complex systems, such as those for CRM or ERP, through a web browser via the Internet (Leavitt, 2009). Software or applications are hosted as services in the clouds, and delivered via browsers once subscribed to by the user. This approach can eliminate the need to install, run, and maintain the application on local computers. SaaS is known for its multi-tenant architecture in which all the users share the same single code base maintained by the provider. Authentication and authorization security policies are used to ensure the separation of user data. Such a sharing mechanism enables the cost and price of SaaS staying competitive as compared to traditional off-the-shelf software.

A prominent example of SaaS is Salesforce's online CRM system, Salesforce.com. This system provides users with complete CRM applications as well as a user side customization platform based on its PaaS by-product Force.com. There are two types of customizations available, one is "point-and-click configuration" that requires no programming, the other is "customize with code" that allows user developers to create new functionalities beyond the constraints of configuration, with Apex - Salesforce.com's own native programming language. Thus on its own website, Salesforce.com declares that there are currently "77,300 Salesforce implementations, all of them unique[3]".

IaaS, PaaS, and SaaS reflect a full spectrum of public cloud services. These three layers of cloud services are naturally inter-related. IaaS providers are the most independent as they operate their own datacenters (e.g. Amazon EC2, IBM Blue Cloud). PaaS providers may build their platforms upon third-party IaaS offerings (e.g. LongJump), or they may have their own IaaS offerings, and extend those businesses by providing application development frameworks (e.g. Microsoft Azure). A SaaS provider can either use the PaaS layer to develop and run its applications or directly use the IaaS layer to deploy already made applications. Moreover, PaaS offerings are most likely subscribed to by IS developers or IT firms possessing confidence and skill in IS development, whereas SaaS may be used more often by non-IT businesses for which infrastructure management is merely a burden.

IS AGILITY AND CLOUD COMPUTING

Cloud providers and proponents often highlight the "agility gain" when promoting cloud services. Oracle provides an online seminar titled "Cloud Computing enables IT agility" (Oracle, 2010), Microsoft promises that adopting cloud services brings "more agility, more freedom, and more choice" (Microsoft, 2010). Some technology writers even suggest that it is "agility, not savings, may be the true value of the cloud" (Mullins, 2010). CIO magazine has been recommending "business strategy based on cloud computing and agility" (Hugos, 2010). However, to date there has been limited academic research explaining if cloud services really enable agility and how this may happen. This section aims to "drill down" into these claims and to provide a systematic analysis.

Sensing, Diagnosing, and Responding Changes in the Cloud

From IaaS to SaaS, from the hardware concentrated layer, to the software concentrated layer, complexity grows, and the changes required may differ. In other words, the agility effect of cloud computing may vary depending on the layer at which cloud solutions are deployed. In an IaaS world, changes can often be straightforward, either increasing or decreasing the number of virtual servers to expand or shrink the computing power or storage resources. Such changes are mostly pre-defined and easily handled by providers. However in a SaaS world, usage changes are often more challenging, because they occur with respect to functionality, where modifications are often more unpredictable and take longer to be understood. Such differences suggest that cloud computing services may not respond equally efficiently and effectively to the changes across all service levels.

Agility at IaaS Level

IaaS has the potential to provide genuine and consistent agility. Changes requested by users at the IaaS level are mostly related to capacity, that is, the allocation and re-allocation of computing and storage resources. The solutions to these capacity changes can be pre-defined. According to technical materials from the cloud providers (e.g. the FAQs page of Amazon EC2), the cloud system is capable of handling these changes by itself, with automatic and self-regulated processes, and no human involvement (though human intervention is needed when setting up the applications and procedures in the first place).

In a typical scenario, an online service gains popularity, which demands more computing and storage capacity than it already has, to handle the growing user requests and to keep a satisfactory QoS (Quality of Service). In this scenario, agility is needed and time is a priority as the longer it takes to expand the capacity, the more dissatisfaction the service users may have due to the decreasing service quality of the online service (e.g. slow response time, discontinuous service). Dissatisfied users may turn to rivals or just leave which in turn undermine the potential growth of the online service.

In a conventional hosting environment, the capabilities of the IT personnel and procedures

they follow play a critical role in responding to such a capacity change. Sensing the change stimulus usually requires manual intervention, e.g., monitoring server utilization or receiving user complaints about slow response of the online service. Diagnosing such a change may also be done manually. IT personnel will need to analyze the issue and decide whether it is a problem of service optimization or a pure capacity limitation. This can be done by collectively examining server logs, application usage history, user complaints, and other relevant observations. Once the diagnosis is done, say, a capacity expansion is necessitated, a response needs to be selected and executed. The response to such a change is also largely manual. Firstly, selecting a solution, perhaps through a meeting, to decide whether to upgrade the existing servers or add new servers. Secondly, executing the solution, say, adding more servers. This can involve activities like purchasing and configuring new servers, connecting them to the old server cluster, and very likely, having a planned outage of the online service to provide a window for testing and rollout. All these processes and activities require intensive human involvement and could take days or even weeks.

On the other hand, in a cloud computing environment characterised by "rapid elasticity" (Mell & Grance, 2009), once an application is deployed upon an IaaS, the sensors, monitors, and hypervisors inside the cloud system will start looking after the resource scheduling and allocating. The workload changes of the applications that may compromise the user's QoS target will be sensed, and diagnosed by the cloud itself (e.g. the Amazon CloudWatch service allows users to define custom metrics and alarms for monitoring their applications). The response will be made automatically and immediately, that is, more virtual servers will be created by hypervisors and then assigned to the demanding applications seamlessly (Lunsford, 2009). The transition from sensing to responding to adjusting capacity may take only a few minutes (as suggested by Amazon EC2[4]), depending on the effectiveness of the resource management algorithm and mechanism employed by the IaaS provider.

The "rapid elasticity" of cloud-based IaaS represents a new generation of automation in capacity scaling and load balancing (Böhm, Leimeister, Riedl, & Krcmar, 2010). Such automation can reduce the user firm's dependency on in-house IT personnel capabilities in terms of provisioning, network configuration and analysis, server maintenance, etc. As suggested by some researchers, the ultimate agility may be found in complete automation which avoids the cognitive limitations of human beings, in this case, of the IT personnel (Pankaj, et al., 2009).

Agility at PaaS Level

PaaS can facilitate the processes of IS development (ISD) by enabling developers to collaborate globally, testing and releasing their products more quickly, and avoiding much non-productive system administration work (Lawton, 2008). Traditionally, developers need a development environment for creating applications, then use a test environment for testing them, and then move to a live environment for production (Gonçalves, 2009). With PaaS, developers can develop, test and release their products on a same platform, and avoid much non-productive system administration work (e.g. integrating database server with web server, synchronizing between live environment and test environment)(Lawton, 2008). However there is not enough evidence showing that PaaS can particularly sense, diagnose, and respond to changes happening at this level. Neither is it obvious that PaaS can generate more agility than the conventional IS development platforms, namely, those on-premise desktop integrated development environments (IDE) such as Visual Studio, JCreator, PowerBuilder, and so forth.

From a user standpoint, changes at the PaaS level are mostly unpredictable, but within the SDLC (System Development Life Cycle) of an application, changes influencing the development progress can be classified into three categories: 1) changes in the application and database developed and deployed by the user, 2) changes in the user's development team, and 3) changes on the development platform itself. Generally the first type of change happens most frequently, the third type appears least frequently, and the second type lies somewhere in the middle (Boehm & Turner, 2003).

Firstly, changes in application and database are often initiated by the end users of the application in response to a fast changing business environment. Handling such changes requires mostly human capabilities instead of infrastructure capabilities; this is not an issue that can be easily solved by solely advanced technologies. Hence agile methods, for example, as a set of principles and practices emphasizing people over process, short iterations, and close collaboration with the clients (AgileAlliance, 2001), are adopted by many ISD teams to cope with unstable business requirements and generate agility in ISD (Fitzgerald, Hartnett, & Conboy, 2006). Technologies provided by PaaS may help to the ISD processes, but the capabilities of IT personnel are still key to generating the actual agility(Sultan, 2011).

Secondly, many organizations aim to minimise changes in the development team, as losing a team member means losing tacit knowledge of the project. However when they happen such changes need to be coped with. To maintain the project schedule, a project member will need to be replaced. The whole process may involve educating the new member, adjusting the collaboration style, and so forth. The agility associated with this type of changes is related more to the technical and inter-personal knowledge and skills of the team, which determines how fast the new team member can be assimilated and work at full speed. PaaS offers no apparent contribution to this type of change.

Finally, changes in the platform itself are less frequent as it has a much longer life cycle than any user development projects happening on it.

PaaS providers prefer to deploy mature and relatively stable IDEs into the cloud to make them publicly accessible platforms (e.g. Microsoft Azure, Google Apps). In fact, from surveying in online developer forums such as the MSDN Visual Studio forums, one can easily see that changing IDE is not a noticeable concern for the developers.

Overall, changes happening at the PaaS level often require substantial human intervention which heavily determines the quality of the outcomes. Technical platforms in the cloud might assist to some degree, but can hardly dominate the processes of sensing, diagnosing, and responding to changes.

Agility at SaaS Level

SaaS has the potential to deliver a certain degree of agility to the user in some aspects. This depends on the circumstances requiring changes, as such potential may be more determined by the capabilities of the provider, and even the user, than the software.

User requested changes at the SaaS level may fall into two categories: 1) changes in capacity, e.g. the application needs to run faster, and keep a short response time even at peak time; 2) changes in the application itself, e.g. the interface needs to be adjusted to fit with the user's new company codes, or the workflow needs to be modified to properly reflect the user's new business processes.

The first type of change is about scalability which is especially critical to new Internet start-ups who may expect sudden surge of user requests associated with increasing popularity. With cloud computing, IaaS is the backbone of anything built upon it, including SaaS. Hence the first type of changes in theory should be handled well given the real-time "rapid elasticity" of IaaS. Ideally, the software system's capacity should be automatically increased or decreased on match demand by adding or removing virtual servers, without the need for any further alteration of application software architecture (Candan, et al., 2009).

Therefore agility can be potentially achieved for this type of change if the SaaS offering is scalable in real time. However, one needs to be aware that, in the current market there are self-proclaimed SaaS providers that do not actually base their software applications on IaaS. Hence software services delivered by such providers may not inherently scale well.

The second type of change relates to user side customization, either configuring the parameters to adjust the layout, or modifying the functionality to support changing business. As mentioned earlier, a key feature of SaaS in the cloud is that it is multi-tenant, meaning all the users share a single code base of the software system maintained by the provider. This is to reduce the operational cost however it also brings up concerns regarding security control, authentication and authorisation. A single code base also means the initial system can only provide common functionalities without ad-hoc designed features. In order to control the development cost, SaaS providers have been pushing the customization work towards the user.

Today a SaaS offering by default should allow the users to configure the software system to some degree, e.g. changing the logo and wording of an entry form. Some providers take one step further by opening up their own development platform to the user (e.g. the CRM system offered by Salesforce.com can be customized using the tools provided by its sibling site Force.com). This makes it a Do-It-Yourself (DIY) approach, where the users are responsible for sensing, diagnosing, and even responding to the system changes. In such a case, the agility in changing the software system lies in the expertise and capabilities of staff on the user side. SaaS providers who don't have their platforms open will have to take the responsibility to customize the system if the users request so. This is more like a traditional outsourcing approach which could take considerable time and effort merely to manage the provider. In such a case, the agility is more dependent on the communication between the user and the provider, as well as on the development capabilities of the provider, than the user side IT expertises. Either using the DIY approach or the traditional outsourcing way, no provider so far has claimed that adopting SaaS makes functionality changes happen fast or on time. They rather direct attention to how "scalable, configurable, multi-tenant-efficient" (Microsoft, 2008) their SaaS offerings could be.

In summary, SaaS has the potential to deliver agility for making capacity changes. However the efficiency and effectiveness of making functionality changes may vary largely across different SaaS providers.

Characteristics of IS Enabling Agility in the Cloud

Having argued the distinct IS agility effects that can be supported by different levels of cloud computing services, elaborating on specific agility-enabling characteristics of IS and the impact of cloud computing on them offers additional insights. The discussion in the last section has already argued that the weight of IT personnel and infrastructure is changing in a cloud environment. This section examines this in more detail.

As explained earlier, three IT personnel capabilities -- business capability, technical capability, and behavioral capability -- are considered important for IS agility. Cloud computing may not help directly to improve these capabilities, but can reduce the importance of them. In other words, cloud computing can potentially make achieving IS agility less dependent on some of

these human capabilities at certain levels. Based on the technical and research literature, Table 5 below summarizes the potential influence of these human capabilities in achieving agility across the three layers of cloud computing services.

- **Technical capability:** From a cloud user's standpoint, high technical capability of staff is strongly required for achieving agility when adopting PaaS, but much less so for adopting IaaS. As discussed before, once applications are deployed, changes at the IaaS level can be handled by the cloud automatically with little human intervention. In contrast, even though PaaS offerings eliminate the system administration burden, designing and developing new business applications on PaaS requires the most human involvement with far more technical knowledge, and the whole process is not at all automatic in today's environment. SaaS provides already made applications running on the Internet which are ready to implement. However, configuring and customizing SaaS business applications does require a certain level of local technical knowledge. Depending on the SaaS provider, the importance of IT personnel technical capability on the user side can vary between low and high. If the customization is mainly delivered by the provider, then the user may have no need to posses advanced technical expertise, rather, should focus mainly on understand-

Table 5. The potential influence of IT personnel capabilities to enable IS agility with cloud computing services

Characteristics of IT Personnel	IaaS	PaaS	SaaS
Technical Capability	Low	High	Low – High (provider dependent)
Business Capability	Low	High	High
Behavioral Capability	Low	High	Low – High (provider dependent)

ing and communicating the business requirements. On the other hand, if the provider offers a DIY approach (e.g. Salesforce.com), then the user does need to have substantial technical expertise to master the proprietary programming languages and tools for efficiently and effectively modifying the applications to accommodate business changes.

- **Business capability:** Achieving agility at the IaaS level requires the least business knowledge due to high automation, whereas it requires much more at the PaaS and the SaaS levels. At the IaaS level, business changes mostly are reflected by the numbers of virtual servers, either more or less, depending on the growth or shrinkage of the business. IT personnel without much business knowledge can still understand the requirements and fulfill the tasks. However, with SaaS, quickly and effectively configuring and customizing a business application requires an in-depth understanding of the business strategies and processes. Without strong business capability it is not achievable. Similarly, with PaaS, IT personnel must grasp the demand of business, and interpret it to technical solutions, in order to efficiently and effectively develop, test, and deploy business applications. To be agile, the development team must be able to rapidly respond to changes in business requirements with appropriate technical solutions. This must be derived from a combination of strong technical capability and business capability.

- **Behavioral capability:** This is most relevant to PaaS, less to SaaS, and almost irrelevant to IaaS. ISD in the cloud involves leadership, authorship, team management and collaboration in a virtual space. Achieving agility at this level relies heavily on the inter-personal and management skills of the development team (e.g., ability

to work effectively in a virtual team, ability to communicate clearly to the clients and other team members, etc.). Such skills have been emphasized especially in agile method literature as a key factor to embrace changes and be agile in ISD projects (Chow & Cao, 2008). At the SaaS level, the importance of behavioral capability to agility may vary between low and high. Depending on the changes required and how they are handled (i.e. either more user DIY customization, or more provider support), interactions can happen between the end users and IT personnel on the user side, and between the IT personnel on the user side and the cloud providers. The behavioral capability can determine how fast one party will respond to a requested change sensed by another party. On the other extreme, according to the providers, adopting IaaS requires minimum human intervention which probably sees lowest value in the behavioral capability of IT personnel.

The six characteristics of IT infrastructure expected to enable IS agility are also discussed in this section. Table 6 below summarizes the availability of each characteristic against each level of cloud computing services.

- **Connectivity:** Connectivity is inherently supported by all three types of cloud services (IaaS, PaaS, and SaaS) owing to the fact that these services are delivered via the Internet using universal protocols (e.g. Http) with high accessibility. The Internet enables various ways to connect systems of business units and partners. For example, though traditional applications are often developed for specific PC or mainframe operating systems, it has become a new norm that online services ought to be connected to any Internet enabled device including mobile phone, PDA, etc.. In this

Table 6. The potential availability of infrastructure characteristics enabling IS agility with cloud computing services

Characteristics of Infrastructure	IaaS	PaaS	SaaS
Connectivity	High	High	High
Compatibility	High	Low	Low
Interoperability	Low	Low	Low
Modularity	High	Low – High (provider dependent)	Low – High (provider dependent)
Standardization	High	Low	Low
Scalability	High	Low – High (provider dependent)	Low – High (provider dependent)

sense cloud computing services can provide better connectivity than many traditional IT solutions.

- **Compatibility:** Compatibility is essential to IaaS but may not be necessary to PaaS and especially SaaS as these two are often proprietary and vendor specific. The extent of variability at the level of hardware systems is far less than at the level of application software. Therefore compatibility is generally better achieved at the hardware level rather than the software level. With IaaS, compatibility is no longer traditional CPU centric but achieved by the uniform virtual representations of the underlying hardware resources. However with SaaS and PaaS, applications and development environments may be built upon proprietary data storage, API, and programming languages. An application developed on one platform may not work on another. Researchers have warned of the potential for the lock-in effect when adopting PaaS for mission-critical development (Lawton, 2008).

- **Interoperability:** Interoperability is currently not provided at all effectively through cloud computing services (Hofmann & Woods, 2010). Cloud vendors normally do not guarantee that applications and/or data

in one cloud will interoperate with another without significant effort. At the SaaS level, for instance, migrating a contact list from Salesforce cloud-based CRM to alternative cloud provided Google Docs is by no means an easy task, requiring substantial time and technical skill. Even at simpler IaaS level, Google's BigTable, Amazon's Dynamo, and Facebook's Cassandra, are all unique and proprietary data storage systems. To solve the problem, a common platform – cloud computing interoperability forum (CCIF)- has been formed (CCIF, 2010) and is planning to come up with a unified cloud interface (a.k.a. cloud broker) to allow clouds interoperate with each other. However with some of the major cloud providers like Microsoft and Amazon rejecting the CCIF offer and pursuing their own interoperability agenda, achieving consensus in interoperability becomes more difficult.

- **Modularity:** This is essential to IaaS but may not be supported by PaaS and SaaS providers. At the hardware and virtual server level, a cloud infrastructure has to be modular to operate effectively. A cloud data center normally has its infrastructure built upon hundreds of self-sufficient container modules that each can house thousands of servers (Katz, 2009). Not only can the container can be easily attached to or removed from the spine infrastructure (feeding network connectivity, power, and water) of the data center, but the individual servers can also be quickly plugged on and off in each container. One level higher, the computing resources are organized into abstract basic units and can be added or removed in the same way with ease. However, with PaaS and SaaS, depending on how much customization is allowed by the provider, the online application may vary from highly modularized SOA style with loosely coupled components to tightly integrated whole package. Though one can argue that more Paas and SaaS providers will consider modularizing their systems due to the interest in user customization and the business competition, by far modularity has not been promoted as an essential feature by the PaaS and SaaS providers.

- **Standardization:** Standardization is relatively better and easier with IaaS than with PaaS and SaaS. IaaS is built based on the virtualisation of commodity PC modules. Standards at the hardware infrastructure and operating system level are mostly well established and obeyed (e.g. Ethernet, PC compatible system-ware), in contrast to those at the development platform level and software application level. PaaS and SaaS involve much more variation and the solutions in market today are largely proprietary without unified industry level standardisation (e.g. the cloud management system and application development environment can vary largely across vendors using different approaches). Standardisation also involves social and legal concerns (standards for privacy, security, and legitimate usage of data across national borders) which are yet to be formalized. There are standardisation efforts underway in the industry. More cloud standardisation groups (e.g. Open Grid Forum, Distributed Management Task Force, and Open Group Cloud) are emerging in the hope to achieve globalised standards. On the government side, the U.S. Federal CIO Vivek Kundra has assigned the NIST the task of accelerating adoption of public cloud standards. NIST in turn has created the Standards Acceleration to Jumpstart Adoption of Cloud Computing (SAJACC) project to collect data. However, one can anticipate that patents and intellectual property (as most clouds today are not open) could be a hurdle for such standardisation process.

- **Scalability:** This is a frequently mentioned selling point for cloud services and is an essential attribute for IaaS. At the IaaS level, as mentioned earlier, the sensors, monitors, and hypervisors work together to check the usage across applications and virtual machines, allocate more resource to demanding applications and revoke resource from unexacting ones. However, scalability at software level is more complex and may not be necessarily fully supported by PaaS and SaaS providers. Ideally they should, but owing to the limitation of underlying relational databases, some applications are inherently not scalable even when deployed on a scalable IaaS. The fact is that traditional RDBMS (Relational Database Management Systems), which many business applications today rely on, do not scale well across large number of server nodes (Hofmann & Woods, 2010), no matter whether they are on-site or in the cloud. Those scalable cloud applications (like Facebook and its add-ones) are mostly based on key-value stores and NoSQL data structure. Hence in reality scalability at the PaaS and the SaaS levels is again largely provider-dependent and can vary between low and high across providers.

CONCLUSION

To achieve IS agility with cloud computing, businesses must recognize and understand the differences between the three levels of cloud offerings, and treat each service level individually. At the IaaS level, successful changes do not rely greatly on the capabilities of the organization's own IT personnel; rather the use of cloud infrastructure has the potential to automate the necessary service level changes. The computing resources provided by IaaS are scalable, modular, and cheap, hence particularly suitable for Internet start-ups, which expect to start small and grow rapidly. Large companies may find IaaS less attractive due to the lack of interoperability, but small businesses with limited IT expertise can take advantages of IaaS and enjoy "quick wins."

On the other hand, though the cloud service model eliminates the cost for managing and maintaining local infrastructures, changes happening at the PaaS and the SaaS levels still require substantial human intervention. Such intervention introduces human cognitive limitations and organizational complexity, which means that the capabilities of IT personnel partly determine IS agility. For example, in the case of system development, many of the issues traditionally experienced with IS development and project management are likely to remain important when the project is "lifted up to the cloud." Developing business applications in the cloud may in turn bring in new challenges, such as learning "how to" on the new platforms regarding version control, project management, auditing for governance, quality assurance, issue tracking, and even the new programming languages that some PaaS providers have developed (Lawton, 2008).

Moreover, unlike IaaS, wherein scalability and modularity are mandatory characteristics, some of today's self-proclaimed SaaS market offerings may not support these capabilities by default, which makes changing SaaS business applications a potentially difficult task. Even though some have suggested that to compete, it is imperative for SaaS providers to make their offerings modular and scalable (Catalyst_Resources, Feb 2009), the reality is determined by the technologies the provider has already developed. Firms demanding IS agility should be aware of such provider dependency and choose providers that allow them to customize and expand inexpensively and easily. Furthermore, with more and more SaaS offerings opening up their own platforms, SaaS users have to prepare themselves technologically for making system changes in a DIY manner.

This chapter has analyzed the concept of IS agility, and how cloud computing services may enable it. The discussion was intended to provide insights for business practitioners who are seeking opportunities with cloud computing, and for researchers seeking to conceptualize IS agility and cloud computing. The analysis presented in this chapter can also serve as a basic framework for furthering research in this area. In particular, an empirical application of the framework is called for, to evaluate whether cloud computing services do contribute to IS agility as promised. Furthermore, future research in this domain should carefully discriminate each layer of the cloud computing services, as each layer does exhibit notably different features, implying different impacts on aspects of IS agility.. Finally, this study was conducted from a user perspective. It would be interesting to investigate the same issues, but from a cloud provider standpoint.

REFERENCES

AgileAlliance. (2001). *Manifesto for agile software development*. Retrieved 20 April, 2008, from http://www.agilemanifesto.org/

Bhatt, G., Emdad, A., Roberts, N., & Grover, V. (2010). Building and leveraging information in dynamic environments: The role of IT infrastructure flexibility as enabler of organizational responsiveness and competitive advantage. *Information & Management, 47*(7-8). doi:10.1016/j.im.2010.08.001

Boehm, B. W., & Turner, R. (2003). *Balancing agility and discipline*. Boston, MA: Addison-Wesley Pearson Education.

Böhm, M., Leimeister, S., Riedl, C., & Krcmar, H. (2010). Cloud computing - Outsourcing 2.0 or a new business model for IT provisioning? In Keuper, F., Oecking, C., & Degenhardt, A. (Eds.), *Application management service management and service creation* (pp. 2–26). Gabler. doi:10.1007/978-3-8349-6492-2_2

Bondi, A. B. (2000). *Characteristics of scalability and their impact on performance*. Paper presented at the 2nd International Workshop on Software and Performance.

Byrd, T. A., & Turner, D. E. (2000). Measuring the flexibility of information technology infrastructure: Exploratory analysis of a construct. *Journal of Management Information Systems, 17*(1), 167.

Camarinha-Matos, L., Afsarmanesh, H., & Rabelo, R. (2003). Infrastructure developments for agile virtual enterprises. *International Journal of Computer Integrated Manufacturing, 16*, 235. doi:10.1080/0951192031000089156

Candan, K. S., Li, W.-S., Phan, T., & Zhou, M. (2009). *Frontiers in information and software as services*. Paper presented at the Data Engineering, 2009. ICDE '09. IEEE 25th International Conference on.

Caswell, N. S., & Nigam, A. (2005, 19 July 2005). *Agility = change + coordination*. Paper presented at the Seventh IEEE International Conference on E-Commerce Technology Workshops, 2005.

CCIF. (2010). *Cloud computing interoperability forum*. Retrieved 10th October, 2010, from http://code.google.com/p/unifiedcloud/

Chang, M., He, J., & Castro-Leon, E. (2006). *Service-orientation in the computing infrastructure*. Paper presented at the IEEE International Symposium on Service-Oriented System Engineering.

Chonko, L. B., & Jones, E. (2005). The need for speed: Agility selling. *Journal of Personal Selling & Sales Management, 25*, 371.

Chow, T., & Cao, D.-B. (2008). A survey study of critical success factors in agile software projects. *Journal of Systems and Software, 81*, 961–971. doi:10.1016/j.jss.2007.08.020

Christopher, M. (2000). The agile supply chain: Competing in volatile markets. *Industrial Marketing Management, 29*(1), 37. doi:10.1016/S0019-8501(99)00110-8

Dove, R. (2001). *Response ability: The language, structure and culture of the Agilie enterprise*. New York, NY: Wiley.

Drucker, P. F. (1968). Comeback of the entrepreneur. *Management Today, April*, 23-30.

Fink, L., & Neumann, S. (2007). Gaining agility through IT personnel capabilities: The mediating role of it infrastructure capabilities. *Journal of the Association for Information Systems, 8*, 440.

Fitzgerald, B., Hartnett, G., & Conboy, K. (2006). Customising agile methods to software practices at Intel Shannon. *European Journal of Information Systems, 15*, 200–213. doi:10.1057/palgrave.ejis.3000605

Foster, I., Yong, Z., Raicu, I., & Lu, S. (2008). *Cloud computing and grid computing 360-degree compared*. Paper presented at the Grid Computing Environments Workshop, GCE '08.

Gallagher, K., & Worrell, J. (2008). Organizing IT to promote agility. *Information Technology Management, 9*, 71. doi:10.1007/s10799-007-0027-5

Goldman, S., Nagel, R., & Preiss, K. (1995). *Agile competitors and virtual organizations.* New York, NY: Van Nostrand Reinhold.

Goldman, S., Preiss, K., Nagel, R., & Dove, R. (1991). *21st century manufacturing enterprise strategy: An industry-led view.* Bethlehem, PA: Iacocca Institute, Lehigh University.

Gonçalves, V. (2009). *Adding value to the network: Exploring the software as a service and platform as a service models for mobile operators* (pp. 13–22). Mobile Wireless Middleware, Operating Systems, and Applications - Workshops. doi:10.1007/978-3-642-03569-2_2

Goodhue, D. L., Chen, D. Q., Boudreau, M. C., Davis, A., & Cochran, J. D. (2009). Addressing business agility challenges with enterprise systems. *MIS Quarterly Executive, 8*(2), 73–87.

Hobbs, G., & Scheepers, R. (2009). *Identifying capabilities for the IT function to create agility in information systems.* Paper presented at the PACIS2009. Retrieved from http://aisel.aisnet.org/pacis2009/20

Hofmann, P., & Woods, D. (2010). Cloud computing: The limits of public clouds for business applications. *IEEE Internet Computing, 14*(6), 90. doi:10.1109/MIC.2010.136

Huff, S. L., Munro, M. C., & Martin, B. H. (1988). Growth stages of end user computing. *Communications of the ACM, 31*(5), 542–550. doi:10.1145/42411.42417

Hugos, M. (2010). Business strategy based on cloud computing and agility. *CIO.* Retrieved from http://advice.cio.com/michael_hugos/14230/business_strategy_based_on_cloud_computing_and_agility

Hugoson, M.-A., Magoulas, T., & Pessi, K. (2009). *Architectural principles for alignment within the context of agile enterprises.* Paper presented at the European Conference on Information Management & Evaluation.

IT Governance Institute. (2007). *COBIT 4.1: Framework, control objectives, management guidelines, maturity models.* Rolling Meadows, IL: IT Governance Institute.

Izza, S., Imache, R., Vincent, L., & Lounis, Y. (2008). An approach for the evaluation of the agility in the context of enterprise interoperability. In Mertins, K., Ruggaber, R., Popplewell, K., & Xu, X. (Eds.), *Enterprise interoperability III - New challenges and industrial approaches* (pp. 3–14). London, UK: Springer. doi:10.1007/978-1-84800-221-0_1

Katz, R. H. (2009). Tech titans building boom. *IEEE Spectrum, 46*(2), 40. doi:10.1109/MSPEC.2009.4768855

Lawton, G. (2008). Developing software online with platform-as-a-service technology. *Computer, 41*(6), 13–15. doi:10.1109/MC.2008.185

Leavitt, N. (2009). Is cloud computing really ready for prime time? *Computer, 42*(1), 15–20. doi:10.1109/MC.2009.20

Lee, D. M. S., Trauth, E. M., & Farwell, D. (1995). Critical skills and knowledge requirements of IS professionals: A joint academic/industry investigation. *Management Information Systems Quarterly, 19*(3), 313. doi:10.2307/249598

Luftman, J., & Ben-Zvi, T. (2010). Key issues for IT executives 2009: Difficult economy's impact on IT. *MIS Quarterly Executive, 9*(1), 46–59.

Lunsford, D. (2009). Virtualization technologies in information systems education. *Journal of Information Systems Education, 20*, 339.

MacCormack, A. (2008). Building the agile enterprise: Myths, perceptions, and reality. *Cutter Benchmark Review, 8*(4), 5–13.

Mathiassen, L., & Pries-Heje, J. (2006). Business agility and diffusion of information technology. *European Journal of Information Systems, 15*(2), 116–119. doi:10.1057/palgrave.ejis.3000610

McKinsey. (2006). *Building a nimble organization: A Mckinsey global survey*. Retrieved from http://www.mckinseyquarterly.com/Building_a_ nimble_organization_A_McKinsey_Global_Survey_1808

Mell, P., & Grance, T. (2009). *The NIST definition of cloud computing*. Retrieved from http:// csrc.nist.gov/groups/SNS/cloud-computing/ index.html

Mell, P., & Grance, T. (2010). The NIST definition of cloud computing. *Communications of the ACM, 53*(6), 50.

Microsoft. (2008). *Architecture strategies for catching the long tail*. Retrieved 24 November, 2010, from http://msdn.microsoft.com/en-us/ library/aa479069.aspx

Microsoft. (2010). *Cloud services*. Retrieved from http://download.microsoft.com/ download/7/0/B/70B05EA3-233E-4677-A921-DA409B4EADF6/Microsoft_CloudServices.pdf

Mullins, R. (2010). Agility, not savings, may be the true value of the cloud. *Network Computing*. Retrieved from http://www.networkcomputing. com/data-center/agility-not-savings-may-be-the-true-value-of-the-cloud.php

Nazir, S., & Pinsonneault, A. (2008). The role of information technology in firm agility: An electronic integration perspective. *AMCIS 2008 Proceedings*.

Ngo-Ye, L., & Ahsan, M. (2005). *Enterprise IT APPLICATION SYSTEMS AGILITY AND ORGANIZATIONAL AGILITY*. Paper presented at the AMCIS 2005.

Oosterhout, M., Waarts, E., & Hillegersberg, J. V. (2006). Change factors requiring agility and implications for IT. *European Journal of Information Systems, 15*(2), 132–145. doi:10.1057/ palgrave.ejis.3000601

Oracle. (2010). *Increase business performance through IT agility*. Retrieved 1st November, 2010, from https://landingpad.oracle.com/webapps/ dialogue/ns/dlgwelcome.jsp?p_ext=Y&p_dlg_ id=8920806&src=7011677&Act=8

Overby, E., Bharadwaj, A., & Sambamurthy, V. (2006). Enterprise agility and the enabling role of information technology. *European Journal of Information Systems, 15*(2), 120–131. doi:10.1057/ palgrave.ejis.3000600

Pankaj, H. M., Ramaprasad, A., & Tadisina, S. K. (2009). Revisiting agility to conceptualize information systems agility. In M. D. Lytras & P. O. de Pablos (Eds.), *Emerging topics and technologies in information systems* (pp. 19-54). Hershey, PA: IGI Global.

Resources, C. (Feb 2009). *The imperative for modular reusable UI in SaaS*. Retrieved 15th June 2010, from http://www.catalystresources. com/saas-blog/the_imperative_for_modular_reusable_ui_in_saas/

Sambamurthy, V., Bharadwaj, A., & Grover, V. (2003). Shaping agility through digital options: Reconceptualizing the role of information technology in contemporary firms. *Management Information Systems Quarterly, 27*(2), 237.

Sengupta, K., & Masini, A. (2008). IT agility: Striking the right balance. *Business Strategy Review, 19*(2), 42. doi:10.1111/j.1467-8616.2008.00534.x

Seo, D., & Paz, A. I. L. (2008). Exploring the dark side of IS in achieving organizational agility. *Communications of the ACM, 51*(11), 136–139. doi:10.1145/1400214.1400242

Setia, P., Sambamurthy, V., & Closs, D. (2008). Realizing business value of agile IT applications: Antecedents in the supply chain networks. *Information Technology Management, 9*, 5. doi:10.1007/s10799-007-0028-4

Sharifi, H., & Zhang, Z. (2001). Agile manufacturing in practice: Application of a methodology. *International Journal of Operations & Production Management, 21*(5/6), 772. doi:10.1108/01443570110390462

Sull, D. (2010). Competing through organizational agility. *The McKinsey Quarterly*, 48.

Sultan, N. A. (2011). Reaching for the "cloud": How SMEs can manage. *International Journal of Information Management, 31*(3), 272–278. doi:10.1016/j.ijinfomgt.2010.08.001

Tassey, G. (2000). Standardization in technology-based markets. *Research Policy, 29*(4,5), 587.

Tiwana, A., & Konsynski, B. (2010). Complementarities between organizational IT architecture and governance structure. *Information Systems Research, 21*(2), 288(217).

Truong, D. (2010). How cloud computing enhances competitive advantages: A research model for small businesses. *Business Review (Federal Reserve Bank of Philadelphia), 15*, 59.

Wang, L., Tao, J., Kunze, M., Castellanos, A. C., Kramer, D., & Karl, W. (2008). *Scientific cloud computing: Early definition and experience.* Paper presented at the 10th IEEE International Conference on High Performance Computing and Communications, 2008. HPCC '08.

Weill, P., Subramani, M., & Broadbent, M. (2002). Building IT infrastructure for strategic agility. *MIT Sloan Management Review, 44*(1), 57.

ADDITIONAL READING

Armbrust, M., Fox, A., Griffith, R., Joseph, A. D., Katz, R., & Konwinski, A. (2010). A view of cloud computing. *Communications of the ACM, 53*(4), 50–58. doi:10.1145/1721654.1721672

Borenstein, N., & Blake, J. (2011). Cloud computing standards: Where's the beef? *IEEE Internet Computing, 15*(3), 74. doi:10.1109/MIC.2011.58

Brynjolfsson, E., Hofmann, P., & Jordan, J. (2010). Economic and business dimensions cloud computing and electricity: Beyond the utility model. *Communications of the ACM, 53*(5), 32. doi:10.1145/1735223.1735234

Buyya, R., Yeo, C. S., Venugopal, S., Broberg, J., & Brandic, I. (2009). Cloud computing and emerging IT platforms: Vision, hype, and reality for delivering computing as the 5th utility. *Future Generation Computer Systems, 25*(6), 599–616. doi:10.1016/j.future.2008.12.001

Byrd, T. A., Lewis, B. R., & Turner, D. E. (2006). The impact of IT personnel skills on IS infrastructure and competitive IS . In Khosrow-Pour, M. (Ed.), *Advanced topics on information resources management* (*Vol. 5*). Hershey, PA: Idea Group Inc. doi:10.4018/978-1-59140-929-8.ch004

Camarinha-Matos, L., Afsarmanesh, H., & Rabelo, R. (2003). Infrastructure developments for agile virtual enterprises. *International Journal of Computer Integrated Manufacturing, 16*, 235. doi:10.1080/0951192031000089156

Conboy, K. (2009). Agility from first principles: Reconstructing the concept of agility in information systems development. *Information Systems Research, 20*(3), 329–354. doi:10.1287/isre.1090.0236

Conboy, K., Coyle, S., Wang, X., & Pikkarainen, M. (2011). People over process: Key challenges in agile development. *IEEE Software, 28*(4), 48. doi:10.1109/MS.2010.132

Desouza, K. C. (2007). *Agile information systems: Conceptualization, construction, and management.* Oxford, UK: Butterworth Heinemann.

Erdogmus, H. (2009). Cloud computing: Does Nirvana hide behind the nebula? *IEEE Software, 26*(2), 4–6. doi:10.1109/MS.2009.31

Grossman, R. (2009). The case for cloud computing. *IT Professional, 11*(2), 23. doi:10.1109/MITP.2009.40

Johnson, J. L. (2009). SQL in the clouds. *Computing in Science & Engineering, 11*(4), 12–28. doi:10.1109/MCSE.2009.127

Lee, G., & Xia, W. (2010). Toward agile: An integrated analysis of quantitative and qualitative field data on software development agility. *Management Information Systems Quarterly, 34*, 87–114.

Li, A., Yang, X., Kandula, S., & Zhang, M. (2011). Comparing public-cloud providers. *IEEE Internet Computing, 15*(2), 50. doi:10.1109/MIC.2011.36

Lin, G., Fu, D., Zhu, J., & Dasmalchi, G. (2009). Cloud computing: IT as a service. *IT Professional, 11*(2), 10. doi:10.1109/MITP.2009.22

Louridas, P. (2010). Up in the air: Moving your applications to the cloud. *IEEE Software, 27*, 6. doi:10.1109/MS.2010.109

Lyytinen, K., & Rose, G. M. (2006). Information system development agility as organizational learning. *European Journal of Information Systems, 15*(2), 183–199. doi:10.1057/palgrave.ejis.3000604

Marston, S., Li, Z., Bandyopadhyay, S., Zhang, J., & Ghalsasi, A. (2011). Cloud computing - The business perspective. *Decision Support Systems, 51*(1), 176. doi:10.1016/j.dss.2010.12.006

Miller, H., & Veiga, J. (2009). Cloud computing: Will commodity services benefit users long term? *IT Professional, 11*(6), 57. doi:10.1109/MITP.2009.117

Owens, D. (2010). Securing elasticity in the cloud. *Communications of the ACM, 53*(6), 46. doi:10.1145/1743546.1743565

Sengupta, K., & Masini, A. (2008). IT agility: Striking the right balance. *Business Strategy Review, 19*(2), 42. doi:10.1111/j.1467-8616.2008.00534.x

Sterling, T., & Stark, D. (2009). A high-performance computing forecast: Partly cloudy. *Computing in Science & Engineering, 11*(4), 42–49. doi:10.1109/MCSE.2009.111

Vouk, M. A. (2008). Cloud computing - Issues, research and implementations. *Journal of Computing and Information Technology, 4*, 235–246.

Wei, Y., & Blake, M. (2010). Service-oriented computing and cloud computing: challenges and opportunities. *IEEE Internet Computing, 14*(6), 72. doi:10.1109/MIC.2010.147

Zhang, Q., Cheng, L., & Boutaba, R. (2010). Cloud computing: State-of-the-art and research challenges. *Journal of Internet Services and Applications, 1*(1), 7–18. doi:10.1007/s13174-010-0007-6

KEY TERMS AND DEFINITIONS

Cloud Computing: A computing model that delivers shared and rapidly scalable IT resources (e.g. servers, databases, applications) via the Internet to the user in an on-demand, self-service manner.

IaaS: Also known as "infrastructure as a service", is the bottom layer of cloud computing services. IaaS offers computing and storage infrastructure (e.g. virtual servers) which can be rented by users for implementing applications or storing data.

IS Agility: The ability of an IS function to sense, diagnose, and respond to IS changes in real time.

PaaS: Also known as "platform as a service", is the middle layer of cloud computing services. PaaS offers integrated development and deployment environments which can be rented by users for developing, testing, and deploying software applications.

SaaS: Also known as "software as a service", comprises the top layer of cloud computing services. SaaS consists of completed software applications which can be rented by users and used directly for production.

ENDNOTES

[1] While there are a number of variants of cloud computing (private, hybrid, etc.), this study focuses on the most common and influential type of these variants, public cloud computing.

[2] This study considers agility as distinct from flexibility, though they are both related to change.

[3] http://www.salesforce.com/platform/customization/ accessed on 20th April 2011, this figure was 82,400 in December 2010.

[4] See http://aws.amazon.com/ec2/faqs/#How_quickly_can_I_scale_my_capacity_both_up_and_down

Chapter 5

Holistic Investment Framework for Cloud Computing:
A Management–Philosophical Approach Based on Complex Adaptive Systems

Marc Rabaey
University of Hasselt, Belgium

ABSTRACT

Cloud computing is a new technology which puts whole or partial parts of the Information Technology (IT) infrastructure and services in a virtualized environment inside and/or outside the traditional IT center perimeter. It touches every level of the IT architecture and thus has a big influence on the way the internal and external users via their business processes are interacting with this architecture. Security is a big issue in this context and a lot of business and IT people are reluctant to move to the Cloud. Besides the security, business and architectural issues may increase the risks and create more uncertainties for these kinds of projects. For this reason, the chapter presents an investment framework, which takes into account the global, the business, the IT and the operational strategies, so that cloud computing projects have more chance to succeed. The need for flexibility in the investments is addressed by the real option valuation, which is placed in the context of the chapter's holistic investment framework for cloud computing.

INTRODUCTION

Cloud computing is a hot topic today amongst business and IT (Information Technology) leaders for its potential to transform IT service delivery (Abrams, 2010) and to galvanize service-oriented architecture (SOA). Some people even state that just like electricity and telephone systems; IT

will be transformed into a commodity or the fifth form of utility.

A survey of Industry Week (IW, 2010) showed that there is a lot of fear surrounding Cloud Computing in the business world to step into the Cloud. Research shows that intuitively they want to make the move, but that they need more accurate data to do it (Benaroch, 2007). So the technology of cloud computing forces the top management of

DOI: 10.4018/978-1-4666-2187-9.ch005

organizations to think more carefully about competition and collaboration, be it now in relation to the customers, suppliers, government or "traditional" competitors. Brandenburger et al. (1995) are talking about "Co-opetition"; a combination of Cooperation and Competition in the evolution of game theory, which through strategic games can generally be applied in the investment decision process and more specifically in IT.

With Cloud Computing, applications and data can be stored all over the world. Thus trust becomes a very important issue. Trust is already en important issue in SOA but Cloud Computing has brought it to the forefront. There has to be a trade-off between cost and confidentiality, which is culturally influenced.

But more important is the strategic context of the organization. Nowadays the business has moved from a "safe and slow" market toward a complex even chaotic fast moving society (not only the markets have changed). The theory of Complex Adaptive Systems (CAS) which describes the internal and external connections of the organization in such an environment will help leaders and managers in companies, governments and non-profit organizations to evolve in this context. Cloud Computing is part of that system.

Therefore there is a need for a new Business Thinking Model. It may not be solely technology driven (otherwise hype) but also business driven. A combination of both should already be implemented in the development of the Grand Strategy. Only in this way can the new paradigm be proliferated into business strategy and resources strategy (like IT-strategy), resulting in an awareness at the operational level (business processes and projects).

Consequently the investment methodology has to follow this new concept where adequate tools provided by the game theory (strategic interaction), and real options analysis (uncertainty, risk, flexibility) can be used.

The purpose of this chapter is to present a holistic investment framework for IT and in particular Cloud Computing. The term holistic refers to the fact that profit and non-profit organizations should take all aspects of the organization, business and resources, into consideration to avoid suboptimization in a domain instead of optimization in the larger whole.

In this way the possible economies of an implementation or an extension of Cloud Computing in the organization, along with the risks, are assessed in the business and technology context of that organization. Concepts like real options and game theory are introduced in this holistic investment framework to tackle issues of strategic interaction, uncertainties, and risks thus grounding investment decisions on proven decision methodologies.

CLOUD COMPUTING AND REAL OPTION VALUATION (ROV)

Cloud Computing Defined

Although terms related to Cloud Computing are being defined (National Institute of Standards and Technology (NIST)), some commercial companies are redefining some terms to suite their sales or marketing model. We will give an overview of the definitions and characteristics of cloud computing as defined by NIST. The quoted parts are extracted from NIST (2011).

The Characteristics of Cloud Computing

"On-demand self-service. A consumer can unilaterally provision computing capabilities, such as server time and network storage, as needed automatically without requiring human interaction with each service's provider." This demands that the service provider's management processes must be as much as possible automated to deliver quick service. However in reality in the case that important parts of the infrastructure or applications are requested, companies want Service Level Agreements (SLA). Therefore negotiated contracts are more the rule than the exception.

"Broad network access. Capabilities are available over the network and accessed through standard mechanisms that promote use by heterogeneous thin or thick client platforms (e.g., mobile phones, laptops, and PDAs)."

"Resource pooling. The provider's computing resources are pooled to serve multiple consumers using a multi-tenant model, with different physical and virtual resources dynamically assigned and reassigned according to consumer demand. There is a sense of location independence in that the customer generally has no control or knowledge over the exact location of the provided resources but may be able to specify location at a higher level of abstraction (e.g., country, state, or datacenter). Examples of resources include storage, processing, memory, network bandwidth, and virtual machines." This can be a situation for confidentiality and security of data (CSA, 2010).

"Rapid elasticity. Capabilities can be rapidly and elastically provisioned, in some cases automatically, to quickly scale out, and rapidly released to quickly scale in. To the consumer, the capabilities available for provisioning often appear to be unlimited and can be purchased in any quantity at any time." This gives an enormous flexibility to the customer's IT-services.

"Measured Service. Cloud systems automatically control and optimize resource use by leveraging

a metering capability at some level of abstraction appropriate to the type of service (e.g., storage, processing, bandwidth, and active user accounts). Resource usage can be monitored, controlled, and reported, providing transparency for both the provider and consumer of the utilized service." This is necessary for the pay per use business model.

The Service Models

"Cloud Software as a Service (SaaS). The capability provided to the consumer is to use the provider's applications running on a cloud infrastructure. The applications are accessible from various client devices through a thin client interface such as a web browser." It can be considered as a complete outsourcing of an application, but based on pay-per-use.

"Cloud Platform as a Service (PaaS). The capability provided to the consumer is to deploy onto the cloud infrastructure consumer-created or acquired applications created using programming languages and tools supported by the provider. The consumer does not manage or control the underlying cloud infrastructure including network, servers, operating systems, or storage, but has control over the deployed applications and possibly application hosting environment configurations."

"Cloud Infrastructure as a Service (IaaS). The capability provided to the consumer is to provision processing, storage, networks, and other fundamental computing resources where the consumer is able to deploy and run arbitrary software, which can include operating systems and applications." This reduces the upfront capital cost and it enables companies to start small and quick, without having to invest in possible future capacity performance (CAPEX becomes OPEX).

We consider also Business Process -as-a-Service (BPaaS). BPaaS is pre-assembled business processes which are provided via cloud application platforms to the consumers (Marks et al., 2010).

The Deployment Models

"Private cloud. The cloud infrastructure is operated solely for an organization. It may be managed by the organization or a third party and may exist on premise or off premise."

"Community cloud. The cloud infrastructure is shared by several organizations and supports a specific community that has shared concerns (e.g., mission, security requirements, policy, and compliance considerations). It may be managed by the organizations or a third party and may exist on premise or off premise."

"Public cloud. The cloud infrastructure is made available to the general public or a large industry group and is owned by an organization selling cloud services."

"Hybrid cloud. The cloud infrastructure is a composition of two or more clouds (private, community, or public) that remain unique entities but are bound together by standardized or proprietary technology that enables data and application portability (e.g., cloud bursting for load balancing between clouds). "

Evolution, Not Revolution

Whereas the NIST's definition is quite strict, Cloud Computing is usually used as a "catch all" concept. The term became a buzz word, referring also to existing techniques like virtualization: old wine in new bottles.

However the term seems to be evolving in the minds of people toward the mutualization of computing resources thanks to remote transfer and access techniques on a "on demand" and instantaneous access basis (Laurent, 2011).

HOLISTIC INVESTMENT FRAMEWORK FOR CLOUD COMPUTING

The Need for a Holistic Approach

This new mindset, especially in the domain of SaaS and BPaaS, is influencing the approach of assessing "IT investments." IT-systems which use Cloud Computing touch every aspect of the organization: business and resources, thus we are encouraged to have a more holistic approach.

The fact that a company's data (or part of it) can be stored anywhere on the internet makes confidentiality and security an important topic (CSA, 2010; Abrams, 2011; Laurent, 2011; Soenen and Palante, 2011). The laws applying to the data will differ from country to country (legal aspects).

Judicial risks lie in the domain of confidentiality of the data, especially with reference to the customers of the organization. For instance, if the

cloud service provider has a cloud data center in China (primary storage or backup storage), then the organization should be aware that data has to cross unencrypted the Chinese border.

Putting data and/or processes in the Cloud is one aspect, getting them out again, or even deleting them and being sure that they are really deleted, is another (security of data). Moreover, integrating Cloud data (off-premise) with data in the company (on- premise) may present difficulties (IT-technical issues, business inefficiency). Certainly the "easy" access to Cloud Computing services is resulting in quick solutions that can be "difficult" to integrate later with other Cloud Computing services and/or legacy systems. We have seen these same problems with Enterprise Application Integration (EAI), but finding solutions now with the Cloud is proving even more challenging. It was a similar problem in the 80's with the introduction of the pc in companies. People were buying stand alone systems that later needed to be integrated into the existing company's applications: here 'bad' wine in new bottles.

The employees and collaborators of a company are confronted more and more with the situation that they are working less on-premise, and more at home (legal aspects, insurance, human resources) and are thus themselves on the internet. Therefore their IT-environment (pc, mobile, devices) should be secure and as such share the responsibility of the IT-security (off-premise).

So the acquisition (here also the financial question of CAPEX and OPEX) of Cloud Computer services cannot and may not be solely assessed from the perspective of the IT-department of a company or organization, but must employ a holistic approach: legal, human resources, material resources, IT, financial, logistics, business, etc. Even in the calculation of the Total Cost of Ownership (TCO) Abrams, Kirwin, Guptill and Odell (2011) a holistic approach is necessary because TCO is not a formal financial model but is a holistic view of IT costs across enterprise boundaries over time. Therefore a holistic framework called Strategic Interdisciplinary Forum (S2IF) is being proposed.

From Strategy to Service

Concept

In the case of Cloud computing S2IF defines the process "from Strategy to Service."

Rabaey et al (2007a) use the Art of War to derive a system which aligns projects and processes -and thus investments- in the case of integration of businesses. The Grand Strategy is the art of combining all the resources of an organization or alliance into a dynamic adaptable plan to achieve its (political) goals. Since the Grand Strategy is the result of the balance between goals and means, the business strategies (goals) and the resources strategies (like IT) are distinguished from each other and are derived from the Grand Strategy. IT will develop the main stream use of IT in the organization, while the business strategy will define the environment in which they would like to attain the business objectives.

Resources and business strategies will be considered together again in the S2IF (Figure 1) where the business processes will be proposed together with the needed resources (allocation). A business process is a logical set of activities that consumes resources to attain its objectives. In the organization of the business processes, we have the second alignment of goals and means. The resource managers and the business unit managers will discuss the operational use of resources (organization) in an interdisciplinary forum; interdisciplinary because of the multitude of functional domains (see above).

The result is the providing of the resources and their service levels (SLA= Service Level Agreement). The decision unit will decide on the proposals and will select the best solution. IT will adapt its SLA-plan and the steering plan of IT.

For the latter, enterprise architecture is proposed (Rabacy, 2012) (see below).

If the organization is now profit or non-profit, Cloud Computing has considerable advantages, not only for the organization but also for its partners, customers and service providers. These advantages along with challenges and opportunities (risks) of Cloud Computing are being brought into frame and placed in the context of S2IF. From a business perspective, a resource or service provider will be evaluated on the delivery of the service (SLA) and the quality of service (QoS), which is defined scalability, availability and reliability.

COMPLEX ADAPTIVE SYSTEMS (CAS)

Characteristics of CAS

Another argument for a holistic approach is found in the complexity theory and the theory of CAS. Complexity theory deals with systems that are large collections of interacting agents. Despite their diversity, complex systems share certain fundamental behaviors (Gore, 1996; Lowe and Ng, 2006):

- **Emergence:** Interactions among agents in complex systems may lead to emerging global (or system-wide) properties that are very different from the behaviors of individual agents.

These properties which cannot be predicted from prior knowledge of the agents, in turn affect the environment that each agent perceives influencing its behavior m a synergetic feedback loop. Thus the "whole" of a complex system is far greater than the sum of its parts and the whole has properties not held by its consisting agents. Therefore the analysis of complex systems requires a holistic approach. An organization may not

Figure 1. Strategic interdisciplinary investment forum

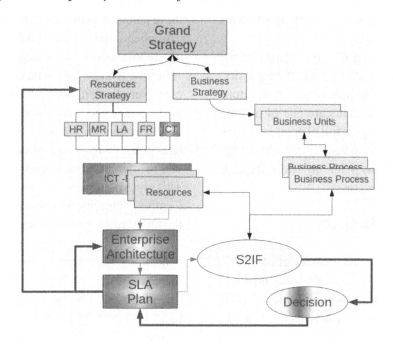

only be decomposed into business units (business agents). The support of the business processes of these business agents is delivered by resources agents (like human resources, material resources, IT). They have also their culture, goals and processes and therefore must also be considered in the "whole."

- **Adaptive Self-Organization:** Complex systems tend to adapt to their environments and to self-organize. Rather than tending toward disorder or entropy, complex adaptive systems spontaneously crystallize into more highly ordered states but with few leverage points.
- **Information Processing:** Complex systems exhibit the ability to process information sensed from the environment and react to it based on internalized models. Information processing is closely related to a system's ability to learn and adapt near the edge of chaos. It creates interacting feedback loops which cause highly

non-linear behavior (Bowser, Cantle and Allan, 2011). If the CAS is an organization then the management will be confronted with counter-intuitive and non-intended consequences.

- **Evolution to the Edge of Chaos:** All dynamic systems exist in one of three regimes:
  ○ A stable regime. in which disturbances tend to die out;
  ○ A chaotic regime (the province of chaos theory);
  ○ The phase transition between stability and chaos.

Whereas increasing disturbances in the environment cause some systems to move from stability to chaos, complex systems learn from their environments and add new functions to cope with previously unknown situations (cause and symptoms are separated in time and space). Thus they increase their complexity and adapt along the edge of chaos. According to complexity theorists the same type of growth in complexity occurs in nature, man-made systems as well as societies, business and economies.

Mauboussin (2011, p. 89) gives in his Harvard Business Review article "Embracing Complexity" the ant colony as an example of a CAS in nature: "Complex adaptive systems are one of nature's big solutions, so biology is full of great examples. Ant colonies are solving very complicated, very challenging problems with no leadership, no strategic plan, no Congress."

CAS and Organizations

Hovhannisian (2001) and Bowser et al. (2011) state that organizations are CAS. Organizations are segmented rather than monolithic in which information flows and interactions between the agents occur. The way it happens is very relevant in the understanding of the working of the whole and its components because it influence the culture (and subcultures), the hierarchy and the structure and it has an impact on the speed of communication and interpretation of the (internal and external) information.

Hovhannisian (2011) points out that if only the components are analyzed (Taylorian decomposition) and not the whole then analysts are not getting the full picture and are missing the links, the interconnections between agents, and how the whole interacts with its environment. Bowser et al. (2011) emphasize that the study of CAS is interdisciplinary (so must be applicable tools) and that emergence requires a holistic approach before studying the parts.

In this context we can refer to the Chaos theory (Glenn, 1996) upon which the complexity theory has been built.. A Chaos system (as a whole) can be controlled by parameters ("control knobs") although the system is not fully described. So, in the case of organization where a traditional command and control hierarchy exists, if that organization has more than one parameter to control the system (functioning) then it should coordinate the

parameterization in the system, otherwise one or more parameters may destabilize its functioning. This phenomenon is also known in CAS (Lowe et al., 2006): "A direct consequence of a Complex Adaptive System's structural heterogeneity and characteristic nonlinear interactions is that some of the nodes and links have a stronger influence on the system by virtue of more or stronger interactions, or by virtue of occupying a point in one or more feedback loops within the system. This gives rise to the concepts of Leverage Points, Centres of Gravity, and the well-known heuristic, the 80/20 rule." (See also Janssen et al.; 2006).

In the left part of Figure 2 we see that the controlling parameters X and Y are separately managed respectively by components A and B. The proposed Strategic Interdisciplinary Investment Forum (S2IF) will monitor the whole and harmonize the input of both parameters, so that no instability a priori is attained. However since organizations are CAS, emergence exists. Later in the chapter, we will discuss how the agents responsible for the command and control should react.

Related to the "Edge of Chaos"; systems exist on a spectrum ranging from equilibrium to chaos. The most productive state to be in is at the edge of chaos where diversity, variety and creativity are at the maximum, leading to new possibilities (see later Cynefin framework). Controls, such as simple rules (Esienhardt et al., 2001) and regulations or institutional and budgetary restrictions, ensure that an agent's behaviors are limited, thus changing the aggregate behavior and helping the CAS to behave in a predictable way (Janssen et al., 2006).

The use of the different levels of strategy does not imply very complicated and complex rules or processes of developing, maintaining and disseminating these strategies, on the contrary. Eisenhardt and Sull are advocating the use of simple rules (in CAS): "Most managers quickly grasp the concept of focusing on key strategic processes that will position their companies where the flow

Figure 2. S2IF as coordination (harmonizing)

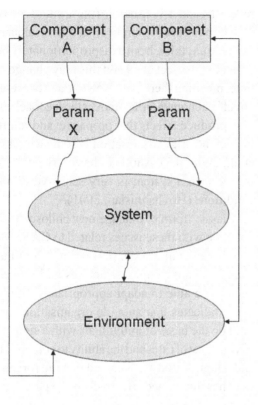
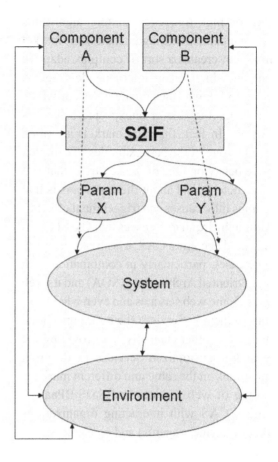

of opportunities is most promising. But because they equate processes with detailed routines, they often miss the notion of simple rules. Yet simple rules are essential. They poise the company on what's termed in complexity theory "the edge of chaos," providing just enough structure to allow it to capture the best opportunities. It may sound counterintuitive, but the complicated improvisational movements that companies like [Amazon, Google, Cisco] make as they pursue fleeting opportunities arise from simple rules." (2001, p. 110).

CAS and Cloud Computing

Capital markets are CAS (Mauboussin, 2011). James Urquhart (2010) justly links the "flash crash" as an example of behavior of a CAS and

links this to Cloud Computing.. On May 6, 2010 several financial indexes experienced a sudden and precipitous drop, losing around 8 percent of their value at the beginning of the day in a matter of minutes. While there has been no definitive cause identified for the day's events, many financial market experts have identified the increasing presence of automated trading and electronic exchanges as a key cause of this "flash crash."

He continues; "High-frequency trading is performed by automated systems that attempt to beat out competition to the best matches of buyers and sellers for particular stocks. These systems are deployed in the same data centers as the exchange systems themselves, and the success of a system is often dependent on shaving milliseconds off of network and computing latencies.

What is critical to note, however, is that the number of high-frequency trading algorithms operating independently against the same market environment creates a sort of complex adaptive system, in which many interdependent agents adhering to known rules create a system which exhibits unpredictable or unexpected behaviors as a whole. In fact, financial markets are often heralded as one of the best examples of complex adaptive behavior. One of the key traits that science has determined about these systems is that sometimes little causes can trigger giant effects."

Although Urquhart foresees that Cloud Computing could become a CAS, it is already a reality in some cases, particularly in combination with Service Oriented Architecture (SOA) and its web services. Some web services and even whole collections of them in Services (be it through Cloud Computing or other channels) are providing the same and/or customized services to different organizations on the same and different markets. Cascading of web services and SaaS/BPaaS is creating a CAS with interacting organizations (market or business agents) and consumers.

So not only is Cloud Computing supporting CAS, but can also be itself a CAS, which makes investing in Cloud Computing a complex process. To better understand this complexity of Cloud Computing, we will go more in depth into the management of a CAS and the implication of it on how to invest (in general, and in Cloud Computing in particular).

CAS AND S2IF

Command and Control (C2)

The concept of CAS is important for the Command & Control (C2) of an organization (military or civilian). Lowe et al. (2006) state that good military commanders have intuitively understood the nature of complexity and nonlinearity on the battlefield. In turn, the science of complexity may reveal the underlying basis of these intuitive truths.

The nonlinearity implies that a given input may produce anything from a disproportionately large effect to no effect at all and this may change over time, meaning there is no Newtonian "cause-and-effect" phenomenon. Moreover the feedback loops may produce effects that propagate and return to impact the original causation in some way (Lowe et al., 2006, p.5). Another characteristic of CAS is that such a system is very sensitive to initial conditions (Hovhannisian, 2001).

Classic "formal" management philosophy does not cope with these issues related to CAS. That's why Lowe et al. (2006, p.9) write: "Continuous change means people, structures and processes need to be able to adapt appropriately. Study of CAS indicates that an agile organisation can be built on the basis of individuals with a simple but effective set of rules and the ability to communicate and adapt. A study ... showed that the [organization] has functioned effectively in the past through the use of informal networks. ... Organisational rigidity has been seen by those within the system as a restriction that reduces effectiveness to some extent. Rather than attempting to address this by finding the perfect C2 structure, CAS ideas promote the use of individual initiative through informal networks as part of our C2 culture and not just as a tolerated 'work-around'."

Weijnen, Herder and Bouwmans (2007) in their paper with the pertinent title "Designing Complex Systems, A Contradiction in Terms" confirm that a classic C2 is not anymore accepted since no agent is superior to any other, therefore a very good communication system is necessary. Furthermore the authors state that aside from the C2, the content-based management by 'expertise of management' is also unlikely to succeed; rather decisions will be based on a negotiated knowledge, which can deteriorate to "negotiated nonsense." (See also Janssen et al. 2006). To avoid this situation Rabaey (2011, 2012a) proposes a framework of intelligence creation and dissemination where experts (knowledge workers) can still play their role.

Cynefin Framework

Not all systems are CAS and components of CAS are not always complex. In their article in Harvard Business Review Snowden and Boone (2007) state that wise executives should tailor their approach for decision making to fit the complexity of the circumstances they are faced with:

- **Simple context:** Here fits the classical C2 where clear cause-and-effect can be detected. The leader should sense the problems, categorize them and then respond with the best practices. It is the domain of the known knowns, however there is a danger to oversimplify the situation. Leaders often become complacent and too often react too late which can be catastrophic. That's why in the Cynefin framework below, an arrow is drawn from simple systems to chaotic systems.

- **Complicated context:** Here also the context is ordered and cause-and-effects exist, but not everybody can see these relationships and therefore experts are needed to detect them. The leaders should sense, analyze and respond. But in this domain of known unknowns, the experts can be overconfident in their own solutions. The so-called "maverick" solutions of non-experts are mostly rejected.

The first two contexts are ordered and the philosophy is based on "cause-and-effect." Mauboussin (2011, p. 90) states that this prevents leaders and managers from dealing effectively with complexity. "The biggest issue, in my mind, is that humans are incredibly good at linking cause and effect—sometimes too good. Ten thousand years ago most cause and effect was pretty clear. And

our brains evolved to deal with that. But it means that when you see something occur in a complex adaptive system, your mind is going to create a narrative to explain what happened—even though cause and effect are not comprehensible in that kind of system. Hindsight's a beautiful thing. Also, we have a tendency to think that certain causes will lead to particular effects. …. And we just don't know. I think that's the biggest single bias."

The two following contexts (See Figure 3) are unordered and don't have this bias. "Complex context" has unknown unknowns and it is the domain to which much of contemporary business has shifted. There are no right answers and leaders should probe, sense and respond, meaning that the organization should look at emergent, patterns. Snowden et al. (2007, p. 74) warn "If [the managers] try to overcontrol the organization, they will preempt the opportunity for informative patterns to emerge. Leaders who try to impose order in a complex context will fail, but those who set the stage, step back a bit, allow patterns to emerge, and determine which ones are desirable will succeed."

"Chaotic context" is the realm of unknowables. A bit counterintuitive, in this case the leader has to act first to create order, so that he can sense where stability is or not to make it possible to transform the situation from chaos to complexity; thus act, sense and respond. So in this case a leader has not much time to think and act quickly. In this context George S. Patton can be quoted "A good plan violently executed now is better than a perfect plan next week'. In this domain the leader can find inspiration from Naturalistic Decision Making (NDM) (See also (Brooks, 2007; Berryman, 2007; Rabaey, 2011; Shattuck, Miller, 2006).

Companies should refer to these contexts because they help provide the best opportunities. Eisenhardt and Sull write about this phenomenon in their HBR-article "Strategy as Simple Rules" (2001, p. 108): 'The secret of companies like Yahoo! is strategy as simple rules. Managers of such companies know that the greatest opportunities

Figure 3. Cynefin framework

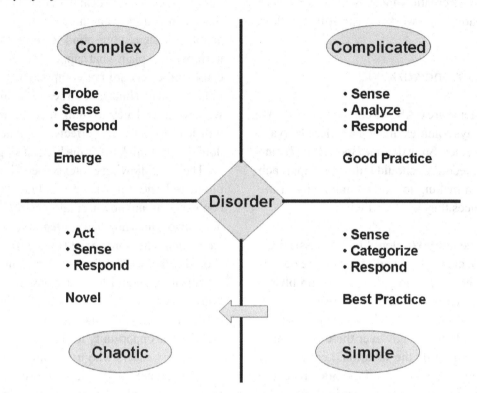

for competitive advantage lie in market confusion, so they jump into chaotic markets, probe for opportunities, build on successful forays, and shift flexibly among opportunities as circumstances dictate. But they recognize the need for a few key strategic processes and a few simple rules to guide them through the chaos." This does not imply that no strategy at all is needed. "Each company follows a disciplined strategy - otherwise, it would be paralyzed by chaos. And, as with all effective strategies, the strategy is unique to the company. But a simple-rules strategy and its underlying logic of pursuing opportunities are harder to see than traditional approaches." (Eisenhardt et al., 2001, p.109)

The fifth context is "disorder" The authors recommend breaking down the situation into constituent parts and assigning each to one of the other realms. In this way leaders can make decisions and intervene in contextually appropriate ways.

Risk and Uncertainty

In literature, "Risk" and "Uncertainty" are interchanged because of the fact that the outcome is the same (expected values) (Aven, 2010, p.55), but semantically they are very different in the approach regarding decision-making. Organizations have to make important decisions (like investments) without complete information in a complex and fast changing environment. Uncertainty is a state in which the outcomes are unknown and perhaps unknowable, the more distant in time (future), the greater the uncertainty (Funston, 2010, p. xxiii). The decision horizon is farther at the strategic level than at the operational or tactical levels of the organization. For most of the organizations in this ever faster changing environment, the time line at the strategic level is from the present until the long term (at least a year), while the operational level is from now until short term (couple of weeks or months at most).

The most important difference is that risk is a measurable unknown factor that will have an unpleasant consequence for the person or the organization if it happens. Risk is based on previously collected statistical (objective) analyses on the issue. Uncertainty is a non-measurable factor. However based on experience (thus subjective) one can estimate what the chances are that it will happen or not. So, the most significant difference is that in the case of risks, the chance that something will happen is based on objective statistical data, while in the case of uncertainty, the chances that it will happen is based on subjective experiences or reasoning. The latter can be further divided into known-unknown (one is aware of the existence) and unknown-unknown (non-awareness). So both are expressed in "chances," but the underlying base is significantly different, which is important to remember when assessing investments.

At all levels of the organization uncertainty exists. However the closer the highest strategic level of the organization, the higher the uncertainty. This is because of the decision time horizon (see above). The highest strategic level of an organization must give the general direction to which the whole organization has to evolve, not only in the environment (business strategy), but also internally (organization and allocation of resources).

Thus it must be noted that uncertainties and risks are not always external to the organization but can also be internal. Techniques as Baldrige (Baldrige, n.d.), Common Assessment Framework (CAF, n.d.) are used to assess the internal organization and to improve its working, which comes down to obtaining the right knowledge and information for meeting the objectives of the organization and to use its resource. in a rational way.

In an economical context, rationality has more to do with the ratio of benefits to costs versus the philosophical meaning of reasoning (Wikipedia Rationality, n.d.). It is not a surprise that even the first principle of the Art of War is to have the right balance between goals (benefits) and means

(costs) to decide which is the best strategic plan to adopt for preserving the best interest of a nation. The only but obligatory rule of this principle is the permanent collection of intelligence (Bernard, 1976). So to reduce its uncertainties for better decision making, the organization will collect intelligence.

Regarding risk, the organization will collect better statistical data, and of course it will look for better methods to avoid or reduce the risks. Fulton et al. (2010, p. xxiii) write that the risk intelligent enterprise recognizes that risk intelligence and risk management are not ends in themselves but a means toward the end of creating and preserving value and surviving and thriving in uncertainty (non-measurable unknown).

Investment Techniques

Different kinds of investment techniques exist and just like in the Cynefin framework, the range goes from simple to very complex techniques. It is not directly the subject of the investment that determines the technique, but rather the context (as described above) that determines the investment technique. In the same way the move of a corporate datacenter infrastructure towards a private cloud can be simple or complicated for company A, while for company B it can be complex and even chaotic (due to a competitive disadvantage that can cause the downfall of the company).

The discussion of all possible investment techniques is out of the scope of this chapter. Only a few will be handled to show the necessary balance between the contexts and investment techniques.

Capital budgeting methods based on the discounted cash flow (DCF) have been the primary instruments for investment decision making. The most commonly used DCF-based method is the net present value (NPV). NPV discounts all cash flows (incoming and outgoing) related to the project or process to the present value (PV). If the sum of discounted cash flows is positive then the project is a candidate to invest in. This technique is suited to a simple context (everything is known). "Under static circumstances, DCF-based methods provide reliable results. However, the real world situations are seldom static. Especially in cases of large investments with long economic lives the static DCF-based methods fail to present a highly reliable picture of the profitability" (Wang and Lee, 2010, p. 696).

What about the issue of moving from CAPEX to OPEX? (See also OG (2010) and Abrams (2011)). For fiscal and accounting these are two different expenditures that are treated differently. However related to DCF, CAPEX is a cost which cannot be deducted in the (tax) year in which it is paid or incurred and must be capitalized. The capital expenditure costs are then amortized or depreciated over the life of the asset which has been acquired. From the point of view of cash flow, the yearly amortized or deprecated amounts are incoming cash flows. As such, CAPEX and OPEX can be used in the same context and be compared to each other.

If business is in a more complex context then it is hard to predict the future, so what about the future cash flows? "[In] a rapidly changing environment, we don't really know how things are going to unfold, so it's difficult to make forecasts or budgets going many years into the future." (Mauboussin, 2011, p. 92)

Shen (2009, p. 712) and Huang, Kao and Li (2007, p. 688) write that indeed the evaluation of (IT-) investments are not trivial, because the costs and benefits may involve uncertainty and vagueness, which make return on investments difficult. Further (IT-)projects are assessed from various dimensions and criteria, which need advanced decision tools to aid. Thirdly, (IT-)solutions may be bundled with some special constraints about the system architecture, budgets, decision preferences, and so on (see also S2IF). The authors are proposing a fuzzy multi-objective decision approach for evaluating IT-projects. Fuzzy sets are used because the expertise of specialized people from different domains has to be combined together along with their level of expertise (see also fuzzy Real Options Valuation below and Tolga and Kahraman (2008)). We refer to Thomaidis, Nikitakos and Dounias (2006) for the theory and case studies based on Fuzzy Sets and Lauria and Duchessi (2006) based on Bayesian Belief Network (BBN).

In the complicated context, this classic investment methodology (DCF) is lacking in every way the flexibility that management need to be able to postpone, delay, start, and abandon projects. Cobb and Charnes (2007) state that managerial flexibility has value. "The assumption that all investments are irreversible is a fundamental weakness of most DCF methods. ... The ability of their managers to make smart decisions in the face of volatile market and technological conditions is essential for firms in any competitive industry."(p. 173). Real Option Analysis (ROA) or Real Option Valuation (ROV) gives management this flexibility and it tackles the problem of uncertainty and risk related to each investment (Trigeorgis, 2002; Fichman, 2004; Brach, 2003; Mun, 2006). Options are the right but not the obligation to execute an action (sell or buy). Translated to real option, it means that management can decide to postpone, stop, start, restart or put on hold a project. The reasons may be because of the lack of relevant information, or to wait for results of some pilot projects. Table 1 gives an overview of possible real options.

Although ROV is known in the IT-world (for example Pendharkar (2010)), most of the time ROI (Return On Investment) and NPV are used to assess investments (For example: (Marks et al., 2010; Spínola, 2009; OG, 2010; Abrams, 2011; Abrams et al., 2011). A possible reason is that most of the books on this subject are written by technology people. For a more in-depth analysis of the use of ROV in Cloud Computing (investment, risk assessment), we refer to Rabaey (2012).

In his study, von Helfenstein (2009) advocates the use of ROV when complexity and risks are involved. Since most of the business has shifted towards complex contexts, it is surprising that

Table 1. Types of real options

Option	Description
Postpone	Wait to determine whether to implement certain modules (hardware, software, network,...) without imperiling the potential benefits.
Abandon	Abandon the project (terminate at the current stage) (exit)
Switch	Re-arrange the sequence of installing/updating/finishing modules
Scope up	Add new modules not scheduled previously or increase quality
Scope down	Remove already installed modules or reduce quality
Explore	Investing in a prototype to explore the possibilities
Stage	Flexibility to stop and resume modules in progress

ROV is not used more in investment appraisals. General Helmuth von Moltke said once: "No plan survives contact with the enemy." As a matter of fact ROV has a common drawback with the classic investment techniques, being that it does not take into account the interaction of the organization with its environment (market, government, etc.) (Grenadier, 2000; Smit et al., 2009; Ferreira et al., 2009). The solution is to combine ROV with game theory, which results in the theory of option games. However option games demands a lot of intelligence and computing power and can only be justified in some cases (see below). The organization can play different games (game theory) at the same time in different domains and/or different levels. Moreover, the underlying organizational elements (agents) can themselves play different games regarding the mother organization (the whole) and regarding each other, even for a same project: IT can collaborate with third parties, while human resources are in competition with these parties. If there is no superstructure (like project management or business unit), then contradictory signals are sent to the market. So, there is no such thing as a unique strategic game to play. Thus if game options are used, in every node more than two (solution) paths may exist, which may quickly lead into a Chaos system (Glenn, 1996; Rabaey, 2011).

Collan et al. (2009) remark another disadvantage of (probabilistic) ROV by stating that real options are commonly valued with the same methods that have been used to value financial options, that is, with Black-Scholes option pricing formula, with the binomial option valuation method, or with Monte-Carlo-based methods. Most of the methods are complex and demand a good understanding of the underlying mathematics, which make their use difficult in practice. Moreover the pure (probabilistic) real option rule characterizes the present value of expected cash flows by a single number, which is not realistic in many cases (Lee and Lee, 2011). In addition these models are based on the assumption that they can quite accurately mimic the underlying markets as a process, an assumption that may hold for some quite efficiently traded financial securities, but not for investments of a 'singular' organization where every investment is intimately linked to the organization and not to a market.

However, if ROV is not used, but classic investment techniques are then their integration with flexibility and risk are more complex than with ROV (example see (Misra et al., 2011)).

To overcome the above mentioned problems Carlson et al. (2000), Collan (2008), Collan et al. (2009), Lee et al. (2011), Wang, and Lee (2010) and Tolga et al. (2008) are proposing fuzzy sets to overcome these problems. (See also Wikipedia Fuzzy Pay-Off Method for Real Option Valuation, n.d.), (Bednyagin et al., n.d.)).

So if enough statistical data is available then ROV can be used (most of the time in complicated contexts). If not then fuzzy ROV is preferred (complicated and complex contexts). Moreover Fuzzy ROV is also better suited for making decisions in groups (Tao, Jinlong, Benhai and Shan, 2007).

In general, "[d]ecision analysis methods have been used for capital budgeting, and several researchers have proposed an integration of decision analysis tools [as shown above] and ROV. The combination of these concepts may allow models that produce a solution for the value of a project and an optimal investment decision rule more intuitively and efficiently." Whatever combination is used with ROV "the optimal strategies suggested are usually the same" (Cobb et al., 2007, p. 178).

S2IF Demands a Cyclic "Awareness" Process

In the case of a lesser degree of interdependency of business and IT, real options can be used for BPaaS and SaaS. However Benaroch et al. (2007) have observed that mainly two camps of thinking (philosophies) on ROV exist. The first camp favors rigor and the technical aspects of valuing investments using option pricing models. It often overlooks the complexities of applying real options to IT projects. The second camp is more strategy focused and therefore in favor of real options thinking based on managerial heuristics. This camp recognizes the complexities of applying real options in practice. Both camps are confronted with the need to monitor on a permanent base the business environment to assess what should be done with the real options (Weeds, 2006), which certainly is needed in the complex and chaotic contexts (Cynefin framework).

Benaroch et al. (2006) observed that managers are following a logic of real options thinking in managing the risk of their IT investments, but based on intuition. The danger of this intuitive real option thinking may lead to suboptimal or counterproductive results. To the authors, intuition ought to be supplemented by the ability of a formal ROV model to "quantify the value that options add to IT investments in relation to their creation cost and to the mitigations they enable. This ability is a prerequisite to approaching IT risk management from an economic optimization perspective."

Benaroch et al. (2006, 2007) are proposing a framework, called Option-Based Risk Management (OBRiM) whose purpose is to control risk and maximize value in information technology investment decisions. Starting from a business case analysis based on NPV or ROI, first a risk assessment is made. Secondly they identify the options to embed by mapping the identified risks to viable real options that can be embedded in the investment in order to control the risks. Subsequently based on these identified options, they design plausible investment configurations using different subsets in the options. Next the ROV is executed to pick the most economically valuable configuration.

The empirical study (Benaroch et al., 2007) showed that the main benefits of OBRiM are the ability to generate meaningful option-bearing investment structures, simplification of the complexities of real options for the business context, accuracy in analyzing the risks of IT investments, and support for more proactive planning.

However, the main flaw is that it is not iterative and this is necessary since the organization needs to permanently screen the environment (Weeds, 2006) and integrate the results in the intelligence base so that the course of actions can be adapted with new updates (Shattuck et al., 2006).

Mun (2006) presents a similar approach, but the iterative process is only driven by the risk management, not by strategic management (grand, business). Although real options are strategy oriented, not all strategic issues will be handled, certainly when it has not been incorporated in the proposed risk management.

Sub-Optimality of Investments

Lowe et al. (2006, p. 7) show that optimal investments are not likely with CAS. There is a trade-off between robustness and optimization. "Real CAS are often sub-optimal, meaning that their effectiveness is not maximised, just good enough to continue to survive. This has a couple of consequences. Firstly, any optimality is transient. Since change is never-ending and uncertainty is unavoidable, any optimisation is true only briefly. Thus, it is rarely worth the effort to create maximum efficiency. Secondly, sub-optimality permits robustness and adaptability. Being sub-optimal and just good enough means that the system can allocate resources to maintaining reserves and variety so that the system can be more robust, resilient and adaptive. However, greater variety tends to generate greater complexity and less efficiency, so that an appropriate balance must be found. As a result, there is no optimum state or perfect design, and designers should not attempt to chase the mirage of maximum efficiency too far."

In a war not all units are fighting at the same moment. The commander keeps units in reserve to cope with unexpected actions of the enemy. They continue to make an analogy with financial investments. "This is analogous to the principle of diversification as a strategy for investment. Diversification is the technique of spreading your investment across (and within) different asset classes (typically cash, bonds, property and shares). It is based on the notion that a poor return in one investment can potentially be offset by a better return in another investment. This is done to reduce the risk and smooth volatility of the overall investment at the expense of maximum potential performance. In other words, the optimal financial performance is traded for greater robustness in investment returns."

CLOUD COMPUTING AND S2IF

Positioning of IT in an Organization

As already mentioned IT does not exist just for itself; it must serve a purpose of facilitating the working and managing of an organization. This organization and its environment are characterized by complexity and IT itself does not escape this phenomenon, on the contrary. This complexity drives organizational shifts in systems, processes, culture and value (Lowe et al., 2006). The challenges that IT with Cloud Computing is facing are "not simple." Formal structures coexist with and are supporting informal structures. The non-Cloud IT has trouble supporting this, because security policies and user management are quite strict and do not permit informal structures. Even virtual groups are still subject to these rules. As a matter of fact, handling complexity in an efficient way encourages culture and processes of devolving control. Moreover the diversity in processes and capabilities is increasing. Through Cloud Computing, business users are able to define and use "Services" in a flexible way. IT-strategy should only give simple rules for acquiring and using this flexibility. So, IT indeed becomes a commodity and utility.

The private Cloud and hybrid Cloud are just a transitional phase towards a global public Cloud. The early adopters are now facing issues like confidentiality and security, however in a CAS every agent has to adapt very quickly to the changes external to the organization (market, government, customers) and internal to the organization (changing relationships, changing structure, etc.) so that even if data is stolen the information will be passé. This does not imply that security can be non-existent, but security may not be a reason to slow down the co-evolution of the (whole) organization and its (heterogeneous) components (agents).

S2IF should reflect this concern and force IT to shift from a centrally controlling information system manager (although systems can be decentralized) to a facilitator/coach of Cloud services for the whole organization (expertise).

On the level of the individual (user, employee, manager, etc.) complexity drives individual demands on knowledge, approach and interactions (Lowe et al., 2006). The IT with Cloud Computing must enable the individual in CAS to operate in a dynamic and uncertain environment. So not only a group of people (forming an agent) but also an individual must be quickly served. All of these individuals have a diversity of knowledge, skills and experience. This implies that the traditional service delivery and programming in IT cannot be used anymore, because it has to serve every individual in the most efficient way. Although investments in CAS are suboptimal (for reason of robustness) this diversity is too big to be served in a centralized way. A consequence for S2IF is that it may not only handle agents' requests but it should also satisfy individual needs in the formal and informal structure. How these needs are expressed is in function of the culture and the structure (ad hoc) of the organization and will therefore be unique (just like the strategy is unique in complex context).

In the domain of Cloud Computing it is impossible for the IT or even the S2IF to foresee everything for everybody. Initiatives will be bottom up, so the general strategy (and its derived resources strategy and business strategy) will only be able to give the general directions by determining the boundaries. Is it typical for Cloud Computing? For Janssen et al. (2006) it is not, because in their CAS perspective on Enterprise Architecture (see below) in e-Government, they state that (IT) system architectures should emerge from the local level, instead of trying to define them at a national level. These authors are discussing classic but nevertheless CAS IT-systems and come to the same conclusion, so that one can state that Cloud Computing has the characteristics of a CAS, and therefore the investments in Cloud Computing should be handled on every level with respect to the characteristics of CAS, which S2IF does in a (w)holistic way.

Service Models

Cloud computing can be an investment in relation to resources (IT) strategy, be it widespread (all levels of cloud computing services) or more related to the infrastructure (IaaS, PaaS). In other cases, cloud computing can be situated on the operational level (SaaS or BPaaS). These services can be stand alone, or can be built upon IaaS or PaaS (acquired or to be acquired). It is however very important that the investment decision of cloud computing be located in the right domain (IT-strategy or operational strategy). This will determine on the one hand if the CIO has more or less freedom of action in making decisions on cloud computing and on the other hand which financial (investment) techniques can be used to assess these investments. In the case of SaaS and BPaaS it is possible that (as mentioned above) the CIO has no say in the matter other than of how it should be assessed or integrated.

Abrams et al. (2011) see three possible ways to implement SaaS. The first one is "Rip-and-Replace." The conditions are that at least 20% cost benefit should be attained and that minimal operational changes are required. "New SaaS" is the second case where the company has a new business model or is exploring new markets, new customers. Or perhaps another reason may be that the existing solutions suffer from technological obsolescence. The third way is the hybrid solution (from the first two ways). Reasons may be:

- Reliance on existing software/solutions/systems;
- New capabilities unaffordable with traditional solutions;

- Extension of business;
- Filling functional or operational gaps

This implies a lot of business assessment and (business and technological) risk mitigation before choosing the best possible solution. Although Rabaey (2012) treats the implementation of a Government Cloud (GovCloud), the proposed method is also applicable for profit and other non-profit. The condition sine qua non is to have a form of Enterprise Architecture (see below).

There is no "logical" path to move into the Cloud like the sequence of IaaS, PaaS and SaaS. One organization can move from SaaS to PaaS when it has developed (or acquired) a software that yields a competitive advantage.

So, it sounds like a paradox but with the introduction of such a technological concept as Cloud Computing in an organization, business gains more freedom in relation to IT, because IT becomes a commodity.

Classic IT-View

Is Private Cloud really a Cloud deployment model? A characteristic of Cloud Computing is an "On demand Self Service" where a consumer pays as he uses services. However if the private cloud is fully bought and maintained by a company then the employee (consumer) does not pay as he uses.

In a fully private cloud the company is the owner (CAPEX) of all hardware, operating systems, system software, applications, network, personnel, etc. As a matter of fact there is no difference between a fully private cloud and a static data center, only the organization of the services is different. The company however can still chose between "buy it or lease it" for one or more components. But the whole management including for example capacity planning and management is the sole responsibility of the company.

Figure 4 shows that a company with a fully private cloud may encounter serious problems (like a static data center). The technological risks for a first implementation are a considerable issue, particularly for the private cloud because all of the risks stays in the organization and it remains a capital investment (CAPEX), and not an operational cost (OPEX) (Marks et al., 2010). Due to this, the private cloud is also more sensitive to economical fluctuations (negative). In addition, since public cloud is another form of outsourcing, the performance of the cloud service provider is something that the organization does not control except through SLA and penalties (Spínola, 2009).

So, the investments of private clouds in relation to capacity are discrete which means that for a certain period the data center has an overcapacity of resources. In the case that the needed capacity drops then this overcapacity increases. So a part of the CPU-cycles, disks and software licenses are not used and it is a loss for the company. This lost money could have been used for other purposes (opportunity costs). The accumulated overcapacity figure gives an impression of how this may evolve over time (accumulated loss in cash flow also).

Another far more dangerous situation is that there is not enough capacity (due to wrong business estimates or problems with the supplier of hardware and/or software), which may results in clients of the companies moving away. If the policy of the company permits it, then a solution can be to (pay as you) use extra capacity off-premise for a certain period, meaning hybrid cloud solution.

As a matter of fact, the only advantage of a "private cloud managed" data center is that it is more efficiently run than non-cloud datacenter.

A first move towards the real cloud philosophy is the "Shared Infrastructure Private Cloud." It is IaaS but the infrastructure is completely (virtualized) separated from the other customers of the Cloud Service Provider. This solves the hardware capacity problem and only licenses (system software and applications) have to be managed

Figure 4. Capacity problem full private cloud

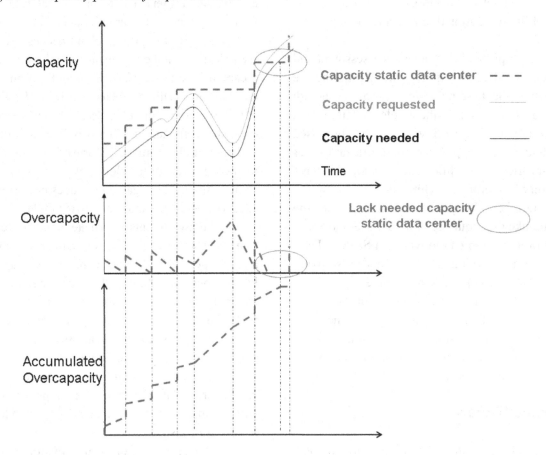

by the company itself, which can also be partly reduced with PaaS.

Big Cloud Service Providers like IBM offer contracts for a "Shared Private Cloud." It is a SLA-driven solution which gives security and flexibility to the customers.

If a company moves directly towards public cloud then this can be cheap (for example credit card clouds) but as already mentioned, it can be very unsafe. For this reason companies are asking more security, confidentiality what means that they are asking for SLA which are compatible with their policies.

In the near future both deployment models, shared private cloud (with SLA) and public cloud (with SLA), will join into one Cloud deployment SLA-model. At that point, IT as commodity will be a fact.

CAS IT-View

In previous point the classic IT-view states implicitly that a centrally managed IT does not give enough flexibility in a fast changing and complex environment and may cause opportunity costs (since alternatives exist now with public and/or shared private cloud. However if the organization is large enough (like a government), where advantages of scale can be attained then it may be worthwhile to have a private cloud. As a matter of fact, a part of the organization becomes a Cloud Service Provider, in which case another dynamic business model is applicable. Another example is Defense (operations), where not only IT but also energy, transport, etc. are provided by Defense itself (reason of autonomy and freedom of action).

From the point of view of CAS-theory, the heterogeneous agents need a lot of flexibility and autonomy (within well defined and simple boundaries). So a centralized management IT is out of the question. The IT-management is rather an enabler of interoperability (processes) and interconnectivity (network, security, access management). IT management is the advisor in accordance with the Enterprise Architecture (see next point) of the different agents in the (mother) organization. Therefore the solution of the public cloud (with SLA) and the solution of the shared private cloud (with SLA) will be the same and is the way to go.

Enterprise Architecture

The strategy of the project itself has to be aligned with the higher strategies, which in the case of CAS are a set of simple strategic rules and boundaries. In a CAPEX situation, the existing investments should also be taken into account, because most of them are irreversible investments and therefore are sunk costs.. The new project may change the investment plan, thus flexibility and adaptability are demanded. For that reason, real options are very useful.

Since IT performs an increasingly important role, it is necessary to have a framework in which IT can be situated in function of the business. Enterprise Architecture (EA) is such a framework. The Enterprise Architecture Research Forum defines Enterprise Architecture (EARF, (n.d.)) as "the continuous practice of describing the essential elements of a socio-technical organization, their relationships to each other and to the environment, in order to understand complexity and manage change."

Janssen et al. (2006, p. 2) relate EA in the context of CAS: "The term "enterprise" refers to the scope of the architecture, dealing with the organization as a whole or multiple agencies rather than with a certain organizational part or individual components and/or projects. The architecture is based on statements of how an enterprise wants to use IT, not on what and how information has to be made available. The strategic aspects of IT systems provide the contexts for the architectural design choices and decisions. Enterprise architecture models provide ways to deal with the complexity including work (who, where), function (how), information (what) and infrastructure (how to)."

Therefore Enterprise Architecture should consist of distinguished levels. The naming of the distinguished levels may differ but in general at least EA should consist of Business Architecture, Information Architecture, Application Architecture and Infrastructure Architecture (Rabaey et al., 2007a).

Rabaey (2012) proposes to add an additional layer, namely Knowledge Architecture, because IT with Cloud Computing will become a utility (commodity) and competitive/collaborative advantage will become almost fully dependent on the capability of producing intelligence for decision-making and knowledge management (in systems, processes and human resources). Some investment techniques use Knowledge units (Housel, 2001) or Knowledge Value Added (KVA) to assess investment probabilities (Mun et al., 2006).

Conforming to the Cynefin framework which states that to avoid disorder limits/boundaries must be set to CAS, Janssen et al. (2006, p. 2) write that "[t]he idea of enterprise architecture is that it can be used to guide design decisions and limits the solution space by setting constraints. Architectural principles are textual statements that describe the constraints imposed upon the organization, and/or the decisions taken in support of realizing the business strategies. Principles restrict architectures and set the direction for the future. Architectural descriptions can form the basis for the implementation and transformation of existing structure into the desired architecture."

For a more in-depth analysis of the role of EA in Cloud Computing, we refer to Rabaey (2012) who concludes that the implementation of Cloud Computing without EA increases the chances of failure (not effective) and/or inefficient investments.

IT-Governance for Cloud Computing

Soenen and Palante (2011) in their work "Cloud Governance is ... more than Security" presented at the conference "Cloud Law or Legal Cloud" warn that the main issue with Cloud Computing is not security (and the related legal aspects). Governance indeed is more than security. So, can S2IF in the context of Cloud Computing be used to integrate IT/Cloud Governance?

The authors' concept of Cloud Governance is based on the IT-governance methodologies like COBIT. The general points of attention are the following ones. "Cloud Context" which defines the managing and the monitoring processes with the roles and responsibilities in the IT-domain. Through CAS, S2IF broadens this set of roles and responsibilities to the whole business. This is possible with the implementation of an Enterprise Architecture.

"Strategic alignment" is embedded in S2IF.

"Value creation" in S2IF is implemented by discussing the contribution to the business by examining the services (immediacy, availability), the SLA, cost (pay for use), scalability and mobility.

"Risk mitigation" for Cloud Computing is handled by the use of ROV (see Rabaey (2012) for more details) and/or should be in an Enterprise Risk Management (ERM) (Bowser et al., 2011; Orros and Cantle, 2010; Ratcliffe, 2011).

"Resources Optimization" is not possible in CAS because of the trade-off between optimization and robustness (see above), however S2IF is seeking by combing all domains (business and resources) for the best possible solution.

"Communication and Information": all business (units) and resources managers are present and should therefore be capable of communicating with and informing all stakeholders. Moreover the

interconnectivity of all agents in a CAS demands a sharing of information and intelligence.

"Monitoring and Evaluation" is equally embedded in S2IF, but attention should be giving to the influence of feedback loops in CAS.

Thus S2IF supports the concept of Cloud Governance, even in the complex context of a CAS. However, it can not be stressed enough that the existence of an Enterprise Architecture is a condition sine qua non for governing Cloud Computing (Rabaey, 2012).

Freedom of Action for IT

"What you don't see, you are not aware of" can be said for IaaS and PaaS because they are below the interactive application view of the clients, therefore IT has more liberty of action to choose the solution. For the business people the cost reduction is quite attractive (Marks et al., 2010), as is transforming CAPEX to OPEX (Etro, 2010; Bradshaw, 2010). From the level of SaaS and above, the influence of the business people increases, and aspects as effectiveness, efficiency are important (Table 2).

The consequences are that for the investments in IaaS en PaaS the SLA is enough, but it is not enough for SaaS or BPaaS. Therefore the possible options are more determined (influenced) by the business then for IaaS and PaaS. So, from the point of view of IT in relation to Cloud Computing, the flexibility and even the volatility is lower for BPaaS and SaaS, which reduces the usefulness of real options in these cases. This may looks like a paradox, but it is not, because the flexibility and volatility has been brought to the business level where other resource strategies' risks and uncertainties are also integrated. For this reason alone, enterprise architecture is a must for the effective and efficient investments in IT.

Figure 5 shows the volatility θ for IaaS and PaaS which is consistently bigger then for IT in each business scenario for SaaS and BPaaS. For the latter the interactive and iterative building of

Table 2. Influence of business on investment decision of cloud computing services

Type of Service	Influence Business on DM	Perspective Business
IaaS	Low	Cost Reduction
PaaS	Low	Cost Reduction
SaaS (Corporate)	Medium	Efficiency
SaaS (Core)	High	Efficiency/Effectiveness
BPaaS	High	Effectiveness/Efficiency

business scenarios in S2IF (in a cycle) is very important. The intelligence process must be flexible and stable to support the development and assessment of the different business scenarios.

In the case of CAS, the intelligence cells in the agents will not be in a hierarchal structure but rather in a networked configuration (see also above C2).

OVERVIEW

Cloud computing is a new paradigm, which requires careful planning to move the organization into the Cloud. We are presenting the Strategic Interdisciplinary Investment Forum (S2IF) to align IT-strategy (responsible for the Cloud Computing architecture) with the Grand Strategy on the one hand, and to allocate IT-resources in the business processes (operational strategy) on the other hand.

To fully understand the new business organization and its interaction with the environment (society and markets), we have introduced the concept of Complex Adaptive Systems. Already at the business level the CAS concept caused a new way of business thinking. Furthermore Cloud Computing itself is a CAS which implies a rewriting of the role of IT-management in the organization. Initiatives are coming from the agents and IT-management can only "guide" the use of Cloud Computing in the organization.

As a consequence, the traditional DCF-based investment techniques are not effective anymore. Real Option Valuation is more suited to support IT-investments; especially the fuzzy sets based ROV.

The use of real options, the right but not the obligation to realize projects permits management to introduce flexibility (start, delay, stop, resume, hold) and risk management into these projects. In the case of Business Process-as-a-Service (BPaaS) or Software-as-a-Service (SaaS), option

Figure 5. Volatility reduction by using scenarios

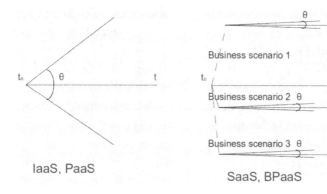

IaaS, PaaS

SaaS, BPaaS

games might be useful if business processes are equal to the information system applications. Infrastructure-as-a-Service (IaaS) and Platform-as-a-Service (PaaS) are more situated in the domain of IT-strategy self.

The framework of Cloud Computing is still in movement and by taken CAS into account, this framework will produce a model which will combine a public cloud (with SLA) with a shared private (with SLA).

The new paradigm shift demands the use of the Enterprise Architecture in which IT can be situated in function of the business.

FUTURE RESEARCH DIRECTIONS

The need for information to produce intelligence comes from the fact that the actual reality is ever changing at an increasing pace. In the literature on decision making in crisis situations (like for firemen and military), we have retained the Naturalistic Decision Making (NDM). NDM studies how people are making decisions and are performing cognitively complex functions in crisis or demanding situations. This research can be used to give structure at the intelligence processes in organizations which find themselves in a similar situation (continuously and fast changing environment in which it is necessary to collect intelligence to adjust the course of action).

A second domain is the theory of fuzzy sets. The classical techniques of real options are very complex because of the correlations between decision variables and the amount of (historical) data to support the ROV. Fuzzy sets have been proposed in this domain with Fuzzy ROV as the result. In the framework of S2IF, fuzzy ROV should be introduced, not to replace the classical ROV, but to complement it. Thus S2IF can extend its arsenal of financial investment techniques to handle investment issues where not much data is available and where a priori there does not seem

to be clear (cor)relations amongst the decision variables.

A third domain is the option games valuation. The purpose of option games is to bundle the advantages of real options and game theory. However, the resulting disadvantage is the increased numbers of decision tree branches due to the fact that in one node multiple games may have to be evaluated. Even in the case of a single game, there are always at least four possibilities: invest/not invest for two players.

We are proposing a way to avoid this, along with the reduction of volatility per scenarios. Research can be done for option games in the domain of the chaos theory. At a certain point in time the number of possible options will be so big that it can become a chaotic system. The question is to know if it can become chaotic and if so, which type it could be and if attractors can be determined, because in the affirmative way, being deterministic, then a large set of initial conditions will lead to orbits that converge to a chaotic region.

CONCLUSION

Cloud Computing is not a hype, but the way to go. Through the process of standardization and virtualization, the IT and the processes or units it supports, gives the organization flexibility (time to market) and cost reduction. However the implementation of cloud computing or the migration to the cloud is not obvious and needs careful assessment of risks and opportunities.

We argued that the classical investment techniques could not integrate the flexibility and risk management into the investment valuation. Real option valuation has this capability.

We introduced Complex Adaptive Systems (CAS) into the discussion because of the fact that the environment of an organization is complex. The Cynefin framework helps determine in which context the organization is in, and what it should do to obtain or keep control. Each context has its characteristics and the used investment techniques need to be aligned to that context.

Cloud Computing itself is a CAS; what implies that the organization is not only confronted with a non-linear external phenomenon but also an internal. To guide investments in Cloud Computing an Enterprise Architecture is needed.

Thus the evaluation of cloud computing must be placed on the one hand in the context of the organization and the allocation of its resources, and on the other hand the environment. For this, we have proposed the Strategic Interdisciplinary Investment Forum (S2IF), where the allocation of inter alia IT-resources (like cloud computing) in business processes (operational strategy) is decided in function of the business goals (business strategy).

In the case of IaaS and PaaS, the investments are more likely in the resources (IT) strategy, while SaaS and BPaaS which are interacting directly with the users (business processes) and are therefore mostly situated in the operational strategy. Anyway, since both (operational and IT-strategy) are derived respectively indirectly and directly from the Grand Strategy, the cloud computing investments are completely placed into the context of the organization.

As already mentioned, ROV is the best suited financial method to support management in the decisions about cloud computing. However real options have some negative points. The first one is the need to screen permanently the environment to allow S2IF to decide upon the actions to be taken.

Another critique on ROV is that it lacks strategic interaction. Amongst others, Ferreira et al. (2009) are proposing option games, which is a combination of real options theory and game theory. We have showed that in some cases like BPaaS, option games can be applied. In the other situations, it is more effective and efficient (reduce complexity) to use real options in the context of business (interactive) scenarios.

Finally, classical ROV can be hard to apply because of the lack of (historical) data and/or a priori correlations. Fuzzy ROV, based on fuzzy sets, can solve this problem, but needs more attention in the financial literature. Another technique to investigate is Bayesian Networks actually most used to assess risks.

The framework of Cloud Computing is still in movement and by taken CAS into account, this framework will produce a model which will combine a public cloud (with SLA) with a shared private (with SLA).

Our conclusive remark is that organizations should not be afraid to move to the "Cloud," as long as they plan it carefully. In this chapter we have proposed a generic framework of S2IF to support these decisions and planning. The organization can instantiate its own framework in function of its capabilities and culture.

REFERENCES

Abrams, R. (2011). *Bringing the Cloud down to Earth: How to choose, launch, and get the most from cloud solutions for your business.* Palo Alto, CA: Planning Shop.

Abrams, R., Kirwin, B., Guptill, B., & Odell, B. (2011). *The cloud bottom line: Calculating ROI for business applications in the cloud.* Webcast of October 6, 2011. Retrieved from http://www. EntepriseEfficiency.com

Aven, T. (2010). *Misconceptions of risk.* Chichester, UK: John Wiley & Sons. doi:10.1002/9780470686539

Baldrige (n.d.). *Baldrige performance excellence program.* Retrieved April 10, 2011, from http://www.nist.gov/baldrige/

Bednyagin, D., & Gnansounou, E. (n.d.). *Real options valuation of fusion energy R&D programme.* (Paper). Lausanne, Switzerland. *Ecole Polytechnique Fédérale.*

Benaroch, M., Jefferery, M., Kauffman, R. J., & Shah, S. (2007). Option-based risk management: A field study of sequential information technology investment decisions. *Journal of Management Information Systems*, *24*(2), 103–140. doi:10.2753/MIS0742-1222240205

Benaroch, M., Lichtenstein, Y., & Robinson, K. (2006). Real options in information technology risk management: An empirical validation of risk-options relationships. *Management Information Systems Quarterly*, *30*(4), 827–864.

Bernard, H. (1976). *Totale Oorlog en Revolutionaire Oorlog* (*Vol. I*). Brussels, Belgium: Royal Military Academy. [course]

Berryman, J. M. (2007). Judgments during information seeking: A naturalistic approach to understanding of enough information. *Journal of Information Science*, *20*(10), 1–11.

Bowser, M., Cantle, N., & Allan, N. (2011). *Unraveling the complexity of risk*. Presented at Open Forum of The Actuarial Profession (January 21, 2011). London.

Brach, M. (2003). *Real options in practice*. Hoboken, NJ: John Wiley & Sons.

Bradshaw, S., Millard, C., & Walden, I. (2010). *Contracts for clouds: Comparison and analysis of the terms and conditions of cloud computing services (paper)*. London, UK: University of London, Queen Mary.

Brandenburger, A., & Nalebuff, B. (1995). *The right game: Use game theory to shape strategy. Harvard Business Review*. July-August.

Brooks, B. (2007). The pulley model: A descriptive model of risky decision-making. *Safety Science Monitor*, *11*(1), 1–14.

CAF. (n.d.). *Common assessment framework*. Retrieved March 3, 2011, from http://www.eipa.eu/en/topic/show/&tid=191

Carlsson, C., & Fullér, R. (2000). *On fuzzy real option valuation*. Turku, Finland: Turku Centre for Computer Science.

Chang, V., Bacigalupo, D., Wills, G., & De Roure, D. (2010a). *A categorisation of cloud computing business models (Paper)*. Southampton, UK: University of Southampton.

Chang, V., Wills, G., & De Roure, D. (2010). *A review of cloud business models and sustainability (Paper)*. Southampton, UK: University of Southampton.

Cobb, B., & Charnes, J. (2007). Real options valuation. In S. G. Henderson, B. Biller, M.-H. Hsieh, J. Shortle, J. D. Tew, & R. R. Barton (Eds.), *Proceedings of the 2007 Winter Simulation Conference,* (pp. 173-182). IEEE.

Collan, M. (2008). *A new method for real option valuation using fuzzy numbers. (Research Paper)*. Turku, Finland: Institute for Advanced Management Systems Research. Retrieved April 12, 2011 from http://ideas.repec.org/p/amr/wpaper/466.html

Collan, M., Fullér, R., & Mezei, J. (2009). A fuzzy pay-off method for real option valuation. *Journal of Applied Mathematics and Decision Sciences*, *1*, 1–14. doi:10.1155/2009/238196

CSA. (2010). *Cloud security alliance: Top threats to cloud computing,* v1.0. Retrieved April 12, 2011, from http://www.cloudsecurityalliance.org

EARF. (n.d.). *Completed projects*. Retrieved April 11, 2001, from http://earf.meraka.org.za/earfhome/our-projects-1/completed-projects/

Eisenhardt, K., & Sull, D. (2001). Strategy as simple rules. *Harvard Business Review*, (January): 106–116.

Etro, F. (2010). *Introducing cloud computing: Results from a simulation study*. Venice, Italy: Ca' Foscari

Fereira, N., Kar, J., & Trigeorgis, L. (2009). Option games: The key to competing in capital-intensive industries. *Harvard Business Review, March.*

Ferson, S. (n.d.). *Fuzzy arithmetic in risk analysis.* Retrieved March 23, 2011, from http://www.ramas.com/fuzzygood.ppt

Fichman, R. (2004). Real options and IT platform adoption: Implications for theory and practice. *Information Systems Research, 15*(2), 132–154. doi:10.1287/isre.1040.0021

Funston, F., & Wagner, S. (2010). *Surviving and thriving in uncertainty: Creating the risk intelligent enterprise.* Hoboken, NJ: John Wiley & Sons.

Glenn, E. J. (1996). *Chaos theory: The essentials for military applications.* Newport, RI: Naval War College.

Gore, J. (1996). *Chaos, complexity, and the military. Newport, RI.* USA: National Defense University.

Grasselli, M. (2007). *The investment game in incomplete markets.* Buzio, Brazil: RIO.

Grenadier, S. (2000). Option exercise games: The intersection of real options and game theory. *Journal of Applied Corporate Finance, 13*(2), 99–107. doi:10.1111/j.1745-6622.2000.tb00057.x

Housel, T., & Bell, A. (2001). *Measuring and managing knowledge.* New York, NY: McGraw-Hill/Irwin.

Hovhannisian, K. (2001). *Exploring on the technology landscapes: Real options thinking in the context of the complexity theory.* Paper presented at the DRUID Winter Conference (January 17-19, 2002), Aalborg, Denmark.

Huang, C., Kao, H., & Li, H. (2007). Decision on enterprise computing solutions for an international tourism. *International Journal of Information Technology & Decision Making, 6*(4), 687–700. doi:10.1142/S0219622007002666

IW. (2010). *Risks of cloud computing outweigh benefits: New survey reveals low appetite for IT-related risk in 2010.* Retrieved April 10, 2011, from http://www.industryweek.com/articles/risks_of_cloud_computing_outweigh_benefits_21526.aspx

Janssen, M., & Kuk, G. (2006). *A complex adaptive system perspective of enterprise architecture in electronic government.* Paper presented at the 39th Hawaii International Conference on System Sciences.

Laurent, P. (2011). *Towards a cartography of the legal aspects of cloud computing.* Paper presented at JuriTIC Conference Cloud Law or Legal Cloud (September 30th, 2011). Brussels, Belgium.

Lauria, E., & Duchessi, P. (2006). A Bayesian belief network for IT implementation decision support. *Decision Support Systems, 42*, 1573–1588. doi:10.1016/j.dss.2006.01.003

Lee, Y., & Lee, S. (2011). The valuation of RFID investment using fuzzy real option. *Expert Systems with Applications, 38*, 12195–12201. doi:10.1016/j.eswa.2011.03.076

Lowe, D., & Ng, S. (2006). *The implications of complex adaptive systems thinking for future command and control.* Paper presented at 11th International Command and Control Research and Technology Symposium (September, 2006), Cambridge, UK.

Marks, E., & Lozano, R. (2010). *Executive's guide to cloud computing.* Hoboken, NJ: John Wiley & Sons.

Mauboussin, M. (2011). Embracing complexity. *Harvard Business Review*, (September): 89–92.

Millard, C. (2010). *Cloud computing: Opportunities and risks.* Paper presented at the Meeting of International Bar Association Annual Meeting 2010. London, UK: University of London.

Misra, S., & Mondal, A. (2011). Identification of a company's suitability for the adoption of cloud computing and modelling its corresponding return on investment. *Mathematical and Computer Modelling, 53,* 504–521. doi:10.1016/j.mcm.2010.03.037

Mun, J. (2006). *Real options analysis versus traditional DCF valuation in layman's terms.* (White Paper). Retrieved April 9, 2011, from http://www.realoptionsvaluation.com/download.html#casestudies

Mun, J., & Housel, T. (2006). *A primer on return on investment and real options for portfolio optimization.* Monterey, CA: Naval Postgraduate School.

NIST. (2011). *National Institute of Standards and Technology.* Retrieved March 25, 2011, from http://www.nist.gov/itl/csd/cloud-020111.cfm

OG. (2009). *Cloud cube model: Selecting cloud formations for secure collaboration.* Retrieved April 9, 2011, from http://www.opengroup.org/jericho/publications.htm

OG. (2010). *Building return on investment from cloud computing.* Retrieved April 9, 2011, from http://www.opengroup.org/cloud/whitepapers/ccroi/index.htm

Orros, G., & Cantle, N. (2010). *ERM for strategic and emerging risks.* Presented at Risk and Investment Conference 2010, (June 14; 2010). Edinburgh, UK.

Pendhakar, P. (2010). Valuing interdependent multi-stage IT-investments: A real options approach. *European Journal of Operational Research, 201,* 847–859. doi:10.1016/j.ejor.2009.03.037

Rabaey, M. (2011). *Game theoretic real option approach of the procurement of department of defense: Competition or collaboration.* Paper presented at the 8th Annual Acquisition Research Symposium (May 10-12, 2011). Monterrey, CA, USA.

Rabaey, M. (2012). A public economics approach to enabling enterprise architecture with the government cloud in Belgium. In Saha, P. (Ed.), *Enterprise architecture for connected e-government: Practices and innovations.* Hershey, PA: IGI Global.

Rabaey, M. (2012a). Framework of knowledge and intelligence base: From intelligence to service. In Ordoñez de Pablos, P., & Lytras, M. D. (Eds.), *Knowledge management and drivers of innovation in services industries.* Hershey, PA: IGI Global. doi:10.4018/978-1-4666-0948-8.ch017

Rabaey, M., Tromp, H., & Vandenborre, K. (2007). Holistic approach to align ICT capabilities with business integration. In Cunha, M., Cortes, B., & Putnik, G. (Eds.), *Adaptive technologies and business integration: Social, managerial, and organizational dimensions* (pp. 160–173). Hershey, PA: Idea Group Publishing.

Rabaey, M., Vandijck, E., & Hoffman, G. (2005a). *An evaluation framework for enterprise application integration.* Paper presented at the 16th IRMA International Conference. San Diego, CA

Racheva, Z., Daneva, M., & Buglione, L. (2008). *Complementing measurements and real options concepts to support inter- iteration decision-making in agile projects.* Paper presented at the 34th EUROMICRO Conference on Software Engineering and Advanced Applications 2008, Parma (Italy), September 3 - 5, 2008.

Ratcliffe, W. (2011). *Embedding ERM into your business.* Presented at Health and Care Conference (May 18-20, 2011), Edinburgh.

Shattuck, L., & Miller, N. (2006). Naturalistic decision making in complex systems: A dynamic model of situated cognition combining technological and human agents. *Organizational Behavior: Special Issue on Naturalistic Decision Making in Organizations, 27*(7), 989–1009.

Shen, C. (2009). A Bayesian networks approach to modeling financial risks of e-logistics investments. *International Journal of Information Technology & Decision Making, 8*(4), 711–726. doi:10.1142/S0219622009003594

Smit, H., & Trigeorgis, L. (2009). Valuing infrastructure investment: An option game approach. *California Management Review, 51*(2), 79–100.

Snowden, D., & Boone, M. (2007). A leader's framework for decision making: Wise executives tailor their approach to fit the complexity of the circumstances they face. *Harvard Business Review*, (November): 68–76.

Soenen, P., & Palante, J.-P. (2011). *Cloud governance is ... more than security.* Paper presented at JuriTIC conference Cloud Law or Legal Cloud (September 30th, 2011). Brussels, Belgium.

Spínola, M. (2009). *An essential guide to possibilities and risks of cloud computing.* Retrieved March 24, 2011, from http://www.mariaspinola.com/cloud-computing/

Subashini, S., & Kavitha, V. (2011). A survey on security issues in service delivery models of cloud computing. *Journal of Network and Computer Applications, 34*, 1–11. doi:10.1016/j.jnca.2010.07.006

Tao, C., Jinlong, Z., Benhai, Y., & Shan, L. (2007). *A fuzzy group decision approach to real option valuation.* Wuhan, China: Huazhong University of Science and Technology. doi:10.1007/978-3-540-72530-5_12

Thomaidis, N., Nikitakos, N., & Dounias, G. (2006). The evaluation of information technology projects: A fuzzy multicriteria decision-making approach. *International Journal of Information Technology & Decision Making, 5*(1), 89–122. doi:10.1142/S0219622006001897

Tolga, A., & Kahraman, C. (2008). Fuzzy multiattribute evaluation of R&D projects using a real options valuation model. *International Journal of Intelligent Systems, 23*, 1153–1176. doi:10.1002/int.20312

Triantis, A. (2000). Real options and corporate risk management. *Journal of Applied Corporate Finance, 13*(2), 64–73. doi:10.1111/j.1745-6622.2000.tb00054.x

Trigeorgis, L. (2002). *Real options and investment under uncertainty: What do we know?* Brussels, Belgium: Nationale Bank van België. doi:10.2139/ssrn.1692691

Urquhart, J. (2010). *What cloud computing can learn from 'flash crash'.* Retrieved October 3, 2011, from http://news.cnet.com/8301-19413_3-20004757-240.html

von Helfenstein, S. B. (2009). *Real options 'in' economic systems: Exploring systemic disturbance causes and cures.* Boston, MA.

Wang, S., & Lee, C. (2010). A fuzzy real option valuation approach to capital budgeting under uncertainty environment. *International Journal of Information Technology & Decision Making, 9*(5), 695–713. doi:10.1142/S0219622010004056

Weeds, H. (2006). *Applying option games: When should real options valuation be used? (Paper).* Colchester, UK: University of Essex. Retrieved April 10, 2011, from http://privatewww.essex.ac.uk/~hfweeds/

Weijnen, M., Herder, P., & Bouwmans, I. (2007). *Designing complex systems: A contradiction in terms.* Paper presented at a Congress on Interdisciplinary Design (April 4th, 2007). Delft, The Netherlands.

Wikipedia. (n.d.). *Fuzzy pay-off method for real option valuation.* Retrieved April 10, 2011, from http://en.wikipedia.org/wiki/Fuzzy_Pay-Off_Method_for_Real_Option_Valuation

Wikipedia. (n.d.). *Rationality.* Retrieved March 24, 2011, from http://en.wikipedia.org/wiki/Rationality

Section 2
Cloud Services Development and Framework

Chapter 6
A Systems Approach to Cloud Computing Services

Anil Aggarwal
University of Baltimore, USA

ABSTRACT

Cloud services are becoming part of every company's "right"mare. They know it is the future but are afraid to jump on the cloud computing bandwagon. This may be due to lack of standardization, evolving technology, and/or fear of loss of privacy and security. However, every emerging technology has its root in early adopters who defy the common wisdom, take chances, and help it to evolve into something marketable. They get the first advantage before it becomes a norm. History is full of such examples: e-commerce, m-commerce, online banking, check in through kiosk, et cetera. Companies who were early adopters still have an advantage over late adopters. Amazon.com and eBay are prime examples of this. As technology evolves, it transfers from "push" to "pull" cycle. Cloud services are in their infancy and still evolving around "push" cycle. The number of companies offering cloud services is multiplying exponentially. This chapter presents a systems approach to cloud computing services. Specifically, it examines issues in the context of the system development life cycle (SDLC). For completeness purposes, the chapter discusses issues in relation to SDLC; however, in practice, each user has to customize this approach to suit their own application(s).

INTRODUCTION

As the cloud service concept is still evolving, theories and applications are emerging. Cloud services require knowledge from multiple disciplines, such as information systems, computer science, management science, statistics, social sciences, international management, and leadership. It is almost impossible for one individual to have expertise in so many domains, which makes this a very challenging but rewarding area of research. Given the richness and research potential of this area, it is becoming important to brainstorm and to bring diverse points of view to develop underlying theory and frameworks.

Cloud services are gaining momentum and are expected to grow exponentially. Cloud computing is not a buzz word anymore; it is becoming a norm as users see practical applications and

DOI: 10.4018/978-1-4666-2187-9.ch006

resulting benefits. Cloud computing is becoming lucrative, and according to Forrester Research, it is expected to become a $159 billion market by the year 2020. Given this astronomical number, it is not surprising that cloud computing is in transition from a "push" to a "pull' technology. A push concept/technology is pushed by vendors on customers, and once it gains traction, customers start demanding better products, and then it becomes a pull concept/technology. The question, of course, arises, "What are cloud services?" Before we can define cloud services, we need to define cloud computing. The best way to understand cloud computing is to look at electrical consumption at home. We pay for only the amount of electricity we use, and we do not have to be concerned about how or where the electricity is generated. In the process, however, we lose control of how much electricity we are allowed to use. In peak periods, utilities may restrict usage, or power outage may occur, or our individual line may be affected. In this case, we have to rely on utilities to restore them, which can take a long time. The concept behind cloud computing is quite similar. We pay for whatever computing resources we use, and we do not have to worry about how or where the computer power is generated. However, we may lose control of our data, privacy and security.

Researchers have provided different definitions of cloud computing. We will use the definition provided by the National Institute of Standards and Technology (NIST). They define cloud computing as a "model for enabling convenient, on-demand network access to a shared pool of configurable computing resources (e.g., networks, servers, storage, applications, and services) that can be rapidly provisioned and released with minimal management effort or service provider interaction." Cloud computing is changing the way companies will perform computing in the future.

Cloud services imply cloud computing with added-value services. We can compare cloud services to services provided by telephone com-panies. They offer telephone equipment, provide installation, and the dial tone to make the telephone operational. In addition, they add value by offering line maintenance, call forwarding/waiting, mail boxes, caller ID, etc. Cloud computing vendors, in addition to providing basic cloud computing capability, can also add value by offering maintenance, policy management, customized portability, security, programming, etc. Cloud computing is already a norm, whereas cloud services are still emerging. We will concentrate on cloud computing in the remainder of this chapter and cloud services wherever appropriate.

The architecture of cloud computing is comprised of many different layers. We classify them as primary and secondary layers. Primary layers support the backbone of cloud computing, whereas secondary layers add value to cloud computing. Primary layers consist of: Infrastructure as a Service (IaaS): comprised of servers, hypervisor, storage, networks and other basic computer resources; Platform as a Service (PaaS): development environment, including database, programming tools, integration and development tools, all ready to use in minutes; and Software as a Service (SaaS): readymade applications hosted on providers' clouds, and secondary (or value) layers consisting of Policy as a Service (PlaaS), Database as a Service (DaaS), Storage as a Service (SaaS): also used for software as a service, Business Process as a Service (BPaaS), Mobility as a Service (MaaS), Communication as a Service (CaaS), Integration as a Service (InaaS) and Security (ScaaS) as a Service (though many will argue security to be a primary layer). In addition, there are different types of clouds: private, public, hybrid, and community clouds, with different capabilities and requirements. As with any new area, cloud computing raises many conceptual, technical and managerial issues that need to be addressed by both academicians and practitioners. The next section discusses the systems approach for designing cloud computing services. The approach presented is general and will need to be customized for individual applications. In addition, we look only at public and hybrid clouds in this chapter.

THE SYSTEMS APPROACH

The systems approach has been used for some time and is referred to as system development life cycle (SDLC) (Laudon and Laudon, 2012). Since its inception, many variations of SDLC have emerged; namely agile, waterfall, eXtreme, etc. We have modified the traditional SDLC approach for cloud computing (See Table 1).

EXPLORE

Readiness of the Company

When a company is looking to move to the cloud, they need to think of their readiness, since cloud services involve a complete change of business computing models. At a minimum, the company

should look into the company's readiness in the following areas:

- Management understanding and support for cloud services
- Fundamental change in computing
- Employee resistance

Any major shift and/or change cannot be successful without upper management support. Dorsey listed top management support as the top factor in a project success. According to Dorsey, "Every study ever done about system success or failure has identified top management support as a critical success factor. Without full commitment from top management, when problems arise on a project (as they inevitably do), the project will collapse." Mooney, Mahoney, and Wixom (2008) went a step further in identifying factors that constitute top management support and identified them as the commitment of necessary resources and political support to the project.

Management must understand the basic concepts of cloud computing, how it can affect their bottom line, and their necessary commitment. In

Table 1.

Modified SDLC	Steps in Modified SDLC

Explore	• Readiness of the company
	• Identify opportunities/Applications for cloud
	• Develop plan
	    o Identify stakeholders
	    o Identify platforms
	    o Identify constraints

Analyze	• Gather Application specifications/requirements • Identify vendors • Write Service Level Agreement (SLA)

Simulate and Test	• Simulate/Develop the system
	• Test the system for
	    o Functionality
	    o Completeness
	    o Robustness

Migrate to the Cloud	• Train stakeholders • Operationalize the system
Document	• Develop operational and regulatory documents

many cases, cloud services may not show favorable returns for a long time, and management should understand that. Every time a new application or a new service is added, it can incur start up costs delaying return on investment. It must be understood by everybody that cloud services will change how computing is done, especially in a hybrid or public cloud environment, since the company loses control of its assets and operations to some extent. Though most end users may not be impacted by cloud migration, information service department and personnel will be most affected, since it changes the IT infrastructure from in-house to the cloud. Just like an airplane, data can move anywhere in the cloud. This may require change in computing processes. For example, data access procedures may have to be changed, or parts of a process may be automated and migrated to the cloud, requiring only partial user interaction with the process. Application development procedures may have to be changed, if applications are residing in the cloud.

Change can result in employee resistance. There is an abundance of literature on this. In a recent article, Fedor, Caldwell, and Herold (2006) studied "how organizational changes in 32 different organizations (public and private) affected individuals' commitment to the specific change and their broader commitment to the organization. Their results indicate that both types of commitment may be best understood in terms of a 3-way interaction between the overall favorableness (positive/negative) of the change for the work unit members, the extent of the change in the work unit, and the impact of the change on the individual's job". Since cloud services may involve at least two factors, change in the work unit and change in individual's job, it is necessary to overcome this resistance before moving to the cloud. Nickols (2010) suggests some mixture of four strategies to overcome employee resistance to change. He identified these strategies as: Rational Empirical, Normative-Reeducative, Power-coercive, and Environmental-Adaptive. Readers

are directed to the reference for more information on these strategies. Companies should be ready for "cloud-centric" environment.

Irrespective of how carefully an organization plans and prepares, disasters can still occur, as was evidenced by the recent failure of Amazon's cloud-based services ("EC2") in 2011. The failure lasted for a day, putting many services in the dark. It is necessary for companies to have their own disaster recovery plans, in addition to cloud service provider plans, in case of such failures.

Identify Opportunities (Drivers)

Cloud migration is not a choice but a necessity in this century. Since cloud services reduce technology cost, provide flexibility, automate processes and reduce development time; it may be tempting to migrate all computing to the cloud. This, however, may be overkill for most companies, since cloud services are evolving, and security is still an overriding issue. An iterative approach which starts with non-critical applications and iteratively moves applications to the cloud may be more desirable. Paula Klein of Microsoft suggests following check marks before jumping on the cloud services bandwagon:

1. Reassess your workload, business processes and data center infrastructure before you get started. Analyze patterns and data center requests. What are your goals for cloud computing?
2. Virtualization is usually a prerequisite for software as a service (SaaS), and server utilization rates should be analyzed and documented. Take an inventory of assets.
3. Answer some basic questions: What is your core business, and does the business want to put major investments into IT infrastructure at this time?
4. Test one app before buying a lot of capacity. Once you go live and build maturity, you may decide to bring the app in-house. Hosting a

small app is a good way to deliver services quickly or to build up app development platforms.

5. Find an older app that's used by fewer than 25 people or in one geographic region, and farm that one out first. It's probably not economical to host it in-house.

6. Consider the cloud when you need extra CPU cycles for a short burst of activity, such as a product launch or an annual event.

7. Cost equations are not black and white. Average cost may look cheap until you scale over time and add more workloads. Keep reassessing.

In a recent survey, Black, Mandelbaum, Grover, and Marvi (2010) reported that companies are migrating collaboration applications like Web conferencing and e-mails, with the hope of migrating critical applications like customer resource management and customized applications at a later stage. For an organization to move to the cloud, they should create a list of IT resources and applications and rank them from critical to non-critical. As the technology evolves, everything is becoming available on the cloud, from the central processing unit to complete platforms. Following are only some examples of available cloud services:

- Server
- CPU
- Storage
- Band width
- Database
- Application
- Security
- Policy

These can be grouped in three major (IaaS, PaaS, SaaS) and other value added services, such as Daas, ScaaS, S(torage)aaS, CaaS, MaaS, PlaaS, BPaaS, InaaS. (note: definitions of these terms are given in several chapters in this book). Typically,

CPU, bandwidth, server and storage, etc. (IaaS) is migrated to clouds first as technology is improving and vendors have mastered the economics of "sharing", "scalability" and "dynamic" virtualization. Data migration is still in its infancy as companies realize they may be completely migrating or splitting data with someone's cloud which may be residing anywhere in the world. This creates security concerns. Data migration, therefore, will remain an issue as long as security and site failure concerns are not adequately addressed. Once IT resources are ranked, next applications should be ranked as critical and non-critical and as standard and customized. These lists, then, should be verified by stakeholders and management. Once verified, a cost-benefit analysis should be done in the context of the level of risk managers are willing to assume. These resources (IT and application) should be evaluated against factors like:

- **Scalability:** Refers to elasticity of services in terms of up and down flexibility. This is especially useful for businesses with seasonal needs and/or for businesses that do not know their needs in advance. Many retailers experienced outage during cyber Monday in 2008-2009 due to bandwidth problems. This could have been avoided with cloud migration (IaaS) and pay per use model.

- **Portability:** Refers to moving of data/application or other resources between cloud service providers. For example, if a company needs to link its supplier to its supply chain management (SCM) systems, it would be necessary for both clouds to talk to each other. However, if that's not feasible, the organization may not reap full benefit of cloud migration. Currently, there are no industry standards, making portability difficult.

- **Interoperability:** The IEEE defines interoperability as, the ability of two or more systems or components to exchange information and to use the information that has been exchanged. In the cloud environment, this may mean exchange of resources between legacy systems and clouds. In hybrid systems, this could be a problem if two systems work on different standards or platforms.

- **Security:** Refers to reliability against unauthorized access to resources. This is always an issue with the cloud, especially where data security is concerned. Since a cloud service provider's model is based on economy of scale, many users are sharing the services at any given point in time. This makes matters worse, since these servers may be spread all over the world, making a security breach even more likely.

- **Availability:** Refers to 24/7 accessibility from any place any time. What guarantee does contract provide in terms of service up (availability) time?

- **Performance:** Cloud services can provide information in real time due to 24/7 accessibility and scalability. This typically can improve efficiency of structured tasks resulting in better performance, at least for structured tasks. For mission critical tasks, cloud services can provide information in real time; however, performance depends

on individual's capacity to use that information for one's advantage.

- **Agility:** Refers to organization's ability to expedite development of applications using cloud services. In many cases, this agility is obtained when pay "what you use" process is automated. This cuts the bureaucracy and reduces the migration time. For example, a user may use a financial package from 9:00 am to noon and an inventory management program from 1:00-2:00 pm. The user does not have to be concerned with installment, selection or any cost associated with this.

Table 2 shows the relationship between cloud services and their importance to organizations in terms of desirable factors. Organizations can decide what is more important based on their rankings of critical and non-critical IT services and applications.

Cloud hosting services are becoming less expensive as competition is growing. For example, companies like godaddy.com are advertising their services in bundles as Economy ($5.99 for 10 B+), Deluxe ($6.99, 150GB+) and ultimate ($9.99 with unlimited space+) (February, 2012), where + are value added options like bandwidth, e-mail accounts and mySQL database. At a

Table 2. Relationship between cloud services and their importance to organizations in terms of desirable factors

	Scalability	Interoperability	Availability	Portability	Security	Performance	Agility
IaaS							
PaaS							
SaaS							
Daas							
ScaaS (security)							
SaaS (storage)							
CaaS							
Etc.							

minimum, companies should take advantage of Web hosting, cloud-based services (IaaS). As already suggested, companies should adopt clouds iteratively and ought to classify IT services and applications as first, second, third, etc. in the order of desired migration.

Once applications and IT services are identified, the next step is to analyze them and to identify cloud and service type.

GATHER SPECIFICATIONS/ REQUIREMENTS FOR CLOUD MIGRATION

All stakeholders, who are associated with each service and application that is to be migrated to the cloud, should be identified. Focus groups and surveys should be conducted to define requirements for each IT service and application. This should provide a necessary, initial estimate of requirements for the types of services (IaaS, PaaS, SaaS, etc.). Typically, the first step is to select a platform. Once a platform is selected, identify data, service, and applications that need to be used with that platform. Requirements will be different for different applications; IT services will depend on the level and type of migration. We will focus on type and services instead of individual application and IT service requirements. Companies need to decide on type of cloud migration (public, private, hybrid or community) and type of service (pay-what-you-use, Plug-n-play, self-service). Requirements for public clouds will be very different than for hybrid clouds.

Migration to Public Clouds

Public cloud migration implies that all IT resources and/or applications that were identified as possible candidates in the previous steps are moved to a public cloud. This migration is suitable for small businesses that do not have the resources to create their own infrastructure. In case of IaaS, scalability is very important, since services may vary based on demand fluctuation. For example, Figure 1(a) and Figure 1(b) shows how the IT environment changes when all applications of a company are migrated to a public cloud. The company needs staff to manage clouds, and all data migration within applications resides in the cloud itself. All data exchange among all applications (1 through k) is done via clouds. This would result in efficiency and cost savings, as companies need only a few people to manage public cloud services. Security provided by a vendor, however, becomes an issue since all data are with cloud provider.

Migration to Hybrid Clouds

Hybrid cloud migration implies that some IT resources and applications are in a public cloud, but some are still with the company. This is appropriate when specific application may not be available from cloud vendors, but some parts like IaaS can still be migrated to public clouds. In circumstances involving highly sensitive customer information and/or legal requirements, companies may decide to keep the data inside their firewalls and use public clouds for other services like IaaS or PaaS. Figure 1(c) shows how computing dynamics change when application1 is migrated to a public cloud but other applications are still in a private cloud. All data related to application1 is moved to a public cloud, and any interaction between application1 and other applications (2 through k) are now done via a public cloud. Application2 to Application k management remains with the company. This results in better control and cost savings, since company does not directly support application1 but still maintains control of applications. For example, Microsoft offers hybrid cloud services that allow front-end application in a cloud, while keeping critical data in a private cloud. However, security provided by vendors becomes a major issue in this case.

A Systems Approach to Cloud Computing Services

Figure 1. Application 1 migration to cloud

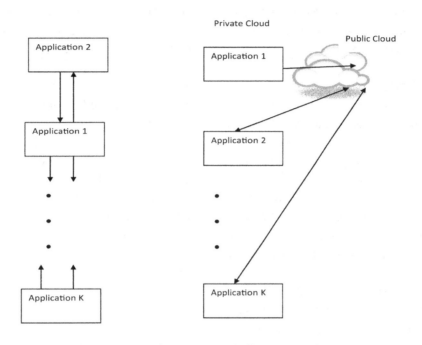

a. Before cloud migration b. After cloud (hybrid) migration

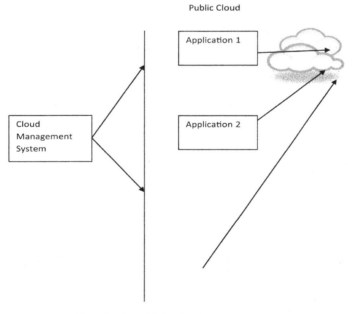

c. After cloud (public) migration

131

At this point, companies need to identify which IT resources and applications can be moved to public clouds and which should remain in hybrid clouds. Next step would be to identify vendors and develop a service level agreement

Identifying Vendors

There is a many-to-many relationship between companies and cloud service providers, implying one cloud service company can serve many companies, or a company may be serviced by many cloud service providers. The more cloud service providers a company chooses, the more complex the migration becomes, due to multiple service level agreements and interoperability among different service providers. In addition, there may be problems between various service providers and the company itself. It is necessary to ensure that there are no compatibility issues and seamless transition can be achieved between clouds and the company. Companies should be wary of companies that are providing "cloud" type services and/or making big interoperability claims. Since cloud computing is based on economy of scale, it is likely that large vendors like Amazon, Google, and Salesforce would be more reliable in terms of uptime, infrastructure improvements, and customer service. Services range from basic CPU to storage, to application as a service. Many companies like Amazon provide basic Web hosting services on one end to Google PaaS on the other end, Vendor longevity and reputation should be checked since new vendors can fail, forcing clients to move to other cloud service providers.

Vendor identification is a two-step process. The first step is to select vendors who meet desirable functionalities in the context of cloud services. Table 3 describes these steps. Note only a sample of vendors is used in the table. All names are proprietary.

A vendor score could be created based on vendor's ratings on each of the above issues in the context of cloud services. Once vendors are ranked next step would be to further prune vendor selection based on vendor reliability propertie, as described in Table 4.

In selecting vendors, companies should be aware of vendor lock-in, which can affect migration to other clouds, or, in some cases maybe be impossible.

Service Level Agreement (SLA)

This is probably one of the most important parts of cloud services. There should be complete understanding of what is included in the contract and what is excluded. According to Frank Ridder of Gartner group, "Cloud markets are generally still very competitive, and it is important for sourcing and procurement executives to leverage competition to optimize negotiations. They should be prepared to walk away from deals, if some of the risk elements are not satisfactorily

Table 3. Vendor identification process

	Scalability	Interoperability	Availability	Portability	Security	Performance	Agility
Amazon							
Microsoft							
Google							
Salesforce.com							
NetSuites							
Databases							

Table 4. Vendor selection process

	Reputation	Longevity	Customer Service	Price	Innovations	Value Added	Management
Amazon							
Microsoft							
Google							
Salesforce.com							
NetSuites							
Databases							

addressed." Since companies have some leverage in negotiation, at a minimum, they should look at the contract in terms of:

- What is provided?
  - At what cost?
  - For how long?
  - At what price (look for hidden costs)?
- Since many companies do business 24/7, look at service level performance. What's the uptime guaranteed, and what are the penalties in case of failure?
- How is data privacy handled? Where will the data be stored? What is covered in case of loss of data? Does the contract guarantee compensation to all individuals affected? Who will inform the customer of a security breach?
- What is excluded from the contract?
- When can a contract be terminated or negotiated?
- Any clause in terms of mid contract adjustments?
- Any restrictions on a move to competition?

Companies should realize they cannot completely avoid risks related to cloud migration but they should mitigate it by reducing or sharing responsibilities with service providers. Once vendors are identified and SLAs are signed, the next step is to simulate and test the migration.

Simulate and Test

Cloud testing is very different than traditional software testing. Cloud testing allows real time testing. Almost all IaaS, PaaS and SaaS vendors provide a test environment which allows users to test before operationalizing the services. These companies provide development platforms on demand, in open source environments. Cloud testing allows actual testing of capabilities of "cloud platforms". Companies need to identify: What needs to be tested? Who needs to test them? Once users, applications and locations are identified, cloud service validation should be performed. If users are distributed in different locations, there may be an option for collaborative testing. Specifically, users need to test for

- Functionality
- Robustness

Functionality refers to a system's performance under stress. A model can be built, using public and/or hybrid clouds, which studies system performance in terms of data aggregation, linking of heterogeneous clouds, application performance, etc. For example, a user could move an application to a cloud and test for data integration, input/output, and its integration with existing data and applications, possibly in private clouds. A user could also test for its interoperability with other models which may reside on user's desktop. A user could study the time it takes for the application to run in the cloud and benchmark it against the time it took on a desktop. If possible, user should also test for demand variation at different times of the day. Test for multi-tenancy visibility and effect on performance. Though tenants share infrastructure, they should not be visible to each other, unless there is prior agreement. Platform should be tested for accessing consistency, irrespective of user's location, implying user should be able to access the cloud from anywhere, any place and any time. Check user interface with the cloud for ease of use. If you are using PaaS and/or SaaS, test for platform flexibility in allowing open architecture platforms that allow authorized users to build their own Web or apps on your platform. In addition, check for security in terms of authentication and authenticity of users. How difficult is it to hack the system? Does it protect individuals' identities and other sensitive information within the platform?

Typically, application testing should be done in two stages:

- Modular
- Complete/Integrated

In modular testing, each service/application module is tested separately for performance under stress. The purpose is to test for functionality and performance under different loads for each part of the jigsaw puzzle. These tests can be used to study factors like input/output, processing speed, and correctness.

Completeness refers to a platform's performance when all components are integrated. Performance is measured against expectations and the applicable SLA. System should be tested for integration of modules and how the complete system works on the cloud platform. In addition, test for import/export of data from multiple sources for any bottlenecks or bureaucracy among modules and among clouds and applications. Another

test would be to examine ease of data integration among applications in public and private clouds. Ideally, this integration should be automatic. For example, test for system behavior during public and private integration in terms of increasing bandwidth demand and/or capacity or decreasing storage. These tests should provide insights into any bottlenecks, performance speed, integration issues or any critical shortcomings. Tests could be used to study factors like portability, interoperability, and agility.

Robustness refers to system performance under unusual circumstances. For example, how the system behaves under unanticipated heavy load, disaster, electric outage, or even faulty design. Does the system crash, or does the system have built-in safety features that back up data and other important information?

The purpose of testing is to test system validation under various stress conditions before operationalization. The next step is actual system migration.

Migrate to the Cloud

Once the cloud-based system is tested, it is ready to be moved to the cloud. Since the system is tested under a real cloud service platform for all services, databases, data integration, functionality and underlying processes, it may be tempting to go live immediately to what some authors (Laudon and Laudon, 2012) have called "crash" implementation. However, if it is an organization's first cloud migration, it is advisable to use what some have called a "phased" approach. The most important aspect would be integration of cloud application to the current IT environment. In this approach, modules are migrated one at a time. This has the benefit of learning as you go. Once one module functions properly, another one is added until the whole application is migrated. Other factors to consider are: personnel requirements and process change.

One of the challenges of cloud migration is personnel training. Cloud migration requires different IT skills than in-house implementation. Murphy (2009) noted comments from Michael Sutton, vice president of security research for Zscaler. Mr. Sutton told CRM Buyer, "Infrastructure as a Service (IaaS), Platform as a Service (PaaS) and Software as a Service (SaaS) provide enterprises with differing levels of control and responsibility when managing the cloud environment," he said. "In general, IaaS would require the most technical skills, while SaaS handles most of the heavy lifting, with PaaS somewhere in between," he remarked. Ultimately, Sutton said, "an ability to interface with and navigate the cloud provider's support system may be something that IT staffers have not previously been required to do. Such skills will be vital as some degree of control is sacrificed in exchange for the efficiencies of outsourcing maintenance of the overall platform." Since cloud migration requires different IT skill sets, it is important to hire or retrain workers in order to maximize return on investment in cloud migration. Personnel can make or break a system hence proper training is a prerequisite for any successful implementation.

As already mentioned, cloud migration requires a process change. It requires a different computing model, since users lose control of their data as applications are migrated to clouds, and users may inadvertently share resources with outsiders. IT departments may disappear or be downsized. In some sense, the "middle" layer support may disappear. The middle layer may consist of help desk, IT department, and/or online training. The middle layer may also be shifted to a cloud service provider. On the other hand, users can respond to changes much more rapidly, since cloud services provide scalability, which can accommodate increases in demand for IT resources. This requires change not only in process but also in corporate culture.

Once processes are reconfigured and users are trained, cloud migration can proceed in phases until all modules are implemented.

Document

This is one of the most important parts of any new system implementation, and it is especially critical in cloud migration. The process changes mean that the old rules change substantially, and users need to learn new protocols for using cloud services. If multiple users are sharing the application from different locations, all access procedures should be spelled out clearly. This also shields a company from employee turnovers. Documents should consist of information on user interface, data access, data integration and hardware and software requirements to function efficiently in the cloud environment.

CONCLUSION

Cloud migration is here to stay. First adopters are already enjoying benefits of this. As lucrative as cloud migration is, it is still in its infancy, and not all applications can or should be moved to cloud. There are some very legitimate concerns in terms of security, multi-tenancy and data portability. Variance in performance on heavy demand periods can also hamper performance. Just like the PC market, cloud computing services are constantly evolving. Vendors are making improvements that customers are demanding. Though cloud computing may be every company's "right"mare, companies, especially small companies, will have no choice but to jump on the bandwagon if they want to survive in this digital and fast-moving economy. This chapter provides a generic systems approach to cloud migration; every company will have to customize this approach to meet organizational requirements.

REFERENCES

Black, L., Mandelbaum, J., Grover, I., & Marvi, Y. (2010). *The arrival of cloud thinking.* Management Insight Technologies. Retrieved from http://www.ca.com/~/media/files/whitepapers/the_arrival_of_cloud_thinking.aspx

Dorsey, P. (2005). *Top 10 reasons why system projects fail.* Retrieved from http://www.hks.harvard.edu/m-rcbg/ethiopia/Publications/Top%2010%20Reasons%20Why%20Systems%20Projects%20Fail.pdf

Fedor, D., Caldwell, S., & Herold, D. (2006). The effects of organizational changes on employee commitment: A multilevel investigation. *Personnel Psychology, 59*(1), 1–29. doi:10.1111/j.1744-6570.2006.00852.x

Klein, P. (2011). *Seven tips for cloud computing.* Retrieved from http://www.microsoft.com/microsoftservices/en/us/article_Seven_Tips_for_Cloud_Computing.aspx

Laudon, K., & Laudon, J. (2012). *Management information systems: Managing the digital firm.* Prentice-Hall.

Mooney, A., Mahoney, M., & Wixom, B. (2008). Achieving top management support in strategic technology initiatives. *Howe School Alliance for Technology Management, 12*(2). Retrieved from http://howe.stevens.edu/fileadmin/Files/research/HSATM/newsletter/v12/f08/MooneyMahoney-Wixom.pdf

Murphy, E. (2009). *Cloud implementation, part 3: Training for the task.* Retrieved February 2, 2012, from http://www.crmbuyer.com/story/66832.html

Nickols, F. (2010). *Four management strategies.* Retrieved February 2, 2012, from http://www.nickols.us/four_strategies.pdf

Chapter 7
Requirements Engineering for Cloud Application Development

Holger Schrödl
University of Magdeburg, Germany

Stefan Wind
University of Augsburg, Germany

ABSTRACT

In industrial practice, cloud computing is becoming increasingly established as an option for formulating cost-efficient and needs-oriented information systems. Despite the increasing acceptance of cloud computing within the industry, many fundamental questions remain unanswered, or are answered only partially. Besides issues relating to the best architectures, legal issues, and pricing models, suppliers of cloud-based solutions are faced with the issue of appropriate requirements engineering. This means eliciting optimal understanding of the customer's requirements and implementing this into appropriate requirements of the solution to be realised. This chapter examines selected, established requirements engineering methods in order to study the extent to which they can be applied to the specific requirements of cloud-based solutions. Furthermore, it develops a comparison framework containing the features of cloud computing. This comparison framework is applied to four established process models for requirements engineering. Recommendations for a requirements engineering process adapted to cloud computing are derived.

INTRODUCTION

While cloud computing has already found its way into practice, deficits in the scientific basis (Leimeister, Böhm, Riedl, & Krcmar) remain. One such shortfall is requirements engineering for cloud computing - as a separate unit with its own different domains. Before elaborating on

the basics of requirements engineering, we take a short insight what encompasses cloud computing and cloud-based solutions.

For the term "cloud computing", a unique definition is not yet established (Armbrust et al., 2010). But the essence of every definition is the intention to provide IT services over the internet from a provider without taking care of the essential

DOI: 10.4018/978-1-4666-2187-9.ch007

resources which are needed to provide this particular service. To distinguish this approach to other service concepts like ASP (Application Service Providing) we draw attention to the dimension of agility. While the ASP concepts focusses on mid- and long-term relationships between provider and user, cloud computing supports on-demand relationships with more agility than a traditional application service providing (R. Buyya, Ch S. Yeo, & S. Venugopal). Therefore, cloud computing is a highly modular service providing concepts. In a classical definition of cloud computing, we consider three levels of services: Infrastructure as a Service (IaaS), Platform as a Service (PaaS) and Software as a Service (SaaS). Cloud-based solutions are software applications, which are combined and/or enhanced with modules from these three levels of service providing, integrated to one single solution (Grossman, 2009).

While some preliminary research initiatives have been carried out under the sub-domain of Software as a Service (SaaS) (c.f. Berkovich, Esch, Leimeister, & Krcmar, 2009, Berkovich, Esch, Leimeister, & Krcmar, 2010), none have yet been carried out for cloud computing in general. Because of its specific characteristics and the different requirements fields, it is necessary to make a distinction between these and established requirements. Forrester Research Consultants has investigated eleven different cloud computing vendor offers with respect to fields of application, costs and commercial benefits, and has drawn a sobering conclusion: many offers do not meet - or only partially meet - customers' requirements (Staten, 2009). The success of cloud computing, therefore, depends a vast understanding on how well customers' and other stakeholders' requirements and wishes are met. The basis for developing successful offers is a requirements engineering system adapted to cloud computing.

The success of development processes and projects essentially depends on whether the results meet the requirements of stakeholders (such as the customer, executive management, legislators etc.). A crucial element here is the implementation of an appropriate and professional requirements engineering tool (Lindemann, 2009; Pohl, 2008; Rupp, 2009). Errors concerning the requirements are one of the main reasons why development projects fail (Aurum & Wohlin, 2010). Evidence of this is provided on a regular basis by the CHAOS study (See Figure 1) carried out by the American consultancy firm, the Standish Group. In a recent study, carried out in 2009 almost 48% of the problems or shortcomings in software development could be traced back to poor requirements engineering (Standish Group, 2010).

Moreover, studies carried out in a wide range of domains (product development, software engineering etc.) show, that errors made while determining requirements include a significant influence on the development process (Hall, Beecham, & Rainer, 2002). And work and costs involved in eliminating the errors increase disproportionately to the time at which they appear (Berkovich, Leimeister, & Krcmar, 2010). The reason for this is the early point in time within the process at which the requirements are defined. It means than any errors occurring at that early stage will affect all the future phases (such as design, implementation etc.) (Pohl, 2008). In his error pyramid, Leffingwell works on the basis that fixing an error at the implementation stage is up to 100 times more difficult, and at the maintenance stage, up to 1000 times more difficult than at the start of development stage (Dörnemann & Meyer, 2003).

Cloud computing is an issue in which, in general, enterprise IT managers are showing a vast deal of interest. According to the latest survey carried out by Sterling Commerce GmbH, a software supplier in Duesseldorf, 87% of all senior IT managers in Germany are planning to move to cloud-based information systems in the B2B sector (Sterling Commerce, 2010). The main driver of such considerations is the study on cost pressures: most companies want to reduce costs by

Figure 1. Results from the CHAOS report 2009 (Pohl, 2008)

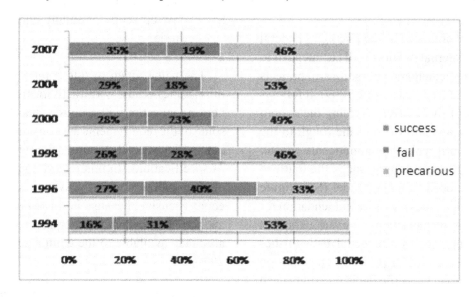

implementing cloud-based IT structures, caused by services accounting based on utilisation.

Other and more wide-ranging aspects are improved deployment of in-house IT staff, a reduction in manual processes, and advance to transparency of processes. However, when considering cloud-based systems, the most prominent feature is to be found in the areas of security and trust (Weinhardt et al., 2009).

REQUIREMENTS ENGINEERING MODELS

Various process models were investigated within a literature research framework to find out the extent to which they are appropriate to provide general support for requirements engineering. To this end, differing groups of models and approaches were identified, which have come about on the basis of individual philosophies, traditions and viewpoints. This included a discussion of monumental and agile process models (Balzert, 2009). From this different viewpoint, typical representatives of a certain class of the method have been chosen. Typical representative means that every selected model represents the core characteristics of the

regarded class and is widely distributed in the industry. Following representatives have been chosen:

- **V-Model:** The model is one of the most well known system development models in Germany (Rupp, 2009). Therefore, it is a typical representative of a monumental model.
- **Rational Unified Process (RUP):** One of the leading system development model which is between the monumental and the agile methods (Barchfeld, Sand, & Link, 2001)
- **Extreme Programming (XP):** A lightly-weighted development method which was positioned as a counter-movement to heavily-weighted methods such as the V-Model (Wolf, Roock, & Lippert, 2005) and acts as a specific method for pure agile methods

Added to these models Volere was added. Volere is a method developed specifically for requirements engineering purposes (Rupp, 2009). This claims to avoid the weaknesses of existing process models.

V-Model

The V-Model produced by the [German] Federal Ministry of Internal Affairs (BMI) is intended to enable the implementation of (software) projects both small and large (Reinhold, 2009). It follows the concept of successively dividing the overall system, refining it down from the rough to the fine detail, until realisable components appear. Requirements engineering is one of the fourteen activities included in the V-Model (See Figure 2), each of which provides a recommendation for handling the implementation of the various project management processes. The model distinguishes according to the type of project: depending on the type of project specific decision points need to be met. In principle, the V-Model provides the following steps in the requirements engineering process:

- Description of the initial circumstances and objectives
- Drawing up functional requirements
- Drawing up non-functional requirements
- Establish risk acceptance
- Draw up draft of life cycle and overall system architecture

- Analyse quality of requirements
- Draw up scope of supply and acceptance criteria.

The name given to this component is quite misleading because not all activities are combined here in connection with requirements. Rather, only some of the requirements are considered, and the contracting client then summarises these into a set of specifications. In this regard, the component dealing with setting up the system is much more comprehensive, because in this case documents and activities for continued requirements handling are made available to the contractor (Reinhold, 2009).

Rational Unified Process (RUP)

The Rational Unified Process (RUP), displayed in Figure 3, is a software development process model, and it consists of two process dimensions (Dörnemann & Meyer, 2003). The time dimension indicates a sub-division into a rough structure (phases) and a refined structure (iterations). The second dimension is concerned with the technical side and divides these into disciplines, of which there are six primary process disciplines (including

Figure 2. V-Modell (Clarus, 2005)

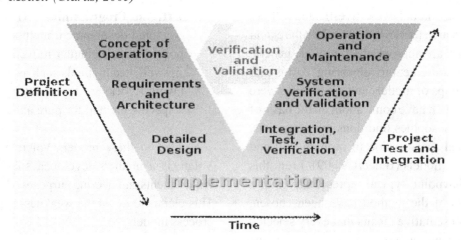

Figure 3. Rational unified process (RUP)

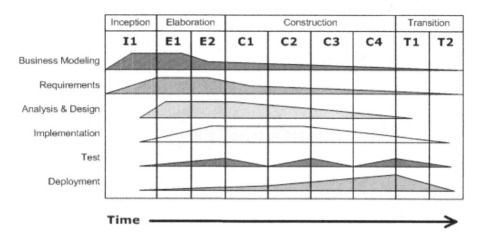

requirement) and three infrastructure disciplines. Each discipline has its own defined workflow.

The requirements engineering discipline pursues the aim of enabling reliable specifications and development, as well as modifications to a system. For example, this means drawing up a uniform picture about the functionality that the system is to perform for all stakeholders, and creating a basis for estimating costs and time parameters (Dörnemann & Meyer, 2003). Essentially, requirements engineering in the RUP consists of the six following principle activities (Heßeler & Versteegen, 2004):

- Analyse the problem
- Understand the stakeholders' needs
- Define the system
- Manage the scope of the system
- Manage changing requirements
- Refine the system definition.

These activities are logically connected to one another and should not be viewed as being merely sequential.

Volere

The Volere approach was developed by Atlantic Systems Guild and is derived from the Italian verb volere (to want, wish) (Dörnemann & Meyer,

2003). The process was developed specifically for requirements engineering (see Figure 4) and, besides techniques for determining requirements, also provide templates for structuring requirements specifications (Robertson & Robertson, 2006). The approach is organised according to the following points:

- Motivation (the purpose of the project or product, user, customer etc.)
- Restrictions and specifications for the project (conditions and assumptions)
- Functional requirements (such as Use Case model, data requirements)
- Non-functional requirements (usability, maintainability, legal requirements, etc.)
- Project information (e.g. risks, costs, task lists)

Volere provides users with a systematic, structured and remarkably comprehensive requirements engineering template.

As opposed to RUP all the information in the templates is held in a single document (monolithic); conversely, the RUP provides various documents (so-called artefacts), each containing relevant information. In order to develop requirements, Volere prefers a requirements template. Quality assurance is an intermediate step (so-called gateway) which is used between requirements

Figure 4. Volere requirement engineering process (http://www.st.cs.uni-saarland.de/edu/se/2009/slides/ volere_reqs_process_complete.jpg)

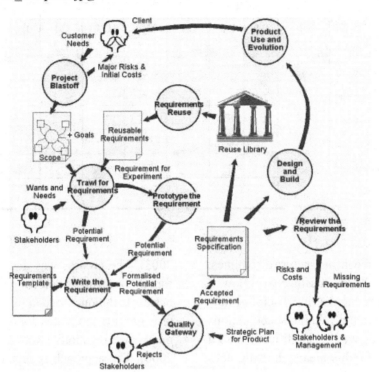

specification and analysis (Robertson & Robertson, 2006). The process should also be considered as being iterative.

Extreme Programming (XP)

XP was developed by Kent Beck, Ward Cunningham and Ron Jeffries and was launched in 1999 with the publication of their book: "eXtreme Programming explained" (Balzert, 2009). XP pursued the objective of formulating software development projects more effectively and more efficiently, by slimming them down significantly and aligning them to the customer as well as to quality issues (Beck & Andres, 2007). As with RUP, XP has an iterative and incremental character. At first glance, XP and a fundamental requirements analysis seem to contradict one another, but XP is concerned with getting an implementable system onto the market (Balzert, 2009; Beck & Andres, 2007).

However, also in this model there are approaches that are well supplemented by requirements analysis. These are User Stories, the Planning Game and the System Metaphor (See Figure 5). For example, User Stories are short reports made by users, which are initially gathered together in an informal manner; details are gradually added and they are then evaluated. It is possible to consider these in comparison with requirements.

REQUIREMENTS ENGINEERING IN CLOUD COMPUTING

A classification system has been developed in order to establish a comparison framework for requirements engineering models in the context of cloud-based solutions. Aim of this comparison framework is to conduct a structured comparison of different requirements engineering model and

Figure 5. eXtreme programming according to (Wells, 1999)

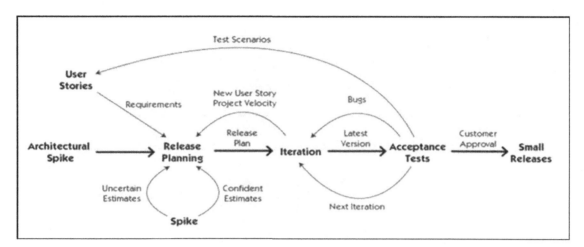

to determine, which of the established models are suitable for the specific requirements of requirements engineering for cloud-based solutions. In general we speak of a classification system if a particular object is first categorised according to certain attributes, and the relevant characteristics are determined for these attributes (Engelien, 1971). No linkage should be made between the various attributes (Knoblich, 1972). Cloud computing in the sense of application development makes use of a four-part conceptual model for the classification developed here (Figure 6). The cloud-based offer is compromised of various services (service A and service B in the Figure 6) and components (component C in Figure 6). Services represent business objects, components represent technical objects. Services and components are linked together through an orchestration level to complex business applications. These complex business applications may be provided by a certain supplier to a single or multiple customer.

Characteristics Relating to the Cloud Offer, from the Customer's Viewpoint

The topmost level of developing a Cloud offer from the customer's viewpoint does not differ significantly from the traditional software engi-neering field. For this reason, to develop a cloud offer, the following established characteristics from the software domain are significant.

The first characteristic is understood to be the requirements specification for the entire cloud offer, which is often subsumed under the term Requirements Elicitation (Kotonya & Sommerville, 1998). This is essential firstly in order to understand the background and motivation of the stakeholders, and secondly to understand the objectives that the cloud solution has to meet. The requirement specification must be supported by means of efficient techniques such as interviews, workshops, scenarios, as well as transaction analyses, and must be able to take into consideration several stakeholders at once (Aurum & Wohlin, 2010; Kotonya & Sommerville, 1998; Rupp, 2009).

A critical characteristic is the requirements analysis and agreement. During this phase, the requirements need to be firmed and consensus obtained from all stakeholders. Therefore, the model must be in a position to deal with conflicts between the different types of requirements, to help to find the solution, and then to contribute towards producing a requirements base supported by all stakeholders (Aurum & Wohlin, 2010; Kotonya & Sommerville, 1998). This is particularly relevant

Figure 6. Conceptual cloud architecture

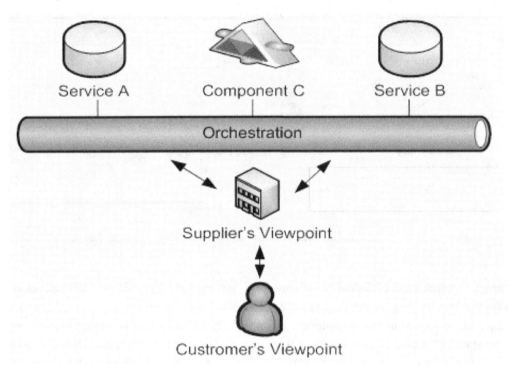

due to the special circumstances in cloud computing, with many different stakeholders and, to some extent, competing requirements.

The third characteristic is the proper documentation and description of the requirements, and this represents the basis of all further activities (Pohl, 2008). Once the requirements have been described, it is possible to assign them to their various sources and to monitor them. The documentation can be implemented in different ways, including essays, Use Cases or style guides (Rupp, 2009).

Characteristics Relating to the Cloud Offer, from the Supplier's Viewpoint

Suppliers of Cloud offers record the customer's requirements and implement them into a specific solution. The idea of cloud computing necessitates that the supplier does not create the complete offer himself, but makes use of the services and components offered within the Cloud, using them to achieve a solution. For this reason, the supplier

must be able to articulate appropriately the requirements of the individual components to be used.

The first characteristic is considered to be the possibility of validating requirements. This is intended to check whether the documentation expresses the stakeholders' requirements (Cheng & Atlee, 2007). The validation process can be helped by using techniques such as reviews, check-lists, prototypes and walk-throughs.

A more fundamental characteristic is the capacity to take account of non-functional requirements. Rupp stresses that this type of requirement is often forgotten and is awarded less value than functional properties (Rupp, 2009). Meeting such criteria opens up many opportunities, such as satisfied customers, increased legal security, and complete specifications. It is precisely in such complex structures as cloud computing that this is given significant weight.

The third characteristic is the existence of a change management system, which verifies any changes in requirements and examines them for any possible effects on existing requirements (Kotonya & Sommerville, 1998). Assurance must be given that changes are documented, analysed and any additional costs that may occur are checked in advance. It should be mentioned here that this criterion differs from change management in the SaaS domain, because it is aimed at changes occurring during project implementation, while with SaaS, the focus is on changes made after the project is completed.

Characteristics Relating to Orchestration

Orchestration is of crucial importance when the Cloud offer is implemented (Ried, 2009). It represents the connecting element between the individual application components, and can therefore be described as the implementation of the solution architecture.

The first characteristic in this area is the architectural capacity of requirements engineering. It must be possible to elicit the requirements of complete information system architecture. In particular, this includes support for formal modelling forms for information system architectures such as ARIS or UML. The second characteristic is the agility of requirements engineering in relation to the description of architecture requirements. A component-based architecture is characteristic for aspects such as reusability, replaceability, extendability and scalability (Vouk, 2008). A third characteristic is identified as being the structured elicitation of infrastructure requirements. These infrastructure requirements must be allocated into areas of service quality, security, and economic dimension (Weinhardt et al., 2009).

Characteristics Relating to SaaS and Applications Components

Within the framework of developing SaaS, it is necessary to take into account specific characteristics such as the integration of multi-discipline components from different domains, or different requirements sources, which affect the requirements engineering process (Berkovich et al., 2010). From this, the following characteristics for requirements engineering models can be derived.

The first characteristic is a coordinated and integrated requirements engineering process for individual components such as software and services, which are mutually dependent upon one another during and after development.

A further characteristic is the proper selection by stakeholders within the development framework, because they have a crucial influence over the success of a target-oriented development project (Pohl, 2008; Rupp, 2009). It is necessary to pay attention to supra-disciplinary coordination of requirements emanating from the software and service areas (Berkovich et al., 2010).

A crucial characteristic for the comparison framework is the comprehensive inclusion of the customer into the entire development process during every phase. Even where this can be difficult (Abramovici & Schulte, 2007), due to different language bases and differing levels of understanding by developers, this must not be abandoned.

Fourthly, in the framework of SaaS it is essential to prepare an optimally functioning change management system for the phase following delivery, in order to be able to implement any modifications in the service area (Berkovich et al., 2010). A clear traceability system for the requirements when implemented is of crucial importance here in order to avoid unwanted counter-effects.

Once development is completed, a complete requirements management system will include, besides the purpose of assuring traceability and validation, a careful statement of the requirements sources. Only thus is it possible to interpret this correctly in its context, even later on.

A further important characteristic is the capacity to be able to obtain the history of the requirement when it is recorded. A more detailed differentiation is necessary because not every elicitation method (workshops, interviews, scenario techniques etc) (Pohl, 2008) is appropriate in equal extent for every type of source (customer, provider, etc). In particular, when ascertaining requirements in the sense of a comprehensive view, it is necessary to consider every possible source, in order, as already mentioned, to assure traceability, validation and a functioning change management system.

The above-mentioned capability is equally vital within the change management framework. The reason for this is the two-way dependency of the system components, which can have an impact on software and services. These must therefore be considered carefully before making any changes.

Solutions and Recommendations

The V-model does not provide general requirements engineering support in the development of cloud computing solutions. A fundamental criticism here is that it is seen as the task of the contracting client to determine the requirements (Balzert, 2009). For this reason, the model does not allow for stakeholders' choices that may extend beyond system limits, but this is extremely important in SaaS. Since the model is kept very broad and is intended to cover any type of project (Reinhold, 2009), it fails to a large extent to provide support in SaaS. One of the indications of this is the fact that there is no supra-disciplinary coordination of requirements emanating from the software and service areas. Furthermore, no support whatsoever is offered for change management in the phase following delivery; the core process of the problem and change management is applied only while the project is in progress. The customer is partially included into the development process because it has to accept documents issued at the various phases of the project.

A further point of criticism is the lack of agility in describing changing architecture requirements. A better picture emerges in the area of the total solution. On one hand, the model aids the process of determining non-functional requirements as a

separate process step. Since the V-model is based on documentation (Reinhold, 2009), it also offers excellent support for requirements documentation. However, its strict rules create an inordinate amount of work.

Since RUP was originally designed for software development, it indicates system problems in other areas, such as in the service environment (Heßeler & Versteegen, 2004). For this reason, it is unable to provide globally optimum support for SaaS. For example, it lacks a coordinated and integrated requirements engineering process for individual components, a change management process for the phase after delivery, and support for managing requirements after the development process is completed in full. It offers only partial support for the selection of appropriate stakeholders beyond domain boundaries and for the inclusion of the customer into the entire development process (this tending to be at the start of the project). In general, the model offers good support in the traditional areas of requirements engineering, including the consideration of non-functional requirements (Dörnemann & Meyer, 2003). Nevertheless it cannot help in the SaaS framework, and especially not in ascertaining the source of requirements. RUP is also lacking in the area of orchestration characteristics, especially in its description of the agility of architecture requirements.

Like the RUP model, the XP model, one of the most well-known representatives of agile methods (Wolf et al., 2005), was originally used for software development. However, as opposed to RUP it offers better support for SaaS which can be traced back to the agile values on which it is based (e.g. strong weighting on customer). Yet XP still does not provide a coordinated and integrated RE for individual components. There is limited support for customer choices that go outside the boundaries of the domain, because XP provides for various roles such as customer, contracting Client etc. Customer integration throughout the entire development process is one of XP's strengths and is supported by the On-site customer practice [21]. Because of XP's objective of delivering executable increments as quickly as possible and then to consider the customer's feedback when planning the next increment, an elementary change management does take place after delivery. But this only applies up until the project has been concluded. For this reason, it provides no management process for requirements after final delivery (e.g. in the form of a library). The ability to determine the source of requirements exists in principle, because the requirements are often ascertained in a joint planning game. It offers the possibility of going into the source in explicit detail. However, in the change management process, consideration of the source is provided only in part, and in the main, this lies with the customer.

In the total solution area, because of the system, the defined characteristics are met only partially as a result of XP's properties. The elicitation of requirements is assisted by means of the planning game. However, XP does not provide sufficient support for documenting requirements, because documentation is produced only in the form of user stories (in principle executable code is prioritised higher than documentation (Beck & Andres, 2007). There is no support for requirements validation or change management. Adaptations to the product are made only until the customer is satisfied. However, due to the specific characteristics of cloud computing, this appears to be difficult. Nor is considering the relevant architectural requirements one of XP's strengths. It is due to this shortfall in its options for offering opportunities to elicit agile architecture requirements, along with a structured elicitation of infrastructure requirements, that XP indicates unsatisfactory possibilities for the implementation of RE for cloud computing.

Compared with those described above, the Volere model was developed especially to handle requirements engineering (Robertson & Robertson, 2006). However, it has weaknesses in the area of SaaS. It does not support a coordinated and integrated requirements engineering system beyond

the domains, because this is not provided within the model. On the other hand, it does support stakeholders' selections beyond domain boundaries in the form of a particular stakeholder management section. This also includes stakeholder integration throughout the entire development process, and this is indicated by frequent stakeholder interaction provided in the model. After delivery the model also offers limited support for change management by means of an active feedback system between customer and supplier. The requirements, together with their sources, are collected into a library, and are also subject to fundamental management after the development work is completed. But there is a lack of specific methods for effective application. Other lacking areas are in the architecture capacity and architecture requirements agility. As expected, it fully supports the traditional tasks of requirements engineering such as eliciting, coordinating, prioritising and documenting, validating and managing requirements, also considering the non-functional requirements.

FUTURE RESEARCH DIRECTIONS

Within the context of this article, cloud computing is understood to be component-based applications development. Since the term cloud computing includes other aspects, the results are seen as limited. If the term cloud computing is extended to include the provision of infrastructure and application, the result could be that the comparison framework has to be expanded. There might also be issues arising solely related to infrastructure issues like network infrastructures, server landscapes and virtualization or related to application issues like security, provisioning or user behaviour. Therefore, to achieve a holistic picture, these investigations have to be extended. A second limitation consists in the choice of the considered models. Typical representatives of a particular type of requirements engineering models were selected for analysis. This option is intended to represent a class of requirements engineering models. But there are a lot more models in software engineering and requirements engineering which are used in practice. An extension to the area of consideration in the meaning of validating the comparison framework could result in additional findings.

This article represents a first step for requirements engineering in cloud computing. It is intended to lay the foundation for a reference model for requirements engineering for cloud-based solutions, which in practice will result in a considerable improvement in the development of customer-specific information systems based on cloud architecture.

CONCLUSION

The objective of this article was to verify established process models for requirements engineering in regard to their suitability for cloud computing. By deriving 16 specific characteristics in four categories, if could be shown that there are some opportunities, bute also some challenges in applying established requirements engineering model to develop cloud-based solutions. The V-model, RUP, XP and Volere process models were evaluated and discussed in more detail. The results enabled us to show that none of the established models is appropriate to cover in full the needs of requirements engineering for cloud computing. Existing shortfalls were identified and recommendations have been derived for cloud computing requirements engineering.

REFERENCES

Abramovici, M., & Schulte, S. (2007). Optimising customer satisfaction by integrating the customer's voice into product development. In *Proceedings of the 16th International Conference on Engineering Design* (pp. 801–802).

Aurum, A., & Wohlin, C. (2010). *Engineering and managing software requirements*. Berlin, Germany: Springer.

Balzert, H. (2009). *Lehrbuch der Softwaretechnik: Basiskonzepte und Requirements Engineering* (3rd ed.). Heidelberg, Germany: Spektrum Akademischer Verlag. Retrieved from http://www.worldcat.org/oclc/647852079

Barchfeld, M., Sand, R., & Link, J. (2001). *XP und RUP - Passt das zusammen?* Retrieved from http://www.fh-wedel.de/archiv/iw/Lehrveranstaltungen/WS2006/SWE/PaperAndrenaObjects.pdf

Beck, K., & Andres, C. (2007). *Extreme programming explained: Embrace change* (2nd ed.). The XP series. Boston, MA: Addison-Wesley.

Berkovich, M., Esch, S., Leimeister, J. M., & Krcmar, H. (2009). Requirements engineering for hybrid products as bundle of hardware, software and service elements - A literature review. In *Tagungsband der 9*. Wien: Internationalen Tagung Wirtschaftsinformatik.

Berkovich, M., Esch, S., Leimeister, J. M., & Krcmar, H. (2010). Towards requirements engineering for "software as a service". In Schumann, M., Kolbe, L. M., Breitner, M. H., & Frerichs, A. (Eds.), *Multikonferenz Wirtschaftsinformatik 2010*. Göttingen, Germany: Universitätsverlag Göttingen.

Berkovich, M., Leimeister, J. M., & Krcmar, H. (2010). Ein Bezugsrahmen für Requirements Engineering hybrider Produkte. In Schumann, M., Kolbe, L. M., Breitner, M. H., & Frerichs, A. (Eds.), *Multikonferenz Wirtschaftsinformatik 2010*. Göttingen, Germany: Universitätsverlag Göttingen.

Buyya, R., Yeo, C. S., & Venugopal, S. (2008). Market-oriented cloud computing: Vision, hype, and reality for delivering IT services as computing utilities, (pp. 5–13). DOI: 10.1109/HPCC.2008.172

Cheng, B. H., & Atlee, J. M. (2007). Research directions in requirements engineering. In L. C. Briand & A. L. Wolf (Eds.), *Future of Software Engineering, FoSE 2007:* 23-25 May 2007, Minneapolis, Minnesota (pp. 285–303). Los Alamitos, CA: IEEE Computer Society.

Clarus. (2005). *Concept of operations.* Publication No. FHWA-JPO-05-072. Retrieved from http://ntl.bts.gov/lib/jpodocs/repts_te/14158_files/14158.pdf

Dörnemann, H., & Meyer, R. (2003). *Anforderungsmanagement kompakt: Mit Checklisten.* Heidelberg, Germany: Spektrum Akad. Verl.

Engelien, G. (1971). *Der Begriff der Klassifikation.*

Hall, T., Beecham, S., & Rainer, A. (2002). Requirements problems in twelve software companies: An empirical analysis. *IEE Proceedings. Software, 149*(5), 153. doi:10.1049/ip-sen:20020694

Heßeler, A., & Versteegen, G. (2004). *Anforderungsmanagement: Formale Prozesse, Praxiserfahrungen, Einführungsstrategien und Toolauswahl.* Berlin, Germany: Springer. Retrieved from http://www.worldcat.org/oclc/248875529

Knoblich, H. (1972). Die typologische Methode in der Betriebswirtschaftslehre. *Wirtschaftswissenschaftliches Studium, 1*(4), 141–147.

Kotonya, G., & Sommerville, I. (1998). *Requirements engineering: Processes and techniques.* New York, NY: John Wiley. Retrieved from http://www.worldcat.org/oclc/38738981

Lindemann, U. (2009). *Methodische Entwicklung technischer Produkte: Methoden flexibel und situationsgerecht anwenden.* Retrieved from http://dx.doi.org/10.1007/978-3-642-01423-9

Pohl, K. (2008). *Requirements engineering: Grundlagen, Prinzipien, Techniken* (2.th ed.). Heidelberg, Germany: Dpunkt-Verl. Retrieved from http://deposit.d-nb.de/cgi-bin/dokserv?id=3086471&prov=M&dok_var=1&dok_ext=htm

Reinhold, M. (2009). V-Modell XT und Anforderungen. In Rupp, C. (Ed.), *Requirements-Engineering und -Management: Professionelle, iterative Anforderungsanalyse für die Praxis.* München, Germany: Hanser Fachbuch Verlag.

Ried, S. (2009). *Market overview: The middleware software market, 2009.* Retrieved from http://www.forrester.com/rb/Research/market_overview_middleware_software_market_2009/q/id/47591/t/2

Robertson, S., & Robertson, J. (2006). *Mastering the requirements process* (2nd). Upper Saddle River, NJ: Addison-Wesley. Retrieved from http://www.worldcat.org/oclc/62697079

Standish Group. (2010). *CHAOS report.* Retrieved from http://www.standishgroup.com/

Staten, J. (2009). *TechRadar™ for infrastructure & operations professionals: Cloud computing, Q3 2009: As much diversity of maturity across categories as confusion among them.*

Sterling Commerce. (2010). *87 Prozent deutscher Unternehmen planen Investitionen in Cloud-Services.* Retrieved from http://www.sterlingcommerce.de/about/news/press-releases/PM_Cloud-Services_10.htm

Vouk, M. A. (2008). Cloud computing - Issues, research and implementations. In *Proceedings of the ITI 2008 30th International Conference on Information Technology Interfaces.*

Weinhardt, C., Anandasivam, A., Blau, B., Borissov, N., Meinl, T., Michalk, W., & Stößer, J. (2009). Cloud-Computing. *Wirtschaftsinformatik, 51*(5), 453–462. doi:10.1007/s11576-009-0192-8

Wells, D. (1999). *Homepage*. Retrieved from ExtremeProgramming.org

Wolf, H., Roock, S., & Lippert, M. (2005). *eXtreme programming* (2nd ed.). s.l: dpunkt.verlag. Retrieved from http://ebooks.ciando.com/book/index.cfm/bok_id/7064

ADDITIONAL READING

Akkermans, J., & Gordijn, J. (2003). Value-based requirements engineering: Exploring innovative e-commerce ideas. *Requirements Engineering, 8*(2), 114–134. doi:10.1007/s00766-003-0169-x

Armbrust, M., Fox, A., Griffith, R., Joseph, A. D., Katz, R., & Konwinski, A. (2010). A view of cloud computing. *Communications of the ACM, 53*(April), 50–58. doi:10.1145/1721654.1721672

Buyya, R., Yeo, C. S., Venugopal, S., Broberg, J., & Brandic, I. (2009). Cloud computing and emerging IT platforms: Vision, hype, and reality for delivering computing as the 5th utility. *Future Generation Computer Systems, 25*(6), 599–616. doi:10.1016/j.future.2008.12.001

Fox, A., Griffith, R., Joseph, A., Katz, R., Konwinski, A., & Lee, G. (2009). Above the clouds: A Berkeley view of cloud computing.

Grossman, R. (2009). The case for cloud computing. *IT Professional. The Case for Cloud Computing, 11*(2), 23–27. doi:doi:10.1109/MITP.2009.40

Hayes, B. (2008). Cloud computing. *Communications of the ACM, 51*, 9–11. doi:10.1145/1364782.1364786

Leimeister, S., Böhm, M., Riedl, C., & Krcmar, H. (2010). The business perspective of cloud computing: actors, roles and value networks. In *ECIS 2010 Proceedings*. Retrieved from http://aisel.aisnet.org/ecis2010/56

Miller, M. (2008, c2009). *Cloud computing: Web-based applications that change the way you work and collaborate online*. Indianapolis, IN: Que. Retrieved from http://www.worldcat.org/oclc/223934946

Pearson, S. (2009). Taking account of privacy when designing cloud computing services. In *CLOUD '09, Proceedings of the 2009 ICSE Workshop on Software Engineering Challenges of Cloud Computing* (pp. 44-52). Washington, DC: IEEE Computer Society. Retrieved from http://dx.doi.org/10.1109/CLOUD.2009.5071532

Rupp, C. (Ed.). (2009). *Requirements-Engineering und -Management: Professionelle, iterative Anforderungsanalyse für die Praxis*. Munich, Germany: Hanser Fachbuch Verlag.

Sommerville, I., & Sawyer, P. (1997). Viewpoints: Principles, problems and a practical approach to requirements engineering. *Annals of Software Engineering, 3*, 101–130. doi:10.1023/A:1018946223345

Wang, L., Laszewski, G., Younge, A., He, X., Kunze, M., Tao, J., & Fu, C. (2010). Cloud computing: A perspective study. *New Generation Computing, 28*(2), 137–146. doi:10.1007/s00354-008-0081-5

Weiss, A. (2007). Computing in the clouds. *netWorker, 16*(25). doi:doi:10.1145/1327512.1327513

Chapter 8
Cloud Computing:
A Decision Framework for Small Businesses[1]

Stephen H. Kaisler
i_SW Corporation, USA

William H. Money
The George Washington University, USA

Stephen J. Cohen
Microsoft Public Sector Services, USA

ABSTRACT

Cloud computing technology is garnering success with marketing-based wisdom-like stories of savings, ease of use, and increased flexibility in controlling how resources are acquired at any given time to deliver computing capability. This chapter develops a preliminary decision framework to assist managers who are determining which cloud solution matches their specific requirements and evaluating the numerous commercial claims (in many cases unsubstantiated) of a cloud's value. This decision framework is the result of the authors' research program in understanding how small to medium-sized businesses can assess the potential benefit from cloud computing helps managers allocate investments and assess cloud alternatives that now compete with in-house data centers that previously stored, accessed, and processed data or with another company's (outsourced) datacenter resources.

INTRODUCTION

Cloud computing is a new computing paradigm in which an IT user does not have to physically access, control (operate), or own any computing infrastructure other than, perhaps, workstations, routers and switches, and, more recently, mobile client devices. Rather, the user "rents or leases" computational resources (time, bandwidth, storage, etc.) in part or whole, from some external entity. The resources are accessed and managed through logical and electronic means. A cloud architecture can be physically visualized as the arrangement of large to massive numbers of computers in distributed data centers to deliver applications and services via a utility model. In

DOI: 10.4018/978-1-4666-2187-9.ch008

a true physical sense, many servers may actually function on a high capacity blade in a single data center.

Confusion exists about the nature of cloud computing. Gartner asserts that a key characteristic is that it is "massively scalable" (DeSisto, Plummer and Smith 2008). Originally, cloud computing was proposed as a solution to deliver large-scale computing resources to the scientific community for individual users who could not afford to make the huge investments in permanent infrastructure or specialized tools, or could not lease needed infrastructure and computing services.

It evolved, rapidly, into a medium of storage and computation for Internet users that offers economies of scale in several areas. The Pew Internet and American Life Project (Horrigan 2008) noted that 69% of Internet users have data stored on-line or use web-based software applications. Examples include various email services (HotMail, Gmail, etc.), personal photo storage (Flickr), social networking sites (FaceBook, MySpace) or instant communication (Skype Chat, Twitter). This approach represents a major shift in the geography of computation analogous to the service bureau concept of the mid-20th century. Recently, large corporations are beginning to develop "private" clouds to host their own applications in order to protect their corporate data and proprietary applications while still capturing significant economies of scale in hardware, software, or support services.

Rather than providing the user with a permanent server to connect to when application execution is required, cloud computing provides "virtualized servers" chosen from a pool of servers at one of the available data centers. A user's request for execution of a web application is directed to one of the available servers that have the required operating environment, tools, and application locally installed. Within a data center, almost any application can be run on any server. The user knows neither the physical server nor, in many cases, where it is physically located, i.e., it is locationally irrelevant.

Most people think of cloud computing as a publicly available resource. We suggest that cloud computing is a viable business computational model for small to medium businesses who cannot afford large investments in permanent infrastructure. For cloud computing to succeed, they must be able to run their own tailored or uniquely configured applications in the cloud, a capability available in the scientific community, but not yet required in the personal and corporate usage community.

As part of our research program in understanding how small to medium-sized businesses can assess the potential benefit from cloud computing, we surveyed over 80 research articles from conferences, symposia, and journals, blogs, white papers, commercial announcements and claims, standards, and books to develop factors to incorporate in a decision model when considering moving to or adopting cloud computing. Our literature review found no single comparative model, but rather competing perspectives that describe the thing referred to as "cloud".

We have identified three broad perspectives in the literature that suggest why no single decision model has emerged to date. These perspectives have been used to construct a decision framework that assesses: services offered, vendor strategies, and cloud technical/architectural evolution. An analogy may help make the point. If you wish to serve a salad at a meal, you have many choices of ingredients, but that may not be the critical issue. You can buy all of your own ingredients, and mix yourself as required by the guests or you can buy a prepackaged bag of mix, and add some special treats (walnuts, tomatoes, carrots, etc.). Alternatives are greatly influenced by what is offered by a vendor (and vendor margins). Shop at a big store, and get premixed salads or buy the individual items when offered. As cloud proponents assert, any of the above options may be more efficient (and cheaper) than buying and managing your own vegetable farm (unless you already own the farm and have the land and resources to make it productive).

Thus, this chapter first examines the services or enabling technologies of cloud computing (products and services). Then, the it examines example commercial organizations to assess how the services and components are packaged for a successful cloud deployment. Finally, it presents several decision matrices – examples of key architectural and business questions a company should ask in considering the move to cloud computing.

Many authors tout the benefits of the computing technologies involved with a cloud strategy, but few address the technical risks, limitations, and disadvantages. It is clear that some major service providers have rolled out or are rolling out bundled services as products described as "cloud computing offerings" with multiple features and pricing plans. The complexity of the offerings makes it imperative that small-to-medium businesses use a clear and well understood decision process to

1. Asses the need to acquire services;
2. Contract/commit through a vendor's "cloud computing" offering; and
3. To select/commit to an cloud architecture initially and evolve toward over time.

The hypothetically newly captured corporate value (from the cloud) is that resources are no longer idle most of the time, and are now much more fully utilized (with lower unit costs). This reduces high ownership and support costs, improves capital leverage, and delivers increased flexibility in the use of resources. However, we noted other values that have been perceived to accrue including reallocation of resources, reduced fluctuation in operating costs, reduced time to addition of compute resources, access from outside corporate boundaries, and improved continuity of operations. Clearly, the perceived value of the cloud depends on the business objectives and goal of the individual organization.

Cloud computing has rapidly evolved to be an essential element of enterprise architecture consideration, system development and enterprise application implementation. Software architecting is historically viewed as a set of design decisions (Jansen and Bosch 2005). These decisions are dependent upon an organization's business strategy, risk tolerance, cost/benefit assessments, and available offerings.

Adopting a cloud computing environment (CCE) as a integral component of an organization's computing infrastructure is a major step away from traditional IT architectures. An organization contemplating such a move should consider:

*   When, how, and how many services should move to a CCE: public, private, or hybrid?
*   How will capital and operational expenses be managed over time?
*   What is the optimal mix of cloud services and how will it be achieved?
*   How does the organization assure that the CCE provider is compliant with application regulations and laws, and what Service Level Agreement (SLA) enforcement mechanism(s) exist?
*   How will the organization control the flow of data to and from the CCE and system architecture components?

BACKGROUND

The cloud computing concept arises from the notion of "software as a service" (SaaS). A set of services are provided on a set of platforms at various locations. The user determines the service he requires and shops for the best deal on that service that he can obtain subject to defined criteria. As Figure 1 depicts, the computing services provided by a cloud computing environment are most popularly accessed in four ways.

Figure 1. Cloud computing models

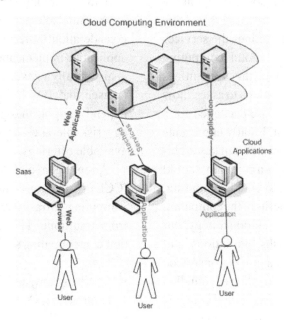

The first model is Software as a Service in which the application runs entirely in the cloud. The local client is typically a web browser or lightweight client. Email and search engines such as Google, are exemplars. The second model is attached services in which a local application acquires common services that allow it to interoperate with other applications or users at other sites.

One example is Apple's iTunes where the local app plays music and allows the user to manage a playlist while the attached service allows the user to buy new audio content. Microsoft's Exchange Hosted Content is another example. The third model treats cloud platforms as application execution engines, e.g., Hardware as a Service, that communicates with locally-based applications. This approach drives SETI@Home, where the cloud application parcels out signals to be analyzed by an application on an idle personal computer. Recently, a fourth use has emerged where the user "rents" a platform in the cloud for application development along with the associated system development kits.

But, multiple technical definitions and perspectives exist for 'cloud computing' as shown in Table 1. NIST (Mello and Grance 2011), which is most frequently cited, defines cloud computing as Software-as-a-Service (SaaS), Platform-as-a-Service (PaaS), or Infrastructure-as-a-Service (IaaS). However, Linthicum (2009) offers ten comprehensive views, which include the three NIST categories.

The technical definitions highlight the key idea behind cloud computing - the delivery of customer services in a flexible, scalable, and useful way. In our research, we surveyed over 80 conference, symposia papers, academic journal articles, laboratory white papers, commercial discussions, and blogs to understand how cloud computing is perceived and the range of decisions that organizations face when considering "cloud."

Cloud computing is often described with a generic control descriptor: cloud computing: public, private, and hybrid. Amazon's cloud service is an example of a public service that employs Amazon's infrastructure to store, access, and process data. A hybrid cloud setup is a mix of public and private cloud functions or services depending on

Table 1. Multiple perspectives on cloud computing

Category	Admin	Client	Example
Storage-as-a-Service (SaaS)	Limited Control	Access Only	Amazon S3
Database-as-a-Service (DaaS)	DB Management	Access Only	Microsoft SSDS
Information-as-a-service (INaaS)	DB Management	Access Only	Many
Process-as-a-Service (PRaaS)	Limited Control	Access Only	Appian Anywhere
Application-as-a-Service (AaaS) [Software-as-a-Service]	Total Control	Limited Tailoring	SalesForce.com Google Docs Gmail
Platform-as-a-Service (PaaS)	Total Control	Limited Programmability	Google App Engine
Integration-as-a-Service (IaaS)	No control (except VM)	Total Control (except VM)	Amazon SQS
Security-as-a-Service (SECaaS)	Limited Control	Access Only	Ping Identity
Management/Governance-as-a-Service (MGaaS)	Limited Control	Access Only	Xen, Elastra
Testing-as-a-Service (TaaS)	Limited Control	Access Only	SOASTA

what information needs to be stored and passed through public networks. Private clouds leverage equipment owned by the client itself or an external third party that can ensure information privacy.

Security, a critical aspect of cloud computing, continues to remain problematic, and must be considered with regard to legal requirements of data protection, company trade secrets, partner information, customer data, and sharing data with business partners. Recently, the public cloud providers have begun to implement security mechanisms including SAML for authentication and exchange of data. Amazon, Microsoft, and Google have all implemented some form of 'sandboxing' to isolate one user's processes from another user's processes. Nevertheless, significant security concerns remain to be addressed. Private clouds provide greater control and enable companies to shape how their data is stored and controlled.

Another challenge is rapid deployment within a cloud infrastructure without having to analyze, price, and plan for the integration of many cloud service components. Customers can obtain a com-

plete package for a fixed price that is immediately available for deploying applications and services.

What is Replaced by "Moving to the Cloud"?

Decision makers and managers must view and understand that "cloud computing" in its many forms is a set of enabling services and technologies for creating target platforms on which to host services. It is not a single accepted mechanism for specifying the explicit technologies to be used in implementing a cloud to support a particular business environment. Confusing the two aspects of business (solutions) architecture development can lead to poor business solutions! A common set of five service layers can be used to define a cloud offering, with some clouds offering services at higher layers than others as depicted in Figure 2.

One version of the first three layers has been ubiquitously referred to as the LAMP stack – Linux, Apache, MySQL, PHP. It can be technically compared to similar grouping of competing

Figure 2. Five layers of cloud computing

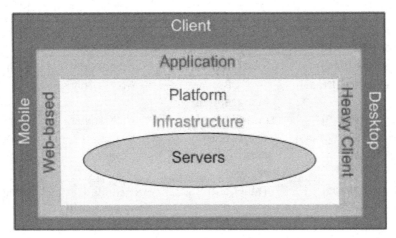

technologies such as Win server, IS server, SQL server on the Microsoft platform. This is the minimum configuration to provide deliverable content over a network. However, as new products and services emerge, the structure and features of this stack are expected to evolve.

Each service layer builds upon the next to form a fabric the encompasses the various services and technologies employed by an organization (See Table 2). Multiple instances of one service layer can work together to provide one instance of the next service layer. Thus, many servers can be integrated with additional required devices to provide different virtual datacenters or infrastructure configurations. The datacenters can host different platforms (i.e. Windows with IIS and SQL Server and Linux with Apache and MySQL) or just redundant instances of the same platform with the multiple instances of the platform layer all combined to present a common environment for the application service layer which could itself serve a variety of cloud clients. The novelty arises from the composition of existing technologies combined with new business models for software and service provisioning.

Virtualization software is the true critical technology enabler to cloud computing. Virtualization software (VMware vSphere, the open-source Xen Hypervisor, and closed-source Enter-prise-level virtualization management tools, and Microsoft's Hyper-V) creates and manages virtual servers that each have an OS and required additional software. Many virtual servers (virtual machines) may exist within an OS on a single physical device (server). The virtualization software also provides additional tools and features to effectively manage such virtualization.

One confusing question that is raised is how cloud computing will replace service-oriented architecture (SOA). As Linthicum has noted, this perspective indicates a misunderstanding of the basic ideas presented above. SOA is an architectural pattern. It is a specification for creating an architecture in which services are bound together to create business solutions. Cloud computing as shown above may involve many enabling technologies for creating target platforms on which to host SOA implementations. SOA is a mechanism for specifying the explicit technologies to be used in implementing a cloud to support a particular business environment. Confusing the two aspects of business (solutions) architecture development can lead to poor business solutions (and suboptimal decisions).

Table 2. Cloud computing layers

Cloud Computing Layers
Server: This layer provides individual server services or server hosting. Typically this service involves the delivery of a *virtual machine* (a single virtualized instance of a server that typically is not aware that it is *not* a tangible, physical server).
Infrastructure: A virtualized data center providing computing, storage, communications, security, and management resources and services. (Iaas)
Platform: The software foundation including the OS and system software (e.g., DBMSs, web services, visualization services). (PaaS)
Application: This layer includes pre-built, network-accessible applications and services (e.g., Google Docs, Salesforce, etc.). (SaaS)
Client: This layer provides end-user access methods to deliver the computing experience such as thin-provisioned clients or slim laptops using a web browser with minimal OS.

A Critical Question: How Are They Packaging the Cloud?

Although many hope for a simple comparison model that enables potential customers to uniformly describe, compare, and assess the features of all the products, this is not presently possible because of the architectural, packaging and, and service differences in cloud offerings.

Four competitive global cloud providers; IBM, Microsoft, Google, and Amazon illustrate this point, and show how the original sale and delivery of "cloud" services began with large providers servicing the easily understood business decision to purchase volumes of scalable services. The business decisions today have morphed into far more complicated assessments with a number of new vendors entering an expanding competitive and specialized industry that tailors architectures and services to customer needs, and requires significantly more decision making expertise to compare and acquire highly differentiated (rather than similar) service offerings. The new entrants (rapidly formed via acquisition and partnerships) are contrasted with the traditional competitors to illustrate the decision complexity.

HDS targets clients needing to search and access large amounts of data residing in cloud storage devices within the HDS Unified Computing Platform solution for cloud infrastructure. Hitachi Data Systems (HDS) provides cloud storage strategies for public, private and hybrid cloud environments. HDS purchased Comstock Systems in 2002, Archivas in 2007, and ParaScale in 2010 – all cloud services providers. Comstock developed software that manages network attached storage (NAS), switches, and routers; Archivas developed software that allows immediate access to protected, archived data; ParaScale provides a service for direct access to cloud storage. These services are combined to deliver technology for searching and managing structured and unstructured data, and delivering storage infrastructure. Microsoft System Center Operations Manager, Virtual Machine Manager, and Microsoft Windows Server 2008 R2 with Hyper-V software are also integrated into the infrastructure.(http://www.hds.com/solutions/storage-strategies/cloud/)

Microsoft Corporation has the Windows Azure platform. Azure is an Internet-scale cloud computing and services platform hosted in geographically distributed, Microsoft data centers. While the internals of the Azure platform have been purpose-built in-house by Microsoft, the platform it provides is an open, standards-based, interoperable environment with support for multiple internet protocols, including HTTP/HTTPS, REST, SOAP, and XML.

The Windows Azure platform is comprised of 3 large grain segments; First, Windows Azure is the cloud services operating system that serves as the development, service hosting, and service management environment for the Windows Azure platform. Windows Azure provides on-demand compute and storage to host, scale, and manages web applications and services. Next, Windows Azure AppFabric provides applications with a common infrastructure to name, discover, expose, secure, and orchestrate Web services. Last, Microsoft SQL Azure can provision and deploy relational databases with manageability, high availability, and scalability baked in.

Hewlett Packard (HP) cloud computing targets large solution oriented enterprises using a hybrid cloud model, needing access between public and private clouds and business decision support. (www.hp.com/go/cloud) HP purchased EDS, a technology services company, in 2008 to provides information technology and business process outsourcing services; 3com in 2009, for networking, switching, routing, and security; 3par in 2010, for utility storage solutions; Vertica in 2011, for a real-time data analytics platform built for physical, virtual, and cloud environments facing business intelligence decisions; and ArcSight Inc., for new security solutions for the cloud. HP only recently (March 2011) announced its plans for cloud computing.

International Business Machines (IBM), offers many hybrid cloud computing infrastructure platforms that include performance, storage, and virtualization for any industry. Its offerings are built via the acquisition of software companies such as BigFix, Cast Iron Systems, Coremetrics, Datacap, Guardium, Intelliden, Netezza, Internet Security Systems, and Sterling Commerce. These companies offer specialties like: software management, cloud application integration, business analytics, enterprise content management, database monitoring and protection, network detection, security, and control, analytic data warehousing, and security. IBM differentiates itself from Microsoft and Amazon by seeking customers who want to transform their business with cloud computing through support of development infrastructure.

Other large firms, such as Oracle, are entering the marketplace. Oracle is marketing a "Cloud in the Box" solution, which can be set up to operate at and scale into any of the cloud service layers from Infrastructure to Application. Considering Oracle's market share of corporate applications (such as Enterprise Resource Planning or Supply Chain Management software), many corporations may be convinced to use Oracle's solution instead if they already use Oracle's software, and thus benefit from the bundling discounts that Oracle would likely provide.

As we drafted this chapter, Apple has promoted its cloud offering which will connect its iPods, phones, and iPods to provide a ubiquitous 24x7 computing experience - anywhere, anytime, anyplace (well, assuming you have connectivity). Given Apple's extensive history of innovation within the IT marketplace, this may lead to revolutionary new ways to use the cloud.

An Example of Vendor Marketing of the "Cloud"

VCE is attempting to provide an integrated service that provides its customers with a complete solution for client Iasi needs. They are attempting to differentiate themselves from the competition by the completeness (the internally-integrated nature) of the solution they provide, the one-call available support and other value-added products and services available for their service, and their solution's performance capabilities.

VCE (http://www.vce.com/) is actually a company formed as a joint venture of VMware, Cisco Systems, and EMC^2, offers a virtual cloud environment that can be scaled from test and development lab environments up to large environments with 3000 virtual machines. The combined company offers a single solution by integrating the various participating company services and a catalog of add-on products, and allowing customers to integrate with their cloud of choice, (as long as the cloud uses VMware vSphere 4.1).

The integration offering stresses simplification by integrating the Nexus series switch line into the offering to deliver control in a top-to-bottom fashion; ten gigabyte fiber channel over Ethernet to consolidate networking and reduce cabling; software switching; a blade chassis supporting Intel and AMD base platforms depending on the client's request; and one interface to backend storage management via VMware, Cisco, and EMC.

The VCE pre-integrated solution markets itself as a combination of off-the-shelf hardware and software that can be tailor built or assembled by converting user systems, offering a possibly money saving solutions to clients who already have some components or are willing to risk just buying missing components. The solution "key" is the VCE single 1-800 number for support minimizing the troubleshooting of datacenter issues.

DECISION FRAMEWORK FOR CLOUD COMPUTING ADOPTION

Acquiring systems resources is a significant commitment for most businesses. Cloud computing offers the advantage of reducing portions of this significant investment by using cloud data center resources – servers, software, networks, infrastructure, people – to support the purchasing organization's business operations. Whether private or public cloud (due to protected business data, client privacy, and security concerns) an initial investment would be sized to the current workload (plus a growth factor). Cloud usage either is or averts a major cost with a significant learning curve.

Moving to the Cloud or Not

Our survey revealed that deciding to use cloud computing is often not made with rigorous analysis. Rather, many organizations decide to experiment with cloud computing, to implement a small low risk application to assess cloud computing. In part, the availability of web-accessible CCEs makes it easy to try cloud computing. A formal approach to deciding to use cloud computing requires the assessment and combination of many decision criteria in an eventual decision.

We formulated a three-tier decision model (See Figure 3) for assessing the types of decisions required to move services to the cloud either wholly or partially or, perhaps, not at all. The model follows our literature analysis and research findings and addresses the requirements for services, commercial offerings (vendor cloud packaging), and architectural decisions (short and long term). In descending order, an organization must decide the importance of numerous factors (not all shown) in how it approaches the cloud adoption decision.

We believe that these decisions must be made in a structured fashion – with exit points when benefits can be realized and future costs are either unknown or very great. To this end, we have begun to articulate a decision framework for adopting cloud computing to address some of these decisions. Currently, we perceive many of these decisions are made in a qualitative manner. Quantifying the basis for these decisions will likely be a unique activity for many businesses. Further research is required to develop a foundation for quantifying these decisions. Version 1, discussed in the following sections, is based on synthesizing key areas of concern form our literature survey.

Decision Framework

Our framework (Figure 4) addresses 15 decision categories which we have selected based on our literature survey and research findings. The first step is to assess cloud computing and determine if it is a viable architectural model for enterprise applications and if the application is adaptable to cloud computing. Clearly, large to massive data analysis programs can benefit from cloud computing using a map-reduce algorithmic formulation. Less clear is whether many business operations, such as order processing and payroll could benefit if they have unique tailored process components. Some of the issues raised by Kaisler and Money (2010) should be answered positively to yield a decision to move to cloud computing as an enterprise architecture platform.

A few issues that affect viability include the following. Applications may not fully utilize the resources of the servers. Cloud computing service demands can vary widely, so the cloud must be sized to support peak demands even though it may often be underutilized. IDC (2007) reported that server overcapacity is costing IT organizations over $140 billion. Inability to meet demand requirements can ripple through the organization and affect multiple work and processing schedules. While virtualization can provide scaling benefits, it is often constrained by other infrastructure components (VLANs, ACLs, network domains, etc.) that create barriers to agility. The fact that each VM runs its own operating system often results in significant duplication and inefficiency compared to symmetric multiprocessing.

Moving to a CCE requires decisions in three architectural categories: service, system, and application. Service architecture – how the service is provided - assesses the user's view of the CCE. System architecture – how the application uses the CCE - assesses infrastructure issues and application architecture – how the application is mapped to the CCE - assesses how the application is mapped to the infrastructure. Selected decisions are identified in the following sections based on our literature survey. We also identify models associated with each decision area.

SERVICE ARCHITECTURE

This category assesses access to the cloud computing environment through four dimensions. Two observations relative to privacy are of significant concern. Many users seemed not to be aware of privacy issues or blithely ignore the implications of placing so much personal data on the Web (e.g., FaceBook, MySpace, YouTube, Twitter, etc.). These sites have been targeted for various scams and are the subject of many child safety concerns. Although CC providers often assert compliance with federal regulations, there is often no explicit way for users to tell that they actually comply and the degree to which they comply.

Allowing a third party to have custody of personal or corporate documents raises significant questions about control and ownership of information. Some of the questions that a user must consider include:

- If the user moves to a competing service provider, can you take your data with you?
- Do you lose access (and control and ownership) of your data if you fail to pay your bill?
- What level of control over your data do you retain: for example, the ability to delete data that you no longer want?
- If your data is subpoenaed by a government agency, who surrenders the data (e.g., who is the target of the subpoena)?
- If a customer's information/data reside in the cloud, does this violate privacy law?
- How does an organization determine that a CCE provider is meeting the security standards it espouses?

Figure 3. Decision model

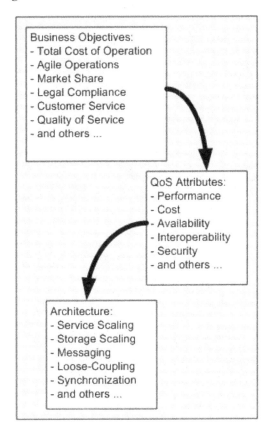

- What legal and financial provisions are made for violations of security and privacy laws on the part of the CCE provider?
- Will users be able to access their data and applications without hindrance from the CCE provider, third parties, or the government?

Regardless of the service agreement between the cloud host and the user regarding governing law, several jurisdictions might claim authority over the data. For example, law enforcement officials in the location in which a particular server is housed likely would assert jurisdiction over the server, even if neither the user nor the cloud host has a major presence in that locale. Users may be surprised to discover that their documents and images stored in the cloud could be subject to laws not of their home state, but instead—or in addition to—some distant state or country with, perhaps, more or less protective laws. This is similar to the situation today in which the U.S. asserts criminal jurisdiction over offshore website operators that accept online gambling from users located in the U.S. Resolving these issues may have significant economic and financial implications for both providers and users.

Placing corporate assets, such as data or applications, into the custody of service providers raises several legal issues. Service agreements and contracts must be tightly written to assign liability in the event data is lost, stolen, or corrupted and to protect the intellectual property embedded in applications. For example, the DOD may require contractors to have plans for continuity of operations in case of catastrophic events. Cloud computing provides a possible solution.

Information stored in the cloud is much more accessible by a private litigant or the government. Traditionally, if an enterprise has information in its possession that a government wants, the government must come directly to the owner of the information to get it. But if the information is in the custody of a third party, the information potentially could be released without the owner's knowledge. The government, for example, can demand the release of the information without the owner of the information being able to object to the disclosure let alone even know their information has been released.

A further problem is the location of cloud resources. Different rules and laws apply in the European Union versus the United States. This will apply to both data and applications residing at a cloud site. Within the US, different state's privacy laws may apply which further muddles the picture. Thus, an organization will have to be very cautious in its usage of cloud computing.

Privacy law is well-established in the United States and many Western European countries, but less so in other parts of the world. As cloud

Figure 4. Decision framework for adopting cloud computing

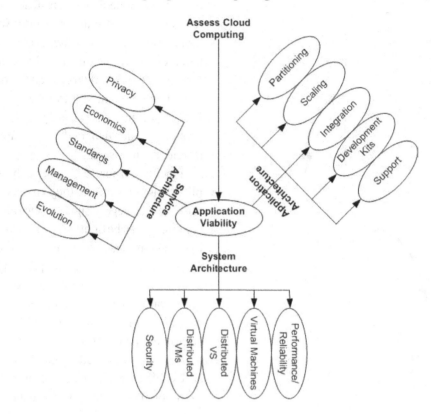

computing becomes a global enterprise due to economic issues, an organization's data may be put at greater risk. The risk is great if there is a breach of privacy. But, the mechanisms do not appear to be in place to track such breaches and notify the right people – victims, responders, oversight officials – with any degree of certainty. With respect to standards, standards need to be developed across all perspectives of cloud computing. Kaisler and Money (2010) offer an initial model for a suite of standards.

With respect to pricing and economics, the diversity of plans which continually change with the evolving competitive marketplace makes it hard to compare them. Current cloud pricing seems to be fixed for certain levels and utilization of resources. Evolving competition and greater model diversity, as evidenced by Linthicum's taxonomy, will yield variable pricing that will potentially undercut fixed

rate cloud pricing. We noted, however, that the cost to convert business operations applications to a cloud computing paradigm is not easily quantified. This will become more difficult as different models and different cloud architectures evolve.

The initial investment in cloud computing varies if one wants to believe the Big Four providers. Organizations wishing to experiment with cloud computing can gain experience for relatively little cost with these providers. A commitment to using cloud computing for many or all of an organization's major applications can become expensive when factoring in servers, storage, communications, security, and programming costs.

As large CCE providers form alliances with professional services firms, the cost to "get on" the cloud will grow substantially. Businesses must make a quantitative decision between the costs of an in-house IT staff versus the use of a professional services firm. Careful analysis is required to determine where the cost of the former exceeds the latter. But, this is just one cost factor. Others include retained knowledge of applications, immediate access to knowledgeable applications developers, understanding of a business's operations, etc. Quantifying these factors makes the decision a complex one. Accordingly, unlike some pundits, we do not believe that private IT staffs will wholly disappear. Rather, we think there will be division of labor based on the complexity of business operations knowledge embedded in an organization's applications. Thus, apps like CRM, HRM, sales management, etc can be farmed out to professional services firms while core business apps containing proprietary information will continue to be developed and maintained in-house.

The last aspect is management from the perspective of the user or client of cloud computing. From our perspective, management is about the amount of user control over the environment. Then environment includes, if a SaaS or other model is selected, provisioning of software applications to the client. The user needs to be aware of the current versions of software relative to the organizational data. It is not uncommon for new versions of software to be installed by the CCE that cause other applications to break. The user must insist upon thorough testing before new versions are installed as well as maintenance and continued provisioning of older versions. In Table 3, we describe some of the decisions to be made in the service architecture.

SYSTEM ARCHITECTURE

Given Linthicum's model, there are a large number of choices for designing system architecture that overlays cloud computing instances (See Table 4). For example, simple three-tier architecture of application, database, and use interface can be distributed across three cloud computing sites.

A distributed cloud computing implementation requires loose coupling among the components in order to ensure that components can be moved to different CCE platforms as well as to scale with workload.

Performance is one of the greatest challenges in managing a cloud-based application. In (distributed) multiprocessor systems, communication between the nodes, depending on the application requirements, can be a significant time component of the overall computation time. With cloud computing, the communication occurs between virtualized nodes which may add time (seen by the user as a lag time), depending on the physical deployment of the processors involved which is, in a cloud scenario, out of the scope of control of the calling operation, to the interaction between application processes.

There may be inherent performance limitations due to software architecture design that will introduce "knees" in performance curves (where performance increases, due to additional processors, degrade significantly) due to design and implementation decisions made for smaller user populations. The authors and other observers have noted these problems in previous projects (e.g., the first author's work in scaling applications and algorithms from 16 to 64 or 128 processors on the BBN Butterfly Parallel Processor). We noted, during our literature review, that this problem has not been adequately addressed in the research community. This issue potentially poses a critical problem in the scaling up or out of SaaS applications if the ability to scale is not considered during the initial design (as it is often not).

Virtualization, which reduces the number of physical servers, can lead to a single point of failure which affects multiple applications, if the business applications are not properly architected and designed for cloud based execution. The tradeoff is to replicate the server hardware, storage, and networking in an alternate data center and increase the operational complexity by implementing an automatic failover capability. Multiple VMs often share one NIC, which means that its capacity is divided among the VMs and thereby reduces their individual performance.

Many cloud implementations assign a suite of physical servers, which may have local memory as well as shared memory, to run a user's application. Recently, some cloud providers now assign virtual machines which may run on a single processor, on a closely coupled set of processors, or may be distributed across multiple symmetric multiprocessors or geographically networked SMPs. Virtual machines often make assumptions about their environment such as the characteristics of the network segments and the storage systems. Conversely, the hypervisor makes assumptions about the VM's behavior. When VMs are replicated on a single host (uni- or multiprocessor), these concerns are resolved through site-specific and non-portable customizations. When VMs are to be replicated across multiple hosts, additional requirements must be considered and adjudicated. For example, consider firewalls with different rules which must often be manually adjusted through communication among multiple administrators.

Many legacy systems utilize a local, centralized storage model, but which may be prone to disk and host failures even when implemented on a multiprocessor system. Distributed virtual storage (DVS) offers scalability and resilience to disk and host failures, but often requires significant modifications to applications to adapt to the DVS model. As CCEs begin to encompass a diverse array of platforms, including cell phones, FLASH drives, and laptops, the DVS must continue to support an application even if some of its storage resources are off-line for periods of time. Thus, a DVS will require peer-to-peer replication across the many storage nodes. Moreover, the DVS will need to ensure consistency in the face of silent replica divergence due to failed nodes or disks and communications corruption. And, the DVS must be optimized for random and mostly exclusive block accesses to large and sparsely populated virtual disk files. The tradeoff between these extra mechanisms to ensure consistency and the need for robust performance given scalability and resilience is yet to be resolved.

Security is a continuing concern in cloud computing, not the least of which is how a CCE provider assures clients that their data and applications are secure – both when they are executing and when they are not. Perhaps the biggest security issue with cloud computing is that an organization's applications and data are no longer located in an environment that it controls. Even though we know that determined attackers can penetrate almost any computer system, there is a perceived protection in knowing that critical and sensitive corporate data is hidden behind the doors of "home".

Within CCEs, the organization's critical data is out in "public"; data storage has been outsourced. CCE providers must instill in their customers the sense of 'home', that their applications and data are protected even though they no longer reside under the organization's roof. An analogy that most organizations may be comfortable with is that of a bank within which our money and financial information are kept. Banks may be robbed or collapse, yet we trust that our money is protected (as a last resort, by the Federal Government's sovereign guarantees, such as FDIC).

Note that this potentially opens a new class of insurance that could be offered to users. In the U.S., homeowner's insurance protects, in a limited fashion, the possessions of one's children who may be residing at college. Similarly, an organization's business insurance could be extended to protect outsourced data.

Providing organizations with that same sense of protection is essential to their perception of the safety of their applications and the data.

Table 3. Selected service architecture decisions

Decision Area	Decisions
Privacy	What are the privacy controls provided by the CCE?
	What are the rules of the jurisdictions where my data might be stored, how do they affect my business operations, and my data?
Economics/ Pricing	How does total cost compare w/ dedicated clusters?
	How easy is it for a user to pay for access to public clouds?
	How many & what types of pricing strategies are offered to the user?
	Can CCE components be purchased piecemeal?
Standard services	What services are provided by the CCE?
	Does the CCE guarantee a service level agreement (SLA)?
	How does the SLA correlate with the services provided?
	What is the guarantee of data access (retention) if a CCE goes out-of-business?
Management	How easy is it for the user to manage an instance?
	Does the organization have the talent to assemble the CCE components at a cost less than acquiring the service from a vendor?
Product/Service Evolution	How often are products & services updated?
	How often are new products & services introduced to meet new customer needs?
	How do you ensure that product/service upgrades will not conflict with each other with a VM environment? With your applications?

APPLICATION ARCHITECTURE

Business applications must often be redesigned to map to the cloud computing environment. In some cases, new applications must be written to replace legacy structures and algorithms that are oriented towards uniprocessors. Scaling and partitioning are closely related (See Table 5).

Cloud computing allows scaling of execution and storage resources as the computational and storage needs of the application grow. Currently, most CCEs require specification of the number of processors and storage units prior to executing an application. Once a processor allocation is made, it is usually static. With virtualization, dynamic scaling becomes possible, because ad-ditional virtual machines and virtual storage can be created and assigned as needed.

An Independent Service Vendor (ISV) might be able to "scale up", "scale out", or both. Scaling up is effected by increasing the computational and storage capabilities of the hardware platform. But, there is a physical limit to this enhancement, even with the current suite of symmetric multiprocessors. Scaling out is affected by expanding the number of independent hardware platforms on which the service runs. While theoretically unlimited, coordination and communication issues among instances of the service can overwhelm the gains in population served. In addition, service application software architectures that were suitable for small populations of users may not be amenable to scaling without imposing significant performance

Table 4. Selected system architecture decisions

Decision Area	Decisions
Performance/ Reliability	How can you perform repeatable benchmarking experiments to gauge scalable performance? To support SLAs? What is the performance 'hit' due to virtualization? Are there algorithmic "knees" that limit the benefits of scaling up? How does one measure reliability versus liability when a CCE provider assumes the responsibility for running "mission-critical" apps?
OS/VM Technology	Are several VM offerings supported, e.g., Xen, etc.? Are several OS offerings supported: Linux, Windows, etc.? How do you determine the best fit between an OS and a VM technology?
Distributed Virtual Storage	Is DVS implemented independent of the compute servers? Does the CCE charge separately for data storage? What is the best communications path to transfer applications and, perhaps, data to the CCE with the best cost-benefit?
Distributed VMs	Does the CCE support a federation of servers across multiple clouds to address scaling and performance? What happens in the cloud (or at a selected service provider) when the set of service demands exceeds the available computational resources? [Is there an analogy to hotel or airline overbooking?]
Security	How do you minimize the risks associated with "living in the cloud"?

constraints. Chong and Carraro (2006) note that the SaaS application must be well-designed to support scaling out.

While many firms are moving entire applications with their associated data to the cloud, others are reluctant to permanently move their proprietary applications and vital data to a public cloud. Integration between in-house applications running on dedicated servers or private clouds and applications running in the public cloud is an emerging area of research and legal concern. A recent evolution is the interoperation of multiple CCEs as organizations distribute functionality across multiple cloud providers per the Linthicum model. This approach allows geographic distribution of cloud services that provides additional benefits, but requires increased complexity and raises additional legal, security, and privacy concerns.

Many cloud computing applications are pieced together as a patchwork of open source software (OSS). While there are benefits to using OSS code, integration of independently written and tested modules introduces many interfaces where security, performance, and reliability can be compromised.

Today, many CCEs provide an implementation of cloud computing based on best practices in standard ways, e.g., "one approach fits all". This seems to work well for many common applications such as CRM, HRM, etc. Complex applications with extensive embedded business operation knowledge or those that provide significant competitive advantage, such as travel reservation systems, may not be easily implementable on the cloud's flexible, but rigid services and platforms. This paradoxical situation may act as a deterrent to moving to the cloud. We expect that as experience with the cloud grows, CCE providers will develop customizable platforms and services that will enable businesses to move mission-critical unique applications to the cloud.

Integration of multiple heterogeneous components raises additional problems: the organization must maintain separate service contracts for each equipment and software vendor, different system management software, additional personnel with specific areas of expertise in multiple hardware and software product vendors, and other recurring costs brought about by a heterogeneous mix of datacenter infrastructure – both hardware and software.

MIGRATION IN THE CLOUDS

Clouds seem to be implemented top-down and, currently, are designed to serve a limited, specific set of use cases and usage modes (Kaisler and Money 2011). Typically, these are web-based applications used by a large interactive community. Presently, cloud computing cannot support users who cannot switch from legacy applications because equivalent cloud applications do not exist. In Kaisler and Money (2011), we suggested an alternative approach where the user is allowed to migrate services to the cloud (under his/her own licenses) provided there is compatibility between the cloud architectures and the applications to be migrated. We proposed that a user be able to migrate data and applications to and from the cloud using a hybrid architecture using the PaaS model. We called this approach "Service Migration".

Table 5. Selected application architecture decisions

Decision Area	Decisions
Partitioning	How do you re-architect your applications to adapt them to the cloud? Is Map-Reduce a viable scheme for your application? Are alternate parallel environments available: MPI, PVM, etc.?
Scaling	Can servers be dynamically (de)allocated as workload varies? What is the increment/decrement of servers or other resources when scaling up or down?
Integration	Is the cloud offering a self-contained or open system? Does the CCE support integration with existing legacy apps? Does the CCE support interoperability with other CCEs? Does the CCE vendor support integration from a heterogeneous mix of components?
Development Kits	What SDKs exist to support application development? Do the SDKs correspond to the applications developed by the organization?
Support	What support services are offered by the CCE vendor? Training? Application development?

We believe that cloud computing is a viable business computational model for small to medium businesses who cannot afford large investments in permanent infrastructure. The scalability, flexibility, pay-as-you-go and minimal upfront investment make CCEs an attractive option for computing services. But, for cloud computing to succeed, they must be able to run their own tailored or uniquely configured applications in the cloud, a capability available in the scientific community, but now becoming available in the personal and corporate usage community.

Cloud computing offers a significant advance in user's and organization's abilities to acquire diverse computing services and data storage at marginal but varying costs. However, unlike an Enterprise Information Technology Architecture (Cohen, Money and Kaisler 2009), which exists (typically as a more standardized single set of co-ordinated resources) for a single corporate entity, a cloud architecture is can be both flexible and heterogeneous in resources: hardware, software, personnel, and legal entities. Cloud computing resource needs for an organization are not actually "simple" and services are not truly standardized. We believe this introduces additional, but tractable, complications when considering the service migration concept.

In Table 6, we introduce a simple model and hypothesis comparing the relative cost/speed for data and service migration in a cloud computing environment (CCE). For data migration, the user sends data into the cloud to be processed by an available server using standard applications. A user can choose the server through one of several mechanisms, including auction, advertised price, guaranteed service, etc. For information migration, the user sends information, which can carry with it its own schema and processing requirements, to a broker who selects the best location based on the processing requirements. In service migration, the user sends applications (perhaps, along with data) to the cloud for processing. The applications transferred may be unique or proprietary to the organization. Finally, in autonomic migration, user services and data reside somewhere in the cloud along with additional information about processing requirements.

The first two migration types implement the Hardware-as-a-Service (HaaS) and Software-as-a-Service (SaaS) concepts, which represent the state-of-the-art.

Service Migration

A service is an integrated application that provides specific functionality to a client. The service provides an API that, among other things:

- Provides a mechanism by which it receives data from the client and emits data to the client
- Provides a mechanism for broadcasting specified attributes and characteristics of the service.
- May provide a mechanism for self-configuration at the client site.

Service migration involves the transport of the service application from a provider to a client for a specified duration. However, numerous issues and challenges must be resolved in order to implement and utilize services within this service migration model. The client's environment must provide certain capabilities and resources to support the service. And, a service migration protocol needs to be established to facilitate service acquisition, installation, operation, and eviction.

In order to enforce the service contract, and enable the service code to know it meets participative conditions, additional infrastructure will be required.

This infrastructure requires a subsystem that:

- Exposes candidate services
- Enables the transaction between provider and consumer to be pre-defined, limited if necessary, and documented

- Applies the service in accordance with the consumers operational context
- Manages the services' life-time including clean-up and removal.

Additionally, it may provide performance feedback and utilization information to the service owner.

Environment Knowledge

A service application should logically incorporate assumptions about the nature of the environment into which it will be integrated to provide the user selection or choice criteria. These assumptions need to be accessible through querying by the putative user prior to contracting for the service or provided as part of the initial service contract, perhaps through the service acquisition protocol. The client, as part of its selection process, needs to know what the service's requirements are to operate correctly and efficiently at the client's site.

If the service is functionally self-configurable, it needs access to an API that allows it to obtain knowledge about it environment and the constraints the environment will impose upon it. Once configured for the host, the service must also exclude operation within an environment other than the one originally contracted. This would prevent the client, for example, copying the service to another processor to use it.

Installation and Migration

Installation and integration encompasses the activities related to accessing a communications endpoint, gaining and leveraging the necessary level of access to operate, persisting the service to the appropriate user store, executing one-time or pre-execution actions either directly on the host operating environment or via a previously installed service support service, pre-execution

validation, and exposing the running service to the host monitoring subsystems.

Linking service application code into a user's computing environment is a challenge. Downloading a service onto a platform is relatively easy. Given the infrastructure mentioned above, it can be invoked using standard OS functions, monitored, and erased when the service contract is fulfilled. Data provisioning and user access issues need to be resolved.

Service Removal

Service removal has two connotations – normal and abnormal termination – but both lead to the same issues. When a service is to be removed from a computer system, the operating system at the CCE site must be able to locate and remove all components of the service. We will assume here a service that is not malicious. From a security perspective, no remnant of the service should remain once it has been evicted from the system.

When a service terminates normally, it should behave in a consistent and predicable manner. It should adhere to the principles and policies that are specified for the platform within which it is operating. Additionally, a terminating service should always invoke its runtime framework, service coordinator, and as necessary, engage the service user to ensure the sequence of shutdown activities acquiesces to other running services.

When a service terminates abnormally – either due to an error condition or because of OS intervention, the service should follow clearly published, well known, and agreed upon sequence of operations as defined by the service contract. This may include, but not necessarily be limited to, sudden termination with data loss, timed termination with user intervention, user informed and termination delayed until the user intervenes, and state-safe partial writes before termination completes.

Table 6. Migration in the cloud

Type of Migration	Cost/Speed
Data Migration Manual Movement	High Slow
Information Migration (Data+Schema+Context) Semiautomatic Movement	Medium Slow
Service Migration Automatic Movement of Data and Information Manual Movement of Applications	High/Low Medium to Slow
Autonomic Migration Automatic Movement of Data, Information and Applications	Low Fast

Security Implementation

Security issues that arise from the dynamic nature of migrating a service can be addressed by making the CCE and its services adhere to the basic Bell-LaPadula axioms of computer security. This means the user must be assured that the downloaded service uses a combination of pre-execution, runtime, and post-execution directive.

Prior to execution, a service contract might require the user to be added to a membership list by an administrator for either the local infrastructure or the service provider or both. As the service loads, its authenticity can be verified via certificate or key exchange. At runtime the service must comply with local execution policies and emit a local system visible trace for logging. Post execution the service should provide user visible signatures, certificates, or keys for return data to be, independent of the service, verified for source and manipulation.

If the client "pushes" the service to the cloud, the service provider system has to be identified to the Client's security system in order to allow the service application code to pass through the firewall and other security systems, including antivirus and spyware checking programs.

Although the client and the service provider have signed a contract, the service provider and client must still be authenticated to each other in order to complete the transaction. Depending on whether the service application code is "pushed" or "pulled", the service provider or client must be approved to access the other's system.

Service Reporting

Owner equities and protections will be important parts of the services. For control (and possible billing verification or validation), a service is likely to report back to its owner the duration or number of times it has been used (or some other similar metric). Client and owner must agree in the contract on what is reported, how often, and what mechanisms are put in place to prevent leakage of information from the client system.

CONCLUSION AND FUTURE WORK

This paper has discussed the challenges that may limit the viability of cloud computing for small to medium-sized businesses where technology, privacy, security, and proprietary information concerns are key to competitive success and efficient operation. We analyzed these concerns through three classes of architectural decisions, and presented a preliminary decision model with the types of decisions that small-to-medium businesses should consider in deciding to move wholly or partially to a cloud computing environment.

This model has raised some interesting research and positioning questions to be addressed from a business operations perspective, including:

1. What impact will public cloud computing services have on organizations' traditional IT infrastructure and processes over the next five years?,
2. What percentage of organizations' current applications are being delivered via a SaaS model? How will this change over time? and
3. Will organizations move to a distributed cloud architecture such as represented by Linthicum's model?

If an organization is going to compete and expand in the cloud marketplace, it has to make decisions about where and how it will compete and attract a sufficient and stable customer base to continue operations. Large businesses seem to be moving to private clouds in order to gain the scalar benefits of cloud computing. Small and medium-sized businesses as well as individuals form the biggest customer base for public cloud computing. For small to medium businesses, early applications for cloud computing include customer resource management (CRM), human resource management, collaboration, and other front office functions. At present we find no likely killer apps for the cloud, rather, easy application integration that delivers cost-effective computing will be the dominating feature. (Social networking app evolution and tactics might change a future assessment.)

We have not addressed how service migration will affect the consumer's ecosystem, e.g., by the transition to service provision and data/information storage in the cloud. We hypothesize that this capability will yield new business models and, perhaps, accelerate a transition from brick and mortar offices to more mobile and distributed organizations. Another aspect of service migration is how multi-enterprise (B2B) interactions and technologies will be affected by service migration. We hypothesize that autonomic migration will enable B2B interactions in interesting ways that need to be explored.

The tradeoff between virtualization versus multicore processing in a private data center from a cost, application development, and resource utilization perspective needs to be quantified. For example, high energy utilization due to increased workload and increased cooling requirements often results during virtualization.

Cloud computing is a new business environment and is a business itself; it is becoming an industry on its own. Thus, business use of CCEs is becoming a business-to-business activity.

We conclude that small private clouds can allow small to medium-sized businesses to assess the use of cloud computing and make the eventual transition of their critical applications to a public CCE easier to accomplish. In particular, micro data centers that support cloud computing applications, traditional business operations applications, and transitional applications are a feasible approach for many small to medium businesses. However, the more issues raised in this and earlier papers that are unresolved by management – technical, legal, operational – should delay, rather than hasten, the move to cloud computing. As a result, we are evolving our model to assist small to medium business in tier decisions on whether or not to move to cloud computing.

REFERENCES

Chong, F., & Carraro, G. (2006). *Architecture strategies for catching the long tail*. Retrieved from http://msdn.microsoft.com/en-us/library/aa479069.aspx

Cohen, S., Money, W. H., & Kaisler, S. H. (2009). *Service migration in an enterprise architecture*. 42nd Hawai'i International Conference on Systems Sciences, Big Island, Hawaii

Desisto, R. P., Plummer, D. C., & Smith, D. M. (2008). *Tutorial for understanding the relationship between cloud computing and SaaS*. Gartner Corporation, G00156152.

Horrigan, J. (2008). *Use of cloud computing applications and services*. Pew/Internet Memorandum.

IDC. (2007). *Virtualization and multicore innovations disrupt the worldwide server market*. IDC Doc# 206035

Jansen, A., & Bosch, J. (2005). Software architecture as a set of architectural design decisions. *Proceedings of the 5th Working IEEE/IFIP Conference on Software Architecture* (WICSA'05). Washington, DC: IEEE Computer Society.

Jha, S., Merzky, A., & Fox, G. (2008). Programming abstractions for clouds. *Concurrency and Computation, 21*(8), 1087–1108. doi:10.1002/cpe.1406

Kaisler, S., & Money, W. (2010). *Dynamic service migration in a cloud architecture*. ARCS 2010 Workshop, Said Business School, University of Oxford, England, June 1, 2010.

Kaisler, S., & Money, W. (2011). *Service migration in a cloud computing architecture*. 44th Hawaii International Conference on System Sciences, Poipu, Kauai, Hawaii, January 8, 2011.

Linthicum, D. (2009). Defining the cloud computing framework: Refining the concept. *Cloud Computing Journal*. Retrieved from http://cloud-computing.sys-con.com/node/811519

Mell, P., & Grance, T. (2011). *The NIST definition of cloud computing. (Draft), SP800-145*. Gaithersburg, MD: National Institute of Standards and Technology.

Sun Microsystems. (2009). *Introduction to cloud computing architecture*. White Paper.

Zimmerman, O., Gschwind, T., Kuster, J., et al. (2007). Reusable architectural decision models for enterprise architecture development. *Proceedings of the 3rd International Conference on Quality of Software-Architectures: Models and Architectures* (QoSA), (pp. 157-166).

ENDNOTES

[1] An earlier version of this paper was presented at HICSS-46. It has been extended and enhanced with additional material for this volume.

Chapter 9
Integrating the Cloud Scenarios and Solutions

Venky Shankararaman
Singapore Management University, Singapore

Lum Eng Kit
Singapore Management University, Singapore

ABSTRACT

Cloud computing adoption is on the rise due to reduced infrastructure resources and a need for agility in meeting IT demands. However, many organizations will still have on-premise applications along side with applications in the cloud, and will have to deal with the challenges that arise from integrating all these applications. In this chapter, the authors briefly introduce the various cloud computing architecture layers, provide detailed cloud integration scenarios, and discuss some of the challenges and present some integration solutions. They also provide points for consideration to help organizations decide appropriate integration solutions to suit their needs.

BACKGROUND

Cloud computing provides a number of benefits that act as key drivers for their adoption. These drivers include optimizing use of hardware infrastructure, offloading the burden of managing various computing resources and thus minimizing IT management overhead, reducing capital and operating costs by obtaining resources on a need to basis and paying for what is used, and ensuring business agility by dynamically meeting the IT needs of the business by scaling up or down to suit rapidly changing market demands of the consumer (Amrhein and Scott, 2009), (Plummer and Smith, 2009) and (Mell and Grance, 2009).

The above drivers have encouraged a number of organizations to adopt cloud computing as a paradigm for offering enterprise solutions.

As more and more enterprise applications are moved to the cloud infrastructure it will lead to a number of integration challenges. For example, organizations will still have a lot of business applications that are not moved to the "cloud" due

DOI: 10.4018/978-1-4666-2187-9.ch009

to regulatory constraints such as HIPPA (Health Insurance Portability and Accountability Act), GLBA (Gramm–Leach–Bliley Act), and general security and NPPI (Non-Public Personal Information) issues. As a result, these on-premise applications have to be integrated with those in the cloud. Additionally, organizations must also face the challenge of integrating cloud-to-cloud applications. An example would be integrating a best of breed SaaS application (e.g. CRM) with another best of breed SaaS application (e.g. ERP).

In the past this best of breed systems architecture problem in which an organization chooses to select the best application software for each of its business functions has often resulted in the need to integrate these silo applications. This led to the emergence of EAI (Enterprise Application Integration) middleware (Linthicum, 2003). EAI supports the creation of new integrated business solutions by enabling applications, databases, interfaces and people to exchange business-critical information in batch mode and in real-time. It includes both the process of creating the solution and the tools and services required to develop the solution. EAI middleware provides capabilities for data transformation, information routing, connectors for invoking services in enterprise applications, process design and process execution. With the maturity of technology most EAI is currently achieved at the data, application and process levels. At the data level, data from various sources is aggregated into a single view. At the application level one application invokes the API (Application Programming Interface) of another application. At the process level, organizations are interested in increasingly looking to streamline entire business processes. A business process is implemented in the process engine component of the EAI middleware and activities in this process invoke services in other applications (Caforiol et. al., 2005). More recently EAI middleware has adopted the web services standards and integration among applications has been achieved through web services

invocation through the SOA framework (Cao et. al., 2007) and (Gu and Zhang, 2010). Within the practice community some refer to this standard based EAI middleware as Enterprise Service Bus (ESB). ESBs help bind the services together within a Service Oriented Architecture (García-Jiménez et. al., 2010). They eliminate point-to-point connection between service provider and service consumer by providing capabilities such as intelligent routing, data transformation, load balancing, and security while also coordinating the flow of service calls. Conceptually, ESBs provide similar functionality to EAI middleware but through leveraging the web services standards and the SOA framework. With the emergence of cloud computing, integration faces a number of new challenges such as limited access to the applications hosted on the cloud through their APIs, additional difficulty in handling version changes to the integration middleware, performance issues due to data latency and security issues due to multi-tenancy and information flow across geographical boundaries.. In Section 3, we give a brief overview of the different cloud computing architecture layers and provide some examples of current vendor offerings for each layer. Section 4 discusses some integration scenarios that organizations are most likely to face. Section 5 highlights some integration challenges that arise within these scenarios. In Section 6, we present the various integration solutions along with some points for consideration when selecting them. Section 7 concludes by highlighting the future trends in integration solutions for the cloud.

CLOUD COMPUTING ARCHITECTURE LAYERS

The traditional layers of a typical IT solution include hardware, software for building applications, software for integrating applications and enterprise applications (e.g. CRM, ERP, small business accounting, etc.). All these layers can be offered as services in the cloud (Zhang and Chen, 2010) as shown in Figure 1.

Infrastructure as a Service (IaaS)

Basic storage, compute capability and network are offered as a service on demand. This may include physical servers, storage systems, network switches and routers. Leveraging this layer, an organization can create an 'image" of the business application including the presentation, application logic and data and deploy on the IaaS cloud. For example, Amazon EC2 and Joyent provide cloud computing infrastructure services. It eliminates the need to buy, install, configure and upgrade hardware, storage devices, and other infrastructure that is used to build applications. This has a direct impact in reducing the capital outlay for IT projects.

Platform as a Service (PaaS)

The software to build a solution is offered as a service on demand. This comprises of two sub-layers namely Application Development and Integration Middleware. However, in some PaaS offerings, these two sub-layers may not be distinct and there is bound to be overlap between these two sub-layers.

Application Development sub-layer helps in building applications and may include IDE tools and standard development environments such as J2EE or.Net. Leveraging this sub-layer, an organization can build custom business applications that run on cloud infrastructure resources. For example, Oracle offers the Oracle WebLogic Server on the Amazon EC2 cloud infrastructure; Windows Azure platform from Microsoft and SaleForce.com offers Force.com. This sub-layer leverages the IaaS layer. It eliminates the need

Figure 1. Cloud computing architecture layers

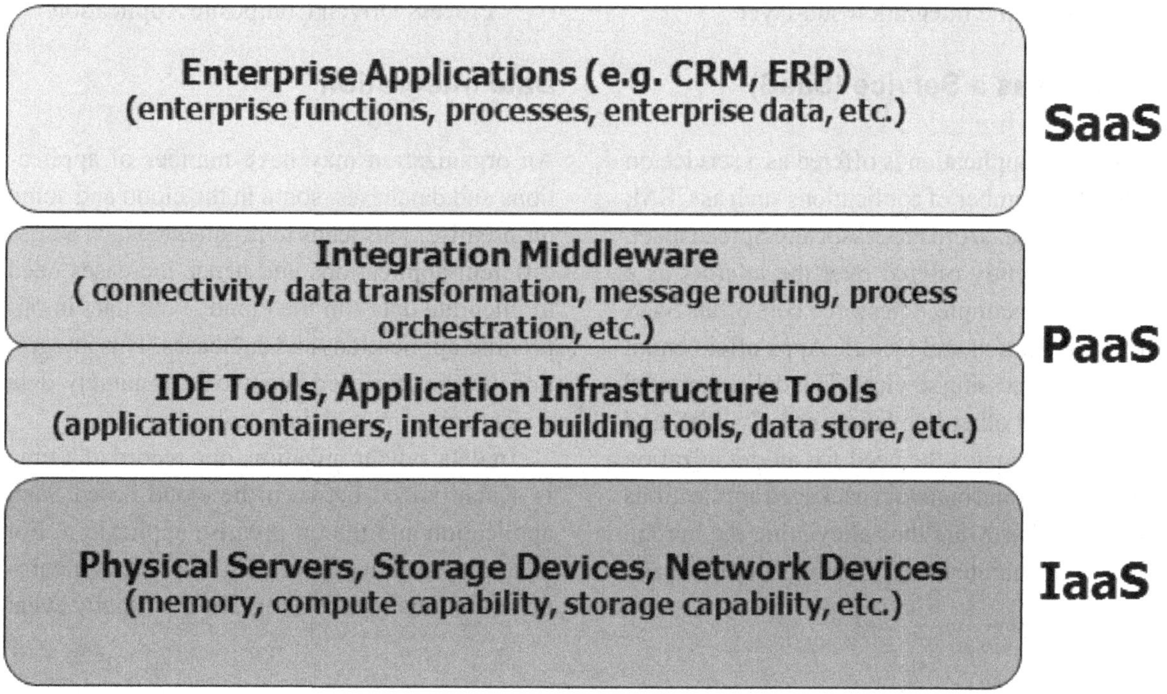

to buy, install, configure and upgrade software that is used to build applications. However, the organization has to spend effort in building the custom applications on the platform and then deploy them in the cloud.

Integration sub-layer can be realized as a software or hardware appliance that helps in integrating applications. This sub-layer provides various integration services such as data transformation, data mediation, routing, and business process orchestration. This sub-layer can be provided as a standalone on top of IaaS. For example, Informatica offers the Informatic on-demand services for data mediation and migration across applications in the cloud, and Dell Boomi offers Atompshere, a cloud based integration service for integrating applications in the cloud. Alternatively the integration sub-layer can be tightly integrated with the application development sub-layer. For example, Microsoft offers the Appfabric as a part of the Windows Azure platform. Appfabric provides some of the integration middleware features such as data transformation. Force.com provides web service APIs for enabling integration with other applications. The remaining sections of this paper will focus on the Integration sub-layer.

Software as a Service (SaaS)

A complete application is offered as a service on demand. A number of applications such as CRM, ERP, Database, Word Processor and Spreadsheet, etc. are currently offered over the internet as a service. For example, Salesforce.com offers SaaS CRM application and Google Apps offers email and word processing services. This delivery model leverages the other two layers namely, IaaS and PaaS. It eliminates the need for an organization to buy, install and maintain packaged applications on its own hardware thus alleviating the burden of software maintenance, ongoing operation, and support.

INTEGRATION BUSINESS SCENARIOS IN THE CLOUD

In order to understand the various integration scenarios in the cloud, let us introduce a fictitious company Zoko. Zoko is a major auto spare parts manufacturer and retailer. Though Zoko is a fictitious company, the scenarios presented are relevant to the automobile supply chain reference framework presented in (Yinglei and Lei, 2011).

Zoko currently uses CRM from Salesforce. com for managing its customers. This is a front office application that manages customer information, opportunity and leads information, quotes, sales information, etc. The back office system is a SAP ERP application that manages inventory, production planning, general ledger and accounts payable. Additionally, Zoko hosts its centralized Oracle Data Warehouse on the Amazon EC2 cloud.

In the context of Zoko, we discuss four different scenarios namely:

- Data Integration
- Point-to-Point Composite Application
- Mashup Composite Application
- Process Driven Composite Application

Data Integration

An organization may have number of applications and databases, some in the cloud and some on-premise. This leads to fragmented data across different applications and hence increases need to integrate data "in the cloud" with data in on-premise applications and databases. This integration may be classified into two types namely, data synchronization and data replication.

In data synchronization, one record at a time is synchronized between the cloud based SaaS application and the on-premise application. For example, customer information updates synchronization. This type of integration is usually event driven, such as when the customer data is updated in the SaaS application, this event triggers the updated record to be copied to the on-premise application. In some instances, data synchronization is also done on a schedule basis such as every two minutes.

In data replication, a large number of records are replicated between the cloud based SaaS application and the on-premise application. For example, copy all cloud-based data from the cloud to on-premise database for ensuring regulatory compliance, disaster recovery, or for reporting and analysis. This type of integration is usually scheduled, such as once every day, week or fortnight depending on the business requirement.

In the Zoko context (see Figure 2), following are some data integration use cases:

- Every time the customer account information is updated by the accounting role in the SAP ERP, the corresponding customer account record in the Salesforce CRM is updated automatically. This ensures real-time consistency of information between Salesforce CRM and SAP ERP (Data Synchronization). Thus the sales team at Zoko has the latest information on customers.
- Every Sunday night millions of rows of customer data are replicated from the Salesforce CRM into the Oracle database. This data is loaded into the appropriate tables to enable reporting and analysis (Data Replication).

Composite Application

Composition is an emerging approach to delivering enterprise solutions by assembling functionality from prebuilt components. This is analogous to getting a prefabricated house assembled rather than having it custom-built. The emphasis is on

Figure 2. Zoko application landscape

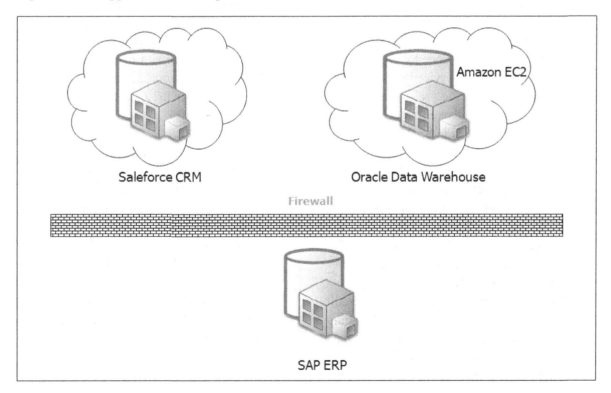

reusing enterprise application functionality instead of building it from scratch (Shankararaman and Eng Kit, 2010). A composite application is one that is composed from existing functionality residing in different distributed applications. Currently, the general trend is to expose functionality in an application as a web service. This enables other applications to consume this functionality by invoking the service. Since there are number of ways to develop a composite application, we present three different integration scenarios namely, point-to-point composite, mashup composite, process driven composite

Point-to-Point Composite Application

In this scenario, only two applications are to be integrated. Each application is able to invoke the functionality (service) of the other application though appropriate service interfaces. In the Zoko context, following are some use cases:

- New customers are created in Salesforce CRM on a regular basis. However, once that customer opportunity reaches a certain stage, the customer needs to be created in SAP. This can be done by invoking the "Create Customer" service in SAP ERP.
- Before creating the sales order, the sales team can invoke "Check Product Availability" service in SAP ERP. This invocation will provide up to date information regarding product availability such as which plant has how many products.
- When converting a sales opportunity in the Salesforce CRM to a sales order, the "Create Sales Order" service in SAP ERP is invoked. The actual sales order is created in the SAP ERP.
- Salesforce users can view customer credit information stored in SAP ERP by invoking the "Read Credit Management Account" service in the SAP ERP. Additionally, the Saleforce user can change the credit limit

of the customer directly from Saleforce by invoking "Create Credit Limit Change Request" service in SAP ERP.

- Once the sales order is created, other services can be invoked in SAP ERP from the Salesforce CRM to enable the sales representatives to monitor orders as they move through fulfillment and billing directly from Salesforce CRM. Furthermore, the sales representative can in real time monitor subsequent related customer transactions in the SAP ERP such as payments, refunds, credit ratings, etc.

Mashup Composite Application

A Mashup is an application that uses content from more than one source that is combined to create single new service that is displayed to the user though graphical users interface (Engrad, 2009). A mashup may require different levels of integration depending on whether the data is read only or can be edited. Usually, the interface is highly interactive. For example, the user can view different content by selecting data from drop down lists. One of the most popular types of mashup composite is a map mashup, where data from different sources are displayed on a geographical map. In the Zoko context following are some use cases:

- Mashup of the sales data from Salesforce CRM with location data from Google map. Thus providing a visual representation of sales target for various geographical regions which are displayed on the map.
- Mashup of the account and opportunity data from Salesforce CRM with order management data from SAP ERP. Thus displaying accounts with open orders.
- Mashup inventory data from SAP ERP with location data from Google map. Thus displaying available material inventory for the various plant lcoations on the map.

Process Driven Composite Application

A process driven composite application comprises a sequence of activities that invoke functionality in different distributed applications. An activity in the process can be human or automated. Human activities require a human to perform an interactive task through an appropriate user interface such as "Approve a Purchase Requisition". Automated activities require the invocation of functionality in an application through a service interface, such as a "Create Purchase Order" in the ERP. The process driven composite application usually requires a BPM tool for modeling and configuring the process details (e.g. activities, service interfaces, etc.), designing the user interfaces, deploying and executing the process. For a more detailed hands-on tutorial on developing process driven composite application, the user may refer to reference (Shankararaman and Eng Kit, 2010). In the Zoko context following is an example use case:

- A Sales Integration Process that integrates Saleforce CRM, a human approval role and SAP ERP. The detail steps for this process are shown in Figure 4.

INTEGRATION CHALLENGES IN THE CLOUD

A summary of challenges faced in the above scenarios are as follows (Pittaro, 2008):

1. An organization's IT team has complete access to its on-premise custom applications hence the IT team can develop integration hooks even when the application has not been "designed to integrate". However, this is not the case with SaaS applications and those custom applications that have been developed and hosted on PaaS. With cloud computing, the IT team has to entirely rely on the APIs provided by the vendor hosting the application. Additionally, integrating one PaaS (e.g. Salesforce Force.com) with another PaaS (e.g. Microsoft Azure) can be quite daunting.

2. When all applications are running on on-premise hardware, operating systems and application platforms, it is easier to handle the impact of version changes. The IT team can adapt and upgrade the integration hooks appropriately to suit the newer versions of operating system and platform. However, with cloud computing, the application, platform and operating system versioning are no longer under the control of the IT team. This situation can become even more challenging when the hardware is hosted by one vendor (e.g. Amazon EC2), the platform from another vendor (e.g. Oracle Weblogic) and the operating system from yet another vendor (e.g. Microsoft Windows).

3. In most cases, traditional on-premise integration is contained within the corporate network. Hence the IT team has a better understanding and control over the network and thus can tune the network to suit integration requirements. Therefore, performance is more predictable. However, with cloud computing, the network distances between the various applications that are integrated are no longer under the control of the IT team. Service Level Agreements (SLAs) with multiple vendors can be different hence it is difficult to optimize the network to suit the integration requirements. Though bandwidth may not be the limiting factor, data access latency will be major issue. The IT team can no longer assume a high performance local access when designing the integration solution. Round trip data exchange between on-premise and SaaS can be an order of magnitude higher than accessing a local database. When large amount of data has to be exchanged between on-premise and SaaS applications through a secure channel, the

implications on performance can be even more profound.

4. As more applications are moved to the cloud, security will become a major concern when data is being exchanged between applications on the cloud with the on-premise applications. This is particularly significant due to the fact that now information flow will have to be controlled across multiple logical and geographical boundaries. Furthermore, use of multi-tenancy implies a need for policy-driven enforcement, segmentation, isolation and governance of security. In order to overcome these security challenges some researchers have proposed security frameworks (Takabi et. al., 2010) and security solutions that can be offered as a service in the cloud (Lan, 2010).

INTEGRATION SOLUTIONS FOR THE CLOUD

There are a number of solutions that can be adopted to satisfy the requirements of the integration scenarios presented above (Pittaro, 2008). We can broadly classify these solutions into the following:

- Enterprise Application Integration Tools
- API Based Integration
- Integration as a Service

Enterprise Application Integration Tools (EAI Tools)

A number of EAI tools such as integration brokers, message brokers, integration appliance, and business process orchestration engine and enterprise service bus (Gu et. al., 2011) are currently being used to integrate applications within and between organizations. Examples of these tools include TIBCO Business Works, SAP Netweaver Composition Environment, IBM Websphere Integration Server, Oracle Fusion Middleware, etc. These tools provide extensive functionality for

data transformation, message routing, adapters for connecting to enterprise systems, graphical interface for modeling and orchestrating complex processes involving both human and automated activities. Additionally, they are proven technologies and have been widely used by many organizations. These tools can also be used to integrate on-premise application with those applications hosted in the cloud through the use of special connectors or adaptors.

There are two deployment options namely, hosting the tools on-premise, or hosting the tools in the cloud (See Figures 3a and 3b). Though the tools are installed on the cloud, very rarely these tools exhibit the cloud characteristics such as elasticity, and multi-tenancy.

The on-premise deployment option is better suited for organizations that already have enterprise integration tools that are currently being used to integrate on-premise applications and looking for options to integrate the newly developed or acquired cloud applications. Moreover such organizations will also have adequate skilled professionals who are trained in installing and configuring the integration tools. The on-cloud deployment option is better suited for organizations that do not have existing integration tools and looking for a solution where they do not have to worry about buying hardware and installing the integration software. This option may also be adopted by systems integrators who develop integration solutions for customer organization where one of the requirements is that no software is installed at the customer site.

Either of the above options is limited by the fact that the enterprise application integration tools were not designed for the cloud and hence may not fully address earlier discussed integration challenges in cloud such as performance, security, dynamic resource allocation and versioning. However, more integration vendors are enhancing and adapting their existing enterprise application integration tools to incorporate the features and functionality required for cloud solutions.

Figure 3. (a) On-premise enterprise integration tools; (b) On cloud enterprise integration tools

Figure 3. (a)

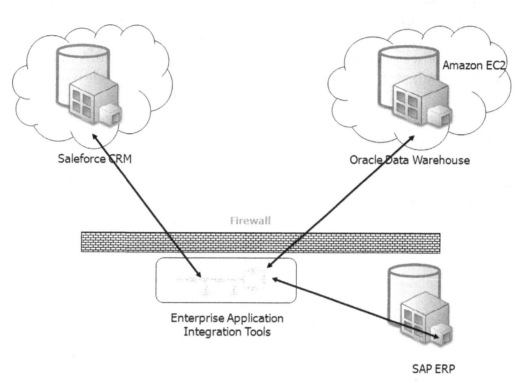

Figure 3. (b)

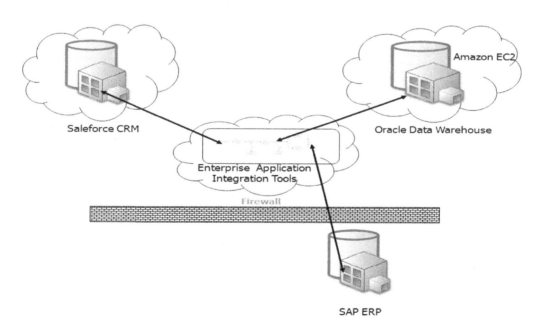

Example

In the Zoko context, the following is an example of a process-driven composite application use case. This use case can leverage the BPM feature provided by the enterprise application integration tool. The process flow is as shown in Figure 4.

The Sales Staff enters a Customer Order in Salesforce CRM application (Human Activity: Enter Customer Order). Following this, the composite application then retrieves the customer credit record from the SAP ERP (Automated Activity: Retrieve Customer Credit). A business rule then verifies if the customer credit is currently below a

Figure 4. Zoko sales integration process

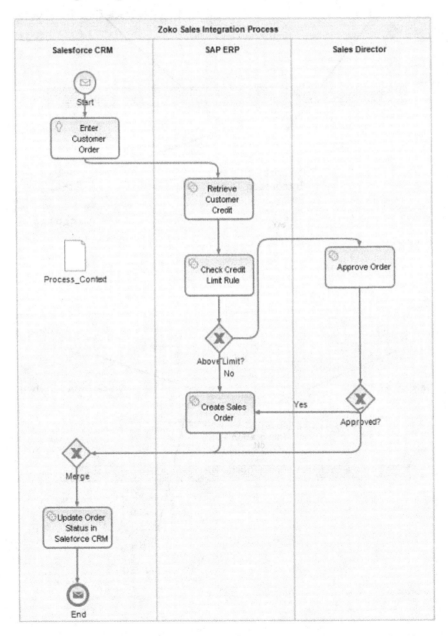

certain credit limit (e.g. $10000) that has been set in the SAP ERP (Automated Activity: Check Credit Limit Rule). If below the limit the process moves to the next activity of creating a Sales Order in the SAP ERP system (Automated Activity: Create Sales Order). The Customer Order is updated in the Saleforce CRM indicating a new Sales Order with Order ID has been created in the SAP ERP (Automated Activity: Update Order in Saleforce CRM). If the credit has exceeded above the limit then the order request is routed for approval by the Sales Director (Human Activity: Approve Order). If the Sales Director approves the order, the Sales Order is created in the SAP ERP system and the Salesforce CRM is updated with Sales Order ID (Automated Activity: Update Order in Saleforce CRM). If the Sales Director does not approve the order then no Sales Order is created and the Salesforce CRM is updated with the appropriate comment from the Sales Director (Automated Activity: Update Order in Saleforce CRM). As seen from Figure 4, the Process_Context object stores data pertaining to the process instance in a persistent store. Hence long lived processes that can extend over a period of time can be supported.

API Based Integration

Many SaaS vendors offer APIs to help integrate back end systems with their SaaS applications. For example Salesforce.com provides APIs to integrate Saleforce.com CRM with the organization's ERP, finance systems or the organization's portal. The APIs offer opportunity for customized integration but at the cost of additional effort to code the APIs. In fact, the APIs only open a secure access to the data and functions, and require a lot of hand coding to handle data translation, routing and process automation. This option is best suited for organizations that have IT savvy professionals who can understand the APIs provided by the SaaS vendors and do some low level coding to integrate them with the on-premise back end applications. In any case, relying purely on APIs without using any integration middleware will lead to point-to-point solutions that can become messy when more than four applications are to be integrated.

In some instances, the API based integration solutions developed by user communities are packaged into application connectors and are sold or made available through the community portals. For example, AppExchange from the Saleforce

Figure 5. Point-to-point integration from Salesforce.com CRM to SAP ERP

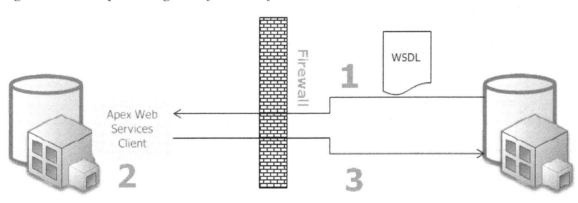

has prebuilt connectors for Outlook, SAP, Google Map, etc. Using these prebuilt connectors can save time and cost. However, over a due course of time the organization may end up having a lot of connectors which are serviced by different small vendors and thus leading to maintenance and upgrade problems.

Example

In the Zoko context, the following is a point-to-point Composite Application use case. We shall illustrate a point-to-point integration between the Salesforce.com CRM cloud application and the

Figure 6. Code generated by Apex – WSDL2Apex (incomplete)

```
public class Binding_T_HTTP_A_HTTP_ECC_CUSTOMERIDQR_DEFAULT_PROFILE {
    public String endpoint_x =
'http://erp.esworkplace.sap.com/sap/bc/srt/pm/sap/ecc_customeridqr/800/default_profile/2/bindin
g_t_http_a_http_ecc_customeridqr_default_profile';
    public Map<String,String> inputHttpHeaders_x;
    public Map<String,String> outputHttpHeaders_x;
    public String clientCertName_x;
    public String clientCert_x;
    public String clientCertPasswd_x;
    public Integer timeout_x;
    private String[] ns_map_type_info = new String[]{'http://sap.com/xi/APPL/SE/Global',
'CustomerERPByIDQuery', 'http://sap.com/xi/SAPGlobal20/Global', 'CustomerERPByIDQuery'};
    public CustomerERPByIDQuery.CustomerERPByIDResponseMessage_sync
CustomerERPByIDQueryResponse_In(CustomerERPByIDQuery.CustomerSelectionByID_element
CustomerSelectionByID) {
        CustomerERPByIDQuery.CustomerERPByIDQueryMessage_sync request_x = new
CustomerERPByIDQuery.CustomerERPByIDQueryMessage_sync();
        CustomerERPByIDQuery.CustomerERPByIDResponseMessage_sync response_x;
        request_x.CustomerSelectionByID = CustomerSelectionByID;
        Map<String, CustomerERPByIDQuery.CustomerERPByIDResponseMessage_sync>
response_map_x = new Map<String,
CustomerERPByIDQuery.CustomerERPByIDResponseMessage_sync>();
        response_map_x.put('response_x', response_x);
        WebServiceCallout.invoke(
          this,
          request_x,
          response_map_x,
          new String[]{endpoint_x,
          'CustomerERPByIDQueryResponse_In',
          'http://sap.com/xi/APPL/SE/Global',
'CustomerERPByIDQuery.CustomerERPByIDResponseMessage_sync'}
        );
        response_x = response_map_x.get('response_x');
        return response_x;
    }
...
```

Figure 7. Custom view of an account record in a Visualforce user interface

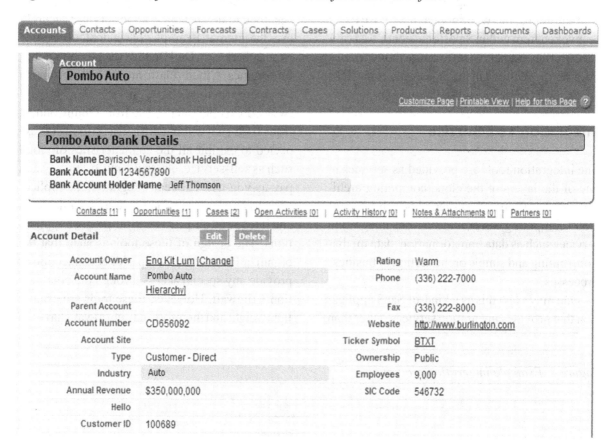

on-premise SAP ERP application using the Web services API.

Salesforce.com CRM is built on the Force.com platform where applications can be customized using a Java-like programming language called Apex that provides integration with Web services utilizing Simple Object Access Protocol (SOAP) and Web Services Description Language (WSDL), or HTTP (RESTful) services.

SAP ERP runs on the SAP NetWeaver platform which enables enterprise application functionality to be exposed as SOAP-based Web services.

For example, suppose we want to retrieve further information about the customer such as the bank details from within a Salesforce.com CRM application, a query can be made to a back-end system like SAP ERP that stores the required information. This integration can be achieved in three steps (see Figure 5).

Step 1: Obtain the relevant web service's WSDL file from SAP ERP. In this example, we can use the Read Customer (CustomerERPBy-IDQueryResponse_In) web service; we shall also assume that the customer ID of the customer stored in SAP ERP is stored in Salesforce.com CRM Account number field in order to make the reference.

Step 2: Upload the WSDL file into Force.com to generate the Apex code stubs that will automatically handle all the logic to construct and parse the XML of the web service messages. Modify the code stubs if required. Following is a snippet of the code generated.

Step 3: Write Apex code (See Figure 6) to call the Web service using the generated code stubs.

That's it; after setting the required security configurations, the Web service in SAP ERP can be invoked from within Salesforce.com CRM (in a user interface or otherwise) to return the necessary information required in the Salesforce.com CRM application (See examaple in Figure 7).

Integration as a Service

The integration tools are provided as services in one of the layers of the cloud computing architecture. As discussed earlier, this sub-layer of cloud computing can provide various integration services such as data transformation, data mediation, routing and simple orchestration of business processes.

One may view this as a kind-of SaaS application that provides integration services rather than business application services. These tools are designed to deliver integration services securely over the internet. Examples of vendor tools include Atomsphere from Dell Boomi (www.boomi.com), Informatica Cloud Platform from Informatica (www.informatica.com), Silver from TIBCO (www.tibco.com) and Cast Iron OmniConnect from IBM (www.ibm.com). These tools are expected to exhibit all the characteristics of cloud such as self-service, elasticity, multi-tenancy and pay-as-you-use. They can integrate cloud applications to on-premise, cloud-to-cloud applications and if required on-premise to on-premise applications. The design of these tools is such that the organization need not setup a VPN connection or provide any special access through the organization's firewall. However, these tools are usually lightweight and therefore may not always have the

Figure 8. Example integration process

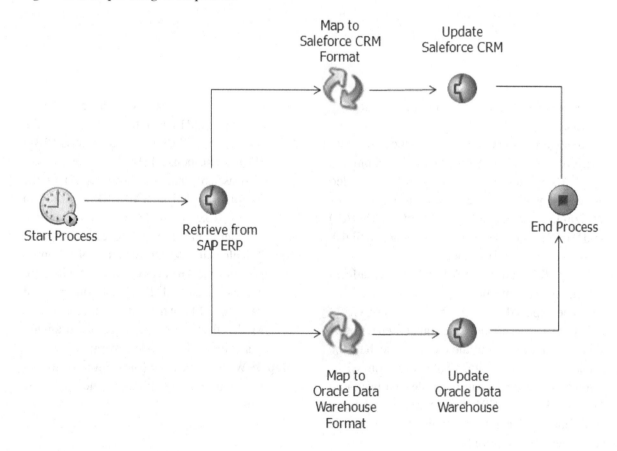

Table 1. Summary of integration solutions

Criteria	Integration Solution
➢ Organization with existing investment in Enterprise integration tools and hardware ➢ Enterprise integration tools form the backbone of the enterprise architecture ➢ Organization with a large pool of IT integration specialists who have delivered a number of integration projects using the enterprise application integration tools ➢ Organization that has very few applications in the cloud (e.g. <2)	➢ Enterprise application integration tools hosted on premise ➢ API based integration, including the prebuilt connectors from the community
➢ Organization with no investment in enterprise application integration tools but seeking to leverage systems integrators to host complex integration solution in the cloud ➢ Organization that are not keen to invest in their own hardware ➢ Organization that do not have sufficient skilled integration specialists ➢ Organization that has some applications in the cloud (e.g. < 4)	➢ Enterprise application integration tools hosted in the cloud and outsourced to be managed by system integrators ➢ Integration as a Service
➢ Organizations that have limited number of skilled integration professionals ➢ Small and medium sized organizations that are not keen to minimize upfront investment in integration software and hardware ➢ Larger organizations that are exploring cloud computing for specific department applications ➢ Organization that have many applications in the cloud (e.g. > 4) ➢ Organizations that aim to automate processes that do not have human activities	➢ Integration as a Service

extensive set of features available in the enterprise application integration tools discussed earlier. For example, most of the enterprise application integration tools provide ability to handle long running processes, which is essential for business processes involving human activities.

This option is best suited for organizations that have limited number of skilled integration professionals and therefore looking for ease of use, minimum maintenance and shorter time to deployment. Mostly, this will fit smaller organizations or to satisfy narrow integration requirements of one department within a larger organization.

Example

In this example we present a scenario from Zoko where SAP ERP is integrated with Saleforce CRM and Oracle Data Warehouse using integration as a service tool (see Figure 8). At 9 pm every day the customer account information from SAP ERP is retrieved and uploaded to the Saleforce CRM and Oracle Data Warehouse. In this process, there is no human role and all the activities are automated. The process is triggered by a Start activity that is scheduled to execute at 9 pm every day. A connection to the SAP ERP is established through a prebuilt SAP connector that is available from the integrations service provider. At the end of each day, recently changed customer account records are retrieved from the SAP ERP. This retrieved data is then mapped to the format of Saleforce CRM and Oracle Data Warehouse applications respectively. In the next step the account data is then added to the corresponding applications, again through the use of prebuilt Salesforce CRM and Oracle Data Warehouse connectors. The integration process is modeled using a GUI and no coding is required to achieve this integration. The integration process is deployed on to the engine in the cloud.

Deciding which solution is the most appropriate for an organization is not that easy and in many cases more than one solution may fit the requirements. Selecting the right approach will depend on a number of factors such as:

- The scope and complexity of the project- is it a strategic project with enterprise wide impact or is it a prototype exploration project with minimum impact
- The approach to managing IT resources- is it mostly outsourced or is there a large pool of in-house IT professionals
- The future strategy of the organization in terms of leveraging the cloud computing paradigm- will future applications be delivered in the cloud or are their regulatory and security requirements restricting where certain applications can be hosted

Table 1 provides a summary of the integration solutions and some pointers to help decide which solution to select based on an organization's needs (Boomi, 2009) and (Lheureux, 2008).

CONCLUSION

As more organizations leverage the cloud computing paradigm, an important consideration will be how to integrate data and functions in the applications in the cloud with those applications on-premise. This integration requirement brings about number of challenges such as limited accessibility to SaaS applications and those custom applications that have been developed and hosted on PaaS; adapting and updating integration hooks to suit the version changes imposed by the SaaS and PaaS; lack of control over the network that makes it difficult for optimizing the network to suit the integration SLA requirements; and need for extra pre-caution to ensure secure integration of applications across the networks. In order to address these challenges a number of integration solutions are available namely enterprise application integration tools that can either be deployed in the cloud or on-premise, API based integration which requires substantial coding, integration as a service tools which are provided as services as part of one of the layers of the cloud computing architecture layers. No one integration solution will be appropriate for all organizations, hence organizations must take into consideration various factors such as available in-house skills, nature and extent of integration, scope of the integration project, existing investment in integration tools and infrastructure to decide the most suitable choice of integration solutions. With further experience gained from real world cloud integration implementations future work will be directed towards developing a Cloud Integration Framework.

REFERENCES

Amrhein, D., & Quint, S. (2009, 8 April). Cloud computing for the enterprise: Part 1: Capturing the cloud. *IBM Websphere Developer Technical Journal.*

Boomi. (2009). *Integration strategies for ISVS.* White Paper. Retrieved from www.boomi.com

Caforiol, A., Corallo, A., & Marco, D. (2005). A framework for interoperability in an enterprise. In Khosla, R. (Eds.), *KES 2005, LNAI 3681* (pp. 97–103). Heidelberg, Germany: Springer-Verlag.

Cao, Y., Chen, Y., & Shen, Y. (2007). The research and application of web services in enterprise application integration. In L. Xu, A. Tjoa, & S. Chaudhry (Eds.), *IFIP International Federation for Information Processing, Volume 254, Research and Practical Issues of Enterprise Information Systems II* (pp. 201-205). Boston, MA: Springer.

Engrad, N. C. (Ed.). (2009). *Library mashups: Exploring new ways to deliver library data.* Information Today.

García-Jiménez, F. J., Martinez-Carreras, M. A., & Gomez-Skarmeta, A. F. (2010). Evaluating open source enterprise service bus. *IEEE International Conference on E-Business Engineering,* November 2010, (pp. 284-291). IEEE Computer Society.

Gu, C., & Zhang, X. (2010). An SOA based enterprise application integration approach. *International Symposium on Electronic Commerce and Security*, July 2010, (pp. 324-327). IEEE Computer Society.

Gu, P., Shang, Y., Chen, J., Deng, M., Lin, B., & Li, C. (2011). ECB: Enterprise cloud bus based on WS-notification and cloud queue model. *IEEE World Congress on Services,* 2011, (pp. 240-246). IEEE Computer Society.

Lan, U. (2010). OpenPMF SCaaS: Authorization as a service for cloud & SOA applications. *IEEE International Conference on Cloud Computing Technology and Science,* 2010, (pp. 634-643). IEEE Computer Society.

Lheureux, B. J. (2008). *SaaS integration: How to choose the best approach.* Gartner ID Number: G00161672.

Linthicum, D. (2003). *Next generation application integration.* Addison-Wesley, 2003.

Mell, P., & Grance, T, (2009). *The NIST definition of cloud computing,* NIST, Version 15, 10-7-09.

Pittaro, M. (2008). *Connecting clouds – Integration and cloud computing.* Retrieved from http://www.snaplogic.com/blog/?cat=23

Plummer, D. C., & Smith, D. M. (2009). *Three levels of elasticity for cloud computing expand provider options.* Gartner ID Number: G00167400.

Shankararaman, V., & Eng Kit, L. (2010). *Create a process driven composite application with CE7.2-introduction.* SAP Community Network. Retrieved from http://www.sdn.sap.com

Takabi, H., Joshi, J. B. D., & Ahn, G.-J. (2010). SecureCloud: Towards a comprehensive security framework for cloud computing environments. *34th Annual IEEE Computer Software and Applications Conference Workshops*, 2010, (pp. 393-398). IEEE Computer Society.

Yinglei, B., & Lei, W. (2011). Leveraging cloud computing to enhance supply chain management in automobile industry. *International Conference on Business Computing and Global Informatization,* 2011, (pp. 150-153). IEEE Computer Society.

Zhang, W., & Chen, Q. (2010). From e-government to c-government via cloud computing. *International Conference on E-Business and E-Government*, 2010, (pp. 679-682). IEEE Computer Society.

Section 3
Security and Legal Issues in Cloud Computing

Chapter 10
Cloud Computing:
Security Concerns and Issues

Shantanu Pal
The University of Calcutta, India

ABSTRACT

In a cloud ecosystem, most of the data and software that users use reside on the remote server(s), which brings some new challenges for the system, especially security and privacy. At present, these security threats and attacks are the greatest concern for the service providers towards delivering a more secure cloud infrastructure. One of the major concerns is data security, implemented by the most effective means possible and the protection of stored data from unauthorized users and hackers. When considering these security issues, trust is one of the most important means to improve the system's security and enable interoperability of current heterogeneous cloud computing platforms. The objective of this chapter is to discuss and understand the basic security and privacy challenges of a cloud computing environment as the security of cloud computing is the greatest challenge for delivering a safer cloud environment for both the service providers and the service customers. With this in mind, this chapter will introduce the risks and possible attacks in a cloud computing environment. The major goal is to specify the security risks and attacks and consider trust of cloud service users for delivering a safer and innovation business model.

INTRODUCTION

Nowadays computer computation has changed immensely. In recent years, the term Cloud has emerged rapidly over the Internet towards faster and more innovative business environments. From the small investor to the big IT (Information Technology) companies, many of whom are now relying on this system. Cloud has several advantages such as its ease of use and maintenance, the relatively low power consumption, unlike other systems and the reductions in overhead for storing and servicing data for companies. However, in spite of these advantages cloud also suffers from different security threats and attacks.

When we sit in a car and start it we don't analysis what is going on under the hood of the car. We do not think about how the motor starts nor are we concerned about the services provided

DOI: 10.4018/978-1-4666-2187-9.ch010

that work the mechanics of the car such as the lights or the brakes or even the radio. We may not consider how the accelerator works or how it causes the vehicle to move fast or slow when we push on or release the pedal. The same thing is going on in the modern computing environment, where we only need the services according to our choices and financial supports available for it. These new type of paradigms are known as Cloud Computing.

In 1969, Leonard Kleinrock said (Buyya, Pandey, & Vecchiola, 2009): "As of now, computer networks are still in their infancy, but as they grow up and become sophisticated, we will probably see the spread of 'computer utilities' which, like present electric and telephone utilities, will service individual homes and offices across the country." In recent years, the term cloud has gained remarkable popularity due to the economical and technical benefits provided by this new way of delivering computing resources, and the pervasive availability of high-speed networks. Businesses can offload their IT infrastructure into the cloud and benefit from the rapid provisioning and scalability. This allows an on-demand growth of IT resources in addition to a pay-as-you-go pricing scheme. This scheme does not require a high up-front capital investment for setup a cloud infrastructure for their businesses. These benefits are in particular more attractive to small industries/ business that prefer to avoid intensive up-front capital investment for their IT infrastructure. However, the benefits of cloud computing is not limited to such small business, from governmental services to defense sectors is deploying their services into cloud platform. These general principles of cloud computing can be implemented on different abstraction levels. While Infrastructure as a Service (IaaS), such as Amazon EC2, provides virtual machines, storage and networks, higher abstractions include Platform as a Service (PaaS) and Software as a Service (SaaS) that provide the actual Web-based applications to the end-users (Cloud Service User or CSU).

In a cloud computing environment, most of data and software that users use resides on the one or more remote server(s), which brings new challenges for the system, especially security and privacy. One major concern is data security, and the most effective ways to protect these sensitive data from unauthorized users and hackers. When considering these security issues, trust is one of the most important means to improve the system's security and enable interoperability of current heterogeneous cloud platform. To date there are several security and trust mechanisms has been proposed to deliver a more secure cloud based application, but many of them are not effective enough to prevent the unauthorized users accesses of the cloud data and also to reduce vulnerabilities in a cloud computing application.

The rest of the chapter is organized as follows: very fist a brief discussion of cloud computing is made to understand the basic architecture of present heterogeneous cloud environment. Then advantages and disadvantages of cloud computing is discussed. Issues, service layers, mode of cloud computing and virtualization are also briefly discussed. Difference security risks and attacks, threats and storage security in cloud data are broadly discussed in this chapter. A view of cloud market orientation is also presented. Finally, the chapter ends with a brief conclusion and future direction.

SECURITY IN CLOUD COMPUTING

Cloud computing is the result of combining Service Oriented Architecture (SOA) and Internet Technologies, mainly Web services and virtualization (Brock & Goscinski, 2010). While cloud computing has made resources accessible to the end users, this technology made resources vulnerable (primarily from sharing same resources and virtualization) for different security threats and attacks. Research is ongoing for the improvement of performance, reliability or scalability in a cloud platform; security becomes an important issue for delivering a safer business environment to the users.

Since cloud computing is an instantiation of distributed computing it brings its own inherent set of security problems. In particular: data privacy and access control. There is also a risk of data theft from machines in a cloud environment, by rogue employees of CSP or by data thieves breaking into service providers' machines, or even by other customers of the same service if there is inadequate separation of different customers' data in a machine that they share in the cloud. These problems belong among three basic security concerns (Brock & Goscinski, 2010) in a cloud computing environment: Resource protection (that is strongly associated with the identity administration); User provisioning (communication and storage security) and Authentication.

Security Issues and Privacy Challenges

Security development for cloud computing is still in its initial stage, and the biggest obstacle is data security. One of the major security challenges is how to guarantee the authenticity of cloud service users (CSU) in a cloud computing environment (Hwang, 2010). There are several security threats and attacks that are possible in cloud (Sedayao, Su, Ma, Jiang, & Miao, 2009) can be defined as: (1) Protection of private data towards user side. (2) Protection of private data towards service provider side and (3) Protection of sensitive and private information in the server place or cloud storage. Several attacks are possible that can breaks the security of a cloud computing environment, such as leakages of data (Papadimitriou & Garcia-Molina, 2011) by service provider, security threats at cloud storage; even misuse of others private data due to the lack of separation in cloud data warehouse.

Securing cloud storage (Mowbray, Pearson, & Shen, 2010) is suffering from a bulletproof

methodology which can protect sensitive information effectively and efficiently from unauthorized users at cloud storage (Subashin & Kavitha, 2011). Basic concerns for providing cloud security is to establish trust with the end users and CSP in a cloud computing environment (Chow, Golle, Jakobsson, Masuoka, Molina, Shi, & Staddon, 2009; Zhu, 2010). There is no such basic solution exists for assuring data security between the end users and service providers at present heterogeneous cloud computing environment.

Security of user's data can be reflected in the following rules of implementation (Zhu, 2010) as follows:

- **Privacy of User's Storage Data:** Cloud storage cannot be viewed or changed by other people or user including the CSP.
- **User Data Privacy at Runtime:** User data cannot be viewed or changed by other people or user at runtime (loaded to system memory).
- **Privacy when Transferring User's Data through Network:** It includes the security of transferring private data in cloud computing center Intranet and Internet. It cannot be viewed or changed by other people or user as well.
- **Authentication and Authorization:** These are needed for users to access their data. Users can access their data through the right way and can authorize other users to access the same.

System Management Challenges

The flexibility and adaptability offered by cloud, facilitates the focus of businesses on their core objectives, rather than becoming heavily involved in strategic IT decisions regarding infrastructure. Whilst easing system management in this respect the cloud computing paradigm also presents some challenges for this system management issues

(Dodda, Smith, & Moorsel, 2009). Whereas from the management's perspective, the following three characteristics are essential for any enterprise cloud which can be defined as follows:

- **Dynamic and Automated Configuration:** Configurations are dynamic and automated (or semi-automated) in varying and unpredictable ways and possibly even include event-driven conditions.
- **Scalable System Management:** Systems management technologies are scalable so that they are manageable in aggregate conditions (such as integration of business constraints with infrastructure constraints).
- **Secure Information Assurance Capabilities:** A cloud should secure and has the necessary information assurance capabilities.

Security Risks and Attacks

Security risks and attacks may be caused due to the (1) Internet Problem (bugs of storage system), (2) Power failure, (3) Communication Problems. Man-in-middle attacks, Dictionary attacks are very well known attacks in this case. Rootkit and system files attacks (Zhang, Xu, Liu, Zhang, & Shen, 2006) are also important issues for securing cloud data storage.

There is no slandered organization or specification set for the cloud computing security consideration (Li & Ping, 2009; Bleikertz, 2010; Hamid, Nezhad, Stephenson, Singhal, & Castellanos, 2009). Even PaaS and SaaS don't have related cloud computing standards yet. Most current systems exploit mature protocols and have variety kinds of service forms. But remark on this issue is that, it is quite impossible to provide standardization for any specific the cloud services. Because this is an emerging field of technology and it is impossible to predict or maintains standardization for this specific service oriented infrastructure.

In numerous studies different security risks of cloud computing environment are discussed. But all agrees with the fact that, this new model of delivering services suffers from numerous attacks and risks. These risks inherent in cloud computing are similar irrespective of the cloud model in use; however, there are unique security and information assurance requirements for each cloud deployment model. Like, security requirements for private clouds are different from that of a public cloud environment.

Security Threats in Cloud Computing

Among the requirements of disseminating the cloud computing services, acquiring reliability, availability and compatibility are in active discussion in present computing community (Oh, Lim, Choi, Park, Lee, & Choi, 2010). Different types of system architectural and service deployment models are present in a cloud computing environment where security risks in each model are also different from each other (Bamiah & Brohi, 2011; Martignoni, Paleari, & Bruschi, 2009). Use of virtualization is the source of a significant security concern as multiple VM run on the same server. Therefore a new concept for removing the virtualization layer is presented in (Keller, Szefer, Rexford, & Lee, 2010; Szefer, Keller, Lee, & Rexford, 2011).

Cloud computing is about gracefully losing control while maintaining accountability even if the operational responsibility falls upon one or more third parties. But even though, as clouds do have benefits, they still have security challenges that need to be addressed effectively as follows:

- **Privileged User Access:** Sensitive data processed outside the enterprise brings with it an inherent level of risk about how their data is being processed and handled so that sensitive data should not be exposed to un-privileged CSUs.

- **Regulatory Compliance:** It is clear that the customers are ultimately responsible for the security and integrity of their own data, even when it is held by a CSP. Traditional service providers are subjected to external audits and security certifications. It is also necessary for the cloud customer to pay precautious attention to the terms and conditions that CSP should give the services (through Service Level Agreement or SLA) of customer compliance according to their policies (Casola, Mazzeo, Mazzocca, & Venticinque, 2004).
- **Data Location:** CSP will be responsible for storing customer's sensitive data but the customer or the CSUs not aware of process that are running insider the service provider machines and where these data are stored. Customer should inquiry the service provider about commitment for protects their sensitive data and should obey service provider's policies.
- **Data Segregation:** Data in cloud storage is typically in a shared environment alongside with the data from other customers. Encryption is effective but is not to provide cure-all protection. It should find out what is done to segregate data at rest (cloud storage).
- **Recovery in the Case of Disaster:** Even if customers do not know where their data is stored, the CSP should inform the customers about what will happen to data and service in case of a disaster.
- **Long-Term Viability:** Ideally, CSP will never go broke or get acquired and swallowed up by a larger organization. But customers must be sure their data will remain available even after such an event.

Trust and Reliability in Cloud Computing

In a cloud application, information crosses the traditional boundaries and passes through non-trusted users/ clouds. Generally, clouds are non-trusted since the guarantee provided regarding the origin and the transformations are minimal, unclear or unreliable. So provenance can be forged or tampered by the unauthorized CSUs. Following security elements (Sakka, Defude, & Tellez, 2010) are the most important means to ensure trustworthy or provenance in a cloud computing environment.

- **Integrity:** Integrity is the assurance that provenance data is not tampered. Any forgery or tampering in provenance records should be detected by the system.
- **Availability:** An auditor can check the integrity and the correctness of provenance information in cloud.
- **Confidentiality:** Provenance information should not be public, only authorized authorities (such as trusted CSU) can access it. This means that the systems must have the confidentiality of data.
- **Atomicity:** At storage time, both provenance and data should be stored or neither should be stored.
- **Consistency:** At retrieval time, data returned should be consistent with provenance.

Trust in cloud computing is also discussed in literature (Rooy, 2010). A privacy regulation in emerging technologies surrounded by uncertainty is discussed (Ruiter & Warnier, 2011) where authors clarify the uncertainty relating to privacy regulations with respect to cloud computing and to identify the main open issues that need to be addressed for its further research. Some of the key features of evolving future Internet business-driven services as follows can be addressed as follows (Lee & Crespi, 2010):

- **Ubiquity:** For providing anywhere-anytime service with 'connecting to anything' feature, such as, seamless mobility between heterogeneous networks using convergence devices. Cloud computing archi-tecture maintains the same to deliver its services to the end users.

- **Personalization:** For personalizing fea-tures of application and services in a cloud environment.
- **Handy Access:** For easing access to servic-es through various terminals using simple, intuitive and consistent user interface(s).
- **Intelligence:** For providing convenient services with automatic recognition and recommending of user's interests and preferences.
- **Broadband Services:** For delivering mul-timedia information including data with large traffic volume due to increase of con-nected devices and increase of bandwidth required by services and applications.
- **Quality and Convergence:** For providing customizable QoS (Quality of Services) from end-to-end across the different pro-vider networks and for offering services in an integrated way.

DATA SECURITY IN CLOUD STORAGE

As it has already discussed that the most important part is to provide data security in cloud platform for delivering a safer and innovative business ap-plication. Many proposed techniques are available at present and those will be discussed categori-cally in this section with the view of data security, privacy and resource protection.

Authentication and Trust Development

Trust development can assure a safely data transac-tion in a cloud computing environment but it is not enough to prevent data leakages during the com-munication. In literature (Li & Ping, 2009) authors

reviews and analyze several trust models (focused on dynamic trust model) and then uses domain trust concept in their proposed model. Proposed method separates the client (or customers) and server (or providers) in the system; then designed different trust strategies for them. It is a domain based (trust domain) model which introduced a novel cloud trust approach to solve the security issues in a cross-clouds environment in which cloud customer can choose different providers services and resources in heterogeneous domains (relations between trust domain and open cloud environment). In this model, trust recommenda-tion is treated as one type of cloud services just like computation or storage.

Author's claim that this model successfully established a large scale 'trust recommendation' in a cross cloud platform; achieves both identity and behavioral authentication. This model can also be used in a large-scale and completely distributed cross-clouds environment. But data security for client data and stored data at the server side not discussed in this literature. No vulnerabilities issues are mentioned against this trust model. Authors might secure the authenticity but how to maintain the integrity of data, not reflected in this model. It is also noted that recommendation factor and a threshold value for trust decision is used in the model. To establish a cross cloud security prototype system and implement the proposed model is in the test-bed; as referred the future work for this approach.

Secure Document Service

Basic objectives of 'data security' for user's data residing in a cloud computing environment are discussed in (Xu, Huang, Huang, & Yang, 2009). Authors have proposed a new conceptual architec-ture where they separates contain and format from a document, before handling and storing its data into a remote cloud server(s) (because the most important information's of a document is stored in the content and format part, particularly in content part). They optimized authorization methods (using encryption functions) for access of data base for the authorized CSUs. This model provides an efficient methodology to guarantee the privacy of user's sensitive data in a heterogeneous cloud computing environment. Authors also claimed that their proposed 'secure document service mechanism' in a cloud environment is authentic. They focused on data leakage and hacking from an unauthorized user. It is also mentioned that partitioning of the document prior to handling and only updating the modified partition could reduce the overhead of document service and the possibility of the whole document being damaged and hacked. This model established a reliable approach for protecting cloud's data from being hacked or leakage and optimized an authorization method to authenticate CSUs. But it is a theoretical concept; no experimental results are given. It is also difficult for handling large documents by this approach, so it is not been possible to apply this service model to huge data bases. If the handling of data that only changed punctuation or a letter happened in a very large partition, the efficiency of transferring and storing document would also be affected. Moreover for the authentication part public-key cryptography is used.

Cryptographic Cloud Storage

Federated identity management (which is a public key encryption technology) together with Hierarchical Identity-Based Cryptography (HIBC) is used (Yan, Rong, & Zhao, 2009) to secure the cloud services. As current solutions have some disadvantages (in terms of security and privacy), authors depicted the principles of identity-based cryptography and hierarchical identity-based cryptography then try to find out how the properties of HIBC will fit well with the security demands in a present cloud platform scenario.

Authors showed that using this method not only key distribution but also the mutual authentication can be greatly simplified in a cloud computing environment. In their proposed model user and server that reside in cloud have their own unique identities. Authors also pointed how the users and servers in the cloud can generate secret session key without message exchange and authenticate between each other with a simple way using identity-based cryptography. The approach simplifies the public key distribution between the client and the server.

More over federated identity is a standard mechanism for different organization to share identity between them and it can enable the portability of identity information across different networks. Using HIBC user and server do not need to ask for a public key directory to get the public key of other users and servers, as in traditional public key schemes.

A discussion on the problem of building a secure cloud storage service on top of a public cloud infrastructure is drawn (Kamara & Lauter, 2010) where the service provider is not completely trusted by the customers. They described a possible architecture for a cryptographic storage service at a high level. This includes data processor (DP), data verifier (DV) and token generator (TG). This paper described both consumer and enterprise scenarios with the benefits of cloud storage in cryptographic manner. Enterprise and customer model described in this approach are conceptually strong.

The core properties of cryptographic storage are:

1. Control of data is maintained by the customer and
2. The security properties are derived from cryptography.

But this paper does not focus on the dynamic approaches for the cloud storage, or any other distributed system environments to protect the cloud resources. Security vulnerabilities associated with customer or vendor's perspective is still missing in this literature. It only described the traditional cryptographic approaches for storage and to access data from data warehouse. Moreover no experimental results are given against their approach in spite of few examples.

Securing Data at Rest

Security approach for 'data at rest'; which is simply data or information stored in a disc in a cloud computing environment (Sedayao, Su, Ma, Jiang, & Miao, 2009). Proposed model protects data from other users in the system as well as ensure the data security from the 'system administrator' or service provider who may read the user's private data (one of the most important concerns towards security challenges in cloud computing environment). This technique protects data at rest or disc while being easy and cheap to implement. Users are in exclusive control of the private key, which the CSP has no view or control over. Authors mentioned that their proposed method can solve confidentiality of data, stored on a cloud computing infrastructure (a key barrier for enterprise cloud adoption).

But this model does not protect the modification of data stored at rest. Therefore this model achieves the confidentiality but not integrity. It does have some notable limitations, this model works only for a process that produces data on a host (virtual or real) that is collected for use by some other host (because concept of public and private key). This model use traditional cryptographic concept and nothing is mentioned about how this model would fit for a dynamic cloud environment.

Security issues in the cloud computing is discussed in (Onwubiko, 2010). Author described the need for cloud computing with basic cloud architecture and proposed cloud security

relationship framework to assess cloud offerings, provides a systematic assessment of cloud computing services based on cost, capability and security perspectives. As a whole this literature discussed risk and security issues but no prototype or practical implementation are given to support the statement.

Securing Data, Respect to Dynamic and Web Approaches

Implementation of a secure dynamic trust mechanism for ad hoc type's networks, to secure a data transfer from a non-trusted party is discussed in (Zhang, Xu, Liu, Zhang, & Shen, 2006). This paper is about Trust Extended Dynamic security model (TED)' which is based on well known BLP and Biba model.

Proposed model imports the concept of reliability to reflect the trustworthiness of subjects and objects. Authors analyzed Rootkit and System Files attack regarding security issues. These are the examples of such attacks that involving processes and objects respectively. Proposed model successfully fits to prevent these (Rootkit and System Files) attacks. No doubt, this model provides a new security design concept; provided by trusted computing. Process (here subject) in conventional security models inherits the security properties of the user who runs it, but the trustworthiness of the running process itself and input data is ignored in this approach. This security models cannot resist running malicious codes. Moreover, most of this model does not satisfy the requirements of some high-assurance environments, in which confidentiality and integrity are needed at the same time.

Literature (Tobarra, Cazorla, Cuartero, & D´ıaz, 2005) described the protocol, uses and examples of traditional Web Service Security (WS Security). This literature presents a Web service application (a software license server) that studies security issues by means of WS-Security. In order to analyses of this Web service security, authors built the SOAP (Simple Object Access Protocol) messages exchanged policy by the client and the server and then translated these messages into Casper syntax in order to verify some security properties. The WS-Security must guarantee the following results:

1. Confidentiality of username and password in the requesting message, and the product key or code element in the response message and
2. Integrity of the full SOAP envelope (Tsai, Wei, Chen, Paul, Chung, & Zhang, 2007).

As the paper focused on WS-Security; a protocol is implemented that extends SOAP in order to implement message integrity and confidentiality. Building a model of the system which allows proving that WS-Security (working together with other protocols such as WS-Addressing and/ or WS-Reliable Messaging) is a good option in guaranteeing the security of Web services (including replay attacks); illustrated as the future work for this research.

A trust approach for Web security is proposed in (Garcia & Felgar, 2008). This approach integrates WS-Trust with standards policy and ontology, which are used to preserve privacy and to develop a suitable Web security for business markets or enterprises. Proposed approach in this literature is suitable for establishment of trust relationships among software systems representing organizations in the dynamic Web service environment such as token service (trusted third-party authorities) or policy based mechanism used for trust establishment.

Approaches in this proposed trust model looks towards dynamic service environments with a view that combines WS-Trust, WS-Policy and OWL introducing to support the establishment of trust relationships with privacy preservation in Web service technology. Main contribution of this paper is extending the trust management approach for Web services with the use of semantic policies to enable service participants and to establish trust relationships in conformity with privacy policies. Where the current approaches does not offer a mechanism for integrating trust and privacy policy management. But no case study or experimental results are given to support this approach. There may be a chance to work with this approach in future with a suitable case study and the constraints against this model can be measured. Moreover In this approach, the establishment of trust relationships is controlled by using policies that are used during different phases of Web service life cycle as:

1. At design time, service providers define policies describing privacy preservation properties of their Web services and tokens, that must be presented and proved by the consumers and
2. At runtime, service consumers define policies stating their tokens and privacy preservation properties that should be offered by the Web services.

Policy-Based Mechanism

A policy-based obfuscation and de-obfuscation mechanism used (Mowbray, Pearson, & Shen, 2010) to secure cloud data. In this paper, authors described a privacy manager for cloud computing that controls policy-based obfuscation and de-obfuscation of personal, sensitive, or confidential data within cloud service provision. Author's claims that, using this approach cloud computing users may reduce the risk of their private data being stolen or misused, and in addition assistance may be given to cloud computing providers for helping them to conform privacy law. They have also described different possible architectures for such privacy management approach in case of a cloud computing environment with algebraic description of obfuscation features provided by their proposed privacy manager. How the policies may be defined to control such obfuscation is also discussed. But the proposed solution is not suitable for all cloud applications.

In literature (Casola, Mazzeo, Mazzocca, & Venticinque, 2004) a policy-based approach is presented to manage security and personalization. They designed a hybrid infrastructure based on Web services in which policy enforcer mechanisms are managed both in a centralized way by the registry server and in a distributed way, such as each service implements security mechanisms to authenticate and authorize users. Authors focused on the issue of security measures when to integrate several distributed systems. To address this problem, they first introduced the adoption of policy-based approaches which are able to split security and application specific problems. They also investigated two security models for managing policies to finally propose their application over a hybrid security mechanism. This literature also focused on Web services and introduces two architectural choices as:

1. Centralized security mechanisms, enforced on the access point,
2. Distributed security mechanisms, enforced on each single service provider.

Proposed hybrid security mechanism overcomes the limitation of classical models (e.g. the pure centralized one and the pure distributed one) and to allow the exploitation of more flexible authentication and authorization mechanisms.

Authors focused on security at application level, in particular on:

1. Identification and Authentication and
2. Access Control Authorization, focused on distributed environment.

But this is an extended model of the well known UDDI (Universal Description, Discovery and Integration) register. This model not mentioned anything about the modification and delete or change of information. It only authenticates and manages the distribution of databases (in several distributed systems) over the users. How several vulnerabilities and attacks can be handled through this model is not discussed. Therefore this model proves authenticity but not integrity. In future it may be possible to work with this literature to measures the different security attacks against this model.

Web Threats and Data Security with Agent-Based Systems

It has been already discussed in previous sections that cloud computing is an emerging technology (Qian, Luo, Du, & Guo, 2009) over the Internet, hence we should be careful about the secure Web applications to enhance the data security and confidentiality in a cloud computing environment for both the users and service provider's perspectives. This section will discussed about Web threats and agent-based system architecture for securing data communications in a heterogeneous cloud computing environment.

In (Panda & Mangla, 2010) authors mentioned about the malware-related data breaches which reached pandemic proportions, resulting criminals discover that Internet crime is easy to commit and highly lucrative. It can be predicted that with a few hundred dollars, a cyber criminal can begin a career of breaking into computers to steal identity and confidential data. This paper covers the current and emerging trends of stealth malware e.g. moving primarily to the Web, since most organizations allow Web traffic into the network. They also mentioned about the advances in network security technologies that use multi-phase heuristic and VM analysis to detect as well as mitigate the damages that are the results from malware-related data thefts.

In (Bhuiyan, 2010) authors presents an overview of Online Social Networks (OSN) based on their most recent research work. They mentioned that rapidly growing Internet is facing enormous challenges due to the unauthorized data uses and leakages through the non-trusted users during transmission. In this literature, authors have reviewed the state-of-the-art technology on the trust in online social networks and presented the result of their survey in the relationship between trust and interest similarity groups, which strongly justify their proposed study. The experimental results support the assumed hypothesis of positive relationship between the trust and interest similarity of the users.

A trust model for multi-agent recommender systems is presented in (Lorenzi, Baldo, Costa, Abel, Bazzan, & Ricci, 2010). A user's request for a travel recommendation (taken as an example) is decomposed into several subtasks by the system, corresponding to the travel services. Agents select tasks autonomously, and accomplish them using knowledge derived from previous solutions or with the help of other trusted-agents. Agents maintain local knowledge bases and when requested to support a user in a travel planning task, they may collaborate exchanging information stored in their local knowledge bases. During this exchange process trusting other agents is fundamental. It helps agents to improve the quality of the recommendations and to avoid communication with unreliable agents in the system. In the proposed model, trust is used to allow agents to become experts for a particular subtasks and helping them to generate better recommendations. Authors also proposed and validate a multi-agent trust model showing the benefits of such model in a travel planning scenario. The proposed model has two important features as:

1. Agents become experts in specific types of tasks during the recommendation cycles, using the computed confidence degree and

2. The communication process between agents is improved using the trust degree, i.e., avoiding unnecessary communication.

One of the major disadvantages found in this research is that, calculation of trust degree is not done uniformly. Authors did not take successive iteration to measure updated trust value for any users. Trust degree decreases for any successive communication but not increases after any successful communication.

Some agent-based software development models are discussed (Boss, Malladi, Quan, Legregni, & Hall, 2007; Madejski, 2007) where security issues involved and propose protocols for securing agent migration. Trust evaluation for Web application is discussed in literature (Costa, de Oliveira, & Braga, 2007). Trust in multi-agent system is presented in literatures (Liau, 2003; Ramchurn, Huynh, & Jennings, 2005; Lu, Lu, Yao, & Yip, 2009). An integrated trust and reputation model for open multi-agent systems is presented in literature (Huynh, Jennings, & Shadbolt, 2006). Authors introduced a reputation multi-agent system (Wang, Zeng, & Yuan, 2006), SemTrust, which enable Semantic Web to utilize reputation mechanism based on semantic similarity between agents. In (Szczypiorski, Margasiński, Mazurczyk, Cabaj, & Radziszewski, 2008) TrustMAS: Trusted Communication Platform for multi-agent systems is discussed. Literature (Kramer & Rybalchenko, 2010) pointed about a multi-modal framework for achieving accountability in multi-agent systems. In (Montaner, L´opez, & Rosa, 2002) development of trust in recommender agents is discussed in details. A review is presented (Talib, 2010) on security framework of cloud data storage, based on a multi-agent system architecture and development.

Cloud Computing and Internet Data Center

There is no doubt that the emergence of the cloud computing paradigm promises flexibility and adaptability through the on-demand provisioning of compute resources. In contrast to the conventional approach of provisioning compute resources as physical entities, the cloud computing paradigm facilitates the provisioning of logical compute resources from a given provider accessible over the infrastructure of the World Wide Web (Dodda, Smith, & Moorsel, 2009).

Internet is on the edge of another revolution, where resources are globally networked and can be easily shared. Cloud is one of the main components of this paradigm (Lombardi & Pietro, 2010) that renders the Internet a larger position where resources are available to everyone as services. In particular, cloud nodes are increasingly popular even though unresolved security and privacy issues are slowing down their adoption and success. Indeed, integrity, confidentiality and availability concerns are still open problems that call for effective and efficient solutions. Cloud nodes are inherently more vulnerable to cyber attacks than traditional solutions, given their size and underlying service-related complexity that brings an unprecedented exposure to third parties of services and interfaces.

In (Cavoukian, 2008) privacy issues of cloud computing is discussed. Thais paper explores the possible technological solutions to ensure that individuals will be able to exercise informational self-determination in an era of network grid computing, exponential data creation, ubiquitous surveillance and rampant online fraud. In literature (Sakka, Defude, & Tellez, 2010) authors presents information provenance challenges in cloud computing environment and determined how it can serve to enhance the information integrity, which

focused on services for electronic documents; more precisely storage and archival services.

In (Zheng, Sun, & Zhou, 2009) authors explores a framework about the applications of cloud computing in Internet Data Center (IDC) with the target of building a public information factory, proposes the framework of cloud computing based in IDC and probe into how to build cloud services over the cloud platform in IDC with a target of building a public information factory from the viewpoint of telecom operators.

Cloud Computing and Networking Security

In (Oh, Lim, Choi, Park, Lee, & Choi, 2010) a survey and recommendations of networking security analysis is described in detailed. Authors also mentioned the way to build up an improving security approaches for a cloud computing environment. To improve security in a cloud computing environment, companies and academia joined together and formed several groups and alliances to address this issues. The common goals for those groups (European Network and Information Security Agency (ENISA)) and alliances are to enhance and improve security for cloud computing through education and by encouraging the use of best practices for providing security in cloud.

In (Wang, 2010) authors mentioned that storing and sharing databases in cloud of computers raise serious concern of individual privacy. In their literature they have considered two kinds of privacy risk, one is presence leakage, by which the attackers can explicitly identify individuals in (or not in) the database, and another is association leakage, by which the attackers can unambiguously associate individuals with sensitive information.

Some mechanisms and solutions have been built to encrypt confidential data when it is stored in data repositories (Mowbray, Pearson, & Shen, 2010). But most of these solutions focus on confidentiality and access control aspects, and have little flexibility in providing policy-driven mechanisms encompassing aspects beyond authentication and authorization. In (Svantesson & Clarke, 2010) privacy and consumer risks that are associated with cloud computing is discussed in details. Authors separated cloud computing into two forms as: Domestic clouds and Transborder clouds. Domestic clouds will not give rise to any cross border issues, but, however, such clouds can still give rise to privacy issues concerning to their businesses. Transborder clouds are associated with additional privacy issues and in approaching those privacy issues; it is useful to draw a distinction between issues associated with transborder cloud operators and issues associated with transborder cloud users. In literature (Sangroya, Kumar, Dhok, & Varma, 2010) data security risks in cloud computing is elaborated. A risk analysis approach is also presented in this literature.

CONCLUSION

Cloud computing has made resources accessible to the end users with a pay-as-you-go manner at anytime, anywhere; this act has immediately made resources vulnerable to intruder attacks and break the system. This challenge is primarily from sharing, virtualization and the use of Web services. Security is a major inhibitor of cloud computing adoption on all levels of abstraction. One of the top risks exposed in numerous studies is the failure of data protection in a cloud computing environment and its becoming an increasingly complex environment due to more systems are sharing the same physical resources. The dynamic and agility in the cloud environments also provides security challenges. In a cloud computing environment it is necessary to validate the identity of services, Cloud Service Providers (CSU) and Cloud Service Users (CSU). There are several proposed

methodologies based on traditional key based encryption and decryption techniques, dynamic security approaches, agent-based system for this purpose, but they are not smart enough to provide a bulletproof security mechanism for the system.

Research is ongoing to deliver a safer cloud environment to the users and there are several proposed architectures for the same. However, there is no doubt that cloud computing has emerged with considerable potential as well as a revolutionizing the IT industries; but still these unique challenges need to be carefully addressed for delivering a safer and innovative business model to the cloud users.

REFERENCES

Bamiah, M., & Brohi, S. (2011). Seven deadly threats and vulnerabilities in cloud computing. *International Journal of Advanced Engineering Sciences and Technologies*, *9*(1), 87–90. Retrieved from http://www.ijaest.iserp.org/archieves/15-Jul-15-31-11/Vol-No.9-Issue-No.1/16.IJAEST-Vol-No-9-Issue-No-1-Seven-Deadly-Threats-and-Vulnerabilities-in-Cloud-Computing-087-090.pdf

Bhuiyan, T. (2010, November). A survey on the relationship between trust and interest similarity in online social networks. *Journal of Emerging Technologies in Web Intelligence*, *2*(4), 291–299. doi:10.4304/jetwi.2.4.291-299

Boss, G., Malladi, P., Quan, D., Legregni, L., & Hall, H. (2007, October). *Cloud computing*. In Workshop in IBM Corporation, Organization: High Performance On Demand Solutions (Hi-PODS), Version 1.0, 08 October 2007. Retrieved September 26, 2011, from http://download.boulder.ibm.com/ibmdl/pub/software/dw/wes/hipods/Cloud_computing_wp_final_8Oct.pdf

Brock, M., & Goscinski, A. (2010, May). Toward a framework for cloud security. In *ICA3PP 2010 Proceedings of the 10th International Conference on Algorithms and Architectures for Parallel Processing, Part II, LNCS Vol. 6082*, (pp. 254-263). Berlin, Germany: SpringerLink. doi: 10.1007/978-3-642-13136-3_26

Buyya, R., Pandey, S., & Vecchiola, C. (2009, December). Cloudbus toolkit for market-oriented cloud computing. In *CloudCom 2009 Proceedings of the 1st International Conference on Cloud Computing, LNCS Vol. 5931*, (pp. 24-44). Berlin, Germany: SpringerLink. doi: 10.1007/978-3-642-10665-1_4

Casola, V., Mazzeo, A., Mazzocca, N., & Venticinque, S. (2004, June). Design of policy-based security mechanisms in a distributed web services architecture. In *PARA 2004 Proceedings of the Workshop on State-of-The-Art in Scientific Computing, LNCS Vol. 3732*, (pp. 454-463). Berlin, Germany: SpringerLink. doi: 10.1007/11558958_54

Cavoukian, A. (2008, December). Privacy in the clouds. *Identity in the Information Society, 1*(1), 89–108. doi:10.1007/s12394-008-0005-z

Chappell, D. (2008, August). A short introduction to cloud computing: An enterprise-oriented view. *Lecture at the Microsoft Corporation*. Retrieved August 25, 2011, from http://www.davidchappell.com/CloudPlatforms--Chappell.pdf

Chow, R., Golle, P., Jakobsson, M., Masuoka, R., Molina, J., Shi, E., & Staddon, J. (2009, November). Controlling data in the cloud: Outsourcing computation without outsourcing control. In *CCSW'09 Proceedings of the ACM Cloud Computing Security Workshop*. doi: 10.1145/1655008.1655020

Costa, L., de Oliveira, B., & Braga, A. (2007). Trust evaluation for web applications based on behavioral analysis. In Venter, H., Eloff, M., Labuschagne, L., Eloff, J., & von Solms, R. (Eds.), *Approaches for security, privacy and trust in complex environments (Vol. 232*, pp. 61–72). Boston, MA: Springer. doi:10.1007/978-0-387-72367-9_6

Dodda, R., Smith, C., & Moorsel, A. (2009). An architecture for cross-cloud system management. In *IC3 2009 Proceedings of the International Conference on Contemporary Computing*, CCIS Vol. 40, (pp. 556-567). Berlin, Germany: SpringerLink. doi: 10.1007/978-3-642-03547-0_53

Garcia, D. Z. G., & Felgar de Toledo, M. B. (2008). An approach for establishing trust relationships in the web service technology. In *IFIP 2008 International Federation for Information Processing (Vol. 283*, pp. 509–516). Boston, MA: Springer. doi:10.1007/978-0-387-84837-2_53

Hamid, R., Nezhad, M., Stephenson, B., Singhal, S., & Castellanos, M. (2009, November). Virtual business operating environment in the cloud: Conceptual architecture and challenges. In *ER 2009 Proceedings of the 28th International Conference on Conceptual Modeling, LNCS Vol. 5829*, (pp. 501-514). Berlin, Germany: SpringerLink. doi: 10.1007/978-3-642-04840-1_37

Huynh, T., Jennings, N., & Shadbolt, N. (2006, March). An integrated trust and reputation model for open multi-agent systems. In *Auton Agent Multi-Agent Sys (2006)*, Vol. 13, (pp. 119–154). Springer Science+Business Media, LLC 2006. doi: 10.1007/s10458-005-6825-4

Hwang, K. (2010, December). Security, privacy, and data protection for trusted cloud computing. In *CloudCom2010: The 2nd International Conference on Cloud Computing.* Keynote Address. Indiana, USA, December 3, 2010. Retrieved from http://salsahpc.indiana.edu/CloudCom2010/slides/PDF/Keynotes/Security,%20Privacy,%20and%20Data%20Protection%20for%20Trusted%20Cloud%20Computing.pdf

Kamara, S., & Lauter, K. (2010, January). Cryptographic cloud storage. In *RLCPS'10 Proceedings of the Financial Cryptography: Workshop on Real-Life Cryptographic Protocols and Standardization.* Retrieved from http://research.microsoft.com/pubs/112576/crypto-cloud.pdf

Keller, E., Szefer, J., Rexford, J., & Lee, R. (2010, June). Nohype: virtualized cloud infrastructure without the virtualization. In *ISCA'10 Proceedings of The 37th Annual International Symposium On Computer Architecture*, Vol. 38(3). doi: 10.1145/1815961.1816010

Kramer, S., & Rybalchenko, A. (2010, August). *A multi-modal framework for achieving accountability in multi-agent systems.* Retrieved September 15, 2011, from http://www7.in.tum.de/~rybal/papers/2010-lis-accountability.pdf

Lee, G., & Crespi, N. (2010, October). Shaping future service environments with the cloud and internet of things: Networking challenges and service evolution. In *ISoLA 2010 Proceedings of the 4th International Symposium on Leveraging Applications of Formal Methods, Verification and Validation, Part I, LNCS Vol. 6415*, (pp. 399-410). Berlin, Germany: SpringerLink. doi: 10.1007/978-3-642-16558-0_34

Li, W., & Ping, L. (2009). Trust model to enhance security and interoperability of cloud environment. In *CloudCom 2009 Proceedings of the 1st International Conference on Cloud Computing, LNCS Vol. 5931,* (pp. 69-79). Berlin, Germany: SpringerLink. doi: 10.1007/978-3-642-10665-1_7.

Liau, C. (2003). Belief, information acquisition, and trust in multi-agent systems—A modal logic formulation. *Elsevier Journal of Artificial Intelligence, 149*, 31–60. doi:doi:10.1016/S0004-3702(03)00063-8

Lombardi, F., & Pietro, R. (2010). Secure virtualization for cloud computing. *Elsevier Journal of Network and Computer Applications, 34*(4). doi:doi:10.1016/j.jnca.2010.06.008

Lorenzi, F., Baldo, G., Costa, R., Abel, M., Bazzan, A., & Ricci, F. (2010, November). A trust model for multi agent recommendations. *Journal of Emerging Technologies in Web Intelligence, 2*(4), 310–318. doi:10.4304/jetwi.2.4.310-318

Montaner, M., Lopez, B., & Rosa, J. (2002, July). Developing trust in recommender agents. In *AAMAS'02 Proceedings of the First International Joint Conference on Autonomous Agents and Multiagent Systems.* doi: 10.1145/544741.544811.

Mowbray, M., Pearson, S., & Shen, Y. (2010, March). Enhancing privacy in cloud computing via policy-based obfuscation. *Springer Journal of Supercomputing, 61*(2). doi:doi:10.1007/s11227-010-0425-z

Oh, T., Lim, S., Choi, Y., Park, K., Lee, H., & Choi, H. (2010, September). State of the art of network security perspectives in cloud computing. In *SUComS 2010 Proceedings of the First International Conference on Security-enriched Urban Computing and Smart Grid*, CCIS Vol. 78, (pp. 629-637). Berlin, Germany: SpringerLink. doi: 10.1007/978-3-642-16444-6_79

Onwubiko, C. (2010). Security issues to cloud computing. In Antonopoulos, N., & Gillam, L. (Eds.), *Cloud computing: Principles, systems and applications*. London, UK: Springer-Verlag Computer Communications and Networks. doi:10.1007/978-1-84996-241-4_16

Panda, S., & Mangla, V. (2010, May). Protecting data from the cyber theft – A virulent disease. *Journal of Emerging Technologies in Web Intelligence, 2*(2), 152–155. doi:10.4304/jetwi.2.2.152-155

Papadimitriou, P., & Garcia-Molina, H. (2011, January). Data leakage detection. *IEEE Transactions on Knowledge and Data Engineering, 23*(1), 51–63. doi:10.1109/TKDE.2010.100

Qian, L., Luo, Z., Du, Y., & Guo, L. (2009, December). Cloud computing: an overview. In *CloudCom 2009 Proceedings of the 1st International Conference on Cloud Computing, LNCS Vol. 5931*, (pp. 626-631). Berlin, Germany: SpringerLink. doi: 10.1007/978-3-642-10665-1_63

Rooy, D. (2010, June). Opportunities, trust, privacy and security challenges in cloud computing. In *Lecture: Moving to the Cloud: Risks and Opportunities, ICT 2010*, Brussels, 8 June 2010. Retrieved from http://www.security-round-table.eu/doc/20100611_cloud_presentations/Dirk_van_Rooy.pdf

Ruiter, J., & Warnier, M. (2011). Privacy regulations for cloud computing: Compliance and implementation in theory and practice. In S. Gutwirth, et al (Eds.), *Computers, privacy and data protection: An element of choice*, 1st ed., (pp. 361-376). Springer Science+Business Media, B.V. doi: 10.1007/978-94-007-0641-5_17

Sakka, M., Defude, B., & Tellez, J. (2010, June). Document provenance in the cloud: constraints and challenges. In *EUNICE 2010 Proceedings of the Networked Services and Applications–Engineering, Control and Management, LNCS Vol. 6164*, (pp. 107-117). IFIP International Federation for Information Processing. doi: 10.1007/978-3-642-13971-0_11

Sangroya, A., Kumar, S., Dhok, J., & Varma, V. (2010, March). Towards analyzing data security risks in cloud computing environments. In *ICISTM 2010 Proceedings of the International Conference on Information Systems, Technology, and Management*, CCIS Vol. 54, (pp. 255-265). Berlin, Germany: SpringerLink. doi: 10.1007/978-3-642-12035-0_25

Sedayao, J., Su, S., Ma, X., Jiang, M., & Miao, K. (2009). A simple technique for securing data at rest stored in a computing cloud. In *CloudCom 2009 Proceedings of the 1st International Conference on Cloud Computing, LNCS Vol. 5931*, (pp. 553-558). Berlin, Germany: SpringerLink. doi: 10.1007/978-3-642-10665-1_51

Subashin, S., & Kavitha, V. (2011). A survey on security issues in service delivery models of cloud computing. *Elsevier Journal of Network and Computer Applications, 34*, 1–11. doi:10.1016/j.jnca.2010.07.006

Svantesson, D., & Clarke, R. (2010). Privacy and consumer risks in cloud computing. *Computer Law & Security Report, 26*, 391–397. doi:10.1016/j.clsr.2010.05.005

Szczypiorski, K., Margasiński, I., Mazurczyk, W., Cabaj, K., & Radziszewski, P. (2008, November). TrustMAS: Trusted communication platform for multi-agent systems. In *OTM 2008 Proceedings of the On the Move to Meaningful Internet Systems, Part II, LNCS Vol. 5332*, (pp. 1019 – 1035). Berlin, Germany: SpringerLink. doi: 10.1007/978-3-540-88873-4_7

Talib, A. (2010, November). Security framework of cloud data storage based on multi agent system architecture: Semantic literature review. *Journal of Computer and Information Science, 3*(4), 175–186. Retrieved from http://www.ccsenet.org/journal/index.php/cis/article/view/7133/6130

Tobarra, L., Cazorla, D., Cuartero, F., & Díaz, G. (2005). Application of formal methods to the analysis of web services security. In EPEW 2005 *Proceedings of the European Performance Engineering Workshop*, LNCS Vol. 3670, (pp. 215-229). Berlin, Germany: SpringerLink. doi: 10.1007/11549970_16

Tsai, W., Wei, X., Chen, Y., Paul, R., Chung, J., & Zhang, D. (2007). Data provenance in SOA: Security, reliability, and integrity. In SOCA (2007) *Service Oriented Computing and Applications*, Vol. 1, (pp. 223-247). Berlin, Germany: SpringerLink. doi: 10.1007/s11761-007-0018-8

Wang, H. (2010, May). Privacy-preserving data sharing in cloud computing. *Journal of Computer Science and Information Technology, 25*(3), 401-414. Springer Science+Business Media, LLC & Science Press. *China*. doi:doi:10.1007/s11390-010-9333-1

Wang, W., Zeng, G., & Yuan, L. (2006, August). A reputation multi-agent system in semantic web. In *PRIMA 2006 Proceedings of the 9ᵗʰ Pacific Rim International Workshop on Multi-Agents, LNAI Vol. 4088,* (pp. 211 – 219). Berlin, Germany: SpringerLink. doi: 10.1007/11802372_22

Xu, J., Huang, R., Huang, W., & Yang, G. (2009, December). Secure document service for cloud computing. In *CloudCom 2009 Proceedings of the 1st International Conference on Cloud Computing, LNCS Vol. 5931,* (pp. 541-546). Berlin, Germany: SpringerLink. doi: 10.1007/978-3-642-10665-1_49

Yan, L., Rong, C., & Zhao, G. (2009, December). Strengthen cloud computing security with federal identity management using hierarchical identity-based cryptography. In *CloudCom 2009 Proceedings of the 1st International Conference on Cloud Computing, LNCS Vol. 5931,* (pp. 167-177). Berlin, Germany: SpringerLink. doi: 10.1007/978-3-642-10665-1_15

Zhang, X., Xu, F., Liu, Y., Zhang, X., & Shen, C. (2006, December). Trust extended dynamic security model and its application in network. In *MSN 2006 Proceedings of the Second International Conference on Mobile Ad-Hoc and Sensor Networks, LNCS Vol. 4325,* (pp. 404-415). Berlin, Germany: SpringerLink. doi: 10.1007/11943952_34

Zheng, J., Sun, Y., & Zhou, W. (2009, December). Cloud computing based internet data center. In *CloudCom 2009 Proceedings of the 1st International Conference on Cloud Computing, LNCS Vol. 5931,* (pp. 700-704). Berlin, Germany: SpringerLink. doi: 10.1007/978-3-642-10665-1_75

Zhu, J. (2010). Cloud computing technologies and applications. In B. Furht & A. Escalante (Eds.), *Handbook of cloud computing*, (pp. 21-45). Springer Science+Business Media, LLC. doi: 10.1007/978-1-4419-6524-0_2

Chapter 11
Security in Cloud Computing

Alpana M. Desai
University of Alaska Anchorage, USA

Kenrick Mock
University of Alaska Anchorage, USA

ABSTRACT

Cloud computing has recently emerged in prominence and is being rapidly adopted by organizations because of its potential and perceived benefits of flexibility and affordability. According to surveys conducted in 2008 and 2009 by International Data Corporation (IDC) of IT executives and CIOs, security was cited as the top concern for the adoption of cloud computing. Enterprises that plan to utilize cloud services for their infrastructure, platform, and/or software needs must understand the security risks and privacy issues related to cloud computing. This chapter discusses the technical, legal, and policy/ organizational security risks of cloud computing, and reviews recommendations/strategies for managing and mitigating security threats in cloud computing. It also presents vendor-specific solutions and strategies that cloud service providers are implementing for mitigating security risks in cloud computing.

INTRODUCTION

The benefits of cloud computing include easy and fast deployment, pay-as-you-go model, benefits of scale, and less in-house IT staff and costs. According to a 2008 survey conducted by International Data Corporation (IDC), a global provider of market intelligence, advisory services, and events for the information technology, telecommunications and consumer technology markets, security and performance were the top two challenges of cloud computing that were cited

by senior IT executives and CIOs, (IDC, 2008b). IDC conducted another survey in 2009 and the top concern was still security but availability was the second top concern and performance moved from the second top concern in 2008 to the third top concern in 2009 (IDC, 2009). The projected increase of spending on public IT cloud services is expected to increase from $16.5billion in 2009 to $55 billion in 2014, (IDC, 2010).

Cloud computing is rapidly being adopted not just domestically but also globally. The European Network and Information Security Agency

DOI: 10.4018/978-1-4666-2187-9.ch011

(ENISA), an EU agency, launched a survey of the actual needs, requirements and expectations of Small and Medium Enterprises (SMEs) for cloud computing services. As per this survey the top two concerns of SMEs were information security and liability. In particular the major concerns of SMEs were confidentiality of their information and liability for incidents involving the infrastructure, (ENISA, 2009).

Thus it is important to understand risks associated with adoption of cloud computing. Enterprises utilize cloud services for their infrastructure, platform, and/or software needs. In this chapter, security risks and security benefits of cloud computing are discussed. Technical, legal, and organizational security risks of cloud computing are also presented as are security risks in the traditional context and as related to cloud computing in particular. Some of the security issues that are discussed in this chapter are insecure interfaces and APIs; risks associated with multi-tenancy; data leakage; malicious insider; data protection risks; data ownership and accountability; compliance risks; and customer lock-in issues.

Several strategies exist and are being proposed by vendors and groups to mitigate security risks in cloud computing. Solutions and strategies that cloud service providers are implementing for mitigating security risks in cloud computing are presented. To convey reliability and security of their cloud services, vendors seek and maintain compliance with existing security standards. Some of these security standards that are already in place and are in development stages are discussed in this chapter.

DEFINITION OF CLOUD COMPUTING

Cloud computing has been defined differently by various groups (comprising of industry, academia, and government). Armbrust, et al., (2009) state that "cloud computing is a new term for a long-held dream of computing as a utility" due to its pay-as-you-go characteristic. They refer to cloud computing as "both the applications delivered as services over the Internet and the hardware and systems software in the datacenters that provide those services."

IDC (2008a) makes a distinction between cloud services and cloud computing by first defining cloud services with eight specific attributes (off-site/third party provider; accessed via the internet; minimal/mo IT skills required to implement; provisioning; pricing model; user interface; system interface; and shared resources/common versions) and then defining cloud computing as consisting of "a growing list of technologies and IT offerings that enable cloud services as defined by its eight characteristics."

In this article, we use NIST's (National Institute of Standards and Technology) definition of cloud computing. NIST defines cloud computing as a model for enabling convenient, on-demand network access to a shared pool of configurable computing resources (e.g., networks, servers, storage, applications, and services) that can be rapidly provisioned and released with minimal management effort or service provider interaction, (Mell & Grance, 2009)

This cloud model promotes availability and it is composed of five essential characteristics, three service models, and four deployment models.

The five essential characteristics are on-demand self-service, broad network access, resource pooling, rapid elasticity, and measured service. A sixth characteristic that is not considered essential but is often discussed as such and is identified as an important element of cloud computing by the Cloud Security Alliance (CSA) is multi-tenancy (Cloud Security Alliance, 2009). A tenant refers to a user's application that runs on the cloud and requires some degree of security or exclusivity. Multi-tenancy refers to multiple tenants running on some shared infrastructure within the cloud. Such sharing could occur at different levels, for example, tenants could share the same hardware separated via virtualization, or tenants could share the same database separated by access permissions. Of paramount importance is a hypervisor that manages which services a tenant is allowed to access and prevents information from leaking from one tenant to another.

The three computing service models are Cloud Software as a Service (SaaS), Cloud Platform as a Service (PaaS), and Cloud Infrastructure as a Service (IaaS) and the four deployment models are private clouds, community clouds, public clouds, and hybrid clouds.

RELATED LITERATURE ON CLOUD SECURITY

Kaufman provides a broad overview of the security issues surrounding cloud computing (2009) and asks many questions that do not have easy answers. For example, is there more risk if private data is stored in a single data center, which offers centralized control, or in multiple data centers, which offers redundancy but more points of failure or attack? Who is responsible for confidentiality, integrity, and availability of data and services? Responsibility could conceivably rest with either the customer or the vendor and may need to be specified in a Service Level Agreement (SLA). New legal issues also arise, such as regulatory compliance and auditing, which may not have been an issue in a non-cloud environment. These situations become even more complex if data on the cloud crosses international boundaries and jurisdiction needs to be determined. These are some of the many open-ended questions in which laws and standards are still being developed.

The European Network and Information Security Agency categorizes cloud security in terms of technical, legal, and organizational risks and we follow a similar approach in this chapter (ENISA, 2009). Betcher uses the same framework in a literature review of cloud security papers published from 2007 to 2009 (Betcher, 2010). Strategies to mitigate security concerns focus on audit controls to determine security compliance, policies and procedures such SLAs, and governance procedures to establish standards and a market exchange for cloud services. On a more practical level, several books on cloud computing offer advice for cloud computing tenants on how to establish appropriate encryption, data security, backup plans, and identity management protocols along with procedures to assess risk for different cloud architectures (Sosisinky, 2011; Winkler, 2011).

Zhou et al. provide a complementary framework to analyze cloud security (2010). Their framework centers on the aspects of availability, confidentiality, data integrity, control, and audit capabilities. Availability refers to the ability of the cloud to be accessible at any time from any place. Confidentiality is the requirement for user data to be kept private, typically through encryption. Data integrity ensures that data is preserved reliably, often through a RAID-like system. Control is the ability to regulate use of the system and audit capabilities allow customers to watch what happened in the cloud.

Foundation reading for academic researchers in cloud computing security can be found in the Proceedings of the ACM Workshop on Cloud Computing Security (Sion & Song, 2009; Perrig & Sion, 2010). Topics range from designs for secure file systems; empirical studies of SSL certificates; managing the security of virtual machines; data harvesting detection; and the availability of cloud services for mission critical applications, such as those required by the US Department of Defense. For applications such as these that involve national security implications, Kim et al. propose a hybrid architecture that uses community clouds as an interface between private and public clouds. These clouds could establish national security communities of interest that could be rapidly created, provisioned, and destroyed as needed (Kim et al., 2010).

RISKS AND CHALLENGES OF CLOUD COMPUTING

Security Challenges and Risks

In this section, we discuss security risks that need to be considered when enterprises plan to utilize cloud services for their infrastructure, platform, and/or software needs. We will discuss the technical, organizational, and legal security risks of cloud computing. Some of the security risks occur in traditional environments as well as in clouds. For each security risk that is presented, we also discuss specific strategies that can be used to alleviate that risk.

Technical Risks

Insecure Interfaces and APIs

Customers use interfaces and APIs to manage and interact with cloud services. These interfaces are used to provision, manage, orchestrate, and monitor processes running in the cloud environment. The customer management interfaces of public cloud providers are Internet accessible and Application Programming Interfaces (APIs) or software interfaces are used to access cloud services. Two categories of web-accessible APIs are used by cloud service providers: SOAP (based on web services) and REST (based on HTTP). Security and authentication mechanisms are not robust in REST style APIs but some cloud providers offer these since they allow for rapid development. These APIs are easy targets for man-in-the-middle or replay attacks. Hence cloud interfaces must have secure authentication, access control, encryption

and activity monitoring mechanisms to prevent any malicious attack. It is recommended to monitor the authentication and access control and other associated encryption and activity monitoring policies to prevent any malicious attack. For example, in March 2009 a flaw was discovered in Google Docs that allowed a user's document to be inadvertently shared (Wauters, 2009). The flaw resulted from an error in the software that controlled sharing permissions. There exists many ways in which a breach can be prevented (Cloud Security Alliance, 2010). Experts recommend the following ways to prevent security breaches due to this threat:

- Security model analysis of cloud APIs
- Strong authentication and access controls
- API dependency chain evaluation

Many efforts are being made to develop open and proprietary APIs. Open API efforts done by Open Cloud Computing Interface Working Group, Sun's Open Cloud API, VMware's DMTF-submitted vCloud API. Proprietary APIs include Amazon EC2 API, Rackspace API, GoGrid's API. DMTF's Open Virtualization Format (OVF) is being developed to help with portability and interoperability issues.

Risks Associated with Multi-Tenancy

Physical resources are shared among cloud computing users through common software virtualization layers. A virtualization hypervisor provides access between users' operating systems and physical compute resources. These physical resources such as CPU caches, GPUs, etc. that make up the infrastructure do not offer strict isolation for multi-tenancy.

These shared environments propagate security risks by allowing inappropriate access to the underlying platform. Cloud users are not aware of whom they are sharing their physical resources with and what their intentions are – their neighbor's virtual machine could be malicious.

Since common storage hardware is used to house different cloud consumers' data, negligent access management or malicious attack can compromise data. The possibility of a side-channel attack in a cloud environment where an attacker could insert malicious code into a neighbor's VM environment with minimal chance of detection was presented in a joint paper published by MIT and UCSD in November 2009 entitled "Hey, You, Get Off of My Cloud: Exploring Information Leakage in Third-Party Compute Clouds". Amazon Web Services issued a security bulletin that reported that the Zeus Botnet was able to install and successfully run a command and control infrastructure in the cloud environment (Trend Micro, 2010).

The Cloud Security Alliance recommends a defense in depth strategy that should include compute, storage, and network security enforcement and monitoring. Best practices for installation and configuration must be implemented and enforced. Cloud environment must be monitored for unauthorized changes and activities. Strong compartmentalization should be employed to ensure that individual customers do not impact the operations of other tenants running on the same cloud provider. Customers should not have access to any other tenant's actual or residual data, network traffic, etc. Strong authentication and access control for administrative access and operations must be promoted. Service level agreements for patching and vulnerability remediation must be enforced. Vulnerability scanning and configuration audits must be conducted on a timely and scheduled basis.

Data Leakage/Data Remanence

It is very common for cloud service providers to recycle storage resources but no clear standard is followed on how to recycle memory or disk space (Trend Micro, 2010). When hardware resources are not reused properly, there is a high risk of

misuse as previous tenants' data could still be accessible to new tenants. Data deletion is more problematic in clouds due to multi-tenancy. From a customer standpoint, data stored on dedicated hardware is less risky than data stored in a cloud (ENISA, 2009).

To safeguard their interests, cloud customers must insist on contractual provisions that clearly outline the standards and guidelines used by cloud providers for data deletion.

Malicious Insider

This is a general threat to all architectures but it is amplified for cloud services because of general lack of transparency of procedures and processes of cloud providers. Cloud providers' guidelines of employees' access policies for physical and virtual assets may not be known. Provider's guidelines on employee monitoring and hiring standards and organizational policy compliance may not be known to the cloud customer. Some of the remediation steps include enforcing transparency into overall information and management practices and specifying human resource requirements as part of legal contracts (Cloud Security Alliance, 2010).

Legal Risks

Data Protection Risks

Cloud computing causes several data privacy and data confidentiality risks for cloud customers and providers. This problem is intensified specially in cases of numerous transfers of data. This risk is categorized as a high risk. Cloud providers may not be practicing secure and safe data handling and may not have proper data controls in place. Inversely, cloud providers may not be aware if the data collected by the customer was done in a lawful manner.

Strategies to minimize data protection risks include implementing strong API access control, encrypting and protecting integrity of data, and including stipulations in contract pertaining to lawful data collection on the part of the customer and secure data handling practices on the part of the cloud provider.

Data Ownership and Accountability

Another risk associated with customers' data is that of data ownership and accountability. Legal complications arise due to the mobile nature of data residing in clouds. To facilitate 24/7 accessibility to customers, data is replicated and stored virtually anywhere. EU Privacy Act does not allow for data processing or storage of customers' data in foreign data centers. Cloud providers must have stringent data controls in place to ensure legal compliance (Trend Micro, 2010).

Policy and Organizational Risks

Compliance Risks

Organizations that have earned certifications to either meet industry standards or regulatory requirements or to gain competitive edge are at risk when migrating to clouds if the cloud provider does not adhere to their own compliance requirements and if the cloud provider does not allow audit by the cloud customer (ENISA, 2009).

Customer Lock-In Issues

Customers face lock-in issues when they are unable to move their data and/or processes away from the cloud provider, (Armbrust, et al., 2009). Cloud customers face major portability challenges when they have to change their cloud service provider, either because the cloud service provider is out of business or the company's dissatisfaction with the providers' service or due to some other reason. Portability challenges are compounded due to the fact that standards and procedures for data and service portability are still evolving. Lock-in may be favorable to providers but customers become vulnerable to price increases, reliability issues, acquisition of providers, or when provid-

ers go out of business. Lock-in challenges differ with different cloud types (IaaS, PaaS, HaaS, or SaaS) of cloud services. SaaS lock-in affects both data and application. If the provider does not offer a routine or process for data migration, the customer has to develop programs to export data and import it to the new provider. Application lock-in is not specific to clouds and occurs both in cloud and traditional environments. Providers have customized applications and if a customer has a large user base it can incur very high switching costs, (ENISA, 2009). PaaS lock-in occurs at the API and component levels. Different providers offer different APIs and it is the customer's responsibility to develop compatible code that uses the provider's custom APIs. IaaS lock-in occurs at the application and data levels. Migration between providers is a major concern due to lack of portability standards.

The risks discussed in this section are high-category risks. Other risks have also been identified but most are medium or low risks and hence have not been included in this article. The reader is referred to the references listed at the end of this article for further discussion on other security risks in cloud computing. In this section, after discussion of each risk we also presented specific remediation steps that must be considered to lessen that risk. In the next section, we discuss general mitigation strategies.

General Mitigation Strategies for Management of Security Risks

Recommendations for protecting organizations' assets against security threats and challenges: It is important for organizations to evaluate and classify the importance of their assets. Assets could be data and/or applications, functions, and processes. Organizations must assess the confidentiality, integrity, and availability (CIA) for their assets and if that asset is moved to the cloud how the CIA for these assets are affected. For assets, it is imperative to determine the specific cloud deployment option that will be pertinent for that asset. It may be a good strategy for highly sensitive data to reside in a private cloud.

ENISA (2009) has published a set of key recommendations that can be used by cloud customers and cloud providers. They recommend a set of assurance criteria that should be used to determine risks associated with the adoption of cloud services, to compare and evaluate various offers by cloud providers, to obtain assurance from cloud providers, and to reduce the assurance burden on cloud providers.

This set of information assurance criteria includes a checklist that encompasses general IT environments as well as those specific to cloud environments, (ENISA, 2009). The information assurance requirements and checklist must contain questions that evaluate

- Personnel security
- Supply-chain assurance
- Operational security (software assurance, patch management, network architecture controls, host architecture, application security for PaaS and SaaS, and resource provisioning)
- Identity and access management (authorization, identity provisioning, management of personal data, key management, encryption, etc.)
- Asset management
- Data and services portability
- Business continuity management
- Physical security
- Environmental controls
- Legal requirements

Cloud customers need to pay special attention to data protection, data security, data transfer, intellectual property, confidentiality, and non-disclosure when assessing the service level agreements, (ENISA, 2009).

Vendor-Specific Mitigation Strategies for Management of Security Risks

In this section, we present vendor-specific solutions and strategies that cloud service providers are implementing for mitigating security risks in cloud computing. To convey reliability and security of their cloud services, vendors seek and maintain compliance with existing security standards. We discuss some of these security standards in this section.

While cloud computing affords convenient and scalable data processing we have seen that the cloud computing model raises a host of issues regarding security, privacy, and trust. With multi-tenant virtualization could information leak from one customer to another? If another customer's host or application is compromised will that affect the reliability for other customers sharing the same hardware? How can customer privacy be ensured? Given the complexities surrounding these issues cloud computing vendors are implementing a number of approaches to allay customer concerns. Most of these approaches apply to IT security in general, although some are specific to cloud computing.

Security Standards, Statutes, and Recommendations

One of the most common strategies to convey system security is to seek certification or accreditation in known security standards. For example, vendors that process credit cards are required to meet the Payment Card Industry Data Security Standard (PCI DSS) (PCI Security Standards Council 2010). Certification requires the vendor to demonstrate their network is secure, that steps are in place to protect cardholder data, and that an information security policy is in place with strong (at least 128 bit) security measures. Cloud vendors can go a step further and become a PCI validated service provider, which means that the vendor has been audited by an independent Qualified Security Assessor. Compliance to the PCI standard does not require a single-tenant environment.

PCI DSS is designed around the security of payment card transactions. More generally, many vendors seek ISO/IEC 27001 (International Organization for Standardization and International Electrotechnical Commission) certification which covers more general information security principles and practices (International Organization for Standards 2008). Certified companies can claim to have implemented a systematic, comprehensive, and holistic security management program. ISO 27001 is a formal specification with mandated requirements that can be audited. For example, Amazon's EC2 PaaS cloud is certified by Ernst & Young CertifyPoint while Microsoft's Azure cloud is certified by the British Standards Institute. The ISO 27001 certification requires the vendor to develop an Information Security Management Systems (ISMS) plan and ensure that it implements the "Plan-Do-Check-Act" cycle that includes planning, implementation, and assessment. In the Plan phase the ISMS is defined, the Do phase implements the ISMS, the Check phase reviews and evaluates the ISMS, and the Act phase implements changes back to the ISMS based on the Check.

Several cloud vendors have also announced compliance with regulatory statutes such as HIPAA (Health Insurance Portability and Accountability Act), SOX (Sarbanes–Oxley Act), or attestations with SAS 70 (Statement on Auditing Standards No. 70). For example, HIPAA's privacy rule prohibits the unencrypted transmission of protected health information while HIPAA's security rule requires controls to access protected health information. Cloud vendors can map their internal controls to meet HIPAA requirements and consequently host medical applications. SAS 70 provides guidance for an auditor to assess the internal controls of an organization. The SAS 70 audit attests that the controls are in place for effective financial reporting, such as those specified by SOX. However, the

SAS 70 report is not proof of security or compliance, although some vendors mischaracterize it as a security certificate (Gartner 2010).

The National Institute of Standards and Technology (NIST) publications comprise another set of security recommendations for which cloud vendors may seek compliance, especially if there is the intent to host federal applications. NIST 800-53, "Recommended Security Controls for Federal Information Systems," documents recommended baseline security controls and processes. For example, processes include auditable events, contingency plans, and procedures to update security controls. Examples of security controls include access enforcement and wireless access restrictions. Other appropriate NIST guidelines include NIST 800-86, "Guide to Integrating Forensic Techniques into Incident Response", NIST 800-30, "Risk Management Guide for Information Technology Systems," and NIST 800-61, "Computer Security Incident Handling Guide" (NIST 2007). Terremark is one cloud vendor that has specifically designed their multi-tenant environment to meet federal General Services Administration regulations up to the TS/SCI-clearance (Top Secret / Sensitive Compartmented Information) level. As an example of the extra steps taken to achieve this level, their Culpepper data center includes over 250 motion sensitive cameras; Department of Defense approved fences, blast-proof exteriors, multi-factor authentication, and 128 bit encryption (Hoover 2009). Some cloud vendors also offer to host private clouds on dedicated hardware or manage dedicated hardware at the customer's site, although these arrangements limit the on-demand scalability aspect of the cloud computing model.

Implement Common Information Security Practices

In terms of specific security practices and controls, virtually all cloud vendors offer basic packages of firewalls, VPN tunnels, VLAN access, and full data encryption. Some vendors offer additional security based on one-time tokens or hardware keys. For example, Fujitsu's cloud service offers one-time passwords provided via SMS (Okuhara, Shiozaki and Suzuki 2010) while Amazon's EC2 supports multi-factor authentication with the option to require a hardware device in addition to standard login credentials (Amazon.com 2010). For authentication exchange between security domains, both the Security Assertion Markup Language (SAML) and WS-Federation are being promoted.

Teach Customers How to Use Security Architectures

Many cloud vendors have published white papers describing their security architecture. Amazon's white paper describes multiple levels of security. Multi-factor authentication is required to access the host and SSH2 to access the guest operating system. Amazon's customized hypervisor isolates different customer instances on a virtual machine (VM) to ensure that each customer has access only to their virtual memory and virtual disk (Amazon. com 2010). Applications are developed using Amazon services. SimpleDB provides domain level access controls for authenticated users. The RDS service allows customers to easily build relational databases and the SQS service supports messaging. By providing these services with appropriate security controls, Amazon PaaS applications transparently enforce security constraints to authenticated user accounts. Windows Azure follows a similar approach by providing services such as AppFabric for messaging and SQL Azure for data storage which support several types of access controls (Microsoft n.d.).

Many PaaS and IaaS vendors also give advice to their customers on how to develop cloud applications securely. Microsoft recommends cloud applications to be developed using the Security Development Lifecycle (Microsoft n.d.). Similar to the software development lifecycle, the security development lifecycle encompasses the phases of Training, Requirements (analyze security risks), Design (threat models, attack analysis), Implementation, Verification (testing, threat models), Release (security review), and Response (to security issues). Specific coding advice is also given. For example, the recommendation is made to use the Gatekeeper / Keymaster design pattern (Marshall, et al. 2010). The name of this pattern may be inspired from the Ghostbusters movie in which a portal could only be opened with the cooperation of both the Gatekeeper and the Keymaster. In this pattern the Keymaster and Gatekeeper run on different VM's. The Gatekeeper interfaces with the Internet and validates input. It has partial trust and interfaces internally with the Keymaster, which has full trust. The Keymaster can decide to process only certain types of requests from the Gatekeeper (for example, reads but not writes). This affords some protection in the event that the Gatekeeper is compromised.

Provide Access Controls

Access control and authentication are central components to any security architecture, and this is one area where cloud vendors offer different approaches. For example, Fujitsu plans to utilize open ID management frameworks (Okuhara, Shiozaki and Suzuki 2010). Windows Azure's access control uses claims-based authentication. In this approach, the client presents a token of claims issued by identity providers (active directory, Facebook, Google, etc.). The token is provided in a common format through the AppFabric Access Control Service and applications can process them as desired in a uniform representation (Microsoft n.d.).

Provide Auditing and Security Monitoring Tools

Another approach to address a customer's security concerns is to provide audits and regular security reports. Amazon Web Services will conduct penetration testing at the request of the user. This can provide valuable information to a customer regarding the effectiveness of security measures currently in place. Tools also exist to help customers visualize their cloud security and are important to keep the customer apprised and comfortable with security arrangements. Visualization tools can depict the efficiency and security coverage in terms of requirements met, measures in place, or highlight suspicious activity. For example, ArcSight's security monitoring tools analyze and correlate events such as logins, file accesses, database queries, etc. to find security risks or compliance violations and summarize them in an understandable report (ArcSight n.d.).

Data Privacy

Throughout this section there has been little mention of data privacy and this is no accident. Aside from addressing privacy mandates such as those included in HIPAA or PCI DSS, cloud vendors have focused on the security component and have left data privacy primarily to the realm of the business client by supplying basic tools such as the option to encrypt data. The client is left to implement their applications as desired to address customer privacy. This also seems to match what customers want. In a study conducted by Fujitsu, customers were concerned about their data but do little to actively protect it. Moreover, data is very personal. Individual responses varied by country, age, gender, and race on what aspects of their data should be private. For example, some did not want to divulge their GPS location but for providing real-time traffic reports, most were in favor of the risk given the reward. As data becomes more personal it has more value and is thus more vulnerable and subject to privacy concerns. The study concludes that no single approach to data privacy will work and that cloud companies should think globally but act locally when it comes to data privacy (Fujitsu Research Institute 2010).

Cloud Vendors Provide Expertise in Security

Finally, although the cloud computing model brings with it new security concerns, there is a strong argument that overall security is increased as more customers adopt the cloud model. It is very easy for businesses to put a web application online using their own host with little regard to security, maintenance, or audit tracking. Moving these hosts to a cloud service provider consolidates customers under an umbrella that is presumably maintained by security experts with considerable resources devoted to security and privacy issues. Adherence to the cloud provider's security protocols will eliminate many basic security problems while provisions for information privacy and compliance can bring attention to ensure that standards are followed.

FUTURE RESEARCH DIRECTIONS

Cloud computing is an evolving paradigm with a vast scope for research in this area. Security is still one of the major areas of concern for a customer migrating to the cloud. Standards related to cloud computing are either nonexistent or in draft versions. When cloud customers want to switch providers they face lock-in issues. It is imperative to have portability and interoperability standards for data and applications in the cloud. While cloud vendors are addressing security concerns, there is still great variation in the depth, breadth, and implementation of security measures.

The efforts of the Trusted Computing Group (TCG) may also have a significant influence on cloud security. The TCG is an initiative with the backing of large technology firms such as Intel, Microsoft, IBM, and Hewlett Packard that aims to create hardware meeting the Trusted Platform Module (TPM) specification. The TPM supports machine authentication, securing data via encryption, secure key storage, and attestation at a hardware level. Attestation is particularly relevant to cloud computing security because it provides a secure report on what is running on a machine and could be used to detect malware or to provide hardware-based verification that the hypervisor is properly separating tenants (Trusted Computing Group, 2010).

On the legal front, many issues such as those surrounding data privacy have yet to be well-defined. Another important research area is to identify the metrics to measure security in cloud computing. Finally, there is also a need for research that explores mechanisms for forensics and evidence collection.

Another area of cloud security that is important and is expected to grow considerably in the recent future is the area of Security as a Service. Several security vendors are using cloud to deliver security solutions including solutions for business continuity and disaster recovery, web and email security, encryption, network security, and intrusion management. The growth in this area will lead to numerous research opportunities. Some research initiatives in this area include efforts by the Security as a Service working group of the Cloud Security Alliance organization. The purpose of this working group is to provide greater clarity in the Security as a Service area by providing clear definitions and identifying main categories in this area. This working group recently published a white paper that discusses major categories of security services and includes a non-exhaustive list of cloud and non-cloud vendors that offer security solutions in these categories (Cloud Security Alliance "Security as a Service" Version 1.0, 2011).

CONCLUSION

The focus and objective of this article is to discuss the most critical security risks and threats to cloud computing and to present general mitigation strate-gies and vendor-specific mitigation strategies that are used to manage security challenges in cloud computing. Technical risks include insecure interfaces, multi-tenancy, data leakage, and malicious insiders. Many of these risks can be mitigated by adopting common information security principles such as defense in depth, access controls, encryption techniques, and auditing tools. Special care must be taken on behalf of the vendor and customer to address cloud specific risks such as multi-tenancy. Legal risks include data protection, data ownership, and accountability. Strong data handling practices and conformance to laws and regulations such as the EU Privacy Act must be considered. Finally, policy and organizational risks include compliance and lock-in issues. Lock-in is particularly problematic as vendors have already introduced proprietary architectures and portability standards are lacking.

We also presented an information assurance framework and legal recommendations that need to be considered before migrating to the cloud. The framework provides criteria that can help a prospective cloud customer assess the security and policy risks and tradeoffs in the different cloud architectures. Key IT decision-makers must use a formal methodology with well-defined metrics to determine if cloud computing is a viable solution for their unit/organization.

REFERENCES

Amazon.com. (2010, 8). *Amazon Web services overview of security processes whitepaper.* Retrieved 12 27, 2010, from http://aws.amazon.com/security

ArcSight. (n.d.). *ArcSight - Protect your business.* Retrieved December 28, 2010, from http://www.arcsight.com

Armbrust, M., Fox, A., Griffith, R., Joseph, A. D., Katz, R. H., Konwinski, A., et al. (2009). *Above the clouds: A Berkeley view of cloud computing.* Retrieved March 15, 2011, from http://www. eecs.berkeley.edu/Pubs/TechRpts/2009/EECS-2009-28.pdf

Betcher, T. (2010). *Cloud computing: Key IT-related risks and mitigation strategies for consideration by IT security practitioners.* Retrieved September 11, 2011 from https://scholarsbank. uoregon.edu/xmlui/handle/1794/10207

Cloud Security Alliance. (2009). *Security guidance for critical areas of focus in cloud computing.*

Cloud Security Alliance. (2010). *Top threats to cloud computing V1.0.*

Cloud Security Alliance "Security as a Service" Version 1.0. (2011). *Defined categories of service 2011.*

ENISA. (2009). *Cloud computing: Benefits, risks and recommendations for information security.*

Fujitsu Research Institute. (2010). *Personal data in the cloud: A global survey of consumer attitudes.* Retrieved December 28, 2010, from http:// www.fujitsu.com/downloads/SOL/fai/reports/ fujitsu_personal-data-in-the-cloud.pdf

Gartner. (2010, 6 25). *SAS 70 is not proof of security, continuity or privacy compliance.* Retrieved December 28, 2010, from http://www.gartner. com/DisplayDocument?ref=clientFriendlyUrl& id=1390444

Hoover, J. N. (2009, July 28). Inside Terremark's secure government data center. *Information Week.*

IDC. (2008, September 23). *Defining "cloud services" and "cloud computing".* Retrieved December 12, 2010, from http://blogs.idc.com/ ie/?p=190

IDC. (2008, October 2). *IT cloud services user survey, pt.2: Top benefits & challenges.* Retrieved December 11, 2010, from IDC eXchange: http:// blogs.idc.com/ie/?p=210

IDC. (2009, December 15). *New IDC IT cloud services survey: Top benefits and challenges.* Retrieved December 12, 2010, from http://blogs. idc.com/ie/?p=730

IDC. (2010, July 1). *IDC's public IT cloud services forecast: New numbers, same disruptive story.* Retrieved April 2, 2011, from IDC eXchange: http://blogs.idc.com/ie/?p=730

International Organization for Standards. (2008). *ISO/IEC 27001:2005.*

Kaufman, L. (2009). Data security in the world of cloud computing. *Security & Privacy, 7*(4).

Kim, A., McDermott, J., & Kang, M. (2010). Security and architectural issues for national security cloud computing. *IEEE 30th International Conference Distributed Computing Systems Workshops,* (pp. 21-25).

Marshall, A., Howard, M., Bugher, G., & Harden, B. (2010). *Security best practices for developing Windows Azure application.* Retrieved December 28, 2010, from http://go.microsoft. com/?linkid=9751405

Mell, P., & Grance, T. (2009). *The NIST definition of cloud computing.* Retrieved March 16, 2011, from http://csrc.nist.gov/groups/SNS/cloud-computing/cloud-def-v15.doc

Microsoft. (n.d.). *Security development lifecycle.* Retrieved 12 28, 2010, from http://www.microsoft. com/security/sdl/

Microsoft. (n.d.). *Windows Azure, Microsoft's cloud services platform.* Retrieved 12 28, 2010, from Microsoft: http://www.microsoft.com/ windowsazure/

NIST. (2007). *NIST, computer security division, computer security resource center*. Retrieved December 27, 2010, from http://csrc.nist.gov/publications/PubsSPs.html

Okuhara, M., Shiozaki, T., & Suzuki, T. (2010). Security architectures for cloud computing. *Fujitsu Scientific and Technical Journal, 46*(4), 397–402.

Owens, D. (2010, June). Securing elasticity in the cloud. *Communications of the ACM, 8*(5), 46–51. doi:10.1145/1743546.1743565

PCI Security Standards Council. (2010). *PCI DSS v2.0.*

Perrig, A., & Sion, R. (2010). *CCSW '10: Proceedings of the 2010 ACM Workshop on Cloud Computing Security*. ACM.

Sion, R., & Song, D. (Eds.). (2009). *CCSW '09: Proceedings of the 2009 ACM Workshop on Cloud Computing Security*. ACM.

Sosinski, B. (2011). *Cloud computing bible*. Indianapolis, IN: Wiley.

Trend Micro. (2010). *Addressing data security challenges in the cloud.*

Trusted Computing Group. (2010). *Cloud computing and security – A natural match*. Retrieved September 11, 2011, from http://www.trustedcomputinggroup.org/files/resource_files/1f4dee3d-1a4b-b294-d0ad0742ba449e07/cloud%20computing%20and%20security%20whitepaper_july29.2010.pdf

Wauters, R. (2009). *More security loopholes found in Google Docs*. Retrieved September 11, 2011, from http://techcrunch.com/2009/03/26/more-security-loopholes-found-in-google-docs/

Winkler, V. (2011). *Securing the cloud*. Waltham, MA: Elsevier.

Zhou, M., Zhang, R., Xie, W., Qian, W., & Zhou, A. (2010). Security and privacy in cloud computing: A survey. *Sixth International Conference on Semantics, Knowledge, and Grids*. IEEE, (pp. 105-112).

ADDITIONAL READING

Buyya, R., Yeo, C. S., Venugopal, S., Broberg, J., & Brandic, I. (2008). *Cloud computing and emerging IT platforms: Vision, hype, and reality for delivering computing as the 5th utility*. Elsevier. doi:10.1016/j.future.2008.12.001

Creeger, M. (2009). CTO roundtable: Cloud computing. *Communications of the ACM, 52*(8), 50–56. doi:10.1145/1536616.1536633

Davis, R., & Kennedy, D. (2009). Working in the cloud. *ABA Journal, 95*, 31–32.

Finnie, S. (2008). Peering behind the cloud. *Computerworld*, 22.

Gatewood, B. (2009). Clouds on the information horizon: How to avoid the storm. *Information & Management, 43*(4), 32–36.

Hayes, B. (2008). Cloud computing. *Communications of the ACM, 51*(7), 9–11. doi:10.1145/1364782.1364786

Kandukuri, B., Paturi, V., & Rakshit, A. (2009). *Cloud security issues*. IEEE International Conference on Services Computing, SCC 2009.

Kim, W. (2009). Cloud computing: Today and tomorrow. *Journal of Object Technology, 8*(1), 65–72. doi:10.5381/jot.2009.8.1.c4

Krebs, B. (2008) Amazon: Hey spammers, get off my cloud! *Washington Post.*

Lasica, J. (2009). *Identity in the age of cloud computing: The next-generation Internet's impact on business, governance and social interaction*. Washington, DC: Aspen Institute.

Leavitt, N. (2009). Is cloud computing really ready for prime time? *Computer*, *42*(1), 15–25. doi:10.1109/MC.2009.20

Nelson, M. (2009). The cloud, the crowd, and public policy. *Issues in Science and Technology*, *25*(4), 71–76.

Owens, D. (2010). Securing elasticity in the cloud. *Communications of the ACM*, 46–51. doi:10.1145/1743546.1743565

Rai, S., & Chukwuma, P. (2009). Security in a cloud. *Internal Auditor*, *66*(4), 21–23.

Rangan, K. (2008, May 7). *The cloud wars: $100+ billion at stake*. Tech. rep., Merrill Lynch.

Vogels, W. (2008). *A head in the clouds—The power of infrastructure as a service*. In First Workshop on Cloud Computing and in Applications (CCA '08).

KEY TERMS AND DEFINITIONS

Hybrid Cloud: This type of deployment is a mix of private and public cloud options where some services and/or infrastructure are provided over a private cloud and others are provided over a public cloud.

Infrastructure as a Service: This is a provision model in which a cloud service provider owns the infrastructure and is responsible for hosting and managing the infrastructure and outsources it to the customer.

Multi-Tenancy in Cloud Computing: This term refers to multiple tenants running on shared infrastructure within the cloud.

Platform as a Service: This is a provision model where the cloud service provider owns the operating system, hardware, storage, and network capacity and makes it available to customers over the Internet.

Private Cloud: In this type of deployment, service and/or infrastructure are provided over a private network.

Public Cloud: In this type of deployment, service and/or infrastructure are shared by multiple organizations.

Software as a Service: This is a provision model in which hosted software applications are made available to customers over the Internet.

Chapter 12
Cloud Computing Security and Risk Management

Yoshito Kanamori
University of Alaska Anchorage, USA

Minnie Yi-Miin Yen
University of Alaska Anchorage, USA

ABSTRACT

Cloud computing is changing the way corporate computing operates and forcing the rapid evolution of computing service delivery. It is being facilitated by numerous technological approaches and a variety of business models. Although utilizing the infrastructure of existing computing and networking technologies, different cloud service providers (CSPs) are able to unite their efforts and address a much broader business space. As a result, confusion has emerged and questions have risen from both Information Technology (IT) and business communities. How cloud environments differ from traditional models, and how these differences affect their adoption are of major importance. In this chapter, the authors first clarify misperceptions by introducing the new threats and challenges involved in cloud environments. Specifically, security issues and concerns will be depicted in three practical scenarios designed to illuminate the different security problems in each cloud deployment model. The chapter also further discusses how to assess and control the concerns and issues pertaining to the security and risk management implementations.

INTRODUCTION

Cloud computing is a new, rapidly evolving model of computing service delivery and has been receiving more and more attention from the IT industry. Although cloud computing integrates the latest computing and networking technologies – which are also used in non-cloud (or traditional) IT infrastructures – it has the potential to deliver more cost-effective and flexible management mechanisms to the IT industry, especially when compared to the traditional, dedicated server hosting model. One of the major characteristics of cloud computing is "Resource Pooling", where a cloud service provider (CSP) pools resources (e.g., computational power, storage space) in a server farm, or datacenter, to run on-demand virtual instances of their customers' servers. Companies can purchase software, platforms, or infrastructures

DOI: 10.4018/978-1-4666-2187-9.ch012

from the CSP through the Internet only when they need it, while the CSP charges the companies based on the amount of services used. Companies can reduce their hardware and software needs, which in turn can reduce their IT staffing requirements. However, this promising technology also brings security and privacy challenges, to not only IT and auditing professionals, but to the business leaders who need to make decisions on whether to adopt a cloud computing model (Armbrust, et al., 2009; Takabi, Joshi, & Ahn, 2010).

In this chapter, security and privacy challenges in the cloud computing environment are discussed. Instead of simply listing the challenges, specific security issues and concerns are depicted in three practical scenarios designed to illuminate the different security problems in each cloud deployment model in the next section. In the third section, the common security issues are discussed in all cloud models. Security and risk management implementation issues will be briefly introduced in the fourth section. Finally, our conclusion and recommendation are given in the last section.

THREATS AND SECURITY CHALLENGES

One of the primary challenges cloud computing faces is data security. When users store their sensitive data on public cloud servers, security will always be a great concern. The major problem behind the data security issue is that cloud servers and data owners are not within the same trusted domain (Yu, Wang, Ren, & Lou, 2010). So, it is difficult for customers to assess the security measures existing in the public cloud service provider (CSP) environment (Choudhary, 2007). For example, when a customer uses a web application provided by a third party to process data, the processed data may be temporarily stored on the third party's server. The customer expects the third party to be in compliance with the regulations required for the customer's business (e.g., HIPAA (HHS, 1996).) However, there is no easy way to

verify how the third party actually processes and stores its customer data. The more third party applications a customer uses, the more threats and challenges that customer will face in the cloud environment.

In the following three scenarios, the security issues and challenges in cloud environments are illustrated based on three key cloud deployment models – private, public, and hybrid clouds – using three distinct delivery models – Software as a Service (SaaS), Platform as a Service (PaaS), and Infrastructure as a Service (IaaS) (Mather, Kumaraswamy, & Latif, 2009; Krutz & Vines, 2010).

Three Cloud Computing Scenarios

In all scenarios, a company provides users with two web applications: (1) an Audio Editor (AE); and (2) a Movie Editor (ME), which uses the AE as an external component to edit the movie's audio track. Since movie editing in general requires a large amount of computations, the ME application copies the user's data as the input and returns edited data to the user. The company has internal users who use the applications, developers who develop the applications, and administrators who manage the company's IT infrastructure. These web applications are also available to customers (i.e. external users). A database is used to manage user account information, including the internal users, and customer or external user information. Customers in the scenarios use the web applications over the Internet. Cloud Service Providers (CSPs) deliver cloud services (i.e., SaaS, PaaS, and IaaS) to the company.

The first company, Company X, uses the private cloud model for its internal users while making the applications available through the public cloud for customers (see Figure 1). The second company, Company Y, utilizes the public cloud for both its internal users and development, as well as for its external users (see Figure 2). The third company, Company Z, uses the hybrid cloud with a combination of services provided by more than one CSP (see Figure 3).

Figure 1. Private cloud (for internal users) and public cloud (for customers)

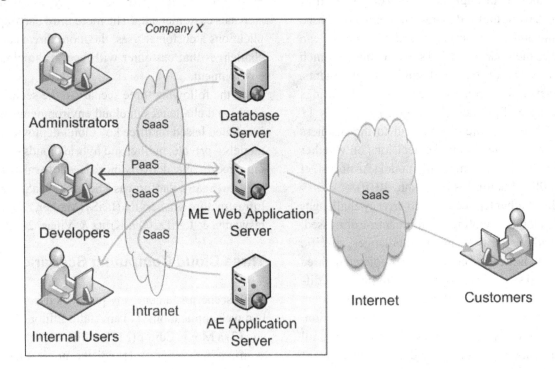

Scenario 1: Private Cloud for Internal Users while Public Cloud for External Users

According to the definition of "Private Cloud" by NIST (Mell & Grance, 2011), "The cloud infrastructure is operated solely for an organization. It may be managed by the organization or a third party and may exist on premise or off premise." Thus, in the private cloud, the data owners can store their data on their organization's servers or on vendors' servers operated solely for the data owners. However, the vendor is restricted by custom Service Level Agreements (SLAs) and contractual clauses with security and compliance while the customer organization must trust the vendor's security model.

Infrastructure and Operation

In Company X, all data and source code are stored on its servers and desktop computers.

The developers use development software (e.g., MS's Visual Studio) on their desktop computers and upload their source code or compiled application files to servers owned by Company X. Administrators use network management software (e.g., MS's Active Directory), which includes a central authentication service (e.g., RADIUS, Kerberos) and directory services to manage the access control for the company's assets (such as data and computers). Thus, administrators have full control over all of the servers and the data stored on them. The developers have full control over their source code files, which is an important asset for the company. The databases, which have sensitive data for Company X, can be accessed only by administrators, developers, and the ME web application.

Security Concerns

There will be no particular security concern caused by the private cloud environment compared with

Figure 2. Public cloud model

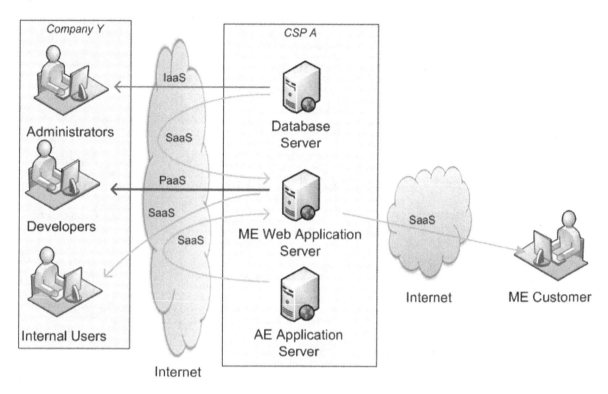

the traditional dedicated server hosting model. Company X allows internal users to use the ME application (SaaS) to process movie data. Since all data stay within the company's boundary, this SaaS would not cause particular security issues through the use of a private cloud environment. However, traditional security issues (such as exploitation of the vulnerabilities in servers and applications) will still exist. All user authentications and authorization processes are handled by Company X's central authentication server. Since the ME web application is also available for their customers (i.e., external users), Company X implements network and web application security protection against intrusions from the Internet, which include both internal and external firewalls in their demilitarized zone (DMZ) where the ME web application server is placed. In case of an incident or disaster, Company X backs up all critical business data, including their databases

and the application source code, to a server owned by Company X. Although the ME web application uses both the database and AE application, which run on different servers in Company X, access control is managed by Company X's central authentication service.

Scenario 2: Public Cloud for Both Internal and External Users

Infrastructure and Operation

Company Y uses only a public cloud. The developers install the software development kit provided by the CSP (such as Google App Engine SDK (Google, n.d.)) on their local computers. They upload the source code and database to the CSP's servers. The ME customers face the same security issues as they do with Company X in Scenario 1. The customers do not know how Company

Figure 3. Hybrid cloud with two CSPs

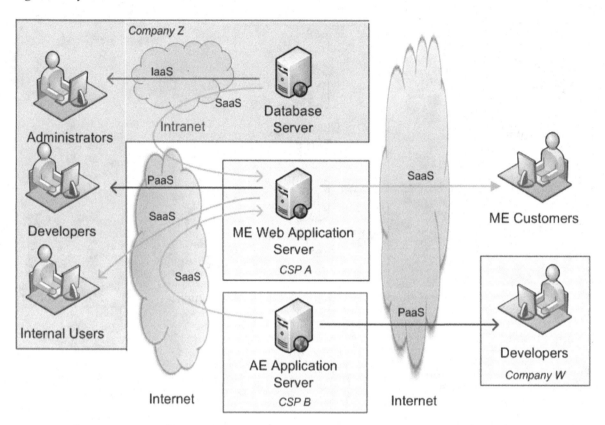

Y processes and stores its data in detail. Worse, Company Y may not know where the data is processed and stored on the Internet.

Security Concerns

Location Independence and Auditability

One of the essential characteristics of cloud computing is its "resource pooling" (Mell & Grance, 2011), where computational resources are pooled as physical and virtual resources in the CSP facilities and the CSP dynamically assigns and reassigns the computational resource to its consumers on demand. It will not only enable "rapid elasticity," another cloud computing characteristic, but also provide a sense of location independence in that the users generally do not have knowledge regarding the exact location of their resources. Also, CSPs

typically use redundancy to improve the availability of services. Large CSPs offer geographic redundancy in their cloud system. For example, Google distributes more than one million machines in 36 datacenters across the world (Zhou, Zhang, Xie, Qian, & Zhou, 2010) and Amazon EC2 (Amazon EC2, n.d.) is hosted in five regions: Northern Virginia, Northern California, Ireland, Tokyo and Singapore (Goldman, 2011).

Therefore, in this example, both the ME customer's data and Company Y's data may be stored in different countries from where Company Y is located. When data are stored in a different country, the CSP may be required to satisfy the security requirements and legal obligations of that country while Company Y may be expecting the CSP to satisfy the requirements and obligations of the country where Company Y is located. Since the location of both Company Y's data and the customer's data may be changed from time to time, it is difficult for the CSP to be compliant with specific regulations required for Company Y and the customer.

Furthermore, the location independence issue makes incident investigation more difficult because the data related to the incident may be located in multiple datacenters in different countries. Even if Company Y has contractual agreements with the CSP regarding the secrecy of private corporate information, such as non-disclosure agreements (NDAs), Company Y has no way to verify that their sensitive data are not being monitored by the CSP or some national agency in the country where the CSP facility is located.

Confidentiality

Compared with the private cloud case (Scenario 1), there are many more Internet data transfers for Company Y. The customers' data are accessed by the ME web application over the Internet. Also, the customers' audio data are transferred back and forth between the ME and the AE applications over the Internet. The customers' data and the web applications are more likely to be exposed to attack. Therefore, it is critical for CSPs and the application customers to use data transfer protocols with encryption schemes (e.g., HTTPS, FTPS) for any data transfer in the cloud.

In this public cloud environment, a customer's confidential data may be stored with other customer data in a datacenter or multiple datacenters. Cloud applications usually have mechanisms to prevent unauthorized access, but the mechanisms can fail due to exploitation of application vulnerabilities (Mather, Kumaraswamy, & Latif, 2009). The most obvious solution for this issue is to encrypt customers' data with different keys. The CSP can require the customers to encrypt their data before placing them in the CSP's public cloud. This approach may work well for some cloud services such as a web data storage service (e.g., Amazon

S3 (Amazon, n.d.),) but it is not always feasible. In Scenario 2, it is not practical for Company Y to encrypt the web application itself because the application code always needs to be decrypted before its execution. Although the data in the database can be encrypted, it will constrain some database functionalities (such as a data search) and significantly degrade performance due to the need to decrypt data prior to processing each query.

Responsibility for Security

The responsibility for security in the public cloud depends on both the cloud delivery modes (i.e., SaaS, PaaS, IaaS) and the SLA between a CSP and its' customers. In this scenario, Company Y uses PaaS for its web applications and IaaS for its database. For ME and AE web applications, the CSP provides the developers in Company Y with an entire application development platform over the Internet so that the developers do not manage or control the infrastructure (e.g., network, server, operating system, and storage). Company Y is responsible for the web application security for ME and AE applications. The developers have to harden the web applications from a variety of attacks, such as cross site scripting (XSS), SQL injection, session hijacking, hidden field manipulations, and so on. The CSP should be responsible for hardening the servers (e.g., applying patches, installing antivirus software) and providing both detective and preventive controls against the attacks directly on the CSP's network and server (e.g., SYN-flooding DOS attack, network intrusion). Company Y would also expect the CSP to offer some security features which cannot be managed by a PaaS customer, such as user authentication, Single Sign-On, and APIs for SSL/TLS configuration.

For the database server, the CSP provides Company Y's administrators with a virtual instance of a host server. In this case, the CSP will be responsible for physical security, environmental security, and virtualization security while the host security responsibilities are transferred to Company Y. Therefore, the administrators are responsible for making its network infrastructure secure by managing prevention and detection controls, such as firewalls and intrusion detection systems, and are also required to harden the database operating system. The developers are responsible for the basic database security (such as data confidentiality, data integrity, and access control).

Scenario 3: Hybrid Cloud for Both Internal and External Users with More Than One CSP

Infrastructure and Operation

In order to illustrate basic security issues, only three trust domains (Company Y, CSP A, Customers) were introduced in Scenario 2. To make a more realistic scenario, five trust domains: CSP A, CSP B, Company Z, Company W, and Customers are introduced here.

Company Z uses both private and public cloud models. The company places its database server on a private cloud due to privacy concerns and the risk that sensitive data may be held hostage by the CSP if a dispute arises with the public CSP (Zhou, Zhang, Xie, Qian, & Zhou, 2010). Although Company Z can place the private cloud infrastructure with a third party to reduce maintenance costs (e.g., hardware upgrades, regular back up operation), it places the private cloud infrastructure on its own network since the risk of information disclosure is too great when its data are stored on someone else's server. Since Company Z has full control over the database, including the infrastructure, and also knows the physical location of the server, it is easier for Company Z to be compliant with national and international regulations.

The ME web application is in CSP A's public cloud and uses the AE application through the SaaS provided by Company W, which developed and stored the application files in the CSP B's public cloud.

Security Concern

Trust and Single Point of Failure

As the number of trust domains in a scenario is increased, the risk of failures in the trust relationships among the domains requires more attention. When all domains are located in different countries, the situation becomes even more complicated. Similar to the problems in offshore outsourcing and international corporate partnerships, if any one of the entities in a trust domain does not follow the contractual agreement, either intentionally or by accident, the service may not be provided as designed or may be compromised.

For example, ME customers expect the web application to work as advertised by Company Z, which is responsible for the security of the ME application. However, Company Z must rely on the security mechanisms provided by CSP A because they have no control over CSP A's public cloud infrastructure which is hosting the ME application. Similarly, Company W is responsible for the security of the AE application and trusts the web server's security controls provided by CSP B. In this case, the database server on the private cloud and the application servers on different public clouds must use compatible protocols and application interfaces to communicate with each other even if the underlying cloud infrastructures are built with different technologies. Also, each CSP must guarantee the throughput of data processing on the web server with SLAs. Any failure of the preconditions would cause the single point of failure. The more external components an application has, the greater the risk of single point of failure.

OTHER COMMON SECURITY CHALLENGES

Since the cloud is built with Internet technologies, security issues are shared. In addition to traditional

Internet security issues and some common threats and security challenges faced by cloud computing described in Section II, it is important to address other concerns that may prevent companies from incorporating the cloud models.

Performance Stability

The servers in the cloud are virtual machines (guest OSs) on high capacity physical host servers located in datacenters. Large CSPs may use hundreds of host servers for thousands of guest OSs while small CSPs may use a few host servers for a hundred of guest OSs, so the data processing throughput of each host server and the network throughput vary with the CSPs. Additionally, it may be difficult for the small CSPs to manage host server load balancing since some guest OSs may require a huge amount of resources for varying short periods of time. Therefore the performance of their guest OSs may vary from time to time, so customers must rely on the SLAs to guarantee the performance of their guest OSs. (For example, Google Apps guarantees 99.9% uptime with penalties for non-fulfillment by the SLA (Google Apps, n.d.)) Although the SLAs stipulate penalties for the CSPs when they violate the contract terms, the compensation may not equal the resulting damage to their customers' reputations by performance degradations (Khan & Malluhi, 2010).

Attacks against Virtualization Technologies

Virtualization is one of the key elements of cloud computing. Virtualization technology enables "resource pooling" and "rapid elasticity" (Mell & Grance, 2011), which are essential cloud characteristics and the major advantages of the cloud. Virtualization also introduces critical security risks. Virtual machines run as guest operating systems on the host server operating system with the virtual machine monitor (VMM). However, several critical vulnerabilities were found in Virtual PC (Microsoft, 2007), VMware (VMware, 2007) and Xen hypervisor (Secunia, 2007, Secunia, 2008) that have been utilized by Amazon EC2 (Amazon, 2008). One vulnerability allows a guest OS to run code on the host or another guest OS, while another vulnerability allows a guest OS to access the host's complete file system and create or modify executable files. Yet another vulnerability allows "root" users of a guest OS to execute arbitrary commands.

Another potential issue with virtualization is the difficulty of forensic investigations (Chow, et al., 2009). In traditional digital forensics, the equipment (such as a hard disk drive) is seized and the media copied for detailed analysis and data recovery. With virtualization technologies, a virtual machine can be cloned for offline forensic analysis and reverted to the recovery state without downtime. However, since virtual machines may be regularly moved to other servers (i.e., different hard disk drives) to enhance the performance of the guest OSs (e.g., with vMotion (VMware, n.d)), traditional forensic techniques may not be sufficient to collect all legal evidence from the virtual machines.

Reputation Sharing

Cloud models not only share computational resources, but also the cloud's service reputation for reliability and security (Armbrust, et al., 2009). For example, if a company's CSP-hosted website suffers a security breach due to vulnerability in the CSP's security mechanism or application interface, all hosted websites and applications in the same cloud may be considered unreliable or lacking secure services even if they are provided by different companies. When a CSP stops its cloud services due to datacenter disk failures, hundreds of companies who use the cloud may find their business continuity plans questioned even if those companies have good continuity plans.

Impact of Denial of Service Attack

Denial of service (DoS) attacks on the cloud may have different impacts on CSPs and their customers (Jensen, Schwenk, Gruschka, & Iacono, 2009). In DoS attacks, attackers send thousands or millions of requests to the target server to overload its processing capability so it cannot perform regular operations. If a DoS attack compromises a guest OS in the cloud, it will not only stop the service on the target server but it may also stop or degrade the services on other guest OSs on the same physical server because those OSs are sharing the same physical resources (e.g., CPU, memory). Although the DoS attack may not be able to stop the service on the guest OS entirely due to the "rapid elasticity" of the cloud infrastructure, the DoS attack can still damage the customer. Unlike desktop application software, the CSP charges customers based on usage (e.g., CPU time, storage requirements). A customer pays more when the customer's website or web application has more visitors. Therefore, if a customer's website suffers a DoS attack, they have to pay for the resources used by the DoS attacks, too. The CSP may set the upper limit of the CPU usage for each guest OS to protect their cloud, but it also helps the DoS attack to succeed.

Malicious Cloud Service (Provider)

Like traditional malware models, there may be malicious cloud services and/or malicious CSPs (Jensen, Schwenk, Gruschka, & Iacono, 2009). An attacker creates its own malicious service or application component (as SaaS, PaaS or IaaS) and makes it available on the cloud for free or as a commercial web service. The attacker may then be able to collect user data without being detected as long as the component works as expected since reverse engineering a cloud service is difficult, if not impossible, for the customers. Legal authorities may also have trouble investigating suspicious

cloud services due to the obscurity and diversity of the data location (e.g., partial data stored on different datacenters in different countries).

RISK MANAGEMENT AND SECURITY CONTROLS

In spite of these risks and security concerns, the evolution of cloud computing also presents enormous benefits and opportunities. However, unless the risks and security issues which are involved in the day-to-day interactions between cloud users and CSPs, as well as between CSPs themselves, are addressed and the required management processes are implemented, the cloud computing community cannot ensure successful growth of the paradigm. Therefore, when organizations are conducting strategic discussions about cloud deployment, it is important to introduce risk management processes and security controls into the whole cloud computing domain and these treatments must be performed at all three layers: service, data and infrastructure.

Many of today's enterprise organizations are familiar with traditional IT controls. Much of the auditing guidelines and security frameworks that have existed for years and are considered mature can also be applied to cloud computing environments. These IT controls are frequently used to evaluate the operational or service delivery risks of an IT environment including its operational stability, availability, protection and recovery. If an organization and its CSPs can demonstrate their compliance with existing guidelines in risk assessment and information system controls, then a portion of the risk assessment should be covered (SANTA FE, 2010). These standards and guidelines included ISACA's COBIT 4.1, ISACA Risk IT Based on COBIT, ISO 27001, Standardized Information Gathering questionnaire (SIG) and Agreed Upon Procedures (AUP), NIST 800-53A, or PCI-DSS, etc. For example, Google and Amazon EC2 attain the Auditing Standards No. 70: Service Organizations, Type II (SAS70 Type II) certification (Amazon, 2008; Google, n.d.). The available threats and risks mitigation techniques used currently for cloud environments are frequently originated and adapted from traditional IT infrastructure security. For example, Amazon EC2 provides protection to ensure that non-authorized systems or users can access the data stored in Amazon EC2, including mandatory inbound firewall, host-based firewall to prevent IP spoofing and Port scan. They also implement standard distributed denial-of-service (DDoS) mitigation techniques (e.g., SYN cookies) and protection mechanisms against packet sniffing and ARP cache poisoning (Amazon, 2008).

However, the characteristics of a cloud computing environment which include but are not limited to virtualization, multi-tenant platforms, data locations and privacy, service orientation and delivery have emerged with different degrees of flexibility and involved new distinct risks. In this section, we will cover some high risk control areas that have particular relevance to cloud computing and whose audit mechanisms and risk mitigation processes are less mature and need more attention and discussion.

Specific IT and Business Management Control

Security controls fundamentally encompass three common goals: confidentiality, integrity and availability. In addition to these overall security controls, organizations will face certain management challenges when trying to deliver their applications and services in the cloud. Identity management, access control, Web application development and management, log management and backup control are always in the first tier of controls and management when a comprehensive cloud computing strategic plan is being developed.

Identity and Access Management

The enterprise authentication and authorization framework does not naturally extend into the cloud. It is important to recognize that with heterogeneity and diversity of services, as well as the diverse domains, management should be flexible enough to capture dynamic access requirements and at the same time, enforce the principle of least privilege (Takabi, Joshi, & Ahn, 2010). Identity and access management systems also need to be easily managed and efficiently administered. Major challenges faced in adoption of the cloud are how a company can meld its existing framework to include cloud resources and how an enterprise can merge cloud security data with its own security metrics and policies (Chow, et al., 2009). (e.g., an on-premise server infrastructure with public cloud services while meeting the criteria and policies for both Federated Identity Management and Single Sign-On.)

Ideally, an employee or a customer/user should not need an additional username and password to access data or services that are managed by the CSPs. Unified identity management is an important and essential component of the cloud, from a business usability and security perspective. Significant progress has been made in this area in recent years with the advent of Identity-as-a-Service (IDaaS) providers, that provide open, federate standards such as SAML and OpenID to permit transparent user sign on (SSO) among CSPs in cloud environments. It is important for an organization and its CSP to determine what protocol (SAML, ID-FF, WS-Federation, etc.) should be used for communication among identity management solutions. How to address the issue of using different protocols given that communication is critical for supporting activities such as provisioning, access management, identity management and security monitoring is a challenge yet to be solved.

Web Application Development and Management

Cloud computing is typically an open environment. Due to the fact that CSPs are usually exposing an increasing number of web interfaces and APIs to the Internet, which is far more than traditional closed on-premise solutions, the risk of application attack is increasing significantly. Since CSPs often provide application services, these applications need to have constant software development process reviews, code reviews, and penetration-test programs in place in order to keep up with the regular software delivery releases. Therefore, a tremendous amount of effort needs to be devoted to building and maintaining an adequate level of application experience and maturity to achieve a satisfactory level of cloud security. CSPs must excel in application security, and must be able to demonstrate that they have the application security team, knowledge, and processes in place to protect user data in the cloud (SANTA FE, 2010).

It is important for organizations to evaluate the depth and capability of the CSP's application security team and evaluate the application firewalls implemented by the CSP. Creating and reviewing the "sanity checklist", pre-and post-deployment, to assure CSPs utilize sufficient application security inspections is recommended. For example, basic checks such as having a secure code review before shipping to production, no password appearing in clear-test format, appropriate permissions having been made for the source code, and no password appearing in database connection strings should be included. To review and ensure sufficient hardening procedures exist for web and application servers and having application security integrated at every phase of software development life cycle (SDLC) are essential components of internal controls.

Log Management, Backup, and Recovery Controls

As described in the Other Common Security Challenges Section one of the fundamental characteristics of cloud environments is the shared infrastructure upon which the services run and where the data is stored. In cloud computing, the majority of logical separation controls are not physical (i.e., separate servers). Virtualization technology enables us to create a virtual version of servers, storage devices and network navigation devices. When referring to data in transmission, cloud computing evolved in the new paradigm of multi-point to multi-point in many different physical locations compared to the traditional point-to-point approach. Although this results in tremendous economies of scale, it also introduces risks, such as data scoping, and greater difficulties in tracking and protecting data. There are typically fewer controls in place to prevent the copying of a virtual image than there are to prevent the copying of server data to a backup tape (SANTA FE, 2010).

It is important to address the controls in place around hypervisor as it manages the virtual environment. Procedures must be implemented to confirm that the CSPs have controls in place to ensure that only authorized snapshots are taken and always request copies of the CSPs' virtualization-hardening guides and policies. The National Institute of Standards and Technology's Guide to Security for Full Virtualization Technologies (Scarfone, Souppaya, & Hoffman, 2011) provides a good starting point and any discrepancies against industry standards and controls will need to be identified and a gap assessment will need to be conducted.

It is essential to evaluate how user actions and system events will be audited and monitored and whether user organizations have access to their information and their logs. Continuous review of the functionality and usefulness of dashboards, reports, and application programming interfaces

(APIs) that the CSPs will provide to their users will ensure they meet user requirements and provide adequate control and monitoring capabilities.

The bottom line for cloud users, when they move any services or data into the cloud, is that they must be confident the CSP will protect their data from loss or compromise. Data protection controls need to be applied to all phases of the data cycle, from loading and copying data, to day-to-day data management, to removing or destroying the data at the end of the contract. Organizations must ensure CSPs have superior operational, change management, disaster recovery and business continuity plans and controls, and their procedures are in compliance with general standards included in the Information Technology Infrastructure Library (ITIL).

Additional Risk Management and Risk Mitigation Processes

Based on the Risk Management Standard (IRM, 2002) published on the Institute of Risk Management site, the entirety of risk management is governed by an organization's strategic objectives, and can be split in the following processes:

1. **Risk Assessment:** The overall process of risk analysis and evaluation.
2. **Risk Reporting:** The communication of risk to different levels within the organization and to its stakeholders on a regular basis.
3. **Risk Treatment:** The implementation and selection of risk-aware policies, as well as measurements, actions, and controls needed to face organizational risks.
4. **Risk Monitoring:** The review of all the above risk areas.

After certain risks are identified, analyzed and evaluated through auditing and investigation by following these standards and processes, how to treat and mitigate the risks through policies,

contracts, legality, and management procedures will be major responsibilities and tasks for an organization and its business leaders.

As with traditional technology outsourcing procurement, the process of obtaining cloud computing technologies also begins with a procurement request followed by an RFP (Request for Proposal) being sent to possible vendors. Next, sourcing strategies and measurement methods will be established in order to evaluate these prospective vendors. After completing the negotiation and selection phases, an organization will be able to initiate its contracts with CSPs based on agreed service levels.

In addition to the security controls discussed in the previous section, trust management and service and operation level agreements for the purpose of risk management and risk mitigation in cloud computing need to be addressed. Through the processes of trust management, contract negotiation and initiation, organizations should be able to apply their risk management strategies when dealing with critical and unacceptable levels of risk. For example, risk avoidance can be practiced by rejecting a new cloud service. Also, risk reduction can be attained by executing application redundancy on different cloud resources or by joining trust federations, for minimizing possible negative impacts due to SLA violations, service disruptions, and performance losses.

Trust Management

In a cloud computing environment, service requirements can drive the interactions between different service domains to be dynamic, transient, and intensive. To develop a trust framework that allows a generic set of parameters for establishing trust while also managing evolving trust interaction and sharing is challenging (Takabi, Joshi, & Ahn, 2010). One workable and ongoing solution is to establish a trust management system through the development of a trust federation where Identity

Providers, Service Providers and those who provide Access and Identity Management Services all work together.

Federated identity allows information about users in one security domain to be provided to other organizations in a federation. This allows for cross-domain Single Sign-On (SSO) and removes the need for content providers to maintain user names and passwords. Identity providers (IdPs) supply user information while service providers (CSPs) consume this information and allow users to obtain access to secure contents without additional login procedures. Federations greatly simplify and streamline the management of relationships and interoperability with multiple partners. These federations have been formed in many countries around the world to build trust structures for the exchange of information using Security Assertion Markup Language (SAML) and Shibboleth software (Internet2, n.d). Many major content providers support Shibboleth-based access. Currently, it is estimated that there are over four million students, staff, and faculty in these federations. SAML has been deployed worldwide in private and public sectors as well as in universities and research centers (SAML XML.org) while Shibboleth is seeing adoption worldwide in primarily research and education communities (Internet2, n.d.).

Contract Negotiation and Initiation

Due to the characteristics of cloud computing, new control areas are required to address the use of new technologies and significant new service models. There are nuances in how these controls apply to cloud computing environments. A Service Level Agreement (SLA) is a part of most service contracts where the level of service is formally defined. It is a negotiated agreement between cloud users and CSPs. The SLA records a common understanding about services, priorities, responsibilities, guarantees and warranties.

The SLA may specify the levels of availability, serviceability, performance, operation, or other attributes of the service, such as billing. The "level of service" can also be specified as "target" and "minimum," which allows customers to be informed what to expect (at a minimum), while providing a measurable (average) target value that shows the level of organizational performance and any additional arrangements. However, for most current well-known CSPs, customers can only accept standard, non-customizable SLAs. In these SLAs, CSPs offer certain guarantees like uptime, but other aspects like data location are not mentioned or guaranteed. For instance, Google Apps offers only one standardized SLA for all its customers (Kupferman, 2006), Salesforce.com does not have an SLA at all and Microsoft Office 365 did not provide an SLA during its beta phase. Office 365 promises that it will provide European Union (EU) data protection guarantees when the product is past the beta phase. Microsoft just made an announcement that Office 365 Complies with EU and U.S. Standards for Data Protection and Security in December, 2011. In some SLA contracts, penalties may be agreed upon for incidents of non-compliance. The SLAs commonly include sections to address the following areas: a definition of services, performance measurements, problem management, customer duties, warranties, disaster recovery, termination of agreement, etc.

For risk management and mitigation purposes, it is important to incorporate the key areas of a comprehensive security and audit program into SLAs and consider inserting a risk, controls and preparedness addendum specifying key policies that the CSP is required to implement. Cloud procurement is comparable to the process used for acquiring a traditional software product or outsourcing technology services. Both are dependent on a scalable due-diligence process to assess vendor viability, including a review of vendor financial stability and the ability of the vendor to support the product and/or service adequately.

However, further training in cloud computing will help to ensure the business/IT evaluation team considers the areas of vendor management, process improvement, risk management, quality control, business continuity, project management, security, compliance, internal control, audit and others in order to effectively evaluate cloud offerings. The contract must include terms and conditions that allow the organization to conduct a periodic assessment and audit for performance, risk, compliance and other purposes or other standards to determine CSPs compliance with organizational standards and policies.

Another issue related to the contractual relationship in cloud computing is that "multi-vendor" environments are becoming increasingly common in organizations and in particular with different CSPs. Integrating the various back-end and front-end components of a managed solution is no small task. It is important to keep it under one service contract and make sure the CSP's and its vendors' support service delivery model for the organization is covered under one maintenance contract. Also, requiring contract provisions that track the physical locations of data is important. Contract arrangements with different vendors are likely to become problematic if customers are required to engage each CSP separately. The CSP should provide consistent quality of service with a single point of contact, a single contract and a single point of accountability should things go wrong.

The customer organization needs to make monitoring the CSP's environment part of its regular security routine and risk management responsibilities. Ensuring that sufficient governance and risk management oversight exists within the user's organization in order to effectively manage and monitor the relationship with the CSP and its vendors is important. Ultimately, it is still the customer organization's data and services and it is the organization's responsibility to safeguard itself even if they are hosted or directly managed by the CSPs (SANTA FE, 2010).

IT Auditing Standards and Regulations Compliance

The safeguards of any risk management and security control system of an organization are dependent upon its own internal controls and assurances system. A system usually consists of the security and risk management policies, standards, and procedures designed and developed by the organization and at the same time, compliance with regulations and laws. COSO (Committee of Sponsoring Organizations of the Treadway Commission) (COSO, n.d.) and COBIT (Control Objectives for Information and related technology) frameworks are widely used as guidelines for audits in organizations and also for information technology governance purposes (Mishra & Dhillon, 2008).

In a cloud computing environment, the need to quantify penalties for various risk scenarios in SLAs and the possible impact of security breaches on reputation, motivate more rigorous internal audit and risk assessment procedures (Catteddu, 2010). According to "The Role of Internal Audit in Cloud Computing" (Ernst &Young, 2009), internal auditors play important roles in supporting activities in the following areas: identifying control requirements, vendor selection support, vendor management review, data migration assessment, project management, controls review and assessment. How to evaluate controls and procedures implemented by CSPs for managing these vendor relationships (e.g. through SLAs/OLAs) and how to deal with their compliance with different legislation from different countries and standards, are new challenges for its adopters.

In addition to the traditional ITIL (the IT Infrastructure Library) and client-server/on-premise ISO/IEC 27001/27002, a number of laws and regulations are important for the customer concerning compliance. Cloud computing not only affects SAS-70 and Sarbanes-Oxley (SOX) compliance, but also Gramm-Leach-Bliley (GLBA),

Payment Card Industry Data Security Standards (PCI DSS), and the Health Insurance Portability and Accountability Act (HIPAA). Compliance with such regulations and standards requires varying degrees of security, and the data will likely need to be handled differently. Some major laws, regulations and/or standards that may need to be considered in cloud computing environments include:

1. **Health Insurance Portability and Accountability Act (HIPAA) (HHS, 2002; HHS, 2003):** This US legislation has recently been expanded to include privacy clauses and security requirements for healthcare and insurance organizations.

2. **Sarbanes-Oxley Act (Sox) (Congress, 2002):** The US legislation that was enacted as a reaction to a number of major corporate and accounting scandals. It requires companies to manage their IT in such a way that software produces correct financial reports, and changes in software are logged.

3. **Payment Card Industry Data Security Standard (PCI DSS) (PCISSC, n.d.):** This is an information security standard for organizations that handles cardholder information for debit and credit cards. The standard was created to increase controls to reduce credit card fraud. Validation of compliance is done annually, by an external assessor for organizations handling large volumes of transactions, or by a self-assessment questionnaire for companies handling smaller volumes.

4. **SAS 70 (PGP, 2008):** This is a widely recognized auditing standard developed by the American Institute of Certified Public Accountants (AICPA). SAS No. 70 is the authoritative guideline that allows service organizations to disclose their control activities and processes to their customers and their customers' auditors in a uniform reporting format. The issuance of a service auditor's

report prepared in accordance with SAS No. 70 signifies that a service organization has had its control objectives and control activities examined by an independent accounting and auditing firm. The service auditor's report, which includes the service auditor's opinion, is issued to the service organization at the conclusion of a SAS 70 examination.

5. **EU Directive 95/46/EC (EC Data Protection Directive) (PGP, 2008):** This directive applies to companies which process sensitive and private data within the borders of the European Union.

6. **Wet Bescherming Persoonsgegevens (Wbp) (Wikipedia, n.d.):** This is the Dutch implementation of the EU Data Protection Directive. The processing of personal data should be reported to the "CBP, (formerly known as "Registratiekamer"), which stores the registrations in a public register and monitors compliance with Wbp.

There are other new important initiatives (Chung, 2011) to be considered including "Cloud Computing Information Assurance Framework" (ENISA) (ENISA, 2009), "Top Threats to Cloud Computing" (CSA, 2010), "Security Guidance for Critical Areas of focus in Cloud Computing" (https://cloudsecurityalliance.org/csaguide.pdf), "Controls Matrix (CM) ", "Consensus Assessments Initiative", "Trusted Cloud Initiative (TCI)" from (CSA, Cloud Security Alliance) and "Cloud Computing: Business Benefits With Security, Governance and Assurance Perspective" (ISACA) (ISACA, 2009).

It is the responsibility of both business managers and internal auditors, together with their IT professionals, to ensure that appropriate processes are in place to support these complex and high-risk projects for obtaining the greatest benefit. Additionally, significant new vendor relationships must be managed to maximize the value the company will receive from that relationship.

CONCLUSION AND RECOMMENDATION

Without a doubt, cloud technologies can deliver cost-effective and flexible solutions to organizations while providing a significant opportunity to leverage economies of scale. A company can minimize the size of its IT infrastructure by placing many components of the infrastructure in the cloud. Consequently, security and risk management can be simplified when customers rely on a CSPs' security controls, such as dedicated forensic servers and well-trained security personnel to protect their cloud. However, security and other associated risks are still major concerns for many organizations adopting or planning to adopt cloud computing (Armbrust, et al., 2009; Zhou, Zhang, Xie, Qian, & Zhou, 2010). As discussed in this chapter, there are many security concerns and privacy challenges to be solved. When sensitive data is placed in the public cloud, customers rightly have apprehensions about the confidentiality, integrity, and availability of their data. The bottom line for any cloud users when they move services or data into the cloud is that they must be confident the CSP will protect their data from loss or compromise. This is especially true when the CSP has data centers in different countries. Therefore, it is essential for cloud users to evaluate the depth and capability of the CSP's security controls by scrutinizing the Service Level Agreements (SLAs), which are a part of most service contracts where the level of service is formally defined.

Most well-known CSPs only provide standard SLAs that are not as customizable as cloud users would expect. In these SLAs, CSPs guarantee certain service properties (e.g., uptime), but they do not guarantee or mention the properties where the security issues we discussed in this chapter arise. (e.g., data location) Therefore, it is essential to introduce risk management processes and security controls into the whole cloud computing domain for an organization in their cloud deployment strategic discussion and this domain should cover three layers: service, data, and infrastructure. The safeguards provided by the risk management and security control system of an organization are also dependent upon its own internal controls, including policies, standards, and procedures designed to be compliance with applicable regulations and laws. It is our belief and recommendation that security concerns about the use of cloud computing in an organization can be reduced by clarifying the trust domains in the cloud, increasing the transparency of CSPs' SLAs and audit abilities, and through implementing appropriate risk management best practices.

REFERENCES

Amazon. (2008). *Amazon Web services: Overview of Security processes, 2008.* Retrieved October 15, 2011, from http://s3.amazonaws.com/aws_blog/AWS_Security_Whitepaper_2008_09.pdf

Amazon EC2. (n.d.). *Amazon Elastic compute cloud.* Retrieved October 15, 2011 from http://aws.amazon.com/ec2/

Amazon. (n.d.). *Amazon Simple storage service (Amazon S3).* Retrieved October 15, 2011, from http://aws.amazon.com/jp/s3/

Armbrust, M., Fox, A., Griffith, R., Joseph, A., Katz, R., Konwinski, A., et al. (2009). *Above the clouds: A Berkeley view of cloud computing.* Technical Report No. UCB/EECS-009-28, University of California at Berkley, USA.

Catteddu, D. (2010). Cloud computing – Benefits, risks and recommendations for information security. *Communications in Computer and Information Science, 72*(Part1, 17).

Choudhary, V. (2007). *Software as a service: Implications for investment in software development.* The 40th Hawaii International Conference on System Sciences (HICSS). Waikoloa, Hawaii.

Chow, R., Golle, P., Jakobsson, M., Shi, E., Staddon, J., Masuoka, R., et al. (2009). *Controlling data in the cloud: Outsourcing computation without outsourcing control*. The 2009 ACM workshop on Cloud computing security.

Chung, M. (2011). *Risk and compliance, new paradigm of automation*. Retrieved October 15, 2011, from http://www.vrisbi.nl/index.php/Download-document/23-New-Paradigm-of-Automation-KPMG.html

Congress. (2002). *Public law 107-204-Sarbanes-Oxley Act of 2002*. Retrieved October 15, 2011, from http://www.gpo.gov/fdsys/pkg/PLAW-107publ204/content-detail.html

COSO. (n.d.). *Committee of Sponsoring organizations of the treadway commission*. Retrieved October 15, 2011, from http://www.coso.org/

CSA. (2010). *Top threats to cloud computing, v1.0*. Retrieved October 15, 2011 from https://cloudsecurityalliance.org/topthreats/csathreats.v1.0.pdf

ENISA. (2009). *Cloud computing information assurance framework*. Retrieved October 15, 2011, from http://www.enisa.europa.eu/act/rm/files/deliverables/cloud-computing-information-assurance-framework

Ernst & Young. (2009). *Cloud computing – The role of internal audit*. Retrieved October 15, 2011, from http://www.isaca-oregon.org/docs/Cloud%20Computing%20-%20The%20role%20of%20Internal%20Audit.pdf

Goldman, D. (2011). *Why Amazon's cloud Titanic went down*. Retrieved October 15, 2011, from http://money.cnn.com/2011/04/22/technology/amazon_ec2_cloud_outage/index.htm

Google. (n.d.). *Top ten advantages of Google's cloud*. Retrieved October 15, 2011 from Google Apps for Business: http://www.google.com/apps/intl/en/business/cloud.html

Google. (n.d.). *What is Google app engine?* Retrieved October 15, 2011 from Google Code: http://code.google.com/intl/en/appengine/docs/whatisgoogleappengine.html

Google Apps. (n.d.). *Google apps service level agreement*. Retrieved October 15, 2011 from Google Apps: http://www.google.com/apps/intl/en/terms/sla.html

HHS. (1996). *The Health Insurance Portability and Accountability Act of 1996 (HIPAA) privacy and security rules*. Retrieved October 15, 2011 from http://www.hhs.gov/ocr/privacy/hipaa/understanding/index.html

HHS. (2002). *Standards for privacy of individually identifiable health information; final rule*. Retrieved October 15, 2011, from http://www.hhs.gov/ocr/privacy/hipaa/administrative/privacyrule/privrulepd.pdf

HHS. (2003). *Health insurance reform: Security standards; final rule*. Retrieved October 15, 2011 from http://www.hhs.gov/ocr/privacy/hipaa/administrative/securityrule/securityrulepdf.pdf

Internet2. (n.d.). *Shibboleth*. Retrieved October 15, 2011 from http://www.shibboleth.internet2.edu/

IRM. (2002). *The risk management standard*. Institute of Risk Management (IRM), The Association of Insurance and Risk Managers (AIRMIC) and Alarm (The Public Risk Management Association), 2002; also adopted by the Federation of European Risk Management Associates (FERMA). Retrieved October 15, 2011, from http://www.theirm.org/publications/documents/Risk_Management_Standard_030820.pdf

ISACA. (2009). *Cloud computing: Business benefits with security, governance and assurance perspectives*. Retrieved October 15, 2011, from http://www.isaca.org/Knowledge-Center/Research/ResearchDeliverables/Pages/Cloud-Computing-Business-Benefits-With-Security-Governance-and-Assurance-Perspective.aspx

ISACA. (n.d.). *COBIT framework for IT governance and control.* Retrieved October 15, 2011, from http://www.isaca.org/Knowledge-Center/COBIT/Pages/Overview.aspx

Jensen, M., Schwenk, J., Gruschka, N., & Iacono, L. (2009). On technical security issues in cloud computing. *2009 IEEE International Conference on Cloud Computing,* (pp. 109-116).

Khan, K. M., & Malluhi, Q. (2010). Establishing trust in cloud computing. *IT Professional, 12*(5), 20–27. doi:10.1109/MITP.2010.128

Krutz, R. L., & Vines, R. D. (2010). *Cloud security: A comprehensive guide to secure cloud computing.* Wiley.

Kupferman, J. (2006). *Service level agreements in web services.* Retrieved October 15, 2011, from http://www.cs.ucsb.edu/~jkupferman/docs/WS-SLA.pdf

Mather, T., Kumaraswamy, S., & Latif, S. (2009). *Cloud security and privacy: An enterprise perspective on risks and compliance.* O'Reilly Media.

Mell, P., & Grance, T. (2011). *The NIST definition of cloud computing (Draft).* Retrieved October 15, 2011, from http://csrc.nist.gov/publications/drafts/800-145/Draft-SP-800-145_cloud-definition.pdf

Microsoft. (2007). *Vulnerability in virtual PC and virtual server could allow elevation of privilege (937986).* Microsoft Security Bulletin MS07-049. Retrieved October 15, 2011, from http://www.microsoft.com/technet/security/bulletin/ms07-049.mspx

Mishra, S., & Dhillon, G. (2008). Defining internal control objectives for information systems security: A value focused assessment. *16th European Conference on Information Systems,* (pp. 1334-1345). Galway, Ireland.

PCISSC. (n.d.). *PCI data security council.* Retrieved October 15, 2011 from https://www.pcisecuritystandards.org/

PGP. (2008). *PGP® compliance brief - E.U. data protection directive 95/46/EC.* Retrieved October 15, 2011, from http://download.pgp.com/pdfs/regulations/EUD_compliance_brief-080618.pdf

SAML XML. org. (n.d.). *List of organizations using SAML.* Retrieved October 15, 2011, from SAML XML.org: http://saml.xml.org/wiki/list-of-organizations-using-saml

Sangroya, A., Kumar, S., Dhok, J., & Varma, V. (2010). Towards analyzing data security risks in cloud computing environments. *International Conference on Information Systems, Technology, and Management (ICISTM),* (pp. 255–265). Springer-Verlag. Santa Fe. (2010). *Evaluating cloud risk for the enterprise: A shared assessments guide.* Retrieved from http://www.sharedassessments.org/media/pdf-EnterpriseCloud-SA.pdf

Scarfone, K., Souppaya, M., & Hoffman, P. (2011). *Guide to security for full virtualization technologies.* The National Institute of Standards and Technology (NIST), Special Publication 800-125. Retrieved October 15, 2011, from http://csrc.nist.gov/publications/nistpubs/800-125/SP800-125-final.pdf

SEC. (n.d.). *Safeguarding of asset.* U.S Securities and Exchange Commission. Retrieved from Retrieved October 15, 2011, from http://www.sec.gov/rules/pcaob/34-49544-appendixc.pdf

Secunia. (2007). *Secunia advisory SA26986: Xen multiple vulnerabilities.* Retrieved October 15, 2011, from http://secunia.com/advisories/26986

Secunia. (2008). *Secunia advisory SA28405: Xen multiple vulnerabilities.* Retrieved October 15, 2011, from http://secunia.com/advisories/28405

Suess, J., & Morooney, K. (2009). Identity management and trust services: Foundations for cloud computing. *EDUCAUSE Review, 44*(5), 24–43.

Takabi, H., Joshi, J., & Ahn, G. (2010). Security and privacy challenges in cloud computing environments. *Security & Privacy, IEEE, 8*(6), 24–31. doi:10.1109/MSP.2010.186

VMware. (2007). *Critical VMware security alert for Windows-hosted VMware workstation, VMware player, and VMware ACE.* Retrieved October 15, 2011, from http://kb.vmware.com/kb/1004034

VMware. (n.d.). *VMOTION - Migrate virtual machines with zero downtime.* Retrieved October 15, 2011, from http://www.vmware.com/products/vmotion/features.html

Wikipedia. (n.d.). *Wet bescherming persoonsgegevens* (in Dutch). Retrieved October 15, 2011 from http://nl.wikipedia.org/wiki/Wet_bescherming_persoonsgegevens

Yu, S., Wang, C., Ren, K., & Lou, W. (2010). *Achieving secure, scalable, and fine-grained data access control in cloud computing. INFOCOM* (pp. 1–9). San Diego, CA: IEEE.

Zhou, M., Zhang, R., Xie, W., Qian, W., & Zhou, A. (2010). Security and privacy in cloud computing: A survey. *Sixth International Conference on Semantics, Knowledge and Grids*, (pp. 105-112).

KEY TERMS AND DEFINITIONS

IT Controls: A procedure or policy that provides a reasonable assurance that the information technology used by an organization is in compliance with applicable laws and regulations.

Location Independence: Customers generally have no control or knowledge over the exact locations of the system resources provided by CSPs.

Rapid Elasticity: A capability of rapidly and elastically increasing or releasing system resources (e.g., data storage, processing, memory) as necessary.

Risk Management: A systematic approach includes the identification, assessment, and prioritization of risks followed by coordinated and economical application of resources.

Risk Mitigation: A systematic mechanism can be used to reduce in the extent of exposure to a risk and/or the likelihood of its occurrence.

Security Controls: Security controls are the mechanism used to avoid, counteract or minimize security risks and safeguard the assets.

SLA: A Service Level Agreement (SLA) is a part of most cloud computing service contracts which records a common understanding about services, priorities, responsibilities, guarantees and warranties between cloud users and Cloud Service Providers (CSPs).

Trust Domain: A domain where a security policy is shared among the data systems and network systems.

Section 4
Legal Issues in Cloud Computing

Chapter 13
Key Legal Issues with Cloud Computing:
A UK Law Perspective

Sam De Silva
Manches LLP, UK

ABSTRACT

The chapter considers the key legal issues with cloud computing, including: (1) liability for service failure; (2) service levels and service credits; (3) intellectual property issues; and (4) jurisdiction and governing law.

INTRODUCTION

Cloud computing is designed to offer on-demand access to a flexible IT facility at reduced cost. This is attractive to a customer with pressures on budgets and possible uncertainty about predicting its IT requirements. However, cloud computing also carries certain additional risks. The chapter considers the key legal issues with cloud computing including:

- Liability for service failure;
- Service levels and service credits;
- Intellectual property issues; and
- Jurisdiction and governing law.

Data protection issues are also relevant for cloud computing. However, given the complexity of the subject matter and the coverage which would

be required to explain the issues, data protection is beyond the scope of this chapter.

In this chapter the service providers who are providing the cloud services are referred to as service providers and the customer is the party in receipt of the benefit of the cloud services.

This chapter is based on the law as at 1 December 2011.

EXISTING RESEARCH

There has been only a limited amount of research and writing from a UK law perspective on the topic of general legal issues related to cloud computing (with the exception of data protection). Whilst there are numerous short articles (less than 5 pages) on this topic (Tayyip 2011), the number of detailed articles and studies are limited. Marchini

DOI: 10.4018/978-1-4666-2187-9.ch013

has explored the legal issues, covering such areas as security in the cloud, data protection, service levels, and contractual issues (Marchini 2011). Kemp and Anderson have considered the legal issues in respect of cloud based service contracts (Kemp and Anderson 2010). In addition there has been a survey of a different number of service providers comparing their terms and conditions (Bradshaw, Millard and Walden 2010). There has been a considerable amount of research in relation to data protection issues and cloud computing (Hon, Millard and Walden 2011a). In a KPMG survey on cloud computing, 51% of participants expressed that legal issues were a key risk area (Chung and Hermans 2010).

LIABILITY FOR SERVICE FAILURE

Background

Liability provisions are, without doubt, the most contentious and fiercely negotiated provisions in almost any technology contract (and cloud computing contracts are no exception). The most obvious reason for this approach is the immediate financial impact that contractual failures have on the businesses that they support and, crucially, the extent to which the resulting financial damage is out of proportion to the level of fees being paid under the cloud computing contract itself. Both customers and service providers seem to vary enormously in the extent to which they expect the other party to accept liability or seek to exclude liability, respectively. Customers are keen for the service provider to be "on the hook" for the potential damage which can be caused by the failure of a business critical IT service or system. Service providers, on the other hand, argue with some justification that it would only be a matter of time before they were out of business if they accepted unlimited liability on every transaction.

Liability under Contract

Under contract law, a contracting party is entitled to damages for reasonably foreseeable losses that were caused by the other party's breach of the contract. Damages are the money that a court decides is to be paid by one person to another person as compensation for loss or damage sustained by that other person in consequence of the actions or omissions of the first person (Chitty and Beale 2011). The object of an award of damages is to place the wronged party in the position they would have been in had the contract been performed (*Gates v City Mutual Life Assurance Society Ltd* (1986) 160 CLR 1).

Generally, there are two types of losses arising from a breach of contract: direct losses and indirect losses.

Direct Loss

Direct losses are:

- Losses which arise naturally from the breach; or
- Losses that arise that would reasonably have been considered to be in the contemplation of the parties as a probable result of the breach.

In summary, if losses do not arise "naturally", or where not reasonably contemplated by the parties at the time the contract was made as a probable result of the breach, then they are not recoverable. These losses are generally categorised as indirect or consequential losses (see below).

Exclusions of Liability: Indirect or Consequential Loss

Service providers will usually argue that an exclusion of consequential or indirect loss is needed because the amount of such losses is related to the nature of the business, the manner in which the customer runs its business and the profitability of the business. The service provider's justification for excluding consequential or indirect loss is on the basis that it has no control over these matters. Service providers usually also wish to be certain of their total liability exposure under a contract, by excluding consequential loss and indirect loss and capping other losses.

Unfortunately the meaning of "indirect" or "consequential" loss is not entirely clear under English law. There have been a number of English cases where the scope and meaning of these words have been considered. Generally, the English cases appear to equate "indirect" loss to "consequential" loss. What is clear is that the English courts have construed what is "consequential" in a legal context very narrowly and, as a result, such an exclusion tends to exclude very little. Certainly such an exclusion provides the service provider very little protection. It is important to understand that claims for loss of profit, while commonly thought to fall within the category of indirect or consequential loss will often be regarded as a loss which is a direct and natural consequence of the breach. The cases of *Hotel Services Limited v Hilton International Hotels (UK) Limited* [2000] BLR 235 and *Deepak Fertilisers v Davy McKee* 1998] 1 Lloyd's Rep 387 are examples of this position.

The recent Court of Appeal decision in *GB Gas Holdings Limited v Accenture (UK) Limited and others* [2010] EWCA Civ 912 confirmed that whether a loss is a direct loss or an indirect/consequential loss is context-specific - what might be a direct loss in one scenario may be indirect/consequential loss in another.

In addition, as there are differences in the legal positions regarding the interpretation of liability provisions in various countries, care should be taken in selecting which law will govern the agreement. For example, if State of New York law is to be the governing law, the parties should consider the meaning of the words "indirect" and "consequential" under New York law (as those terms have specific meaning under New York law).

Approach to Direct Losses Adopted by Cloud Computing Contracts

It appears that all US based cloud providers surveyed in the study as part of the Cloud Legal Project at the Centre for Commercial Law Studies (CCLS), within the School of Law at Queen Mary, University of London (the "CCLS Study") seek to limit liability for direct damage as far as possible, be it in very general terms or phrased as relating to the consequences of inability to access data (Bradshaw, Millard and Walden 2010). In this context "direct liability" is taken to mean liability for losses to the customer relating to the loss or compromise of data hosted on the cloud service.

Cloud providers based in Europe tend to be less overt about seeking to exclude direct liability. This presumably is on the basis that in most European legal systems it is difficult to do so. Such exclusions as there are tend to be based on, for instance, force majeure (Bradshaw, Millard and Walden 2010).

Approach to Indirect/Consequential Losses Adopted by Cloud Computing Contracts

Exclusions against indirect liability, such as for indirect, consequential or economic losses arising from a breach by the cloud provider, appear to be even more common. This is no doubt due to the potentially very large scope of such damages. It may prove difficult to quantify the direct loss, if any, resulting from the deletion of customer data by a cloud provider. However, if that data is essential to, for instance, the operation of a busy online retail system, the resulting loss of business may be very large. As such, with the exception of one cloud provider which did not make a specific reference to such indirect or consequential losses, every single provider surveyed in the CCLS Study specifically excluded such losses (Bradshaw, Millard and Walden 2010).

Practical Application

The issue relating to liability is not academic. Effective cloud architecture should be robust. However, it is not possible to guarantee that the service will be immune to outages. Amazon's Simple Storage Service (S3) suffered two outages during 2008 (one in February and another in July) (Brodkin 2008) and salesforce.com's service was interrupted for nearly an hour in December 2008 (Ferguson 2009). During both of these outages customers were unable to access information and data stored with the products. In the case of Amazon, the interruption caused many customers' websites to be unavailable or have reduced functionality.

Every service (whether run in a cloud or in-house) is susceptible to outages or technical difficulties. However, limitations on both the power to control the technical solution and the ability to obtain remedies against the cloud provider may cause some customers to reconsider using cloud services or restrict the parts of its business for which it uses them.

It is extremely unlikely that any cloud provider will be prepared to guarantee compensation for all business disruption that it causes customers. However, the limitations of liability those cloud providers currently offer are unlikely to provide a financial incentive for the providers to invest in highly resilient infrastructure. This may be a particular concern given the lack of contractual assurances from many providers concerning the cloud architecture. In the current environment, while cloud computing establishes itself, the best assurance for a customer is to deal with a cloud computing service provider with a:

- Good track record;
- Commitment to remain in the cloud computing market; and
- Reputation to protect.

SERVICE LEVELS AND SERVICE CREDITS

The performance and quality of cloud-computing services are primarily monitored by service level and service credit mechanisms. Service levels provide objective and measurable assessments of key elements of the service (Strum, Morris and Jander 2000). As a result, they are probably the most important part of the cloud-computing contract, although they are not always included within the service provider's standard terms.

For example, many service providers are currently offering their products only on an "as is" basis. Many are excluding any warranties regarding performance of the service, including any warranties:

- That the service will function as described in its marketing material; and
- Regarding the reliability, availability, quality, or accuracy of the service (Bradshaw, Millard and Walden 2010).

In addition, some providers retain the right to suspend their service at any time due to any unanticipated downtime or unavailability (Bradshaw, Millard and Walden 2010).

Service credits provide a financial mechanism for customers to put pressure on service providers and ensure that the services meet the service levels (see under the heading "Service credits"). In a software-licensing arrangement the customer can make a technical assessment of the software to be provided and decide whether or not the software meets the customer's needs. By contrast, in a cloud-computing arrangement (as in IT-outsourcing arrangements) the customer is completely reliant on the contractual services descriptions which form the basis of the service to be provided to the customer. Negotiating adequate service level and service-credit arrangements is therefore particularly important in cloud-computing arrangements.

Service Availability

Service availability service levels seek to measure the extent to which the cloud-computing service is available to users as a percentage of the time during which the service provider is contracted to provide the service to the customer. There are a number of issues that need to be considered when negotiating service availability service levels for cloud computing service arrangements, including:

- Point of measurement;
- Service measurement period; and
- Application availability.

The point of measurement of service availability can be at a variety of points. For example, it can be at:

- The service provider's servers that host the application;
- The cloud-termination point (where the link is made between the cloud service and the customers' IT infrastructure); and
- The user's computers.

Service providers normally aim to establish the point of measurement at their servers, but this argument should not be accepted without question by the customer. Where the transmission is over the internet, there are many different types of internet service provision and the service provider should not be allowed to adopt a potentially low-quality and low-cost approach, with the inevitable impact on service quality, unless the customer understands the approach and has agreed to it.

From the customer's perspective, service availability measurement at the user's computer is attractive because the measurement assesses the extent to which the cloud computing service is available to the user. However, this may not be possible if there is no technological method of assessing service availability at the user's computer. A customer needs to have a reasonably sophisticated system infrastructure to make the measurement, but the necessary tools are no longer uncommon.

A service provider can be expected to argue that the service availability measurement at the user computer level is inappropriate as this will introduce downtime (when the service is not available) resulting from the customers' infrastructure failure, rather than from the failure of the cloud service. The service provider may therefore suggest that the point of measurement should be the cloud termination point at the customer's premises. However, if service availability is measured at this point, it will be more difficult for the customer to assess service availability at an individual-user level rather than at the aggregate level relating to all of the users to whom the service is provided.

The period when service availability service levels will be assessed needs to be specified because the choice of the service measurement period has an impact on the calculation of service-level assessment. Whilst a 24/7 service might appear to be attractive (particularly for global organisations), in practice this can lead to a need for considerable downtime before service credits are incurred. For example, a 98% service level would mean nearly 15 hours of downtime in a 31 day month before it was failed, whereas on an 8.00 am to 6.00 pm weekday service, around 4 hours of downtime might be sufficient to trigger service credits. Customers should consider the impact that taking either approach would have on their operations. Downtime that does occur out of hours can be more difficult to rectify quickly as engineers are less likely to be available. With the focus of cloud computing on flexible anytime, anywhere access, out of hours downtime can soon have a detrimental effect on a service that would otherwise have met its service availability targets and which in all other respects is acceptable.

At its most basic, a service provider may provide a bundled cloud service comprising, for example, e-mail, internet browsing and office applications (such as word processing and presentation applications). The service availability service level, therefore, should relate not just to the overall cloud computing service availability, but also to the availability of the individual software applications.

Service Credits

As mentioned above, service credits are an attempt to incentivise the service provider and compensate the customer in a pre-agreed manner for levels of performance which are not perfect but not disastrous either. Service credits are by no means appropriate for all degrees of failure. Where service credits apply they will generally be in full and final settlement of all claims related to performance falling within the scope of the service credit regime. In other words no other remedies will be applicable whether by way of damages or termination (De Silva and Golding 2005).

The customer needs to decide whether it favours a service credit regime and, if so, how extensive it should ideally be. Of course, it will always have to be negotiated and agreed with the service provider. Service credit regimes have the advantage to both the customer and service provider of certainty and of keeping risk to identifiable and manageable levels. Pre-agreed service credits also avoid disputes about applicable compensation occurring on an ongoing basis. Service credits are also useful where it is particularly difficult to quantify the loss which has been suffered as a result of specific breaches.

From the customer's perspective the exclusive remedy nature of service levels may be a problem particularly if they are not sufficiently sensitive to reflect poor performance or if they cover too broad a scope of poor performance such that the customer is not left with a meaningful remedy or threat to secure improvements. Also, as mentioned above, service credit regimes can lead to service providers wrongly concentrating on simply avoiding incurring credits to the detriment of the service overall.

Conversely, if service credits are too sensitive in their operation the service provider will be overly punished for relatively minor breaches and will be left with an unprofitable contract and with significant disincentives to perform well.

In order to be enforceable, service credits must be a genuine pre-estimate of loss. They must also not be unduly "oppressive". If they are a penalty they will be unenforceable in their entirety. A English case, *McAlpine v Tilebox* [2005] EWHC 281 (TCC) suggests that a court will be slow to interfere with a liquidated damages clause negotiated at arms length between commercial parties. In that case even though the liquidated damages amount was quite significant (£45,000 per week), it was still not held to be a penalty. In practice, the circumstances in which a customer could negotiate a regime which amounts to a penalty is likely to be quite rare. The English courts have certainly begun to incorporate this requirement for a liquidated damages clause to amount to "oppression" before it would be unenforceable in a contract negotiated between commercial entities.

Nevertheless, from a practical perspective, when negotiating the amount of service credits it is prudent for the customer to retain evidence indicating how the predetermined sum was calculated and any evidence demonstrating how that sum was negotiated. This is particularly important if it is difficult to calculate likely losses with precision.

The service credits may be a lump sum, a percentage of the monthly charge, or the product of a more complex formula. Whatever the calculation, the amount of service credits involves implicit or explicit weighting based upon the importance of a particular function or service to the customer's business. The more significant the failure, the more it will cost. Repeated or multiple failures may cost even more (for example, if the same failure recurs, or more than one critical service level is missed in a single month).

Of course a customer could decide not to go for a service credit regime at all. This means that the service provider is immediately at risk of damages at large (according to common law principles) subject to any applicable exclusions/limitations upon liability contained within the outsourcing contract. This can represent quite a significant incentive as against a service credit regime which is not sufficiently sensitive (i.e. the formula does not adequately compensate the customer/incentivise the service provider). However, it does mean that for levels of performance which are poor but not disastrous there is effectively no remedy short of the "nuclear" option of going to court and claiming damages. Since court action is very much a last resort it probably means most service providers get away without paying compensation in such circumstances unless performance deteriorates to such low levels as to be completely intolerable.

INTELLECTUAL PROPERTY ISSUES

Licensing

Although cloud-computing contracts relate to the provision of services rather than to the supply of software to customers, appropriate software licences still need to be granted to the customer. This is because users have online use of software at a computer and, without a licence, this would amount to copyright infringement. These licences are usually very narrowly defined and limited to use of the online application for their own business purposes. Customers have no rights to make copies of or modifications or enhancements to the software, and they cannot sub-license to third parties (Marchini 2011).

The service provider will not always own the intellectual property rights ("IPR") in the software that is the subject of the cloud-computing service. Where this is the case, the service provider will need to arrange for the right to sub-license the software to its customers, or for a direct licence to be entered into between the customers and the relevant third-party licensor. For the purposes of contractual simplicity, it is preferable (and most common) for the service provider to sub-license the customer's use of the third-party software. All of the contractual arrangements will then be between the service provider and the customer.

However, software licensors often require a direct licence agreement to be entered into between the customer and the third-party licensor. In these circumstances, the cloud-computing contract should make it clear that the service provider is responsible for the management of the third-party licences, together with the payment of any licence fees. The third-party licensor should also be informed that the licence arrangements relate to licensing only. All other issues relating to the provision of the software, such as delivery, installation and configuration requirements, should be dealt with in separate agreements between the customer and the service provider.

Content Licensing

The standard terms and conditions offered by many service providers in the consumer market include a broad licence from the customer to the service provider allowing them to use any content stored on its servers. These licences are often expressed as being perpetual and irrevocable. The uses to which the service provider can put the content are usually limited but there are often rights to pass the content to third parties or use it for the purpose of promoting the cloud computing service. This may not be appropriate for much of the information customers would be looking to store (such as personal data, third-party IPR or confidential information contained in or attached to e-mails).

Customers should take particular care in identifying any rights they are agreeing to provide to the service provider. Licences may be implied by necessity or business efficacy, however a better and more certain approach is to have an express licence in place that is broad in scope and covers the full range of likely activities.

Content Issues

The service provider will look to exclude all liability for content stored or posted on its services and will normally include a right in its standard terms to remove any data from its servers. This is because under:

- Directive 2001/29/EC of the European Parliament and of the Council on the harmonisation of certain aspects of copyright and related rights in the information society;
- Directive 2000/31/EC of the European Parliament and of the Council on certain legal aspects of information society services, in particular electronic commerce, in the Internal Market; and the Digital Economy Act 2010

Internet service providers (ISPs) can be liable for failing to take down offensive, defamatory or IPR-infringing content, and cloud-computing applications often blur the line between public and private networks. In these circumstances, corporate customers should seek an indemnity for any loss suffered as a result of material being unnecessarily deleted or moved and should look to impose a requirement to be notified in advance if any content is to be removed.

IPR Indemnities

It is standard practice in all IT contracts to include an IPR indemnity for the customer's benefit in the event that a third party makes a claim that the use of IT products by the customer (particularly software) infringes the third party's IPR. The inclusion of IPR indemnities in cloud-computing contracts remains important because customers have to rely on the service provider to ensure that software licensing issues have been resolved so as to entitle the customer to use the software as part of the service. One of the benefits of cloud-computing arrangements is that the burden of the upkeep of software licensing arrangements is generally lifted from the customer. However, if the arrangements are not properly made, the customer may still infringe the IPR of a third party even though it may have no knowledge of the infringement.

Cloud-computing users need to be aware of the possibility of patent infringement through the use of cloud-computing arrangements. Patent protection is increasingly available for computer software in the US and, to a lesser extent, in the EU. Where cloud-computing arrangements are established on an international basis, the IPR indemnity needs to be sufficiently broad to protect the cloud services' customers in all jurisdictions in which the software will be used.

Protecting IPR

Following recent case law, there has been some discussion on the threat to suppliers' IPR in their own software and the extent to which customers may take advantage of know-how gained in a short-term contractual relationship, which may be terminated on short notice by a customer.

Computer programs and the preparatory design material behind them are subject to copyright protection as literary works under the Copyright, Designs and Patent Act 1998. However, it is important to draw the distinction between the idea for a computer program and the expression of that idea for the purposes of determining whether copyright exists. Under common law, copyright will cover the expression of an idea, but not the idea itself. The application of this principle in relation to computer programs has been enshrined in EU law, which confirms that "ideas and principles which underlie any element of a computer program, including those which underlie its interfaces, are not protected by copyright" (Article 2(1), Council Directive 91/250/EEC on the legal protection of computer programs).

This means that there is a risk that users of cloud services could produce simulations of the functionality in a cloud offering in order to build a competing cloud service (although the terms and conditions might seek a contractual undertaking to only access the solution for the purposes of using the service).

The courts recently considered this principle in a software provision rather than a cloud context, in *SAS Institute v World Programming Ltd* [2010] EWHC 1829 (Ch). In this case, the defendant used the claimant's publicly available manuals together with a learning edition of its software to produce its own program, which emulated the core functionality of the claimant's system. The claimant alleged that, while the defendant had not accessed the original software in creating its program, it had infringed the claimant's copyright through use of the manuals and the learning edition. The court did not share the claimant's view and held that there had been no infringement. In its judgment, the court expanded on the principle that copyright could not subsist in mere ideas, stating that the programming language, interface and functionality of a computer program also fell outside the scope of protection.

The judgment may prove to be highly significant to service provider, who will now fear that the non-protected elements of their product can now be freely emulated.

JURISDICTION AND GOVERNING LAW

It is common for service providers and their customers to be located in different jurisdictions. Where this is the case, two separate issues need to be considered: applicable governing law and jurisdiction.

Governing law relates to the law that governs the contract. Jurisdiction relates to courts of the country which is to resolve any dispute.

In each case, the cloud contract may stipulate choice of law and jurisdiction. However, there may also be separate and different rules on applicable law and jurisdiction which apply irrespective of provisions in the contract, for example, data protection, which has its own free-standing rules on applicable law and jurisdiction.

In relation to the governing law of the contract, the parties will usually expressly provide that the cloud-computing contract is to be governed in accordance with the laws of a particular country. Where the parties have not expressly chosen a legal system, various rules such as Regulation (EC) 593/2008 of the European Parliament and of the Council on the law applicable to contractual obligations ("Rome I") will apply.

In the case of non-contractual obligations, such as tort, unfair competition or IP infringement, Regulation (EC) 864/2007 of the European Parliament and of the Council on the law applicable to non-contractual obligations ("Rome II") will apply.

The application of Rome I and Rome II is complex and beyond the scope of this chapter.

Of the 31 terms and conditions in the CCLS Survey, 15 claim to be governed by the law of a US state, usually California, although the laws of Massachusetts, Washington, Utah and Texas were also invoked. Of the other 16, 8 either specified English law generally, or stated that it would apply for a U.K. or European customer (Bradshaw, Millard and Walden 2010).

If the cloud computing contract is a set of non-negotiable terms and conditions, the choice of governing law for non-contractual obligations may be ineffective. This is because this right of choice (provided by Article 14(1)(b) of Rome II) applies to agreements that are freely negotiated. Although the meaning of "freely negotiated" has not been defined in Rome II, its requirement creates uncertainty over whether a governing law clause in standard form agreements that covers a non-contractual obligation will be effective.

Customers often take the view that the cloud-computing contract should be governed by their local law as this is the legal system of which they have greatest knowledge. However, this will be difficult to negotiate (as service providers will not want a range of contracts across a global client base governed by different legal systems), although if the customer is dealing as a consumer, Rome I provides that certain protection provisions of the law of the consumer's country of habitual residence cannot be contracted out of.

Further, the above approach may not necessarily be the most advantageous position. If the service provider does not have a sizeable presence in the customer's jurisdiction then any court order that might be obtained will be difficult to enforce in the service provider's jurisdiction. This applies particularly between EU customers and US service providers and where there is a need to obtain emergency remedies against a service provider, for example, if the customer considers that its data has been misused by the service provider. In these circumstances, obtaining emergency remedies will generally be more straightforward if the governing law of the contract is the local law of the service provider.

Where the customer is a multi-national corporate entity, additional jurisdictional issues arise, including:

- Local law; and
- Conflict of laws; and
- Encryption regulation,

all of which are beyond the scope of this chapter.

SUMMARY AND OVERALL RECOMMENDATIONS

The four key legal issues outlined at the beginning of this chapter highlight the main areas of contention between customers and service providers in relation to cloud computing contracts. Each issue is likely to be the subject of fierce negotiation, with the outcome influenced by the negotiating strength of both parties.

Exclusion of liability for service failure in cloud computing contracts is an extremely important issue. Service providers are very prudent in excluding liability for both direct and indirect/consequential loss, although it is recognised that this is more difficult within the European legal systems. Given the lack of contractual assurances from service providers, cloud customers will have to take a less formal approach to risk management by only dealing with the most reputable service providers who have a firm commitment to remaining in the cloud computing market whilst it develops.

Service levels allow customers to monitor the availability of the cloud-computing service. The "point of measurement" is a key issue and will generally determine the standard of service required of a service provider. Generally, both parties will settle for the "cloud termination point" as a common ground for the point of measurement. Service credits are a compensation mechanism usually insisted upon by customers as an attempt to incentivise the service provider to provide pre-agreed levels of performance. If a service provider fails to meet the required standard, they will be required to pay the customer liquidated damages at a pre-agreed level. Customers seeking to rely on service credits must ensure that they are a genuine pre-estimate of loss which does not amount to an "oppressive" or penalty figure.

Customers need to ensure that they are granted the appropriate software licence(s) even though they are being provided with a service. In addition, customers should be aware that the standard terms offered by many service providers usually include a broad licence allowing the use of any content that is stored on its servers. This may not be appropriate where the content to be stored is of a highly sensitive and confidential nature. Service providers will look to include a right to remove any content stored on their servers in order to comply with any "take down" notices they are issued. Corporate customers should seek an indemnity for any loss suffered as a result of material being unnecessarily deleted or moved.

Service providers should be aware of the risks in operating a cloud computing service. As copyright laws will only cover the expression of an idea and not the idea itself, there is a risk that cloud users could produce simulations of the functionality in a cloud offering in order to build a competing cloud service.

An advantage of cloud computing is that the customer and service provider need not necessarily operate from the same country. However, this does raise problematic applicable law and jurisdictional issues. These problems may be avoided if both parties expressly provide that the cloud computing contract is to be governed in accordance with the laws of a particular country. In the absence of agreement between the parties, customers may find it difficult to negotiate in favour of a particular country's laws as a service provider will not want a range of contracts spread across different legal systems.

To manage some of these legal risks the parties should check that all of the following issues are covered in a cloud-computing agreement.

- Core Services
  - Basic monthly service charge;
  - Any separate licence fee(s) or other mandatory charges; and
  - Core service features and limits (for example, seats/users, storage).
- Cost variations
  - Price per additional seat/user;
  - Pricing for additional storage. This should be benchmarked over time (storage cost trends are usually downwards);
  - Volume discount bandings;
  - Features and pricing of basic support/ maintenance charge;
  - Features and pricing of premium support/maintenance; and

- Details and pricing of other chargeable elements.
- Pre-contract due diligence
  - Service construction (for example, is infrastructure subcontracted?);
  - Service locations;
  - Service and security accreditations and certification;
  - Customer references;
  - Data models and formats for migration (in and out);
  - Service provider's access management processes (that is, which supplier employees will have access);
  - Service provider's product/service development plan (for example, new features that are planned); and
  - Interoperability with customer's other systems.
- Customer retained risks
  - Details of who can authorise which changes to service (for example, taking additional functions);
  - Details of customer security obligations (for example, password management);
  - Note and manage for unwarranted risks (for example, data loss).
- Implementation
  - Details and pricing of training and configuration assistance;
  - Trial and acceptance periods (and when payments commence or will be refunded); and
  - Integration with customer's other systems.
- Service arrangements
  - Access management arrangements and self-provisioning tools;
  - Service levels, service credits and termination thresholds;
  - Support, governance and service management arrangements;

- ◦ Invoicing and payment systems, including service reports and query management; and
- ◦ Internal customer governance policies (for example, support, password provision and withdrawal).
- Service continuity and disaster recovery
  - ◦ Service provider contingency and disaster recovery procedures;
  - ◦ Price for extra storage back-up and business continuity;
  - ◦ Any options and pricing for escrow of object code, source code and data.
- Exit and transition arrangements
  - ◦ Features and pricing of transition services at termination/expiry.

REFERENCES

Balboni, P. (2010). *Data protection and data security issues related to cloud computing in the EU.* Securing Electronic Business Processes - Highlights of the Information Security Solutions Europe Conference 2010; Tilburg Law School Research Paper No. 022/2010. Retrieved May 13, 2011, from http://ssrn.com/abstract=1661437

Bradshaw, S., Millard, C., & Walden, I. (2010). *Contracts for clouds: Comparison and analysis of the terms and conditions of cloud computing services.* Queen Mary School of Law Legal Studies Research Paper No. 63/2010. Retrieved May 13, 2011, from http://ssrn.com/abstract=1662374

Brodkin, J. (2008). *More outages hit Amazon's S3 storage service.* Network World. Retrieved 13 May from http://www.networkworld.com/news/2008/072108-amazon-outages.html

Chitty, J., & Beale, H. G. (2011). *Chitty on contracts.* London, UK: Sweet & Maxwell.

Chung, M., & Hermans, J. (2010). *From hype to future.* KPMG's 2010 Cloud Computing Survey. KPMG. Retrieved May 13, 2011, from http://www.kpmg.com/AR/es/IssuesAndInsights/ArticlesPublications/KPMGInternacional/Document/Cloud_Computing_Survey_2010.pdf

Copyright, Designs and Patent Act. (1998). UK Parliament.

Council Regulation (EC) 44/2001 on jurisdiction and the recognition and enforcement of judgments in civil and commercial matters. (2001). Retrieved May 13, 2011, from http://eur-lex.europa.eu/LexUriServ/LexUriServ.do?uri=OJ:L:2001:012:0001:0023:EN:PDF

De Silva, S., & Golding, P. (2005). Outsourcing contracts: Lessons learned. *Commonwealth Law Bulletin, 31*(2), 1–51. doi:10.1080/03050718.2005.9986678

Deepak Fertilisers v Davy McKee. (1998). 1 Lloyd's Rep 387

Digital Economy Act. (2010). UK Parliament.

Directive 2000/31/EC of the European Parliament and of the Council on certain legal aspects of information society services in particular electronic commerce, in the internal market. (2001). Retrieved May 13, 2011, from http://eur-lex.europa.eu/LexUriServ/LexUriServ.do?uri=CELEX:32000L0031:EN:HTML

Directive 2001/29/EC of the European Parliament and of the Council on the harmonisation of certain aspects of copyright and related rights in the information society. (2001). Retrieved May 13, 2011, from http://eur-lex.europa.eu/LexUriServ/LexUriServ.do?uri=OJ:L:2001:167:0010:0019:EN:PDF

Directive 91/250/EEC on the legal protection of computer programs. (1991). Retrieved May 13, 2011, from http://eur-lex.europa.eu/LexUriServ/LexUriServ.do?uri=CELEX:31991L0250:EN:HTML

Directive 95/46/EC of the European Parliament and of the Council of 24 October 1995 on the protection of individuals with regard to the processing of personal data and on the free movement of such data. (1995). Retrieved May 13, 2011, from http://eur-lex.europa.eu/LexUriServ/LexUriServ.do?uri=CELEX:31995L0046:en:HTML

Ferguson, T. (2009). *Salesforce.com outage hits thousands of businesses.* CNET News. Retrieved 13 May from http://news.cnet.com/8301-1001_3-10136540-92.html

Gates v City Mutual Life Assurance Society Ltd. (1986). 160 CLR 1.

GB Gas Holdings Limited v Accenture (UK) Limited and others. (2010). EWCA Civ 912.

Hadley v Baxendale. (1854). 9 Ex 341 at 354.

Hon, W. K., Millard, C., & Walden, I. (2011a). *The problem of 'personal data' in cloud computing - What information is regulated? The cloud of unknowing, part 1.* Queen Mary School of Law Legal Studies Research Paper No. 75/2011. Retrieved May 13, 2011, from http://ssrn.com/abstract=1783577

Hon, W. K., Millard, C., & Walden, I. (2011b). *Who is responsible for 'personal data' in cloud computing? The cloud of unknowing, part 2.* Queen Mary School of Law Legal Studies Research Paper No. 77/2011. Retrieved May 13, 2011, from http://ssrn.com/abstract=1794130

Hotel Services Limited v Hilton International Hotels (UK) Limited. (2000). BLR 235.

Kemp, R., & Anderson, R. (2010). *Cloud computing: The rise of service-based computing.* Retrieved May 13, 2001, from http://www.kemplittle.com/PDFs/HotTopicArticle_Cloud-Computing_Feb2009.pdf

Marchini, R. (2010). *Cloud computing. A practical introduction to the legal issues.* London, UK: British Standards Institute.

McAlpine v Tilebox. (2005). EWHC 281 (TCC).

Regulation (EC) 593/2008 of the European Parliament and of the Council on the law applicable to contractual obligations. (2008). Retrieved May 13, 2011, from http://eur-lex.europa.eu/LexUriServ/LexUriServ.do?uri=OJ:L:2008:177:0006:0016:En:PDF

Regulation (EC) 864/2007 of the European Parliament and of the Council on the law applicable to non-contractual obligations. (2007). Retrieved May 13, 2011, from http://eur-lex.europa.eu/LexUriServ/LexUriServ.do?uri=OJ:L:2007:199:0040:0040:EN:PDF

SAS Institute v World Programming Ltd. (2010). EWHC 1829 (Ch).

Strum, R., Morris, W., & Jander, M. (2000). *Foundations of service level management.* SAMS publishing.

Tayip, D. (2011). Navigating the cloud: Solutions for a cloud computing age. *Computers and Law Magazine of SCL, 21*(5), 14–18.

ADDITIONAL READING

Armbrust, M., Fox, A., Griffith, R., Joseph, A., Katz, R., Konwinski, A., et al. (2009). *Above the clouds: A Berkeley view of cloud computing.* University of California, UC Berkeley Reliable Adaptive Distributed Systems Laboratory. Retrieved May 13, 2011, from http://www.eecs.berkeley.edu/Pubs/TechRpts/2009/EECS-2009-28.pdf

Balboni, P., Mccorry, K., & Snead, D. (2009). *Cloud computing – Key legal issues.* In Cloud Computing Risk Assessment. European Networks and Information Security Agency (ENISA). Retrieved May 13, 2011, from http://www.enisa.europa.eu/act/rm/files/deliverables/cloud-computing-riskassessment/at_download/fullReport

Borland, J. (2008, August 7). Cloud computing's perfect storm? *Technology Review*. Retrieved May 13, 2011, from http://www.technologyreview.com/computing/21180/

Daniele, C., & Giles, H. (2009). *Cloud computing: Benefits, risks and recommendations for information security.* European Network and Information Security Agency (ENISA) Report. Retrieved May 13, 2011, from www.enisa.europa.eu/act/rm/.../cloud-computing-risk.../fullReport

Dean, D., & Saleh, T. (2009*). Capturing the value of cloud computing: How enterprises can chart their course to the next level.* The Boston Consulting Group. Retrieved May 13, 2011, from http://www.bcg.com/documents/file34246.pdf

Hall, M. (2009). The limits of SaaS. *Computerworld*. Retrieved May 13, 2011, from http://www.computerworld.com/action/article.do?command=viewArticleBasic&articleId=334951

Jackson, J. (2009). Data location not the overriding factor in cloud security. *Government Computer News*. Retrieved May 13, 2011, from http://www.gcn.com/blogs/tech-blog/2009/06/cloud-security.aspx?s=gcndaily_030609

Jaeger, P. T., Lin, J., & Grimes, J. (2008). Cloud computing and information policy: Computing in a policy cloud? *Journal of Information and Politics*, 5(3), 269–283. doi:10.1080/19331680802425479

Mell, P., & Grace, T. (2009). *The NIST definition of cloud computing*. National Institute of Standards and Technology. Retrieved May 13, 2011, from http://csrc.nist.gov/groups/SNS/cloud-computing/cloud-def-v15.doc

Poullet, Y., Van Gyseghem, J., Gérard, J., Gayrel, C., & Moiny, J. (2010). *Cloud computing and its implications on data protection.* Council of Europe. Retrieved May 13, 2011, from http://www.coe.int/t/dghl/cooperation/economiccrime/cyber-crime/Documents/Reports-Presentations/2079_reps_IF10_yvespoullet1b.pdf

Snyder, B. (2008). Cloud computing: Tales from the front. *CIO*. Retrieved May 13, 2011, from http://www.cio.com/article/print/192701.

Sunosky, J. T. (2000). Privacy online: A primer on the European Union's Directive and the United States' Safe Harbor privacy principles. *International Trade Law Journal*, *9*, 80–88.

Trauth, J., & Hovey, R. (2009). *The 2009 cloud consensus report—Bringing the cloud down to Earth* (Sponsored by the Merlin Federal Cloud Initiative). July 28, 2009. Retrieved May 13, 2011, from http://www.meritalk.com/pdfs/The-2009-Cloud-Consensus-Report.pdf

KEY TERMS AND DEFINITIONS

Consequential Loss: Whilst the meaning is not entirely clear, the phrase takes its meaning from a statement in a landmark English case (*Hadley v Baxendale)* that, where there has been a breach of contract by one party, the other party is entitled to damages to cover losses that fall under either of two "limbs" of loss, being: losses such as may fairly and reasonably be considered arising naturally, i.e. according to the usual course of things, from such breach of contract itself (the "first limb"); or losses such as may reasonably be supposed to have been in the contemplation of both parties, at the time they made the contract, as the probable result of the breach of it (the "second limb"). "Consequential" (or "indirect" or "special") losses are those losses that fall within the second limb. Direct loss - "Direct", "normal" or "general" losses refer to those losses within the first limb (see definition of "consequential loss").

Force Majeure: The happening of events outside the control of the parties, for example, natural disasters or the outbreak of hostilities. It is usual for parties to provide in a contract that such events will not make the defaulting party liable if they prevent it from performing its obligations.

The concept is derived from civil law and is not fully recognised under common law; therefore it should always be fully defined.

Indemnity: Under English law, an indemnity places a higher level of obligation upon a party than that under general contract law. In the absence of an indemnity a party claiming loss would usually have to prove its loss (for example, through potentially lengthy and expensive court proceedings), take steps to mitigate (i.e. minimise) its loss, and may not be able to recover all or any of its ancillary costs or expenses. It will also have to show that the loss has been caused as a result of a breach by the other party, i.e. the claim is subject to a "test of remoteness". By contrast, an indemnity: is a promise to reimburse the other party for a particular type of liability, should it arise; is a guaranteed remedy (pound-for-pound); removes the usual obligation upon the claiming party to mitigate (i.e. minimise) its loss; and importantly, may also allow for recovery of costs and expenses that may not otherwise have been recoverable.

Intellectual Property: Intangible property rights which are a result of intellectual effort. Intellectual property rights include patents, trademarks, designs and copyright.

Service Credit: A deduction from the contract price payable by the customer in response to a service provider's failure to meet a service level.

Service Levels: The levels of services expected from the service provider.

Chapter 14
The Legal Implications of Cloud Computing

Michael L. Kemp
University of Richmond, USA

Shannon Robb
University of Richmond, USA

P. Candace Deans
University of Richmond, USA

ABSTRACT

The purpose of this chapter is to examine the current legal environment of cloud computing. As the cloud platform continues to evolve, companies will find the need to address the business risks, particularly legal issues which will be of paramount concern. This chapter discusses the legal dimensions of cloud computing from the perspective of three L's: Location, Litigation, and Liability. Most of the current issues can be evaluated as part of one of these categories. Although the legal aspects of the cloud lag behind the business and technology side, prior case law is discussed as it applies to issues arising from various implementations of cloud computing applications. This discussion provides a road map for CIOs and other managers as they deal with emerging issues and legal ramifications of cloud computing. The chapter also provides direction for research in this realm.

INTRODUCTION

Cloud computing is the oft-lauded new wave in business. But few outside of the legal profession have stopped to consider the implications associated with what is, in reality, a quite complex network of players. A seamless transition to the cloud will require compliance with a "patchwork" of federal and state privacy laws that can confound even the most focused researcher (Mills, 2009). No responsible CIO should rush to jump on the cloud computing bandwagon without first analyzing and assessing the risks involved.

The goal of this chapter is to provide an awareness of the types of issues that might arise in interactions with a cloud service provider, and to suggest questions that might be appropriate for a CIO to consider. While the aim of this chapter is to illuminate the most common issues a firm

DOI: 10.4018/978-1-4666-2187-9.ch014

might face in its efforts to employ a cloud service provider, it is not possible for every issue to be addressed. To help the reader remember the kinds of issues involved, the chapter is separated into three major sections that are referred to as the "three L's:" Location, Litigation, and Liability. This chapter will address each "L" in turn, and hopefully leave the reader more cognizant of potential dangers lurking in the shadows of this new trend.

The chapter is intended to provide a synthesis of the legal issues companies should be aware of as they deal with the various aspects of cloud computing. It should be noted, however, that this chapter does not constitute legal advice, and is intended for informational purposes only. Legal pitfalls in this area of technology abound, and every contract is different. As such, consultation with legal counsel when negotiating contracts always is recommended.

LITERATURE REVIEW

Very little academic work in the business and information technology (IT) literature has addressed issues related to cloud computing. This is due partly to the relatively short time in which cloud computing has been an issue for companies to consider. Some of the early work has addressed high-level issues related to emerging cloud technology as a platform for business operations (e.g.; Hayes, 2008). Fingar (2009) published one of the first books that addresses the business implications of cloud technologies. Some consulting firms have published work that addresses risks and legal implications of cloud computing (e.g.; Logan, 2009; Plummer, 2010; Bittman, 2011; Casper, 2011).

A massive amount of literature has emerged from the business and IT trade publications related to cloud computing in general. Cloud computing is a high-priority issue on the radar screen of most CIOs today. Most of the current popular press focuses on cost savings of cloud implementations, selection criteria for cloud vendors, and implications of cloud computing for the organization. Security also has been a significant issue that has been covered extensively in blogs, presentations, and publications. Only recently has this discussion turned to the legal aspects that should be considered (e.g., Nash, 2010; Golden, 2009). This is likely due to the lack of awareness and understanding of the potential legal impacts. More emphasis on the legal aspects are likely to emerge as the issues become more relevant and the technology develops.

The legal research on cloud computing is also in its infancy. Some research has appeared recently in the academic literature (e.g., Couillard, 2009; Forsheit, 2010; Robison, 2010; Ryan & Loeffler, 2010). As with the business and IT literature, much of the legal discussion is in the trade publications, blogs and presentations (e.g.; Mills, 2009; Pinguelo & Muller, 2011; Jaeger, Lin, Grimes & Simmons, 2009). Journal articles only recently have begun to shift from broad, overarching analyses of privacy issues to addressing more esoteric issues such as cloud computing's interplay with Fifth Amendment law, the law of contracts, and copyright enforcement (Colarusso, 2011; Eisner & Oram, 2010; Melzer, 2011). Most journals still recognize cloud computing as a new and emerging technology, using terms such as "a coming storm" and "a new era," and recognize that "the law cannot keep up with the pace of change in computer networking" (Robison, 2010; Tsilas, 2010). In short, legal research in this area has yet to reach the level of nuance and sophistication seen in some other areas.

LEGAL DIMENSIONS OF CLOUD COMPUTING

The following sections provide a discussion of the current state of legal issues related to cloud computing. The layers of complexity make it difficult to get a thorough understanding of the many dimensions and risks involved. To simplify the discussion, the three "L" model of Location, Litigation, and Liability provides a framework to more easily understand the many issues and laws that may impact cloud computing. A summary of the issues addressed in the three L model can be found in Figure 1, below.

Location

One of the most obvious - and trickiest - problems associated with using a cloud service provider precipitates out of the nebulous (pun intended) nature of the cloud. To understand why location is a problem, one must first analyze the structure of a cloud. When a user does business with a cloud service provider, the user submits data for storage at a remote location. The cloud service provider's Terms of Service may or may not specifically name the location where the data will be stored, and, even if it does, the data may be subject to transfer at any time without notice to the user (Gellman, 2009). Once data is stored in the cloud, it eventually must be used. When a user draws on the data, the data will find its way to a physical server in a specific location (Gellman, 2009). Once the data reaches that location, that location's laws may govern the use and subsequent transfer of the data (Gellman, 2009). As the above illustration shows, the physical location of three key elements is vital to understanding exposure to risk - the location of the user, the location of the cloud service provider, and the location of the data at any given time.

The fluid nature of information in a cloud can have serious legal implications. Primarily, the storage and transfer of data between parties may result in the data having multiple simultaneous legal locations. In addressing this issue, a recent World Privacy Forum report outlined the possible legal locations of cloud data as follows:

"The legal location of information placed in a cloud could be one or more places of business of the cloud provider, the location of the computer on which information is stored, the location of a communication that transmits the information from user to provider and from provider to user, a location where the user has communicated or could communicate with the provider, and possibly other locations." (Gellman, 2009)

Figure 1. Summary of chapter topics

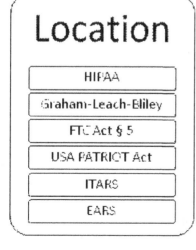

Maintaining multiple simultaneous locations can have unexpected jurisdictional consequences in a litigation context. The ease with which data can spread from jurisdiction to jurisdiction is demonstrated in Figure 2, below. Litigation aside, however, this also exposes the user to the laws and regulations of any given state or country in which any of the aforementioned elements are located. The following sections will address the implications of dealing with domestic and foreign cloud service providers.

United States Cloud Service Providers

Currently, cloud computing largely is unregulated in the United States (Mills, 2009). However, firms looking at using cloud computing should be aware that the law in this area is in a state of flux. Multiple pieces of proposed legislation, such as the Cybersecurity Act of 2009 and the Cloud Computing Advancement Act, aim to extend privacy protections to the cloud, empower the National Institute of Standards and Technol-

Figure 2. A little information goes a long way

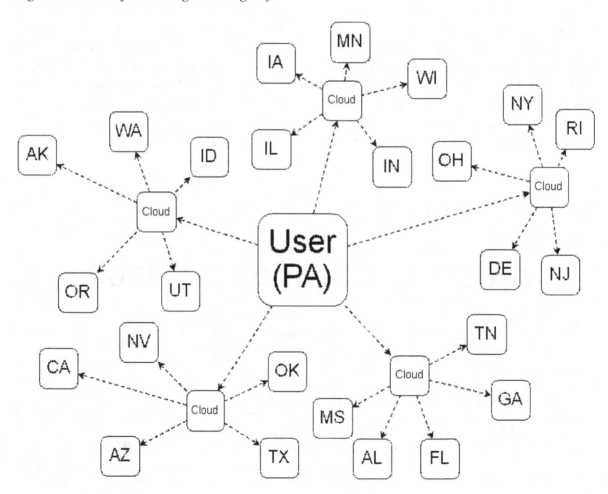

ogy to promulgate cybersecurity guidelines, and strengthen the rights and remedies available to cloud service providers in the event of a breach (Tsilas, 2010). As the field becomes more legislated, highly regulated U.S. industries will find it increasingly more difficult to do business with cloud providers. Currently, firms — either foreign or domestic — that are looking to do business with a United States cloud service provider need to be aware that existing government regulations may inhibit the transfer or storage of some types of information. Firms in specific industries or that deal with specialized types of data still are subject to the requirements of acts such as the Health Insurance Portability and Accountability Act ("HIPAA") and the Graham-Leach-Bliley Act.

For example, a firm looking to transfer health-related information to a cloud service provider should be aware that it must first enter into a business associate agreement with that provider. In these cases, the firm should be careful to analyze the service provider's Terms of Service, as they may be in direct conflict with the requirements of HIPAA (e.g., if the cloud provider reserves the right to publish the information stored on its servers). In this case, employing the cloud service provider may be a violation of HIPAA (Gellman, 2009). Additionally, financial services firms look-

ing to enter the cloud should be aware that the Graham-Leach-Bliley Act imposes restrictions on the transfer of financial information. While Graham-Leach-Bliley does not specifically restrict the disclosure of financial information to a service provider, the Terms of Service of the agreement may alter how the cloud provider is classified, thus affecting the legality of the data's storage or use (Gellman, 2009). Additionally, the Graham-Leach-Bliley Act imposes on the firm seeking to enter the cloud the responsibility to find a service provider that is capable of implementing "appropriate safeguards," and to require the service provider by contract to implement those safeguards (Forsheit, 2010).

Beyond specific federal regulations, the Federal Trade Commission (the "FTC") has taken to enforcing privacy issues by using its power to regulate unfair and deceptive business practices under Section 5 of the Federal Trade Commission Act (Eisner & Oram, 2010) (See Figure 3). While the FTC initially only pursued businesses for violating security promises after a breach occurred, the commission recently has taken enforcement actions for a variety of failures to diligently guard consumer information. According to Eisner and Oram (2010), recent cases outline five possible breaches of FTC Section 5(a) - allowing easy

Figure 3. Summary of the Federal Trade Commission act issues and solutions

Federal Trade Commission Act § 5(a)						
Breaches				Corrections		
Easy Network Access	No Breach Detection	Weak Encyption	Failure to Defend	Info Security Measures	Bi-annual Audits	Maintain Records

network access, failing to implement a breach detection system, storing unnecessary information, maintaining weak encryption or password protections, and failing to adequately defend against known attacks.

In essence, the FTC seems to be concerned with negligent failures to maintain adequate security that verge on a willful disregard for data privacy. Given the widely known risks associated with free access to the Internet (Trojan horses, spyware, etc.), a failure to limit access is irresponsible. With the sheer amount and sensitivity of data that some firms possess, failing to assess security weaknesses and to actively seek out potential breaches can be costly. With the speedy evolution and spread of viruses, a company's failure to employ adequate safeguards to known attacks practically begs for a security breach. In response to all five of the cases, the FTC outlined three possible corrective actions:

1. Establish and maintain a comprehensive information security program;
2. Obtain independent bi-annual, third-party audits to certify the sufficiency of existing security measures; and
3. Maintain records and copies of documents relating to compliance, reporting any changes in corporate structure to the FTC (Eisner & Oram, 2010).

Foreign firms looking to do business with a U.S. cloud service provider also should be aware of the effects of the embattled USA Patriot Act (the "Patriot Act"). Under the Patriot Act, the Federal Bureau of Investigation essentially may obtain any business record stored in the United States (Greene, 2009) using a National Security Letter (Mills, 2009). A National Security Letter is essentially an administrative subpoena for records that was authorized by court order (Gellman, 2009). Due to the nature of National Security Letters, third parties in receipt of a letter are limited in their ability to disclose that they have even received it (Gellman, 2009). As such, a firm looking to work

with a U.S.-based cloud service provider should be cognizant of the fact that it may not be made aware of any inquiries by federal authorities. This dynamic has caused some international firms to fear that the U.S. government will use the Patriot Act to trump mutually agreed upon privacy rules. Firms in countries such as Canada, for example, are limited in their ability to deal with U.S.-based cloud service providers due to a fear that this could put Canadian data in danger of exposure (Greene, 2009).

In addition to federal laws and regulations, some state laws impose general security guidelines and contractual requirements that could affect contract negotiations (Ryan & Loeffler, 2010). Firms looking to do business with U.S. cloud service providers should recognize that state laws also vary according to the state in which the cloud provider is located.

Foreign Cloud Service Providers

When dealing with a cloud provider located in a foreign country, it is important to recognize that differences in privacy rules and laws governing the transfer of information may make the use of some foreign cloud providers particularly unpalatable to the firm's customers. A good example of the difficulties inherent in dealing with cloud providers can be found in a review of European Union data privacy regulations.

In comparison to the United States, the European Union has extremely strict rules governing the movement of certain types of data across borders (Mills, 2009). One example of this type of foreign regulation is EU Directive 95/46/EC. Directive 95/46/EC ("the Directive") comes into play whenever any personally identifiable information is furnished to a cloud provider located in an EU member country, a state in the European Economic Area, Switzerland, Russia, or any other jurisdiction with data protection laws modeled after the Directive (Forsheit, 2010). The Directive imposes strict limitations on the storage and transfer of personally identifiable information.

The upshot of this is that once a U.S.-based firm furnished personally identifiable information to a country under the guidance of the Directive or its kindred, this strict protection attaches to the data, and its movement to another country – including to the United States - may be limited or prohibited (Gellman, 2009). In essence, a U.S. firm could furnish data to a cloud provider in the EU, and then be prohibited from accessing that data. Once the Directive's protection attaches to the furnished data, there is no clear way of eliminating its influence (Gellman, 2009).

Another issue to consider if data is to be sent overseas is that some export regulations apply to more than just goods. Exporting certain kinds of controlled data, specifically military or so-called "dual use" items that possess both a commercial and military or proliferation application, without a proper regulatory compliance framework can result in fines of between $250,000 and $1 million per violation, or even criminal charges (McClafferty, 2010). These hefty fines can certainly add up considering that a firm unwittingly could be committing a violation every time it saves data to a cloud server located in a foreign country. If a firm wishes to do business with a foreign cloud service provider, it should first review and understand the provider's plan to comply with all Export Administration Regulations ("EAR") and International Traffic in Arms Regulations ("ITAR").

Litigation

The risks inherent in utilizing a cloud service extend beyond the mere physical location of the service provider. "Litigation" risks, for the purposes of this chapter, can be defined both as risks inherent to criminal investigations and/or prosecutions and risks inherent in civil discovery and/or litigation. This section will address cloud computing issues associated with criminal and civil trials. Mainly, the focus will be on issues associated with jurisdiction, search and seizure and civil discovery, and intellectual property protection.

Jurisdiction

Under the law of civil procedure, United States courts are not free to hear any case they choose without regard to where the litigants reside or conduct business. A court may hear a case only if it has jurisdiction over the parties involved. The rule that a court must establish jurisdiction over the subject matter and the parties involved in the litigation can be traced back to the Fifth and Fourteenth amendments to the U.S. Constitution. Federal courts are required to establish jurisdiction by the Fifth Amendment Due Process Clause, which states that "[n]o person shall be... deprived of life, liberty or property, without due process of law... (U.S. Const., amend V)." This same clause is specifically extended to the states in the Fourteenth Amendment Due Process Clause ("[N]or shall any State deprive any person of life, liberty, or property, without due process of law....") (U.S. Const., amend XIV). While a jurisdictional analysis can be broken down into both personal and subject matter jurisdiction, the focus here will be on personal jurisdiction as it relates to cloud computing.

According to the seminal case of *Hanson v. Denckla* (1958), three forms of personal jurisdiction exist - *in personam* jurisdiction, *in rem* jurisdiction, and *quasi in rem* jurisdiction. *Hanson v. Denckla* (1958) succinctly defines each form as follows:

A judgment *in personam* imposes a personal liability or obligation on one person in favor of another. A judgment *in rem* affects the interests of all persons in designated property. A judgment *quasi in rem* affects the interests of particular persons in designated property.

In order to obtain *in personam* jurisdiction, the plaintiff must satisfy a statute. This is generally done by either serving the defendant with process in the state, or by demonstrating, for example, that the defendant conducts a certain amount or type of business in the state. The current constitutional personal jurisdiction analysis is based on the case of *International Shoe Co. v. Washington* (1945), which states that a court may exercise personal jurisdiction if the defendant has "certain minimum contacts with [the forum] such that the maintenance of the suit does not offend 'traditional notions of fair play and substantial justice'" (Spencer, 2005). This formulaic approach to establishing personal jurisdiction is demonstrated in Figure 4.

A recent case out of New York provides some insight into how courts might interpret jurisdictional rules as they relate to cloud computing. In 2008, the New York Supreme Court decided the case of *Forward Foods LLC v. Next Proteins, Inc.* (2008). In that case, a Delaware business based in New York and its subsidiary, a Delaware business based in Nevada, sued a potential acquisition target in a New York state court for intentionally misleading them regarding the viability of its business (*Forward Foods LLC v. Next Proteins, Inc.*, 2008). The defendants moved to dismiss the suit under New York's "long-arm" statute for lack of personal jurisdiction (*Forward Foods LLC v. Next Proteins, Inc.*, 2008).

The plaintiffs argued that a cloud system established by the defendant to facilitate the sale constituted sufficient minimum contacts to allow the exercise of long-arm jurisdiction (*Forward Foods LLC v. Next Proteins, Inc.*, 2008). The defendant would upload documents related to the sale of its business to this "virtual data room" for the plaintiff and its subsidiary to view at their offices in New York and Nevada (Pinguelo &

Muller, 2011). Judge Jane S. Solomon, writing for the New York Supreme Court, agreed that these were indeed sufficient contacts to establish jurisdiction: "Plaintiffs correctly argue that Defendants maintained sufficient contacts with the state of New York and have clearly transacted business within the state such that the personal jurisdiction over Defendants under CPLR § 302(a)(1) would be appropriate (*Forward Foods LLC v. Next Proteins, Inc.*, 2008)."

While the *Forward Foods* case eventually was dismissed on a claim of *forum non conveniens* - the doctrine that, although a court is competent to entertain the suit in question, it should pass the case off onto another forum of competent jurisdiction for the convenience of the parties involved (Black's Law Dictionary, 2004) -, the result is a clear indication of the possible risks a firm faces in using a cloud service. The obvious conclusion of this is that use of a cloud does indeed increase the number of "contacts" for the purposes of an *International Shoe* analysis, and can expose the user to more risk than it might be willing to undertake (Pinguelo & Muller, 2011).

Search and Seizure/Discovery

One particularly unexpected area of risk arises in criminal investigations and prosecutions out of a firm's possible exposure to more relaxed search and seizure laws. The Fourth Amendment to the

Figure 4. The formula for personal jurisdiction

U.S. Constitution establishes the law of searches and seizures in the United States. The Fourth Amendment (U.S. Const., amend IV) reads as follows:

"The right of the people to be secure in their persons, houses, papers, and effects, against unreasonable searches and seizures, shall not be violated, and no Warrants shall issue, but upon probable cause, supported by oath or affirmation, and particularly describing the place to be searched, and the persons or things to be seized."

The most relevant question for our purposes, then, is "what constitutes an unreasonable search?" The seminal case defining what constitutes an unreasonable search is the 1967 case of *Katz v. United States*.

In *Katz*, the government employed an electronic device placed on the top of a telephone booth to overhear a conversation held by the defendant (*Katz v. United States*, 1967). In his concurrence with the majority's decision that the government had in fact executed an unreasonable search in violation of Mr. Charles Katz's constitutionally protected right to privacy, Justice John M. Harlan set forth the oft-quoted, two-part test for determining the reasonableness of a search: A person must have (1) an actual (subjective) expectation of privacy (2) that society is prepared to recognize as reasonable (*Katz v. United States*, 1967). "What [a person] seeks to preserve as private, even in an area accessible to the public," the Court reasoned, "may be constitutionally protected (*Katz v. United States*, 1967)."

However, the court in *Katz* also noted that "[w]hat a person knowingly exposes to the public, even in his own home or office, is not subject to Fourth Amendment protection" (*Katz v. United States*, 1967). This principle has been extended to a variety of cases in which an individual voluntarily shares information with a third party, starting four years later with *United States v. White*, (1971). In *White*, the defendant voluntarily

gave incriminating information to a confidential informant who was wearing a wire (*United States v. White*, 1971). The Supreme Court determined that the police's use of the informant's recording was not an unreasonable search, as anyone's friend could, without warning or reason, turn to the police with incriminating evidence told in confidence during a private conversation (*United States v. White*, 1971).

While there is currently no case law applying directly to cloud computing, the basic principles of cases such as *Katz* and *White* have been carried forward into a trio of cases dealing with the voluntary deliverance of data to a third party that is subsequently subpoenaed. In *Couch v. United States* (1973), Couch regularly delivered various business and tax records to an independent accountant who kept the records in his continuous possession. Due to the nature of the disclosure, the court held that Couch had no reasonable expectation of privacy in the data turned over to the accountant (*Couch v. United States*, 1973). The same held true in *United States v. Miller* (1976), in which the Supreme Court found no reasonable expectation of privacy in checks and deposit slips (both "voluntarily conveyed to the banks and exposed to their employees in the ordinary course of business"), and, in *Smith v. Maryland* (1979), in which it found no reasonable expectation of privacy in the numbers dialed by the defendant and stored by the telephone company (*United States v. Miller*, 1976; *Smith v. Maryland*, 1979).

Although there is no case law on point, these cases may provide some guidance in determining the amount of exposure a firm transferring data to a cloud provider might face. While some provisions in the Electronic Communications Privacy Act might ameliorate the effects of cases such as *Miller*, it is extremely difficult to tell which kinds of data will be protected (Gellman, 2009). If it is difficult for a user to pre-emptively tell which data is protected, then one can imagine that a cloud provider facing a subpoena will likely be unable — or unwilling — to make the same determination. While a user in control of his or her own data would be able immediately to challenge a subpoena that he or she believes violates his or her constitutional rights, a cloud provider has no motivation to even inform the user that his or her data is being sought.

That having been said, most major cloud service providers have policies in place regarding when and how customer data should be turned over to law enforcement (Gantz, 2010). For example, Google's website openly states that it will "compl[y] with valid legal process," though it will attempt to notify users whenever "possible and legally permissible" (Google, Inc.). Before entering into a service agreement, it is important to know how data is stored and protected, and who may have access. It is important to understand the cloud provider's document retention and destruction policies in order to fully assess risk exposure during criminal investigations or discovery (Ryan & Loeffler, 2010).

Intellectual Property Protection

Firms looking to transfer protected intellectual property to the cloud must deal with a few extra layers of risk. According to the Uniform Trade Secrets Act, a trade secret must be "the subject of efforts that are reasonable under the circumstances to maintain its secrecy" (Uniform Trade Secrets Act). In the event that the trade secret is misappropriated or sought by a legal adversary from a cloud provider, questions may arise as to what constitutes "reasonable efforts" to maintain secrecy. Entering into a contract with a cloud service provider that retains the right to see, use, or disclose data potentially could constitute a waiver of trade secret protection (Gellman, 2009).

Additionally, a firm looking to employ a cloud service provider should be aware of the provider's loyalties and motivations. As mentioned above, a firm in receipt of a subpoena for a protected document could seek to quash the subpoena. A

cloud service provider, however, has no motivation outside of its contract to fight subpoenas or to inform the user of requested documents. Potential cloud users should engage in open conversation with the service provider in an effort to mitigate this risk.

Liability

When negotiating a service contract with a cloud vendor, there are a host of liability-related issues a user should consider. This section will address potential liability from poorly or incompletely drafted contracts. Specifically, this section will address contractual provisions that a user should specifically consider when addressing security and compliance, operations, and indemnification.

Security and Compliance

As mentioned above, regulatory compliance can be a major issue — especially when dealing with a U.S.-based cloud service provider. A firm looking to employ a cloud service provider should make every effort to select one that either agrees, or is willing to agree, to comply (and remain in compliance) with all laws and regulations generally applicable to the user's business (Ryan & Loeffler, 2010). Firms should be aware, however, that a simple agreement to comply might not be sufficient. As laws and regulations are ever changing — especially in emerging areas of technology such as this — it is important that the cloud service provider be able to produce a strategy to address changes in laws, including a plan to migrate off of the cloud if necessary to remain in compliance (Ryan & Loeffler, 2010).

A firm desiring to employ a cloud service provider needs to understand any and all applicable federal and state data security regulations, as these may affect contractual negotiations. Many of the issues raised by these statutes can be addressed via thorough and well-thought out definitions of key terms such as "security" and "sensitive information." Forsheit (2010) mentions that many data security regulations require a firm to take "reasonable steps to select and retain third-party service providers that are capable of maintaining appropriate security measures," and require those service providers to maintain such measure via contract. Examples of these provisions in state law include Massachusetts 201 CMR 17.03(2)(f):

[A user must] [o]versee service providers by (1) [t]aking reasonable steps to select and retain third-party service providers that are capable of maintaining appropriate security measures to protect such personal information consistent with these regulations and any applicable federal regulations; and (2) requiring such third-party service providers by contract to implement and maintain such appropriate security measures for personal information....

A business that discloses personal information about a California resident pursuant to a contract with a nonaffiliated third party shall require by contract that the third party implement and maintain reasonable security procedures and practices appropriate to the nature of the information, to protect the personal information from unauthorized access, destruction, use, modification, or disclosure.

In the face of such regulations, a firm should agree that "security" is more than just "reasonable security." It should be "security" consistent with all laws, regulations, and standards applicable to the industry.

Also, while it is important to assess future contracts with cloud service providers, it is equally important to assess existing contracts for any potentially problematic contractual obligations related to privacy or data security. Before migrating into the cloud, it is crucial to do the following:

1. Update any potentially conflicting privacy policies (Ryan & Loeffler, 2010).
2. Consider what will happen in the event that a cloud provider's security is breached.
3. Review existing insurance coverage and contracts governing liability to determine possible exposure to claims arising from breaches of customer privacy (Mills, 2009).

Operations

Dealing with a third party introduces another layer of complexity into the chain of operations. While a firm's customers may be accustomed to or, in fact, may require by contract certain levels of uptime or certain structures of downtime (e.g., 60 minutes once a month versus 15 minutes per week), a cloud service provider may maintain a different structure. A firm seeking to retain a cloud service provider should establish acceptable service levels and appropriately allocate risk in the event of a server crash. Additionally, the firm should understand the service provider's backup and disaster recovery policies to ensure that all data is adequately protected from unexpected disasters. The firm also should review the service provider's document retention and destruction policies. This might be a point of contention, as some cloud providers may not wish to retain documents for as long as firms may require due to contract or laws and regulations (Mills, 2009).

Indemnification

According to Forsheit (2010), this is perhaps the most important part of a contract with a cloud provider. When negotiating indemnification provisions in a contract with a cloud service provider, a firm should be sure to delineate exactly what is covered in the event of a breach. A firm should be cognizant of the differing levels of exposure that may result from a breach. The firm may incur

1. Expenses outside of a claim or lawsuit even if the aggrieved party does not pursue a claim or lawsuit;
2. Fees and expenses in connection with a claim or lawsuit; and/or
3. Fines and penalties (Forsheit, 2010).

In order to fully asses exposure to risk, it is important to understand just how far the cloud provider is willing to go to indemnify the firm for expenses incurred in the event of a breach, and under what circumstances such provisions would come into play. A firm should keep in mind that not all damages are pecuniary. The damage a security breach can cause to a firm's reputation can be far more crippling than the estimated average $204 per individual cost of a breach (Forsheit, 2010).

IMPLICATIONS FOR THE CIO

If this chapter has achieved its purpose, the reader will understand the importance of being informed. In order to effectively make the decision to migrate to the cloud, the CIO will need to ask as many questions as possible. As such, a list of questions have been formulated based the three "L's" discussed in the paper:

Location

- Where is the cloud provider located?
- Where are the data subjects located?
- Where are potential users within your organization located?
- Where are the servers located that will store the data?
- Will the data be transferred? If so, where and under what circumstances?
- What laws and regulations are applicable to the industry in potential legal locations? Is the cloud provider currently in compliance with those laws and regulations? What is the cloud provider's plan to remain in compliance with those laws and regulations?
- If data is to be transferred overseas, how does the cloud service provider plan to deal with export regulations?

Litigation

- Based on answers to all the questions above, will use of this cloud provider potentially increase "minimum contacts" within other jurisdictions? Could this expose your firm to litigation in those jurisdictions?
- What is the provider's data retention/destruction policies?
- What is the provider's policy for handling document requests by law enforcement officials?
- What is the provider's policy for handling document requests by adversaries in litigation?
- What kind of data will be stored, processed, or maintained in the cloud? Is any of it protected intellectual property?
- Who owns the cloud provider?
- What rights is the cloud provider retaining with respect to the data? Will the provider's rights potentially put your intellectual property rights at risk?

Liability

- If you are in a highly regulated industry or deal with specialized laws or regulations, does the cloud service provider have a written security policy that satisfies the requirements of the applicable laws, regulations, and industry standards?
- What does the cloud service provider's contract say about privacy and data protection?
- Has the cloud provider ever suffered a security breach? If so, to what result? How

did the provider respond? To what extent did the provider indemnify the client? How and to what extent will the provider indemnify your firm?

- What is the landscape of your existing third-party contracts? Do any of the privacy clauses in existing contracts need to be reworked to accommodate a cloud framework? Do their acceptable service levels differ from the cloud service provider's?
- What is the cloud provider's backup and restoration policy?
- Does the cloud provider undergo any regularly scheduled third-party audits of its security? Does it keep records of those audits?

While this list certainly is not exhaustive, albeit exhausting, it is intended to get CIOs thinking of the kinds of questions that might be relevant to his or her firm. The legal issues surrounding cloud computing are numerous, elusive, and, in many cases, require specialized knowledge in order to fully comprehend and address. CIOs should be aware of the rocky terrain that they are likely to face in migrating to a cloud service, and should work in close tandem with their firm's legal department or outside counsel to ensure as smooth a transition as possible.

FUTURE RESEARCH DIRECTIONS

Research opportunities abound that address an array of issues, opportunities and challenges associated with cloud computing and related legal issues. The impact of cloud implementations on business processes, organizational dynamics, cost savings, and revenue generation largely is unknown today. These issues and others will become more important as the cloud movement continues to evolve and to reach mainstream status in companies. Currently, there is a need

for research that sets the stage and provides a platform from which others can build. The door is wide open for studies that identify best practices, critical success factors, and other implementation issues. Studies examining strategic alignment and impacts on business operations and work flow also will be important.

As the cloud movement evolves, more examples will emerge as legal debates proliferate and vendor and client disputes are assessed. Even now, several cases are working their way through the federal courts that might provide greater insight into how courts will treat cloud computing issues (Arista Records LLC v. Usenet.com, Inc., 2009; Columbia Pictures, Inc. v. Bunnell, 2007; In re Boucher, 2009; State v. Bellar, 2009; United States v. Gavegnano, 2009; United States v. Kirschner, 2010). While these cases range from prosecutions of individuals for child pornography to civil disputes with cloud service providers over copyright infringement, the basic premises should help demonstrate the court's views of this emerging technology. These developing opinions on cloud computing should help flesh out some of the more fledgling areas of scholarly research, and will lend credence to some current theories.

There is much legal research to accomplish related to the three L's of Location, Litigation, and Liability presented in this paper. This research will be accomplished as cloud technology continues along its evolutionary path.

CONCLUSION

The intention of this chapter is to show that the legal implications of cloud computing are complex, and that the laws, as always, lag behind the technology. It is imperative that companies consider the legal implications of entering cloud computing before moving ahead with ambitious plans.

Cloud computing is changing the way companies do business and eventually will move toward mainstream adoption. Most CIOs either have already adopted some form of cloud computing or are evaluating the potential benefits for their companies. Given the wide-reaching implications for the firm's operations, it is important that companies allocate the resources for legal expertise and work in partnership with their lawyers when making decisions about potential cloud service providers and when negotiating contracts.

This is a critical aspect of business operations and it is essential that good decisions be made from the outset. If problems arise down the road, having the right people involved and the right measures in place from the start will make the resolution quick, painless, and inexpensive. Putting in the requisite amount of time and patience at the front end doubtless will pay off in peace of mind down the road.

REFERENCES

Arista Records LLC v. Usenet.com, Inc., 633 F.Supp.2d 124 S.D.N.Y. *(2009)*.

Bittman, T. (2011). *Key issues for private cloud computing, 2011*. Retrieved April 16, 2011, from Gartner Research: http://www.gartner.com

California Civil Code § 1798.81.5(c).

Casper, C. (2011). *Privacy in the cloud*. Retrieved April 16, 2011, from Gartner Research: http://www.gartner.com

Colarusso, D. (2011). Heads in the cloud-A coming storm: The interplay of cloud computing, encryption, and the fifth amendment's protection against self incrimination. *Boston University Journal of Science and Technology Law, 17*(1).

Columbia Pictures, Inc. v. Bunnell, 245 F.R.D. 443 C.D. Ca. *(2007)*.

U.S. Const., amend IV.

U.S. Const., amend V.

U.S. Const., amend XIV.

Couch v. United States, 409 U.S. 322. (1973).

Couillard, D. A. (2009). Defogging the cloud: Applying fourth amendment principles to evolving privacy expectations in cloud computing. *Minnesota Law Review, 93*(6), 2205–2239.

Eisner, R. S., & Oram, M. A. (2010). Clear skies or stormy weather for cloud computing? Critical privacy and security contracting issues for customers of cloud computing. *Intellectual Property Course Handbook*, 1-29.

Fingar, P. (2009). *Dot.Cloud*. Tampa, FL: Meghan-Kiffer Press.

Forsheit, T. L. (2010). Contracting for cloud computing services: Privacy and data considerations. *Privacy & Security Law Report, 9*, 20–23.

Forum non conveniens. (2004). Black's Law Dictionary. 8th. ed. St. Paul, MN: West Print.

Forward Foods LLC v. Next Proteins, Inc., 2008 BL 238516. N.Y. Sup. *(2008)*.

Gantz, S. (2010). *Major cloud computing privacy legal issues remain unresolved*. Retrieved April 5, 2011, from http://blog.securityarchitecture.com/2010/08/major-cloud-computing-privacy-legal.html

Gellman, R. (2009). *Privacy in the clouds: Risks to privacy and confidentiality from cloud computing*. World Privacy Forum.

Golden, B. (2009). *The case against cloud computing- Part one*. Retrieved April 16, 2011, from http://www.cio.com/article/477473/The_Case_Against_Cloud_Computing_Part_One

Google, Inc. (n.d.). *Security and privacy - Google apps help*. Retrieved April 12, 2011, from http://www.google.com/support/a/bin/answer.py?answer=60762

Greene, T. (2009). *The U.S. Patriot Act has an impact on cloud computing*. Retrieved April 5, 2011, from http://www.networkworld.com/newsletters/2009/092909cloudsec1.html

Hanson v. Denckla, 375 U.S. 235, 246 n. 12. (1958).

Hayes, B. (2008). Cloud computing. *Communications of the ACM, 51*(7), 9–11. doi:10.1145/1364782.1364786

In re Boucher, 2009 WL 424718, D. Vermont. (2009).

International Shoe Co. v. Washington, 326 U.S. 310. *(1945).*

Jaeger, P. T., Lin, J., Grimes, J. M., & Simmons, S. N. (2009). *Where is the cloud? Geography, economics, environment, and jurisdiction in cloud computing.* Retrieved April 13, 2011, from http://www.uic.edu/htbin/cgiwrap/bin/ojs/index.php/fm/article/view/2456/2171

Katz v. United States, 389 U.S. 347. (1967).

Logan, D. (2009). *Compliance in the cloud: Whose data is it anyway?* Retrieved April 16, 2011, from http://www.gartner.com

Massachusetts 201 CMR 17.03(2)(f).

McClafferty, E. R. (2010). *Exporting into the cloud: Export compliance issues associated with cloud computing.* Retrieved April 14, 2011, from http://it.tmcnet.com/topics/it/articles/74329-exporting-into-cloud-export-compliance-issues-associated-with.htm

Melzer, M. A. (2011). Copyright enforcement in the cloud. *Fordham Intellectual Property. Media and Entertainment Law Journal, 21,* 403.

Mills, L. H. (2009). *Legal issues associated with cloud computing.* SecureIT. Retrieved April 5, 2011, from http://www.google.com/url?sa=t&source=web&cd=1&ved=0CCYQFjAA&url=http%3A%2F%2Fwww.secureit.com%2Fresources%2FCloud%2520Computing%2520Mills%2520Nixon%2520Peabody%25205-09.pdf&rct=j&q=legal%20aspects%20of%20cloud%20computing&ei=Y6CbTbGtIMnB0QGvoM3bAg&usg=AFQjCNFMpRVM3NigyJkzLYJU_fQZPP_i-Q&sig2=Qr71BOupa6zhHRz2LFtPzg&cad=rja

Nash, K. (2010). *Questions you need answered before going cloud.* Retrieved April 16, 2011, from http://www.cio.com/article/525014/Questions_You_Need_Answered_Before_Going_Cloud

Pinguelo, F. M., & Muller, B. W. (2011). *Avoid the rainy day: Survey of U.S. cloud computing caselaw.* BC Law IPTF Blog. Retrieved April 13, 2011, from http://www.google.com/url?sa=t&source=web&cd=2&ved=0CCIQFjAB&url=http%3A%2F%2Fbciptf.org%2Findex2.php%3Foption%3Dcom_content%26do_pdf%3D1%26id%3D60&rct=j&q=Avoid%20the%20Rainy%20Day%3A%20Survey%20of%20U.S.%20Cloud%20Computing%20Caselaw&ei=V_alTfzsDJCugQeQnrzFCg&usg=AFQjCNFvHZ_okDRD9H-H2DsN5MIDl47XeA&sig2=5HEkU2pgj45E3YaGPd-EuA&cad=rja

Plummer, D. (2010). *Vendor response: How providers address the cloud rights and responsibilities.* Retrieved April 16, 2011, from http://www.gartner.com

Robison, W. J. (2010). Free at what cost? Cloud computing privacy under the stored communications act. *The Georgetown Law Journal, 98,* 1195.

Ryan, M. W., & Loeffler, C. M. (2010). Insights into cloud computing. *Intellectual Property & Technology Law Journal, 22,* 22–28.

Smith v. Maryland, 442 U.S. 735. (1979).

Spencer, A. B. (Ed.). (2005). *Acing civil procedure* (2nd ed.). St. Paul, MN: Thompson/West.

State v. Bellar, 217 P.3d 1094, Ct. App. Or. (2009).

Tsilas, N. (2010, June). Moving responsibility to the cloud to ensure its full potential. *Intellectual Property Course Handbook Series,* 1-12.

Uniform Trade Secrets Act, 11 U.S.C. §§ 332, 363.

United States v. Gavegnano, 305 Fed. Appx. 954, 4th Cir. *(2009).*

United States v. Kirschner, 2010 WL 1257355, E.D. Mich. *(2009).*

United States v. Miller, 425 U.S. 435. (1976).

United States v. White, 401 U.S. 745. (1971).

ADDITIONAL READING

Abramson, F. (2009). *Litigation, privacy and other legal issues in cloud computing.* New York Business Law. Retrieved April 5, 2011, from http://nylawblog.com/2009/10/legal-issues-in-cloud-computing/

Babcock, C. (2010). *Management strategies for the cloud revolution.* New York, NY: McGraw Hill.

Buyya, R., Yeo, C. S., Venugopal, S., Broberg, J., & Branic, I. (2009). Cloud computing and emerging IT platforms: Vision, hype, and reality for delivering computing as the 5th utility. *Future Generation Computer Systems, 25*(6), 599–616. doi:10.1016/j.future.2008.12.001

Gerson Lehrman Group. (2010). *Who has legal jurisdiction in the cloud?* Gerson Lehrman Group: Intelligently Connecting Institutions and Expertise. Retrieved April 13, 2011, from http://www.glgroup.com/News/Who-has-Legal-Jurisdiction-in-the-Cloud--50084.html

Hurwitz, J., Bloor, R., Kaufman, M., & Halper, F. (2010). *Cloud computing for dummies.* Hoboken, NJ: Wiley Publishing, Inc.

Mason, Hayes & Curran. (n.d.). *Cloud computing.* Trinity Business Alumni. Retrieved April 6, 2011, from http://www.tba.ie/resources/partner-content/16-mason-hayes--curren/48-cloud-computing

Miller, M. (2008). *Cloud computing: Web-based applications that change the way you work and collaborate online.* Oue Publishing Company.

Rosenthal, A., Mork, P., Li, M. H., Stanford, J., Koester, D., & Reynolds, P. (2010). Cloud computing: A new business paradigm for biomedical information sharing. *Journal of Biomedical Informatics, 43*(2), 342–353. doi:10.1016/j.jbi.2009.08.014

Shreve, G. R., & Raven-Hansen, P. (2002). *Understanding civil procedure* (3rd ed.). Matthew Bender & Company, Inc.

Sosinsky, B. (2011). *Cloud computing bible.* Indianapolis, IN: Wiley Publishing, Inc.

KEY TERMS AND DEFINITIONS

Cloud Computing: Resources (such as email, software, applications, and databases) available on demand for access from servers in remote locations.

Cloud Service Providers: Vendors that provide services (such as data and file storage, software applications and email) remotely in the cloud.

Section 5
Economic Impact of Cloud Computing

Chapter 15
Business Impacts of Cloud Computing

Cameron Deed
Yellowfin, Australia

Paul Cragg
University of Canterbury, New Zealand

ABSTRACT

While many articles have discussed likely benefits of cloud computing, there have been relatively few empirical reports of the impacts of cloud computing. This study explores the business impacts associated with the adoption of a cloud-based business intelligence application. A generic benefits management framework was adopted to guide the study of five firms. Numerous types of benefit were identified, including strategic, managerial, operational, and functional and support. The results supported the literature in that managerial impacts were strongly correlated with business intelligence functionality. Additionally, operational and functional and support benefits were mainly positive, with some due to the cloud nature of the service.

INTRODUCTION

Cloud computing (CC) has been foreseen as the next potential revolutionary change to the internet and information systems (Sharif, 2010). Cloud computing is a new movement towards computing as a utility (Smith, 2009) as it provides IT services on-demand, through a web browser, over the internet (Aymerich, Fenu, & Surcis, 2008). According to Grossman (2010, p. 25), the use-based pricing model of cloud computing provides "several advantages including reduced capital expenses, a low barrier to entry, and the ability to scale up as demand requires". Therefore, it would seem that cloud computing can provide affordable IT services to businesses, without the need to invest significant amounts of money in in-house resources and technical equipment (Aymerich, et al., 2008).

Clouds can provide on-demand computing such as Software-as-a-Service (SaaS) (Grossman, 2010). Service based solutions such as SaaS are already used by people without perhaps realizing it (Manford, 2008). SaaS software applications are a standard piece of software offered as services

DOI: 10.4018/978-1-4666-2187-9.ch015

over the internet, rather than traditional software packages that are purchased by customers (Motahari-Nezhad, Stephenson, & Singhal, 2009). The growing importance of SaaS as a delivery mechanism is expected to change software buying practices over the next decade (Kugel, 2010). SaaS can provide a diverse range of applications, such as Enterprise Resource Planning (ERP), Customer Relationship Management (CRM) and Business Intelligence (BI) (Dubey & Wagel, 2007).

Existing literature provides limited empirical evidence about SaaS. We argue that the IT industry needs more empirical research on the actual impact of SaaS to understand the value that this type of software delivery can provide. However, at present, much ambiguity and uncertainty still exists in regards to the actual benefits from cloud computing (Greenwood et al, 2010). This chapter helps to address this gap by reporting results from an empirical study of the impacts of a SaaS business intelligence application. A secondary objective is to report organizational differences that influence impacts. The research method involved multiple-case studies. Each case study involved semi-structured interviews with managers and IT professionals.

BACKGROUND

Cloud computing is a new term for a relatively long-held vision of using computing as a utility (Armbrust, et al., 2009). In recent times, cloud computing has been of high interest in the information systems (IS) literature and is perceived as a potentially significant new movement in IS. Although there is no common definition of cloud computing, Armbrust et al (2009) provide a relatively recent definition of cloud computing as:

"The applications delivered as services over the Internet and the hardware and systems software in the data centers that provide those services. The

services themselves have long been referred to as Software as a Service (SaaS). The data center hardware and software is what we will call the cloud" (Armbrust, et al., 2009, p. 1).

The main reason behind the difficulties in defining cloud computing is that the descriptions encompass many pre-existing categories of IT service, of which the most relevant to cloud computing is software-as-a-service (Clarke, 2010).

Some of the cloud computing literature focuses on infrastructure. Generally, hardware and software services are stored on the provider's web servers and accessed through the internet (Aymerich, et al., 2008). The IS literature recognizes that it is unlikely that all businesses will outsource all of their computing requirements to a cloud services provider. Instead, they will set up heterogeneous computing environments which may include more than one public cloud provider (Greenwood, et al., 2010). This means organizations may have a hybrid type infrastructure, including in-house technologies and outsourced technologies and services.

Benefits and Disadvantages of SaaS

Prior literature indicates that SaaS can provide a broad range of benefits and disadvantages to organizations. To help structure the analysis of this literature, we adopted the framework of Farbey et al (1993). Their generic framework applies to IS/IT investments in general rather than specifically relating to cloud computing. A strength of the framework is that it identifies four major types of benefit, with definitions and examples (see Figure 1 and Appendix).

Strategic benefits are benefits that support the strategy, vision, new business models and overall direction for the organization (Ward & Daniel, 2006). One potential benefit identified in the literature, is that some third party cloud infrastructure solutions enable sales and marketing

Figure 1. Four types of IT benefits from IT systems (Farbey et al, 1993)

Strategic Benefits that are abstract, wide ranging, and which affect the organisation as a whole (Farbey, et al.,1993).	**Management** Benefits which support the duties of middle-line managers including collection, aggregation and passing of information, as well as decision making relevant information and the allocation of resources (Farbey, et al., 1993).
Operational Benefits where computer technology was introduce to support the basic work of the organisation (Farbey, et al., 1993).	**Functional & Support** Benefits to support staff and business units that exist to provide support to the organisation outside of its normal operating work flow (Farbey, et al., 1993).

staff to create new product and service contributions (Khajeh-Hosseini, Greenwood, & Sommerville, 2010). Additionally, reducing the IT resources that are managed in-house, may allow businesses to focus their IT efforts on developing new technologies to support their core products and services. The IS literature typically refers to this as focusing on core competences. Also, hiring outsiders to handle information systems is claimed to help an organization focus on improving its services and maintaining a competitive advantage (Grover, Cheon, & Teng, 1994). However, existing literature provides little discussion of strategic impacts of cloud computing.

Management benefits relate to the activities of middle managers within the organization (Farbey, et al., 1993). For SaaS, rather than spending managerial time and resources developing an internal infrastructure, organizations are able to concentrate their efforts on the effective use of information, which can therefore improve management's responsiveness to organizational needs (Grover, et al., 1994). Clouds can also improve efficiency and decision making, therefore making companies more competitive and profitable (Harris & Alter, 2010). Another relevant managerial benefit is flexibility. For example, if the SaaS subscriber is

no longer happy with the service provided then they can easily change to another (Manford, 2008). Also, flexible licensing agreements can provide subscribers more flexibility in the duration of the SaaS application adoption (Manford, 2008). However, there may be concerns with data lock-in (Misra & Mondal, 2010). For example, if the provider manages valuable data, it may become a complex process to switch providers. Also, having unique and proprietary services may mean a business cannot move their applications to another provider without some major changes to software and data (Smith, 2009).

Farbey et al. (1993) consider operational benefits as the benefits associated with the production of goods and services. According to Clarke (2010), the majority of service providers perceive cost-savings as the primary driver for adoption of cloud computing. Cloud Computing enables pay-for-use, requiring no client-side investments in their own technologies (Clarke, 2010); thus, enabling a reduction in an IT resources, including infrastructure and staff. Furthermore, these innovative services can alleviate the costs of purchasing, maintaining, supporting and modernizing infrastructures (Aymerich, et al., 2008). The savings from eliminating costs of servers, software licenses, maintenance fees, floor space, power and IT labor and avoiding large upfront costs, makes the appeal of cloud computing very luring (Harris & Alter, 2010).

One of the technical advantages of cloud computing is its dynamic scalability, meaning consumers can draw as much computing power as necessary on an hourly basis (Smith, 2009). Additionally, processing power of the cloud is considerably more powerful than that of user PC's (Aymerich, et al., 2008). Moreover, staffing and equipment problems can be transferred to a service provider, who is better positioned to manage IT personnel and infrastructures (Grover, et al., 1994). A potential technical disadvantage is service quality. Since many companies are sharing the cloud resources, there will be variations in the quality of service provided (Smith, 2009). Not surprisingly, organizations worry about whether computing services will have adequate availability (Armbrust, et al., 2009). Users are entirely dependent on the service provider to solve problems and ensure availability of service (Clarke, 2 February, 2010). Problems with reliability, performance and other technical issues present a variety of IT-related concerns (Harris & Alter, 2010).

Although the cost savings seem promising, much of the literature reported cost increases. For example, a large amount of bandwidth would be required for data processing and storage in the cloud environment, causing a substantial amount of money spent on bandwidth charges alone (Misra & Mondal, 2010). However, organizations still need to spend time and money to gather essential information such as user requirements, strategic and implementation plans (Clarke, 2010). According to another study of SaaS users, only about half of the respondents reported a positive return on investment from SaaS, whereas, a quarter of respondents found the costs associated were greater than initially anticipated (Harris & Alter, 2010).

The fourth type of impact for Farbey et al (1993) is functional and support, which en-

compasses activities that support the business processes, in relation to the production of goods and services. These support activities can assist human resources, legal, finance and IT services (Ward & Daniel, 2006). SaaS provides users with flexibility as they can use a variety of devices to connect to a cloud service (Aymerich, et al., 2008). For example, SaaS allows mobile users to connect to the cloud using multiple devices, in various locations (Clarke, 2010). Ward & Daniel (2006) perceive these software functions can provide information to staff and allow them to carry out tasks not specific to production of goods or services. Data security has been identified as an issue for organizations, especially firms that have highly sensitive data (Misra & Mondal, 2010). Although threats could emerge in remote storage and transit, effecting the confidentiality, integrity and availability of data (Clarke, 2010), so far there has been no reported cases of client-to-client penetration of software or data in the cloud (Smith, 2009). Additionally, clouds can provide some potential security benefits. Some clouds have the ability to generate audit data and avoid problems associated with updates, such as, implementing patches and rapid security updates (Harris & Alter, 2010).

In summary, the literature indicates that cloud computing is an emerging area of interest. While the concept of SaaS has been around for many years and has recently growing in popularity (Manford, 2008), the majority of Cloud Computing and SaaS studies focus on either cost effectiveness (Kondo, Javadi, Malecot, Cappello, & Anderson, 2009), architecture (Clarke, 31 January, 2010) or general overviews of the concept (Grossman, 2010; Manford, 2008; Sharif, 2010; Smith, 2009). Some address benefits, disadvantages and concerns (Aymerich, et al., 2008; Khajeh-Hosseini, et al., 2010; Smith, 2009); nevertheless, there are no current empirical studies on the business impacts of cloud computing, incorporating tangible and intangible benefits and disadvantages. Enterprises are showing interest in cloud computing, although presently there is ambiguity and uncertainty regarding the realization of actual benefits from it (Greenwood, et al., 2010). Much of the hype around cloud computing is for its cost savings, which are based on simplistic assumptions (Greenwood, et al., 2010).

STUDY DESIGN

The above literature identified a broad range of potential benefits for SaaS. However, many of the benefits were speculated benefits, and not supported by empirical evidence. Thus, in studying this relatively new area of SaaS impacts, a multiple-case study research design was adopted, based on Yin (2003). The Farbey et al (1993) framework was used to guide the research design. Although the Farbey et al (1993) framework was developed as a benefits management guide it includes a diverse range of outcomes from many different business activities. The framework was adopted as it provides a means of categorizing impacts into four types.

With the objective of identifying business impacts, one SaaS provider was selected and data gathered from five of their customers. All five customers were similar in that they were retailers with numerous outlets in different parts of New Zealand. They had also adopted the same business intelligence (BI) application. However, the five firms were not competitors as they were in different industries, as indicated in Table 1. The retailers primarily sell pharmaceutical medicines, office products and equipment and toys. The organizations have between 30 and 50 stores that operate New Zealand wide. Four of the five companies have head offices and a common brand, and the other organization provides marketing and staff training services to a variety of pharmacies. Interviews were conducted with managers in each of the five firms. The interviews were

semi-structured and questions were open-ended, allowing participants to address any impacts they thought were important to themselves or their organization. Company data was also collected through websites, including core products and other company related information.

The SaaS vendor, RPM Retail, provides cloud services to a variety of retail businesses within New Zealand. RPM Retail was established in 2002 and since has developed a unique software service. The product they supply is a Software-as-a-Service Business Intelligence solution for medium-to-large retail chains within New Zealand. The technology provides decision support assistance by supplying firms with information on sales and stock data from multiple branches. It performs sophisticated data analysis to generate insights on potential performance improvements by integrating with existing Point-of-Sale (POS) systems. Like all SaaS solutions, it is accessible via a standard web browser, anywhere in the world.

The BI application is installed on branch computers, which extracts data from the POS terminals and transfers the data via FTP to RPM. The application provides decision support assistance. The technology requires no additional investments in hardware, software or technical expertise. Even though parts of the system are customizable, it is typically implemented in 1-2 months. The application costs approximately $1000 for the initial license fee, then approximately $200 to set up for each branch. On-going costs include $250 per branch, as well as $500 -$1500 per month per supplier.

Business Impacts of SaaS

The results from the eight interviews were grouped into the four quadrants of the Farbey et al (1993) benefits management framework. Disadvantages and negative outcomes are also reported to provide a more complete evaluation of SaaS impacts.

Table 1. Company backgrounds

Company	Industry	Number of Employees (head office)	IT Skill Sources	Participants Interviewed	Duration of using RPM SaaS app.	Number of Stores
FirmA	Pharmaceutical Products	14	Outsourced to external consultants	South Island Regional Manager, GM Marketing and Operations, Senior Category Manager	6 Months +	35
FirmB	Marketing and training support for pharmaceutical retailers	2	External Web Designer	The two founding partners	2+ years	46 (36 use RPM)
FirmC	Office Supplies Retailer	18	Internal IT team of four professionals	Chief Executive	2+ years	38
FirmD	Retailer of Vitamins, Minerals and Supplements	8	An internal IT Employee	Managing Director	5+ years	31
FirmE	Specialist Toy Retailer	4	Outsourced to Melbourne Head office	Operations Manager	2+ years	37

Strategic

While the Farbey et al (1993) framework identifies nine types of strategic impact, the case analysis found evidence of only four of these types of impact (Table 2). Of these four, all five firms acknowledged that the technology supported their business strategies. For example, for FirmA this has been useful in tracking their strategies:

"It reinforces our strategic review, so we had identified the key drivers that we wanted to focus on... RPM has allowed us to track our progress against our strategy."

The results for the other types of impact were diverse. One firm admitted that the service had impacted their long-term viability. For example, according to the Operations Manager at FirmE:

Table 2. Strategic impacts

Strategic	Support for the organization's strategy or vision	Long/short term viability of the organization	Provide customers with unique value propositions	Permit new business models
FirmA	Positive		Positive	
FirmB	Positive			Positive
FirmC	Positive			
FirmD	Positive			
FirmE	Positive	Positive		

Table 3. Managerial impacts

Managerial	Better Control through Information	Meeting Professional Standards	Ease of Operations	Improved quality of working life	Existing Systems inadequate
FirmA	Positive	Positive	Positive	Positive	Positive & Negative
FirmB	Positive		Positive	Positive	Positive & Negative
FirmC	Positive	Positive	Positive & Negative	Positive & Negative	Positive
FirmD	Positive & Negative			Positive	Positive & Negative
FirmE	Positive	Positive	Positive	Positive	Positive

"Yes. If I think has [RPM], or will [RPM] affect our long-term viability, then the answer is yes because it will make the stores more profitable."

Conversely, a manager at FirmA showed a different perspective:

"If we didn't have [RPM] we would still have long term or short term viability."

The majority of the interviewees perceived that the application has not assisted in introducing new products, services or strategies. An interviewee from FirmA summarized this:

"I'm not sure that RPM has helped us develop new strategies but it has certainly assisted us in the implementation of existing strategies."

There was no evidence of other types of strategic impact, i.e., desire to be seen to be innovative, permit new forms of organization, build barriers to entry, lock-in customers and geographic or market expansion appear. Table 2 below demonstrates the areas that have been impacted and the direction of the relationship[1].

Management

The interviews identified many managerial impacts (Table 3). The majority of these impacts were positive, but some negative impacts were identified.

One of the considerable motivations for adopting the technology was the inadequacy of existing systems. In most cases, the functionality provided by the SaaS product was not replacing another IT application although the POS systems at the stores already provided some data. The SaaS application was typically replacing manual processes. According to a manager at FirmA:

"Prior to RPM we used to do a lot of manual reports through (the POS system) and effectively it was difficult to use; With RPM it is a lot more streamlined."

Better control through improved information was another benefit identified at all five firms. For example, a manager at FirmA stated:

"It allows us to focus quite quickly on areas that are under performing."

And also a manager at FirmE quoted:

"Now we have better information available, you can actually make better management decisions."

Improved quality of working life was another managerial impact. The benefits from this category have been diverse. For example, a manager at FirmA claimed that business meetings were now more productive. For FirmB, the flexibility in work activities had been assisted by the mobile characteristics of the applications:

"We can deal with our stores all over New Zealand without having to leave the office, in the company or your own home and without it, it would be almost impossible to do the job."

There were no reported impacts for four of the Farbey et al (1993) managerial categories: increased agility, growing the skills of the workforce, less crises and flatter organisational structure. Table 3 shows the managerial impacts associated with using RPM.

Operational

Seven different types of benefit were identified (See Table 4), based on the Farbey et al (1993) framework. For example, the system helped make more effective use of existing POS systems and only small changes were needed to incorporate the new system into the organization. The new system was also seen as very cost effective. According to a manager at FirmC:

"It's affordable, easy to get up and running, easy to learn and accessible for our members in terms of getting up and running quickly at a low cost."

While the upfront costs of the system were considered to be low, the licensing fees could become a significant on-going cost. Thus costs could increase over time as the number of users increased:

"It's now starting to cost us a fortune as there are so many stores involved".

Some firms also reported reduced head count and reduction in property costs. While none of the firms changed their organizational structure or downsized after implementing the service, the system helped FirmB refrain from employing more staff:

"Until we get to 60 stores we do not need to add any more people because RPM can achieve that for us."

Table 4. Operational impacts

Operational	Effective use of existing IT	Cost Effectiveness	Improved turnaround time	Reduced head count	Reduction in property costs	Increased income from better quality products	Timeliness and accessibility of data
FirmA	Positive	Positive	Positive			Positive	Positive
FirmB	Positive	Positive & Negative	Positive	Positive	Positive		Positive & Negative
FirmC	Positive	Positive	Positive			Positive	Positive & Negative
FirmD	Positive	Positive & Negative					Positive
FirmE	Positive	Positive		Positive	Positive	Positive	Positive & Negative

Similarly, the alternative to a SaaS system, i.e., implementing a traditional in-house system, would increase property costs. According to a manager at FirmE:

"If we wanted a centralised POS system, we would have needed an additional two or 3 people, plus investments in infrastructure and incurred ongoing costs. Although a centralised POS would not have had the functionality and analytics RPM provides, so I would have to go to an external vendor to get that functionality."

Many managers reported impacts regarding timeliness and accessibility of data. The manager at FirmA found:

"It seems to work on any web browser, or I use it at home, I've used it on my pc and it seems to work anywhere anytime."

All of the firms reported timeliness impacts. However, while some were positive, e.g., from receiving real-time data, some of the impacts were negative. Three firms mentioned occasions when they had troubles with the accessibility or speed of the application. Typically, these had been infrequent and resolved quickly.

Functional and Support

Functional and support impacts relate to the activities that are intended to support the core operations of the organization (Ward & Daniel, 2006). The new system had proved to be valuable for not only head office, but also branch owners who could benchmark and compare their store's performance against the performance of the franchised group, as well as track the sales and profitability of a variety of products (See Table 5). The system could also be available to suppliers, thus FirmA aimed to *"Get these suppliers to subscribe so that we can get them to work with the stores to drive sales, as well as the store managers..."*.

The interviews also identified some cases of user resistance. To avoid extra costs from the licensing fee, some branches decided to either fully resist or use the application rarely. This caused some frustrations for the managers at FirmB:

"We have about 10 stores that don't use it partly because they don't want to pay the extra money and they have an internal system of reporting of their own. From our [support office] point of view, that is extremely annoying, we find it a totally invaluable tool."

Table 5. Functional and support impacts

Functional and Support	Employee Self-service	Production of standard reports	Improved communication and collaboration opportunities	Adherence to standards	Compatibility to partner's systems	Identification of best practices	Implementation of Metrics
FirmA	Positive	Positive	Positive			Positive	Positive
FirmB	Positive & Negative	Positive	Positive			Positive	Positive
FirmC	Positive	Positive	Positive			Positive	Positive
FirmD	Positive	Positive					Positive
FirmE	Positive & Negative	Positive	Positive	Positive	Positive	Positive	

User resistance generally originated from store managers. The majority of interviewees saw this as limiting the benefits that can be achieved from using the application. A manager at FirmE didn't find resistance surprising:

"We have had some stores that are resisting using it, but they are resisting using everything."

A business intelligence application can provide metrics, such as Key Performance Indicators (KPI). According to a manager at FirmA, *"Just by point and click I use the benchmarking RPM index, I also use the comparison of the market every month and say this is how you have done and this is how the rest of the stores have done."* Thus, there is little effort required to generate reports and metrics and therefore could save the organization valuable work time.

The system was also viewed as compatible with partners' systems as the data was predominantly collected from the POS systems within the branches. Thus, the SaaS solution does not interact with a supplier's infrastructure and thus there are no compatibility issues. This made the system fast and simple to adopt by additional stakeholders.

User Resistance

Although most impacts were positive, user resistance was experienced at the branch level by some firms. For example, some branches would either avoid using the system or use it only when critically required. For example at FirmB, user involvement varied across the branches:

"Some are better than others, there are some branches that are a lot more techno-literate than others, they understand the data more so it's a lot more meaningful when they themselves use it. There are other branches where for some reason

they don't go into it often enough to make a huge difference but when they do, they get it right."

Four out of five of the firms reported moderate to low levels of user resistance. In part, differences in user resistance were related to who funded the system as the system was funded in different ways across the five firms. For example, head office paid for the operating costs for the new system at FirmD, while at FirmA, FirmC and FirmE the costs were shared between branches and head office. For FirmD, who funded the system from head office, all of the branches had to adopt the technology; yet issues related to the use or lack of use of the system emerged. FirmD funded the system purely from head office, as they did not want branches to view the system as an additional cost and not consider the additional benefits that could be obtained. *"No [the branches] are not [funding the system], we fund it. If they had to fund it, a lot of them would choose not to"*. Despite this, FirmD had some user resistance and sub-optimal utilization rates, partly as a newly installed POS system had eroded some benefits of the BI system.

"A lot of stores prefer to use their POS for some reports because it's not manipulated; they can actually see it in real data."

FirmB does not fund the system, yet it is a requirement to belonging to their group. Whereas, FirmC and FirmE funded the startup costs for RPM but do not fund the system's on-going costs for their branches, thus some branches are choosing not to use the technology. Although there has been user resistance in four of the cases, no user resistance was mentioned in the three interviews with FirmA. FirmE shared the costs across three stakeholders *"storeowners, ourselves and the suppliers"*.

IDENTIFYING SOFTWARE-AS-A-SERVICE AND BI IMPACTS

The Tables above identify many types of impact from the RPM system. This section primarily attempts to identify which impacts were associated with the SaaS service model and which were due to the functionality of the new BI system.

Cost impacts is one area that had a strong link to SaaS delivery rather than the BI system. This is supported by the literature. For example, savings from eliminating costs of servers, software licenses, maintenance fees, floor space, power and IT labor and avoiding large upfront costs, makes the appeal of cloud computing very luring (Harris & Alter, 2010). Moreover, a manager at FirmE had considered but rejected a move to a new centralized POS system based on costs. Finding a SaaS solution with a cheap upfront cost was very appealing to him.

Another SaaS related benefit was the simplicity of setting up and integrating the new system with the existing POS systems. All of the organizations had POS systems in place before adopting RPM. Therefore, once the branch applications were customized and installed, there was little else to do but train users on how to use the system. In contrast, traditional BI applications would require the installation of servers, user PC software and a central data processing application.

For RPM's BI application, no extra workload was required in managing and updating the service for customers, which in turn, avoids some operating costs. However, the cash saved from avoiding upfront investments in infrastructure and maintenance, can be negated by on-going license fees. Therefore, the scalability of the system can make it expensive if a large number of users were to subscribe and there are different economies of scale. As confirmed by a manager at FirmE:

"If we had 500 stores you would probably have a different system, wherein, you have different levels of economy of scale. It's a defined solution that fits with the type of business scale that you in."

The managerial impacts were very strong, which would be expected for a BI –type application as they are useful for decision making and this is typically done at a managerial level (Negash, 2004). The benefits gathered from up-to-date metrics and reports are particularly related to the BI functionality of the application (Negash (2004). Furthermore, increased income from better quality products and identification of best practices are purely correlated with the information delivered from the BI application.

Some of the impacts were due to both SaaS and BI. For example, timeliness and accessibility of data is a result of the combination of the service type and functionality. The information could be accessible through other means; however, the accessibility from anywhere in the world, on any computer with an Internet connection is hugely beneficial for travelers.

FUTURE RESEARCH DIRECTIONS

Cloud computing is a new hot topic in IS research. IS articles are emerging on the various CC service models, including Infrastructure-as-a-Service (IaaS) and Database-as-a-Service (DaaS). The current study was relatively unique for SaaS and unique for SaaS business intelligence applications. Nonetheless, more case study research on the shift from an in-house IT architecture to a Software-as-a-Service solution could be undertaken. This could aim to provide clear evidence of the differences between services and the impacts specifically associated with SaaS. The future is looking bright for SaaS, especially with mobile devices like tablets and cell phones. Apps allow greater access to content so seem likely to be a major part of SaaS in the future, including business intelligence applications.

The major limitation of the above evidence is that the study focused on one type of SaaS application, i.e., a Business Intelligence application, which is only one example of a cloud service. There are many other service types and each with their own distinct characteristics. Therefore one should be careful when attempting to generalize the findings to other forms of cloud computing. Future research could examine whether benefits and disadvantages are related to the type of service implemented. Another limitation is that this study analyzed only one SaaS service provider with one BI application. Other providers and other BI applications could produce different results.

CONCLUSION

This study examined five SaaS adopting firms. The organizations were medium-to-large sized retailers, each selling a variety of products for a diverse range of industries. The benefits management framework of Farbey et al (1993) was used to guide the study to help identify examples of four different types of impact: strategic, management, operational and functional and support. Strategic impacts were relatively small. All organizations felt that using the application helped support monitoring the performance of strategies, and track the performance of new strategies.

Many managerial impacts were associated with the use of this SaaS BI application. It provided better control through information by supplying managers with information collected from point of sale systems, allowing improved decision-making. The application also improved quality of working life as head office did not need to initiate cumbersome communications to gather business data, reports were created automatically and real-time information was available at the click of a mouse. Another important managerial impact was the inadequacy of existing system. All organizations studied perceived their previous means was inadequate, and thus a strong driver to adopt a BI solution.

For operational impacts, the majority of impacts identified were positive outcomes, although a few negative outcomes were encountered. The system made good use of existing POS systems and required only small adjustments from users. Additionally, the system was relatively cheap to rent. It required only a small upfront cost and rather cheap on-going costs for licensing fees. The timeliness and accessibility of data was another beneficial dimension. The information could be accessed through a standard web-browser anywhere in the world. The majority of participants found only minor insignificant issues with the connection that were solved promptly.

In terms of functional and support impacts, employee self-service was a useful feature. Retail branches were able to use information collected from their POS system and other POS systems across their group to compare how they were performing against the market and consider ways to improve their position. These two dimensions were supported by the literature, as companies are eager for applications for a distributed user base, and require little integration with existing applications and limited software customization (Dubey & Wagel, 2007). However, there were cases of user resistance within the branches, in part reflecting who funded the system. Although all of the cases had no previous in-house solution, no reductions in staff or property costs were acknowledged. Additionally, the complexity and functionality of the existing POS Systems had an effect on the outcomes.

The SaaS nature of the software presented a cheap and affordable application, due to the easy set up and low upfront costs. The BI functionality of the application provided a variety of impacts, including better control through improved information, ease of operations, implementation of metrics and production of standard reports. The BI functionality was also strongly associated with Management impacts due to the business value of BI lying within management processes (Williams & Williams, 2003). Additionally, some Functional and Support impacts were related to BI. Conversely, operational impacts, such as reduced cost and timeliness and accessibility of data, were strongly associated with the SaaS delivery mechanism.

Finally, SaaS has provided these businesses with a BI application that for most of them would have been unfeasible by any other means. The SaaS concept is simple and attractive; whereas, the traditional cycle of software buying requires buying software licenses, paying for a maintenance contract and managing time-consuming and expensive upgrades (Dubey & Wagel, 2007).

REFERENCES

Armbrust, M., Fox, A., Griffith, R., Joseph, A. D., Katz, R., Konwinski, A., et al. (2009). *Above the clouds: A Berkeley view of cloud computing.* Technical Report No. UCB/EECS-2009-28. UC Berkley Reliable Adaptive Distributed Systems Laboratory.

Aymerich, F. M., Fenu, G., & Surcis, S. (2008). *An approach to cloud computing network.* First International Conference on the Applications of Digital Information and Web Technologies, ICADIWT 2008. Retrieved from www.chinacloud.cn/upload/2009-04/temp_09042911246387.pdf

Clarke, R. (2 February, 2010). *Computing clouds on the horizon? Benefits and risks from the user's perspective.* Retrieved from http://www.rogerclarke.com/II/CCBR.html

Clarke, R. (31 January, 2010). User requirements for cloud computing architecture. Retrieved from http://www.rogerclarke.com/II/CCSA.html

Clarke, R. (2010). Computing clouds on the horizon? Benefits and risks from the user's perspective. Retrieved February 2, 2010, from http://www.rogerclarke.com/II/CCBR.html

Dubey, A., & Wagel, D. (2007). Delivering software as a service. *The McKinsey Quarterly, Web Exclusive.* Retrieved from http://www.mckinseyquarterly.com/delivering_software_as_a_service_2006

Farbey, B., Land, F., & Targett, D. (Eds.). (1993). *IT investment: A study of methods and practice.* Oxford, UK: Butterworth-Heinemann.

Greenwood, D., Khajeh-Hosseini, A., Smith, J., & Sommerville, I. (2010). *The cloud adoption toolkit: Addressing the challenges of cloud computing adoption.* SICSA 2010 Conference. Retrieved from http://arxiv.org/ftp/arxiv/papers/1003/1003.3866.pdf

Grossman, R. L. (2010). The case for cloud computing. *IT Professional, 11*(2), 23–27. doi:10.1109/MITP.2009.40

Grover, V., Cheon, M. J., & Teng, J. T. C. (1994). A descriptive study on the outsourcing of information systems functions. *Information & Management, 27*(1), 33–44. doi:10.1016/0378-7206(94)90100-7

Harris, J. G., & Alter, A. E. (2010). *Six questions every executive should ask about cloud computing.* Accenture Institute for High Performance, January 2010. Retrieved from http://www.accenture.com/Global/Research_and_Insights/Institute-For-High-Performance/Six-Questions.htm

Khajeh-Hosseini, A., Greenwood, D., & Sommerville, I. (2010). *Cloud migration: A case study of migrating an enterprise IT system to IaaS.*

Kondo, D., Javadi, B., Malecot, P., Cappello, F., & Anderson, D. P. (2009). Cost-benefit analysis of cloud computing versus desktop grids. *IPDPS '09 Proceedings of the 2009 IEEE International Symposium on Parallel & Distributed Processing*

Kugel, R. (2010). *SaaS is breaking out*. Retrieved from http://www.businessintelligence.com/researchi.asp?id=306

Manford, C. (2008). The impact of the SaaS model of software delivery. *21st Annual Conference of the National Advisory Committee on Computing Qualifications (NACCQ)*, (pp. 283-286). Retrieved from www.naccq.ac.nz

Misra, S. C., & Mondal, A. (2010). Identification of a company's suitatbillity for the adoption of cloud computing and modelling its corresponding return on investment. *Mathematical and Computer Modelling, 53*(3-4). doi:doi:10.1016/j.mcm.2010.03.037

Motahari-Nezhad, H. R., Stephenson, B., & Singhal, S. (2009). Outsourcing business to cloud computing services: Opportunities and challenges, Hewlett-Packard Development Company, L.P. *IEEE Internet Computing, Special Issue on Cloud Computing*. Retrieved from http://www.hpl.hp.com/techreports/2009/HPL-2009-23.html.

Negash, S. (2004). Business intelligence. *Communications of the Association for Information Systems, 13*, 177–195.

Sharif, A. M. (2010). It's written in the cloud: The hype and promise of cloud computing. *Journal of Enterprise Information Management, 23*(2). doi:10.1108/17410391011019732

Smith, R. (2009, September 1). Computing in the cloud. *Research Technology Management*. Retrieved from http://207.57.8.178/papers/RSmith_InnovationColumn5.pdf

Ward, J., & Daniel, E. (Eds.). (2006). *Benefits management: Delivering value from IS & IT investments (Vol. 1)*. Padstow, UK: T.J. International.

Williams, S., & Williams, N. (2003). The business value of business intelligence. *Business Intelligence Journal, 8*(4).

Yin, R. (2003). *Case study research* (3rd ed.). Newbury Park, CA: Sage Publications.

ENDNOTES

[1] The relationship may be positive, meaning it is beneficial to the organisation, or negative, a disadvantage to the business or other concerns. Additionally, any blank cell refers to there being no reported impact.

APPENDIX

GENERIC IT BENEFITS FROM IT SYSTEMS

Strategic	**Management**
• Support for the organisation's strategy or vision • Long or short term viability of the organization • Provide customers with unique value proposition • Desire to be seen to be innovative • Permit new business models • Permit new forms of organization • Build barriers to entry • 'Lock in' customers • Geographic or market expansion	• Increased agility • Better control through improved information • Growing the skills of the workforce • Meeting the highest professional standards • Ease of operation, allowing use by less experienced staff • Improve the quality of working life • Existing systems have become inadequate • Less crises • Flatter organizational structure
Operational	**Functional & Support**
• More effective use of existing IT and systems • Improved quality at reduced cost • Improved turnaround time • Reduced headcount • Reduction in property costs • Increased income from better quality products • Timeliness and accessibility of data	• Employee self-service • Improved recruitment and retention processes • Provision of infrastructure systems • Improved communication and collaboration opportunities • Adoption of/adherence to standards • Compatibility with customers' and/or suppliers' systems • Enforcement of regulatory or legal requirements • Identification/promulgation of best practice • Implementation of metrics • Production of standard reports • Business continuity/disaster recovery

(adapted from Farbey et al, 1993)

Chapter 16

An Economic Analysis of Cloud:
"Software as a Service" (SaaS) Computing and "Virtual Desktop Infrastructure" (VDI) Models

Wei Nein "William" Lee
University of Houston, USA

ABSTRACT

Cloud based "Software as a Service (SaaS)" computing and "Virtual Desktop Infrastructures" (VDI) are game changing technologies. Both enable convenient, on-demand access through shared computing resources as opposed to the more rigid and fragmented infrastructures of tethering on specific hardware components for computational processing. The architecture and delivery models of SaaS and VDI offer both superior flexibility and scalability in response to constant changes in organizational business requirements. This chapter provides specific return on investment analysis and business case studies leveraging the application and value proposition of these solutions. In summary, the analysis presented suggests an inevitable shift from legacy network architectures to SaaS and VDI computing is the path forward.

INTRODUCTION

Cloud "Software as a Service (SaaS)" computing and VDI "Virtual Desktop Infrastructure" are new and rapidly evolving models for enabling convenient, on-demand access to shared computing resources (e.g., networks, servers, storage, applications, and services). Both technologies have been getting more and more favorable attention from the IT industry.

"Software as a Service (SaaS)" or Cloud computing delivers the utility of software applications over the Internet, eliminating the need to install and run the application on the customer's own computers and simplifying maintenance and support. Common applications of this type include email hosting and social networking sites. A user of Gmail, Facebook or LinkedIn accesses the application and their data through any browser on any device. User configuration settings and data are stored on in the "Cloud". The user does not need to keep up with anything more than a password; everything is stored and managed in the "Cloud". The user has no idea how the underlying platform works. If they can get to the Internet, they can get to their account and data.

DOI: 10.4018/978-1-4666-2187-9.ch016

VDI stands for "Virtual Desktop Infrastructure" and is a complete virtualization of a desktop, encompassing the hardware and software systems required to support a virtualized environment. Computers are now powerful enough to enable multiple software layers to be incorporated between the physical hardware, operating systems, and the applications they run. In traditional desktop computing, machines running individual application(s) are executed with user interfaces displayed on screens. By introducing virtualization at the desktop level, the direct connection between physical hardware, operating system, application and display is separated.

The common factor between both these models is the use of virtualization technologies which offer tremendous economic advantages. On the server side, Cloud computing simplifies maintenance and support for entire organization infrastructures greatly reducing the total cost of ownership by eliminating redundant systems and the need for administrators in each area. On the client side, with the empowerment of VDI, the user entire environment can be managed and controlled from a central point greatly simplifying operational challenges such as asset management, patches management, and standardized desktop policies implementation across an entire enterprise.

In this paper, the economic advantages in the use of Cloud and VDI solutions are discussed. Google's "Software as a Service (SaaS)" e-mail and productivity solution for the City of Los Angeles will be used as a specific case study to illuminate the value of the Cloud computing model. For VDI solutions, multiple case studies from The Wantagh Union Free School District, The Western Wayne School District in Pennsylvania, The University of Texas in Austin, The Campbell Union High School District, and the Brick Township Public Schools are used to qualify the many economic advantages of this model. Finally, a conclusion is offered on the potential impact of these technologies to the IT industry.

"SAAS" CASE STUDY: (CITY OF LOS ANGELES)

In 2009, the City of Los Angeles entered into a contract with Computer Science Corporation (CSC) to replace the City's entire e-mail system with Google's "Software as a Service (SaaS)" e-mail and productivity solution, which includes:

- Gmail
- Google Calendar
- Google Talk
- Google Docs
- Google Sites
- Google Video
- Google Messaging Security, and
- Google Message Discovery

The City licensed seats for an estimated 30,000 users servicing all City departments. Over the proposed five-year term of the contract, the full budgetary obligation to Google is $24,518,013. Over this five-year term, the "Software as a Service (SaaS)" model is reported to bring approximately $1.5 million in savings to the City, as shown in Exhibits 1 through 4. Areas of savings include:

By moving to a "Software as a Service (SaaS)" e-mail system, 30 of the 90 servers dedicated to the GroupWise system will be retired and not be replaced; the estimated savings by not refreshing these GroupWise servers is estimated to be in the range of $350,000 to $700,000.

By reducing the number of server administrators required, 9 of 13 staff can be reassigned to other functions which results in increased capacity and productivity to other City service areas.

The remaining 60 production servers originally servicing the GroupWise system can be reassigned to other functions creating immediate value at no additional capital costs to the City.

By design the "Software as a Service (SaaS)" solution provides the City with disaster recovery which brings significant value to the City. Under the service level agreement, Google will make available all City data 99.9 percent of the time, even in the event of a disaster. The City did not have such a disaster recovery system for email data as the true cost for such a system is estimated at $1,300,000 with on-going annual costs of $260,000. Thus, the total value proposition to the City is calculated to be $2,340,000 over the five-year term.

Another area of value proposition is the storage space made available on Google servers. The City estimated that to purchase the amount of storage included with the "Software as a Service (SaaS)" solution is $25 per employee per year. Therefore, the City would have had to spend $3,555,000 over the five-year term for comparable storage space.

By using Google's office applications instead of Microsoft Office for 30,000 users, the City expects sizable savings in the licensing costs as a result of the Google implementation.

Video conferencing is a built-in "Software as a Service (SaaS)" application with the Google system. To purchase and implement a comparable enterprise-wide video conferencing solution, the City would have needed to spend $2,000,000 for the first year and $1,720,000 over the subsequent four years for a total value proposition of $3,720,000.

Lastly, a subjective value proposition is the potential of productivity gains from the use of web-based tools instead of desktop based tools. There are no accurate measurements to predict the magnitude of such productivity changes. However, the City estimates that per City employee, a gain of 10 minutes per week is realistic given the elimination of help desk and desktop support for each of the legacy desktop clients related to supporting the Microsoft Office applications. Using an average salary of $71,200 and gain of 10 minutes per week calculates to $44,509,500 in increased productivity benefiting the City over the five-year term.

An analysis of actual costs for the City of Los Angeles / Google solution is located in the addendum of this report.

VDI: Case Studies

VDI - "Virtual Desktop Infrastructure" is an extension of "Cloud" computing concept. However, instead of calling on specific application over the Internet, users call upon an entire virtual machine (e.g. operating system, applications, and data) all of which is hosted as an instance on the local network environment.

Some of the early adopters of VDI are educational institutions. According to Citrix which offers VDI products, more than 400 school districts in the United States have implemented VDI solutions. Further, according to a VDI vendor, NComputing, the school districts that switch to its desktop virtualization products can save up to 70 percent on hardware, 75 percent on maintenance, and 90 percent on energy costs when compared with a traditional technology rollouts.[1]

Some other case studies of academic institutions that have implemented VDI solutions with success are:

- **The Wantagh Union Free School District on Long Island, N.Y.:** Adopted a desktop virtualization model when confronted with the prospect of having to replace aging computers in its elementary school classrooms. The school was using 10-year-old Dells that were over due for a refreshes. Instead of buying new PCs, the district purchased X series devices from NComputing Inc. of Redwood City, Calif. Wantagh elementary schools typically have five computers per classroom. With desktop virtualization, the district only had to purchase new PCs for teachers. Students use a monitor, keyboard, and mouse–along with the VDI devices –to share computing power from the teacher's PC. Depending on the VDI solutions available in the marketplace, the ratio of users supported can be up to 30 users connected to a desktop PC or up to 200 users connected to server grade hardware. A typical desktop PC costs about $500 whereas servers can run about $6,000 to $10,000 apiece. In the end, the district didn't have to replace as many new PCs or servers and with the energy savings, the project will pay for itself in only a few years. Further, this district will save even more money in the future for no longer having to swap out as many PCs every three to five years which was about $3,600 to $3,800 to equip a classroom with six workstations with the devices and monitors now reduced to $1,800 to $2,000 on refresh cycles.

- **The Western Wayne School District in Pennsylvania:** The district installed a server virtualization system from Palo Alto, Calif.-based VMware Inc. along with Wyse thin clients. In addition to saving money on hardware, software, and energy, Microsoft licensing fees were cut reduced because they no longer using all computers at the same time. The overlap on the district's 200 workstations was reduced to only needing 100 copies of Windows XP.

- **The University of Texas in Austin:** By using VMware View and Microsoft's Softricity software to provide 600 virtual desktop "Seats". The virtualization solution allows the university to offer students use of the university's software that was traditionally restricted to the physical computer labs. Now the students can use it anywhere with internet access. The university provides students with a certain amount of disk space, and can purchase more if students need it.

- **The Campbell Union High School District in San Jose, CA:** Spent $300,000 to virtualize 500 desktops and 50 servers. That includes the physical devices and licenses for operating systems and other software. Licensing prices vary from vendor to vendor, depending on the number of users or other factors. But the district saved about $500,000 the first year by not having to spend $250,000 on new PCs and $300,000 on new Servers. And that doesn't include the long-term savings realized by not having to replace computers under a four or five-year refresh cycle. Altogether, the district estimated savings of $4 million over eight years. Additional "soft dollar savings" are realized with virtualization because IT staff can be more effective if they don't have to spend as much time on hardware maintenance and software support. Energy use also declined about 30 percent, partly owing to a centrally managed system that turns off all the desktops at night.

- **Brick Township Public Schools in Ocean County, N.J.:** Virtualized its servers, using a grant from Microsoft to obtain a Hyper-V platform, which is part of Windows Server 2008. That allowed about a dozen servers to run on a single host machine, eliminating about 26 servers. Before, the district had been spending about $2,600 annually to power and cool each of the 53 servers in its data center. The server virtualization resulted in savings of $30,000 just in electrical costs and has reduced rack space by about 50 percent and another $80,000 in hardware replacement costs will be eliminated because of the server virtualization.[2]

The conclusion of this chapter is that Cloud "Software as a Service (SaaS)" computing and VDI "Virtual Desktop Infrastructure" are new and rapidly evolving models which offer tremendous value propositions, flexibility, and economies of scale. Using virtualized technologies, applications and services are not tethered to specific hardware components. Instead, processing is handled across a distributed, globally accessible network of resources, which are dispensed on demand, as a service. The availability of such highly dynamic infrastructures enables corporate data centers to operate with improved flexibility and scalability, ready to respond quickly to changing business requirements. Such flexibility is essential in the fast-paced, constantly changing, globalized world—and even more so in an economic downturn, where rigid and fragmented infrastructures can severely limit an organization's responsiveness. For the global tech industry, the shift to Cloud and VDI computing offers a path out of the economic doldrums. In fact, it may be the largest growth opportunity since the Internet boom.

REFERENCES

Ashford, E. (2010). *Virtual desktops save schools money and hassle*. E-School News, Special Report. Retrieved October 18, 2010, from http://www.eschoolnews.com/2010/03/02/esn-special-report-virtual-desktops-save-schools-money-and-hassle/

Stansbury, M. (2010). *Seven proven ways to save on school budgets*. E-School News. Retrieved October 8, 2010, from http://www.eschoolnews.com/2010/07/28/seven-proven-ways-to-save-on-school-budgets/

APPENDIX

Exhibit 1. Analysis of city of Los Angeles / Google – "Software as a Service (SaaS)"

COMPARATIVE BUDGETARY OBLIGATION FOR GOOGLE AND GROUPWOSE - 30,000 USERS

Cost Elements	2009-10 Cost	2010-11 Cost	2011-12 Cost	2012-13 Cost	2013-14 Cost	Total Costs
Resources Dedicated to Google						
Google Subscriptions	$ 863,860	$ 1,439,700	$ 1,439,700	$ 1,259,700	$ 1,259,700	$ 6,262,660
Implementation Costs	$ 890,900	$ -	$ -	$ -	$ -	$ 890,900
Internet Upgrade - Leases	$ 180,000	$ 180,000	$ 198,000	$ 217,800	$ 239,580	$ 1,015,380
Internet Upgrade - Hardware	$ 16,500	$ 19,800	$ 23,760	$ 28,512	$ 34,214	$ 122,786
Groupwise Licenses	$ 539,400	$ -	$ -	$ -	$ -	$ 539,400
Associated Applications	$ 368,513	$ 36,750	$ 38,588	$ 40,517	$ 42,543	$ 526,910
Office Licenses	$ 1,597,449	$ 1,499,192	$ 1,366,218	$ 758,106	$ 763,162	$ 5,984,126
Servers (refresh, software, power)	$ 4,500	$ 12,371	$ 12,607	$ 12,855	$ 13,115	$ 55,447
Staff	$ 383,222	$ 424,429	$ 437,162	$ 450,277	$ 463,785	$ 2,158,875
Total Cost	$ 4,844,344	$ 3,612,241	$ 3,516,034	$ 2,767,767	$ 2,816,099	$ 17,556,484
Resources Not Dedicated to Google, but Retained Under the Proposal						
Servers Repurposed (refresh, software, power)	$ 87,500	$ 240,538	$ 245,131	$ 249,955	$ 255,019	$ 1,078,143
Staff Reassigned	$ 1,044,361	$ 1,156,658	$ 1,191,358	$ 1,227,098	$ 1,263,911	$ 5,883,386
Total Cost	$ 1,131,861	$ 1,397,195	$ 1,436,489	$ 1,477,053	$ 1,518,931	$ 6,961,528
Total Google Budgetary Obligation	$ 5,976,205	$ 5,009,437	$ 4,952,523	$ 4,244,820	$ 4,335,029	$ 24,518,013
Resources Dedicated to GroupWise						
Groupwise Licenses	$ 539,400	$ 566,370	$ 594,689	$ 624,423	$ 655,644	$ 2,980,525
	$ -	$ 350,000	$ 350,000	$ -	$ -	$ 700,000
Associated Applications	$ 368,513	$ 386,939	$ 406,286	$ 426,600	$ 447,930	$ 2,036,267
Office Licenses	$ 1,706,623	$ 1,728,458	$ 1,751,384	$ 1,162,531	$ 1,187,808	$ 7,536,804
Servers (refresh, software, power)	$ 138,000	$ 379,362	$ 386,607	$ 394,214	$ 402,202	$ 1,700,385
Staff	$ 1,427,583	$ 1,581,087	$ 1,628,519	$ 1,677,375	$ 1,727,696	$ 8,042,261
Total GroupWise Budgetary Obligation	$ 4,180,119	$ 4,992,215	$ 5,117,485	$ 4,285,143	$ 4,421,280	$ 22,996,242

Exhibit 2. Analysis of city of Los Angeles / Google – "Software as a Service (SaaS)"

ANNUAL COSTS AND SAVINGS FROM TRANSITIONING 30,000 USERS TO GOOGLE

Cost Elements	2009-10 Cost	2010-11 Cost	2011-12 Cost	2012-13 Cost	2013-14 Cost	Total Costs
New Google System Costs						
Google Subscriptions	$ 863,860	$ 1,439,700	$ 1,439,700	$ 1,259,700	$ 1,259,700	$ 6,262,660
Implementation Costs	$ 890,900	$ -	$ -	$ -	$ -	$ 890,900
Internet Upgrade - Leases*	$ 180,000	$ 180,000	$ 198,000	$ 217,800	$ 239,580	$ 1,015,380
Internet Upgrade - Hardware	$ 16,500	$ 19,800	$ 23,760	$ 28,512	$ 34,214	$ 122,786
Total Google System Costs	$ 1,951,260	$ 1,639,500	$ 1,661,460	$ 1,506,012	$ 1,533,494	$ 8,291,726
*The cost are funded by departmental savings and no additional funding is required						
Budgetary Savings						
GroupWise Costs						
Groupwise Licenses	$ 539,400	$ 566,370	$ 594,689	$ 624,423	$ 655,644	$ 2,980,525
GroupWise Upgrade	$ -	$ 350,000	$ 350,000	$ -	$ -	$ 700,000
Associated Applications	$ 368,513	$ 386,939	$ 406,286	$ 426,600	$ 447,930	$ 2,036,267
Office Licenses	$ 1,706,623	$ 1,728,458	$ 1,751,384	$ 1,162,531	$ 1,187,808	$ 7,536,804
Servers Retired (refresh, software, power)	$ 46,000	$ 126,454	$ 128,869	$ 131,405	$ 134,067	$ 566,795
Total GroupWise Costs	$ 2,660,536	$ 3,158,220	$ 3,231,227	$ 2,344,959	$ 2,425,449	$ 13,820,391
Google Costs						
Groupwise Licenses	$ 539,400	$ -	$ -	$ -	$ -	$ 539,400
GroupWise Upgrade	$ -	$ -	$ -	$ -	$ -	$ -
Associated Applications	$ 368,513	$ 36,750	$ 38,588	$ 40,517	$ 42,543	$ 526,910
Office Licenses	$ 1,597,449	$ 1,499,192	$ 1,366,218	$ 758,106	$ 763,162	$ 5,984,126
Servers Retired (refresh, software, power)	$ -	$ -	$ -	$ -	$ -	$ -
Total Google Costs	$ 2,505,362	$ 1,535,942	$ 1,404,805	$ 798,623	$ 805,704	$ 7,050,436
Budgetary Savings (GroupWise Costs minus Google Costs)	$ 155,174	$ 1,622,278	$ 1,826,422	$ 1,546,336	$ 1,619,745	$ 6,769,955

Exhibit 3. Analysis of city of Los Angeles / Google – "Software as a Service (SaaS)"

Cost Elements	2009-10 Cost	2010-11 Cost	2011-12 Cost	2012-13 Cost	2013-14 Cost	Total Costs
ANNUAL COSTS AND SAVINGS FROM TRANSITIONING 30,000 USERS TO GOOGLE						
Reallocation of Existing Resources						
GroupWise Costs						
Servers Repurposed (refresh, software, power)	$ 92,000	$ 252,908	$ 257,738	$ 262,810	$ 268,135	$ 1,133,590
Staff Reassigned	$ 1,427,583	$ 1,581,087	$ 1,628,519	$ 1,677,375	$ 1,727,696	$ 8,042,261
Total GroupWise Costs	$ 1,519,583	$ 1,833,995	$ 1,886,257	$ 1,940,184	$ 1,995,831	$ 9,175,851
Google Costs						
Servers Repurposed (refresh, software, power)	$ 4,500	$ 12,371	$ 12,607	$ 12,855	$ 13,115	$ 55,447
Staff Reassigned	$ 383,222	$ 424,429	$ 437,162	$ 450,277	$ 463,785	$ 2,158,875
Total Google Costs	$ 387,722	$ 436,800	$ 449,769	$ 463,132	$ 476,900	$ 2,214,322
Reallocation of Existing Resources (GroupWise Costs minus Google Costs)	$ 1,131,861	$ 1,397,195	$ 1,436,489	$ 1,477,053	$ 1,518,931	$ 6,961,528

Exhibit 4. Analysis of city of Los Angeles / Google – "Software as a Service (SaaS)"

Cost Elements	Groupwise	Google	Costs
FIVE-YEAR COSTS AND SAVINGS FROM TRANSITIONING 30,000 USERS TO GOOGLE			
New Google System Costs			
Google Subscriptions	$ -	$ 6,262,660	$ 6,262,660
Implementation Costs	$ -	$ 890,900	$ 890,900
Internet Upgrade - Leases	$ -	$ 1,015,380	$ 1,015,380
Internet Upgrade - Hardware	$ -	$ 122,786	$ 122,786
		Total Google Costs	$ 8,291,726
			Savings
Budgetary Savings			
Groupwise Licenses	$ 2,980,525	$ 539,400	$ 2,441,125
GroupWise Upgrade	$ 700,000	$ -	$ 700,000
Associated Applications	$ 2,036,267	$ 526,910	$ 1,509,357
Office Licenses	$ 7,536,804	$ 5,984,126	$ 1,552,678
Servers Retired (refresh, software, power)	$ 566,795	$ -	$ 566,795
Total Budgetary Savings (GroupWise Costs minus Google Costs)			$ 6,769,955
Reallocation of Existing Resources			
Servers Repurposed (refresh, software, power)	$ 1,133,590	$ 55,447	$ 1,078,143
Staff Reassigned	$ 8,042,261	$ 2,158,875	$ 5,883,386
Total Reallocation of Existing Resources (GroupWise Costs minus Google Costs)			$ 6,961,528

Chapter 17
The Economics of Cloud Computing

Federico Etro
University of Venice, Ca' Foscari, Italy

ABSTRACT

This chapter examines the economic impact of the diffusion of a new technology as cloud computing. This will allow firms to rent computing power and storage from service providers, and to pay on demand, with a profound impact on the cost structure of all the industries, turning some of the fixed costs in marginal costs of production. Such a change will have a substantial impact on the incentives to create new business, and through this, on: investments and macroeconomic growth, job creation in all industries and job reallocation in the ICT sector, and public finance accounts, through the direct impact on the public sector spending and the indirect one on the tax revenues. In this study, the author investigates the consequences of the diffusion of cloud computing on market structures and competition and tries to disentangle the above mentioned aspects with a particular focus on a simulation run for the European economy.

INTRODUCTION

Cloud computing is a general purpose technology of the IT field which became widely available in the late 2000s. Vaquero *et al.* (2009) define it as "a large pool of easily usable and accessible virtualized resources (such as hardware, development platforms and/or services). These resources can be dynamically reconfigured to adjust to a variable load (scale), allowing also for an optimum resource utilization. This pool of resources is typically exploited by a pay-per-use model in which guarantees are offered by the Infrastructure Provider by means of customized Service Level Agreements".

The diffusion of this new technology appears to follow the pattern of older general purpose innovations. In the course of modern history, the introduction of new technologies has often created initial resistance (think of modern assembly lines), initial diffidence (think of early mobile phones), visionary ideas (think of Bill Gates' claims of bringing a PC in every house), a slow adoption at the beginning (even for electricity),[1] with a mix of clear general benefits and specific costs (think of new energy sources), and finally a process of rapid

DOI: 10.4018/978-1-4666-2187-9.ch017

and generalized adoption. Researchers often talk of a technology adoption lifecycle model: the first group of agents to use a new technology is called "innovators" (and they overcome technological or institutional or coordination barriers to the adoption of the new technology), followed by the "early adopters" (that are typically forward looking), the majority (that simply follows a process of rent maximization) and the "laggards" (that are relatively myopic). This leads to repeated processes of gradual and sometimes slow diffusion of new technologies, even when their net benefits for the society are large and generalized. With the new general purpose technology of the ICT field, cloud computing, the path of adoption is likely to be similar, though different national policies in support of its adoption may induce variable speed of diffusion in different countries.[2]

Cloud computing is an Internet-based technology through which information is stored in servers and provided as a service and on-demand to clients. The impact of its diffusion may be quite relevant, as it happened for the diffusion of telecommunications infrastructures in the 70s and 80s (for a related econometric study on their economic impact see Röller and Waverman, 2001) or the introduction of the Internet in the 90s (for an interesting study on this technological revolution see Varian *et al.*, 2002) and, in general, for the diffusion of computers in the last three decades. In an important article, Jorgenson (2001) has shown how substantial has been the contribution of the adoption of the computer for the accumulation of capital and for the growth process of the US since the 80s.[3]

Through cloud computing, firms will be able to rent computing power (both hardware and software in their latest versions) and storage from a service provider, and to pay on demand, as they already do for other inputs as energy and electricity. This will have a profound impact on the cost structure of all the industries using hardware and software, and therefore it will have crucial consequences on:

- Business creation and macroeconomic performance;
- Job creation in all industries and job reallocation in the ICT sector;
- Public finance accounts, through the direct impact on the public sector spending and the indirect one on the tax revenues.

In this study we try to disentangle these three aspects of the impact of cloud computing with reference to the European economy in the next few years. The first aspect is in line with our earlier results derived in Etro (2009,a) on the basis of recent research on endogenous market structures in macroeconomic models by Etro and Colciago (2010) and more recently Colciago and Rossi (2011): the diffusion of the new technology may create a few hundred thousand new European SMEs with a substantial impact on employment and a reduction of the unemployment rate of a few decimal points. Moreover, the net impact on employment derives from a high ratio between new jobs in all sectors and lost jobs in traditional ICT employment: the problem of reallocation of labor (within IT departments or between these and other IT-related sectors) may be quite limited. Finally, our simulation suggests that the corresponding impact on the deficit/GDP ratio should be around 0.1% in the pessimistic scenario and 0.2% in the optimistic one. Therefore, the introduction of a cost reducing technology as cloud computing, can have a small but not negligible impact on public finances, even if it creates a marginal reduction of the costs of the public sector. This happens because public finances benefit on one side from the direct reduction in costs, and on the other side from the additional tax revenue derived from the boost of the economic activity and the creation of new private business and jobs.

The paper is organized as follows. Section I reviews multiple aspects of the new technology. Section II is about its macroeconomic impact with a special emphasis on the labor market. Section

III examines the social costs and benefits of the process of job creation and destruction associated with the diffusion of cloud computing. Section IV is about the consequence for European public finances. Section V concludes.

BACKGROUND

A new general purpose technology as cloud computing can exert a number of effects on the economy. First of all, it can provide huge cost savings and more efficiency in large areas of the public sector including hospitals and healthcare (especially to provide information and technologies in remote or poorer locations), education (especially for e-learning and universities) and the activity of government agencies with periodic spikes in usage.

A few examples from the European health sector are in order. We start from the most simple applications to move toward more relevant ones. One of the leading Italian hospitals, the Children's Hospital of Bambin Gesù in Rome, has recently switched to an online solution for the email services of its 2500 employees (the switch took place in 2010 in less than four months, created large cost savings and allowed IT specialists to focus on other more relevant tasks for the hospital). The Swedish Red Cross has improved the coordination of its intervention adopting a cloud computing solution which has reduced costs of about 20% and enhanced communication in real time between its employers. A Russian cardiovascular centre, Penza, has adopted a cloud computing solution to coordinate activities, diagnosis and decisions on treatment and surgery between doctors around the country, with crucial gains for the patients. During the H1N1 pandemic, a global cloud computing tool was build and made available in a few days (based on the Microsoft's Windows Azure platform) to centralize and provide information on the diffusion of the flu.

Second, cloud computing can provide cost efficiencies in the private sector, whose exploitation in all industries is directly related to the diffusion of what Lanvin and Passman (2008) call e-business skills in the managerial environment (the capability of exploiting new opportunities provided by the ICT and to establish new business). Liebenau (2010) has been studying the relationship between the character of the cloud and the organizational, financial and managerial changes that businesses need to make to take advantage of what is on offer. He has focused on different kinds of ICT budget issues, noticing that "for many functions the up-front costs can be much lower, reducing the entry barriers for small firms and providing many companies new opportunities for experimentation, prototyping, and containing risks. Organizations can shift from major ICT expenditure on capital goods to spending on operating costs, a change that will have meaning for more than accountants. Budgets that form part of planning and some of the ways incentives are structured are likely to change. This could have major effects upon how firm performance is measured and thereby how companies are valued, stocks traded and other financial services extended. A focus on innovation should become the most important element of these changes."[4]

Beyond cost efficiencies, on which we will return soon, substantial positive externalities are expected from cloud computing because of energy savings: the improvement of energy efficiency may contribute to the reduction of total carbon emissions in a substantial way. The introduction of cloud computing can also create multilateral network effects between businesses and increased productivity within businesses, and it can promote entry and innovation in all the sectors where ICT costs are relevant and are drastically reduced by the adoption of cloud computing.

The Diffusion of Cloud Computing

In a recent research based on the works of Etro and Colciago (2010) and Colciago and Rossi (2011) we have simulated the economic impact of the diffusion of cloud computing in Europe through the incentives to promote business creation. They key point was that, somewhat surprisingly, a big portion of the benefits associated with the diffusion of the new technology derives from indirect mechanisms active in non-ICT sectors rather than from the direct efficiencies in the ICT sector. Here, we report some refinements of this study which take in consideration aspects that were neglected in the earlier work, namely the decomposition of the process of job creation across countries and macrosectors and between job creation and job destruction, and the role of public finances.

Starting from conservative assumptions on the cost reduction process associated with the diffusion of cloud computing over five years, we obtain that the diffusion of cloud computing could provide a positive and substantial contribution to the annual growth rate (up to a few decimal points), helping to create several hundred thousand new jobs every year through the development of a few hundred thousand new SMEs in the whole EU-27. The driving mechanism behind the positive contribution works through the incentives to create new firms, and in particular SMEs. One of the main obstacles to entry in new markets is represented by the high up-front costs of entry, often associated with physical (and ICT) capital spending. Cloud computing allows potential entrants to save in the fixed costs associated with hardware/software adoption and with general ICT investment, and turns part of this capital expenditure into operative expenditure, that is in variable costs. This reduces the constraints on entry and promotes business creation. The importance of such a mechanism is well known at the policy level, especially in Europe, where SMEs play a crucial role in the production structure.

Cloud computing is currently developing along different concepts, focused on the provision of Infrastructure as a Service (IaaS: renting virtual machines), Platform as a Service (PaaS, on which software applications can run) or Software as a Service (SaaS: renting the full service, as for email). In preparation for its introduction, many hardware and software companies are investing to create new platforms able to attract customers "on the clouds". Cloud platforms provide services to create applications in competition with or in alternative to on-premises platforms, the traditional platforms based on an operating system as a foundation, on a group of infrastructure services and on a set of packaged and custom applications. The crucial difference between the two platforms is that, while on-premises platforms are designed to support consumer-scale or enterprise-scale applications, cloud platforms can potentially support multiple users at a wider scale, namely at Internet scale.[5]

Competition Issues in the Provision of Cloud Computing

The introduction of cloud computing is going to be gradual. Currently, we are in the middle of a phase of preparation with a few pioneers offering services that can be regarded as belonging to cloud computing, often derived from internal solutions (turning private clouds into public ones). Amazon Cloud Computing was launched in October 2006, IBM's Blue Cloud in November 2007, followed by cloud solutions by Google and Microsoft. Meanwhile, many large high-tech companies as Amazon, Google, Microsoft, Saleforce.com, Oracle and others keep building huge data centres loaded with hundreds of thousands servers to be made available for customer needs in the near future.[6]

Competition between these companies is probably going to reshape the ICT market structure as PC distribution did in the 80s. This may raise some concern for competition and for the consequences on the users of cloud services.

On one side, the strength of competition for the provision of cloud services suggests that multiple players (as those mentioned above and, possibly, others) would probably share the market for a while avoiding excessive concentration. The importance of cloud computing in changing the prevailing business model in ICT is determining wide investments in innovation by these same players, therefore the ultimate success in the cloud business will be associated with the creation of superior technologies rather than with the exploitation of network effects or barriers to entry.

On the other side, the development of alternative cloud computing solutions could create the risk of being locked-in for potential customers. To avoid this, it is important to promote, especially in this initial phase, agreements between public authorities and industry leaders on a minimum set of technological standards and process standards to be respected in the provision of cloud services to guarantee data security, privacy and portability.

For sure, the diffusion of cloud computing is going to create a solid and pervasive impact on the global economy. The first and most relevant benefit is associated with a generalized reduction of the fixed costs of entry and production, in terms of shifting fixed capital expenditure (CAPEX) in ICT into operative costs (OPEX) depending on the size of demand and production. This contributes to reduce the barriers to entry especially for SMEs, as infrastructure is owned by the provider, it does not need to be purchased for one-time or infrequent intensive computing tasks, and it generates quick scalability and growth. The consequences on the endogenous structure of the markets with largest cost savings will be wide, with entry of new SMEs, a reduction of the mark ups, and an increase in average and total production. In spite of the fact that the relative size of IT cloud services may remain limited in the next few years, they are destined to increase rapidly as a percentage of total IT revenues, and to have a relevant macroeconomic impact, especially in terms of creation of new SMEs and of employment. Cloud platforms and new data centres are creating a new level of infrastructures that global developers can exploit, especially SMEs that are so common in Europe. This will open new investment and

business opportunities currently blocked by the need of massive up-front investments. The new platforms will enable different business models, including pay-as-you-go subscriptions for computing, storage, and/or IT management functions, which will allow small firms to scale up or down to meet the demand needs. This mechanism is going to be crucial in Europe because of the large presence of SMEs and of the higher risk aversion of the entrepreuners compared to their American counterparts (largely because of differences in the capital and credit markets and in the venture capital market): reduction of the fixed costs may reduce the risk of failure and promote entry even more.

Evaluating the Impact of Cloud Computing

To evaluate the impact of cloud computing, we have adopted a macroeconomic approach emphasizing the effects that this innovation has on the cost structure of the firms investing in ICT and consequently the incentives to create and expand new business, on the market structure and on the level of competition in their sectors, and ultimately on the induced effects for aggregate production, employment and other macroeconomic variables. The methodology is based on a dynamic stochastic general equilibrium calibrated model augmented with endogenous market structures in line with recent developments in the macroeconomic literature. The model follows the framework introduced by Etro and Colciago (2010) and recently extended to include the dynamics of the labour market by Colciago and Rossi (2011), and it has been augmented with a public sector producing goods and services and, for the sake of simplicity, being financed with labor income taxation.[7] Such a model is perturbed with a realistic structural change to the cost structure, with the purpose of studying the short and long term reactions of the economy.

Our experiment is focused on Europe taking as given the rest of the world (which is an additional conservative hypothesis). Therefore, all our data derive from official EU statistics (Eurostat), mainly for the number of firms, which is basically equivalent to the number of small and medium size enterprises (SMEs), employment and gross domestic product. In particular, we used data for most of the EU member countries. Moreover, we focused on few aggregate sectors for which we have detailed and comparable EU statistics: manufacturing, wholesale and retail trade; services including hotels and restaurants, transport storage and communication, real estate and other financial and business activities. These aggregate sectors cover the majority of firms in terms of number (more than 17 million firms) and a large part of employment for the European countries (about 114 million workers), and include all the sectors where the effects emphasized in our analysis are relevant, namely manufacturing and service sectors, where the use of ICT capital and the role of entry costs and competition effects are more relevant.[8]

Two key factors for the impact of cloud computing are, on one side, the size of the cost savings in ICT spending and, on the other side, the reduction of the fixed costs of production. On the first point, the business literature emphasizes large savings. IDC (2009) estimated a total cost reduction of about 50% or more in the private sector, but a more prudential estimate in a negative scenario could go down to 20%. Estimates for the public sector are more limited, ranging between a reduction in total costs of 10% in a pessimistic scenario and of 30% in an optimistic one (but West, 2010, suggests a range between 25% and 50% in successful cases). One should also keep in mind that the portion of these potential benefits that will be translated on the private sector will also depend on the level of competition in the provision of cloud services: as mentioned above while discussing the potential antitrust issues, we have reasons to believe that competition in the field will be strong enough to conjecture a wide translation of the cost savings.

On the second point, Carr (2003) suggests that about half of capital expenditure of modern firms

is ICT related, and therefore a large part of it may be eliminated and (partially) turned into operative expenditure. While this may be true in a number of sectors and for advanced companies, following Etro (2009,a) we adopted a more conservative assumption for our macroeconomic investigation. One of the best reviews of the state of ICT in Europe is provided by the e-Business Watch of the European Commission. The 2006 e-Business Report provided a comprehensive survey of ICT adoption and spending, showing that 5% of total costs is spent in ICT. Since only part of the total cost corresponds to fixed costs of production, the average ICT budget must be more than 5% of the total fixed costs of production. Of course, only a part of ICT spending represents fixed costs, and only a part of it will be cut even after the adoption of cloud computing in alternative to a fully internal solution. For this reason, we decided to adopt a conservative assumption and to consider a range of reduction in the fixed costs in the long run between 1% and 5%. The same cost reduction is assumed to take place in the production of goods and services of the public sector. Our main purpose is to show that even such a limited technological change due to cloud computing delivers substantial effects at the macroeconomic level. Needless to say, larger shocks will be associated with wider effects.

THE MACROECONOMIC IMPACT OF CLOUD COMPUTING: WHAT IS THE CONTRIBUTION TO THE REDUCTION OF THE UNEMPLOYMENT RATE?

In this section we report the results of our simulation for the introduction and diffusion of cloud computing in the European economy. We focus on the impact on GDP, business creation and employment (the role of the public sector will be considered in more detail in a subsequent section) in the short term, which is defined as a period of one year since the beginning of the process of adoption of cloud computing (say in 2012), and in the medium term, that is after five years (say in 2016). Two scenarios are considered: slow adoption corresponds to the case of a slow diffusion of the new technology leading to a 1% reduction of the fixed cost, and rapid adoption leading more rapidly to a 5% rapid reduction in the fixed costs. The calibration of the model and of the shock is the same adopted in Etro (2009,a).

The contribution to GDP growth can be hardly differentiated between countries and sectors, therefore we simply summarize our average estimates to the European countries. The range is between 0.1% a year in the short run under slow adoption and 0.4% in the medium run under fast adoption of cloud computing.

Before entering in further details, it is worthwhile to sketch the main mechanism emphasized in our model. The gradual introduction of cloud computing reduces the fixed costs needed to enter in each (non-ICT) sector and increases the incentives to enter. This increases current and future competition in each market and tends to reduce the mark ups and increase production. The associated increase in labor demand induces an upward pressure on wages that induces workers to work more (or new agents to enter in the labor force). The current and expected increase in output affects the consumption / savings behavior. In the short run, the demands of new business creation requires and increase in savings, which may induce a temporary negative impact on consumption. However, in the medium and long run the positive impact on output leads to an increase in consumption toward a higher steady state level. Of course, a faster adoption exerts a large impact on business creation and therefore on output and employment as well.

The simulation confirms our earlier result of a permanent creation of about 400 thousand new SMEs. The largest impact is expected to occur in the aggregate sectors of wholesale and retail trade (about 160 thousand new firms in the medium run under fast adoption) and of real estate and other financial and business activities (plus 150 thousand new SMEs). Our empirical exercise shows a strong impact on the creation of new SMEs, in the magnitude of a few hundred of thousand in the whole EU (again, this is additional to a normal situation without the introduction of cloud computing). Incidentally, this is consistent with the conclusions of studies by IDC (2009) arguing that cloud services could add $ 800 billion in net new business revenues between 2009 and 2013. Notice that the effect is permanent and tends to increase over time: the creation of new SMEs is not going to vanish, but it is going to remain over time with a permanent impact on the structure of the economy. Moreover, the effect is deeper in countries where the diffusion of SMEs is particularly strong (as in Italy) or where ICT adoption has been generally rapid (as in the UK).

We have also examined the impact on employment in each country with a distinction between aggregate sectors. Overall, the results country by country are similar to those found in our earlier study, and are in part affected by differences in labor market conditions, that tend to affect the ability of the economy to react to a positive change through job creation, in the regulatory framework and in the competitive conditions of the goods markets (which create the conditions for a quick business creation)

One should take the estimates on the impact on employment with care. Even if we took in consideration country specific factors related to the labor market conditions, our basic simulations emphasize the impact in terms of hours worked, whose translation in new jobs depends on a number of institutional and structural features of the labor markets and their country-specific regulation. Keeping this in mind, we confirm the spirit of the results of our earlier study. The introduction of cloud computing could create hundreds of thousand new jobs in a permanent way. Our simulation at the EU level suggests an initial creation of about three hundred thousand new jobs under the scenario of a slow adoption and more than a million new jobs under our positive scenario. The positive contribution to employment would be reduced in the following years, with a range between 70 thousand and 700 thousand new jobs created in the fifth year of the adoption process. About two thirds of job creation is expected to occur in the six largest countries (United Kingdom, Germany, France, Poland, Italy and Spain), but each country could enjoy an increase in the work force. The positive contribution of cloud computing to the net creation of new jobs can be translated in a quicker path of adjustment toward the long run equilibrium of the labour market, that is into a more rapid reduction of the unemployment rate. Our estimates of the reduction of the unemployment rate in the European countries due to the introduction of cloud computing remain between 0.1% and 0.3% in the short run and between 0.05% and 0.2% in the medium run. In other words, the process of adjustment of the unemployment rate toward its long run level in the next years could be substantially accelerated by a rapid adoption of the new technology throughout the economy.

While the nature of our experiment (a simulation) suggests that these results should be taken *cum grano salis*, the results also suggest the relevance of the mechanism underlying the diffusion of cloud computing. Most of the new jobs are expected in the manufacturing sector (31% for our countries), followed by the sector of wholesale and retail trade (28%) and the real estate and finance and other business activities (23%), with only a minor contribution by the sector related to transport and communication (10%) and the one including hotel, restaurants, and related activities (8%). Nevertheless, the process of business creation is going to be highly differentiated across countries, for instance with a predominance of the manufacturing sector in industrial countries as Germany and Italy, but also in Eastern European countries with a less developed tertiary sector, of the financial sector in the UK and of trade and

services in a country as Greece. Not by chance, 36% of the new jobs in Germany are expected from the manufacturing sector, 34% in Italy and percentages above 40% in the Czech Republic, Slovakia and Romania. At the same time, only 19% of the new jobs estimated in the UK derive from manufacturing, while 29% of them are expected in the macrosector including real estate, finance and other business activities. Finally, Greece can expect 56% of the new jobs from wholesale and retail trade and from services including hotels and restaurants.

JOB CREATION AND JOB DESTRUCTION: HOW LARGE A THE SOCIAL COSTS OF THE PROCESS OF JOB CREATION AND DESTRUCTION?

The results of our simulation on employment refer to the net creation of jobs, which is the difference between new (non-ICT) jobs created in the economy and (ICT) jobs possibly lost during the process of technology adoption. This leads to crucial questions on the decomposition of these figures between gross job creation and job destruction.

First of all, we need to emphasize that the social problems associated with the crowding out of ICT jobs may be much lower than one may expect. A first reason for this is implicit in the same nature of our results: as mentioned, a crucial benefit of the diffusion of cloud computing is associated with the push of the economy due new business creation, which in turn is by definition creating new firms with the new technology without destroying any jobs associated with the old technologies. For this reason, a lot of the benefits of the adoption of cloud computing are completely unrelated to a process of job destruction.

A second reason is that cloud computing generates a range of innovation opportunities that can only br exploited by ICT departments after a fundamental change of tasks. As noticed by Brynjolfsson, Hofmann and Jordan (2010), "the real strength of cloud computing is that it is a catalyst for more innovation. In fact, as cloud computing continues to become cheaper and more ubiquitous, the opportunities for combinatorial innovation will only grow. It is true that this inevitably requires more creativity and skill from IT and business executives."

In countries with a more rigid labour market, short run costs of reallocation may emerge, and policy intervention in these cases may be useful. However, the results suggest that the problem of reallocation of labour following the diffusion of a new technology as cloud computing may be quite limited.

THE IMPACT ON PUBLIC FINANCES: WHAT WILL BE THE IMPACT ON THE DEFICIT/GDP RATIO?

The adoption of cloud computing in the public sector can also have a fundamental role in the near future. A few business studies have investigated this aspect (see West, 2010) emphasizing a potential for a large impact on cost savings, though lower than in the private sector.

In the U.S. interesting examples are available both for local and central public authorities. The city of Los Angeles has switched to a Google-based online solution for its email services in 2009: the estimated cost reduction was around 25%, only nine jobs were gradually eliminated and almost 100 servers were relocated to a different use within the city administration. A similar switch took place in Washington, D.C. with estimated cost savings around 50%. At a smaller level, the switch to a Microsoft-based online solution of the email services of the Californian town of Carlsbad created cost savings of 40% per year (West, 2010). Even higher were the savings associated

with the adoption of a cloud computing solution for service hosting and mapping technologies of the city of Miami, which also allowed the local authorities to introduce a new and more efficient system of control of the urban area. A SalesForce. com solution was employed by the U.S. State Department for budget information and led to cost reductions around 75%, while private clouds have been adopted by NASA and the U.S. Air Force. In September 2009 the Obama Administration has instituted the FCCI (Federal Cloud Computing Initiative), with the purpose of promoting standards and rules for the adoption of online services to reduce the $ 76 billion spending of the American government in IT.

In Europe, the most advanced country in terms of the adoption of cloud computing in the public sector is definitely the U.K., which is trying to move to the cloud its IT assets at a rate of 10% a year, a wise gradual approach to reduce the £ 16 billion spending of the British government in IT. Many other local public authorities and central ministries have started to switch toward cloud computing solutions. For instance, in 2010 the Ministry of Health of Belgium adopted the SharePoint platform hosted by Microsoft to organize the entire activities of the Presidency of the European Union in the second semester of the year: this has induced high cost efficiency and better organization. Other examples are abundant in public health and education. As mentioned above, in 2010 one of the leading Italian hospitals, the Pediatric Hospital of Bambin Gesù has switched to an online solution for the email services of its 2500 employees. At the same time, a similar switch took place in a university centre based near Florence, the European University Institute (a EU-sponsored research centre in social sciences), which moved to the cloud mailboxes of about 2500 researchers, students and other staff. The switch took about four months, led to a hundred times more storage space and an improved web-based experience at substantial savings (estimated in 43% by EUI).[9]

The costs savings associated with these experiences in the public sector should not be seen as the typical ones because of an endogeneity problem: the early adopters are naturally those who benefit the most. Nevertheless a range of cost savings between 10% and 40% appears reasonable in the public sector.

The introduction of the public sector and of labour taxation in our theoretical model allows us to derive a few more implications. First of all, the mechanism of propagation of the effects of the new technology is slightly different. Following, standard assumptions, a fixed part of the initial income (before the introduction of the cost reducing technology) is destined to the production of public goods (20% as in standard macroeconomic simulations). The introduction of the cost saving technology makes public spending more efficient, which translates in direct savings (of spending needed to create the same amount of public goods), but does not create a multiplier effect (as in the private sector). However, the adoption of distorsive taxation needed to finance public spending introduces new and more realistic mechanisms in the model. In particular, it strengthens the propagation of the technology change (because of a classic substitution effect: higher net wages enhance labor supply) and creates changes in public finance accounts. Since we assume budget balance to start with (which sets the initial tax rate at the level needed to finance the initial amount of public spending), the simulation allows one to derive the impact of the introduction of a cost reducing technology on public finances. As for the simulation of the impact on GDP, we are not able to provide differentiated results for countries and sectors, but we can simply derive a summary result.

It is useful to remind the reader of the thought experiment we have performed. The gradual introduction of cloud computing creates an expansion in the economy through new business creation, additional employment and additional income. For a given tax rate, this increases the tax revenues, which creates a surplus in the public accounts (that is assumed to be redistributed to the consumers). The sum of the direct savings from the adoption of cloud computing and the increased tax revenues represent together the additional amount that the public sector redistributes to the private one (which in turn is consumed and contributes to strengthen the expansion). This sum, expressed as a percentage of total income, can be interpreted as the improvement in the ratio deficit/GDP due to the introduction of the general purpose technology, which is what we are ultimately interested in.

We focus again on the impact in the short term, that is after one year, and in the medium term, that is after five years, in our two scenarios. The model suggests that the corresponding impact on the deficit/GDP ratio is about 0.1% in the pessimistic scenario and 0.2% in the optimistic one. In other words, the introduction of a cost reducing technology as cloud computing can have a small but not negligible impact on public finances, even if it only creates a marginal reduction of the costs of the public sector. This happens because public finances benefit on one side from the direct reduction in costs, and on the other side on the additional tax revenues derived from the boost to the economy and to the creation of new private business.

A back of the envelop calculation confirms these numbers: if ICT spending is about 4% of GDP and a quarter of this (1%) is within the public sector, a cost reduction between 10% may imply an impact of 0.1% of GDP that could be moderately increased because of the indirect impact of the expansion of the private sector on taxation.

CONCLUSION

Part of the positive effects of cloud computing are going to be positively related to the speed of adoption of the new technology. Of course there are a number of factors that may slow down this adoption, as a lack of understanding of the cloud by firms, systemic risk, security, privacy [10] and interoperability issues, reliability, jurisdictional complexity, data governance, loss of IT control and general *status quo* inertia. For this reason, our investigation suggests that policymakers should promote as much as possible a rapid adoption of cloud computing. Concrete interventions include (beyond the expansion of the broadband capacity, of course):

- International agreements in favour of unrestricted flow of data across borders (since datacenters are located in different countries with different privacy laws, data portability remains a key issue for the diffusion of cloud computing);
- Agreements between EU authorities and industry leaders on a minimum set of technological standards and process standards to be respected in the provision of cloud computing services to guarantee data security, privacy and portability, and promote a healthy diffusion of the new technology;
- Introduction of fiscal incentives for the adoption of cloud computing and a specific promotion in particular dynamic sectors (for instance, governments could finance, up to a limit, the variable costs of computing for all the domestic and foreign firms that decide to adopt a cloud computing solution).
- Introduction of public support to the reallocation of employment within the IT field (from IT departments especially of small firms toward different destinations in the IT sector).

These policies may be studied in such a way to optimize the process of adoption of the new technology and to strengthen the propagation of its benefits.

NOTE

This chapter was written while preparing a talk at the Annual Conference on European Antitrust Law 2011. The Future of European Competition Law in High-tech Industries (Brussels, March 3-4, 2011). A preliminary version of this paper has been presented at the Conference organized by Holyrood on "Cloud Computing For the Public Sector" (Edinburgh, September 20, 2010) and at the Government Leaders Forum Europe (London, November 4, 2010). I am thankful to data collection by Sara Pancotti and Amit Kumar and outstanding research assistance and suggestions by Andrea Colciago.

REFERENCES

Ahmad, M. (2010). Security risks of cloud computing and its emergence as 5th utility service. *Information Security and Assurance. Communications in Computer and Information Science*, 76, 209–219. doi:10.1007/978-3-642-13365-7_20

Bilbiie, F., Ghironi, F., & Melitz, M. (2007). *Endogenous entry, product variety, and business cycles*. NBER WP 13646.

Brynjolfsson, E., Hofmann, P., & Jordan, J. (2010). Cloud computing and electricity: Beyond the utility model. *Communications of the ACM*, 53(5), 32–34. doi:10.1145/1735223.1735234

Carr, N. (2003). IT doesn't matter. *Harvard Business Review*, (May): 41–49.

Cecioni, M. (2010). *Firm entry, competitive pressures and the US inflation dynamics. Mimeo*. Bank of Italy.

Colciago, A., & Etro, F. (2010). Real business cycles with cournot competition and endogenous entry. *Journal of Macroeconomics*, 32(4), 1101–1117. doi:10.1016/j.jmacro.2010.04.005

Colciago, A., & Rossi, L. (2011). *Endogenous market structure and labor market dynamics*. Mimeo, University of Milano Bicocca.

David, P. (1990). The dynamo and the computer: An historical perspective on the modern productivity paradox. *The American Economic Review, 80*(2), 355–361.

Economist (2008, October 25).Where the cloud meets the ground. *The Economist, 387*.

Etro, F. (2007a). Endogenous market structures and macroeconomic theory. *Review of Business and Economics, 52*(4), 543–566.

Etro, F. (2009a). The economic impact of cloud computing on business creation, employment and output in the E.U. *Review of Business and Economics, 54*(2), 179–208.

Etro, F. (2009b). *Endogenous market structures and the macroeconomy*. New York, Germany: Springer. doi:10.1007/978-3-540-87427-0

Etro, F., & Colciago, A. (2010). Endogenous market structure and the business cycle. *The Economic Journal, 120*(549), 1201–1233. doi:10.1111/j.1468-0297.2010.02384.x

European Commission. (2007). *The European e-business report, 2006/07. A portrait of e-business in 10 sectors of the EU economy, 5th Synthesis Report of the Sectoral e-Business Watch*. Brussels: European Commission.

Faia, E. (2010). *Oligopolistic competition and optimal monetary policy. Mimeo*. Goethe University of Frankfurt.

Ghironi, F., & Melitz, M. (2005). International trade and macroeconomic dynamics with heterogenous firms. *The Quarterly Journal of Economics, 120*, 865–915.

International Data Corporation. (2008). *IT cloud services forecast -- 2008-2012: A key driver for growth*. Mimeo, October 8.

International Data Corporation. (2009, October 9). *Aid to recovery*. White paper.

Jäätmaa, J. (2010). *Financial aspects of cloud computing business models information systems science. Mimeo*. Department of Business Technology, Aalto University School of Economics.

Jorgenson, D. (2001). Information technology and the U.S. economy. *The American Economic Review, 91*(1), 1–28. doi:10.1257/aer.91.1.1

Lanvin, B., & Passman, P. (2008). Building e-skills for the information age. In *Global Information Technology Report 2007-2008*, WEF.

Lewis, V., & Poilly, C. (2010). *Firm entry and the monetary transmission mechanism. Mimeo*. National Bank of Belgium.

Liebenau, J. (2010, June 8). *Manage the cloud? It's not airy-fairy!* Retrieved from http://microsoft.eu/Posts/Viewer/tabid/120/articleType/ArticleView/articleId/662/Menu/3/Manage-the-cloud-Its-not-airy-fairy.aspx

Parente, S., & Prescott, E. (1994). Barriers to technology adoption and development. *The Journal of Political Economy, 102*(2), 298–321. doi:10.1086/261933

Ranganathan, V. (2010). Privacy issues with cloud applications. *IS Channel, 5*(1), 16–20.

Rappa, M. (2004). The utility business model and the future of computing services. *IBM Systems Journal, 43*(1), 32–42. doi:10.1147/sj.431.0032

O Reilly, T. (2005). *What is Web 2.0? Design patterns and business models for the next generation of software*. Mimeo.

Röller, L.-H., & Waverman, L. (2001). Telecommunications infrastructure and economic development: A simultaneous approach. *The American Economic Review, 91*(4), 909–923. doi:10.1257/aer.91.4.909

Totzek, A. (2011). *Banks, oligopolistic competition, and the business cycle: A new financial accelerator approach.* Mimeo, Christian-Albrechts-University of Kiel.

Vaquero, L. M., Rodero-Merino, L., Caceres, J., & Lindner, M. (2009). A break in the clouds. towards a cloud definition. *Computer Communication Review, 39*(1), 50–55. doi:10.1145/1496091.1496100

Varian, H., Litan, R. E., Elder, A., & Shutter, J. (2002). *The net impact study: The projected economic benefits of the internet in the United States, United Kingdom, France and Germany.* Mimeo 2.0.

West, D. (2010). *Saving money through cloud computing.* Mimeo, Governance Studies at Brookings.

Zittrain, J. (2007). Saving the Internet. *Harvard Business Review*, (June): 49–59.

ENDNOTES

[1] As noticed by David (1990), only with the reinvention of the production process in the factories (which took decades) was the potential of electrification fully realized.

[2] The classic work by Parent and Prescott (1994) has emphasized how differences in the barriers to the adoption of new technologies can heavily affect the growth potential of different countries.

[3] Jorgenson (2001) estimates that computers contributed to 32% of TFP growth and software to 9% of it in the period 1995-1999.

[4] On the financial aspects of cloud computing see also Jäätmaa (2010).

[5] In the business literature, cloud computing has been seen as a step in the commoditization of IT investments (Carr, 2003), as the outcome of an evolution toward a utility business model in which computing capabilities are provided as a service (Rappa, 2004; Brynjolfsson, Hofmann and Jordan, 2010), as the core element of the era of Web 2.0, in which Internet is used as a software platform (O'Reilly, 2005), or simply as an application of the generativity power of the Internet (Zittrain, 2007). See also IDC (2008).

[6] The first mover in the field has been Amazon, that has provided access to cloud solutions with its Amazon Web Services (initially developed for internal purposes). Through this cloud computing service, any small firm can start a web-based business on its computer system, add extra virtual machines when needed and shut them down when there is no demand: for this reason the utility is called Elastic Cloud Computing. Google is also investing huge funds in data centres and Google App engine allows software developers to write applications that can be run for free on Google's servers. Even the search engine of Google or its mapping service can offer cloud application services: for instance, when Google Maps were launched, programmers easily found out how to use their maps with other information to provide new services. Microsoft is also investing a lot in new data centres. In January 2010, the leading software company has launched a cloud platform called Windows Azure that is able to provide a number of new technologies: a Windows-based environment in the cloud to store data in Microsoft data centres and to run applications, an infrastructure for both on-premises and cloud applications (through. NET Services), and a cloud based database (through SQL Data Services, which can be used from different users and different locations). Moreover, Windows Azure provides a browser-accessible portal for customers: these can create a hosting account to run applications or a storage account to store data in the cloud, and they can be charged through subscriptions, per-use fees or other methods.

Another important player is Salesforce.com with its Force.com products. Also Oracle has introduced a cloud based version of its database program.

[7]　See Ghironi and Melitz (2005), Bilbiie *et al.* (2007, 2008,a,b), Etro (2007a), Etro and Colciago (2010), Cecioni (2010), Faia (2010), Lewis and Poilly (2010), Totzek (2011) and Colciago and Rossi (2011). See Etro (2009,b) for a survey.

[8]　We ignored other aggregate private sectors (as electricity, gas and water supply), where we believe that our mechanisms are either weaker or absent, or sectors where comparable data were not available. Country specific heterogeneity and sectoral differences were taken in consideration on the basis of statistics on the labor market and the entry/ competitive conditions at the level of EU countries and their aggregate sectors.

[9]　See http://www.microsoft.com/casestudies/ Microsoft-Active-Directory-Domain-Services/European-University-Institute/ University-Avoids-345-233-in-Messaging-Upgrade-Gains-100-Times-More-Storage/4000009020.

[10]　See Ahmad (2010) on security risk issues and Ranganathan (2010) on privacy issues. The latter suggests that a way to overcome legal problems of privacy protection across countries could rely on technological solutions (including data encryption).

Section 6
Applications and Advances in Cloud Computing

Chapter 18
Patterns of Tactical Networking Services

Alex Bordetsky
Naval Postgraduate School, USA

ABSTRACT

The Cloud Computing services are making their way to the world of tactical networking. According to CDR James Mills (Mills, 2011) the new area of tactical networking, named cloudlets, is shaping up:

"Cloudlets are small, portable appliance-like devices akin to a "data center in a box" and include an embedded compute cluster, wireless access point and battery or alternate source power (e.g., solar, wind, etc.). Cloudlets offer the benefit of offloading computation from mobile devices, reduce latency of mobile devices by being in close proximity to the user's device, and offload data relay costs to the larger cloud/network from the mobile device."

This chapter describes findings and prototypes of emerging tactical networking services, which were identifiable based on unique experimental studies of tactical networking. The described findings would be helpful in structuring tactical cloud services for the variety manned-unmanned sensor networking applications.

EXPERIMENTAL STUDIES OF EMERGING TACTICAL NETWORKING SERVICES

Beginning in 2002, a team of Naval Postgraduate School researchers together with sponsors from the United States Special Operations Command (USSOCOM), and later joined by the Office of the Secretary of Defense (OSD) and the Department of Homeland Security (DHS) S&T Programs, started

a new interagency experimentation program, which is now collectively known as the Tactical Network Testbed (TNT) Experiments (Bordetsky and Netzer, 2010).

In the core of TNT experimentation is a unique testbed, which enables sustainability and evolution of the experimentation process. It provides the adaptation and integration processes between people, networks, sensors, and unmanned systems. It enables plug-and-play tactical-on-the-move sensor-unmanned systems networking capabilities (Bordetsky and Bourakov, 2006) combined with

DOI: 10.4018/978-1-4666-2187-9.ch018

global reach back to remote expert/command sites and augmentation by rapid integration of applied research services.

The TNT interagency experimentation program has two major venues. The first one involves quarterly field experiments with USSOCOM, in which NPS researchers and students as well as participants from other universities, government organizations, and industry investigate various topics related to tactical networking with sensors and unmanned systems as well as collaboration between geographically distributed units with focus on high value target (HVT) tracking and surveillance missions (Figure 1).

The second venue involves Maritime Interdiction Operation (MIO) experiments with Lawrence Livermore National Laboratory, USCG and First Responders (San Francisco Bay, New York/New Jersey), and is supported by Homeland Defense (HLD) and HLS S&T Programs and Department of Energy (DoE) agencies. These experiments are conducted twice a year and are also supported by overseas partners from Sweden, Germany, Greece, and Singapore. This series of experiments is being conducted to test the technical and operational challenges of searching large cargo vessels and interdicting small craft possessing nuclear radiation threats. One goal is to test the applicability of using a wireless network for data sharing during an MIO scenario to facilitate "reach back" (a current technologically challenging operational gap) to experts for radiation source analysis and biometric data analysis (Figure 2).

From the scholarly stand point (Alberts and Hayes, 2007), the TNT testbed represents a unique field model for learning complex relationships between man and machine in the emerging environment of tactical networking and collaboration.

Figure 1. Typical cluster of tactical ad hoc mobile networking services

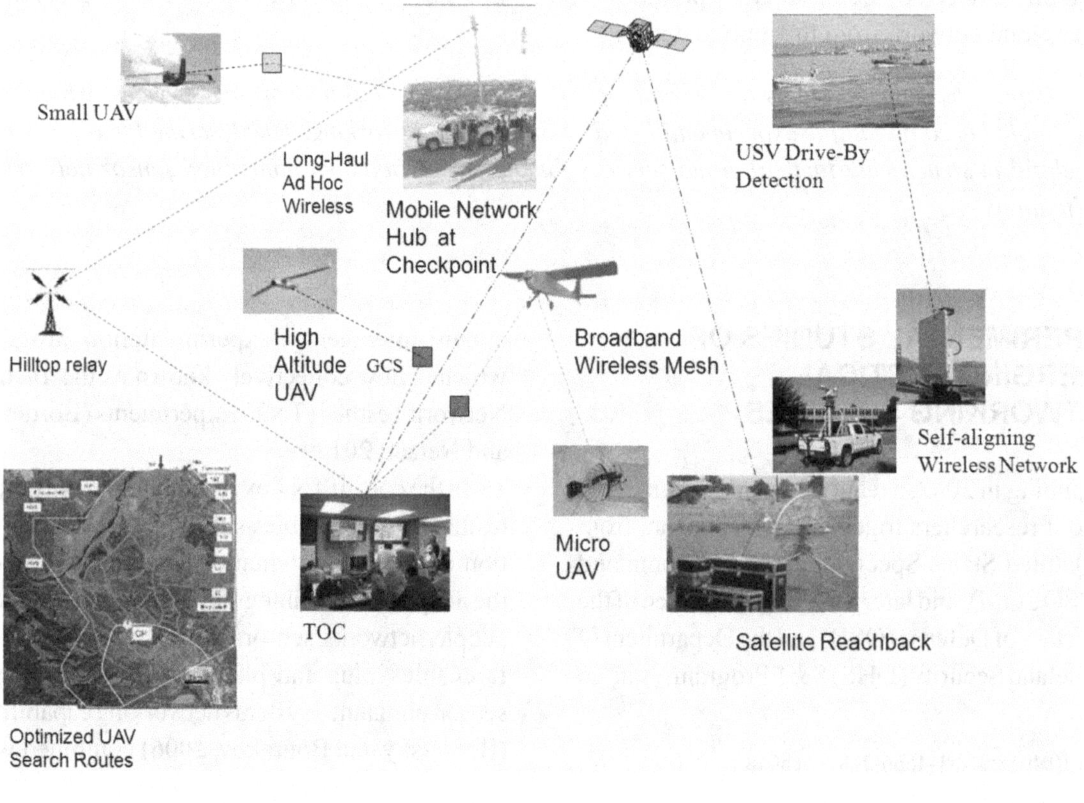

Figure 2. Typical cluster of MIO ad hoc mobile networking services (diagram prepared by Michael Clement and Eugene Bourakov)

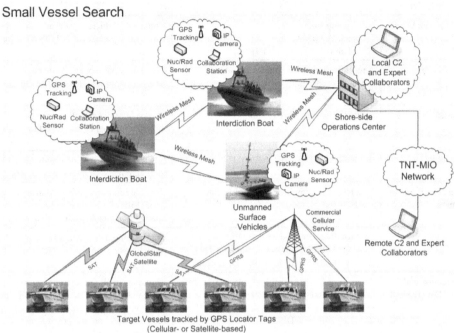

Exploring feasibility and major operational constraints associated with those relationships allowed the TNT experimentation team to identify critical elements of tactical networking and collaboration frontier and identify emerging tactical networking services for such tasks. Tables 1 and 2 illustrate some of our team findings.

NETWORKED UNMANNED SYSTEMS SERVICES

Rapid Allocation of Network Resources On-the-Move

One of the typical operational scenarios, supported by tactical network (Figure 3), is countering the adversary's intend by enabling rapid collaboration between the manned aircraft, UAV, ground station crews, and dismounted unit operators (McGrew, Chen, and Masacioglu, 2009).

On top technical challenges of integrating UAV in the tactical networked environment (Clement, Bourakov, Jones, and Dobrokhodov, 2009), there is a major service management challenge, which tactical level commander needs to address in a matter of several minutes, making multiple tradeoffs between soft and hard constraints on the UAV selection, manned aircraft weapons, dismounted unit response, and networking capabilities. The examples include:

- **UAV Service:** Small UAV Service (low altitude, short distance (5-8km), short flight time); Medium Size UAV Service (low altitude, medium range (40km), medium flight time (6-8h); Large UAV Service (medium altitude (12,00 ft), medium range, medium flight time); High Altitude Large UAV Service (higher altitude (16,000ft), long range (100 km), long time (12h), weapons on board.

Table 1. Findings of sensor and unmanned systems tactical networking services

Emerging Tactical Networking Services	Study Team	Content and First Results
Network and Situation Awareness controlled UAVs, USVs, UGVs	An ongoing study Clement, Bourakov, Jones and Dobrokhodov (2009) and Jones et al. (2009)	Unmanned vehicle is controlled by submitting the way points via tactical N-LOS mesh network
Way Point Information Services	A recently completed study with the University of Bundeswehr, thesis project of Knopp and Shramm (2009)	Computational models for managing way points submission through highly discrete moments of time
Network-on-Target	Bordetsky and Bourakov (2006)	Peer-to-peer links configured from the top of Common Operational Picture interface, self-aligning directional antennas
Hyper-Nodes with 8th Layer	Bordetsky and Hayes-Roth (2007)	Extending tactical self-forming networking nodes to miniature network operations centers
Decision Makers as sensors to unmanned systems	First results accomplished by James Gateau and Bordetsky (2008)	Creating military operator Management Information Base (MIB) for navigating human decision space and making it available to the unmanned system agents
Networking-by-touch	First results accomplished in by Rideout and Strickland (2007), continuing research TNT 08-2 QLR (2008) and TNT 08-4 QLR (2008)	Transmitting data via highly adaptive human network by using physical or electronic touch
GPS denial navigation and Ultra Wideband (UWB) Mesh networking	An ongoing study TNT 07-4 QLR (2007), TNT 08-2 QLR (2008). Since 2009 study team is joined by George Papagonopolus, Ketula Patel, and Greg Blair (ARDEC, Fire Storm group)	Providing small unit operator as well as sensor location by posting alerts from inside the building and from under the deck on-the-move, integrating the UWB link into the peer-to-peer wireless mesh network
Projectile-based Networking:	TNT MIO 07-4 After Action Report (2007)	New data collection and reachback networking technique based on the burst mesh networking with on board sensor or wireless base station node during a few seconds of projectile descend
Small Distributed Unit Private Tactical Satellite Network	Study started by Conrad and Tzanos (2008)	Creating private orbital network for geographically distributed small units
Small Distributed Private Tactical Cellular Network	Study stated with TNT 08-4 QLR (2008)	Creating private cellular network on-the-move for geographically distributed small units. The ground and aerial based macro and micro base stations utilization.

- ○ **Payload:** Each UAV is selected subject to payload configuration: camera, computer board, network relay
- ○ **Weather:** Wind speed, cloud level, extreme temperature, sand storms.
- **Dismounted Units Service:** Tracking only, advising ground commander, independent attack decision.
- **Network Operation Services:** Bandwidth allocation, frequency deconfliction, satellite link availability, access to ground ad hoc mobile mesh.

Executing such services on-the-move requires new robust multiple criteria computational models, such as the nonlinear PSI technique (Statnikov, Bordetsky, Statnikov, 2010), to be executed by geographically distributed cloud of ad hoc mobile tactical handheld devices.

The other new phenomena, associated with networked unmanned services are the need to structure and execute an exchange of way points with unmanned systems autopilots, or in more generalized term autonomous control agents. It could tentatively be named Way Point Informatics or Way Point Information Services.

Table 2. Expert reachback and interagency collaboration services

Expert Reachback and Interagency Collaboration Services	Study Team	Content and First Results
Collaborative networks for rapid interagency data sharing and expert response in Maritime Interdiction Operations (MIO) Collaboration	with An ongoing research with Dougan & Dunlop (LLNL), Bourakov, Hutchins, Looney, Clement, Vega, Hudgens, Bergin-NPS; Friman (Swedish Defence Research Agency), Pickl (University of Bundeswehr)): (Bordetsky et al, 2006), (Hutchins, et.al., 2006), (Bordetsky & Friman, 2007), (Bordetsky & Hutchins, 2008)	Bringing the remote expert advice to an immediate support of the boarding officers
Synergy of social and information networking	Study started with Hudgens, Vega, Koons, Bergin, Bekatoros: (Hudgens and Bordetsky, 2008), (TNT MIO 08-4 Report)	Achieving synergy of interagency response network by creating new weak and strong ties in the workspaces of virtual collaborative environment. Flattening hierarchical relationships in the cyber space of MIO operation
Interoperability of Situational Awareness (SA) and Collaborative platforms, collaboration with Coalitions partners	First results accomplished with Bourakov and Clement (NPS), Reimers (BAE), Poulsen and Cooper (PANYNJ), Hanson and Lindt (Swedish Naval Warfare Center and Kokums, Sweden), Hoy-Petersen and Nielsen (Systematik, Denmark): (TNT MIO 08-2 Report, 2008), (TNT MIO 08-4, Report, 2008)	Propagating alerts between NPS SA tools, Port Authority NY-NJ (PANYNJ) Joint Situational Awareness System (JSAS)

Figure 3. Manned-unmanned teaming tactical services

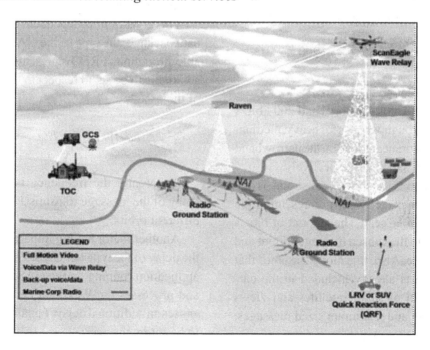

Simple Model of Waypoint Information Services

The study conducted by the University of Bundeswehr students of Professor Stefan Pickl, Markus Knopp and Alexander Schramm during their visiting term at the US Naval Postgraduate School (NPS Advisor, Professor Alex Bordetsky), represents an interesting example of computational model, which would be needed to enable and manage Waypoint Information Services. In this study (Knopp and Schramm, 2009) it is assumed that the waypoints for directing Unmanned Aerial System (UAS) to the area of interest, are received during highly discreet moments of time from the Cube-, Pico-, or other Miniature Satellite passing over the area of action, or by ground vehicle or vessel approaching the areas. The processing of managing Way Point submission and control services requires unique robust models of time delay constraints balancing, such as the constraints described in the sections below.

Service Design Constraints

The first service design restriction is the throughput (tpt), which is described by the following set:

$$tpt = \left\{ 10 \ kbit \ / \ s, \ 80 \ kbit \ / \ s, \ 200 \ kbit \ / \ s \right\}$$

In this set, 10 kbit/s, 80 kbit/s and 200 kbit /s represent data throughput rates for heavy, medium and low contemporaneous load on the narrowband channel of small satellites, respectively.

The second service design constraint is the waypoint data package (wpdp) representing the number of bits to be sent. The amount of bits is directly linked to the chosen message format and the used structure. Also, this model assumes that error correction is already included in the narrowband channel of small satellites and views on the minimum and maximum sized messages.

On these accounts, the Waypoint Data Package is described by the following set:

$$wpflp = \left\{ CoT, \ ASCII \right\}$$

The type t of the employed UAS plays a major role, as well, since its hardware and software affects the outcome and speed of the message transmission.

This also applies to the operating system (os) and the application used to submit the Waypoint messages. There are a lot of different combinations of operating systems and applications, which are not discussed in detail at this point. The effects are described in the functional constraints, where the caused delay of the chosen operating system is evaluated.

Functional Constraints

The functional constraints in this model result from the employed design constraints and can be described as follows.

A restriction within this process is the frequency (freq) to submit the Waypoint messages over the small satellites.

This constraint is dependent on the Waypoint data package, the type of the UAS, and the available throughput. FREQ represents the threshold as a variable to be set in respect to the requirements of the user:

$$freq\left(wpdp, t, tpt\right) \geq FREQ$$

Apparently the frequency is limited by the delay of the message transmission caused by the different orbits.

Another factor having impact on the model is the delay of the type t of UAS. The focus is on the application running on the UAS, which receives and processes the Waypoint data, and therefore causes an additional delay. T again is the threshold to be set by the user:

$$d(t) \leq T$$

The application and operating system (os) used to submit the Waypoint data again take time to execute the commands causing the third delay to be taken into consideration, where OS is the highest delay accepted by the user:

$$d(os) \leq OS$$

Waypoint Service Criteria

The response time of the UAS has to be taken into consideration, when looking at the factors of influence on the delay. This factor describes the actual time the UAS needs to process the received information and execute the task and is the first criterion in this model. The response time of a UAS is a function f of the type of the UAS and the related frequency used for Waypoint submission. X hereby represents the threshold value set by the user.

$$RT_{UAV} = f(t, freq(wpdp, t, tpt)) \leq X$$

On the account of the aforementioned factors and conditions, the overall function g for the actual waypoint transmission delay is influenced by the OS delay and the application delay of the UAV itself. The variable Y again is the threshold value for the by the user accepted Waypoint delay:

$$D_{WP} = g(d(os), d(t)) \leq Y$$

The criteria for optimizing this process is to keep the Waypoint delay and the UAV response time consistent. In other words, the waypoint delay has to be part of the response time in order to minimize the overall delay. Two other factors are found in the provided Duration of Service (DoS) of the used constellation, as well as in the cost of using this specific set of satellites. Given the cost factor effect the service criteria model could look as follows:

$$D_{wp} \rightarrow \min$$

$$RT_{UAV} \rightarrow \min$$

$$DoS(constellation) \rightarrow \max$$

$$Cost(constellation) \rightarrow \min$$

One possible way of conducting Way Point Service Management, which study team started to consider, is to us Multiple Criteria Parameter Space Investigation Model(PSl)4 [SS95].

WAYPOINT SERVICE MANAGEMENT MODEL

In accordance with Multiple Criteria PSI approach, the tactical networking services model would be structured through the interrelated clusters of the design constraints, functional constraints and criteria constraints to be balanced at the Pareto compromise level by Way Point service providers and service consumers.

First, a number of trail points, i.e. setups for the experimental environment, has to be generated by combining the N different design constraints $\alpha_i^* \leq \alpha_i \leq \alpha_i^{**}, i = 1, ..., n$ meeting the requirements as described in the quantitative model and therefore creating the design variable space $\prod$. The generated trial points do not necessarily have to cover all possible combinations, but the most desirable ones in the first iteration. If these trial points do not meet the further requirements, more sets have to be created and evaluated. The functional constraints then have to be applied on every single trial point in order to sort the ones out that do not match their restrictions and leaving a set of trial points N*. The points that did not satisfy the functional constraints are subject to a possible readjustment to meet the requirements, and to be added and evaluated in the criteria space.

In a final step, the trial points N* have to be evaluated within the created criteria space. This space is $\Phi_v(\alpha) \leq \Phi_v^{**}, v = 1, ..., k$ and their corresponding computed values. After this evaluation the user is finally able to decide, if one of the designed setups fits the desires best, or if another iteration has to be run.

Table 3 shows one example of service variables choices to be made along the course of PSI driven rapid experimentation (Knopp and Shramm, 2009) on Way Point service constraints balancing.

DISRUPTION-BASED TACTICAL NETWORKING SERVICES: USING TOUCH, PROJECTILES, AND CUBE SATELLITES

In the section above, while introducing the basic idea of Way Point tactical information services, we've almost inevitably touched on the growing role of disruption-based networking, a need to consider communications unfolding through

Table 3. Variables

Variable	Selected set
tpt	10, 80, or 200 Kbit per sec
wpdp	CoT or ASCII
t	RASCAL or P10
os	MacOS X or MS Windows
FREQ	6 per min
D	100ms
T	20ms
OS	20ms
X	500ms
Y	300ms

highly discrete moments of time. Our ongoing field experimentation with tactical networking environments clearly indicates that the disruption-based networking could become one of the major trends in the emerging tactical services.

The conventional approach to self-organizing tactical networking is based on applying signal/delay adaption and different mesh routing techniques to the ad hoc mobile wireless nodes, such as sensors, unmanned aerial/ground vehicles, and operators on-the-move. The well-known clones of MANET model and recently DARPA initiated Control-Based MANET (CBMANET), are good examples of such solutions. As good as these techniques are in providing adaptive self-organizing routing at Layer 2 and 3 of the OSI stack, they lack capability of negotiating application services and maintaining disrupted transactions, which would be tolerant to minutes long delays and changes in the relay nodes location on the scale of hundreds of miles. Also, maintaining security within the self-organizing sensor networking tactical clusters using continuing shared medium type wireless communications represents a significant challenge.

A new approach to self-organizing tactical networking with sensors, unmanned systems, and operators on-the-move, would deny the need in maintaining wireless time and space communication continuum. Alternatively, the approach would based on delivering significant amount of timely-sensitive tactical situational awareness information through largely disjoint moments of time, by means of human or machine nodes rapidly changing their 3D location across significant distances. The new approach also would take full benefit of integrating social networking in the cooperative process of sensor networking in the battlefield, thus enhancing wireless service delivery network by disruption tolerant capability, and providing new unconventional interfaces between mobile operators and networking devices.

One interesting model of the emerging disruption-based tactical services, which we started to study with the NPS at the Center for Network Innovation and Experimentation (CENETIX), has been identified as Networking-by-Touch (Rideout and Strickland, 2007). It is a new paradigm of tactical self-organizing networking, which applies physical or electronic touch, enabled by human area network and new touch-based devices, to data transfer, collaboration and coordination at the tactical level. The new approach takes benefit of social networking through the moments of "touch" largely disjoint in time to deliver the message or share data when continuing broadband communications on-the-move aren't feasible.

Another disruption-based networking concept, which first came out of TNT MIO experiments, could be described as Projectile-Based Networking (TNT MIO 08-2 QLR, 2008). It is a disruption-based model of networking at high-speed, as well as across unattended locations with no other networking infrastructure in place, in which two-way communication takes place during 2-8 seconds of the grenade type device slowed down descend to the area of interest. The Rafael's Firefly 40 mm LV video round (Israel) is a good example of such prototype. The projectile contains two CCD color video cameras with a resolution of 20 cm per pixel at the maximum altitude of 150 m, at which a coverage of 1,200 m² is provided. The maximum flight time of the projectile is 8 seconds. The signal from the cameras is sent back to a hand-held computer for storage and analysis.

Another very interesting component of the disruption-based services is emerging in the low orbit. It is represented by small, cube level satellites (less than 10kg), capable of process and relaying sensor data to fusion centers and small units on-the-move (Bordetsky and Mantzouris, 2010). Such small data processing satellite could play the role of a "private" ad hoc orbital node that sensor operators and experts could use at their discretion to collect data from unattended sensors, follow on target over the large distances, etc.

NEW TACTICAL APPLICATION SERVICES: MESSAGE ROUTING AND EXPERT REACHBACK

Integrating Sensors with Situational Awareness Interface

In the proposed Testbed detectors and unmanned vehicles could be integrated with other sensors for multiple systems threat adjudication via the applications layer interoperability interface. In our research we'll explore advanced sensor interface solutions based on the Cursor-on-Target (CoT) integration channel. The CoT model for sensor-unmanned systems applications layer networking was initially developed at MITRE (Miller, 2004). Based on this model, the application layer architecture for integrating nuclear detection sensors (mobile or fixed) with other types, such as video surveillance camera on board UAV, biometrics identification sensors, etc camera, would be comprised of the CoT message router and CoT XML adapters for each node needed to be integrated (Figure 4).

The Cursor-on-Target XML-based schema is used for representing positioning, sensor, and other tactically-relevant data; current CoT message routing infrastructure is based upon a simple publish-subscribe model which does not incorporate ontological metadata. The Ontonet (Kopena and Loo, 2008) model represents another advanced solution for efficient dissemination of information based upon message content and ontological reasoning. It leverages OWL, which is an XML-based language for expressing ontologically-tagged information.

Expert Reachback

An immediate delivery of a unique expert knowledge to support front line operator actions becomes an interesting new tactical networking paradigm, in which social and information networking comprise a unified system of tactical knowledge

Figure 4. CoT sensors integration channel (prepared by Michael Clement)

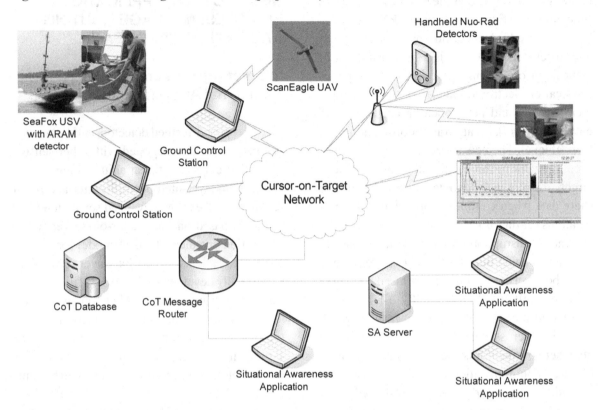

services. The recent analysis of expert-operator collaboration, conducted by Nissen and Bordetsky based on results of the Maritime Interdiction Operations (MIO) experiments, illustrates the profound relationship between expert reachback and team tacit knowledge emergence (Nissen and Bordetsky, 2011). The following is field experimentation example of reachback services, in which geographically distributed experts collaborate with boarding officers in real time as the detection and interdiction of target takes place assisting in adjudicating the level of threat and providing most critical information.

In the series of MIO experiments, conducted during the 2007-2009, which have been focused on interagency collaboration during the cargo vessel search and identification of nuclear radiation threat, the experimentation team observed how the emergency response network is "flattening" itself, trying to execute the required expert reachback

process by means of end-to-end networking and collaboration. These findings represent a good illustration of finding new paths in the knowledge flow transfer (Figure 5).

The experiments with cargo vessel search in San Francisco Bay Area (TNT MIO 07-4 and TNT MIO 09-2) and Port of NY-NJ (TNT MIO 08-4) reveal that during the interagency collaboration with nuclear radiation and biometric identification experts, the response network tends to self-organize based on ubiquitous ad-hoc mobile networking and instantaneous data sharing capabilities (Figures 5 and 6).

Such network-enabled data sharing environment allows the MIO interagency social network to speed up tacit knowledge flow exchange by morphing into the "flattened" infrastructure of committee, team, and group team working clusters, as depicted in Figure 6. These clusters correspondingly represent different topological forms of

Figure 5. "Slow" Hierarchy of reachback process for boarding teams, belonging to different agencies, during the nuclear radiation source detection

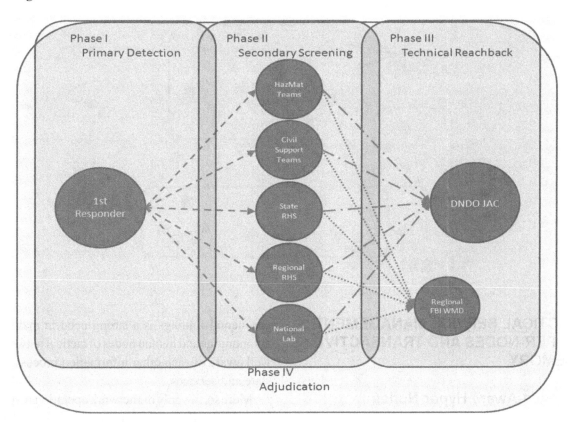

knowledge flow routing driven by MIO response network virtual space morphism.

Our subsequent studies of response network topology (Bekatoros & Bordetsky, 2010) revealed that committees represent an efficient from of tacit-explicit knowledge through the explicit model of applying majority rule to the condition-action constraints satisfaction. In addition, the observations produced collaborative technology features adaptation matrix (Figure 7). The results like this provide vital background for the interagency teams in defining the data sharing requirements for the emerging MIOs.

Another significant finding is the path to tacit knowledge conversion into explicit relationship patterns through the multimedia flow sharing. In Figure 8, the video from the swimmer conduct-

ing detection (lower left frame) becomes immediately available to the nuclear radiological expert (upper right frame), who is evaluating the spectrum (overlapping right frame) in Figure 8. Swimmer control patrol boat and radiological experts share the same log and mapped situational awareness. The swimmer, guided by the patrol boat, can now adjust his distance and detection angle, subject to spectrum shape and its interpretation by the expert. The third party command center (low right frame in Figure 8) is facilitating shared viewing composition and collaborative messaging control.

Figure 10 illustrates how, in terms of the knowledge flow management model (Nissen and Bordetsky, 2011), the new shared tacit knowledge of frontline operators emerges based on the expert reachback (See also Figure 9).

Figure 6. Group, committee, and team topology of MIO response network in the virtual space of collaborative environment

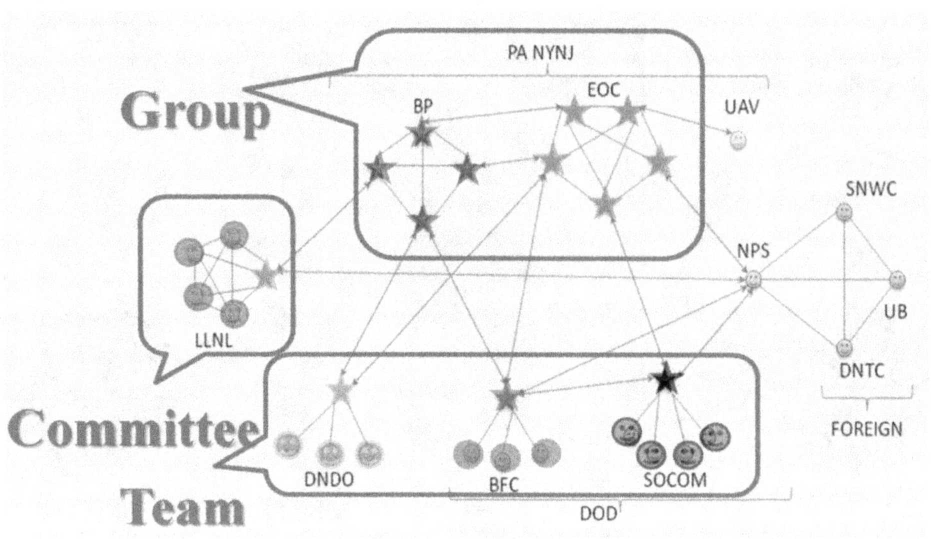

TACTICAL SERVICE MANAGEMENT: HYPER-NODES AND TRANSACTIVE MEMORY

Service-Aware Hyper-Nodes

Management of emerging tactical networks could hardly be kept centralized. One of our major experimental findings is a strong need in making autonomous and human nodes of tactical network well aware of each other information processing state and services.

More so, not only the network operations capability needs to be available to the individual nodes, the duality of distributed network management (Figure 11) requires substantial tacit knowledge

Figure 7. Captured differences in knowledge flows sharing techniques for different MIO entities

		DOD			PORT AUTHORITY NY-NJ				LLNL	DNDO	FOREIGN		
		NPS	SOCOM	BFC	BP1	BP2	UAV	PA EOC		JAC	SNWC	UB	DNTC
DOD	NPS		C,M,F,S	F,M	F,M	F,M		F,M,S	F,M	F,M	C,M,F,S	C,M,F,S	C,M,F,S
	SOCOM	C,M,F,S		F,M	F,M	F,M		F,M	F,M	F,M			
	BFC	F,M	F,M		F,M	F,M		F,M					
PA NY-NJ	BP1	F,M	F,M	F,M		C,M,F,V		C,M,F,V	C,F,M,V	C,F,M,V			
	BP2	F,M	F,M	F,M	C,M,F,V			C,M,F,V	C,F,M,V	C,F,M,V			
	UAV							F					
	PA EOC	F,M,S	F,M,S	F,M	C,M,F	C,M,F				F,M			
LLNL		F,M	F,M										
DNDO	JAC				F,M	F,M		F,M					
FOREIGN	SNWC	C,M,F,S										C,M,F,S	C,M,F,S
	UB	C,M,F,S											C,M,F,S
	DNTC	C,M,F,S											

C: CHAT   V: VIDEO STREAM   M: MESSAGE   F: FILE SHARING   S:SITUATIONAL AWARENESS

Figure 8. Tacit-explicit transformation through sharing collaborative flows (executing path A-C depicted in Figure 10)

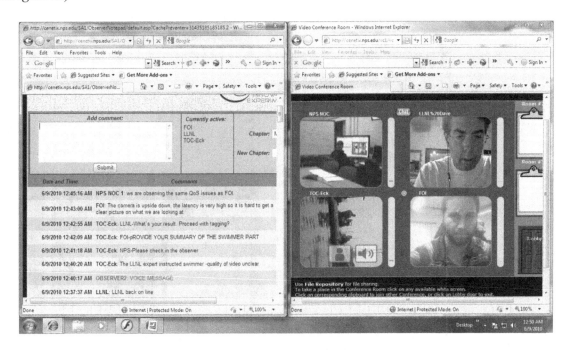

to be involved in the node behavior adaptation. For instance, one can measure the performance of self-forming networks by capturing network (IP) or data link (wireless) layer packet flows (i.e., explicit knowledge on network performance). However, in most practical cases, it is difficult to bring feedback controls directly to these same layers. The most feasible options available to the sensor/unmanned system operator would be limited application load controls (e.g., degraded video, still images only, voice only) at the top most applications layer, or node physical location (mobility) control at the lowest physical layer.

By moving the nodes around, the tactical commander could bring them back to the line-of-sight with the closest neighbors, or change their location for better performance due to improved signal strength. In either case, the effect of such actions on the network performance is implicit. It requires substantial tacit knowledge of how the application load changes, or physical relocation of nodes,

would effect performance of tactical network in a particular node distribution setting.

This could potentially be accomplished by introducing novel self-organizing data network operation architecture, which enables to maintain application service continuity between the touch/projectile nodes that generate and receive data through largely disjoint moments of time in different locations that aren't initially connected. Such architecture would be based on the 8th layer enabled hyper-nodes (Bordetsky and Hayes-Roth, 2008), which contain minimal elements of the network operation center functionality and are capable of negotiating video, text, and sensor data services with their neighbors. The hyper-nodes negotiate service agreements (moments, volume, and path) using the Cursor-on-Target protocol model (Miller, 2007). The minimal set of the hyper-nodes would include ground and surface self-aligning robotic antenna nodes (Bordetsky and Bourakov, 2007), network-controlled UAVs (Clement and

Figure 9. Visualization of tacit expert knowledge formation: pairing detection spectrum with shared event log and situational awareness view (visualizing path A-C depicted in Figure 10)

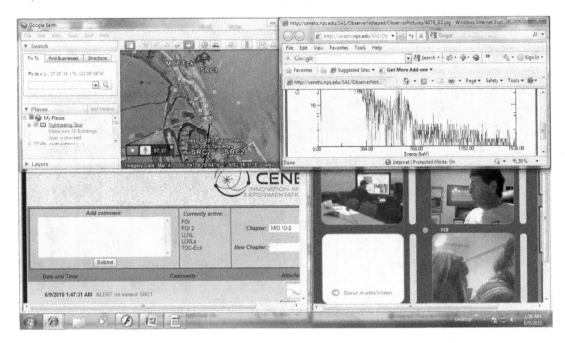

Figure 10. MIO expert reachback service decsribed in terms of tacit-explicit-tacit knowledge transfer

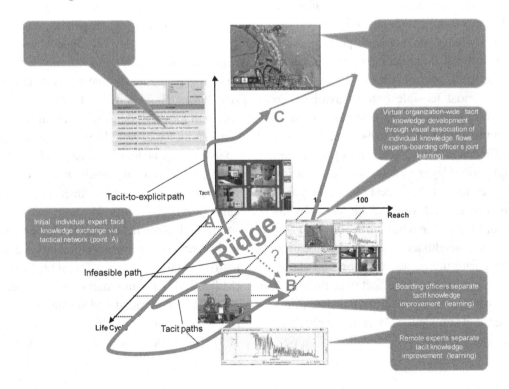

Figure 11. Adaptive network management duality

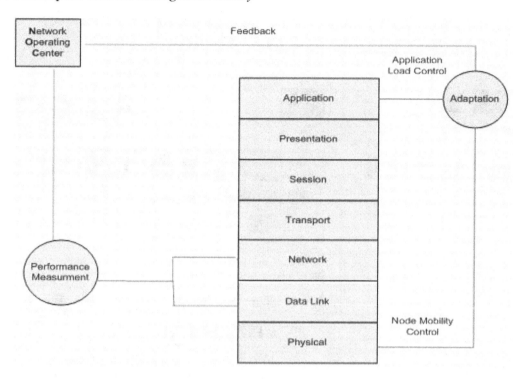

Bourakov, 2009), network-controlled parafoil (Bourakov, Yakimenko, Bordetsky, 2010), and cube satellite type private orbital nodes (Bordetsky and Mantzouris, 2010).

Managing Sensor-Expert Services: Transactive Memory Mechanism

In addition to CoT platform for consolidating the data streams from multiple mobile and fixed detection sensor, surveillance cameras, USV/UAV/UGV sensor feeds and intelligence from field operatives, we propose to develop an Integrated Detection Transactive Memory capable of leveraging remote experts cognitive abilities to detect inconsistencies in multiple threat adjudication, rather than to rely solely on computational data filtering tools.

Dr. Paul Keel (MIT) has recently developed an innovative transactive memory architecture, named: "The Electronic Virtual Transactive

Memory" (EVTM). The system is based on the earlier prototype, named EWall, developed for the Office of Naval Research (Keel, et al, 2008; Keel, 2007).

The NPS team is partnering with Dr. Keel and his EVTM team on adopting it to the tactical ground and maritime interdiction services. Figure 12 illustrates NPS-MIT earlier adaptation of EWall News View component in the tactical services environment. Based on Dr. Keel's model the Workspace View can self-synchronize with dynamic information sources and display interactive content such as, for example, a geographic map that provides real time updates about the current location of field operatives.

The Workspace View (left) displays a personal selection and arrangements of Objects; The News View (right) displays in a subject-time matrix data streams from different sources; Objects can be copied from the News View to the Workspace View. Superimposed on the News View is

Figure 12. The workspace view of transactive memory mechanism

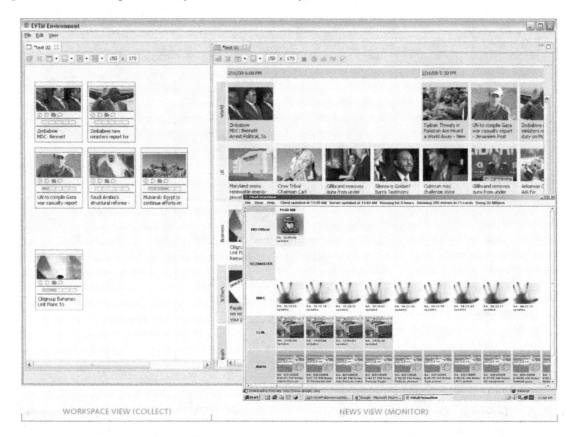

WORKSPACE VIEW (COLLECT)   NEWS VIEW (MONITOR)

earlier tactical adaptation version, representing feeds coming from cargo search active detection sensor (LLNL row), biometrics identification (NBFC row), and command center alerts (Alerts row). The Artificial Intelligence component helps to establish relations between objects and people by inferring associations from their spatial and temporal organization.

CONCLUSION

The presented patterns of emerging tactical networking services illustrate possible taxonomy of emerging tactical services. The waypoint services for networking with and between the unmanned systems could be viewed as a precursor for the future Way Point Cloud. In such a cloud unmanned

tactical nodes would be publishing way point (location and service needed) requests, while the other autonomous aerial, ground, and surface agents will be offering the control to execute the action.

The Disruption-based Services could be viewed as background for a kind of Phantom Tactical Cloud, so that at any given moment of time 3D physical and virtual configuration could change to a different platform. The network is morphing from the wireless terrestrial to orbital overlay, or to even social information transfer, like in the networking-by-touch case. It is an elusive in space and time type service.

The expert reachback services represent another interesting phenomenon. This type of tactical service could be viewed as a foundation Tactical Knowledge or Tactical Memory Cloud. Such a cloud would allow live expert knowledge to be immediately shared with tactical manned-unmanned nodes on the move, so that frontline operators become the remote situational sensors available to "collective brain" of experts, and experts in turn give back the fastest learning experience to the operators.

ACKNOWLEDGMENT

The author would like to thank Eugene Bourakov and Michael Clement for the critical contribution to the research described in this chapter as well as to author's thinking on the subject. Special thanks to COL Ramez Andraus, Brazilian Air Force and COL Steven Mullins (Ret) for the outstanding assistance in producing the chapter.

REFERENCES

Alberts, D., & Hayes, R. (2007). *Planning: Complex endeavors*. Washington, DC: CCRP Publication Series.

Bordetsky, A., & Bourakov, E. (2006). Network on target: Remotely configured adaptive tactical network. In *Proceedings of the 10th Command and Control Research & Technology Symposium*, San Diego, CA

Bordetsky, A., Bourakov, E., Looney, J., Hutchins, S. G., Dougan, A. D., & Dunlop, W. … Lawrence, C. R. (2006). Network-centric maritime radiation awareness and interdiction experiments. In *Proceedings of the 11th International Command and Control Research & Technology Symposium*, Cambridge, UK.

Bordetsky, A., & Dougan, A. (2008). Networking and collaboration on maritime-sourced nuclear threats. In *Online Proceedings of Sixth Security Workshop*, Washington, D.C.

Bordetsky, A., & Dougan, A. (2008). Networking and collaboration on maritime-sourced nuclear threats. In *Online Proceedings of Sixth Security Workshop*, Washington, D.C.

Bordetsky, A., Dougan, A., Foo Yu, C., & Kihlberg, A. (2006). *TNT maritime interdiction operation experiments: enabling radiation awareness and geographically distributed collaboration for network-centric maritime interdiction operations*. Defense Technology and Systems Symposium, 5-8 December, Singapore.

Bordetsky, A., & Friman, H. (2007). Case-studies of decision support models for collaboration in tactical mobile environments. In *Proceedings of 12th International Command and Control Research & Technology Symposium*, Newport, VA.

Bordetsky, A., & Hayes Roth, F. (2007). Extending the OSI model for wireless battlefield networks: A design approach to the 8th Layer for tactical hyper-nodes. *International Journal of Mobile Network Design*, 2(2).

Bordetsky, A., & Hutchins, S. (2008). Plug-and-play testbed for collaboration in the global information grid. In Letsky, M., Warner, N., Fiore, S., & Smith, C. (Eds.), *Macrocognition in teams*. Ashgate.

Bordetsky, A., & Matzouris, G. (2010). Micro and pico satellites in maritime interdiction operations. In *Proceedings of 15th International Command and Control Research and Technology Symposium*, Santa Monica, CA.

Bordetsky, A., & Netzer, D. (2010.) Testbed for tactical networking and collaboration. *International Command and Control Journal*, 3(4).

Bourakov, E., & Bordetsky, A. (2009). Voice-on-target: A new approach to tactical networking and unmanned systems control via the voice interface to the SA environment. In *Proceedings of 14th International Command and Control Research & Technology Symposium*, Washington, D.C.

Clement, M., Bourakov, E., Jones, K., & Do-brokhodov, V. (2009). Exploring network-centric information architectures for unmanned systems control and data dissemination. In *Proceedings of the 2009 AIAA Infotech@Aerospace Conference,* April 6-9, Seattle, WA

Conrad, B., & Tzanos, I. (2008). *A conceptual framework for tactical private satellite networks.* Master Thesis, (Advisor: Dr. Alex Bordetsky), Naval Postgraduate School

Creigh, R., Dash, R., & Rideout, B. (2006). *Collaborative technologies for maritime interdiction operations analysis. Midterm Project Report for IS 4188 Class (Advisor: Dr. Alex Bordetsky).* Naval Postgraduate School.

Gateau, J., & Bordetsky, A. (2008). Extending simple network management protocol (SNMP) beyond network management: A MIB architecture for network-centric services. In *Proceedings of 13th International Command and Control Research & Technology Symposium,* Seattle.

Hudgens, B., & Bordetsky, A. (2008). Feedback models for collaboration and trust in crisis response networks. In *Proceedings of 13th International Command and Control Research & Technology Symposium,* Seattle.

Hutchins, S. G., Bordetsky, A., Kendall, A., Looney, J., & Bourakov, E. (2006). Validating a model of team collaboration. In *Proceedings of the 11th International Command and Control Research & Technology Symposium,* Cambridge, UK. September 26-28, 2006.

Jones, K., Dobrokhodov, V., Kaminer, I., Lee, D., Bourakov, E., & Clement, M. (2009). Development, system integration and flight testing of a high-resolution imaging system for small UAS. In *Proceedings of the 47th AIAA Aerospace Sciences Meeting,* January 5-8, Orlando, Florida

Keel, P., Porter, W., Sither, M., Winston, P., & Wall, E. (2008). Computational support for collaborative sense-making activities. In M. Letsky, W. Norman, S. Fiore, & C. Smith (Eds.), *Macrocognition in teams: Understanding the mental processes that underlie collaborative team activity.* Ashgate.

Keel, P., & Wall, E. (2007). A visual analytics environment for collaborative sense-making. *Information Visualization, 6,* 48–63.

Knopp, M., & Schramm, A. (2009). *Manned-unmanned systems situational awareness using Galileo satellite constellation and small satellites.* Master Thesis, (Advisors: Prof. Dr. Stefan Pickl and Prof. Dr. Alex Bordetsky), University of Bundeswehr and Naval Postgraduate School

Kopena, J., & Loo, B. T. (2008). OntoNet: Scalable knowledge-based networking. In *Proceedings of ICDE Workshop,* (pp. 170-175).

McGrew, T., Chen, H. C., & Masacioglu, M. (2009). *Managing network centric nodes with UAV relay.*

Miller, J., & Page, S. (2009). *Complex adaptive systems: An introduction to computational models of social life.* Princeton University Press.

Miller, W. (2004) Cursor-on-target. *Military Information Technology Online, 8*(7).

Mills, J. (2011). *CDR building cyber competitive advantage: Delivering resilient, threat responsive networks for an information dominant Navy.* CMU, 2011.

Nissen, M., & Bordetsky, A. (2011). Leveraging mobile network technologies to accelerate tacit knowledge flows across organizations and distances. In Trentino, G. (Ed.), *Network technology and knowledge flow.*

Rideout, B., & Strickland, J. (2007). *Military application of networking by touch in collaborative planning and tactical environments.* Master Thesis, (Advisor: Dr. Alex Bordetsky), Naval Postgraduate School

Satcliffe, R. (2009). Web 3.0: Are we there yet? *The Next Wave, NSA Review of Emerging Technologies, 17*(3).

TNT 08-2 QLR, Quick Lookup Report. (2008). Monterey, CA: Naval Postgraduate School. Retrieved from http://cenetix.nps.edu

TNT 08-4 QLR, Quick Lookup Report. (2008). Monterey, CA: Naval Postgraduate School. Retrieved from http://cenetix.nps.edu

TNT MIO 08-2 After Action Report. (2008). Monterey, CA: Naval Postgraduate School. Retrieved from http://cenetix.nps.edu

TNT MIO 08-4 After Action Report. (2008). Monterey, CA: Naval Postgraduate School. Retrieved from http://cenetix.nps.edu

Compilation of References

Abramovici, M., & Schulte, S. (2007). Optimising customer satisfaction by integrating the customer's voice into product development. In *Proceedings of the 16th International Conference on Engineering Design* (pp. 801–802).

Abrams, R., Kirwin, B., Guptill, B., & Odell, B. (2011). *The cloud bottom line: Calculating ROI for business applications in the cloud.* Webcast of October 6, 2011. Retrieved from http://www.EntepriseEfficiency.com

Abrams, R. (2011). *Bringing the Cloud down to Earth: How to choose, launch, and get the most from cloud solutions for your business.* Palo Alto, CA: Planning Shop.

Accenture. (2010). Cloud computing and sustainability: The environmental benefits of moving to the cloud. Retrieved from http://www.microsoft.com/click/services/Redirect2.ashx?CR_EAC=300012377

AgileAlliance. (2001). *Manifesto for agile software development.* Retrieved 20 April, 2008, from http://www.agilemanifesto.org/

Ahmad, M. (2010). Security risks of cloud computing and its emergence as 5th utility service. *Information Security and Assurance. Communications in Computer and Information Science, 76,* 209–219. doi:10.1007/978-3-642-13365-7_20

Alberts, D., & Hayes, R. (2007). *Planning: Complex endeavors.* Washington, DC: CCRP Publication Series.

Amazon EC2. (n.d.). *Amazon Elastic compute cloud.* Retrieved October 15, 2011 from http://aws.amazon.com/ec2/

Amazon. (2008). *Amazon Web services:Overview of Security processes, 2008.* Retrieved October 15, 2011, from http://s3.amazonaws.com/aws_blog/AWS_Security_Whitepaper_2008_09.pdf

Amazon. (n.d.). *Amazon Simple storage service (Amazon S3).* Retrieved October 15, 2011, from http://aws.amazon.com/jp/s3/

Amazon.com. (2010, 8). *Amazon Web services overview of security processes whitepaper.* Retrieved 12 27, 2010, from http://aws.amazon.com/security

Amrhein, D., & Quint, S. (2009, 8 April). Cloud computing for the enterprise: Part 1: Capturing the cloud. *IBM Websphere Developer Technical Journal.*

Appian. (2011). *BPM is the cloud.* Retrieved February 27, 2011, from http://www.appian.com/bpm-software/cloudbpm.jsp

ArcSight. (n.d.). *ArcSight - Protect your business.* Retrieved December 28, 2010, from http://www.arcsight.com

Arista Records LLC v. Usenet.com, Inc., 633 F.Supp.2d 124 S.D.N.Y. *(2009).*

Armbrust, M., Fox, A., Griffith, R., Joseph, A. D., Katz, R. H., Konwinski, A., et al. (2009). *Above the clouds: A Berkeley view of cloud computing.* Retrieved March 15, 2011, from http://www.eecs.berkeley.edu/Pubs/TechRpts/2009/EECS-2009-28.pdf

Ashford, E. (2010). *Virtual desktops save schools money and hassle.* E-School News, Special Report. Retrieved October 18, 2010, from http://www.eschoolnews.com/2010/03/02/esn-special-report-virtual-desktops-save-schools-money-and-hassle/

Aurum, A., & Wohlin, C. (2010). *Engineering and managing software requirements*. Berlin, Germany: Springer.

Aven, T. (2010). *Misconceptions of risk*. Chichester, UK: John Wiley & Sons. doi:10.1002/9780470686539

Aymerich, F. M., Fenu, G., & Surcis, S. (2008). *An approach to cloud computing network*. First International Conference on the Applications of Digital Information and Web Technologies, ICADIWT 2008. Retrieved from www.chinacloud.cn/upload/2009-04/temp_09042911246387.pdf

Balboni, P. (2010). *Data protection and data security issues related to cloud computing in the EU*. Securing Electronic Business Processes - Highlights of the Information Security Solutions Europe Conference 2010; Tilburg Law School Research Paper No. 022/2010. Retrieved May 13, 2011, from http://ssrn.com/abstract=1661437

Baldrige (n.d.). *Baldrige performance excellence program*. Retrieved April 10, 2011, from http://www.nist.gov/baldrige/

Balzert, H. (2009). *Lehrbuch der Softwaretechnik: Basiskonzepte und Requirements Engineering* (3rd ed.). Heidelberg, Germany: Spektrum Akademischer Verlag. Retrieved from http://www.worldcat.org/oclc/647852079

Bamiah, M., & Brohi, S. (2011). Seven deadly threats and vulnerabilities in cloud computing. *International Journal of Advanced Engineering Sciences and Technologies*, *9*(1), 87–90. Retrieved from http://www.ijaest.iserp.org/archieves/15-Jul-15-31-11/Vol-No.9-Issue-No.1/16.IJAEST-Vol-No-9-Issue-No-1-Seven-Deadly-Threats-and-Vulnerabilities-in-Cloud-Computing-087-090.pdf

Barchfeld, M., Sand, R., & Link, J. (2001). *XP und RUP - Passt das zusammen?* Retrieved from http://www.fh-wedel.de/archiv/iw/Lehrveranstaltungen/WS2006/SWE/PaperAndrenaObjects.pdf

Barnett, G. (2010). *The mainframe and the cloud. (No. BC-INF-W-00068UK-EN-00)*. The Bathwick Group.

Beck, K., & Andres, C. (2007). *Extreme programming explained: Embrace change* (2nd ed.). The XP series. Boston, MA: Addison-Wesley.

Bednyagin, D., & Gnansounou, E. (n.d.). *Real options valuation of fusion energy R&D programme*. (Paper). Lausanne, Switzerland. *Ecole Polytechnique Fédérale*.

Belady, C., Rawson, A., Pfleuger, J., & Cader, T. (2008). Green grid data centr power efficiency metrics: PUE and DCiE. Retrieved from http://www.thegreengrid.org/~/media/WhitePapers/White_Paper_6_-_PUE_and_DCiE_Eff_Metrics_30_December_2008.pdf?lang=en

Benaroch, M., Jefferery, M., Kauffman, R. J., & Shah, S. (2007). Option-based risk management: A field study of sequential information technology investment decisions. *Journal of Management Information Systems*, *24*(2), 103–140. doi:10.2753/MIS0742-1222240205

Benaroch, M., Lichtenstein, Y., & Robinson, K. (2006). Real options in information technology risk management: An empirical validation of risk-options relationships. *Management Information Systems Quarterly*, *30*(4), 827–864.

Benioff, M. R., & Adler, C. (2009). *Behind the cloud: the untold story of how Salesforce.com went from idea to billion-dollar company--And revolutionized an industry* (1st ed.). San Francisco, CA: Jossey-Bass.

Berkovich, M., Esch, S., Leimeister, J. M., & Krcmar, H. (2009). Requirements engineering for hybrid products as bundle of hardware, software and service elements - A literature review. In *Tagungsband der 9*. Wien: Internationalen Tagung Wirtschaftsinformatik.

Berkovich, M., Esch, S., Leimeister, J. M., & Krcmar, H. (2010). Towards requirements engineering for "software as a service". In Schumann, M., Kolbe, L. M., Breitner, M. H., & Frerichs, A. (Eds.), *Multikonferenz Wirtschaftsinformatik 2010*. Göttingen, Germany: Universitätsverlag Göttingen.

Berkovich, M., Leimeister, J. M., & Krcmar, H. (2010). Ein Bezugsrahmen für Requirements Engineering hybrider Produkte. In Schumann, M., Kolbe, L. M., Breitner, M. H., & Frerichs, A. (Eds.), *Multikonferenz Wirtschaftsinformatik 2010*. Göttingen, Germany: Universitätsverlag Göttingen.

Berl, A., Gelenbe, E., Di Girolamo, M., Giuliani, G., De Meer, H., & Dang, M. Q. (2009). Energy-efficient cloud computing. *The Computer Journal*, *53*(7), 1045–1051. doi:10.1093/comjnl/bxp080

Bernard, H. (1976). *Totale Oorlog en Revolutionaire Oorlog* (*Vol. I*). Brussels, Belgium: Royal Military Academy. [course]

Berryman, J. M. (2007). Judgments during information seeking: A naturalistic approach to understanding of enough information. *Journal of Information Science*, *20*(10), 1–11.

Betcher, T. (2010). *Cloud computing: Key IT-related risks and mitigation strategies for consideration by IT security practitioners*. Retrieved September 11, 2011 from https://scholarsbank.uoregon.edu/xmlui/handle/1794/10207

Bhatt, G., Emdad, A., Roberts, N., & Grover, V. (2010). Building and leveraging information in dynamic environments: The role of IT infrastructure flexibility as enabler of organizational responsiveness and competitive advantage. *Information & Management*, *47*(7-8). doi:10.1016/j.im.2010.08.001

Bhuiyan, T. (2010, November). A survey on the relationship between trust and interest similarity in online social networks. *Journal of Emerging Technologies in Web Intelligence*, *2*(4), 291–299. doi:10.4304/jetwi.2.4.291-299

Bilbiie, F., Ghironi, F., & Melitz, M. (2007). *Endogenous entry, product variety, and business cycles*. NBER WP 13646.

Bittman, T. (2011). *Key issues for private cloud computing, 2011*. Retrieved April 16, 2011, from Gartner Research: http://www.gartner.com

Black, L., Mandelbaum, J., Grover, I., & Marvi, Y. (2010). *The arrival of cloud thinking*. Management Insight Technologies. Retrieved from http://www.ca.com/~/media/files/whitepapers/the_arrival_of_cloud_thinking.aspx

Boehm, B. W., & Turner, R. (2003). *Balancing agility and discipline*. Boston, MA: Addison-Wesley Pearson Education.

Böhm, M., Leimeister, S., Riedl, C., & Krcmar, H. (2010). Cloud computing - Outsourcing 2.0 or a new business model for IT provisioning? In Keuper, F., Oecking, C., & Degenhardt, A. (Eds.), *Application management service management and service creation* (pp. 2–26). Gabler. doi:10.1007/978-3-8349-6492-2_2

Bondi, A. B. (2000). *Characteristics of scalability and their impact on performance*. Paper presented at the 2nd International Workshop on Software and Performance.

Boomi. (2009). *Integration strategies for ISVS*. White Paper. Retrieved from www.boomi.com

Bordetsky, A., & Bourakov, E. (2006). Network on target: Remotely configured adaptive tactical network. In *Proceedings of the 10th Command and Control Research & Technology Symposium,* San Diego, CA

Bordetsky, A., & Dougan, A. (2008). Networking and collaboration on maritime-sourced nuclear threats. In *Online Proceedings of Sixth Security Workshop*, Washington, D.C.

Bordetsky, A., & Friman, H. (2007). Case-studies of decision support models for collaboration in tactical mobile environments. In *Proceedings of 12th International Command and Control Research & Technology Symposium*, Newport, VA.

Bordetsky, A., & Matzouris, G. (2010). Micro and pico satellites in maritime interdiction operations. In *Proceedings of 15th International Command and Control Research and Technology Symposium*, Santa Monica, CA.

Bordetsky, A., & Netzer, D. (2010.) Testbed for tactical networking and collaboration. *International Command and Control Journal, 3*(4).

Bordetsky, A., Bourakov, E., Looney, J., Hutchins, S. G., Dougan, A. D., & Dunlop, W. … Lawrence, C. R. (2006). Network-centric maritime radiation awareness and interdiction experiments. In *Proceedings of the 11th International Command and Control Research & Technology Symposium,* Cambridge, UK.

Bordetsky, A., Dougan, A., Foo Yu, C., & Kihlberg, A. (2006). *TNT maritime interdiction operation experiments: enabling radiation awareness and geographically distributed collaboration for network-centric maritime interdiction operations*. Defense Technology and Systems Symposium, 5-8 December, Singapore.

Bordetsky, A., & Hayes Roth, F. (2007). Extending the OSI model for wireless battlefield networks: A design approach to the 8th Layer for tactical hyper-nodes. *International Journal of Mobile Network Design, 2*(2).

Bordetsky, A., & Hutchins, S. (2008). Plug-and-play testbed for collaboration in the global information grid. In Letsky, M., Warner, N., Fiore, S., & Smith, C. (Eds.), *Macrocognition in teams*. Ashgate.

Bose, S. (2008). *Gathering clouds of XaaS!* Retrieved March 26, 2011, from https://www.ibm.com/developer-works/mydeveloperworks/blogs/sbose/entry/gathering_clouds_of_xaas?lang=en

Boss, G., Malladi, P., Quan, D., Legregni, L., & Hall, H. (2007, October). *Cloud computing.* In Workshop in IBM Corporation, Organization: High Performance On Demand Solutions (HiPODS), Version 1.0, 08 October 2007. Retrieved September 26, 2011, from http://download.boulder.ibm.com/ibmdl/pub/software/dw/wes/hipods/Cloud_computing_wp_final_8Oct.pdf

Bourakov, E., & Bordetsky, A. (2009). Voice-on-target: A new approach to tactical networking and unmanned systems control via the voice interface to the SA environment. In *Proceedings of 14th International Command and Control Research & Technology Symposium,* Washington, D.C.

Bowser, M., Cantle, N., & Allan, N. (2011). *Unraveling the complexity of risk.* Presented at Open Forum of The Actuarial Profession (January 21, 2011). London.

Brach, M. (2003). *Real options in practice.* Hoboken, NJ: John Wiley & Sons.

Bradshaw, S., Millard, C., & Walden, I. (2010). *Contracts for clouds: Comparison and analysis of the terms and conditions of cloud computing services.* Queen Mary School of Law Legal Studies Research Paper No. 63/2010. Retrieved May 13, 2011, from http://ssrn.com/abstract=1662374

Brandenburger, A., & Nalebuff, B. (1995). *The right game: Use game theory to shape strategy. Harvard Business Review.* July-August.

Brock, M., & Goscinski, A. (2010, May). Toward a framework for cloud security. In *ICA3PP 2010 Proceedings of the 10th International Conference on Algorithms and Architectures for Parallel Processing, Part II, LNCS Vol. 6082,* (pp. 254-263). Berlin, Germany: SpringerLink. doi: 10.1007/978-3-642-13136-3_26

Brodkin, J. (2008). *More outages hit Amazon's S3 storage service.* Network World. Retrieved 13 May from http://www.networkworld.com/news/2008/072108-amazon-outages.html

Brooks, B. (2007). The pulley model: A descriptive model of risky decision-making. *Safety Science Monitor, 11*(1), 1–14.

Brynjolfsson, E., Hofmann, P., & Jordan, J. (2010). Cloud computing and electricity: Beyond the utility model. *Communications of the ACM, 53*(5), 32–34. doi:10.1145/1735223.1735234

Buyya, R., Pandey, S., & Vecchiola, C. (2009, December). Cloudbus toolkit for market-oriented cloud computing. In *CloudCom 2009 Proceedings of the 1st International Conference on Cloud Computing, LNCS Vol. 5931,* (pp. 24-44). Berlin, Germany: SpringerLink. doi: 10.1007/978-3-642-10665-1_4

Buyya, R., Yeo, C. S., & Venugopal, S. (2008). Market-oriented cloud computing: Vision, hype, and reality for delivering IT services as computing utilities, (pp. 5–13). DOI: 10.1109/HPCC.2008.172

Byrd, T. A., & Turner, D. E. (2000). Measuring the flexibility of information technology infrastructure: Exploratory analysis of a construct. *Journal of Management Information Systems, 17*(1), 167.

CAF. (n.d.). *Common assessment framework.* Retrieved March 3, 2011, from http://www.eipa.eu/en/topic/show/&tid=191

Caforiol, A., Corallo, A., & Marco, D. (2005). A framework for interoperability in an enterprise. In Khosla, R. (Eds.), *KES 2005, LNAI 3681* (pp. 97–103). Heidelberg, Germany: Springer-Verlag.

California Civil Code § 1798.81.5(c).

Camarinha-Matos, L., Afsarmanesh, H., & Rabelo, R. (2003). Infrastructure developments for agile virtual enterprises. *International Journal of Computer Integrated Manufacturing, 16,* 235. doi:10.1080/0951192031000089156

Candan, K. S., Li, W.-S., Phan, T., & Zhou, M. (2009). *Frontiers in information and software as services.* Paper presented at the Data Engineering, 2009. ICDE '09. IEEE 25th International Conference on.

Cao, Y., Chen, Y., & Shen, Y. (2007). The research and application of web services in enterprise application integration. In L. Xu, A. Tjoa, & S. Chaudhry (Eds.), *IFIP International Federation for Information Processing, Volume 254, Research and Practical Issues of Enterprise Information Systems II* (pp. 201-205). Boston, MA: Springer.

Carlsson, C., & Fullér, R. (2000). *On fuzzy real option valuation*. Turku, Finland: Turku Centre for Computer Science.

Carr, N. (2003). IT doesn't matter. *Harvard Business Review*, (May): 41–49.

Carr, N. G. (2008). *The big switch: Rewiring the world, from Edison to Google* (1st ed.). New York, NY: W. W. Norton & Co.

Casola, V., Mazzeo, A., Mazzocca, N., & Venticinque, S. (2004, June). Design of policy-based security mechanisms in a distributed web services architecture. In *PARA 2004 Proceedings of the Workshop on State-of-The-Art in Scientific Computing, LNCS Vol. 3732*, (pp. 454-463). Berlin, Germany: SpringerLink. doi: 10.1007/11558958_54

Casper, C. (2011). *Privacy in the cloud*. Retrieved April 16, 2011, from Gartner Research: http://www.gartner.com

Caswell, N. S., & Nigam, A. (2005, 19 July 2005). *Agility = change + coordination*. Paper presented at the Seventh IEEE International Conference on E-Commerce Technology Workshops, 2005.

Catteddu, D. (2010). Cloud computing – Benefits, risks and recommendations for information security. *Communications in Computer and Information Science, 72*(Part1, 17).

Cavoukian, A. (2008, December). Privacy in the clouds. *Identity in the Information Society, 1*(1), 89–108. doi:10.1007/s12394-008-0005-z

CCIF. (2010). *Cloud computing interoperability forum*. Retrieved 10th October, 2010, from http://code.google.com/p/unifiedcloud/

Cecioni, M. (2010). *Firm entry, competitive pressures and the US inflation dynamics. Mimeo*. Bank of Italy.

Chang, M., He, J., & Castro-Leon, E. (2006). *Service-orientation in the computing infrastructure*. Paper presented at the IEEE International Symposium on Service-Oriented System Engineering.

Chang, V., Bacigalupo, D., Wills, G., & De Roure, D. (2010). *A categorisation of cloud computing business models (Paper)*. Southampton, UK: University of Southampton.

Chang, V., Wills, G., & De Roure, D. (2010). *A review of cloud business models and sustainability (Paper)*. Southampton, UK: University of Southampton.

Chappell, D. (2008, August). A short introduction to cloud computing: An enterprise-oriented view. *Lecture at the Microsoft Corporation*. Retrieved August 25, 2011, from http://www.davidchappell.com/CloudPlatforms--Chappell.pdf

Cheng, B. H., & Atlee, J. M. (2007). Research directions in requirements engineering. In L. C. Briand & A. L. Wolf (Eds.), *Future of Software Engineering, FoSE 2007: 23-25* May 2007, Minneapolis, Minnesota (pp. 285–303). Los Alamitos, CA: IEEE Computer Society.

Cherry Tree. (2000, September). *Framing the IT services industry: 2nd generation ASPs*. Spotlight Report, Cherry Tree & Co. Retrieved from www.cherrytreeco.com

Chitty, J., & Beale, H. G. (2011). *Chitty on contracts*. London, UK: Sweet & Maxwell.

Chong, F., & Carraro, G. (2006). *Architecture strategies for catching the long tail*. Retrieved from http://msdn.microsoft.com/en-us/library/aa479069.aspx

Chonko, L. B., & Jones, E. (2005). The need for speed: Agility selling. *Journal of Personal Selling & Sales Management, 25*, 371.

Choudhary, V. (2007). *Software as a service: Implications for investment in software development*. The 40th Hawaii International Conference on System Sciences (HICSS). Waikoloa, Hawaii.

Chow, R., Golle, P., Jakobsson, M., Shi, E., Staddon, J., Masuoka, R., et al. (2009). *Controlling data in the cloud: Outsourcing computation without outsourcing control*. The 2009 ACM workshop on Cloud computing security.

Chow, T., & Cao, D.-B. (2008). A survey study of critical success factors in agile software projects. *Journal of Systems and Software, 81*, 961–971. doi:10.1016/j. jss.2007.08.020

Christopher, M. (2000). The agile supply chain: Competing in volatile markets. *Industrial Marketing Management, 29*(1), 37. doi:10.1016/S0019-8501(99)00110-8

Chung, M. (2011). *Risk and compliance, new paradigm of automation.* Retrieved October 15, 2011, from http://www.vrisbi.nl/index.php/Download-document/23-New-Paradigm-of-Automation-KPMG.html

Chung, M., & Hermans, J. (2010). *From hype to future.* KPMG's 2010 Cloud Computing Survey. KPMG. Retrieved May 13, 2011, from http://www.kpmg.com/AR/es/IssuesAndInsights/ArticlesPublications/KPMGInternacional/Document/Cloud_Computing_Survey_2010.pdf

Cisco. (2008). *Approaching the zettabyte era: Visual networking index - Cisco Systems.* Retrieved February 26, 2010, from http://www.cisco.com/en/US/solutions/collateral/ns341/ns525/ns537/ns705/ns827/white_paper_c11-481374_ns827_Networking_Solutions_White_Paper.html

Cisco. (2009). Cisco cloud computing - Data center strategy, architechture, and solutions. Retrieved April 25, 2011, from http://www.cisco.com/web/strategy/docs/gov/CiscoCloudComputing_WP.pdf

Cisco. (2009). *Cisco VN-link: Virtualization-aware networking.* Retrieved from http://www.cisco.com/en/US/solutions/collateral/ns340/ns517/ns224/ns892/ns894/white_paper_c11-525307.pdf

Clabby Analytics. (2008). *The data center 'implosion explosion'.* Retrieved from http://www-03.ibm.com/press/us/en/attachment/23540.wss?fileId=ATTACH_FILE4&fileName=Clabby%20Analytics%20Implosion%20Explosion.pdf

Clarke, R. (2 February, 2010). *Computing clouds on the horizon? Benefits and risks from the user's perspective.* Retrieved from http://www.rogerclarke.com/II/CCBR.html

Clarke, R. (2010). Computing clouds on the horizon? Benefits and risks from the user's perspective. Retrieved February 2, 2010, from http://www.rogerclarke.com/II/CCBR.html

Clarke, R. (31 January, 2010). User requirements for cloud computing architecture. Retrieved from http://www.rogerclarke.com/II/CCSA.html

Clarus. (2005). *Concept of operations.* Publication No. FHWA-JPO-05-072. Retrieved from http://ntl.bts.gov/lib/jpodocs/repts_te/14158_files/14158.pdf

Clement, M., Bourakov, E., Jones, K., & Dobrokhodov, V. (2009). Exploring network-centric information architectures for unmanned systems control and data dissemination. In *Proceedings of the 2009 AIAA Infotech@ Aerospace Conference,* April 6-9, Seattle, WA

Cloud Computing Use Case Group. (2011). *Open cloud manifesto.* Retrieved January 1, 2011, from http://www.opencloudmanifesto.org

Cloud Security Alliance "Security as a Service" Version 1.0. (2011). *Defined categories of service 2011.*

Cloud Security Alliance. (2009). *Security guidance for critical areas of focus in cloud computing.*

Cloud Security Alliance. (2010). *Top threats to cloud computing V1.0.*

Clouds Standard Customer Council. (2011). *Website.* Retrieved from http://www.cloud-council.org/

Cobb, B., & Charnes, J. (2007). Real options valuation. In S. G. Henderson, B. Biller, M.-H. Hsieh, J. Shortle, J. D. Tew, & R. R. Barton (Eds.), *Proceedings of the 2007 Winter Simulation Conference,* (pp. 173-182). IEEE.

Cohen, S., Money, W. H., & Kaisler, S. H. (2009). *Service migration in an enterprise architecture.* 42nd Hawai'i International Conference on Systems Sciences, Big Island, Hawaii

Colarusso, D. (2011). Heads in the cloud - A coming storm: The interplay of cloud computing, encryption, and the fifth amendment's protection against self incrimination. *Boston University Journal of Science and Technology Law, 17*(1).

Colciago, A., & Etro, F. (2010). Real business cycles with cournot competition and endogenous entry. *Journal of Macroeconomics, 32*(4), 1101–1117. doi:10.1016/j.jmacro.2010.04.005

Colciago, A., & Rossi, L. (2011). *Endogenous market structure and labor market dynamics.* Mimeo, University of Milano Bicocca.

Collan, M. (2008). *A new method for real option valuation using fuzzy numbers. (Research Paper).* Turku, Finland: Institute for Advanced Management Systems Research. Retrieved April 12, 2011 from http://ideas.repec.org/p/amr/wpaper/466.html

Collan, M., Fullér, R., & Mezei, J. (2009). A fuzzy pay-off method for real option valuation. *Journal of Applied Mathematics and Decision Sciences, 1,* 1–14. doi:10.1155/2009/238196

Columbia Pictures, Inc. v. Bunnell, 245 F.R.D. 443 C.D. Ca. *(2007).*

Congress. (2002). *Public law 107 - 204 - Sarbanes-Oxley Act of 2002.* Retrieved October 15, 2011, from http://www.gpo.gov/fdsys/pkg/PLAW-107publ204/content-detail.html

Conrad, B., & Tzanos, I. (2008). *A conceptual framework for tactical private satellite networks.* Master Thesis, (Advisor: Dr. Alex Bordetsky), Naval Postgraduate School

Copyright, Designs and Patent Act. (1998). UK Parliament.

COSO. (n.d.). *Committee of Sponsoring organizations of the treadway commission.* Retrieved October 15, 2011, from http://www.coso.org/

Costa, L., de Oliveira, B., & Braga, A. (2007). Trust evaluation for web applications based on behavioral analysis. In Venter, H., Eloff, M., Labuschagne, L., Eloff, J., & von Solms, R. (Eds.), *Approaches for security, privacy and trust in complex environments* (*Vol. 232,* pp. 61–72). Boston, MA: Springer. doi:10.1007/978-0-387-72367-9_6

Couch v. United States, 409 U.S. 322. (1973).

Couillard, D. A. (2009). Defogging the cloud: Applying fourth amendment principles to evolving privacy expectations in cloud computing. *Minnesota Law Review, 93*(6), 2205–2239.

Council Regulation (EC) 44/2001 on jurisdiction and the recognition and enforcement of judgments in civil and commercial matters. (2001). Retrieved May 13, 2011, from http://eur-lex.europa.eu/LexUriServ/LexUriServ.do?uri=OJ:L:2001:012:0001:0023:EN:PDF

Creigh, R., Dash, R., & Rideout, B. (2006). *Collaborative technologies for maritime interdiction operations analysis. Midterm Project Report for IS 4188 Class (Advisor: Dr. Alex Bordetsky).* Naval Postgraduate School.

CSA. (2010). *Cloud security alliance: Top threats to cloud computing,* v1.0. Retrieved April 12, 2011, from http://www.cloudsecurityalliance.org

CSA. (2010). *Top threats to cloud computing, v1.0.* Retrieved October 15, 2011 from https://cloudsecurity-alliance.org/topthreats/csathreats.v1.0.pdf

Cusumano, M. (2003). Finding your balance in the products and service debate. *Communications of the ACM, 46*(3), 15–17. doi:10.1145/636772.636786

David, P. (1990). The dynamo and the computer: An historical perspective on the modern productivity paradox. *The American Economic Review, 80*(2), 355–361.

De Silva, S., & Golding, P. (2005). Outsourcing contracts: Lessons learned. *Commonwealth Law Bulletin, 31*(2), 1–51. doi:10.1080/03050718.2005.9986678

Deepak Fertilisers v Davy McKee. (1998). 1 Lloyd's Rep 387

Desisto, R. P., Plummer, D. C., & Smith, D. M. (2008). *Tutorial for understanding the relationship between cloud computing and SaaS.* Gartner Corporation, G00156152.

Desizn Tech. (2009). *Top 5 web operating systems.* Retrieved January 26, 2011, from http://desizntech.info/2009/08/top-5-web-operating-systems/

Digital Economy Act. (2010). UK Parliament.

Dijiang, H., Xinwen, Z., Myong, K., & Jim, L. (2010, 4-5 June 2010). *MobiCloud: Building secure cloud framework for mobile computing and communication.* Paper presented at the 2010 Fifth IEEE International Symposium on Service Oriented System Engineering (SOSE).

Directive 2000/31/EC of the European Parliament and of the Council on certain legal aspects of information society services in particular electronic commerce, in the internal market. (2001). Retrieved May 13, 2011, from http://eur-lex.europa.eu/LexUriServ/LexUriServ.do?uri=CELEX:32000L0031:EN:HTML

Directive 2001/29/EC of the European Parliament and of the Council on the harmonisation of certain aspects of copyright and related rights in the information society. (2001). Retrieved May 13, 2011, from http://eur-lex.europa.eu/LexUriServ/LexUriServ.do?uri=OJ:L:2001:167:0010:0019:EN:PDF

Directive 91/250/EEC on the legal protection of computer programs. (1991). Retrieved May 13, 2011, from http://eur-lex.europa.eu/LexUriServ/LexUriServ.do?uri=CELEX:31991L0250:EN:HTML

Directive 95/46/EC of the European Parliament and of the Council of 24 October 1995 on the protection of individuals with regard to the processing of personal data and on the free movement of such data. (1995). Retrieved May 13, 2011, from http://eur-lex.europa.eu/LexUriServ/LexUriServ.do?uri=CELEX:31995L0046:en:HTML

DMTF. (2011). *Cloud: DMTF.* Retrieved Mar 24, 2011, from http://dmtf.org/standards/cloud

Dodda, R., Smith, C., & Moorsel, A. (2009). An architecture for cross-cloud system management. In *IC3 2009 Proceedings of the International Conference on Contemporary Computing*, CCIS Vol. 40, (pp. 556-567). Berlin, Germany: SpringerLink. doi: 10.1007/978-3-642-03547-0_53

Dörnemann, H., & Meyer, R. (2003). *Anforderungsmanagement kompakt: Mit Checklisten.* Heidelberg, Germany: Spektrum Akad. Verl.

Dorsey, P. (2005). *Top 10 reasons why system projects fail.* Retrieved from http://www.hks.harvard.edu/m-rcbg/ethiopia/Publications/Top%2010%20Reasons%20Why%20Systems%20Projects%20Fail.pdf

Dove, R. (2001). *Response ability: The language, structure and culture of the Agilie enterprise.* New York, NY: Wiley.

Drucker, P. F. (1968). Comeback of the entrepreneur. *Management Today, April*, 23-30.

Dubey, A., & Wagel, D. (2007). Delivering software as a service. *The McKinsey Quartely, Web Exclusive.* Retrieved from http://www.mckinseyquarterly.com/delivering_software_as_a_service_2006

EARF. (n.d.). *Completed projects.* Retrieved April 11, 2001, from http://earf.meraka.org.za/earfhome/our-projects-1/completed-projects/

Economist (2008, October 25). Where the cloud meets the ground. *The Economist, 387.*

Economist. (2008). *Down on the server farm.* Retrieved December 21, 2010, from http://www.economist.com/node/11413148

Economist. (2008). *Let is rise.* Retrieved January 10, 2011, from http://www.economist.com/node/12411882?story_id=12411882

Eisenhardt, K., & Sull, D. (2001). Strategy as simple rules. *Harvard Business Review*, (January): 106–116.

Eisner, R. S., & Oram, M. A. (2010). Clear skies or stormy weather for cloud computing? Critical privacy and security contracting issues for customers of cloud computing. *Intellectual Property Course Handbook*, 1-29.

Engelien, G. (1971). *Der Begriff der Klassifikation.*

Engrad, N. C. (Ed.). (2009). *Library mashups: Exploring new ways to deliver library data.* Information Today.

ENISA. (2009). *Cloud computing information assurance framework.* Retrieved October 15, 2011, from http://www.enisa.europa.eu/act/rm/files/deliverables/cloud-computing-information-assurance-framework

ENISA. (2009). *Cloud computing: Benefits, risks and recommendations for information security.*

Erdogmus, H. (2009). Cloud computing: Does Nirvana hide behind the nebula? *Software, 26*(2), 4–6. doi:10.1109/MS.2009.31

Ernst & Young. (2009). *Cloud computing – The role of internal audit.* Retrieved October 15, 2011, from http://www.isaca-oregon.org/docs/Cloud%20Computing%20-%20The%20role%20of%20Internal%20Audit.pdf

Etro, F. (2010). *Introducing cloud computing: Results from a simulation study.* Venice, Italy: Ca' Foscari

Etro, F. (2007). Endogenous market structures and macroeconomic theory. *Review of Business and Economics*, *52*(4), 543–566.

Etro, F. (2009). The economic impact of cloud computing on business creation, employment and output in the E.U. *Review of Business and Economics*, *54*(2), 179–208.

Etro, F. (2009). *Endogenous market structures and the macroeconomy*. New York, Germany: Springer. doi:10.1007/978-3-540-87427-0

Etro, F., & Colciago, A. (2010). Endogenous market structure and the business cycle. *The Economic Journal*, *120*(549), 1201–1233. doi:10.1111/j.1468-0297.2010.02384.x

European Commission. (2007). *The European e-business report, 2006/07. A portrait of e-business in 10 sectors of the EU economy, 5th Synthesis Report of the Sectoral e-Business Watch*. Brussels: European Commission.

Faia, E. (2010). *Oligopolistic competition and optimal monetary policy. Mimeo*. Goethe University of Frankfurt.

Farbey, B., Land, F., & Targett, D. (Eds.). (1993). *IT investment: A study of methods and practice*. Oxford, UK: Butterworth-Heinemann.

Fedor, D., Caldwell, S., & Herold, D. (2006). The effects of organizational changes on employee commitment: A multilevel investigation. *Personnel Psychology*, *59*(1), 1–29. doi:10.1111/j.1744-6570.2006.00852.x

Fereira, N., Kar, J., & Trigeorgis, L. (2009). Option games: The key to competing in capital-intensive industries. *Harvard Business Review, March*.

Ferguson, T. (2009). *Salesforce.com outage hits thousands of businesses*. CNET News. Retrieved 13 May from http://news.cnet.com/8301-1001_3-10136540-92.html

Ferson, S. (n.d.). *Fuzzy arithmetic in risk analysis*. Retrieved March 23, 2011, from http://www.ramas.com/fuzzygood.ppt

Fichman, R. (2004). Real options and IT platform adoption: Implications for theory and practice. *Information Systems Research*, *15*(2), 132–154. doi:10.1287/isre.1040.0021

Fingar, P. (2009). *Dot.Cloud*. Tampa, FL: Meghan-Kiffer Press.

Fink, L., & Neumann, S. (2007). Gaining agility through IT personnel capabilities: The mediating role of it infrastructure capabilities. *Journal of the Association for Information Systems*, *8*, 440.

Fitzgerald, B., Hartnett, G., & Conboy, K. (2006). Customising agile methods to software practices at Intel Shannon. *European Journal of Information Systems*, *15*, 200–213. doi:10.1057/palgrave.ejis.3000605

Forsheit, T. L. (2010). Contracting for cloud computing services: Privacy and data considerations. *Privacy & Security Law Report*, *9*, 20–23.

Forum non conveniens. (2004). Black's Law Dictionary. 8th. ed. St. Paul, MN: West Print.

Forward Foods LLC v. Next Proteins, Inc., 2008 BL 238516. N.Y. Sup. *(2008)*.

Foster, I., Yong, Z., Raicu, I., & Lu, S. (2008). *Cloud computing and grid computing 360-degree compared*. Paper presented at the Grid Computing Environments Workshop, GCE '08.

Fujitsu Research Institute. (2010). *Personal data in the cloud: A global survey of consumer attitudes*. Retrieved December 28, 2010, from http://www.fujitsu.com/downloads/SOL/fai/reports/fujitsu_personal-data-in-the-cloud.pdf

Funston, F., & Wagner, S. (2010). *Surviving and thriving in uncertainty: Creating the risk intelligent enterprise*. Hoboken, NJ: John Wiley & Sons.

Furht, B., & Escalante, A. (2010). *Handbook of cloud computing* (1st ed.). New York, NY: Springer. doi:10.1007/978-1-4419-6524-0

Gallagher, K., & Worrell, J. (2008). Organizing IT to promote agility. *Information Technology Management*, *9*, 71. doi:10.1007/s10799-007-0027-5

Gantz, S. (2010). *Major cloud computing privacy legal issues remain unresolved*. Retrieved April 5, 2011, from http://blog.securityarchitecture.com/2010/08/major-cloud-computing-privacy-legal.html

Garcia, D. Z. G., & Felgar de Toledo, M. B. (2008). An approach for establishing trust relationships in the web service technology. In *IFIP 2008 International Federation for Information Processing* (*Vol. 283*, pp. 509–516). Boston, MA: Springer. doi:10.1007/978-0-387-84837-2_53

García-Jiménez, F. J., Martinez-Carreras, M. A., & Gomez-Skarmeta, A. F. (2010). Evaluating open source enterprise service bus. *IEEE International Conference on E-Business Engineering,* November 2010, (pp. 284-291). IEEE Computer Society.

Gartner. (2007). *Gartner forecasts worldwide communications-as-a-service revenue to total $252 million in 2007.* Retrieved March 1, 2011, from http://www.gartner.com/it/page.jsp?id=518407

Gartner. (2010). *Key issues for cloud computing*

Gartner. (2010, 6 25). *SAS 70 is not proof of security, continuity or privacy compliance.* Retrieved December 28, 2010, from http://www.gartner.com/DisplayDocument?ref=clientFriendlyUrl&id=1390444

Gartner. (2011). *Cloud computing.* Retrieved January 1, 2011, from www.gartner.com/technology/initiatives/cloud-computing.jsp.

Gateau, J., & Bordetsky, A. (2008). Extending simple network management protocol (SNMP) beyond network management: A MIB architecture for network-centric services. In *Proceedings of 13th International Command and Control Research & Technology Symposium,* Seattle.

Gates v City Mutual Life Assurance Society Ltd. (1986). 160 CLR 1.

GB Gas Holdings Limited v Accenture (UK) Limited and others. (2010). EWCA Civ 912.

Gellman, R. (2009). *Privacy in the clouds: Risks to privacy and confidentiality from cloud computing.* World Privacy Forum.

Ghironi, F., & Melitz, M. (2005). International trade and macroeconomic dynamics with heterogenous firms. *The Quarterly Journal of Economics, 120,* 865–915.

Glenn, E. J. (1996). *Chaos theory: The essentials for military applications.* Newport, RI: Naval War College.

Glisic, S. G. (2011). *Advanced wireless communications & Internet: Future evolving technologies* (3rd ed.). Chichester, UK: Wiley. doi:10.1002/9781119991632

Golden, B. (2009). *The case against cloud computing-Part one.* Retrieved April 16, 2011, from http://www.cio.com/article/477473/The_Case_Against_Cloud_Computing_Part_One

Goldman, D. (2011). *Why Amazon's cloud Titanic went down.* Retrieved October 15, 2011, from http://money.cnn.com/2011/04/22/technology/amazon_ec2_cloud_outage/index.htm

Goldman, S., Nagel, R., & Preiss, K. (1995). *Agile competitors and virtual organizations.* New York, NY: Van Nostrand Reinhold.

Goldman, S., Preiss, K., Nagel, R., & Dove, R. (1991). *21st century manufacturing enterprise strategy: An industry-led view.* Bethlehem, PA: Iacocca Institute, Lehigh University.

Gonçalves, V. (2009). *Adding value to the network: Exploring the software as a service and platform as a service models for mobile operators* (pp. 13–22). Mobile Wireless Middleware, Operating Systems, and Applications - Workshops. doi:10.1007/978-3-642-03569-2_2

Goodhue, D. L., Chen, D. Q., Boudreau, M. C., Davis, A., & Cochran, J. D. (2009). Addressing business agility challenges with enterprise systems. *MIS Quarterly Executive, 8*(2), 73–87.

Google Apps. (n.d.). *Google apps service level agreement.* Retrieved October 15, 2011 from Google Apps: http://www.google.com/apps/intl/en/terms/sla.html

Google, Inc. (n.d.). *Security and privacy - Google apps help.* Retrieved April 12, 2011, from http://www.google.com/support/a/bin/answer.py?answer=60762

Google. (n.d.). *Top ten advantages of Google's cloud.* Retrieved October 15, 2011 from Google Apps for Business: http://www.google.com/apps/intl/en/business/cloud.html

Google. (n.d.). *What is Google app engine?* Retrieved October 15, 2011 from Google Code: http://code.google.com/intl/en/appengine/docs/whatisgoogleappengine.html

Gore, J. (1996). *Chaos, complexity, and the military. Newport, RI.* USA: National Defense University.

Grasselli, M. (2007). *The investment game in incomplete markets*. Buzio, Brazil: RIO.

Greene, T. (2009). *The U.S. Patriot Act has an impact on cloud computing*. Retrieved April 5, 2011, from http://www.networkworld.com/newsletters/2009/092909cloudsec1.html

Greenwood, D., Khajeh-Hosseini, A., Smith, J., & Sommerville, I. (2010). *The cloud adoption toolkit: Addressing the challenges of cloud computing adoption*. SICSA 2010 Conference. Retrieved from http://arxiv.org/ftp/arxiv/papers/1003/1003.3866.pdf

Grenadier, S. (2000). Option exercise games: The intersection of real options and game theory. *Journal of Applied Corporate Finance*, *13*(2), 99–107. doi:10.1111/j.1745-6622.2000.tb00057.x

Grossman, R. L. (2010). The case for cloud computing. *IT Professional*, *11*(2), 23–27. doi:10.1109/MITP.2009.40

Grover, V., Cheon, M. J., & Teng, J. T. C. (1994). A descriptive study on the outsourcing of information systems functions. *Information & Management*, *27*(1), 33–44. doi:10.1016/0378-7206(94)90100-7

Gu, C., & Zhang, X. (2010). An SOA based enterprise application integration approach. *International Symposium on Electronic Commerce and Security*, July 2010, (pp. 324-327). IEEE Computer Society.

Gu, P., Shang, Y., Chen, J., Deng, M., Lin, B., & Li, C. (2011). ECB: Enterprise cloud bus based on WS-notification and cloud queue model. *IEEE World Congress on Services*, 2011, (pp. 240-246). IEEE Computer Society.

Hadley v Baxendale. (1854). 9 Ex 341 at 354.

Hall, T., Beecham, S., & Rainer, A. (2002). Requirements problems in twelve software companies: An empirical analysis. *IEE Proceedings. Software*, *149*(5), 153. doi:10.1049/ip-sen:20020694

Hamid, R., Nezhad, M., Stephenson, B., Singhal, S., & Castellanos, M. (2009, November). Virtual business operating environment in the cloud: Conceptual architecture and challenges. In *ER 2009 Proceedings of the 28th International Conference on Conceptual Modeling, LNCS Vol. 5829*, (pp. 501-514). Berlin, Germany: SpringerLink. doi: 10.1007/978-3-642-04840-1_37

Hamilton, J. (2008). *Internet-scale service efficiency*. Paper presented at the Large-Scale Distributed Systems and Middleware (LADIS) Workshop.

Hanson v. Denckla, 375 U.S. 235, 246 n.12. (1958).

Harbert, T. (2011). *New job for mainframes: Cloud platform*. Retrieved April 5, 2011, from http://www.computerworld.com/s/article/9214913/New_job_for_mainframes_Cloud_platform

Harris, J. G., & Alter, A. E. (2010). *Six questions every executive should ask about cloud computing*. Accenture Institute for High Performance, January 2010. Retrieved from http://www.accenture.com/Global/Research_and_Insights/Institute-For-High-Performance/Six-Questions.htm

Hayes, B. (2008). Cloud computing. *Communications of the ACM*, *51*(7), 9–11. doi:10.1145/1364782.1364786

Heßeler, A., & Versteegen, G. (2004). *Anforderungsmanagement: Formale Prozesse, Praxiserfahrungen, Einführungsstrategien und Toolauswahl*. Berlin, Germany: Springer. Retrieved from http://www.worldcat.org/oclc/248875529

HHS. (1996). *The Health Insurance Portability and Accountability Act of 1996 (HIPAA) privacy and security rules*. Retrieved October 15, 2011 from http://www.hhs.gov/ocr/privacy/hipaa/understanding/index.html

HHS. (2002). *Standards for privacy of individually identifiable health information; final rule*. Retrieved October 15, 2011, from http://www.hhs.gov/ocr/privacy/hipaa/administrative/privacyrule/privrulepd.pdf

HHS. (2003). *Health insurance reform: Security standards; final rule*. Retrieved October 15, 2011 from http://www.hhs.gov/ocr/privacy/hipaa/administrative/securityrule/securityrulepdf.pdf

Higginbotham, S. (2009). Google gets shifty with its data center operations. Retrieved November 29, 2010, from http://gigaom.com/2009/07/16/google-gets-shifty-with-its-data-center-operations/

Hobbs, G., & Scheepers, R. (2009). *Identifying capabilities for the IT function to create agility in information systems*. Paper presented at the PACIS2009. Retrieved from http://aisel.aisnet.org/pacis2009/20

Hoffman, R. (2007, March 11). *Why being embarrassed is critical to the success of your startup.* Retrieved from http://www.cambrianhouse.com/blog/startups-entrepreneurship/why-being-embarrassed-is-critical-to-the-success-of-your-startup/

Hofmann, P., & Woods, D. (2010). Cloud computing: The limits of public clouds for business applications. *IEEE Internet Computing, 14*(6), 90. doi:10.1109/MIC.2010.136

Hon, W. K., Millard, C., & Walden, I. (2011). *The problem of 'personal data' in cloud computing - What information is regulated? The cloud of unknowing, part 1.* Queen Mary School of Law Legal Studies Research Paper No. 75/2011. Retrieved May 13, 2011, from http://ssrn.com/abstract=1783577

Hon, W. K., Millard, C., & Walden, I. (2011). *Who is responsible for 'personal data' in cloud computing? The cloud of unknowing, part 2.* Queen Mary School of Law Legal Studies Research Paper No. 77/2011. Retrieved May 13, 2011, from http://ssrn.com/abstract=1794130

Hoover, J. N. (2009, July 28). Inside Terremark's secure government data center. *Information Week.*

Horrigan, J. (2008). *Use of cloud computing applications and services.* Pew/Internet Memorandum.

Hossain, S., & Luby, D. (2010). *Cloud computing in healthcare Industry.* Paper presented at the Annual International Conference on Cloud Computing and Virtualization, Singapore.

Hotel Services Limited v Hilton International Hotels (UK) Limited. (2000). BLR 235.

Housel, T., & Bell, A. (2001). *Measuring and managing knowledge.* New York, NY: McGraw-Hill/Irwin.

Hovhannisian, K. (2001). *Exploring on the technology landscapes: Real options thinking in the context of the complexity theory.* Paper presented at the DRUID Winter Conference (January 17-19, 2002), Aalborg, Denmark.

Huang, C., Kao, H., & Li, H. (2007). Decision on enterprise computing solutions for an international tourism. *International Journal of Information Technology & Decision Making, 6*(4), 687–700. doi:10.1142/S0219622007002666

Hudgens, B., & Bordetsky, A. (2008). Feedback models for collaboration and trust in crisis response networks. In *Proceedings of 13th International Command and Control Research & Technology Symposium,* Seattle.

Huff, S. L., Munro, M. C., & Martin, B. H. (1988). Growth stages of end user computing. *Communications of the ACM, 31*(5), 542–550. doi:10.1145/42411.42417

Hug, M. (2008). *Will cloud-based multi-enterprise information systems replace extranets?* Retrieved Dec 7, 2010, from http://www.infoq.com/articles/will-meis-replace-extranets

Hugos, M. (2010). Business strategy based on cloud computing and agility. *CIO.* Retrieved from http://advice.cio.com/michael_hugos/14230/business_strategy_based_on_cloud_computing_and_agility

Hugoson, M.-A., Magoulas, T., & Pessi, K. (2009). *Architectural principles for alignment within the context of agile enterprises.* Paper presented at the European Conference on Information Management & Evaluation.

Hurwitz, J. D. (2009). *Cloud computing for dummies* (1st ed.). Indianapolis, IN: Wiley Pub., Inc.

Hutchins, S. G., Bordetsky, A., Kendall, A., Looney, J., & Bourakov, E. (2006). Validating a model of team collaboration. In *Proceedings of the 11th International Command and Control Research & Technology Symposium,* Cambridge, UK. September 26-28, 2006.

Huynh, T., Jennings, N., & Shadbolt, N. (2006, March). An integrated trust and reputation model for open multi-agent systems. In *Auton Agent Multi-Agent Sys (2006),* Vol. 13, (pp. 119–154). Springer Science+Business Media, LLC 2006. doi: 10.1007/s10458-005-6825-4

Hwang, K. (2010, December). Security, privacy, and data protection for trusted cloud computing. In *CloudCom2010: The 2nd International Conference on Cloud Computing.* Keynote Address. Indiana, USA, December 3, 2010. Retrieved from http://salsahpc.indiana.edu/CloudCom2010/slides/PDF/Keynotes/Security,%20Privacy,%20and%20Data%20Protection%20for%20Trusted%20Cloud%20Computing.pdf

IBM. (2007). *Virtualization in education*. Retrieved from http://www-07.ibm.com/solutions/in/education/download/Virtualization%20in%20Education.pdf

IBM. (2009). The benfits of cloud computing Retrieved Feb 1, 2011, from http://www-304.ibm.com/business-center/cpe/download0/202011/cloud_benefitsofcloud-computing.pdf

IBM. (2009). *Cloud computing: Save time, money, and resources with a private test cloud*. Retrieved from http://www.redbooks.ibm.com/redpapers/pdfs/redp4553.pdf

IBM. (2009). *IBM point of view: Security and cloud computing*.

IBM. (2010). *IBM smart business development and test cloud*. Retrieved Jan 12, 2011, from http://www-935.ibm.com/services/au/gts/pdf/IBM_Smart_Business_Dev_Test_Cloud.pdf

IBM. (2011). *Cloud computing and IBM LotusLive*. Retrieved January 10, 2011, from https://www.lotuslive.com/styles/tours/cloud_computing_datasheet.pdf

IBM. (2011). *IBM joins forces with over 45 organizations to launch cloud standards customer council for open cloud computing*. Retrieved April 10, 2011, from http://www-03.ibm.com/press/us/en/pressrelease/34198.wss

IBM. (2011). *IBM Poughkeepsie green data center*. Retrieved April 2, 2011, from http://www-01.ibm.com/software/success/cssdb.nsf/CS/LWIS-8FEUFH?OpenDocument&Site=default&cty=en_us

IBM. (2011). *IBM smarter planet*. Retrieved Jun 7, 2010, from http://www.ibm.com/smarterplanet/us/en/

IBM. (2011). *IBM service delivery manager*. Retrieved March 1, 2011, from http://www-01.ibm.com/software/tivoli/products/service-delivery-manager/

IBM. (2011). *Smart business development and test cloud*. Retrieved Jan 15, 2011, from http://www-935.ibm.com/services/us/en/it-services/smart-business-development-and-test-cloud.html

IBM. (2011). *IBM Systems z - News: Cloud computing with System z*. Retrieved Jan 31, 2011, from http://www-03.ibm.com/systems/z/news/announcement/20090915_annc.html

IBM/CISCO. (2008). *Virtualized storage infrastructure solution from IBM and Cisco*. Retrieved from http://www.cisco.com/web/partners/pr67/pr30/pr220/docs/IBM_Cisco_Virtualized_Storage_042808_SB.pdf

IDC. (2007). *Virtualization and multicore innovations disrupt the worldwide server market*. IDC Doc# 206035

IDC. (2008, October 2). *IT cloud services user survey, pt. 2: Top benefits & challenges*. Retrieved December 11, 2010, from IDC eXchange: http://blogs.idc.com/ie/?p=210

IDC. (2008, September 23). *Defining "cloud services" and "cloud computing"*. Retrieved December 12, 2010, from http://blogs.idc.com/ie/?p=190

IDC. (2009, December 15). *New IDC IT cloud services survey: Top benefits and challenges*. Retrieved December 12, 2010, from http://blogs.idc.com/ie/?p=730

IDC. (2010, July 1). *IDC's public IT cloud services forecast: New numbers, same disruptive story*. Retrieved April 2, 2011, from IDC eXchange: http://blogs.idc.com/ie/?p=730

In re Boucher, 2009 WL 424718, D. Vermont. (2009).

International Data Corporation. (2008). *IT cloud services forecast -- 2008-2012: A key driver for growth*. Mimeo, October 8.

International Data Corporation. (2009, October 9). *Aid to recovery*. White paper.

International Organization for Standards. (2008). *ISO/IEC 27001:2005*.

International Shoe Co. v. Washington, 326 U.S. 310. *(1945)*.

Internet2. (n.d.). *Shibboleth*. Retrieved October 15, 2011 from http://www.shibboleth.internet2.edu/

IRM. (2002). *The risk management standard*. Institute of Risk Management (IRM), The Association of Insurance and Risk Managers (AIRMIC) and Alarm (The Public Risk Management Association), 2002; also adopted by the Federation of European Risk Management Associates (FERMA). Retrieved October 15, 2011, from http://www.theirm.org/publications/documents/Risk_Management_Standard_030820.pdf

ISACA. (2009). *Cloud computing: Business benefits with security, governance and assurance perspectives.* Retrieved October 15, 2011, from http://www.isaca.org/Knowledge-Center/Research/ResearchDeliverables/Pages/Cloud-Computing-Business-Benefits-With-Security-Governance-and-Assurance-Perspective.aspx

ISACA. (n.d.). *COBIT framework for IT governance and control.* Retrieved October 15, 2011, from http://www.isaca.org/Knowledge-Center/COBIT/Pages/Overview.aspx

IT Governance Institute. (2007). *COBIT 4.1: Framework, control objectives, management guidelines, maturity models.* Rolling Meadows, IL: IT Governance Institute.

IW. (2010). *Risks of cloud computing outweigh benefits: New survey reveals low appetite for IT-related risk in 2010.* Retrieved April 10, 2011, from http://www.industryweek.com/articles/risks_of_cloud_computing_outweigh_benefits_21526.aspx

IXDA Interaction Design Association. (2007, November 27). Define the "user centered design" process. Retrieved from http://www.ixda.org/node/15599

Izza, S., Imache, R., Vincent, L., & Lounis, Y. (2008). An approach for the evaluation of the agility in the context of enterprise interoperability. In Mertins, K., Ruggaber, R., Popplewell, K., & Xu, X. (Eds.), *Enterprise interoperability III - New challenges and industrial approaches* (pp. 3–14). London, UK: Springer. doi:10.1007/978-1-84800-221-0_1

Jäätmaa, J. (2010). *Financial aspects of cloud computing business models information systems science. Mimeo.* Department of Business Technology, Aalto University School of Economics.

Jaeger, P. T., Lin, J., Grimes, J. M., & Simmons, S. N. (2009). *Where is the cloud? Geography, economics, environment, and jurisdiction in cloud computing.* Retrieved April 13, 2011, from http://www.uic.edu/htbin/cgiwrap/bin/ojs/index.php/fm/article/view/2456/2171

Jansen, A., & Bosch, J. (2005). Software architecture as a set of architectural design decisions. *Proceedings of the 5th Working IEEE/IFIP Conference on Software Architecture* (WICSA'05). Washington, DC: IEEE Computer Society.

Janssen, M., & Kuk, G. (2006). *A complex adaptive system perspective of enterprise architecture in electronic government.* Paper presented at the 39th Hawaii International Conference on System Sciences.

Jennings, R. J. (2009). *Cloud computing with the Microsoft Azure services platform* (1st ed.). Indianapolis, IN: Wiley Pub., Inc.

Jensen, M., Schwenk, J., Gruschka, N., & Iacono, L. (2009). On technical security issues in cloud computing. *2009 IEEE International Conference on Cloud Computing,* (pp. 109-116).

Jha, S., Merzky, A., & Fox, G. (2008). Programming abstractions for clouds. *Concurrency and Computation, 21*(8), 1087–1108. doi:10.1002/cpe.1406

Jones, K., Dobrokhodov, V., Kaminer, I., Lee, D., Bourakov, E., & Clement, M. (2009). Development, system integration and flight testing of a high-resolution imaging system for small UAS. In *Proceedings of the 47th AIAA Aerospace Sciences Meeting,* January 5-8, Orlando, Florida

Jorgenson, D. (2001). Information technology and the U.S. economy. *The American Economic Review, 91*(1), 1–28. doi:10.1257/aer.91.1.1

Juniper. (2010). *Cloud-ready data center reference architecture.* Retrieved from http://www.juniper.net/us/en/local/pdf/reference-architectures/8030001-en.pdf

Juniper. (2010). *Government data center network reference architecture.* Retrieved from http://www.juniper.net/us/en/local/pdf/reference-architectures/8030004-en.pdf

Juniper. (2010). *Network fabrics for modern data center.* Retrieved from http://www.juniper.net/us/en/local/pdf/whitepapers/2000327-en.pdf

Kaisler, S., & Money, W. (2010). *Dynamic service migration in a cloud architecture.* ARCS 2010 Workshop, Said Business School, University of Oxford, England, June 1, 2010.

Kaisler, S., & Money, W. (2011). *Service migration in a cloud computing architecture.* 44th Hawaii International Conference on System Sciences, Poipu, Kauai, Hawaii, January 8, 2011.

Kamara, S., & Lauter, K. (2010, January). Cryptographic cloud storage. In *RLCPS'10 Proceedings of the Financial Cryptography: Workshop on Real-Life Cryptographic Protocols and Standardization*. Retrieved from http://research.microsoft.com/pubs/112576/crypto-cloud.pdf

Katz v. United States, 389 U.S. 347. (1967).

Katz, R. H. (2009). Tech titans building boom. *IEEE Spectrum, 46*(2), 40. doi:10.1109/MSPEC.2009.4768855

Kaufman, L. (2009). Data security in the world of cloud computing. *Security & Privacy, 7*(4).

Keel, P., Porter, W., Sither, M., Winston, P., & Wall, E. (2008). Computational support for collaborative sense-making activities. In M. Letsky, W. Norman, S. Fiore, & C. Smith (Eds.), *Macrocognition in teams: Understanding the mental processes that underlie collaborative team activity*. Ashgate.

Keel, P., & Wall, E. (2007). A visual analytics environment for collaborative sense-making. *Information Visualization, 6*, 48–63.

Keller, E., Szefer, J., Rexford, J., & Lee, R. (2010, June). Nohype: virtualized cloud infrastructure without the virtualization. In *ISCA'10 Proceedings of The 37th Annual International Symposium On Computer Architecture*, Vol. 38(3). doi: 10.1145/1815961.1816010

Kemp, R., & Anderson, R. (2010). *Cloud computing: The rise of service-based computing*. Retrieved May 13, 2001, from http://www.kemplittle.com/PDFs/HotTopicArticle_CloudComputing_Feb2009.pdf

Khajeh-Hosseini, A., Greenwood, D., & Sommerville, I. (2010). *Cloud migration: A case study of migrating an enterprise IT system to IaaS.*

Khan, K. M., & Malluhi, Q. (2010). Establishing trust in cloud computing. *IT Professional, 12*(5), 20–27. doi:10.1109/MITP.2010.128

Kim, A., McDermott, J., & Kang, M. (2010). Security and architectural issues for national security cloud computing. *IEEE 30th International Conference Distributed Computing Systems Workshops,* (pp. 21-25).

Kim, W., Kim, S. D., Lee, E., & Lee, S. (2009). Adoption issues for cloud computing. *The Proceedings of the 11th International Conference on Information Integration and Web-based Applications & Services.*

Klein, P. (2011). *Seven tips for cloud computing*. Retrieved from http://www.microsoft.com/microsoftservices/en/us/article_Seven_Tips_for_Cloud_Computing.aspx

Knoblich, H. (1972). Die typologische Methode in der Betriebswirtschaftslehre. *Wirtschaftswissenschaftliches Studium, 1*(4), 141–147.

Knopp, M., & Schramm, A. (2009). *Manned-unmanned systems situational awareness using Galileo satellite constellation and small satellites*. Master Thesis, (Advisors: Prof. Dr. Stefan Pickl and Prof. Dr. Alex Bordetsky), University of Bundeswehr and Naval Postgraduate School

Kondo, D., Javadi, B., Malecot, P., Cappello, F., & Anderson, D. P. (2009). Cost-benefit analysis of cloud computing versus desktop grids. *IPDPS '09 Proceedings of the 2009 IEEE International Symposium on Parallel & Distributed Processing*

Kopena, J., & Loo, B. T. (2008). OntoNet: Scalable knowledge-based networking. In *Proceedings of ICDE Workshop,* (pp. 170-175).

Kotonya, G., & Sommerville, I. (1998). *Requirements engineering: Processes and techniques*. New York, NY: John Wiley. Retrieved from http://www.worldcat.org/oclc/38738981

Kramer, S., & Rybalchenko, A. (2010, August). *A multi-modal framework for achieving accountability in multi-agent systems*. Retrieved September 15, 2011, from http://www7.in.tum.de/~rybal/papers/2010-lis-accountability.pdf

Krutz, R. L., & Vines, R. D. (2010). *Cloud security: A comprehensive guide to secure cloud computing*. Wiley.

Kugel, R. (2010). *SaaS is breaking out*. Retrieved from http://www.businessintelligence.com/researchi.asp?id=306

Kupferman, J. (2006). *Service level agreements in web services*. Retrieved October 15, 2011, from http://www.cs.ucsb.edu/~jkupferman/docs/WS-SLA.pdf

Lan, U. (2010). OpenPMF SCaaS: Authorization as a service for cloud & SOA applications. *IEEE International Conference on Cloud Computing Technology and Science, 2010*, (pp. 634-643). IEEE Computer Society.

Lanvin, B., & Passman, P. (2008). Building e-skills for the information age. In *Global Information Technology Report 2007-2008*, WEF.

Laudon, K., & Laudon, J. (2012). *Management information systems: Managing the digital firm.* Prentice-Hall.

Laurent, P. (2011). *Towards a cartography of the legal aspects of cloud computing.* Paper presented at JuriTIC Conference Cloud Law or Legal Cloud (September 30th, 2011). Brussels, Belgium.

Lauria, E., & Duchessi, P. (2006). A Bayesian belief network for IT implementation decision support. *Decision Support Systems, 42*, 1573–1588. doi:10.1016/j.dss.2006.01.003

Lawton, G. (2008). Developing software online with platform-as-a-service technology. *Computer, 41*(6), 13–15. doi:10.1109/MC.2008.185

Leavitt, N. (2009). Is cloud computing really ready for prime time? *Computer, 42*(1), 15–20. doi:10.1109/MC.2009.20

Lee, G., & Crespi, N. (2010, October). Shaping future service environments with the cloud and internet of things: Networking challenges and service evolution. In *ISoLA 2010 Proceedings of the 4th International Symposium on Leveraging Applications of Formal Methods, Verification and Validation, Part I, LNCS Vol. 6415*, (pp. 399-410). Berlin, Germany: SpringerLink. doi: 10.1007/978-3-642-16558-0_34

Lee, D. M. S., Trauth, E. M., & Farwell, D. (1995). Critical skills and knowledge requirements of IS professionals: A joint academic/industry investigation. *Management Information Systems Quarterly, 19*(3), 313. doi:10.2307/249598

Lee, Y., & Lee, S. (2011). The valuation of RFID investment using fuzzy real option. *Expert Systems with Applications, 38*, 12195–12201. doi:10.1016/j.eswa.2011.03.076

Lewis, V., & Poilly, C. (2010). *Firm entry and the monetary transmission mechanism. Mimeo.* National Bank of Belgium.

Lheureux, B. J. (2008). *SaaS integration: How to choose the best approach.* Gartner ID Number: G00161672.

Li, W., & Ping, L. (2009). Trust model to enhance security and interoperability of cloud environment. In *CloudCom 2009 Proceedings of the 1st International Conference on Cloud Computing, LNCS Vol. 5931*, (pp. 69-79). Berlin, Germany: SpringerLink. doi: 10.1007/978-3-642-10665-1_7.

Liau, C. (2003). Belief, information acquisition, and trust in multi-agent systems—A modal logic formulation. *Elsevier Journal of Artificial Intelligence, 149*, 31–60. doi:doi:10.1016/S0004-3702(03)00063-8

Liebenau, J. (2010, June 8). *Manage the cloud? It's not airy-fairy!* Retrieved from http://microsoft.eu/Posts/Viewer/tabid/120/articleType/ArticleView/articleId/662/Menu/3/Manage-the-cloud-Its-not-airy-fairy.aspx

Lindemann, U. (2009). *Methodische Entwicklung technischer Produkte: Methoden flexibel und situationsgerecht anwenden.* Retrieved from http://dx.doi.org/10.1007/978-3-642-01423-9

Linthicum, D. (2003). *Next generation application integration.* Addison-Wesley, 2003.

Linthicum, D. (2009). *Defining the cloud computing framework.* Retrieved March 22, 2011, from http://cloudcomputing.sys-con.com/node/811519

Logan, D. (2009). *Compliance in the cloud: Whose data is it anyway?* Retrieved April 16, 2011, from http://www.gartner.com

Lombardi, F., & Pietro, R. (2010). Secure virtualization for cloud computing. *Elsevier Journal of Network and Computer Applications, 34*(4). doi:doi:10.1016/j.jnca.2010.06.008

Lorenzi, F., Baldo, G., Costa, R., Abel, M., Bazzan, A., & Ricci, F. (2010, November). A trust model for multi agent recommendations. *Journal of Emerging Technologies in Web Intelligence, 2*(4), 310–318. doi:10.4304/jetwi.2.4.310-318

Lowe, D., & Ng, S. (2006). *The implications of complex adaptive systems thinking for future command and control.* Paper presented at 11th International Command and Control Research and Technology Symposium (September, 2006), Cambridge, UK.

Luftman, J., & Ben-Zvi, T. (2010). Key issues for IT executives 2009: Difficult economy's impact on IT. *MIS Quarterly Executive, 9*(1), 46–59.

Lunsford, D. (2009). Virtualization technologies in information systems education. *Journal of Information Systems Education, 20,* 339.

MaaS360. (2011). *Mobility-as-a-service.* Retrieved March 30, 2011, from http://www.maas360.com/fiberlink/en-US/mobilityAsAService/

MacCormack, A. (2008). Building the agile enterprise: Myths, perceptions, and reality. *Cutter Benchmark Review, 8*(4), 5–13.

Mall, P., & Grance, T. (2009). Effectively and securely using the cloud computing paradigm. Retrieved January 31, 2011, from http://csrc.nist.gov/groups/SNS/cloud-computing/cloud-computing-v26.ppt

Manford, C. (2008). The impact of the SaaS model of software delivery. *21st Annual Conference of the National Advisory Committee on Computing Qualifications (NACCQ),* (pp. 283-286). Retrieved from www.naccq.ac.nz

Marchini, R. (2010). *Cloud computing. A practical introduction to the legal issues.* London, UK: British Standards Institute.

Marks, E., & Lozano, R. (2010). *Executive's guide to cloud computing.* Hoboken, NJ: John Wiley & Sons.

Marshall, A., Howard, M., Bugher, G., & Harden, B. (2010). *Security best practices for developing Windows Azure application.* Retrieved December 28, 2010, from http://go.microsoft.com/?linkid=9751405

Masahiko, J., & Yukio, T. (2009). *Virtualized optical network (VON) for agile cloud computing environment.* Paper presented at the Optical Fiber Communication Conference.

Massachusetts 201 CMR 17.03(2)(f).

Mather, T., Kumaraswamy, S., & Latif, S. (2009). *Cloud security and privacy: An enterprise perspective on risks and compliance.* O'Reilly Media.

Mathiassen, L., & Pries-Heje, J. (2006). Business agility and diffusion of information technology. *European Journal of Information Systems, 15*(2), 116–119. doi:10.1057/palgrave.ejis.3000610

Mauboussin, M. (2011). Embracing complexity. *Harvard Business Review,* (September): 89–92.

Maximilien, E. M., Ranabahu, A., Engehausen, R., & Anderson, L. C. (2009). *Toward cloud-agnostic middlewares.* Paper presented at the 24th ACM SIGPLAN Conference Companion on Object Oriented Programming Systems Languages and Applications.

McAlpine v Tilebox. (2005). EWHC 281 (TCC).

McClafferty, E. R. (2010). *Exporting into the cloud: Export compliance issues associated with cloud computing.* Retrieved April 14, 2011, from http://it.tmcnet.com/topics/it/articles/74329-exporting-into-cloud-export-compliance-issues-associated-with.htm

McGrew, T., Chen, H. C., & Masacioglu, M. (2009). *Managing network centric nodes with UAV relay.*

McKinsey. (2006). *Building a nimble organization: A Mckinsey global survey.* Retrieved from http://www.mckinseyquarterly.com/Building_a_nimble_organization_A_McKinsey_Global_Survey_1808

Mell, P., & Grance, T, (2009). *The NIST definition of cloud computing,* NIST, Version 15, 10-7-09.

Mell, P., & Grance, T. (2011). *The NIST definition of cloud computing (Draft).* Retrieved October 15, 2011, from http://csrc.nist.gov/publications/drafts/800-145/Draft-SP-800-145_cloud-definition.pdf

Mell, P., & Grance, T. (2010). The NIST definition of cloud computing. *Communications of the ACM, 53*(6), 50.

Mell, P., & Grance, T. (2011). *The NIST definition of cloud computing. (Draft), SP800-145.* Gaithersburg, MD: National Institute of Standards and Technology.

Melzer, M. A. (2011). Copyright enforcement in the cloud. *Fordham Intellectual Property. Media and Entertainment Law Journal, 21,* 403.

Menken, I. (2008, November 20). *SaaS - The complete cornerstone guide to software as a service best practices concepts, terms, and techniques for successfully planning, implementing and managing saas solutions*, (pp. 12, 18, 19, 34, 36, 39). Emereo Pty. Ltd.

Menken, I., & Blokdijk, G. (2009, October 10). Cloud computing best practice guide specialist, software as a service & web applications, (pp. 11-19, 43, 45, 46). Emereo Pty. Ltd.

Menken, I., & Blokdijk, G. (2010, September 8). Cloud computing: SaaS and Web applications specialist level complete certification kit - Software as a service study guide book and online course, (2nd ed, pp. 11-21, 38-42, 43). Emereo Pty. Ltd.

Microsoft. (2007). *Vulnerability in virtual PC and virtual server could allow elevation of privilege (937986)*. Microsoft Security Bulletin MS07-049. Retrieved October 15, 2011, from http://www.microsoft.com/technet/security/bulletin/ms07-049.mspx

Microsoft. (2008). *Architecture strategies for catching the long tail*. Retrieved 24 November, 2010, from http://msdn.microsoft.com/en-us/library/aa479069.aspx

Microsoft. (2010). *Cloud services*. Retrieved from http://download.microsoft.com/download/7/0/B/70B05EA3-233E-4677-A921-DA409B4EADF6/Microsoft_Cloud-Services.pdf

Microsoft. (n.d.). *Security development lifecycle*. Retrieved 12 28, 2010, from http://www.microsoft.com/security/sdl/

Microsoft. (n.d.). *Windows Azure, Microsoft's cloud services platform*. Retrieved 12 28, 2010, from Microsoft: http://www.microsoft.com/windowsazure/

Millard, C. (2010). *Cloud computing: Opportunities and risks*. Paper presented at the Meeting of International Bar Association Annual Meeting 2010. London, UK: University of London.

Miller, W. (2004) Cursor-on-target. *Military Information Technology Online, 8*(7).

Miller, J., & Page, S. (2009). *Complex adaptive systems: An introduction to computational models of social life*. Princeton University Press.

Mills, J. (2011). *CDR building cyber competitive advantage: Delivering resilient, threat responsive networks for an information dominant Navy*. CMU, 2011.

Mills, L. H. (2009). *Legal issues associated with cloud computing*. SecureIT. Retrieved April 5, 2011, from http://www.google.com/url?sa=t&source=web&cd=1&ved=0CCYQFjAA&url=http%3A%2F%2Fwww.secureit.com%2Fresources%2FCloud%2520Computing%2520Mills%2520Nixon%2520Peabody%25205-09.pdf&rct=j&q=legal%20aspects%20of%20cloud%20computing&ei=Y6CbTbGtIMnB0QGvoM3bAg&usg=AFQjCNFMpRVM3NigyJkzLYJU_fQZPP_i-Q&sig2=Qr71BOupa6zhHRz2LFtPzg&cad=rja

Mishra, S., & Dhillon, G. (2008). Defining internal control objectives for information systems security: A value focused assessment. *16th European Conference on Information Systems*, (pp. 1334-1345). Galway, Ireland.

Misra, S. C., & Mondal, A. (2010). Identification of a company's suitatbillity for the adoption of cloud computing and modelling its corresponding return on investment. *Mathematical and Computer Modelling, 53*(3-4). doi:doi:10.1016/j.mcm.2010.03.037

Misra, S., & Mondal, A. (2011). Identification of a company's suitability for the adoption of cloud computing and modelling its corresponding return on investment. *Mathematical and Computer Modelling, 53*, 504–521. doi:10.1016/j.mcm.2010.03.037

Montaner, M., Lopez, B., & Rosa, J. (2002, July). Developing trust in recommender agents. In *AAMAS'02 Proceedings of the First International Joint Conference on Autonomous Agents and Multiagent Systems*. doi: 10.1145/544741.544811.

Mooney, A., Mahoney, M., & Wixom, B. (2008). Achieving top management support in strategic technology initiatives. *Howe School Alliance for Technology Management, 12*(2). Retrieved from http://howe.stevens.edu/fileadmin/Files/research/HSATM/newsletter/v12/f08/MooneyMahoneyWixom.pdf

Motahari-Nezhad, H. R., Stephenson, B., & Singhal, S. (2009). Outsourcing business to cloud computing services: Opportunities and challenges, Hewlett-Packard Development Company, L.P. *IEEE Internet Computing, Special Issue on Cloud Computing.* Retrieved from http://www.hpl.hp.com/techreports/2009/HPL-2009-23.html.

Mowbray, M., Pearson, S., & Shen, Y. (2010, March). Enhancing privacy in cloud computing via policy-based obfuscation. *Springer Journal of Supercomputing, 61*(2). doi:doi:10.1007/s11227-010-0425-z

Mullins, R. (2010). Agility, not savings, may be the true value of the cloud. *Network Computing.* Retrieved from http://www.networkcomputing.com/data-center/agility-not-savings-may-be-the-true-value-of-the-cloud.php

Mun, J. (2006). *Real options analysis versus traditional DCF valuation in layman's terms.* (White Paper). Retrieved April 9, 2011, from http://www.realoptionsvaluation.com/download.html#casestudies

Mun, J., & Housel, T. (2006). *A primer on return on investment and real options for portfolio optimization.* Monterey, CA: Naval Postgraduate School.

Murphy, E. (2009). *Cloud implementation, part 3: Training for the task.* Retrieved February 2, 2012, from http://www.crmbuyer.com/story/66832.html

Nambisan, S. (2001). Why service business are not product businesses. *MIT Sloan Management Review, 42*(4), 72–81.

Nash, K. (2010). *Questions you need answered before going cloud.* Retrieved April 16, 2011, from http://www.cio.com/article/525014/Questions_You_Need_Answered_Before_Going_Cloud

Nazir, S., & Pinsonneault, A. (2008). The role of information technology in firm agility: An electronic integration perspective. *AMCIS 2008 Proceedings.*

Negash, S. (2004). Business intelligence. *Communications of the Association for Information Systems, 13*, 177–195.

Ngo-Ye, L., & Ahsan, M. (2005). *Enterprise IT APPLICATION SYSTEMS AGILITY AND ORGANIZATIONAL AGILITY.* Paper presented at the AMCIS 2005.

Nickols, F. (2010). *Four management strategies.* Retrieved February 2, 2012, from http://www.nickols.us/four_strategies.pdf

Nissen, M., & Bordetsky, A. (2011). Leveraging mobile network technologies to accelerate tacit knowledge flows across organizations and distances. In Trentino, G. (Ed.), *Network technology and knowledge flow.*

NIST. (2007). *NIST, computer security division, computer security resource center.* Retrieved December 27, 2010, from http://csrc.nist.gov/publications/PubsSPs.html

NIST. (2010). *NIST definition of cloud computing* v15. Retrieved May 1, 2011, from http://csrc.nist.gov/groups/SNS/cloud-computing/

NIST. (2011). *National Institute of Standards and Technology.* Retrieved March 25, 2011, from http://www.nist.gov/itl/csd/cloud-020111.cfm

O Reilly, T. (2005). *What is Web 2.0? Design patterns and business models for the next generation of software.* Mimeo.

Oberle, K., Stein, M., Voith, T., Gallizo, G., Ku, X., et al. (2010, 11-14 October). *The network aspect of infrastructure-as-a-service.* Paper presented at the 2010 14th International Conference on Intelligence in Next Generation Networks (ICIN).

OG. (2009). *Cloud cube model: Selecting cloud formations for secure collaboration.* Retrieved April 9, 2011, from http://www.opengroup.org/jericho/publications.htm

OG. (2010). *Building return on investment from cloud computing.* Retrieved April 9, 2011, from http://www.opengroup.org/cloud/whitepapers/ccroi/index.htm

Oh, T., Lim, S., Choi, Y., Park, K., Lee, H., & Choi, H. (2010, September). State of the art of network security perspectives in cloud computing. In *SUComS 2010 Proceedings of the First International Conference on Security-enriched Urban Computing and Smart Grid*, CCIS Vol. 78, (pp. 629-637). Berlin, Germany: SpringerLink. doi: 10.1007/978-3-642-16444-6_79

Okuhara, M., Shiozaki, T., & Suzuki, T. (2010). Security architectures for cloud computing. *Fujitsu Scientific and Technical Journal, 46*(4), 397–402.

Onwubiko, C. (2010). Security issues to cloud computing. In Antonopoulos, N., & Gillam, L. (Eds.), *Cloud computing: Principles, systems and applications.* London, UK: Springer-Verlag Computer Communications and Networks. doi:10.1007/978-1-84996-241-4_16

Oosterhout, M., Waarts, E., & Hillegersberg, J. V. (2006). Change factors requiring agility and implications for IT. *European Journal of Information Systems*, *15*(2), 132–145. doi:10.1057/palgrave.ejis.3000601

Oracle. (2010). *Increase business performance through IT agility*. Retrieved 1st November, 2010, from https://landingpad.oracle.com/webapps/dialogue/ns/dlgwelcome.jsp?p_ext=Y&p_dlg_id=8920806&src=7011677&Act=8

Orenstein, G. (2010). *Show me the gateway - Taking storage to the cloud*. Retrieved December 21, 2010, from http://gigaom.com/2010/06/22/show-me-the-gateway-taking-storage-to-the-cloud/

Orros, G., & Cantle, N. (2010). *ERM for strategic and emerging risks*. Presented at Risk and Investment Conference 2010, (June 14; 2010). Edinburgh, UK.

Overby, E., Bharadwaj, A., & Sambamurthy, V. (2006). Enterprise agility and the enabling role of information technology. *European Journal of Information Systems*, *15*(2), 120–131. doi:10.1057/palgrave.ejis.3000600

Owens, D. (2010, June). Securing elasticity in the cloud. *Communications of the ACM*, *8*(5), 46–51. doi:10.1145/1743546.1743565

Panda, S., & Mangla, V. (2010, May). Protecting data from the cyber theft – A virulent disease. *Journal of Emerging Technologies in Web Intelligence*, *2*(2), 152–155. doi:10.4304/jetwi.2.2.152-155

Pankaj, H. M., Ramaprasad, A., & Tadisina, S. K. (2009). Revisiting agility to conceptualize information systems agility. In M. D. Lytras & P. O. de Pablos (Eds.), *Emerging topics and technologies in information systems* (pp. 19-54). Hershey, PA: IGI Global.

Papadimitriou, P., & Garcia-Molina, H. (2011, January). Data leakage detection. *IEEE Transactions on Knowledge and Data Engineering*, *23*(1), 51–63. doi:10.1109/TKDE.2010.100

Parekh, H. (2011). *Defining what the cloud is not – Myths and misnomers*. Retrieved Jan 15, 2011, from http://hareshparekh.ulitzer.com/node/1772591

Parente, S., & Prescott, E. (1994). Barriers to technology adoption and development. *The Journal of Political Economy*, *102*(2), 298–321. doi:10.1086/261933

Partridge, R. (2011). *Are mainframe the original cloud platform?* Retrieved April 6, 2011, from http://ideasint.blogs.com/ideasinsights/2011/04/are-mainframes-the-original-cloud-platforms.html?utm_source=feedburner&utm_medium=feed&utm_campaign=Feed%3A+IdeasInsights+%28IDEAS+Insights%29

Patrizio, A. (2010). *IDC sees cloud market maturing quickly*. Retrieved December 1, 2010, from http://itmanagement.earthweb.com/netsys/article.php/3870016/IDC-Sees-Cloud-Market-Maturing-Quickly.htmhttp:/itmanagement.earthweb.com/netsys/article.php/3870016/IDC-Sees-Cloud-Market-Maturing-Quickly.htm

PCI Security Standards Council. (2010). *PCI DSS v2.0*.

PCISSC. (n.d.). *PCI data security council*. Retrieved October 15, 2011 from https://www.pcisecuritystandards.org/

Pendhakar, P. (2010). Valuing interdependent multi-stage IT-investments: A real options approach. *European Journal of Operational Research*, *201*, 847–859. doi:10.1016/j.ejor.2009.03.037

Perrig, A., & Sion, R. (2010). *CCSW '10: Proceedings of the 2010 ACM Workshop on Cloud Computing Security*. ACM.

PGP. (2008). *PGP® compliance brief - E.U. data protection directive 95/46/EC*. Retrieved October 15, 2011, from http://download.pgp.com/pdfs/regulations/EUD_compliance_brief-080618.pdf

Ping Identity Corporation. (2011). *Website*. Retrieved March 2, 2011, from http://www.pingidentity.com/

Pinguelo, F. M., & Muller, B. W. (2011). *Avoid the rainy day: Survey of U.S. cloud computing caselaw*. BC Law IPTF Blog. Retrieved April 13, 2011, from http://www.google.com/url?sa=t&source=web&cd=2&ved=0CCIQFjAB&url=http%3A%2F%2Fbciptf.org%2Findex2.php%3Foption%3Dcom_content%26do_pdf%3D1%26id%3D60&rct=j&q=Avoid%20the%20Rainy%20Day%3A%20Survey%20of%20U.S.%20Cloud%20Computing%20Caselaw&ei=V_alTfzsDJCugQeQnrzFCg&usg=AFQjCNFvHZ_okDRD9H-H2DsN5MIDl47XeA&sig2=5HEkU2pgj45E3YaGPd-EuA&cad=rja

Pittaro, M. (2008). *Connecting clouds – Integration and cloud computing.* Retrieved from http://www.snaplogic.com/blog/?cat=23

Plummer, D. (2010). *Vendor response: How providers address the cloud rights and responsibilities.* Retrieved April 16, 2011, from http://www.gartner.com

Plummer, D. C., & Smith, D. M. (2009). *Three levels of elasticity for cloud computing expand provider options.* Gartner ID Number: G00167400.

Pohl, K. (2008). *Requirements engineering: Grundlagen, Prinzipien, Techniken* (2.th ed.). Heidelberg, Germany: Dpunkt-Verl. Retrieved from http://deposit.d-nb.de/cgi-bin/dokserv?id=3086471&prov=M&dok_var=1&dok_ext=htm

Procopio, M. (2011). *Cloud computing does not require virtualization.* Retrieved August 8, 2011, from http://www.enterprisecioforum.com/en/blogs/michaelprocopio/cloud-computing-does-not-require-virtualization

Pultz, J. E. (2009). *10 key actions to reduce IT infrastructure and operations cost structure. (No. G00170304).* Gartner.

Qian, L., Luo, Z., Du, Y., & Guo, L. (2009, December). Cloud computing: an overview. In *CloudCom 2009 Proceedings of the 1st International Conference on Cloud Computing, LNCS Vol. 5931,* (pp. 626-631). Berlin, Germany: SpringerLink. doi: 10.1007/978-3-642-10665-1_63

Rabaey, M. (2011). *Game theoretic real option approach of the procurement of department of defense: Competition or collaboration.* Paper presented at the 8th Annual Acquisition Research Symposium (May 10-12, 2011). Monterrey, CA, USA.

Rabaey, M., Vandijck, E., & Hoffman, G. (2005). *An evaluation framework for enterprise application integration.* Paper presented at the 16th IRMA International Conference. San Diego, CA

Rabaey, M. (2012). A public economics approach to enabling enterprise architecture with the government cloud in Belgium. In Saha, P. (Ed.), *Enterprise architecture for connected e-government: Practices and innovations.* Hershey, PA: IGI Global.

Rabaey, M. (2012). Framework of knowledge and intelligence base: From intelligence to service. In Ordoñez de Pablos, P., & Lytras, M. D. (Eds.), *Knowledge management and drivers of innovation in services industries.* Hershey, PA: IGI Global. doi:10.4018/978-1-4666-0948-8.ch017

Rabaey, M., Tromp, H., & Vandenborre, K. (2007). Holistic approach to align ICT capabilities with business integration. In Cunha, M., Cortes, B., & Putnik, G. (Eds.), *Adaptive technologies and business integration: Social, managerial, and organizational dimensions* (pp. 160–173). Hershey, PA: Idea Group Publishing.

Racheva, Z., Daneva, M., & Buglione, L. (2008). *Complementing measurements and real options concepts to support inter- iteration decision-making in agile projects.* Paper presented at the 34th EUROMICRO Conference on Software Engineering and Advanced Applications 2008, Parma (Italy), September 3 - 5, 2008.

Ranganathan, V. (2010). Privacy issues with cloud applications. *IS Channel, 5*(1), 16–20.

Rappa, M. (2004). The utility business model and the future of computing services. *IBM Systems Journal, 43*(1), 32–42. doi:10.1147/sj.431.0032

Ratcliffe, W. (2011). *Embedding ERM into your business.* Presented at Health and Care Conference (May 18-20, 2011), Edinburgh.

Reese, G. (2009). *Cloud application architectures: Building applications and infrastructure in the Cloud.* Sebastopol, CA: O'Reilly Media, Inc.

Regulation (EC) 593/2008 of the European Parliament and of the Council on the law applicable to contractual obligations. (2008). Retrieved May 13, 2011, from http://eur-lex.europa.eu/LexUriServ/LexUriServ.do?uri=OJ:L:2008:177:0006:0016:En:PDF

Regulation (EC) 864/2007 of the European Parliament and of the Council on the law applicable to non-contractual obligations. (2007). Retrieved May 13, 2011, from http://eur-lex.europa.eu/LexUriServ/LexUriServ.do?uri=OJ:L:2007:199:0040:0040:EN:PDF

Reinhold, M. (2009). V-Modell XT und Anforderungen. In Rupp, C. (Ed.), *Requirements-Engineering und -Management: Professionelle, iterative Anforderungsanalyse für die Praxis.* München, Germany: Hanser Fachbuch Verlag.

Resources, C. (Feb 2009). *The imperative for modular reusable UI in SaaS*. Retrieved 15th June 2010, from http://www.catalystresources.com/saas-blog/the_imperative_for_modular_reusable_ui_in_saas/

Rideout, B., & Strickland, J. (2007). *Military application of networking by touch in collaborative planning and tactical environments*. Master Thesis, (Advisor: Dr. Alex Bordetsky), Naval Postgraduate School

Ried, S. (2009). *Market overview: The middleware software market, 2009*. Retrieved from http://www.forrester.com/rb/Research/market_overview_middleware_software_market,_2009/q/id/47591/t/2

Ried, S., Rymer, J. R., & Iqbal, R. (2008). *Forrester's SaaS maturity model*. Forrester Research.

Rimal, B. P., Eunmi, C., & Lumb, I. (2009, 25-27 Aug. 2009). *A taxonomy and survey of cloud computing systems*. Paper presented at the Fifth International Joint Conference on INC, IMS and IDC, 2009. NCM '09.

Rittinghouse, J. W., & Ransome, J. F. (2010). *Cloud computing: Implementation, management, and security*. Boca Raton, FL: CRC Press.

Riverbed (2011). WAN acceleration. Retrieved April 2, 2011, from http://www.wan-acceleration.org

Robertson, S., & Robertson, J. (2006). *Mastering the requirements process* (2nd). Upper Saddle River, NJ: Addison-Wesley. Retrieved from http://www.worldcat.org/oclc/62697079

Robison, W. J. (2010). Free at what cost? Cloud computing privacy under the stored communications act. *The Georgetown Law Journal*, *98*, 1195.

Röller, L.-H., & Waverman, L. (2001). Telecommunications infrastructure and economic development: A simultaneous approach. *The American Economic Review*, *91*(4), 909–923. doi:10.1257/aer.91.4.909

Rooy, D. (2010, June). Opportunities, trust, privacy and security challenges in cloud computing. In *Lecture: Moving to the Cloud: Risks and Opportunities, ICT 2010*, Brussels, 8 June 2010. Retrieved from http://www.security-round-table.eu/doc/20100611_cloud_presentations/Dirk_van_Rooy.pdf

Ruest, D., & Ruest, N. (2009). *Virtualization: A beginner's guide*. New York, NY: McGraw Hill.

Ruiter, J., & Warnier, M. (2011). Privacy regulations for cloud computing: Compliance and implementation in theory and practice. In S. Gutwirth, et al (Eds.), *Computers, privacy and data protection: An element of choice*, 1st ed., (pp. 361-376). Springer Science+Business Media, B.V. doi: 10.1007/978-94-007-0641-5_17

Russell, D. (2010). *Weather report: Considerations for migrating to the cloud*. Retrieved December 1, 2010, from http://www.ibm.com/developerworks/cloud/library/cl-wr1migrateappstocloud/index.html

Ryan, M. W., & Loeffler, C. M. (2010). Insights into cloud computing. *Intellectual Property & Technology Law Journal*, *22*, 22–28.

SaaS-Attack. (2008). *SaaS business model*. Retrieved from http://www.saas-attack.com/SaaSModel/SaaSBusinessModels/tabid/60/Default.aspx

Sakka, M., Defude, B., & Tellez, J. (2010, June). Document provenance in the cloud: constraints and challenges. In *EUNICE 2010 Proceedings of the Networked Services and Applications–Engineering, Control and Management, LNCS Vol. 6164*, (pp. 107-117). IFIP International Federation for Information Processing. doi: 10.1007/978-3-642-13971-0_11

Sambamurthy, V., Bharadwaj, A., & Grover, V. (2003). Shaping agility through digital options: Reconceptualizing the role of information technology in contemporary firms. *Management Information Systems Quarterly*, *27*(2), 237.

SAML XML. org. (n.d.). *List of organizations using SAML*. Retrieved October 15, 2011, from SAML XML.org: http://saml.xml.org/wiki/list-of-organizations-using-saml

Sangroya, A., Kumar, S., Dhok, J., & Varma, V. (2010). Towards analyzing data security risks in cloud computing environments. *International Conference on Information Systems, Technology, and Management (ICISTM)*, (pp. 255–265). Springer-Verlag. Santa Fe. (2010). *Evaluating cloud risk for the enterprise: A shared assessments guide*. Retrieved from http://www.sharedassessments.org/media/pdf-EnterpriseCloud-SA.pdf

Sarna, D. E. Y. (2011). *Implementing and developing cloud computing applications*. Boca Raton, FL: CRC Press.

SAS Institute v World Programming Ltd. (2010). EWHC 1829 (Ch).

Satcliffe, R. (2009). Web 3.0: Are we there yet? *The Next Wave, NSA Review of Emerging Technologies, 17*(3).

Scarfone, K., Souppaya, M., & Hoffman, P. (2011). *Guide to security for full virtualization technologies.* The National Institute of Standards and Technology (NIST), Special Publication 800-125. Retrieved October 15, 2011, from http://csrc.nist.gov/publications/nistpubs/800-125/SP800-125-final.pdf

SearchSecurity.com. (2011). Retrieved February 20, 2011, from http://searchsecurity.techtarget.com/sDefinition/0,sid14_gci1381571,00.html

SEC. (n.d.). *Safeguarding of asset.* U.S Securities and Exchange Commission. Retrieved from Retrieved October 15, 2011, from http://www.sec.gov/rules/pcaob/34-49544-appendixc.pdf

Secunia. (2007). *Secunia advisory SA26986: Xen multiple vulnerabilities.* Retrieved October 15, 2011, from http://secunia.com/advisories/26986

Secunia. (2008). *Secunia advisory SA28405: Xen multiple vulnerabilities.* Retrieved October 15, 2011, from http://secunia.com/advisories/28405

Sedayao, J., Su, S., Ma, X., Jiang, M., & Miao, K. (2009). A simple technique for securing data at rest stored in a computing cloud. In *CloudCom 2009 Proceedings of the 1st International Conference on Cloud Computing, LNCS Vol. 5931,* (pp. 553-558). Berlin, Germany: SpringerLink. doi: 10.1007/978-3-642-10665-1_51

Sengupta, K., & Masini, A. (2008). IT agility: Striking the right balance. *Business Strategy Review, 19*(2), 42. doi:10.1111/j.1467-8616.2008.00534.x

Seo, D., & Paz, A. I. L. (2008). Exploring the dark side of IS in achieving organizational agility. *Communications of the ACM, 51*(11), 136–139. doi:10.1145/1400214.1400242

Setia, P., Sambamurthy, V., & Closs, D. (2008). Realizing business value of agile IT applications: Antecedents in the supply chain networks. *Information Technology Management, 9*, 5. doi:10.1007/s10799-007-0028-4

Seungseok, K., Jaeseok, M., Jongheum, Y., Seong-Wook, H., Taehyung, C., Ji-man, C., & Sang-Goo, L. (2010). *General maturity model and reference architecture for SaaS service* (pp. 337–346).

Shankararaman, V., & Eng Kit, L. (2010). *Create a process driven composite application with CE7.2-introduction.* SAP Community Network. Retrieved from http://www.sdn.sap.com

Sharif, A. M. (2010). It's written in the cloud: The hype and promise of cloud computing. *Journal of Enterprise Information Management, 23*(2). doi:10.1108/17410391011019732

Sharifi, H., & Zhang, Z. (2001). Agile manufacturing in practice: Application of a methodology. *International Journal of Operations & Production Management, 21*(5/6), 772. doi:10.1108/01443570110390462

Shattuck, L., & Miller, N. (2006). Naturalistic decision making in complex systems: A dynamic model of situated cognition combining technological and human agents. *Organizational Behavior: Special Issue on Naturalistic Decision Making in Organizations, 27*(7), 989–1009.

Shen, C. (2009). A Bayesian networks approach to modeling financial risks of e-logistics investments. *International Journal of Information Technology & Decision Making, 8*(4), 711–726. doi:10.1142/S0219622009003594

Sion, R., & Song, D. (Eds.). (2009). *CCSW '09: Proceedings of the 2009 ACM Workshop on Cloud Computing Security.* ACM.

Smith v. Maryland, 442 U.S. 735. (1979).

Smith, R. (2009, September 1). Computing in the cloud. *Research Technology Management.* Retrieved from http://207.57.8.178/papers/RSmith_InnovationColumn5.pdf

Smit, H., & Trigeorgis, L. (2009). Valuing infrastructure investment: An option game approach. *California Management Review, 51*(2), 79–100.

SNIA. (2011). *SNIA - SNIA cloud storage initiative.* Retrieved March 1, 2011, from http://www.snia.org/cloud

Snowden, D., & Boone, M. (2007). A leader's framework for decision making: Wise executives tailor their approach to fit the complexity of the circumstances they face. *Harvard Business Review*, (November): 68–76.

Soenen, P., & Palante, J.-P. (2011). *Cloud governance is ... more than security.* Paper presented at JuriTIC conference Cloud Law or Legal Cloud (September 30th, 2011). Brussels, Belgium.

Sorenson, P., & Chen, X. (2008 October, 28). *Towards SaaS (software as a service) evaluation model.* Department of Computing Science, University of Alberta. Retrieved from http://ssrg.cs.ualberta.ca/images/3/35/CASCON2008-Sorenson.pdf

Sosinski, B. (2011). *Cloud computing bible*. Indianapolis, IN: Wiley.

Spencer, A. B. (Ed.). (2005). *Acing civil procedure* (2nd ed.). St. Paul, MN: Thompson/West.

Spínola, M. (2009). *An essential guide to possibilities and risks of cloud computing.* Retrieved March 24, 2011, from http://www.mariaspinola.com/cloud-computing/

Sridhar, T. (2009). Cloud computing - A primer part 2: Infrastructure and implementation topics. *The Internet Protocol Journal Cisco, 12*(4).

Sridhar, T. (2009). Cloud computing - A primer part 1: Models and technologies. *The Internet Protocol Journal Cisco, 12*(3), 2–19.

Standish Group. (2010). *CHAOS report*. Retrieved from http://www.standishgroup.com/

Stansbury, M. (2010). *Seven proven ways to save on school budgets*. E-School News. Retrieved October 8, 2010, from http://www.eschoolnews.com/2010/07/28/seven-proven-ways-to-save-on-school-budgets/

State v. Bellar, 217 P.3d 1094, Ct. App. Or. (2009).

Staten, J. (2009). *TechRadar™ for infrastructure & operations professionals: Cloud computing, Q3 2009: As much diversity of maturity across categories as confusion among them.*

Sterling Commerce. (2010). *87 Prozent deutscher Unternehmen planen Investitionen in Cloud-Services.* Retrieved from http://www.sterlingcommerce.de/about/news/press-releases/PM_CloudServices_10.htm

Strum, R., Morris, W., & Jander, M. (2000). *Foundations of service level management.* SAMS publishing.

Subashin, S., & Kavitha, V. (2011). A survey on security issues in service delivery models of cloud computing. *Elsevier Journal of Network and Computer Applications, 34*, 1–11. doi:10.1016/j.jnca.2010.07.006

Suess, J., & Morooney, K. (2009). Identity management and trust services: Foundations for cloud computing. *EDUCAUSE Review, 44*(5), 24–43.

Sull, D. (2010). Competing through organizational agility. *The McKinsey Quarterly, 48*.

Sultan, N. A. (2011). Reaching for the "cloud": How SMEs can manage. *International Journal of Information Management, 31*(3), 272–278. doi:10.1016/j.ijinfomgt.2010.08.001

Sun Microsystems. (2009). *Introduction to cloud computing architecture*. White Paper.

Svantesson, D., & Clarke, R. (2010). Privacy and consumer risks in cloud computing. *Computer Law & Security Report, 26*, 391–397. doi:10.1016/j.clsr.2010.05.005

Szczypiorski, K., Margasiński, I., Mazurczyk, W., Cabaj, K., & Radziszewski, P. (2008, November). TrustMAS: Trusted communication platform for multi-agent systems. In *OTM 2008 Proceedings of the On the Move to Meaningful Internet Systems, Part II, LNCS Vol. 5332*, (pp. 1019–1035). Berlin, Germany: SpringerLink. doi:10.1007/978-3-540-88873-4_7

Takabi, H., Joshi, J. B. D., & Ahn, G.-J. (2010). SecureCloud: Towards a comprehensive security framework for cloud computing environments. *34th Annual IEEE Computer Software and Applications Conference Workshops*, 2010, (pp. 393-398). IEEE Computer Society.

Takabi, H., Joshi, J., & Ahn, G. (2010). Security and privacy challenges in cloud computing environments. *Security & Privacy, IEEE, 8*(6), 24–31. doi:10.1109/MSP.2010.186

Talib, A. (2010, November). Security framework of cloud data storage based on multi agent system architecture: Semantic literature review. *Journal of Computer and Information Science*, *3*(4), 175–186. Retrieved from http://www.ccsenet.org/journal/index.php/cis/article/view/7133/6130

Tao, C., Jinlong, Z., Benhai, Y., & Shan, L. (2007). *A fuzzy group decision approach to real option valuation*. Wuhan, China: Huazhong University of Science and Technology. doi:10.1007/978-3-540-72530-5_12

Tassey, G. (2000). Standardization in technology-based markets. *Research Policy, 29*(4,5), 587.

Tayip, D. (2011). Navigating the cloud: Solutions for a cloud computing age. *Computers and Law Magazine of SCL*, *21*(5), 14–18.

The Green Grid. (2008). Five ways to reduce data center server power consumption. Retrieved from http://www.thegreengrid.org/Global/Content/white-papers/Five-Ways-to-Save-Power

Thomaidis, N., Nikitakos, N., & Dounias, G. (2006). The evaluation of information technology projects: A fuzzy multicriteria decision-making approach. *International Journal of Information Technology & Decision Making*, *5*(1), 89–122. doi:10.1142/S0219622006001897

Tiwana, A., & Konsynski, B. (2010). Complementarities between organizational IT architecture and governance structure. *Information Systems Research, 21*(2), 288(217).

TNT 08-4 QLR, Quick Lookup Report. (2008). Monterey, CA: Naval Postgraduate School. Retrieved from http://cenetix.nps.edu

TNT MIO 08-4 After Action Report. (2008). Monterey, CA: Naval Postgraduate School. Retrieved from http://cenetix.nps.edu

Tobarra, L., Cazorla, D., Cuartero, F., & Díaz, G. (2005). Application of formal methods to the analysis of web services security. In EPEW 2005 *Proceedings of the European Performance Engineering Workshop*, LNCS Vol. 3670, (pp. 215–229). Berlin, Germany: SpringerLink. doi: 10.1007/11549970_16

Tolga, A., & Kahraman, C. (2008). Fuzzy multiattribute evaluation of R&D projects using a real options valuation model. *International Journal of Intelligent Systems*, *23*, 1153–1176. doi:10.1002/int.20312

Totzek, A. (2011). *Banks, oligopolistic competition, and the business cycle: A new financial accelerator approach*. Mimeo, Christian-Albrechts-University of Kiel.

Trend Micro. (2010). *Addressing data security challenges in the cloud*.

Triantis, A. (2000). Real options and corporate risk management. *Journal of Applied Corporate Finance*, *13*(2), 64–73. doi:10.1111/j.1745-6622.2000.tb00054.x

Trigeorgis, L. (2002). *Real options and investment under uncertainty: What do we know?* Brussels, Belgium: Nationale Bank van België. doi:10.2139/ssrn.1692691

TripleTree. (2004). *Software as a service: Changing the paradigm in the software industry*. Washington, DC: SIIA and TripleTree Industry Analysis Series. Retrieved from www.siia.net

Truong, D. (2010). How cloud computing enhances competitive advantages: A research model for small businesses. *Business Review (Federal Reserve Bank of Philadelphia)*, *15*, 59.

Trusted Computing Group. (2010). *Cloud computing and security – A natural match*. Retrieved September 11, 2011, from http://www.trustedcomputinggroup.org/files/resource_files/1f4dee3d-1a4b-b294-d0ad0742ba449e07/cloud%20computing%20and%20security%20whitepaper_july29.2010.pdf

Tsai, W., Wei, X., Chen, Y., Paul, R., Chung, J., & Zhang, D. (2007). Data provenance in SOA: Security, reliability, and integrity. In SOCA (2007) *Service Oriented Computing and Applications*, Vol. 1, (pp. 223-247). Berlin, Germany: SpringerLink. doi: 10.1007/s11761-007-0018-8

Tsilas, N. (2010, June). Moving responsibility to the cloud to ensure its full potential. *Intellectual Property Course Handbook Series*, 1-12.

U.S. Const., amend IV.

U.S. Const., amend V.

U.S. Const., amend XIV.

Uniform Trade Secrets Act, 11 U.S.C. §§ 332, 363.

United States v. Gavegnano, 305 Fed. Appx. 954, 4th Cir. *(2009)*.

United States v. Kirschner, 2010 WL 1257355, E.D. Mich. *(2009)*.

United States v. Miller, 425 U.S. 435. (1976).

United States v. White, 401 U.S. 745. (1971).

Urquhart, J. (2010). *What cloud computing can learn from 'flash crash'.* Retrieved October 3, 2011, from http://news.cnet.com/8301-19413_3-20004757-240.html

Vaquero, L. M., Rodero-Merino, L., Caceres, J., & Lindner, M. (2009). A break in the clouds. towards a cloud definition. *Computer Communication Review, 39*(1), 50–55. doi:10.1145/1496091.1496100

Varia, J. (2008). *Building GrepTheWeb in the cloud, part 1: Cloud architectures.* Retrieved June 30, 2010, from http://aws.amazon.com/articles/1632?_encoding=UTF8&jiveRedirect=1

Varian, H., Litan, R. E., Elder, A., & Shutter, J. (2002). *The net impact study: The projected economic benefits of the internet in the United States, United Kingdom, France and Germany.* Mimeo 2.0.

Velte, A. T., Velte, T. J., & Elsenpeter, R. C. (2010). *Cloud computing: A practical approach.* New York, NY: McGraw-Hill.

VMware. (2007). *Critical VMware security alert for Windows-hosted VMware workstation, VMware player, and VMware ACE.* Retrieved October 15, 2011, from http://kb.vmware.com/kb/1004034

VMware. (n.d.). *VMOTION - Migrate virtual machines with zero downtime.* Retrieved October 15, 2011, from http://www.vmware.com/products/vmotion/features.html

Voas, J., & Zhang, J. (2009). Cloud computing: New wine or just a new bottle? *IT Professional, 11*(2), 15–17. doi:10.1109/MITP.2009.23

von Helfenstein, S. B. (2009). *Real options 'in' economic systems: Exploring systemic disturbance causes and cures.* Boston, MA.

Vouk, M. A. (2008). Cloud computing - Issues, research and implementations. In *Proceedings of the ITI 2008 30th International Conference on Information Technology Interfaces.*

Wainewright, P. (2009). *PRaaS: Process as a service.* Retrieved February 5, 2011, from http://nauges.typepad.com/my_weblog/2009/08/praas-process-as-a-service.html

Wang, L., Tao, J., Kunze, M., Castellanos, A. C., Kramer, D., & Karl, W. (2008). *Scientific cloud computing: Early definition and experience.* Paper presented at the 10th IEEE International Conference on High Performance Computing and Communications, 2008. HPCC '08.

Wang, W., Zeng, G., & Yuan, L. (2006, August). A reputation multi-agent system in semantic web. In *PRIMA 2006 Proceedings of the 9th Pacific Rim International Workshop on Multi-Agents, LNAI Vol. 4088,* (pp. 211–219). Berlin, Germany: SpringerLink. doi: 10.1007/11802372_22

Wang, H. (2010, May). Privacy-preserving data sharing in cloud computing. *Journal of Computer Science and Information Technology, 25*(3), 401-414. Springer Science+Business Media, LLC & Science Press. *China.* doi:doi:10.1007/s11390-010-9333-1

Wang, S., & Lee, C. (2010). A fuzzy real option valuation approach to capital budgeting under uncertainty environment. *International Journal of Information Technology & Decision Making, 9*(5), 695–713. doi:10.1142/S0219622010004056

Ward, J., & Daniel, E. (Eds.). (2006). *Benefits management: Delivering value from IS & IT investments (Vol. 1).* Padstow, UK: T.J. International.

Wauters, R. (2009). *More security loopholes found in Google Docs.* Retrieved September 11, 2011, from http://techcrunch.com/2009/03/26/more-security-loopholes-found-in-google-docs/

Weeds, H. (2006). *Applying option games: When should real options valuation be used? (Paper).* Colchester, UK: University of Essex. Retrieved April 10, 2011, from http://privatewww.essex.ac.uk/~hfweeds/

Weijnen, M., Herder, P., & Bouwmans, I. (2007). *Designing complex systems: A contradiction in terms.* Paper presented at a Congress on Interdisciplinary Design (April 4th, 2007). Delft, The Netherlands.

Weill, P., Subramani, M., & Broadbent, M. (2002). Building IT infrastructure for strategic agility. *MIT Sloan Management Review, 44*(1), 57.

Weinhardt, C., Anandasivam, A., Blau, B., Borissov, N., Meinl, T., Michalk, W., & Stößer, J. (2009). Cloud-Computing. *Wirtschaftsinformatik, 51*(5), 453–462. doi:10.1007/s11576-009-0192-8

Wells, D. (1999). *Homepage*. Retrieved from ExtremeProgramming.org

West, D. (2010). *Saving money through cloud computing*. Mimeo, Governance Studies at Brookings.

Wikipedia. (2011). *Cloud storage*. Retrieved March 1, 2011, from http://en.wikipedia.org/wiki/Cloud_storage

Wikipedia. (2011). *Hypervisor*. Retrieved January 15, 2011, from http://en.wikipedia.org/wiki/Hypervisor

Wikipedia. (2011). *Virtual private server*. Retrieved August 25, 2011, from http://en.wikipedia.org/wiki/Virtual_private_server

Wikipedia. (n.d.). *Fuzzy pay-off method for real option valuation*. Retrieved April 10, 2011, from http://en.wikipedia.org/wiki/Fuzzy_Pay-Off_Method_for_Real_Option_Valuation

Wikipedia. (n.d.). *Rationality*. Retrieved March 24, 2011, from http://en.wikipedia.org/wiki/Rationality

Wikipedia. (n.d.). *Thin client*. Retrieved February 1, 2011, from http://en.wikipedia.org/wiki/Thin_client

Wikipedia. (n.d.). *Wet bescherming persoonsgegevens* (in Dutch). Retrieved October 15, 2011 from http://nl.wikipedia.org/wiki/Wet_bescherming_persoonsgegevens

Williams, S., & Williams, N. (2003). The business value of business intelligence. *Business Intelligence Journal, 8*(4).

Winkler, V. (2011). *Securing the cloud*. Waltham, MA: Elsevier.

Winthrop, P. (2011). *Ruminating on MaaS: Mobility as a service*. Retrieved April 5, 2011, from http://theemf.org/2011/03/16/ruminating-on-maas-mobility-as-a-service

Wolf, H., Roock, S., & Lippert, M. (2005). *eXtreme programming* (2nd ed.). s.l: dpunkt.verlag. Retrieved from http://ebooks.ciando.com/book/index.cfm/bok_id/7064

Wtoll. (2011, April 15). *The SaaS transition and the importance of web performance*. Retrieved from http://blog.yottaa.com/2011/04/the-saas-transition-and-the-importance-of-web-performance

Xu, J., Huang, R., Huang, W., & Yang, G. (2009, December). Secure document service for cloud computing. In *CloudCom 2009 Proceedings of the 1st International Conference on Cloud Computing, LNCS Vol. 5931*, (pp. 541-546). Berlin, Germany: SpringerLink. doi: 10.1007/978-3-642-10665-1_49

Yan, L., Rong, C., & Zhao, G. (2009, December). Strengthen cloud computing security with federal identity management using hierarchical identity-based cryptography. In *CloudCom 2009 Proceedings of the 1st International Conference on Cloud Computing, LNCS Vol. 5931*, (pp. 167-177). Berlin, Germany: SpringerLink. doi: 10.1007/978-3-642-10665-1_15

Yinglei, B., & Lei, W. (2011). Leveraging cloud computing to enhance supply chain management in automobile industry. *International Conference on Business Computing and Global Informatization, 2011*, (pp. 150-153). IEEE Computer Society.

Yin, R. (2003). *Case study research* (3rd ed.). Newbury Park, CA: Sage Publications.

Yu, S., Wang, C., Ren, K., & Lou, W. (2010). *Achieving secure, scalable, and fine-grained data access control in cloud computing. INFOCOM* (pp. 1–9). San Diego, CA: IEEE.

Zhang, W., & Chen, Q. (2010). From e-government to c-government via cloud computing. *International Conference on E-Business and E-Government, 2010*, (pp. 679-682). IEEE Computer Society.

Zhang, X., Xu, F., Liu, Y., Zhang, X., & Shen, C. (2006, December). Trust extended dynamic security model and its application in network. In *MSN 2006 Proceedings of the Second International Conference on Mobile Ad-Hoc and Sensor Networks, LNCS Vol. 4325*, (pp. 404-415). Berlin, Germany: SpringerLink. doi: 10.1007/11943952_34

Zheng, J., Sun, Y., & Zhou, W. (2009, December). Cloud computing based internet data center. In *CloudCom 2009 Proceedings of the 1st International Conference on Cloud Computing, LNCS Vol. 5931,* (pp. 700-704). Berlin, Germany: SpringerLink. doi: 10.1007/978-3-642-10665-1_75

Zhou, M., Zhang, R., Xie, W., Qian, W., & Zhou, A. (2010). Security and privacy in cloud computing: A survey. *Sixth International Conference on Semantics, Knowledge and Grids,* (pp. 105-112).

Zhou, M., Zhang, R., Xie, W., Qian, W., & Zhou, A. (2010). Security and privacy in cloud computing: A survey. *Sixth International Conference on Semantics, Knowledge, and Grids.* IEEE, (pp. 105-112).

Zhu, J. (2010). Cloud computing technologies and applications. In B. Furht & A. Escalante (Eds.), *Handbook of cloud computing,* (pp. 21-45). Springer Science+Business Media, LLC. doi: 10.1007/978-1-4419-6524-0_2

Zimmerman, O., Gschwind, T., Kuster, J., et al. (2007). Reusable architectural decision models for enterprise architecture development. *Proceedings of the 3rd International Conference on Quality of Software-Architectures: Models and Architectures* (QoSA), (pp. 157-166).

Zittrain, J. (2007). Saving the Internet. *Harvard Business Review,* (June): 49–59.

About the Contributors

Al Bento is Professor and Thompson Chair of MIS at the University of Baltimore, and Editor- in - Chief of the *Journal of Information Technology Management,* a publication of the Association of Management. He was on the faculty of Boston University, Bentley University, California State University, and the founder and Chair of the Special Interest Group in Information Security (SIGSEC) of the Association of Information Systems, the premier MIS international academic society. He holds a M.S. in Computer Science and Systems Engineering, and a Ph.D. in Computer Information Systems from UCLA. Prior to his academic career, he worked for nine years at IBM World Trade as Systems Engineer, Budget Manager, and Education and Scientific Affairs Manager. His professional and research focuses on information technology infrastructure (operating systems, networking, Internet, Web, cloud and mobile computing, and technical aspects of security), and management of information and control systems (planning and control systems, budgeting, individual, and organizational performance management).

A. K. Aggarwal is a Fulbright Scholar and Professor in the Merrick School of Business at the University of Baltimore. Dr. Aggarwal has published in many journals, including *Decision Sciences - Journal of Innovative Education, Computers and Operations Research, Decision Sciences, Information and Management, Production and Operation Management, Total Quality Management & Business Excellence, eService, International Journal of Web-Based Learning and Teaching Technologies, Journal of EUC, Transactions of DSS,* and many national and international professional proceedings. He has edited two books on web-based education: Web-Based Teaching: Opportunities and Challenges and Web-Based Education: Learning from Experiences and one book on cloud computing. His current research interests include collaborative systems, web-based teaching, model-based organizational systems, web-based systems and educational issues in MIS.

* * *

Alex Bordetsky is tenured Associate Professor of Information Systems at the Naval Postgraduate School. Professor Bordetsky is Director of the NPS Center for Network Innovation and Experimentation (CENETIX). He is a recipient of Robert W. Hamming Interdisciplinary Research Award for the pioneering studies of collaborative technologies and adaptive networking, featured in the AFCEA *SIGNAL* Magazine, *Via Sat,* and the USSOCOM *Tip of the Spear* Journal, and *Pentagon Channel.* Dr. Bordetsky publishes in major IS journals including *Information Systems Research, Telecommunication Systems Modeling and Analysis, International Journal of Mobile Wireless Communications,* and *International Command and Control Research Journal.*

Cecelia Wright Brown is an Assistant Professor in the Division of Science, Information Arts and Technologies at the University of Baltimore. She is also the President of BEE Engineering Consulting, LLC. Dr. Wright Brown graduated from Morgan State University with a Doctorate of Engineering degree in Civil Engineering, concentration infrastructure and transportation, Masters of Science in Science degree with a concentration in Physics from Morgan State University, and is certified in Homeland Security. She is a board member and supporter of a number of professional organizations. Her career path has included a variety of experiences including being the former Chief Engineer with the American Baptist Churches of the South Mission and Conference Center, a Consulting Engineer with A. Goldberger Control, a Field Engineer for Square D Company and a Research Physicist for the U.S. Army. Dr. Wright Brown has developed and implemented curriculum in Homeland Security and Information Assurance domestically and internationally. She has computer literacy copyrights, conducted workshops, consulted on research/sponsored projects, facilitated courses for educators and presented before government officials in Port au Prince, Haiti on the topic of "Enterprise Resource Planning & Development Role in Decentralization and Civil Reform Programs."

Stephen Cohen is the Chief Architect with Microsoft Public Sector Services, US Public Sector practice focusing on large, complex, command and control systems for the US Government. Mr. Cohen has been the Primary Enterprise Architect and Lead System designer for multiple Federal and State government agency projects. He has had the opportunity to develop low level tools, real-time, high data rate, and large storage, mission, and simulation systems. He has presented for various internal and external groups including Microsoft's Engineering Excellence Group (EEG), the International Association for Software Architecture (IASA), Microsoft's Trustworthy Computing Conference (TwC) as well as the Project Management Institute (PMI). He has several published papers on Architecture and bridging Agile and Formal software development practices. He is an occasional blogger but his full time job as Architect for MCS Public Sector practice keeps him in the trenches combining architecture, art, and technology to support the various missions of government.

Paul Cragg is Professor of Information Systems at the University of Canterbury, New Zealand. He received his PhD from Loughborough University, England. He teaches the management of IS across a wide range of courses from undergraduate through to PhD. He has published his research on IS in small and medium-sized enterprises in numerous journals, including *Information & Management, MIS Quarterly, European Journal of Information Systems, Journal of Strategic Information Systems, Journal of Small Business Management, International Small Business Journal*, and *Total Quality Management and Business Excellence.*

P. Candace Deans is an Associate Professor at the University of Richmond, Robins School of Business. Prior appointments include Thunderbird School of Global Management and Wake Forest University. She received her Ph.D. from the University of South Carolina. Her research interests and publications are at the intersection of information technology and international business. She has extensive international experience consulting with multinational companies, designing study abroad programs and leading executive seminars worldwide. She has received many teaching awards, including one as runner-up for the 2009 Decision Sciences Institute Innovation in Teaching Award.

Cameron Deed graduated at the University of Canterbury in 2010 with an Information Systems Honours degree. His focus for study included information systems change, software-as-a-service, and business intelligence. He now works as a Consultant for an Australian BI software vendor and has worked on a variety of large and small BI implementations worldwide. In his spare time he enjoys attending music concerts and is an avid snowboarder.

Alpana M. Desai is an Associate Professor of Management Information Systems in the College of Business and Public Policy at the University of Alaska Anchorage. She has over 11 years of academic experience. She has taught courses at the undergraduate and graduate level and her research interests and publications are in the areas of information systems security, information systems privacy, mobile analytics, group collaboration systems, mathematical modeling, and information systems education.

Sam De Silva is a Partner and the Head of Technology and Outsourcing Law at leading UK law firm, Manches LLP. Prior to joining Manches, Sam has worked for leading law firms in London, Australia and New Zealand. His main areas of practice are technology and business process outsourcing and technology law topics and is the Chairperson on the Law Society's Technology and Law Reference Group. In addition to his LLB and Masters in Business Law, Sam has post-graduate degrees in information technology and business administration so is well aware of the commercial, business and technical issues facing both users and suppliers of technology. Sam is also one of very few UK solicitors who is a Fellow of the Chartered Institute of Purchasing and Supply (FCIPS), Fellow of the British Computer Society (FBCS) and a Chartered IT Professional (CITP). Sam also has in-house industry legal experience having been seconded to Accenture UK as a senior legal counsel. Sam is a Society of Computers and Law IT Law Accredited member and is Trustee of the Chartered Institute of Purchasing and Supply. Dr. De Silva is a Barrister and Solicitor of the High Court of New Zealand, a Solicitor of the Supreme Court of England and Wales and a Solicitor of the Supreme Court of New South Wales, Australia.

Federico Etro is Professor of Economics at the *University of Venice, Ca' Foscari*. He is an expert of industrial organization and international macroeconomics with academic publications on *American Economic Review, International Economic Review, European Economic Review, Economic Journal* and leading applied works on the economics of cloud computing, online advertising, and antitrust policy for the New Economy. He holds a Laurea *cum laude* from the Catholic University of Milan and a Master's in Economics from the University of California, Los Angeles, has taught at the University of Edinburgh, the University of Milan and Luiss in Rome, and has been Research Assistant for the National Bureau of Economic Research in Boston.

Shamim Hossain achieved a Bachelor of Electrical and Computer Systems Engineering with Telecommunications major (First Class Honours, 2004) from Monash University, Australia. Currently he is working as Senior IT Consultant in Global Business Services, IBM Australia. Besides his full time work he is also pursuing a PhD on "Energy Efficiency of Cloud Computing" with the University of Melbourne. Shamim has published papers in numerous academic and technical conferences and served as a technical program committee member in few technical conferences. Shamim has been active in conducting research besides his full time job. His areas of interests are cloud computing (Cloud Infrastructure, application areas of cloud computing, cloud architecture, networking layer), optical fiber communications (DWDM, MPLS, VPLS), wireless and mobile network design, Radio Frequency Identification, parallel and distributed computing, and enterprise application development. Shamim is a member of Engineers Australia.

Sid Huff is Professor of Information Systems at Victoria University of Wellington, New Zealand. His teaching and research address IS strategy, IT governance, senior management roles in information systems, and IS management. His work has appeared in numerous academic and practitioner journals, including *MIS Quarterly, Information Systems Research, Journal of MIS, Journal of Strategic Information Systems, Communications of the ACM, CAIS* and others. His most recent book is *Managing IT Professionals in the Internet Age,* co-authored with Dr. Pak Yoong. He currently serves as a Senior Editor for *Information Systems Management Journal* and for *Journal of Information Technology,* and as an Associate Editor for *MIS Quarterly.* He has also written over 60 teaching cases for educational use, and was the originator of the IS.

Stephen Kaisler is currently a Senior Scientist with i_SW Corporation, a firm specializing in science, engineering, and technology research, development and integration. Dr. Kaisler has been working with big data, MapReduce technology, and advanced analytics in support of the CATALYST program for the past 15 months. Prior to joining i_SW, he was a Senior Scientist with Logos Technologies and SET Corporation, where he worked at DARPA as a SETA/Deputy Program Manager. Prior to that, he was Technical Advisor to the Sergeant At Arms of the U.S. Senate, where he was responsible for systems architecture, modernization, and strategic planning for the U.S. Senate. He has taught in the Department of Electrical Engineering and Computer Science at George Washington University. Recently, he has also taught enterprise architecture and information security in the GWU Business School. He earned a D.Sc. (Computer Science) from George Washington University, and an M.S. (Computer Science) and B.S. (Physics) from the University of Maryland at College Park. He has written four books and published over 35 technical papers.

Yoshito Kanamori is an Assistant Professor in the Department of Computer Information Systems at the University of Alaska, Anchorage. He received his Ph. D and M.Sc. degrees at the University of Alabama in Huntsville in 2006 and 2002 respectively. He joined the Department of Computer information Systems at University of Alaska Anchorage in 2006. His current research interests include security in cloud computing, web content trust, and quantum information processing. He is a member of the IEEE.

Michael L. Kemp is an attorney in Philadelphia, PA. After receiving a B.S. in Integrative Biology from the University of Illinois at Urbana-Champaign, Michael went on to receive a J.D. and an M.B.A. from the University of Richmond. During his time at U of R, Michael served as an Articles Editor for the University of Richmond Law Review. Michael's coursework at U of R focused on business and corporate law, and his current practice consists of corporate transactions and commercial litigation.

Wei Nein "William" Lee is the Manager of the PMO (Project Management Office) with Oil States International (NYSE: OIS) based in Houston, Texas. He received a Bachelor's degree in Economics from the University of Texas at Austin and is currently pursuing a graduate degree with the University of Houston – College of Technology. In his 18 years of experience, he has served as consultant and full-time management roles with a number of high profile organizations such as Accenture, CNBC.com, SBI, Idea Integration, and public sector entities such as the City of Houston, Sugar Land, Arlington, and the Harris County Flood Control District. In 2008, Mr. Lee's project with the City of Houston was awarded Microsoft Partner of the year in the data visualization category.

Eng Kit Lum is an Instructor at School of Information Systems, Singapore Management University, Singapore, teaching courses in the areas of business processes and enterprise systems. He develops and facilitates hands-on learning exercises for the students in the Enterprise Business Solutions course, which teaches SAP Enterprise Resource Planning (ERP) business processes and Enterprise Services Architecture (ESA). Prior to this role, he has worked for a local mobile operator and a global mobile services provider, developing mobile applications and managing the implementation and deployment of mobile services for his customers, who include large banks, software, and internet companies.

Kenrick Mock is an Associate Professor of Computer Science in the Department of Mathematical Sciences at the University of Alaska Anchorage. He has taught over 20 courses in computing and conducts research in artificial intelligence, complex systems, agent-based systems, computer security, and computer science education. He has over 20 years of programming experience and has co-authored four textbooks on programming in Java and C++. Dr. Mock is also interested in promoting research experiences for undergraduates through grants, student activities, curriculum, and faculty development.

William Money joined the George Washington University School of Business and Public Management faculty September 1992 after acquiring over 12 years of management experience in the design, development, installation, and support of management information systems (1980-92). His publications and recent research interests focus on information system development tools and agile software engineering methodologies, collaborative solutions to complex business problems, program management, business process engineering, and individual learning. He is also developing teaching and facilitation techniques that prepare students to use collaboration tools in complex organizations and dynamic work environments experiencing significant change. Dr. Money has been engaged in a number of significant software development programs as a consultant to the Government and to industry. Dr. Money's academic training includes the Ph.D., Organizational Behavior 1977, Northwestern University, Graduate School of Management; the M.B.A., Management, 1969, Indiana University; and a B.A., Political Science, 1968, University of Richmond. Dr. Money has had numerous publications in professional journals and speaking engagements at professional meetings.

Kofi Nyarko, is an Associate Professor at Morgan State University (MSU), within the Department of Electrical and Computer Engineering. Furthermore, he serves as the president and CEO of K & K Analytics LLC, a software and systems engineering firm. Under the Chesapeake Information Based Aeronautics Consortium (CIBAC), Dr. Nyarko works with engineers at Morgan State University and NASA Langley on aeronautics related research. Dr. Nyarko received his Bachelor of Science degree from Morgan State University in Electrical Engineering in 1997. He stayed on to complete his Master's Degree in 2001, and later Doctorate Degree in Electrical and Computer engineering in 2004. During that period, he held the position of Research Technical Lead of the Engineering Visualization and Semiconductor Characterization Laboratory (EVSC). Upon completion of his Doctorate degree, he was appointed the title of Director of the Engineering Visualization Research Laboratory (EVRL), which maintains active grants and partnerships with several government agencies, including Department of Defense, Department of Energy, Army Research Laboratory, and NASA. Over the course of his career Dr. Nyarko has worked in many technical areas, such as: computational engineering, scientific/engineering simulation & visualization, visual analytics, complex computer algorithm development, computer network theory (including Ad-Hoc Mobile Networks), portable computing design and development, advanced computer display technologies, and avionic system software development.

Shantanu Pal is presently doing his research in the Department of Electrical and Computer Engineering at the Braunschweig University of Technology in Germany. He received his M.Tech in Information Technology from the University of Calcutta, India. Prior to that, he did his B.Tech in Information Technology from the West Bengal University of Technology, India. He was visiting researcher at the Ca' Foscari University the Venezia, Venice, Italy in 2010. His current research interest is in the broad area of distributed computing, computer communications, cloud computing, and networking security. Shantanu has also served in the committees of several international conferences, journals, and magazines including IEEE Potentials. He was the coordinator of the IEEE All India Young Engineers' Humanitarian Challenge for 2010 and 2011.

Marc Rabaey is senior officer in the Belgian Ministry of Defense (MOD) where he fulfilled different functions: IT-manager Medical Service, IT-procurement manager Medical Service, CIO of the Assistant Chief of Staff Evaluation, Technical Director Royal Military Academy. He is now System Manager Education of MOD. His main projects were the migration of the applications of the Belgian Medical Service from Mainframe to Client/Server architecture, the implementation of a imaging, workflow and document management in the Medical Administration and the conceptualization of the information system of Evaluation and Education of MOD. He is now Business IT consultant in Open-Raxit. He holds the degrees of Commercial Engineer (IT) and Master in Social and Military Science. Actually he has a PhD Applied Economics in progress at the University of Hasselt, Belgium. The main subject is the investment of IT, more specifically in the domain of Cloud Computing for public services. His test case is the move of an application of a federal agency into the Cloud.

Shannon Robb is an attorney in Philadelphia, PA. After receiving her B.S. in Business Management from Virginia Tech with Minors in Psychology and Business Leadership, Shannon went on to receive a J.D. and an M.B.A. from the University of Richmond. While at the University of Richmond, Shannon served as Managing Editor of the *Journal of Global Law and Business*. Shannon's primary areas of interest include corporate, commercial, and tax law.

Holger Schrödl work as Research Associate at Otto-von-Guericke University Magdeburg, Germany. After his study of mathematics and informatics at the University of Augsburg, Germany, he worked as entrepreneur and management consultant in numerous IT projects in the area of information systems architectures and business intelligence. After several teaching assignments, he trained as research assistant at University of Augsburg to teach and conduct research in business informatics. Main interests areas are information system architectures and data centre development.

Mary Tate is a Senior Lecturer in Information Systems at Victoria University of Wellington, New Zealand. She has 20 years of experience in the IT industry including channel management, service delivery, project management, and business analysis. Since joining Victoria University in 2001 Mary has embarked on a research career with more than 50 peer-reviewed publications including journals such as the *Journal of the Association of Information Systems,* and *Behaviour and Information Technology.* Mary has served as track chair and AE for e-commerce and research methods tracks in a range of IS conferences including ICIS, PACIS, and ACIS.

Venky Shankararaman is an Associate Professor of Information Systems (Practice) at the School of Information Systems, Singapore Management University, Singapore. His current areas of specialization include business process management, enterprise architecture and enterprise integration. He has over 16 years experience in the IT industry in various capacities as a researcher, academic faculty member, and industry consultant. Venky has designed and delivered professional courses for government and industry in areas such as enterprise architecture, technical architecture, enterprise integration and business process management. Venky also worked as a faculty member at Universities in the UK and Singapore where he was actively involved in teaching and research in the areas of intelligent systems and distributed systems. He has published over 55 papers in academic journals and conferences.

Stefan Wind takes part in an international Master's program in the area of Information Systems at the Otto-Friedrich-University in Bamberg, Germany. During his graduate studies, he focused on e-business, requirements engineering, and project management. Since October 2009 he works on his PhD-work in the area of Cloud Computing.

Haibo Yang is a PhD candidate in Information Systems at Victoria University of Wellington. Haibo's professional background includes online application design, database management, and business intelligence. From an academic perspective his research interest includes understanding the dynamics between technologies and online service delivery. Haibo's recent work focuses on IT agility and cloud computing and has been presented at conferences such as AMCIS and ACIS.

Minnie Yi-Miin Yen is a Professor of Management Information Systems in the Department of Computer Information Systems, University of Alaska Anchorage. She received her Ph.D. in Management Information Systems from University of Houston. Dr. Yen's work has appeared in *IEEE Transactions on Software Engineering, Journal of Database Management, International Journal of Management, Human Factors in Information Systems, Journal of Information Education,* and other journals. Her research interests focus on cloud computing security controls and auditing, human-computer interaction, client-server database systems, e-commerce and web-based learning. She currently teaches Database Management, Client-Server Systems, and Object-Oriented Programming.

Index